MW01618160

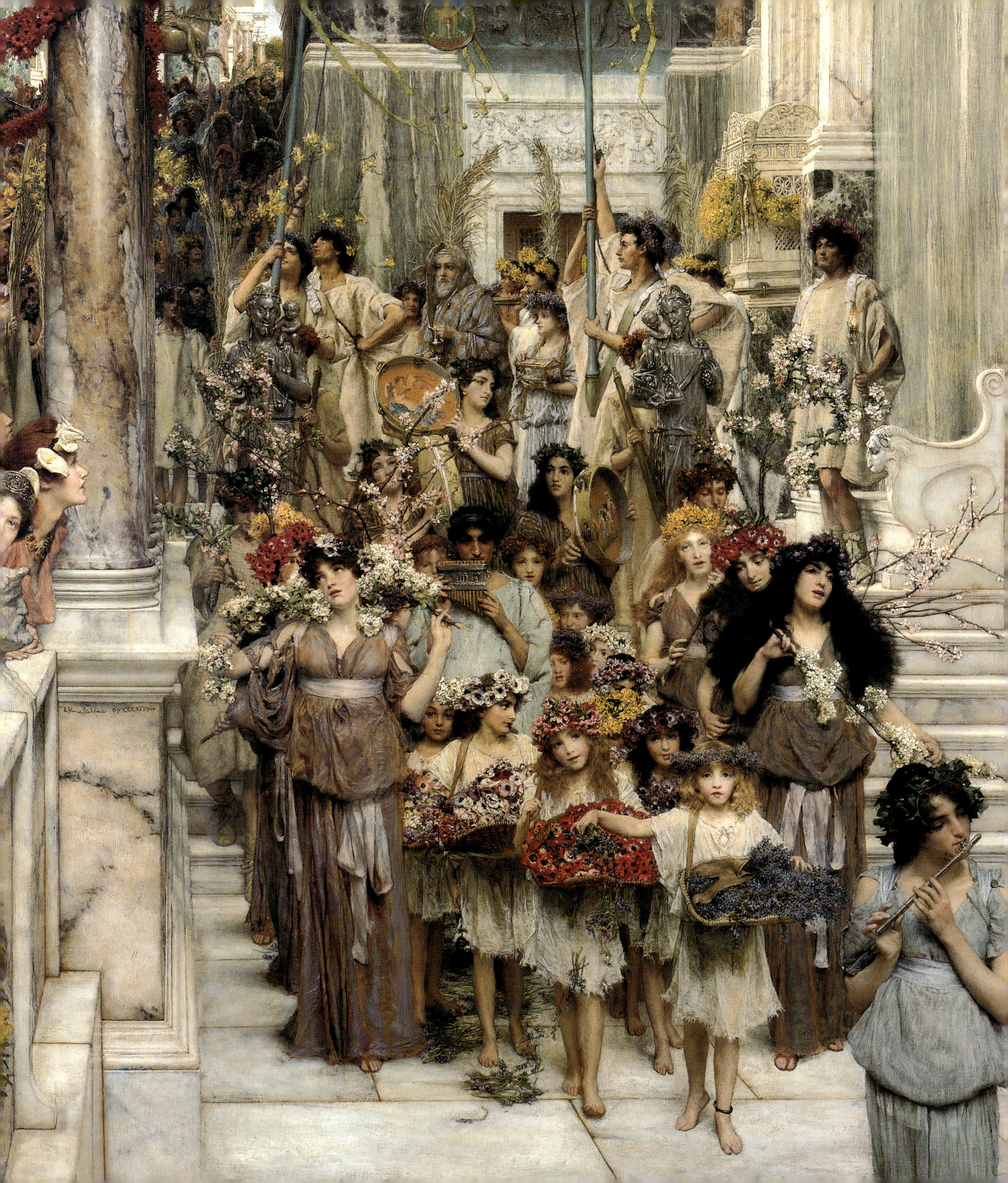

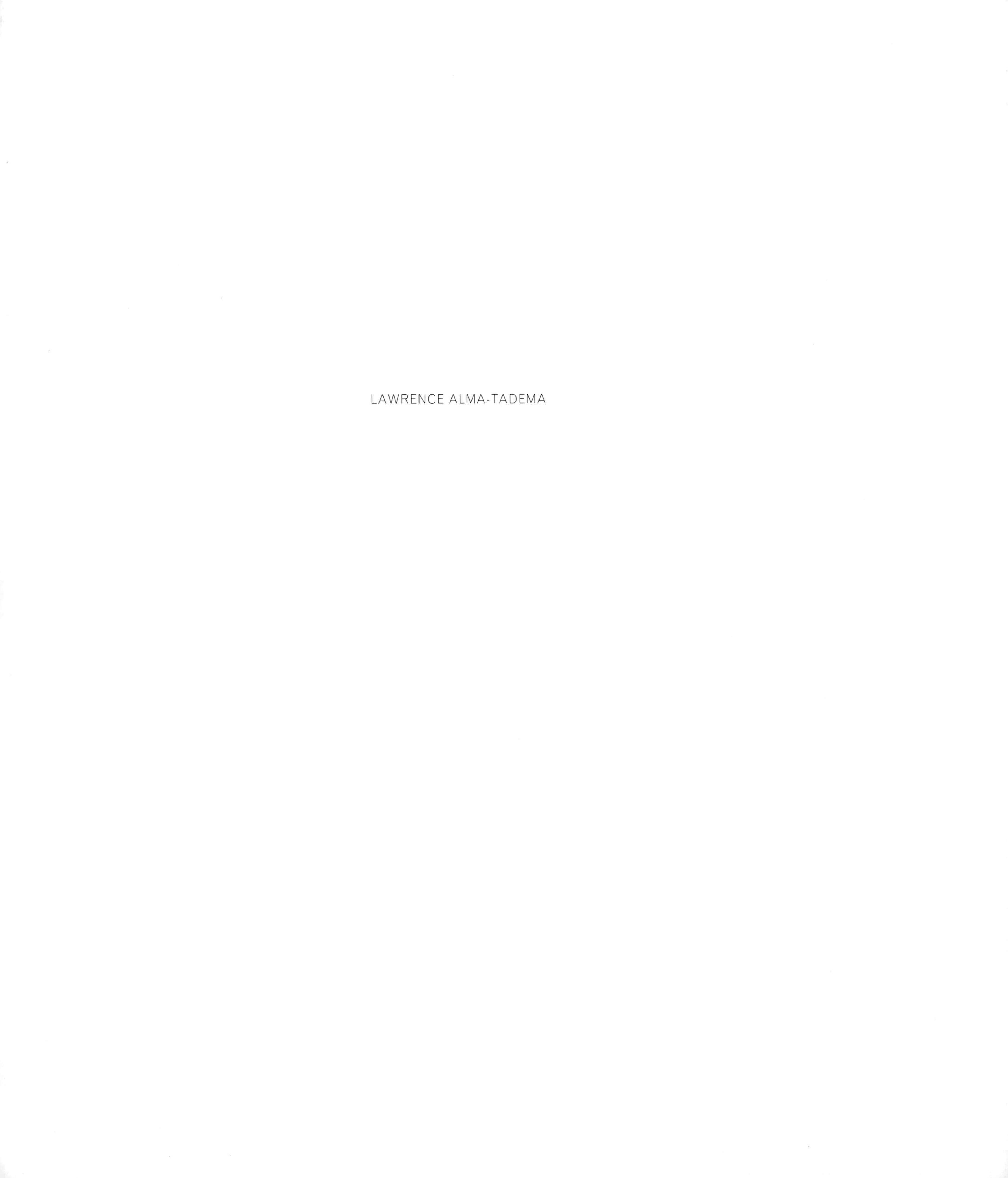

LAWRENCE ALMA-TADEMA

R J BARROW

LAWRENCE ALMA-TADEMA

Φ

Phaidon Press Limited
Regent's Wharf, All Saints Street, London N1 9PA

Phaidon Press Inc.
180 Varick Street, New York, NY 10014

www.phaidon.com

First published 2001

ISBN 0 7148 3918 3

A CIP catalogue record for this book
is available from the British Library.

Typeset in Monotype Grotesque 125 and Apollo
Designed by Phil Baines studio
Printed in Hong Kong

Frontispiece
Spring (detail of Pl.149)

AUTHOR'S ACKNOWLEDGEMENTS

I am grateful to Professor Michael Silk for invaluable and enduring encouragement and guidance; Dr Dominic Montserrat, for much helpful advice, information and kindness; Professor Leonée Ormond, for her commitment and enthusiasm; and Dr Elizabeth Prettejohn for her many useful comments and suggestions. I would like to thank all the students whom I have been fortunate enough to teach, in particular, Sona Bose, Caroline Carter, Victoria Fangen, Ronald Higginson and Catherine Lain, who have provided a stimulating arena for discussion as well as ideas and suggestions. I am grateful to the editor, Bernard Dod, whose judgement and close comments have always proved astute; to the assistant editor, Charlotte Garner; picture researcher, Sarah Hopper; the design team; and all at Phaidon Press who have ensured the completion of this book. Finally, I would like to thank Jean and Tony Lewis.

OPUS NUMBERS

Alma-Tadema assigned opus numbers to his works. This system made forgery difficult and also removed the need to inscribe a date on each painting, thus allowing every work to be exhibited as the artist's latest.

PHOTOGRAPHIC COLLECTION

The artist amassed a collection of photographs throughout his life. The collection is stored in 167 portfolios in the Heslop Room, Main Library, University of Birmingham. Illustrations of these photographs can be identified by the acknowledgement to the University of Birmingham in the captions.

1836–1870: YOUTH, ART TRAINING, EARLY CAREER

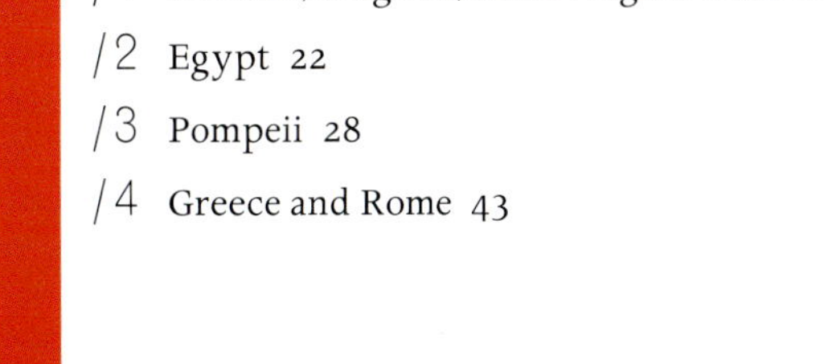

1870–1887: ESTABLISHMENT AND SUCCESS

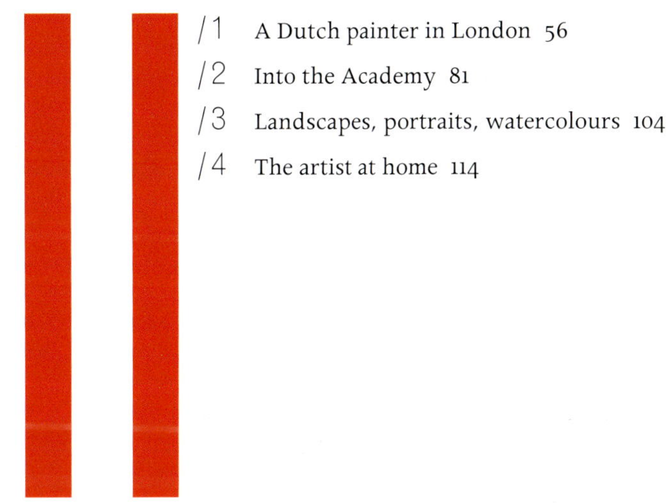

1887–1912: FINAL HONOURS AND THE END OF A CAREER

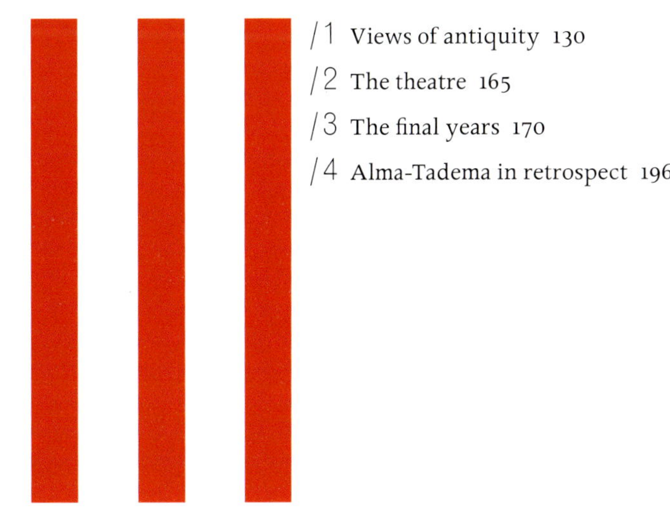

INTRODUCTION

This book seeks to reappraise Lawrence Alma-Tadema's distinctive achievement as an artist within the British tradition and, beyond it, the history of European painting, through a new consideration of his works. At the same time, the artist's life is a phenomenon of considerable interest in its own right. Alma-Tadema's biography was published in book form three times during his lifetime,[1] while many more articles offered a sketch of his life and work. His biographers were all friends of his, and as each repeats the same narrative and the same anecdotes, we must conclude that Alma-Tadema wished to present himself in a particular light: a boy with few advantages who, through hard work and determination, succeeded in pursuing his chosen career. As a mature artist, he became an established figure in the social milieu of Victorian London, and the range of sources relating to his life diversifies. From additional material that has been uncovered in the form of personal letters and contemporary reminiscences,[2] he emerges as a memorable character. Personality and painting aside, his career itself constitutes a remarkable achievement: that a boy from Friesland should grow up to become one of the most admired and successful artists in Victorian Britain.

Highly acclaimed in his own time, Alma-Tadema is once again attracting and stimulating a wide public today. Of all the notable Victorian artists, none is better placed to make an impact on the modern sensibility – visually alert and sensitized to ironies and subversions – at the turn of the third millennium. During his long career he successfully mastered many styles and subjects from Merovingian and Egyptian historical and genre scenes to contemporary portraits and landscapes. However, he is best-known for his pictures of the ancient world: of the four hundred works completed in his working life over three hundred are classical in subject. With their play of light, soft colour-harmonies, gorgeous textures and settings of marbled interiors and sunny Mediterranean sea scapes, it is not surprising that these works exercise a lasting sensuous appeal. But more than this, as a learned and conceptually sophisticated reader of the ancient world, Alma-Tadema presents both a plausible visualization of antiquity and an intriguing construction of ancient political and social life.

At the height of his career, Alma-Tadema offered an interviewer a rare comment on his own art: 'there is not such a great difference between the ancients and the moderns as we are apt to suppose. This is the truth that I have always endeavoured to express in my pictures, that the old Romans were human flesh and blood like ourselves, moved by the same passions and emotions.'[3] In the recent past, this statement has been used to support the notion that in Alma-Tadema's depictions of the ancient world, all we see is 'Victorians in togas'[4]. Given that the reception of antiquity discloses much about the age to which the reception belongs, we can, at least, assume that Alma-Tadema's paintings reflect contemporary attitudes to ancient cultures; even so, his work can be shown to be far more than the representation of Victorian mores in Roman garb. This book aims to present Alma-Tadema's classicism in a more revealing guise: as a strikingly original and often deeply ironic use of themes, motifs and allusions, literary and archaeological. In his work, we are invited to relish and rethink an ancient world constructed from a complicated interplay of sources and informed by contemporary suggestion and nuance. A playful irony becomes apparent as the artist selects and mediates texts and archaeological artefacts which are calculated to draw our attention to the exciting, the corrupt, the risqué and the subversive.

How far his public – viewers and patrons – were able to decipher his imagery is difficult to answer. His critics, certainly, admired his work largely for its stylistic merits and its pure aesthetic appeal. My own reading of the paintings is that they function on several distinct levels – sensual and intellectual, popular and élite – and given the nature of his imageries and his ironies, I would in general have to suppose that this was Alma-Tadema's broad sense of his work too. However, without independent evidence of his intentions or much more in the way of authorial self-revelation by the artist himself, it is impossible to try and articulate his understanding of his own work in any detail. It is of course the case that any attempt, including my own, to relate an artist's life and work is likely to construct some sort of artistic consciousness to connect them, but then it is equally the case that the reconstruction of authorial intentions, where practicable, is fraught with theoretical problems of a distinctive kind. We should, for instance, note that if we had Alma-Tadema's interpretation of a given work, we would not necessarily be satisfied with it, if only because, for reasons of cultural change, our interpretative categories are not necessarily his:

gender issues are a case in point. The question of intention will recur, but my prime concern is a reassessment and a revaluation of the paintings themselves.

Classicism impinged on nineteenth-century culture in a way that is almost unimaginable today, and many artists acquired a precise and extensive knowledge of ancient history, literature and archaeology. While classical-subject movements flourished in most of the European nation states, Alma-Tadema developed his own brand of classicism in which he looked primarily to Roman history, art and architecture for historical genre subjects, often in works of small dimensions. He made at least six long study trips to Italy,[5] and while his great contemporaries Frederic Leighton and Edward Poynter were founder members of the British Hellenic Society, Alma-Tadema reserved his membership for the Roman Society, founded in 1911, a year before his death.

Alma-Tadema's Rome is not the Rome of Caesar and Cicero, Livy and Virgil, not the Rome of militarism, heroism, and triumphant imperialism. Instead, it is a hedonistic society preoccupied with the pleasures of the senses. We are fascinated by the idle rich at their leisure; we are delighted with the revellers who carouse and the lovers who make love; and we marvel at the magnificence, opulence and utter decadence of the imperial circle. Favoured subjects include courtship rituals and a host of activities appropriate to an ancient setting, including bathing, dining and the performance of intriguing pagan rites, which, at the same time, evoke an archetypally wealthy and leisured mode of existence. Such an antiquity is not the artist's invention but is based on a popular notion of Rome which itself looks back to Edward Gibbon's *The History of the Decline and Fall of the Roman Empire*, written at the end of the eighteenth century. In this monumentally influential work, Gibbon forged a connection between material prosperity and the demise of empire and, in doing so, delineated a Rome of luxurious indolence.

The Rome that is recognizable in Gibbon, in the nineteenth-century popular imagination, and in Alma-Tadema too, derives ultimately from the testimonials of her own writers. Throughout Alma-Tadema's career, we can discern the use of a particular group of ancient literary texts. Biographical scenes of Latin poets look to the urbane and witty love poems of Catullus and Horace; historical subjects to the amusing and anecdotal histories of Suetonius and the *Scriptores Historiae Augustae*; genre scenes to the works of Latin moralists and satirists, Pliny, Juvenal, Martial, and the bawdy sophistications of Petronius, all of them rich exposés of the follies and indulgences of Roman life. Unlike Rome's own writers, however, Alma-Tadema takes a detached delight in his subversions: their stock-in-trade is moral outrage; for him, moral agendas are redundant.

From the ostentatious public façade of the city of Rome itself, to the *dolce vita* along the Bay of Naples, Alma-Tadema's Roman life is played out in settings which are calculated to create a distinctive and recognizable mood. Locations change as Pompeian-inspired interiors of bright red walls make way for the white marble buildings of the city of Rome or for terraces overlooking the Mediterranean sea and a world on which the sun always shines. Roman Italy is conceived as an eternal summer: roses are in bloom and marble is freshly polished. At the same time, however, the paintings present us with a series of intellectual challenges as the artist directs the viewer to uncover hidden meanings in his use of obscured inscriptions, half-hidden statues, implicit references to histories and texts. His paintings, then, reconcile the tradition of an idealized antiquity with a world plausibly reconstructed from ancient sources, and, equally, with a subversive vision which must have appealed, in some degree, to contemporary tastes. It is perhaps to this paradoxical relationship between the depiction of the sensual and the appeal to the intellect, that we may trace Alma-Tadema's distinctive power, and, perhaps, also the special elusiveness of his enduring charm.

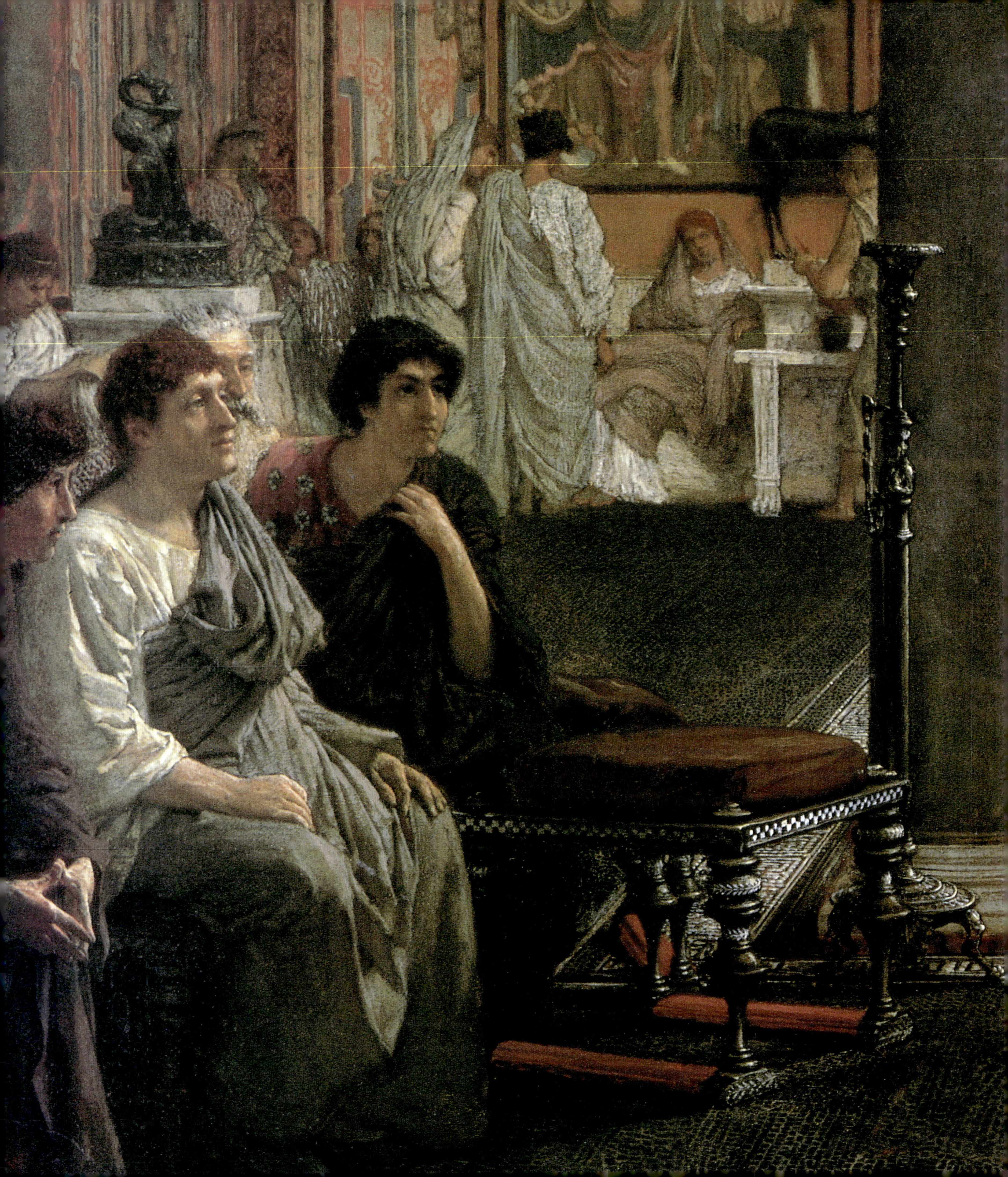

1836–1870
YOUTH
ART TRAINING
EARLY CAREER

1/1

HOLLAND, BELGIUM, MEROVINGIAN GAUL

A self-portrait (Pl.2), painted at the age of sixteen, marks the artist's first entry into the public arena. It shows a half-length figure, his face in three-quarter profile, seated in front of a curtain which has been swept to one side to reveal a receding architectural interior. The polished execution and subdued palette recall the work of the Friesian portraitist and genre painter, Willem Bartel van der Kooi (1768–1836); and, despite some technical awkwardness, it is an admirable effort from a boy who has, as yet, received no formal art training. More arresting, however, is the serious manner in which the boy seeks to project his image as an artist. Seated upright, his head held rigid by a stiff collar, the subject looks sternly out of the canvas, leaving the viewer in no doubt as to the gravity of his purpose. Yet completely at odds with this solemn image are the memories which the mature artist will later associate with it. In 1909 Alma-Tadema was to look back to the portrait's merits as a likeness, summed up by the way that while he was taking his picture home, 'certain small boys of Leeuwarden ... ran after me, crying "Look, he's carrying himself under his arm!"'[6] Once we are aware that the older artist looks back with amusement at an image of his earnest younger self, we can only view the portrait in a new light. We have, inseparably, a commendable early work by an aspiring artist and yet also an ironic comment on a first attempt to assert artistic identity. Dual meanings will become all-important in this artist's work, and the difference here between initial serious intent and the irreverence later attached to it is emblematic of the curious tension between detached and playful irony and serious scholarly or 'painterly' projection which will characterize so much of Alma-Tadema's work.

Lourens Alma Tadema[7] was born on 8 January 1836, in the small village of Dronrijp in Friesland in the north of Holland, the third child of Pieter Jiltes Tadema (1797–1840), the village notary, and Hinke Dirks Brouwer (*c*.1800–63). Pieter Tadema already had three sons by his first wife, Artje Dirks Brouwer, after whose death he married Artje's half-sister, Hinke. Tadema was a traditional Friesian name, while the names Lourens and Alma belonged to the boy's godfather. Alma was incorporated into the surname by the artist for the purpose of having his name appear at the beginning of exhibition catalogues, under A rather than under T.[8]

In 1837 the family moved to the nearby town of Leeuwarden. His father died when Lourens was four, leaving his mother with five children: Lourens, his sister and three boys from his father's previous marriage. A local drawing master was engaged to tutor the older children and Lourens joined them. Enrolled at the Gymnasium at Leeuwarden, he drew in his spare time. As a schoolboy, Lourens is known to have bought two books in a local shop: Leonardo da Vinci's treatise on painting and a seventeenth-century discussion of the rules of perspective, from which he began to teach himself how to draw and paint.[9] His family intended Lourens to follow his father and pursue a legal career, but as the artist later recalled, 'every moment I could steal from work was devoted to drawing and sketching, and my tasks were often neglected in the pursuit of my passion for art.'[10] As a boy he would have his mother wake him at five o'clock in the morning, so that he could continue his art studies before school.

The first opused painting, *Portrait of My Sister, Artje*, completed in 1850 at the age of fourteen, was shown at an exhibition in Leeuwarden. The following year, the young Lourens was diagnosed consumptive; given only a short time to live, his legal preparation was curtailed and he was allowed to spend his remaining days at his leisure, drawing and painting. Thus left to his own devices, the boy regained his health and resolved to pursue a career as an artist. In 1852, at the age of sixteen, he began a formal art training. Rejected by Dutch art schools,[11] he was accepted at the prestigious Royal Academy of Fine Art in Antwerp, where the brother of the local music master was studying and promised to befriend the boy.

At the start of the nineteenth century, Dutch and Belgian painting was dominated by French Neo-classicism and the principles of Jacques-Louis David. From 1795 the Dutch Republic (created in 1648 and comprising both Holland and Belgium) was officially under French control. As the Batavian Republic, modelled on revolutionary France, it survived until 1806, when

1 previous page
A Juggler (detail of Pl.43)

2
Self-Portrait, 1852
Oil on canvas, 55·9 × 48·3 cm (22 × 19⅛ in)
Fries Museum, Leeuwarden

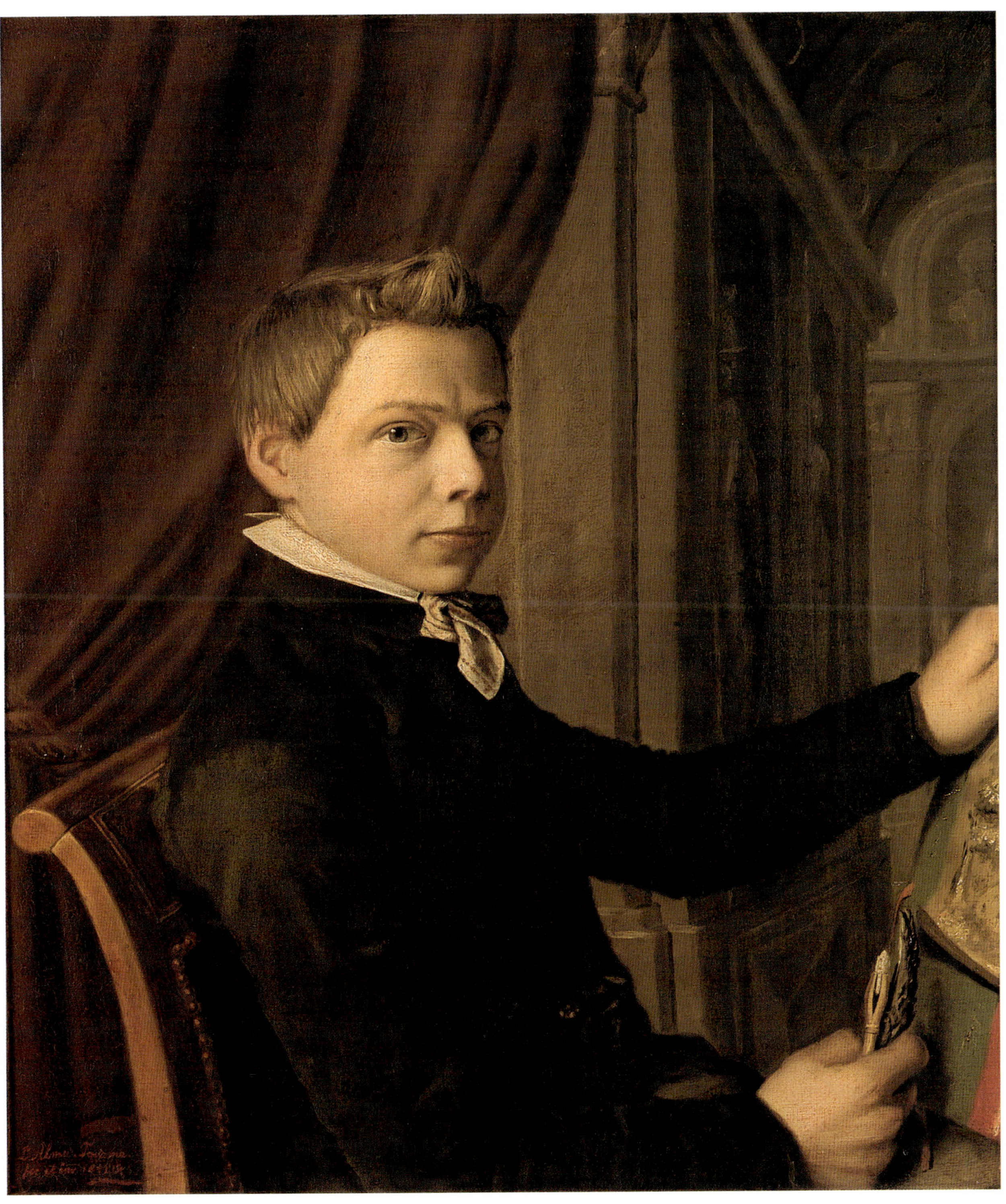

Napoleon converted it to the Kingdom of Holland and four years later incorporated it into the French Empire. French was the language of government, French ideas were absorbed into the culture, and Neo-classicism became the dominant trend in painting. After the fall of Napoleon, independence was restored in 1815, when Prince William Frederick became William I of the United Netherlands. And while Davidian Neo-classicism continued to flourish (David himself had retired as an exile to Brussels in 1816), King William, who strove to forge links between his reign and the earlier history of the Royal House of Orange, patronized court painters who produced propaganda subjects. Paintings such as Joseph François Odevaere's *The Foundation of the Principality of Orange 1579* and Mattheus van Brée's *The Patriotism of P A van der Werff, Burgomaster of Leyden 1576*, created a vogue for costume-history subjects concerned with the history of the Netherlands rather than a classical past.

In 1830 a Belgian uprising led to a declaration of Belgian independence, with Leopold I proclaimed as King. Eight years later the Dutch officially recognized the independence of Belgium, and the two countries were separated. However, the popularity of Orangist history painting under William I encouraged painters in both Holland and Belgium to seek subjects from the sixteenth and seventeenth centuries. The sixteenth-century struggle against Spanish domination and the lives of famous seventeenth-century Flemish painters were popular choices up to 1830 and beyond. At the same time, Davidian Neo-classicism gave way to a Romanticism in the vein of Delacroix as the dominant school in Belgium and Holland alike. Subjects were sought both from national history and from Romantic literature including Walter Scott, Schiller and Victor Hugo. Furthermore, while Neo-classicists placed emphasis on line rather than colour, Romanticists looked to the Dutch old masters in their appreciation of rich colouring and effects of light.

Between 1840 and 1853 the Director of the Royal Academy in Antwerp was the historical painter Gustaaf Wappers (1803–74). By 1830 Wappers had established himself as the leader of Flemish Romanticism, strongly opposed to Davidian Neo-classicism as championed by François Joseph Navez (1787–1869), a pupil of David who had followed him to Brussels. Wappers specialized in historical paintings which strongly affirmed national identity: his *Patriotism of the Burgomaster of Leyden during the Seige of the Spaniards* (1830) is typical. In 1855 he was succeeded by another Romanticist-historical painter, Nicaise de Keyser (1813–87).

Alma-Tadema's early work was fostered in this atmosphere of Flemish nationalism and Romanticism. He produced studies, minor portraits, figure sketches and a number of city scenes on paper, many of them later mounted on canvas,[12] which reflect the teaching of Joseph Laurens Dyckmans (1811–88), a Professor at the Academy and a contemporary and historical genre painter who specialized in architectural scenes. Influenced by Dyckmans's own depictions of picturesque corners of old buildings, these works also serve to illustrate Alma-Tadema's early interest in the traditional Dutch preoccupation with light and shadow in interior architectural settings. Rather different is his first narrative picture in oil, a genre subject, *A Poacher Returning Home after the Hunt* (1855), which was shown at an exhibition of contemporary art at Leeuwarden.

Alma-Tadema spent four years as a student at the Antwerp Academy. Georg Ebers, friend and biographer, describes him as 'a merry young fellow, universally popular, fond of all the pleasures of the gay artist-world to which he belonged, yet full of earnest devotion to study.'[13] Another biographer, Percy Cross Standing, quotes a letter from a contemporary who stresses Alma-Tadema's determination to compensate for his lack of formal training: '[he] did not merely *work* at Antwerp, but *slaved* in his efforts to make up for all the precious time he had lost.'[14] In 1856 the young art student received a private commission from Klaus Tigler Wybrandi, the husband of his aunt, Sjoukje Brouwer, for an oil painting entitled *The Declaration of Love* (1856), showing a cavalier kneeling before a seated lady. The Academy rules stated that an absence of more than three weeks from approved work would lead to automatic expulsion, but Alma-Tadema accepted the commission and ceased to be a regular pupil. No longer a student at the Academy, he continued his training in the studios of established artists.

Towards the end of 1855 Alma-Tadema moved into the house and studio of the historical painter, Louis De Taeye, and, as an apprentice, began to turn to subjects from Dutch and related history. *The Destruction of Terdoest Abbey in 1571* (1857) was the artist's first exhibit at the Salon in Brussels; failing to sell, it was eventually presented to his cook, who used it as an oil-cloth for the kitchen table.[15] In 1857 Alma-Tadema became a member of the 'Cercle Artistique', undoubtedly under the influence of De Taeye who was a prominent member of the group. The 'Cercle Artistique' were particularly interested in the rediscovery of Germanic myth and history, and in this spirit Alma-Tadema painted the watercolour, *Faust and Marguerite* (Pl.3), taking as its subject the sixteenth-century legend of Faust popularized by Goethe. The representation of Gothic architecture against a misty morning is

3
Faust and Marguerite, 1857
Watercolour, 45·2 × 50·1 cm (17¾ × 19¾ in)
John Constable Esq, England

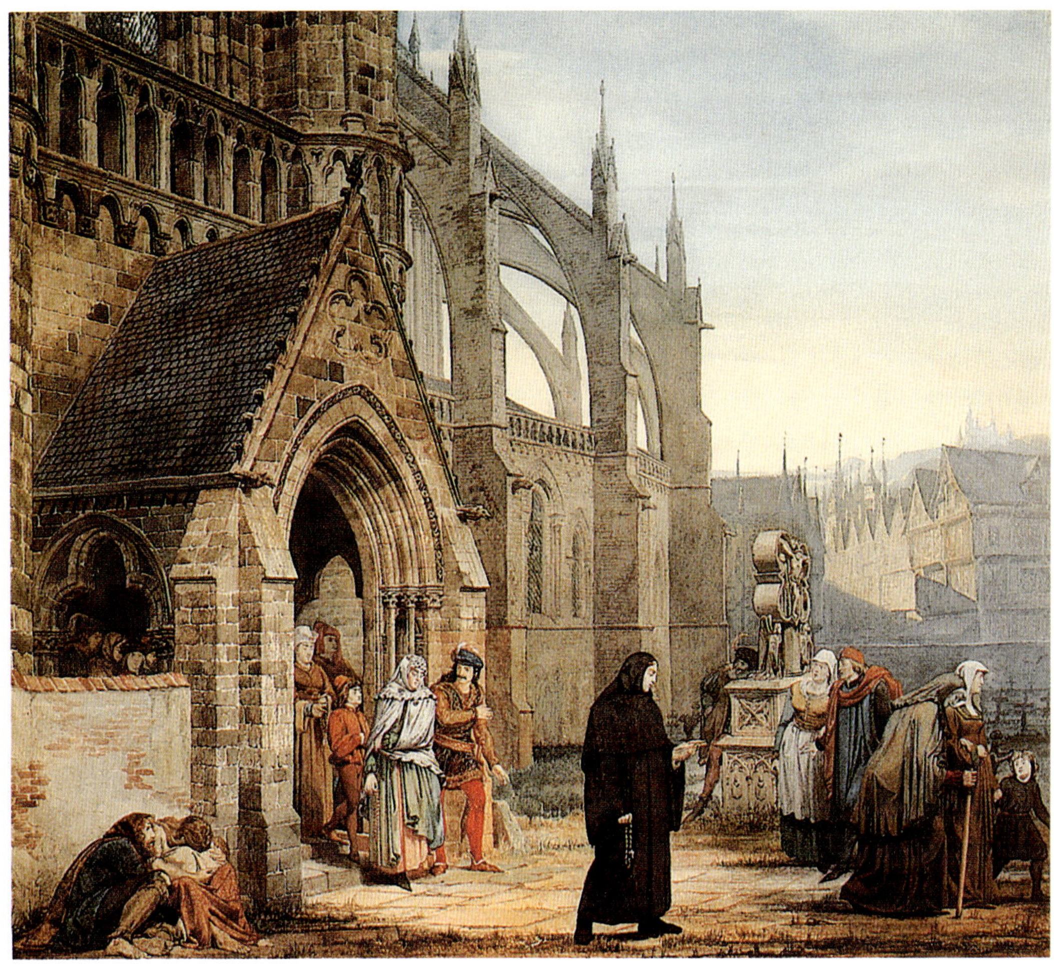

clearly influenced by German Romanticism. Alma-Tadema also completed an oil of the same subject which he later destroyed. Already a perfectionist, he allowed few of his early works to survive, and those which did not meet his exacting standards, including *The Destruction of Terdoest Abbey in 1571* and the oil *Faust and Marguerite*, were destroyed by his own hand. Ellen Gosse tells us that when *House on Fire* (*c.*1859) was returned unsold from an exhibition in Brussels, 'fellow students were asked into the studio of the rejected painter and were invited to jump through the canvas, the owner of it leading the way by leaping, head first, through the oily flames.'[16]

Between 1855 and 1860 Alma-Tadema was chiefly concerned with historical subjects depicting the history of the Low Countries. These included *Triumphal Return of Willem van Saeftingen to the Abbey Terdoest in 1513* (1860) and *Crossing of the River Berizina: 1812* (Pl.4). The latter, one of a large series of paintings depicting events from the history of the Netherlands between AD 40 and 1861 for the Amsterdam lawyer and collector, Jacob de Vos, was to remain Alma-Tadema's only painting that deals with a recent historical event. In 1812 Napoleon, allied with Austria and Prussia, declared war on Russia. The invasion resulted in a disastrous retreat from Moscow. More than 10,000 of Napoleon's troops (including many conscripts from the United Netherlands) died under Russian artillery bombardment while crossing the river Berezina in November 1812.

War was a frequent theme of Dutch–Belgian historical painting and for Alma-Tadema, death, plunder and destruction become a central focus. Examples include the watercolours *The Massacre of the Monks of Tamond* (1855) and *The Death of Attila: AD 453* (*c.*1859) and the oil painting, *The Plundering of Egmond Abbey by the Spanish: 1567* (1859). It is noteworthy that the artist makes a point of including dates in his titles, a practice which he was to continue on and off throughout his career. The dating of subjects contrives to highlight periods of significance and assure the viewer of historical authenticity. *The Plundering of Egmond Abbey by the Spanish: 1567* is set during the oppressive rule of Philip II of Spain over the Netherlands (a period often represented by Dutch and Belgian history painters from the beginning of the nineteenth century). Political disaffection coincided with Protestant revolt against the Catholic Church of Spain. In 1566 riots destroyed Catholic churches, and the following year Philip deployed Spanish troops. The year 1567 marks the beginning of eighty years of war which resulted in independence. *The Death of Attila: AD 453* shows the end of the infamous

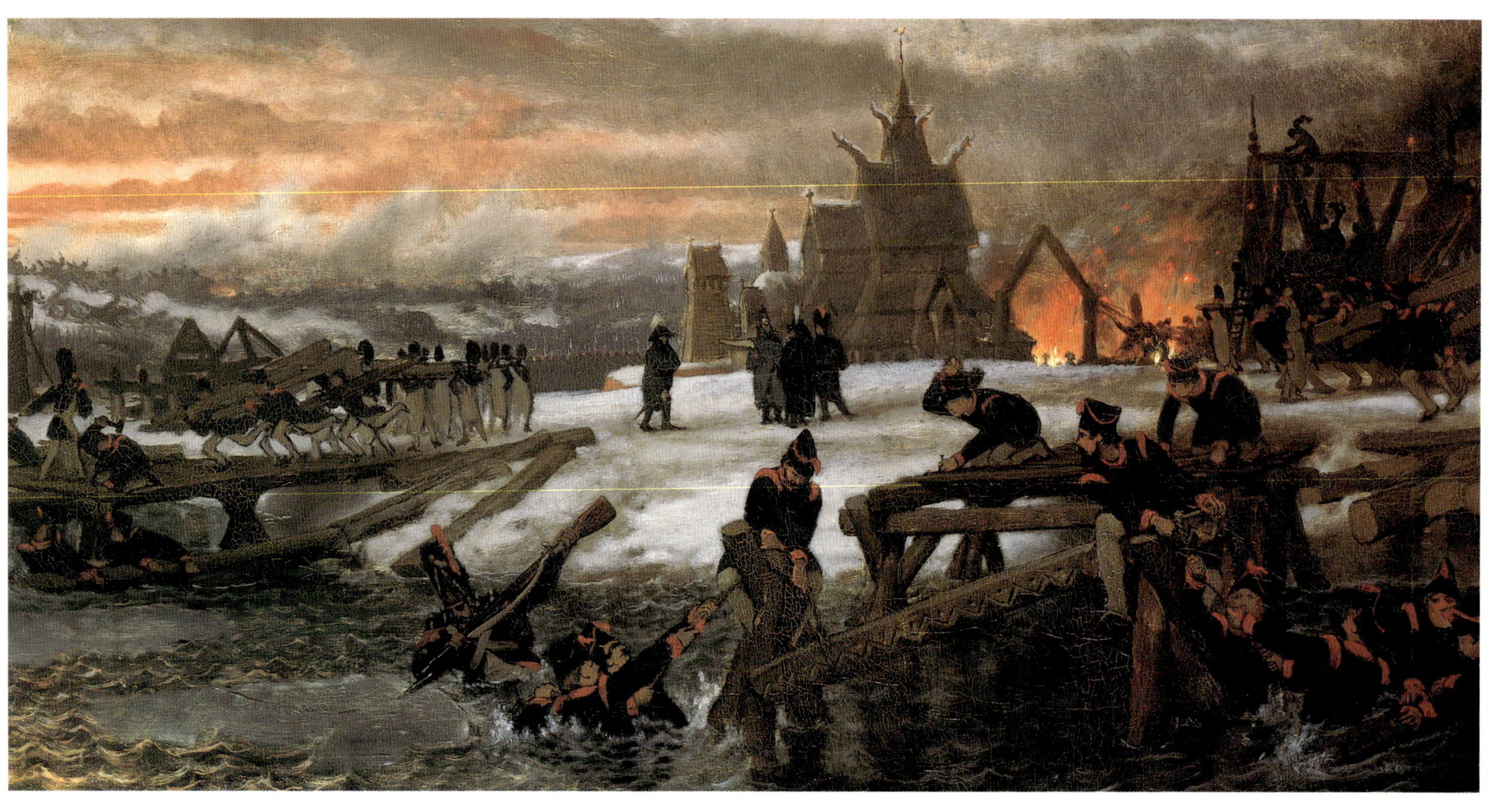

4
Crossing of the River Berizina: 1812, c.1859–69
Oil on canvas, 39 × 73 cm (15⅜ × 28¾ in)
Historisch Museum, Amsterdam

king of the Huns who defeated the Byzantine emperor Theodosius II, conquered much of the old Roman Empire and even invaded Italy itself. He died in 453 preparing for a second invasion of Italy. Although these historical subjects range widely in date from the fall of the Roman Empire to the campaigns of Napoleon, the artist soon turned his attention almost exclusively to one particular time and place: Merovingian Gaul. Having found a subject, Alma-Tadema was now to develop his own painting style and make the transition from student to professional artist.

The history of the Merovingians is that of the Frankish peoples after the fall of the Roman Empire in the fifth century AD. The Franks, a group of Germanic tribes living beyond the river Rhine, migrated into the Roman provinces of Germany and Gaul from the third century AD and divided themselves into two principal groups: the Salians and Ripuarians. The Salians were conquered and allied with Rome in the fourth century. During the early fifth century, the Romans retired from the Rhine, and the Salians established themselves in most of the territory of the Loire valley. Descended from the Salian Franks was the Merovingian dynasty of kings who ruled Gaul from the early-fifth to the mid-eighth century. Their name derives from an early dynast, Merovech, whose grandson Clovis I (481–511) was to become the first important Merovingian ruler. Under Clovis, Salian and Ripuarian Franks were united, the last Roman governor of Gaul, Syagrius, was overthrown, and with the support of the Church, the newly converted Clovis subjugated neighbouring northern peoples until the Frankish kingdom extended from the Pyrenees to Friesland and the Atlantic to the Rhine.

Alma-Tadema once told his friend, Carel Vosmaer, 'they are a sorry lot, to be sure, these Merovingians ... but still they are picturesque and interesting.'[17] The textual sources for his paintings are Gregory of Tours's *History of the Franks*, written in the sixth century AD, and the work of a modern French historian, Augustin Thierry, *Récits de temps Mérovingiens* (1840). Gregory, Bishop of Tours, was a Gallo-Roman aristocrat from Auvergne and his *History of the Franks* is a sober narration of gruesome and bloody events, enlivened with details of contemporary life. Thierry's study, despite a nineteenth-century political agenda, is not dissimilar in tone. In the same spirit, Alma-Tadema concentrates on death and destruction, portraying the Merovingians as a warlike and bloodthirsty people.

Although Merovingian subjects were not popular with other artists, Alma-Tadema's choice must be considered within the context of nineteenth-century Flemish historical painting. Netherlandish and French historical tradition can be traced back to the end of the Roman Empire and the beginning of Merovingian domination in the fifth century AD. Gregory of Tours's *History of the Franks*, which opens with the Biblical Creation and culminates in an account of the Merovingian dynasty, serves, like Virgil's *Aeneid*, to trace the origins of a people and their nation. For Thierry, this nation could ultimately be claimed as French. Alma-Tadema may have chosen this bloody period of Europe's past for different reasons: is he appropriating Merovingian history as a Netherlandish rather than a French foundation myth? Or is he choosing to display the barbarity of the 'French' historical tradition in ironic contrast to the noble antiquity beloved by Neoclassicism?

The fifth century witnessed the last years of a declining Roman Empire, whose end was heralded in 476 by the deposition of the last emperor in the West, Romulus Augustulus. Alma-Tadema's Merovingian subjects, however, are not represented as the periphery of a dominant, if declining, Rome. Following Thierry, his emphasis is on Frankish domination and not Roman demise and his portrayal of Merovingian identity is in clear opposition to a Rome centred view of late antiquity. Much contemporary historical thought, by contrast, was clearly Rome-focused. The norm was still what it had been in Edward Gibbon's *The History of the Decline and Fall of the Roman Empire* (1776–88), which dismisses the Merovingian dynasty as 'long-haired kings' who, by comparison with the urbane and sophisticated Romans, lived a life of rustic simplicity. The reign of Clovis is, for Gibbon, 'a perpetual violation of moral and Christian duties'.[18] Unlike Gibbon, Alma-Tadema neglects fifth-century Latin texts which lament the end of Roman domination and the fall of empire – for example, Rutilius Namatianus' poignant description of his return to Gaul – in favour of the different perspectives of a native of Gaul, Gregory of Tours. All in all, whether Alma-Tadema's Merovingian subjects are to be seen as a celebration of national identity or as an ironic comment on French historical painting, it is apparent that he is willing to subvert traditional views of late antiquity with a significant recentring of Merovingian history. The Merovingian paintings belong to a tradition of nationalism, and yet their unquiet subjects present a new and unconventional reading of historical heritage: Netherlandish or French. As we shall find throughout Alma-Tadema's career, even the most straightforward-looking narrative subjects seem, on inspection, to make way for the ambiguous and the subversive.

The first Merovingian painting, *Clotilde at the Tomb of her Grandchildren* (1858), was painted in the studio of Louis De Taeye. Clotilde, a Burgundian princess, married King Clovis and had three sons with him. After the death of her eldest son, she took care of her two grandchildren. Her two remaining sons, jealous of the attention lavished on the grandchildren, had them murdered. Gregory of Tours relates: 'Queen Clotilde placed the two small corpses on a bier and followed them in funeral procession to the church of Saint Peter, grieving her heart out as the psalms were sung. There she buried them side by side. One was ten years old and the other only seven.'[19] The painting shows Clotilde weeping over the children's grave.

Alma-Tadema left De Taeye's studio in 1858 and returned briefly to his family in Leeuwarden, before joining the studio of Henri Leys (1815–69). The following year, his mother and sister moved to Antwerp to join him, from which point he sought to establish himself among the artistic community of the city. Belgian art education followed a traditional pattern of apprenticeship as students progressed from the Academy to the studio of a recognized painter. Alma-Tadema had already studied with De Taeye and now was fortunate enough to be accepted by Leys into one of the most highly regarded studios in Belgium. Leys was a Romanticist-historical painter, who had himself studied at the Antwerp Academy and under Delacroix in Paris. Leys's works took the form of group compositions in architectural settings. He drew inspiration from seventeenth-century Dutch genre scenes and, after a journey to Germany in the 1850s, also from old German masters and the Nazarenes (a group of artists who formed a brotherhood in 1809 and sought to revive the principles of German religious art), influences which added a sharp, linear quality to his work. His historical and historical genre subjects tend to draw on local history: *Flemish Wedding in the Seventeenth Century* (1839), *Entry of the Duke of Anjou into Antwerp* (1840) and *Albert Dürer Visiting Antwerp 1520* (1855). Among his pupils were Jean-Jacques Tissot, Joseph Lies, Victor Lagye and Ferdinand and Henri de Braekeleer, all destined to become successful artists. Like Alma-Tadema, each was to forge a distinctive artistic personality, but all began their careers with historical and genre painting in the traditional Dutch-Flemish mould.

Leys attributed great importance to precision of historical detail. As a studio assistant, Alma-Tadema was required to paint a table in Leys's *Luther and the Three Reformers*. Dissatisfied with the result, Leys declared: 'that is not my idea of a Gothic table; it ought to be so constructed that everyone knocks his knees to pieces on it.'[20] Accordingly, Alma-Tadema repainted the table to conform to Leys's historically authentic specifications.

In 1861 Alma-Tadema completed his first major painting, a Merovingian subject entitled *The Education of the Children of Clovis* (Pl.5).[21] Although criticized by Leys, who famously compared the marble to cheese,[22] the painting excited much critical attention when exhibited at the Artistic Congress in Antwerp. It was purchased by the Antwerp Society for the Encouragement of the Fine Arts and won in a lottery by King Leopold of Belgium. The subject predates *Clotilde at the Tomb of her Grandchildren* and shows the queen watching her own children being trained in throwing axes. Her design is that they should avenge the murder of her parents by Gondobald, king of the Burgundians. The painting shows a small boy aiming an axe at a wooden target while his younger brother waits his turn. Alma-Tadema deviates from his source – in Gregory of Tours's *History of the Franks* (III.6), Clotilde summoned her three adult sons to do battle with the murderers of her parents – and imagines an earlier scene not described in the text.

Set in clear daylight and using bright, bold colours, the painting challenges any prejudicial notion of the 'Dark Ages'. White marble columns are surmounted by elaborate capitals, a decorative frieze borders the room, painted decoration defines the door, and a marble floor sparkles under foot. The group of onlookers wear bright colours, their gowns are edged with rich embroidery, and their polished armour gleams in the sun. And yet we must remember that despite its cheerful air, the underlying theme of the painting is bloody revenge: it is significant that the solidly wooden and roughly hewn axe target stands out sharply against a background of smooth marble.

In the upper right-hand corner, we catch a glimpse of bright blue sky, while on the left the eye is drawn out of the main building, past greenery, to an architectural structure and blue sky beyond. The device of leading the viewer through an interior to an exterior beyond is characteristic of Dutch painting of the seventeenth century. First used here by Alma-Tadema, this conscious debt to the Dutch tradition was to become a trademark found in many of his works. It is interesting to note that in the same year Leys produced a comparable painting, *The Education of Charles V*, a much grander subject, in which Erasmus, surrounded by the court, instructs the young king in the cathedral at Ghent. The subjects are diametrically opposed: Charles is schooled in humanist learning and the children of Clovis in armed combat. Is Alma-Tadema hinting at an ironic contrast with Leys's painting or is he making a comment on the nature of royal education in general? As we shall see, irony will become a prominent feature in his later works. The painting may even be credited with some personal significance given that Alma-Tadema and Leys were pupil and teacher. Theirs appears to have been an uneasy relationship: Leys's attested comments on his pupil's works are, after all, markedly negative.

Between 1859 and 1862 Alma-Tadema spent much of his time assisting Leys with a series of frescoes for the Hôtel de Ville, Antwerp, depicting the history of the Low Countries, an ambitious project which was never completed. He also worked on *The Institution of the Golden Fleece* which was Leys's principal exhibit at the London International Exhibition of 1862. At the age of twenty-five, his art training nearly at an end, Alma-Tadema decided to travel; in 1861 he visited Germany, and the following year, London. After a period of training which had lasted almost ten years, he was now technically accomplished and on the way to forming his own style. After the success of *The Education of the Children of Clovis*, he was in a position to earn a living as an independent artist and on his return from London he left Leys's studio to establish himself alone.

The newly independent artist continued his exploration of Merovingian history with *Venantius Fortunatus Reading his Poems to Radegonda VI: AD 555* (Pl.6). Venantius Fortunatus, like Gregory of Tours, was a contemporary historian of Merovingian Gaul. Born near Treviso, he studied in Ravenna and travelled to Gaul in AD 564–5. He later settled in Poitiers where he became close friends with Saint Radegonda. Radegonda was captured by the Merovingian king, Lothar, during his conquest of Thuringia in 530 and made his wife. She fled after Lothar's murder of her brother, was consecrated by Saint Medard at Noyons and founded a religious community at Poitiers. Venantius Fortunatus became bishop of Poitiers and concentrated on writing poetry about his religious community. A number of his verses are dedicated to Radegonda and to her abbess, Agnes. The painting shows a reclining Fortunatus declaiming his poems to the two seated women: Agnes and Radegonda.

Alma-Tadema turned to more dynastic intrigue with *Queen Fredegonda at the Death-Bed of Bishop Praetextatus* (1864) and *The Death of Galswintha AD 567* (1865). Fredegonda was the wife of King Chilperic, the grandson of Clovis. She had a reputation for single-minded pursuit of power and married Chilperic only a few days after the death of his first wife, Galswintha, murdered on Chilperic's own order. This subject evidently held a fascination for Alma-Tadema: he was to return to it ten years later in a set of three watercolours entitled *The Tragedy of an Honest Wife* (Pl.7). In the first, Fredegonda watches the marriage of Chilperic and Galswintha, the second

5
The Education of the Children of Clovis, 1861
Oil on canvas, 127 × 176·8 cm (50 × 69⅝ in)
Private collection

6
Venantius Fortunatus Reading his Poems to Radegonda VI: AD 555, 1862
Oil on canvas, 65 × 83·1 cm (25⅝ × 32¾ in)
Dordrechts Museum, Dordrecht

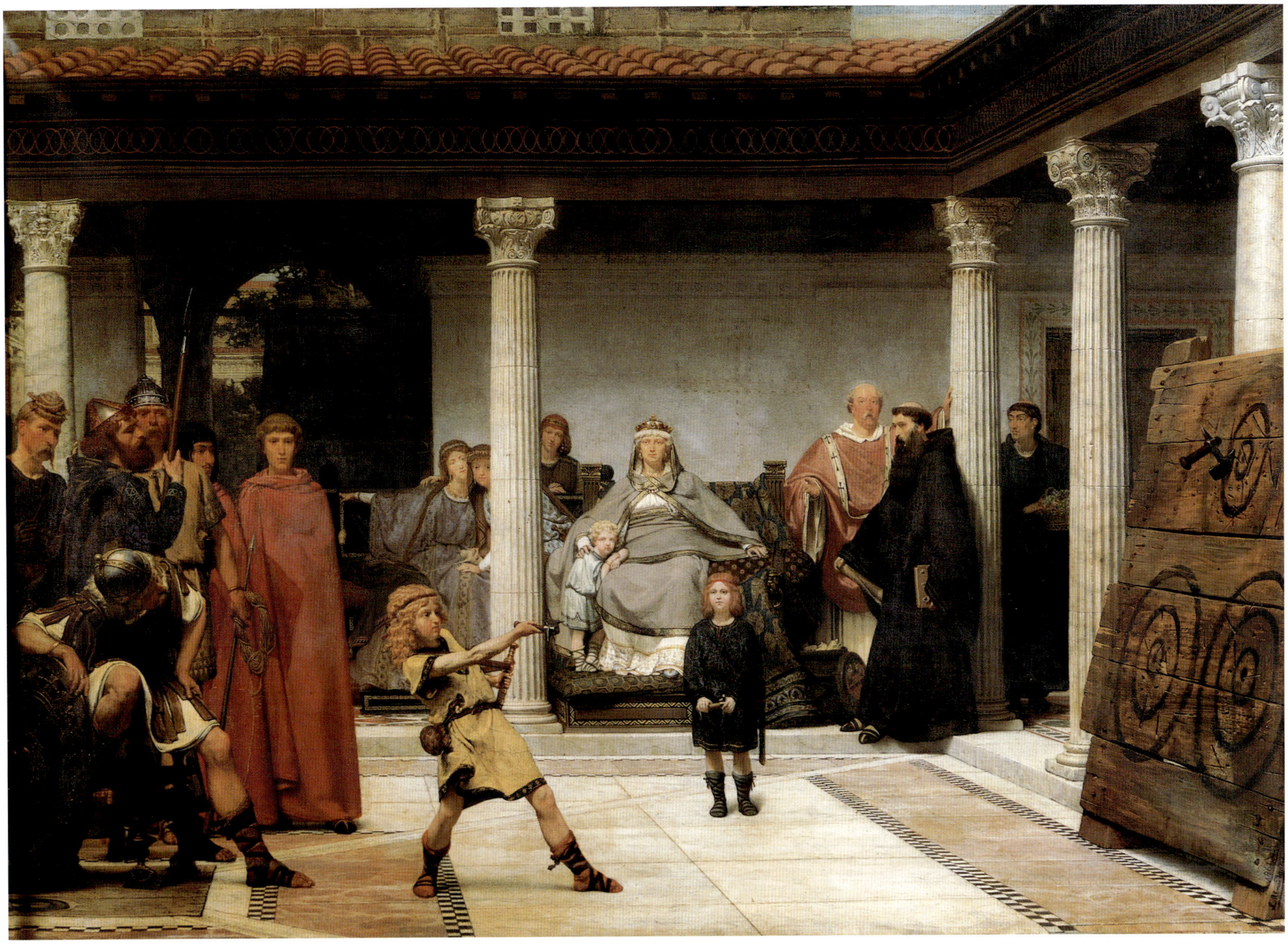

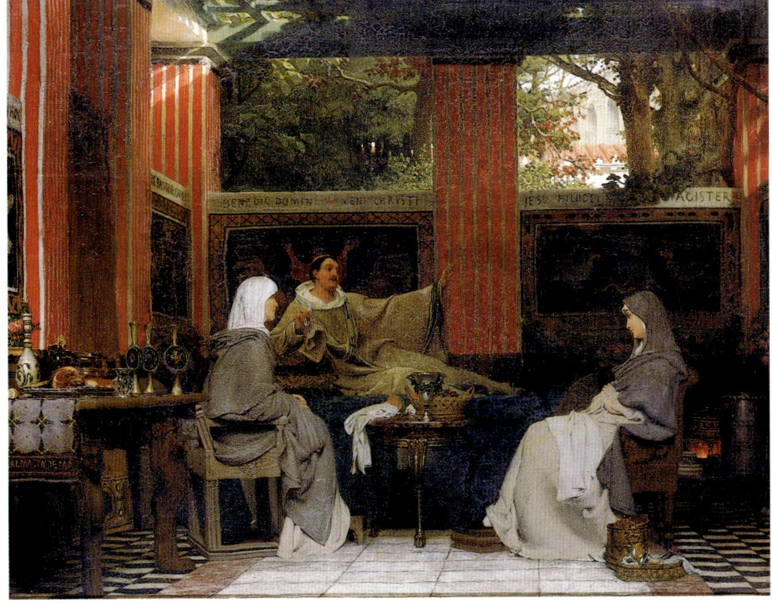

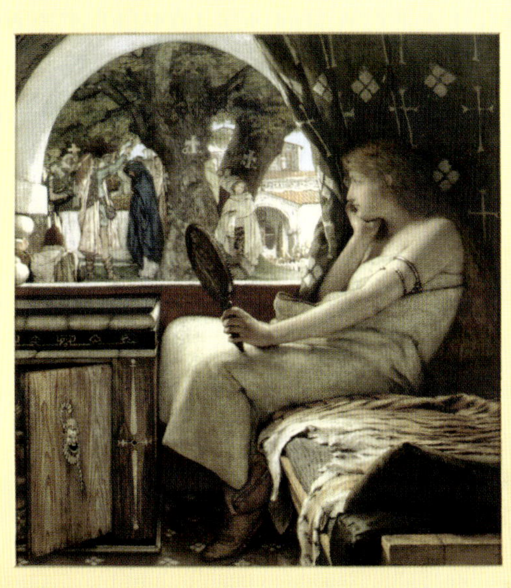

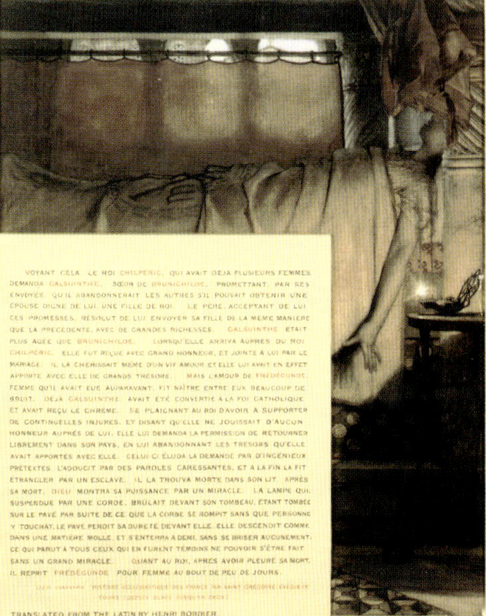

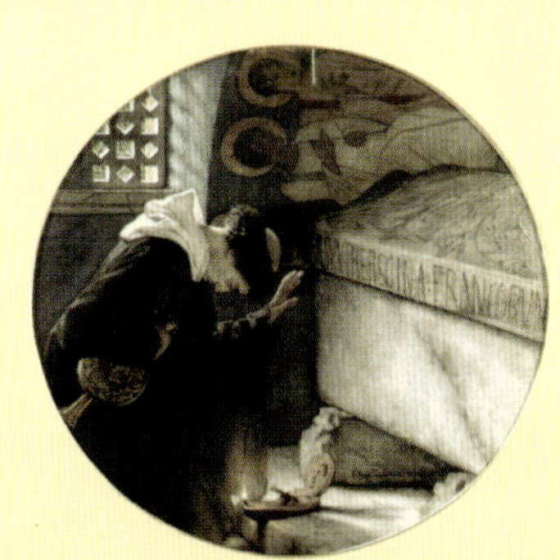

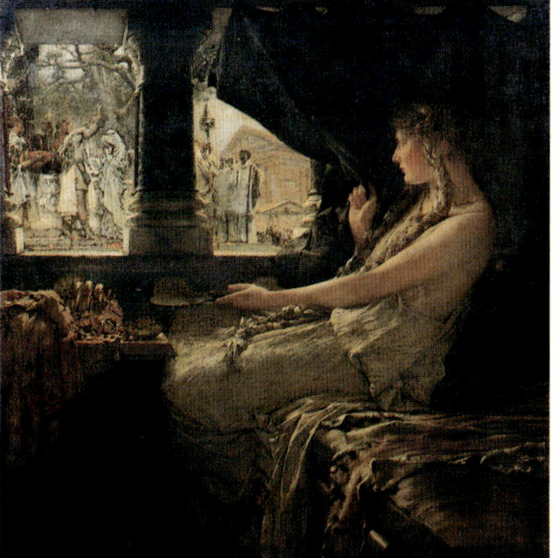

7
The Tragedy of an Honest Wife, 1875
Three watercolours mounted and masked in a frame
Fredegonda, Seated before a Window, Watches Galswintha's Arrival
65·3 × 47·7 cm (25¾ × 18¾ in)
Galswintha on her Deathbed
65·5 × 47·7 cm (25¾ × 18¾ in)
King Chilperic before Galswintha's Tomb, 1875
65·3 × 32·5 cm (25¾ × 12¾ in)
Fogg Art Museum, Harvard University Art Museums, Cambridge MA, Gift of Samuel D. Warren

8
Fredegonda and Galswintha AD 566, 1878
Oil on canvas, 139·8 × 129 cm (55 × 50¾ in)
Gemäldegalerie der Akademie der Bildenden Künste, Vienna

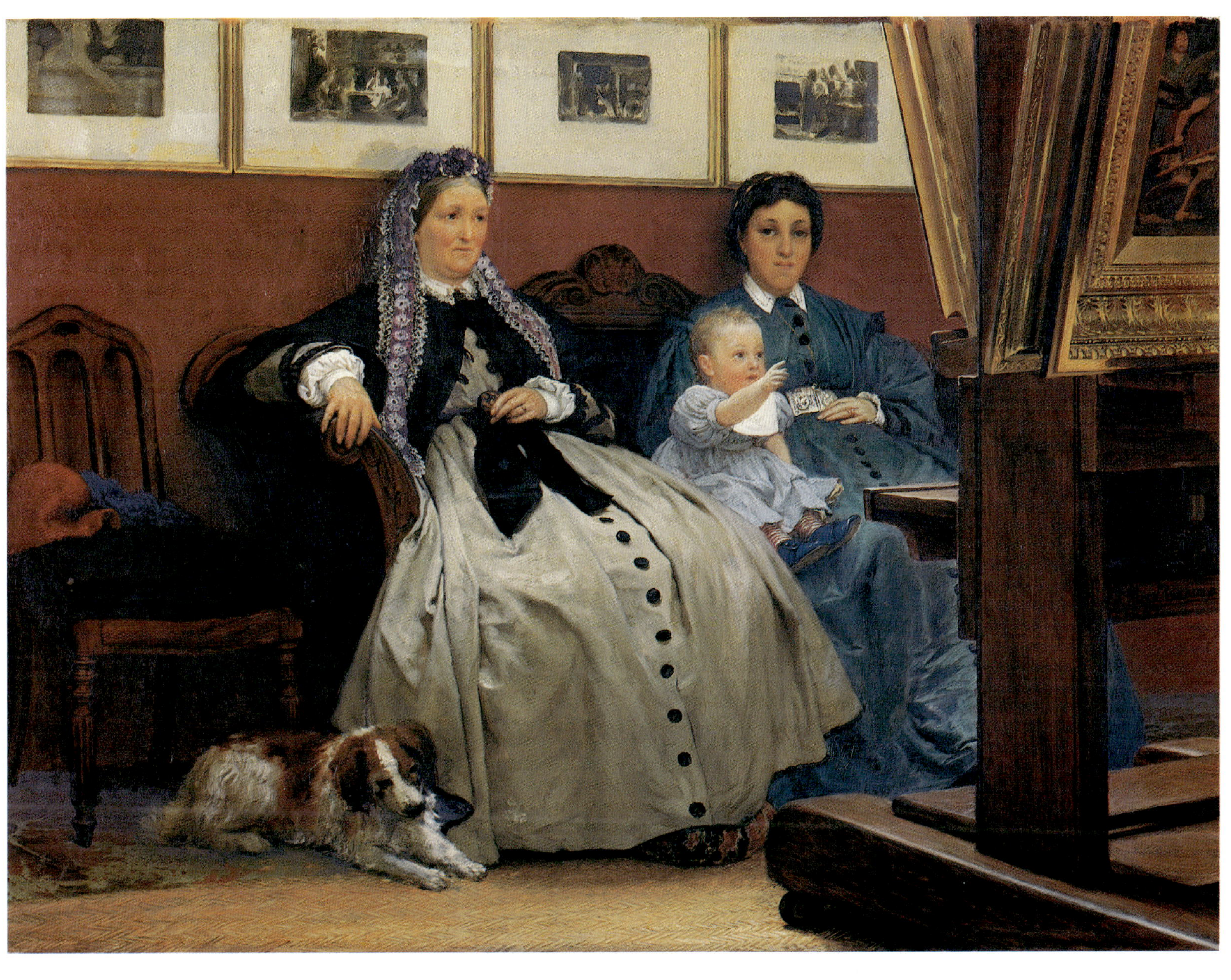

9
My Studio, 1867
Oil on wood, 42·1 × 54 cm ($16\frac{5}{8} \times 21\frac{1}{4}$ in)
Groninger Museum, Groningen

shows Galswintha lying dead, while in the final picture, Chilperic is shown mourning before Galswintha's tomb. A broken cord suspended from the ceiling and a lamp on the floor allude to a miracle described by Gregory of Tours (IV.28), in which a lamp suspended above Galswintha's tomb fell to the floor, but instead of breaking, sank into the ground unharmed. Although the 'honest wife' of the title is Galswintha, the most arresting image from the series is Fredegonda, who, in the first watercolour, is looking out of the window at the marriage of Chilperic to her rival.

In 1878 Alma-Tadema repeated the scene of that first watercolour with an oil painting entitled *Fredegonda and Galswintha AD 567* (Pl.8), which was to prove his last Merovingian subject. The *femme fatale* is an ever-present figure in nineteenth-century art and literature; from Dante Gabriel Rossetti's *Helen of Troy* (1863) to John William Waterhouse's *La Belle Dame Sans Merci* (1893), the cruel and fascinating women of myth and history are paraded endlessly before us, and thus Alma-Tadema's Fredegonda paintings engage with a theme which preoccupies so many painters of his age.

The years 1863–4 mark a turning point in Alma-Tadema's career. His mother died in January 1863, and in September of the same year he married Marie Pauline Gressin Dumoulin de Boisgirard, the daughter of Eugène Gressin, a French journalist living near Brussels. Little is known of Pauline Alma-Tadema. In a published biographical reminiscence in 1909 Alma-Tadema alludes to this period in his life with one laconic sentence: 'I married, in September 1863.'[23] Her portrait appears in *My Studio* (Pl.9) along with the artist's mother-in-law, Madame Gressin-Dumoulin, and the couple's daughter, Laurense. They had two daughters, Laurense, born in 1865 and Anna, two year later. In 1864 a son, Eugène, was born but died a few months later of smallpox.

1863 also saw Alma-Tadema's first trip to Italy, a honeymoon visit with the intention of studying late antique and early medieval visual culture. Alma-Tadema later wrote: 'during my first visit to Italy, at a moment when I was steeped in studies of the Merovingian period, I was mainly preoccupied by the study of early-Christian churches.'[24] While the Italian visit, especially a trip to Pompeii, was to mark a new phase in Alma-Tadema's work,[25] the only painting begun during the holiday was indeed of an early Christian church noted for its mosaics, *Interior of the Church of San Clemente, Rome* (Pl.11). Surprisingly, though, the scene is placed in a contemporary setting, as we gather from the glimpse of a woman in modern dress just disappearing behind one of the columns. Alma-Tadema had avoided travelling scholarships while still a student, and

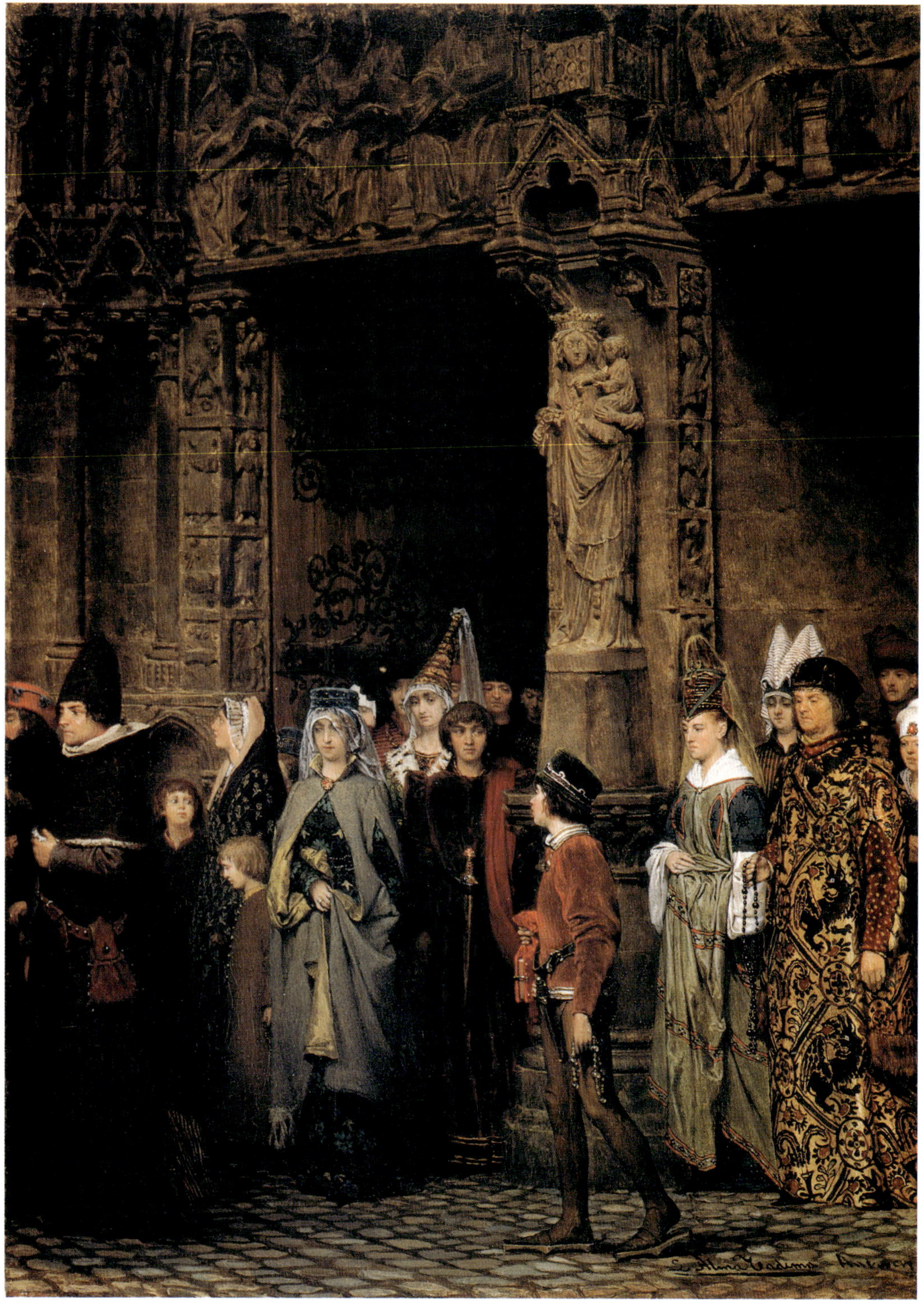

10
Leaving Church in the Fifteenth Century, 1864
Oil on canvas, 57·1 × 39·4 cm (22½ × 15½ in)
Private collection

now his first extended study trip was undertaken at a time when he was well on the way to establishing himself as an independent artist. In later life he consistently maintained the uselessness of study abroad too early in a career:

> With one or two exceptions the Prix de Rome men are not the foremost of their day. Meisonnier, Gérôme, van Leys, remained at home 'till they had become consummate artists. Rembrandt never left Amsterdam, and Rubens, when travelling through Italy, made some sketches after Lionardo da Vinci which might pass as original Rubens, because Rubens was already Rubens when he did them. Vandyck and Velasquez travelled when they were already Vandyck and Velasquez, but not before.[26]

On their return from Italy the couple stopped in Paris, where Alma-Tadema met prominent members of several artistic circles, including Rosa Bonheur (1822–99) and Jean-Léon Gérôme (1824–1904). The work of Gérôme, a painter who distinguished himself with Oriental and classical themes, was to have an influence on Alma-Tadema's own development as an artist. In the same year his fortunes changed dramatically on meeting the Belgian art dealer, Ernest Gambart. Gambart had offices in various European capitals, but was based in England, where he had been presenting European artists to the British public since the 1850s through his French Gallery in Pall Mall. A colourful story accounts for their first meeting. Hearing that Gambart was in Antwerp, Alma-Tadema devised a plan to lure the dealer to his studio. Bound for the house of another artist (sometimes named as Dyckmans, the former Professor at Antwerp Academy), Victor Lagye,[27] a fellow pupil of Leys already exhibiting with Gambart, gave Gambart's coachman Alma-Tadema's address instead. Once he had arrived at the wrong studio, so impressed was Gambart by Alma-Tadema's work that he agreed to purchase a painting on the easel although it was already promised to a buyer. Gambart would, in all probability, already have been aware of the young artist through Rosa Bonheur or through Leys himself, both of whom sold works via the dealer. Whatever the precise character of the encounter with Gambart, it certainly secured Alma-Tadema's future: he was offered a lucrative commission in the form of a contract for twenty-four pictures. The price of his works rose in stages, so that by the time he finished the contract in 1868, each painting earned about £80. Before meeting Gambart, Alma-Tadema had only managed to sell a few works and the largest amount he had received was £64 for *The Education of the Children of Clovis*. Gambart's commission ensured that the artist could now make a comfortable living from his work.

In 1865 the Alma-Tademas moved from Antwerp to Brussels. Brussels was rapidly attracting artists and dealers as an alternative to Paris while at the same time benefiting from a rail link with the French capital. The Brussels Salon was a much larger exhibiting venue than its counterpart in Antwerp, and Alma-Tadema had already had some success there, most notably with *Queen Fredegonda at the Death-Bed of Bishop Praetextatus*, which had been acquired for the tombola of the Triennial Winter Salon of 1864.

Although Alma-Tadema continued to paint Fredegonda until the late 1870s, by the mid-1860s his Merovingian phase was more or less over. The painting that had so impressed Gambart in the artist's studio was *Leaving Church in the Fifteenth Century* (Pl.10), a typical Dutch-Belgian historical genre scene, but his opening commission consisted mostly of Egyptian and Roman pictures. The first of Alma-Tadema's paintings shown by Gambart in London at the Twelfth Annual French and Flemish Exhibition at the French Gallery, Pall Mall, in 1865 were *Birthday Presents in the Sixteenth Century, Pastimes in Ancient Egypt, 3,000 Years Ago* (exhibited under the title, *An Evening Party at Nineveh*) (Pl.14) and *Egyptian Chess Players* (Pl.16): two Egyptian subjects and only one Dutch-Belgian historical painting. Gambart attracted clients from all over Europe as well as Britain, and Merovingian subjects must have seemed very obscure to buyers outside Holland, Belgium or France. It is unknown whether Gambart insisted on subjects which cast a universal appeal or whether Alma-Tadema, influenced by his travels throughout the continent, was eager to expand his repertoire. Whatever the case, the artist, newly allied with an international art dealer, was ready to move away from his Dutch-Belgian origins and to assume a role within European painting.

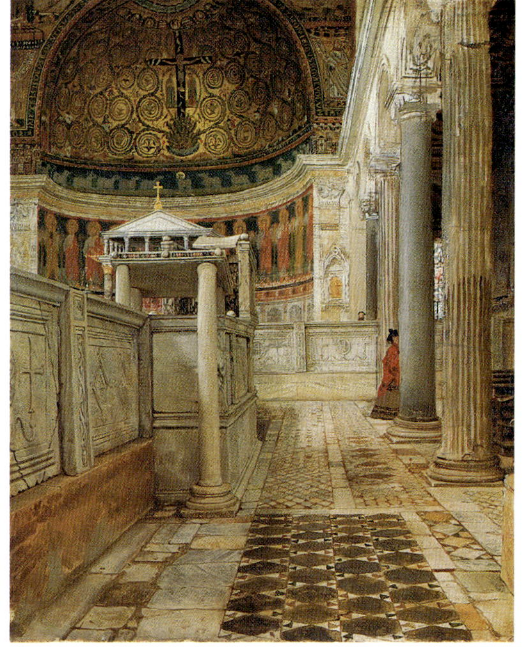

11
Interior of the Church of San Clemente, Rome, 1863
Oil on canvas, 63·5 × 51 cm (25 × 20⅛ in)
Fries Museum, Leeuwarden

1/2
EGYPT

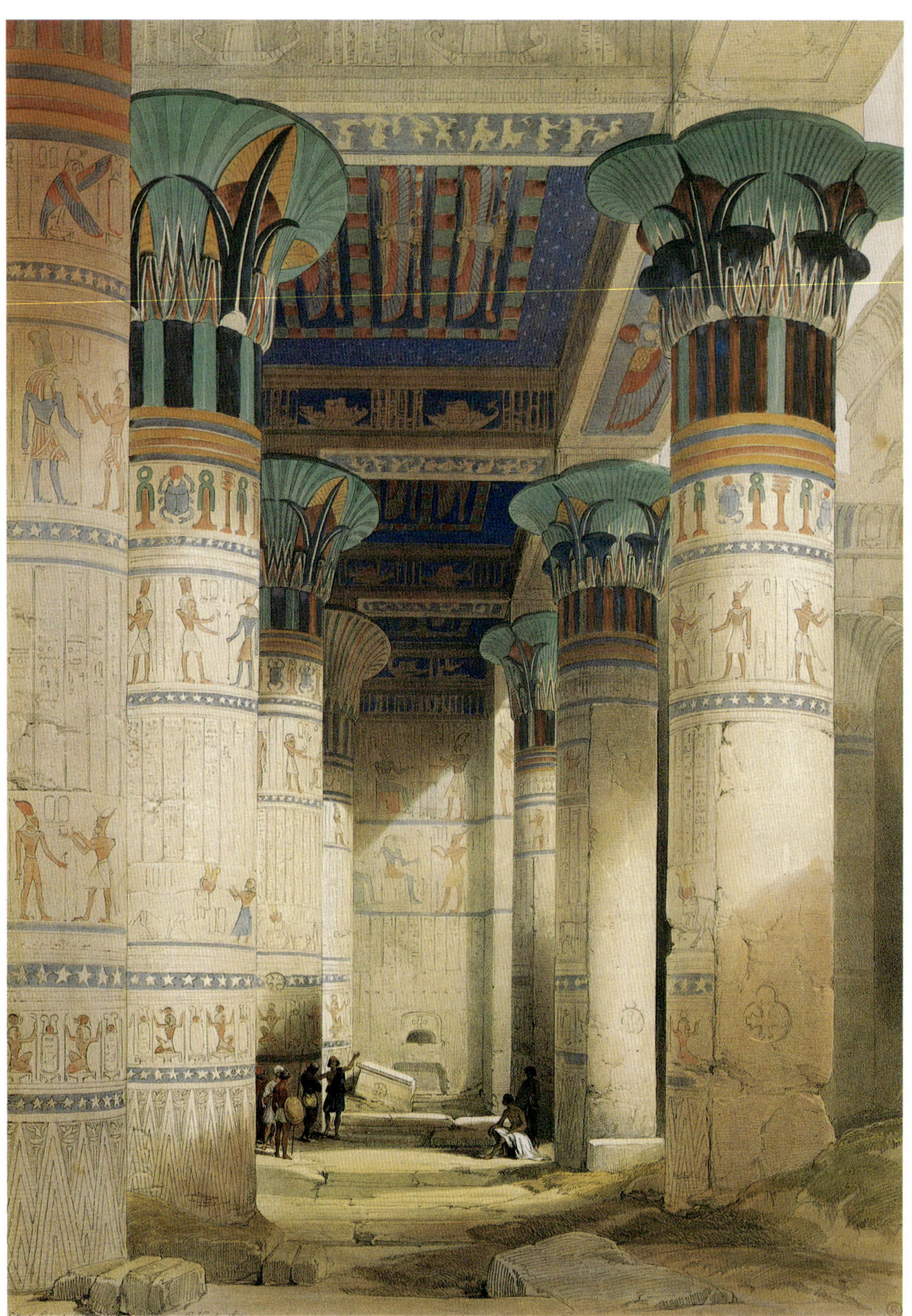

12
David Roberts, *Portico of the Temple of Isis at Philae*, 1851
Oil on canvas, 109·2 × 84·5 cm (43 × 33¼ in)
Private collection

Nineteenth-century theories of artistic progression sited the origins of ancient art in Egypt.[28] Museums displayed ancient sculpture chronologically, often including casts when lacking original pieces, in order to illustrate the whole artistic canon from Egypt to the late Roman Empire. Having turned his attention to the ancient world through Merovingian history, Alma-Tadema now shifted his focus from late to early antiquity, or, in nineteenth-century terms, from the death to the birth of ancient art. Alma-Tadema himself describes his interest in Egyptian subjects in terms of current evolutionary ideas: 'Where else should I have begun ... as soon as I had become acquainted with the life of the ancients? The first thing a child learns of ancient history is about the court of Pharaoh; and if we go back to the source of art and science, must we not return to Egypt?'[29]

In an age of archaeological discovery, Egypt was the focus of much activity. The French occupation of Egypt under Napoleon between 1798 and 1801 marked the beginning of a renewed European interest in Egyptian art and culture and paved the way for systematic excavation and cataloguing. The Napoleonic campaigns also signalled the beginnings of Orientalizing painting by European artists. While some, like Eugène Delacroix (1798–1863), were interested in romantic atmosphere, others, such as Horace Vernet (1789–1863), were preoccupied with realism of contemporary detail. A number of artists sought inspiration by joining the increasing number of Western travellers who journeyed throughout the East. The British artist, David Roberts (1796–1864) (Pl.12), was one of the first painters to visit Egypt independent of an archaeological expedition. Roberts travelled through Egypt and the Middle East in 1838–9, and made enough studies to produce Egyptian landscapes and architectural scenes for the next ten years. Later visitors to the East included British artists David Wilkie (1758–1841), John Frederick Lewis (1805–76), William Holman Hunt (1827–1910), Frederick Goodall (1822–1904) and Jean-Léon Gérôme. In general, these and other Orientalizing painters were concerned with the customs and visual spectacle of a contemporary East or with re-creating biblical scenes in vague landscape settings. In striking contrast, Alma-Tadema's Egypt takes the form of an exploration of social history in archaeologically specific Pharaonic set-

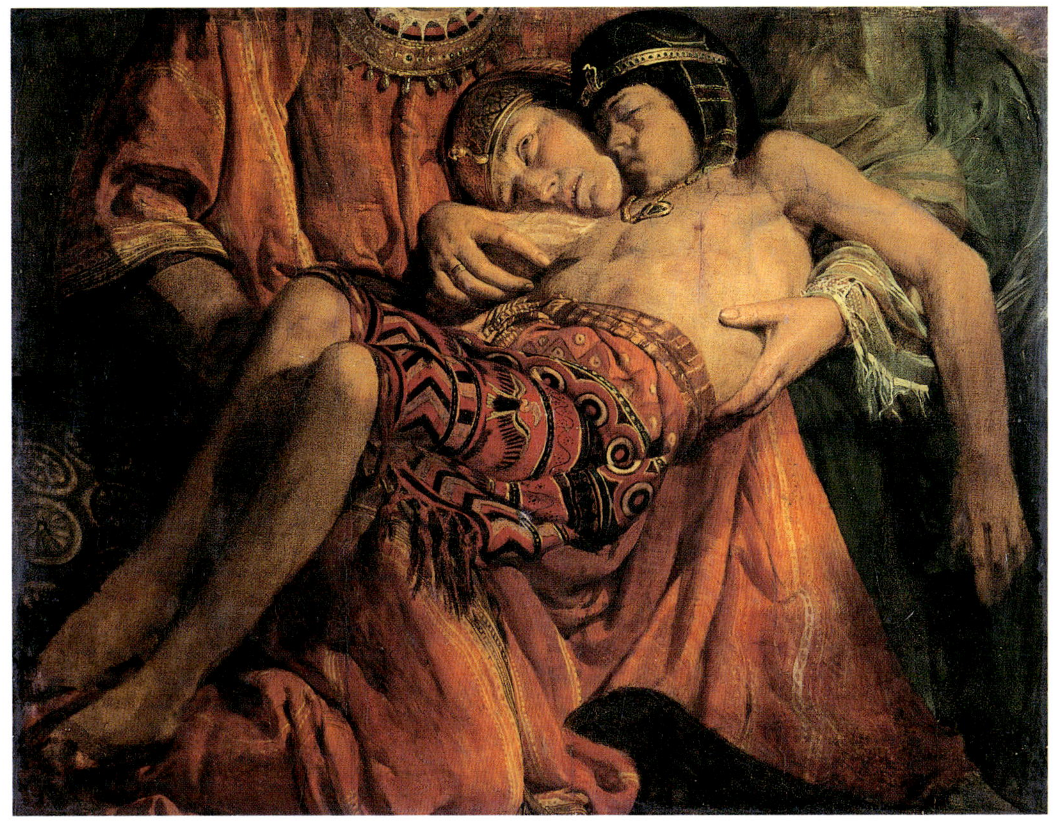

13
The Sad Father, 1859 (fragment)
Oil on canvas, 68·6 × 86.4 cm (27 × 34 in)
Johannesburg Art Gallery

tings. As the young artist strives to create a new approach to his subject, we can see a distinctive artistic personality beginning to emerge. He combines the attention to historical detail found in the paintings of Leys and the Dutch-Belgian historical tradition with a European-wide fascination with Orientalist subjects. From this early stage in his career, a driving force behind Alma-Tadema's work is the desire to present traditional subjects in an innovative manner by drawing on different artistic traditions and manipulating each to suit his purpose.

Alma-Tadema did not visit Egypt until 1902, but he produced his first Egyptian picture, *The Sad Father* (Pl.13), a biblical subject set in a Pharaonic interior, while studying under Leys in Antwerp. Originally a large processional picture in an architectural setting, it was later cut down to a reduced scale showing only three figures.[30] In its fragmentary state, Maarten Raven has identified details as deriving from J. Gardner Wilkinson's influential book, *Manners and Customs of the Ancient Egyptians* (1837).[31] Raven identifies the scarab worn around the neck of the boy from an illustration in Wilkinson.[32] Nevertheless, the scarab is housed in Leiden Museum where the artist may well have seen it for himself. The most influential Dutch Egyptologist of the nineteenth century, Conradus Leemans (1809–93), became Director of Leiden Museum in 1839 where he organized the collection and published a systematic catalogue. It has been assumed by modern art historians that Alma-Tadema was heavily reliant on Wilkinson for his information, yet, given that his library includes a number of Egyptological publications, it is likely that he was collecting information as well as visiting local museums and collections as early as the late 1850s.

Emile de Meester de Ravenstein (1813–89) was a prominent Belgian collector of Egyptian artefacts; he donated his collection to the Musée Royal in Brussels in 1884, although it was most probably available to scholars and artists before this date. Another possible source of inspiration to the artist was the Egyptian temple in Antwerp Zoo, built by Charles Servais in 1855–6 and based on the styles of temples at Philae and Dendera. In 1862 Alma-Tadema was in London and able to witness both the Crystal Palace (inaugurated in 1851) and the British Museum. The Crystal Palace sported the magnificent Egyptian court created by the architect Owen Jones and the Egyptologist Joseph Bonomi. They constructed models of Egyptian monuments ranging from the Pharaonic, Ptolemaic and Roman periods. The British Museum, moreover, housed an impressive Egyptian collection including pieces gathered by Napoleon and confiscated in 1801 when Anglo-Ottoman forces expelled the French, as well as new finds.

After his visit to London, the artist completed his first major Egyptian picture, *Pastimes in Ancient Egypt, 3,000 Years Ago* (Pl.14). In an undated letter to Henry Holiday, Alma-Tadema recalls the complicated history of this painting:

> The picture was painted in 1863 & had its success in Brussels that year. Then the figures were all in white & the background open and in full colour. It was exhibited then under the title of *How people enjoyed themselves 3,000 years ago.*

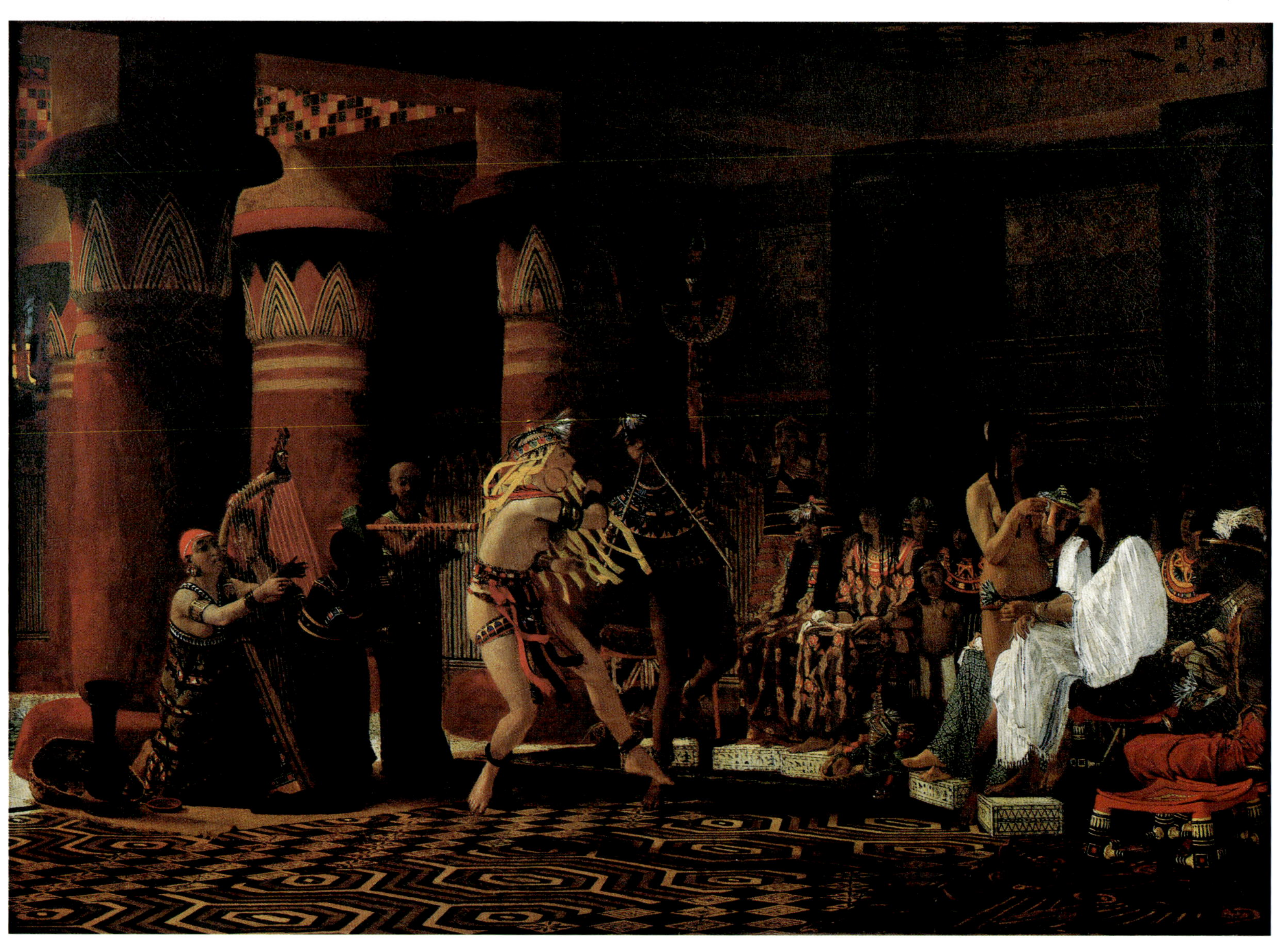

14
Pastimes in Ancient Egypt 3,000 Years Ago, 1863
Oil on canvas, 99·1 × 135·8 cm (39 × 53½ in)
Harris Museum and Art Gallery, Preston

15 opposite
Copy of a wall painting from the tomb of Nebamun in the British Museum, London, 1860s
Pencil on paper, 8.9 × 14.6 cm (3½ × 5¾ in)
University of Birmingham

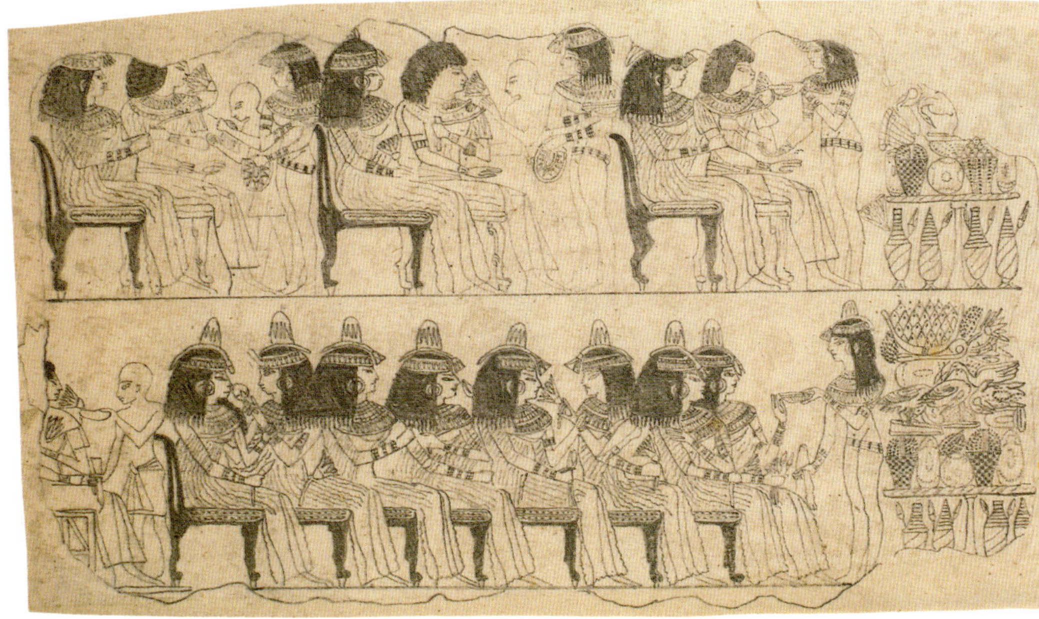

I repainted it as it is now & sent it to the Paris Salon in 1864 under the title of *The 18th Dynasty*, and had the gold medal for it. Gambart bought it in 1865, and exhibited it in the French Gallery in that year [as *An Evening Party at Nineveh*]. In 1866 it was very much damaged in the great gas explosion in Gambart's house 62 Avenue Road. It was restored and touched up by myself.[33]

The artist must have repaired the damage by 1867, as in that year the painting was awarded a second-class medal in the Paris Exposition Universelle. The excellent reviews and awards it elicited helped to consolidate Alma-Tadema's European reputation.

The subject is described in some detail by a contemporary critic:

It is intended to represent an entertainment given in honour of a Nubian ambassador, who is seated in front, and to whom an Egyptian slave is offering some beverage in a cup: on his right, amidst a group of young people, is the host, a priest, named Phtames, the scribe of the great house of the god Phta, at Memphis, whose name appears on the furniture and walls: behind the priest, a little to his right hand, is his standard-bearer: the name of the priest is taken from the column of his tomb, now in the Museum of Leyden. The other leading figures in the composition – musicians and dancers – speak for themselves. The presence of the mummy, in the background on the extreme right, invites the company to be merry, according to the principles of the ancient Egyptians.[34]

The same critic goes on to state that the whole scene 'was suggested by a wall-painting in the British Museum, that M. Alma-Tadema saw there when he visited London in 1862'. The wall painting cited is surely one of a group of eleven paintings from an unidentified tomb from Thebes – often called the tomb of Nebamun – dating from the Eighteenth Dynasty (roughly 3,500 years ago).[35] A number of these paintings were reproduced by the artist in the form of watercolours and sketches (Pl.15). The painting which influenced *Pastimes in Ancient Egypt* shows female entertainers at a banquet scene. Alma-Tadema imitates these female entertainers in the form of the dancers at the centre of his picture. As in the wall paintings, they both wear elaborate collars and head gear while one plays the double flute.

Other details include a harp copied from the Louvre and a chair from the British Museum. A wall painting in the background showing Phtames praying to his ancestors is suggested by the representation of Thutmose I in the room of his ancestors in the Bibliothèque Nationale, Paris, and, like the tomb of Nebamun, dates from the Eighteenth Dynasty. While many of these artefacts have been identified by Maarten Raven as being represented in Wilkinson's *Manners and Customs of the Ancient Egyptians*,[36] they may also have been witnessed by the artist at first-hand during his trips to London and Paris. The precision of archaeological detail relating to the notional date of the scene functions on two levels: as Alma-Tadema had been taught by Leys, archaeologically accurate settings reassure the viewer of historical authenticity and support the notion that we really are presented with a glimpse of ancient life rather than costumed models and studio props. At the same time, references to artefacts in public museums would be familiar to a knowledgeable public and thus the identification of each source becomes an intellectual challenge for the learned viewer. Alma-Tadema painted two versions of his subject: the second smaller version (1867–8) has only a few changes in decorative detail and bears the inscription 'to my friend Andrew Gow'. Gow was a British artist who specialized in historical, genre and military subjects.

In order to understand Alma-Tadema's Egyptian paintings, it will be helpful to consider modern debates surrounding Orientalism. Edward Said's influential *Orientalism* (1978) sees the Western notion of the East as the 'Other' and its expression in nineteenth-century art and literature as a construction emblematic of Western domination. This problematizing has been challenged by John M. Mackensie's *Orientalism: History, Theory and the Arts* (1995) in which the complexity of Western approaches to the East is acknowledged and interpreted as a welcoming celebration of historical parallelism and familiarity. Just as modern notions of nineteenth-century Orientalizing pose these starkly alternative

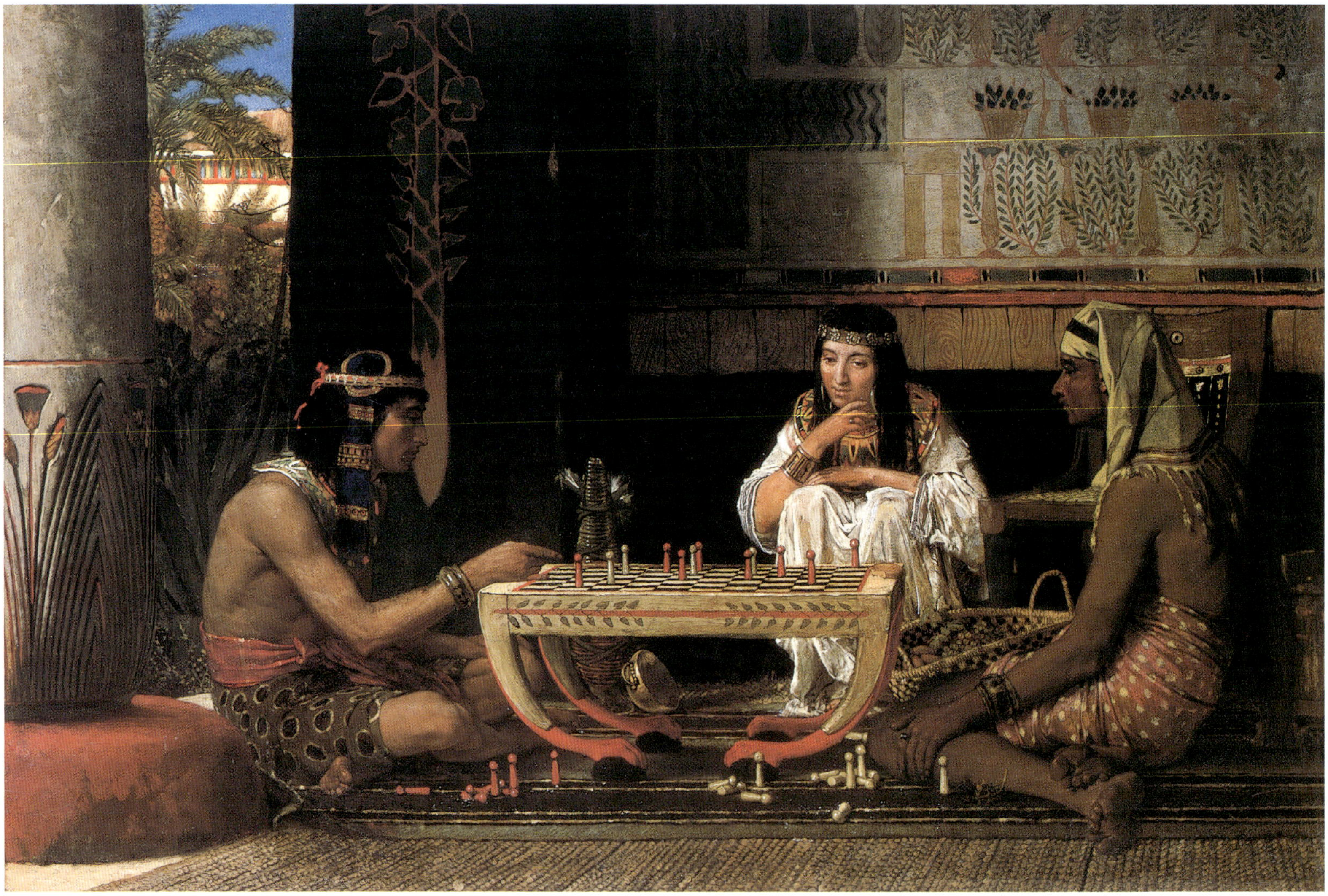

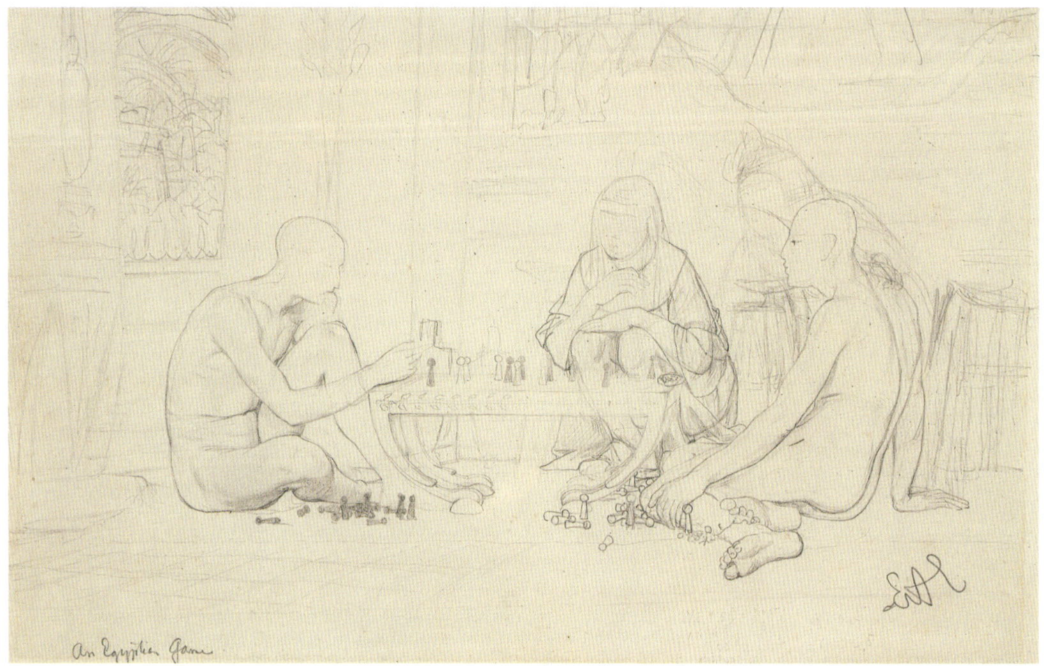

16
Egyptian Chess Players, 1865
Oil on wood, 39·8 × 55·8 cm ($15\frac{5}{8} \times 22$ in)
Private collection

17
Egyptian Chess Players, 1865
Pencil on paper, 25 × 35 cm ($9\frac{7}{8} \times 13\frac{3}{4}$ in)
Rijksmuseum, Amsterdam

views, so nineteenth-century Orientalism itself embraces opposing concepts of the East. On the one hand, Egypt is exotic, dangerous and the purveyor of sexual possibility (as seen in, for example, numerous harem paintings); on the other, Egyptianizing motifs proliferate in European domestic buildings and furniture design, and pyramids, obelisks and hieroglyphic inscriptions become part of private funerary monuments from Père Lachaise to Kensal Green.

Pastimes in Ancient Egypt is remarkable in that it reconciles exoticism and domesticization: the inclusion of the word 'pastimes' in the title reassures us of sameness, while, at the same time, the subtitle, 'three thousand years ago', sets up distance. The painting itself is a genre scene of everyday life, but everyday life in an unfamiliar and exotic setting. Alma-Tadema's next Egyptian painting, *Egyptian Chess Players* (Pl.16), another genre scene, is much more intimate: it shows three figures seated around a low table playing *senet*, a board game comparable to modern chess. A preparatory drawing for the painting (Pl.17) was given by the artist to his friend, the Dutch art critic and writer, Carel Vosmaer. Despite his concern with the archaeological setting of decorated walls and pillar in the painting, the sketch concentrates on figure drawing and leaves the background indistinct. Alma-Tadema continued his exploration of Egyptian themes with *An Egyptian at his Doorway* (1865), *The Mummy in the Roman Period* (1867) and *Grand Chamberlain to Sesostris the Great* (1869).

Egypt, meanwhile, continued to fuel the European imagination. The Exposition Universelle of 1867 in Paris contained two Egyptianizing pavilions: the Pavilion de l'Isthme de Suez and the more scholarly Temple Egyptien inspired by the western temple at Philae. With the opening of the Suez canal in 1869, the East afforded greater accessibility to Western travellers. On a more personal level, Alma-Tadema was influenced by his friendship with Georg Moritz Ebers (1837–98) who became Professor of Egyptology in Leipzig in 1870. He was both an academic Egyptologist and a popular historical novelist who presented his stories in accurate ancient settings, often with full footnotes citing ancient texts and modern authorities. *An Egyptian Princess*, Ebers's most celebrated work, published in German in 1864, had by 1928 sold 400,000 copies in sixteen languages. It is uncertain when the two men first met, but in 1878 Ebers dedicated his novel, *Homo Sum* (set in the fourth century AD), to Alma-Tadema, while a number of Alma-Tadema's paintings were included as illustrations in Ebers's *Egypt: Descriptive, Historical, and Picturesque* (London 1881, published in German, Leipzig 1879–80). Alma-Tadema also contributed a drawing entitled *Paulus und Hermes discus werfend* ('Paul and Hermes throwing a discus') depicting a scene from *Homo Sum* to *The Ebers Gallery* (a book illustrating Ebers's fictional works).[37] The friendship between the two men lasted until Ebers's death in 1898.

Significantly, parallels can be drawn between the work of the two men. The philosopher Friedrich Nietzsche was said to have once described Ebers as regaling 'his readers with the daughters of Leipzig professors in Egyptian dress.'[38] This same charge has, more recently, been levelled against Alma-Tadema.[39] Although these judgements represent the historicities of both as frivolous, in point of fact, each offers a curious and often highly novel combination of the imaginary and the scholarly. Alma-Tadema introduces archaeological data into his paintings and Ebers peppers his popular fiction with erudite footnotes and even allows imaginary conjecture in his academic publications. Such methods suggest that both men sought to reveal an antiquity based on ancient sources rather than on modern fantasies and preconceptions.

Alma-Tadema continued painting Egyptian subjects until the mid-1870s, but by this time popular Orientalizing themes of harems, odalisques and naked slave girls embraced the East as a repository of erotic freedoms. To show how far Alma-Tadema distanced himself from this eroticization of Egyptian subjects, it will be useful to compare two paintings on a similar subject: Alma-Tadema's *Egyptian Chess Players* and Jean-Léon Gérôme's *Almehs Playing Chess* (Pl.18). Both are intimate scenes of individuals absorbed in the game, but whereas Alma-Tadema's painting is of a group of two men and a female spectator, Gérôme's shows two women. The title, *Almehs Playing Chess*, adds an erotic frisson absent in Alma-Tadema's painting. Almehs were female entertainers or 'belly-dancers', and the painting of these women enjoying their free time recalls Toulouse-Lautrec's paintings later in the century which show prostitutes waiting between clients. Alma-Tadema's preoccupations are, on any reckoning, quite different. Shortly after his first Egyptian phase in the mid-1860s, he turned to the classical past and to the Roman subjects which were to dominate his œuvre for the rest of his career.

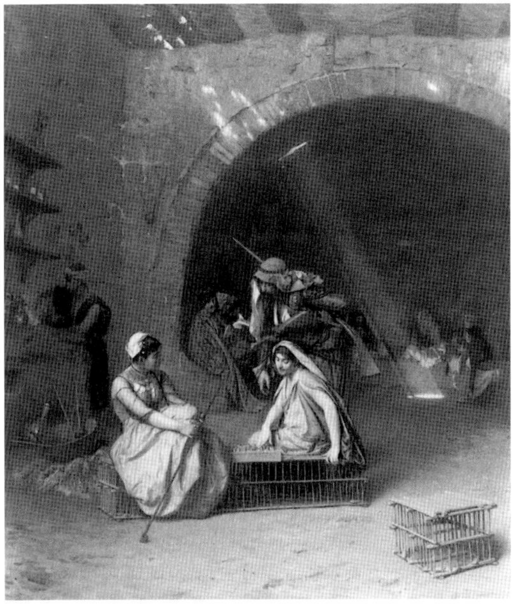

18
Jean-Léon Gérôme, *Almehs Playing Chess*
Oil on canvas, 63·4 × 53·3 cm (25 × 21 in)
Private collection

1/3

POMPEII

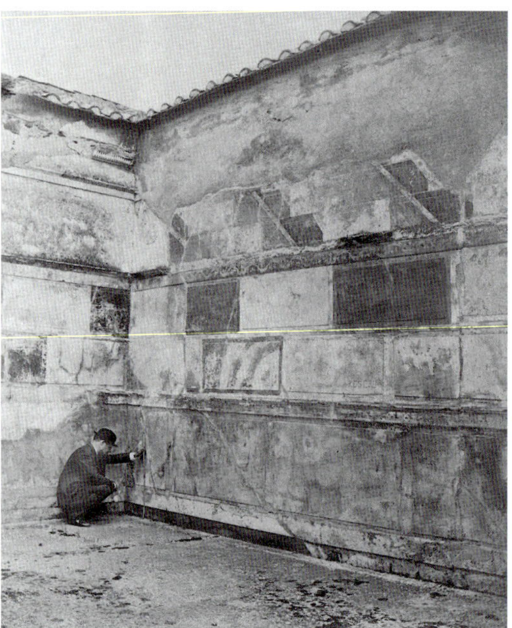

19
Lawrence Alma-Tadema in the House of Sallust, Pompeii, 1862–3
University of Birmingham

The artist had already experimented with classical subjects while studying under Leys (as seen with the Greek mythological painting, *The Death of Hippolytus*, and a Roman historical canvas, *Marius on the Ruins of Carthage*), but from 1865 the representation of Roman genre scenes presented in settings of a broadly Pompeian cast predominated. The first of these Roman subjects, *Gallo-Roman Women* (Pl.20), was painted in Antwerp before the family's move to Brussels. As with the Merovingian subjects, the title places this scene in late-antique Gaul; however, in direct contrast to Merovingian-centred history, this painting shows a Romanized Gaul. Two richly dressed and bejewelled women, posed in intimate conversation, lean over a marble parapet. Leisured women in couples or groups and the juxtaposition of dark and fair models was to become a familiar formula.

The impetus behind Alma-Tadema's change to Roman subjects has long been cited as his honeymoon visit to Italy in 1863. The rediscovery of the Roman towns of Herculaneum in 1738 and Pompeii in 1748, both buried by the eruption of Mount Vesuvius in AD 79, provided the modern world with a unique view of antiquity. Both sites yielded not just a plethora of art objects – wall paintings, mosaics, statues, statuettes and decorative items – but a glimpse of domestic life in a provincial town. At Herculaneum, submerged in a torrent of mud which hardened to tufa, the preservation of timber (burned at Pompeii) even allowed a new understanding of the construction of a Roman house.

Alma-Tadema's visit to the sites coincided with the beginning of the first systematic excavations under Giuseppe Fiorelli. Fiorelli, as director of excavations at Pompeii between 1860 and 1875, carefully surveyed the site before digging commenced, and excavation, which had formerly been only of individual houses, was now of entire blocks. Excavations unearthed a wealth of information relating to the ordinary life of the ancient Romans. Fiorelli also supervised the excavation of Herculaneum between 1869 and 1875, although large-scale excavations did not begin until the twentieth century. During this exciting period of archaeological activity, Fiorelli himself, Heinrich Nissen and other scholars brought out important publications. In 1873 August Mau transformed the study of Roman wall painting with a classification of the different phases in painted decoration.[40] Excavations at Pompeii continued throughout the 1880s and the 1890s, and some of the most significant finds, including wall paintings in the House of the Vettii and a superb collection of silver plate at a country house near Boscoreale, were not uncovered until the end of the century.[41]

Although the itinerary of Alma-Tadema's Italian trip had been chosen with the purpose of studying the visual remains of late antiquity, his experiences of classical Rome, and Pompeii in particular, are often described as a kind of epiphany. His biographer, Percy Cross Standing, explained: 'For him the ugliness and pitiless squalor of Merovingia's history – of cloistered queens and slaughtered kings – as in a flash began to make itself manifest ... He would no more of it; of that he became most speedily convinced. To him henceforward the classic school should be dedicate.'[42] While the artist was content to have his adoption of classical subjects elucidated in terms of the new revelation of Roman art, of equal importance are his trips to London and Paris and his subsequent entry into cosmopolitan art circles. Whereas his Merovingian subjects would be of relevance to only a local audience, representations of a classical past cast an appeal even wider than paintings of Egypt. Orientalist subjects were a relatively recent addition to the European artist's œuvre but Greek and Roman subjects looked back to a high art tradition inherited from the Renaissance and to a universally recognized classical past.

Romano-Pompeian genre scenes had been popularized by the works of French Néo-Grec artists. Following Jean-Dominique Ingres's representation of a Pompeian-type interior in *Antiochus and Stratonice* (1840), throughout the late 1840s and 1850s, Néo-Grec artists (mostly pupils of Paul Delaroche and Charles Gleyre, including Jean-Léon Gérôme, Gustave Boulanger (Pl.21), Jean-Louis Hamon and Henri-Pierre Picou), began to concentrate on scenes from daily Roman life within precise archaeological settings inspired by finds from Pompeii and Herculaneum. Comparisons can be made between the work of Alma-Tadema and Gérôme, in particular, although Alma-Tadema was to go on and transform the type of classical genre painting pioneered by the French artist.[43] From the mid to late 1860s British artists also began to produce Roman genre subjects.[44] Gambart, acutely aware of artistic currents throughout the continent, may well have contributed to Alma-Tadema's change in subject:

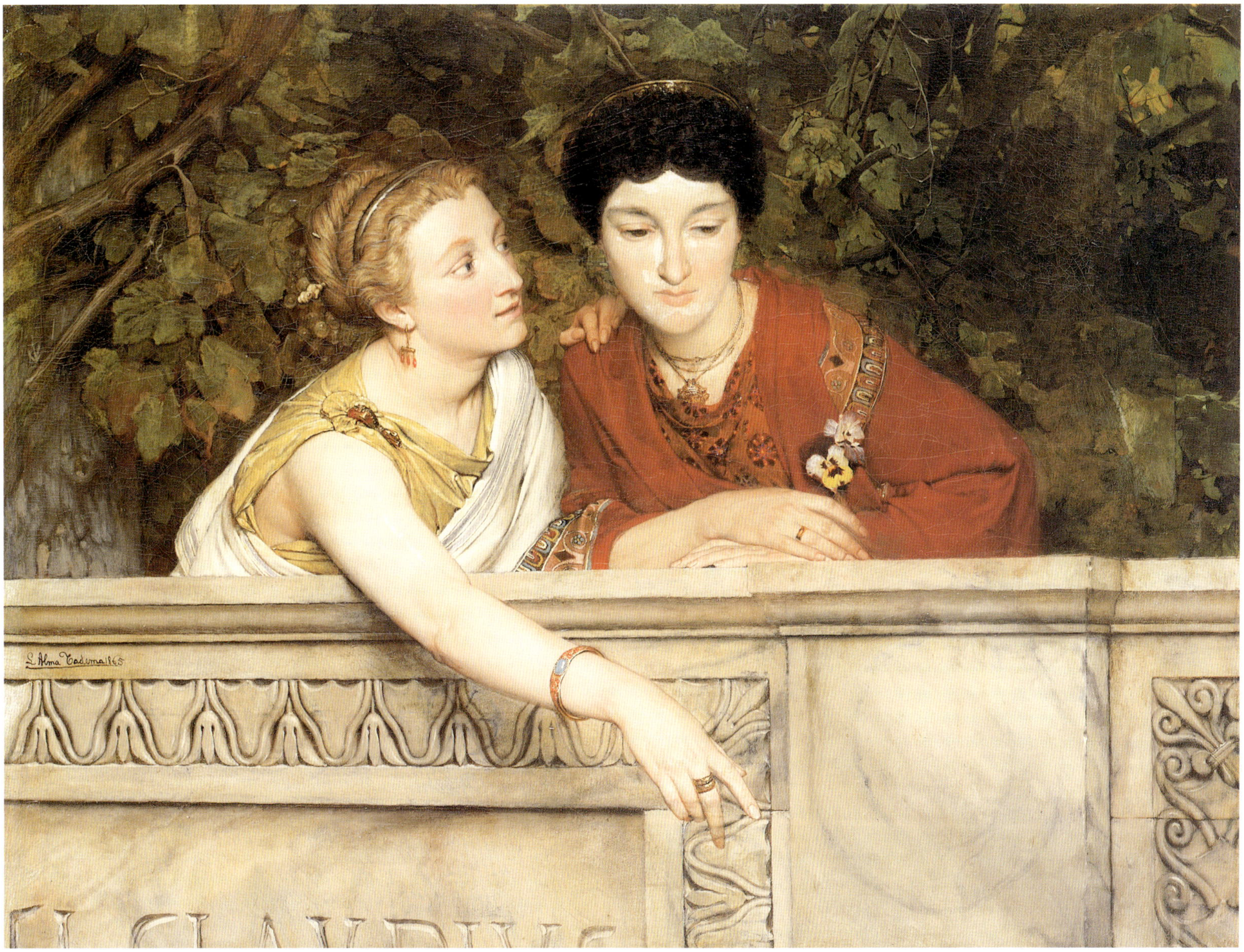

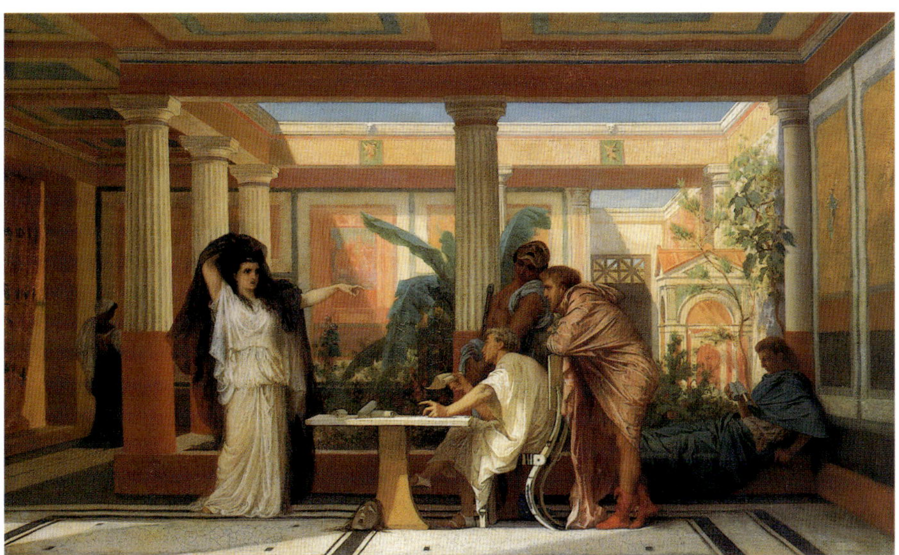

20
Gallo-Roman Women, 1865
Oil on canvas, 80·6 × 101·6 cm (31¾ × 40 in)
Private collection

21
Gustave Boulanger, *The Rehearsal in the House of the Tragic Poet*, 1855
Oil on canvas, 48 × 76 cm (18⅞ × 30 in)
State Hermitage Museum, St Petersburg

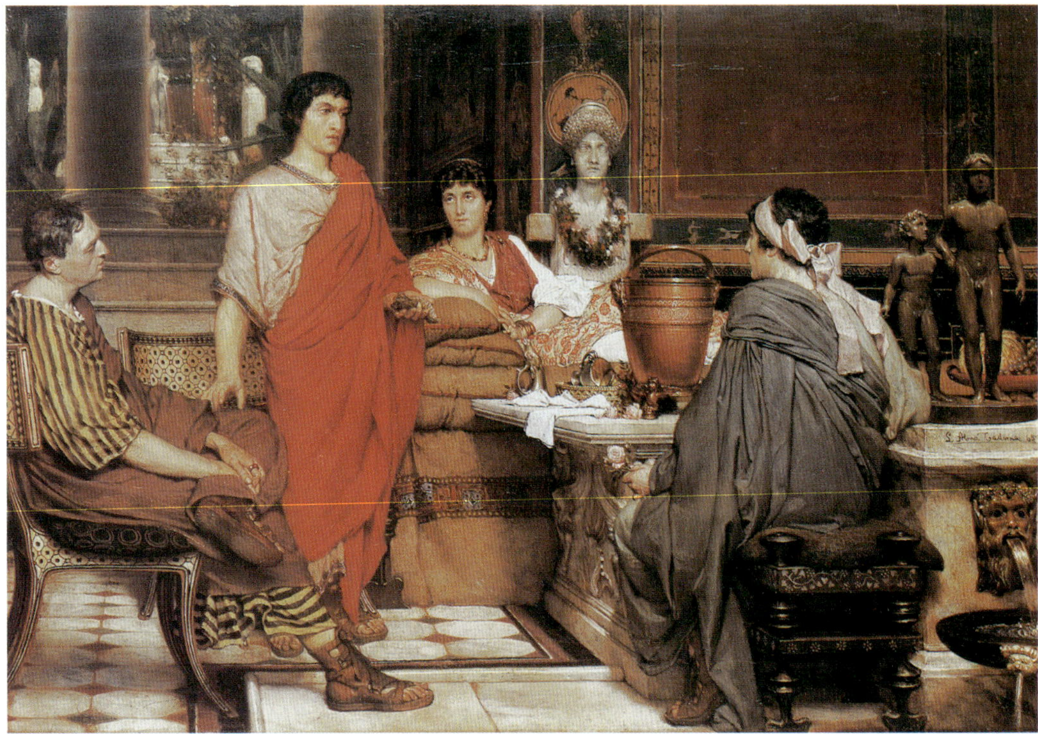

work by a young artist which looked both to new art movements and to a long-established tradition was, after all, a highly saleable product.

After his move to Brussels, Alma-Tadema completed his first series of Roman pictures in 1865: *Catullus at Lesbia's* (Pl.22), *A Chat, A Roman Scribe Writing Dispatches* and *Returning Home from Market*. Set in Pompeian-type interiors characterized by vibrant red walls, these Roman pictures make use of ancient architecture, decoration and accessories, as well as Latin literature. From the time of his first visit to Pompeii, he began collecting commercial photographs of artefacts and sites as well as commissioning his own. Over time he accumulated a vast collection of over five thousand photographs, which encompassed a wide range of subjects, including Greek, Roman, Etruscan, Egyptian, Japanese and Islamic art and architecture.[45] The photographic collection forms part of the artistic process as the artist looks to them as primary source material, and many artefacts included in paintings are recognizable from photographs in the collection. He also accumulated a vast collection of books which, by the end of his life, numbered over four thousand volumes.[46] This private library consisted mostly of classical texts and translations and classical-archaeological publications by modern authorities. Throughout his career, he endeavoured to familiarize himself with up-to-date scholarly discussions of the ancient world.

Catullus at Lesbia's is the most striking of his first Pompeian pictures. It shows the Latin poet Catullus (*c*.84–*c*.54 BC) and his fictional lover, Lesbia. French paintings such as Thomas Couture's *Horace and Lydia* (1843) and Charles-Francois Jalabert's *Virgil, Horace and Varius at the House of Maecenas* (1844–6), set the example for biographical studies of the Latin poets. Catullus' personal life, particularly the intriguing question of the identity of his lover, Lesbia, was a topic of intense interest among mid-nineteenth-century scholars. In 1862, a German scholar, Ludwig Schwabe, proposed a Catullan biography in which he assumed Lesbia to be Clodia Metelli, the sister of the tribune, Publius Clodius and wife of the nobleman, Q. Metellus Celer.[47] Clodia was a cultured, fashionable and married aristocrat who seemingly knew how to enjoy herself. The Latin orator and moralist, Cicero, describes her behaviour as a catalogue of indulgences: 'debauchery, amours, misconduct, trips to Baiae, beach-parties, feasts, revels, concerts, musical parties, pleasure-boats.'[48]

Alma-Tadema represents his Lesbia as cultured, refined and liberated. She reclines on a couch attended by the poet himself and two other male guests in a richly decorated Pompeian interior cluttered with expensive gold and silver

22
Catullus at Lesbia's, 1865
Oil on wood, 39·5 × 54·5 cm (15½ × 21½ in)
Private collection

plate and statuary. On a marble lion-legged table rest a silver ram's head *rhyton* or drinking cup, a silver cup and a bronze *situla* or drinking bucket, while an ornate bronze statuette stands to the right. All these objects are of a type excavated at Pompeii and housed at the Archaeological Museum, Naples. The bronze stool with disc-decorated legs derives from a Pompeian couch of which Alma-Tadema owned a photograph (Pl.23).

Behind Lesbia, a female bust sports an elaborate coiffure of curls, a hairstyle popular on portrait busts of women in the Flavian period (69–98 AD) (Pl.24). Although the hairstyle is anachronistic in the late Republican setting, Lesbia's own hairstyle imitates that of the bust, connecting her with a recognizable image of aristocratic Roman womanhood. A garland obscures the inscription accompanying the bust, but the first letter can be recognized as a 'C', suggesting that is does indeed read 'CLODIA'.

Catullus at Lesbia's itself is based on the famous poem Catullus 3 in which the poet laments the death of Lesbia's pet sparrow:

> Grieve, O Venuses and Loves
> And all the lovelier people there are:
> My girl's sparrow is dead.[49]

Alma-Tadema's Catullus arrives at Lesbia's house with the dead sparrow in his hand. He appears much more concerned than either Lesbia, who is reclining blithely on a couch, or her other male guests. Might the death of the sparrow in Catullus 3 signify the death of love and the end of the poet's affair? This, it would seem, is Alma-Tadema's construction. His is a desolate Catullus, evidently supplanted in Lesbia's affections by the two other men in the painting, presumably her new lovers. The meticulously groomed young man holding a rose may also evoke Catullus 51, in which the poet is consumed with envy by a rival who sits opposite Lesbia, listening to her 'sweet laugh'. In the poem, Catullus is deprived of speech ('But my tongue's paralysed') and correspondingly, in the painting, he stares speechless at the seated young man.

An extraordinary detail is the wall painting, glimpsed above the bust of Lesbia (or Clodia), showing a satyr anticipating copulation with a goat. Although the painting does not appear to derive from any particular prototype, it recalls the famous marble sculptural group from Herculaneum of Pan copulating with a she-goat (Pl.25). Such unmistakably risqué eroticism evokes the sexual intrigue which Cicero ascribes to the historical Clodia. The conflation of Catullan biography and text, and their enactment in a credible archaeological setting, is based on Néo-Grec painting, but the inclusion of a half-hidden reference to a powerful (even bestial) sexuality is

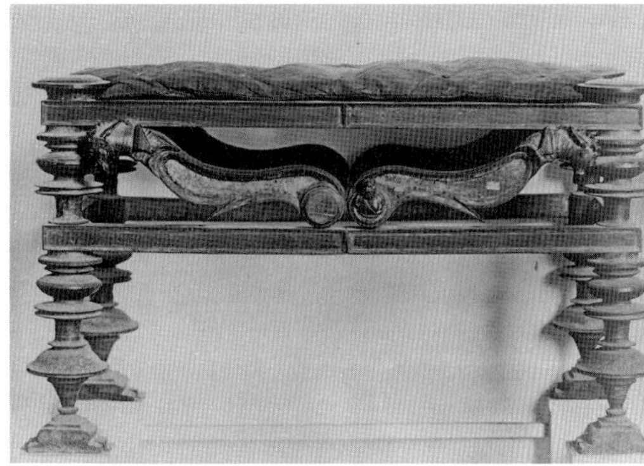

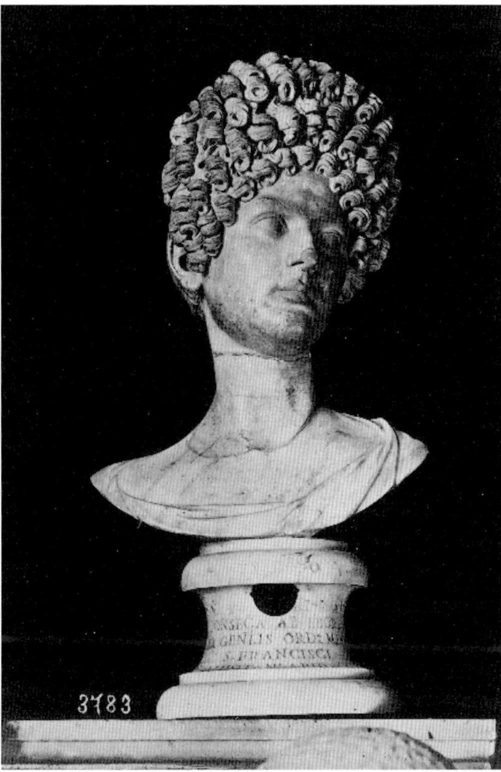

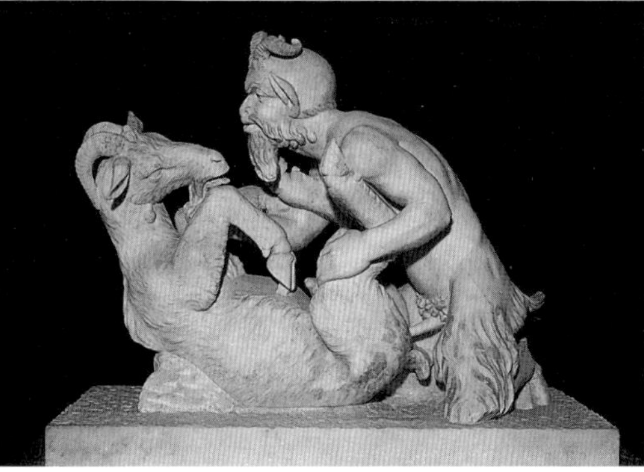

23
Pompeian Disc-legged Couch
Bronze, Archaeological Museum, Naples:
University of Birmingham

24
Female Portrait Bust with Flavian hairstyle, 2nd century AD
Marble, Capitoline Museum, Rome:
University of Birmingham

25
Pan and She-Goat
Roman, Marble
Archaeological Museum, Naples

Alma-Tadema's own innovation. From now on, archaeological detail acts as signifier of historical authenticity, an intellectual challenge to the educated viewer and an invitation to uncover added meanings. The Roman world which is ultimately revealed is one of sexual intrigue. This same construction of Rome was found in nineteenth-century historical novels; from Edward Bulwer Lytton's *The Last Days of Pompeii* (1834) to Henryk Sienkiewicz's *Quo Vadis?* (1896), the popular imagination is captivated by the excesses of a corrupt world. While other paintings – most notably, Thomas Couture's *Romans of the Decadence* (1843) – portray the unofficial side of Roman life, Alma-Tadema rarely directly represents erotic abandon[50] and instead points to such a reading of Rome through nuance, suggestion and archaeological allusion.

Alma-Tadema returned to the life and poetry of Catullus with *Lesbia Weeping over her Sparrow* (1866) which once again evokes Catullus 3, and *Catullus Reading his Poems at Lesbia's House* (Pl.26) in which the poet is depicted declaiming poetry to Lesbia and her assembled guests. *Catullus Reading his Poems at Lesbia's House* recalls Alma-Tadema's own *Venantius Fortunatus Reading his Poems to Radegonda*. Both paintings show men reading poetry to a female audience (although Catullus is also reading to seated men, it is Lesbia to whom the poems are addressed). Nevertheless, the mood of the two paintings is very different: the solemnity of Merovingian history painting has made way for a light-hearted genre scene and a late-antique religiosity for the pleasure-seeking society of the late Roman Republic. The choice to reject his former preoccupation with sombre historical subjects may, once again, have been prompted by commercial reasons. Alma-Tadema's genre scenes painted on small or moderate-sized canvases were sold to private buyers, and a painting depicting wealthy Romans at play would seem more suited to a private gallery or drawing room than the gloomy preoccupations of Merovingian monarchs.

Another Roman poet reading to his mistress is represented in *Tibullus at Delia's* (Pl.27). Tibullus (*c*.50–19 BC) belongs to a generation younger than Catullus but the poems of both construct a witty, urbane and carefree Roman world. In Book One of Tibullus' *Elegies*, the poet presents himself as devoted to Delia, who, like Lesbia, is a married woman who has other lovers as well as the poet. The configuration is similar to *Catullus Reading his Poems at Lesbia's House*: the poet recites his verse in the house of his lover. An effete Tibullus reclines on the couch next to Delia while a male audience listens attentively. The interior is once again cluttered with Pompeian-type artefacts: a bronze stove found at a villa near Stabiae and a bronze folding table from Pompeii, both based on prototypes in the Archaeological Museum, Naples, as well as more generic objects such as bronze candelabrum, oil lamp, stool and a silver jug which appears in a number of paintings.

The artist alludes to another genre of Latin literature in *Entrance to a Roman Theatre* (Pl.28). This exterior scene depicts the social life of wealthy Pompeii with an audience gathering outside the theatre before a dramatic performance. The inscription on the right identifies characters – Dromo, Byrrhia, Glycerium, Mysis – from Terence's comedy, *The Girl from Andros*. This is an entirely plausible choice of play on Alma-Tadema's part: Terence (*c*.186–159 BC), the leading Latin comic poet of his day, continued to be much admired in later ages of Rome.

On the right-hand side of the canvas, most of a carriage is abruptly cut off and we sense that the artist has caught a small part of a larger scene which continues beyond the confines of the canvas. This compositional device is in direct contrast to Neo-classical painting in which figures are framed in the centre of the canvas. Alma-Tadema, after all, was trained in Antwerp under Wappers, the opponent of French Neo-classicism. Cut-off figures and buildings continue to figure in Alma-Tadema's paintings and, later in the century, when the device comes to be used in photography, we can see the artist's photographic collection assisting his paintings in respect of both precision of archaeological detail and also composition.

The women in *Entrance to a Roman Theatre* are identified as being of the same social standing as Lesbia and her circle by their Flavian hairstyles. The face of the woman on the left is obscured by her companion and all that is visible of her is a false front of curls, dyed a dramatic red. Women's vanity was the target of much ancient satire and, Ovid, in particular, reveals:

> A woman flaunts in yards
> of purchased curls;
> Failing her own, she buys another girl's.[51]

Alma-Tadema's painting, a genre scene showing theatre-goers in ancient Rome, contains an ironic subtext: the fashionable audience are more concerned about being seen appropriately dressed and coiffured than about the performance they are to attend.

If we apply Alma-Tadema's statement 'that the old Romans were human flesh and blood like ourselves, moved by the same passions and emotions'[52] to this painting, we see that rather than allying the manners and customs of respectable nineteenth-century society with those of ancient Rome, the artist exposes follies and foibles common to both. In *Entrance to a Roman Theatre*, then, the vanity of a wealthy audience attending

26
Catullus Reading his Poems at Lesbia's House, 1870
Oil on wood, 39·3 × 48·2 cm (15½ × 19 in)
Private collection

27
Tibullus at Delia's, 1866
Oil on wood, 43·9 × 66 cm (17¼ × 26 in)
Museum of Fine Arts, Boston

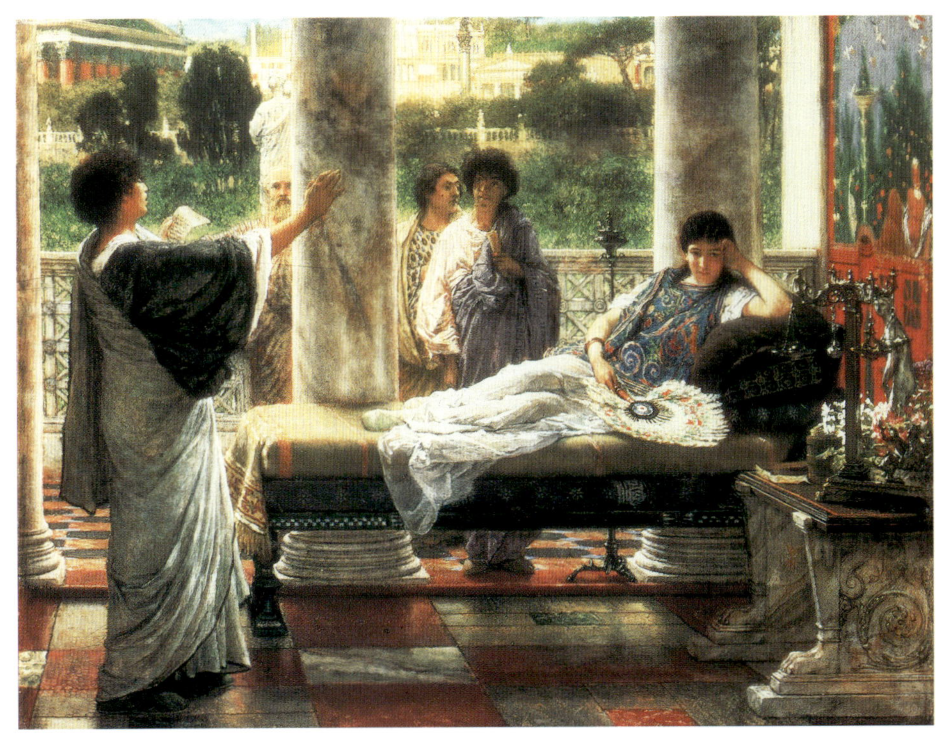

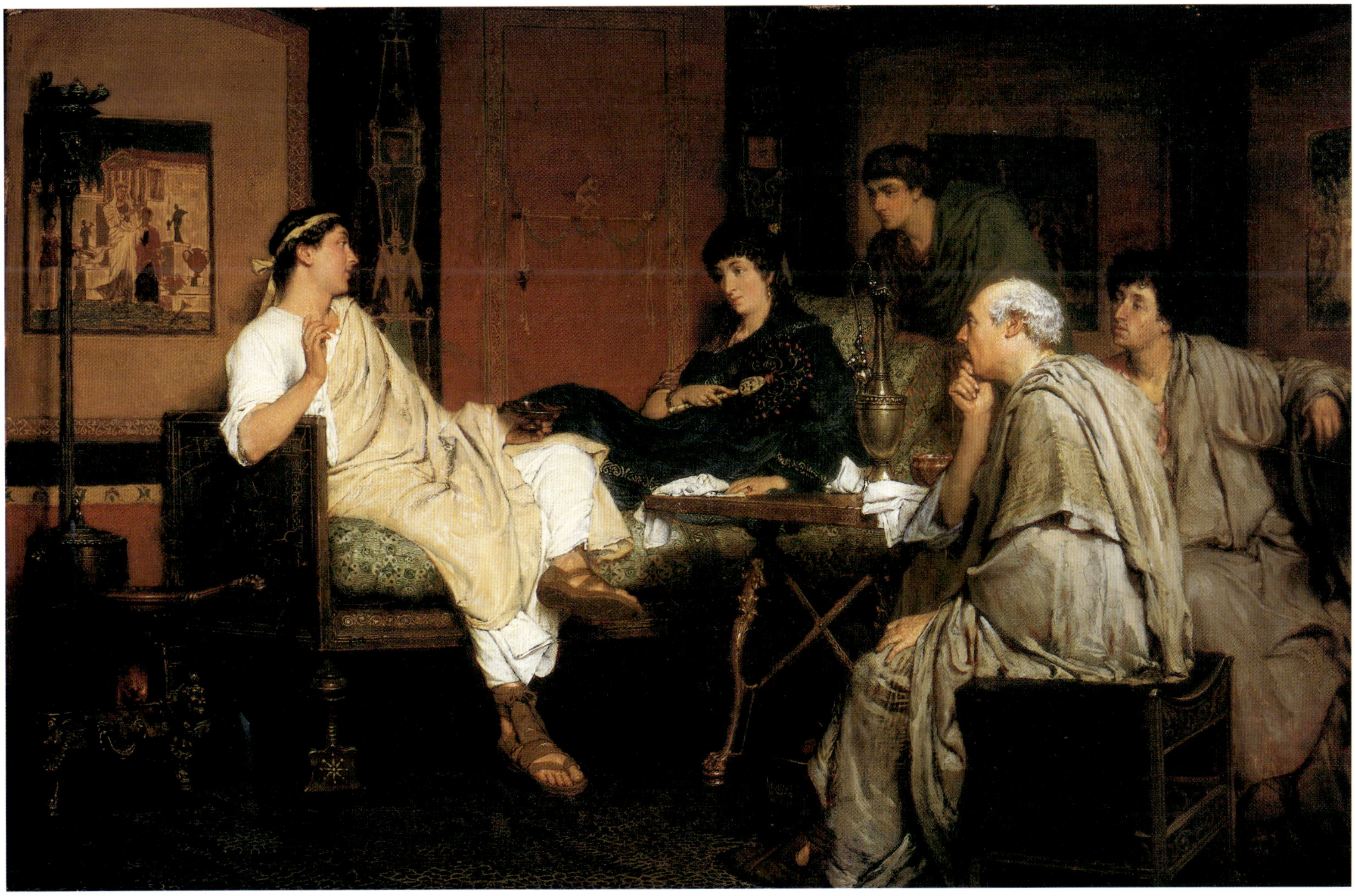

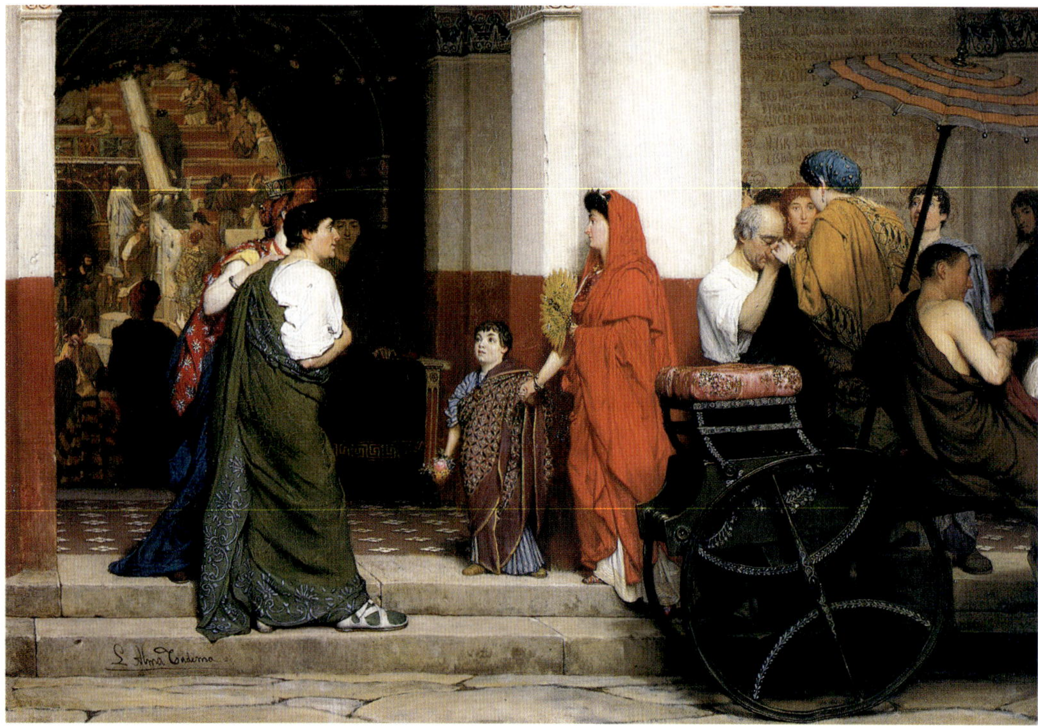

28
Entrance to a Roman Theatre, 1866
Oil on canvas, 70·4 × 98·4 cm (27¾ × 38¾ in)
Private collection

a fashionable show is presented as little different from that found in European society circles.

Alma-Tadema continued his Roman genre paintings placed in Pompeian settings. In *An Exedra* (Pl.29), painted in 1869, the artist moves his scene to the outskirts of Pompeii and the tomb of Mamia, erected in the form of an *exedra* or semicircular bench, on the Via dei Sepulcri (Street of the Tombs). Two men admire the view over the Bay of Naples, another two sit chatting on the bench while a third dozes. The foreground figure is a slave, identified from the lettering on his tunic as belonging to the Holconii, a prominent family from historical Pompeii. This figure with his hunched shoulders and slouched position, shaved head and bare feet provides a rare glimpse of the underbelly of Roman life. Bored and tired, he makes a piquant comparison with the wealthy sightseers. Although many painters of Rome pursue no earnest agenda or high-minded purpose, a vast arena of Roman life is usually left untouched and the institution of slavery and the interminable cruelty suffered by individual slaves remains unacknowledged. Slave scenes tend to form Orientalist fantasies, as in Gérôme's *A Roman Slave Market* (1884), where naked slave girls are offered up to the viewer. Alma-Tadema's *An Exedra*, by contrast, is one of the few paintings to touch on the degradation of slavery. This slave's plight is made all the more poignant by the understated way in which Alma-Tadema has approached his subject: no heart-wrenching depiction of cruelty, but an everyday event of a slave, parasol in hand, impassively awaiting his master's instructions.

Although Alma-Tadema's early paintings are mostly historical genre subjects in which anonymous Romans are engaged in everyday activities, he was also interested in Roman historical themes. The first historical painting, *Agrippina Visiting the Ashes of Germanicus* (1866), is a touching depiction of Agrippina the elder, grand-daughter of Augustus, in private grief as she mourns her dead husband, the Roman general Germanicus. The notion of Agrippina as an embodiment of female stoicism and virtue – drawn from the sympathetic account of her life and character by the Roman historians Suetonius and Tacitus – was a popular subject in eighteenth-century Neo-classical history painting which generally looked to historical episodes illustrative of moral edification (*exempla virtutis*).

The second historical painting, *Tarquinius Superbus* (1867), is drawn from the early history of Rome, a period conventionally chosen for depictions of *exempla virtutis*. In striking contrast to traditional notions of history painting, however, *Tarquinius Superbus* illustrates no heroic ideal and is instead the artist's first exploration of historical corruption. Cicero cites the reign of the Roman king, Tarquinius Superbus, as an example of the degeneration of monarchy,[53] while his very name, 'Superbus' (proud), was acquired through arrogance and tyranny. Alma-Tadema illustrates an anecdote related by the Roman historian, Livy. At war with Gabii and unable to overcome the city by force, Tarquinius sent his son, Sextus, to the enemy with a story that he was being ill-treated by his father. Sextus was so convincing that the city entrusted him with a position of command and he promptly sent a message to his father for further orders. When the messenger arrived, 'the king, as if absorbed in meditation, passed into the garden of his house, followed by his son's envoy. There, walking up and down without a word, he is said to have struck off the heads of the tallest poppies with his stick.'[54] Sextus interpreted his father's actions correctly and banished or murdered all the leading citizens of Gabii, after which the city soon fell. To ensure an authentic look to the early Roman setting, Alma-Tadema has reproduced Etruscan tomb paintings on the rear wall.

Tarquinius Superbus is a decisive departure from traditional history painting. It subverts the notion of early Roman history as a paradigm of self-sacrifice and heroism – exemplified by David's *Oath of the Horatii* – by deliberately choosing an episode which points to tyranny and deceit.

Alma-Tadema's concern with Livian history was short-lived. He turned his attention, instead, to the Roman Empire. As a period vividly documented by classical writers and boasting an almost limitless array of colourful personalities engaged in corrupt, extravagant and licentious behaviour, the Empire offered him a new and extensive range of possibilities for the pursuit of his chosen themes. The imperial period, further-

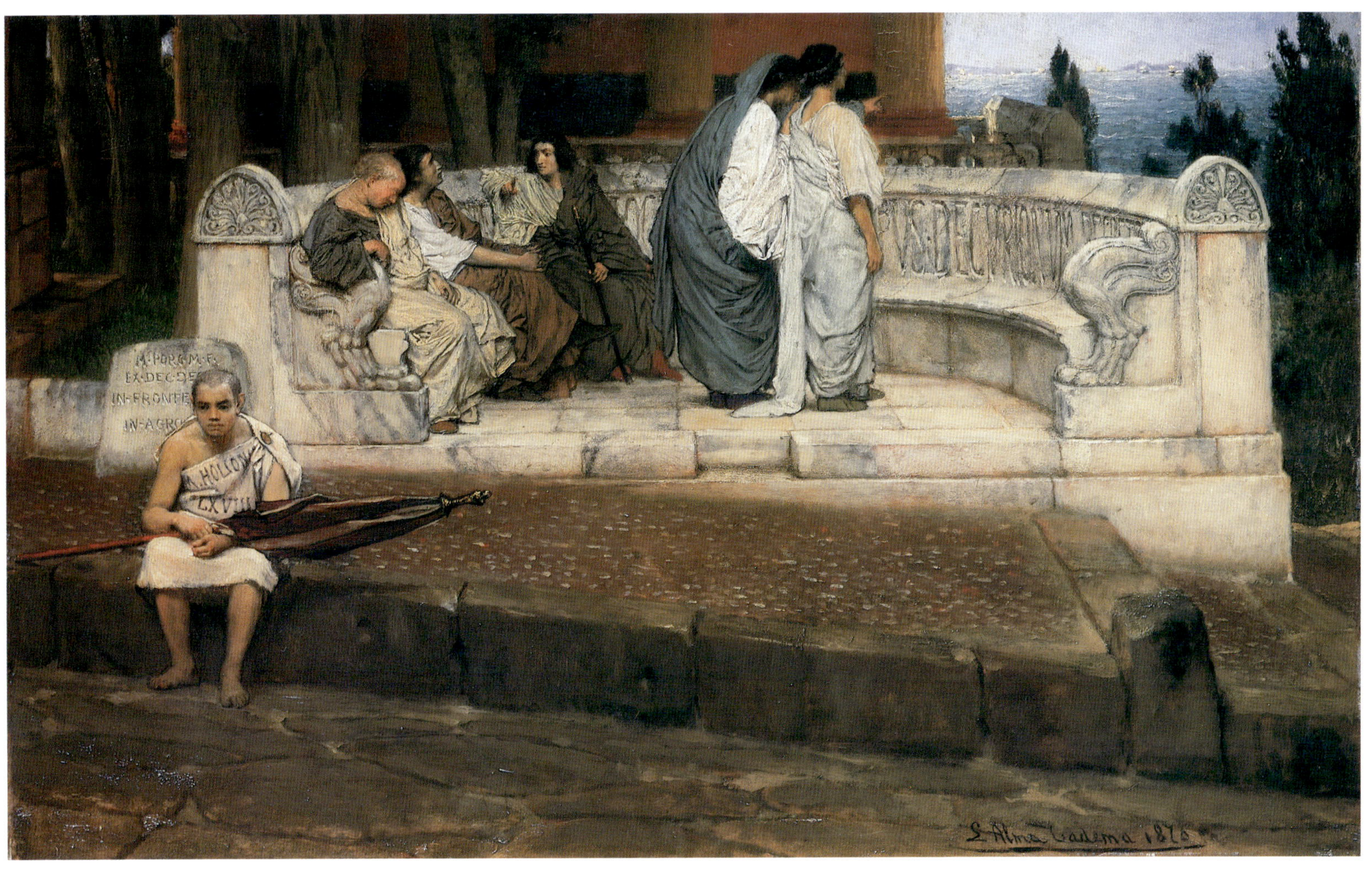

29
An Exedra, 1869
Oil on wood, 38 × 59·8 cm (15 × 23½ in)
Frances Lehman Loeb Art Center,
Gift of Mrs Avery Coonley

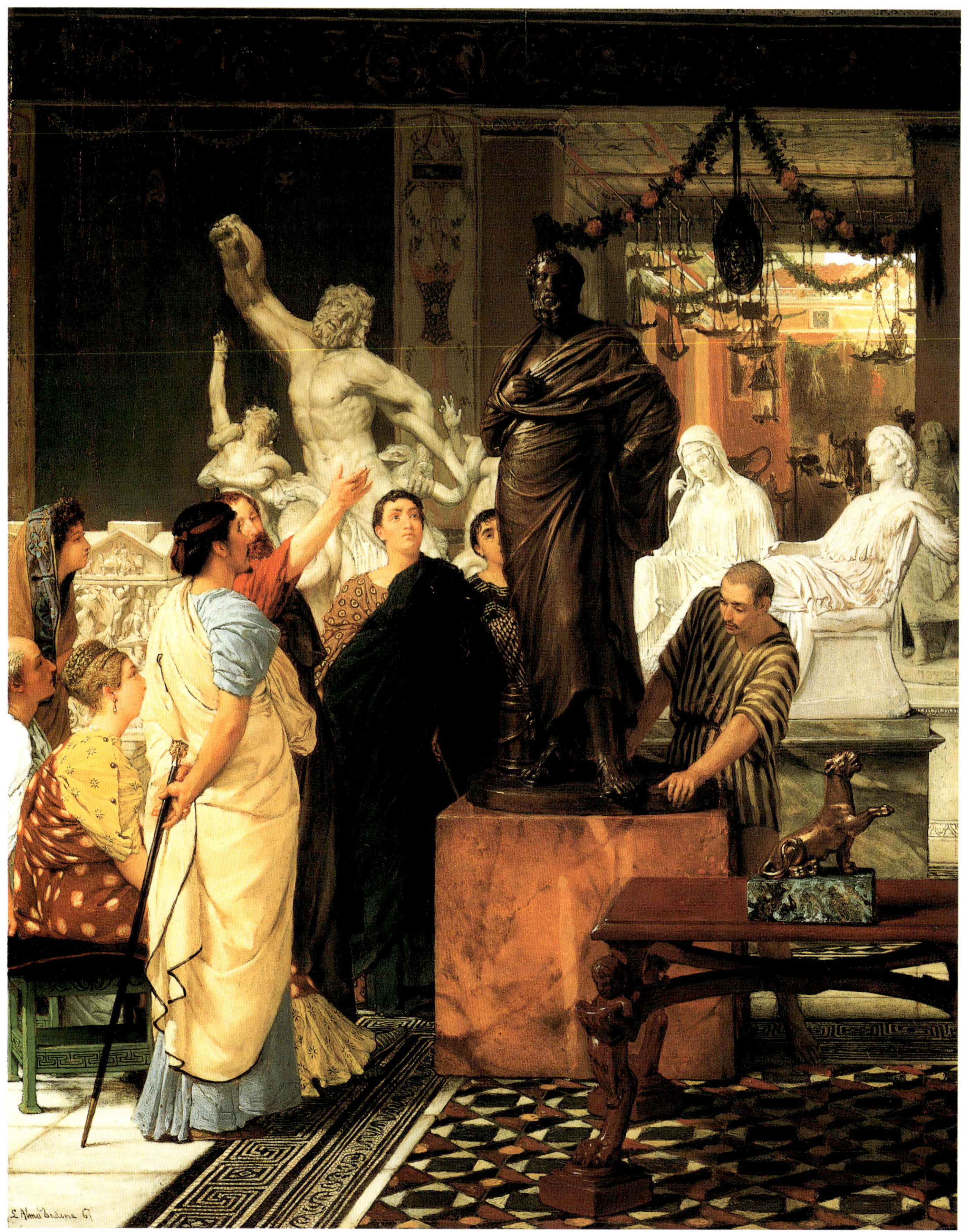

LAWRENCE ALMA-TADEMA 36

more, was familiar from the numerous popular historical novels set during the reigns of the most notorious emperors: Tiberius in Lew Wallace's *Ben Hur* (1880), Nero in Henryk Sienkiewicz's *Quo Vadis?* (1896) and Domitian in Ernst Eckstein's *Quintus Claudius, a Romance of Imperial Rome* (1882).[55] Such novels, viewed as low-brow by serious critics, were easily available and widely read, and, as such, both reinforced and reflected popular notions of a decadent Rome.

Proclaiming Claudius Emperor (1867) is Alma-Tadema's first depiction of imperial intrigue. The subject is suggested by the Roman historian, Suetonius, who offers a droll account of the murder of Caligula and the proclamation of his uncle, Claudius, as Emperor of Rome by the Praetorian Guard. The artist was to return to the same inglorious episode twice more with *A Roman Emperor AD 41* (1871)[56] and *Ave Caesar! Io Saturnalia* (1880). From this point onwards, themes of infamy and death underlie most of Alma-Tadema's Roman historical paintings. However, unlike the Merovingian paintings which deal with comparable themes, these Roman subjects depict a bloody and corrupt world which is, at the same time, strangely glamorous. The attraction of Alma-Tadema's historical paintings is analogous to that of the popular historical novels: gladiators fight, crowds roar, revellers carouse and lovers make love. Novelists often pursue a moral agenda whereby we are persuaded to identify with (as it might be) the Christian martyr in Nero's Rome, and yet, we cannot help but be captivated by the excesses of the imperial circle and even of the Emperor himself. For Alma-Tadema, the lure of Rome remains the same, but, unlike the novelists, he dispenses with all moral comment.

In the winter of 1867–8, the Alma-Tadema family travelled throughout Europe and once again visited Italy. On his return, the artist continued with his Roman subjects. Little is known about this period in his life except that he worked consistently in order to fulfil the terms of his contract with Gambart. One of his major new themes was Roman luxury centred around the notion of ancient connoisseurship and art collecting. Collecting as an organized activity began in the second century BC with the conquest of Greek lands. By the end of the Republic (late first century BC), a market had developed for copies of Greek originals as well as for Greek statuary itself. Alma-Tadema follows descriptions by ancient authors of wealthy Romans admiring and acquiring works of art purely for value and status,[57] and accordingly, his paintings emphasize wealth and acquisition rather than discernment and taste. The first works on this theme are a pair of large pictures, *A Sculpture Gallery in Rome at the Time of Augustus* (Pl.30) and *The Collector of Pictures at the Time of Augustus* (Pl.32). *A Sculpture Gallery* displays a dealer's shop cluttered with statuary. Customers are being shown a large bronze, copied from a marble statue of Sophocles (Pl.31). Other identifiable statues, including Agrippina (now known as a Roman matron: Capitoline Museum, Rome), Penelope (Vatican Museum, Rome) and the famous Laocöon group (Vatican Museum, Rome), are displayed in the background.

The Laocöon, admired as one of the most celebrated statues from antiquity since its discovery in 1506, has a much higher status in any modern art-historical perspective than the Sophocles, which stands centre stage. Yet the artist has transformed the Sophocles from the marble of the Vatican statue to bronze. Are we to take this as the original Greek bronze which stood in the Theatre of Dionysus at Athens (of which the Vatican marble is a probable copy), or is Alma-Tadema suggesting that a statue's importance is based on its material?[58] The Roman writer, Pliny, claims that bronze was valued highly in statues and statuettes and other decorative items, including cauldrons, hanging lamps and candelabra.[59] In the back of Alma-Tadema's shop we see a wealth of such bronzes, obviously a speciality of this dealer. Corinthian bronze was deemed the most precious form of the metal. Pliny, once again, states that it was more highly prized than silver,[60] and the Roman satirist, Martial, relates the amusing anecdote of the would-be connoisseur, Mamurra, who could tell Corinthian bronzes merely by their smell.[61] One curious facet of this painting about the shortcomings of wealthy Rome is the inclusion of portraits of the artist and his friends. The bearded figure of Alma-Tadema pointing at the statue of Sophocles is accompanied by recognizable likenesses of his fellow artists, Jan Verhaus, Felix Moscheles and Alfred Verwee. As in *Entrance to a Roman Theatre*, Alma-Tadema exposes the follies of contemporary society by relating them to those of ancient Rome, and yet the inclusion of his friends, and even himself, suggests that his purpose is tongue-in-cheek irony rather than scurrilous satire.

The companion painting, *The Collector of Pictures at the Time of Augustus*, shows clients viewing paintings at a dealer's shop. All the paintings are based on Pompeian wall paintings or mosaics, which themselves derive from Greek originals.[62] Although only a few inches are visible of a picture on the far left, the detail of spears meeting at an angle in the corner identifies it as the *Battle of Issus*, a Pompeian mosiac thought to be a copy of a famous Greek painting. Next to this is an architectural scene of the type found in Pompeian wall

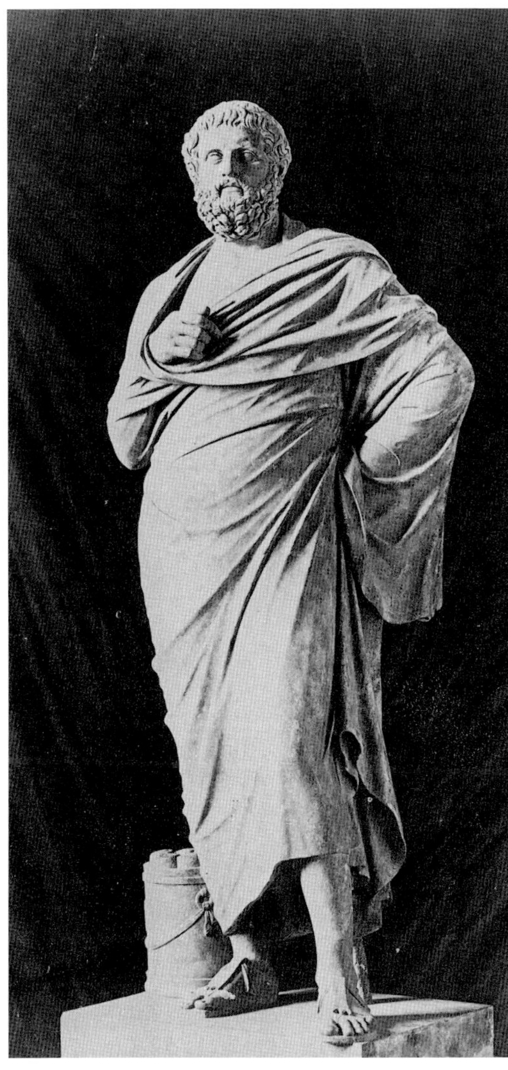

30 opposite
A Sculpture Gallery in Rome at the Time of Augustus, 1867
Oil on wood, 62·2 × 46·9 cm (24½ × 18½ in)
Montreal Museum of Fine Arts, Horsley and Annie Townsend Bequest

31
Sophocles, Roman copy of a 4th-century BC original
Marble, Vatican Museum, Rome:
University of Birmingham

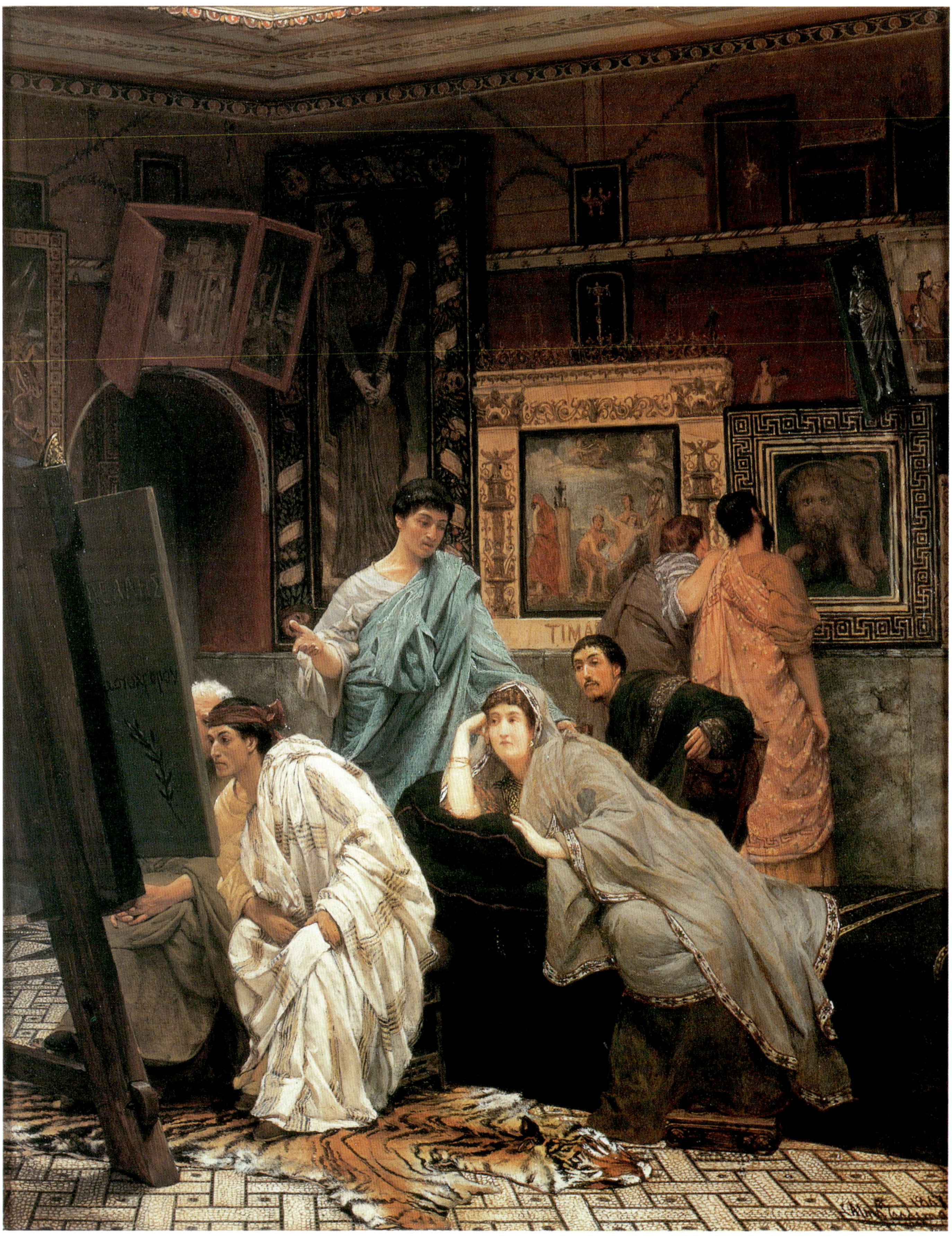

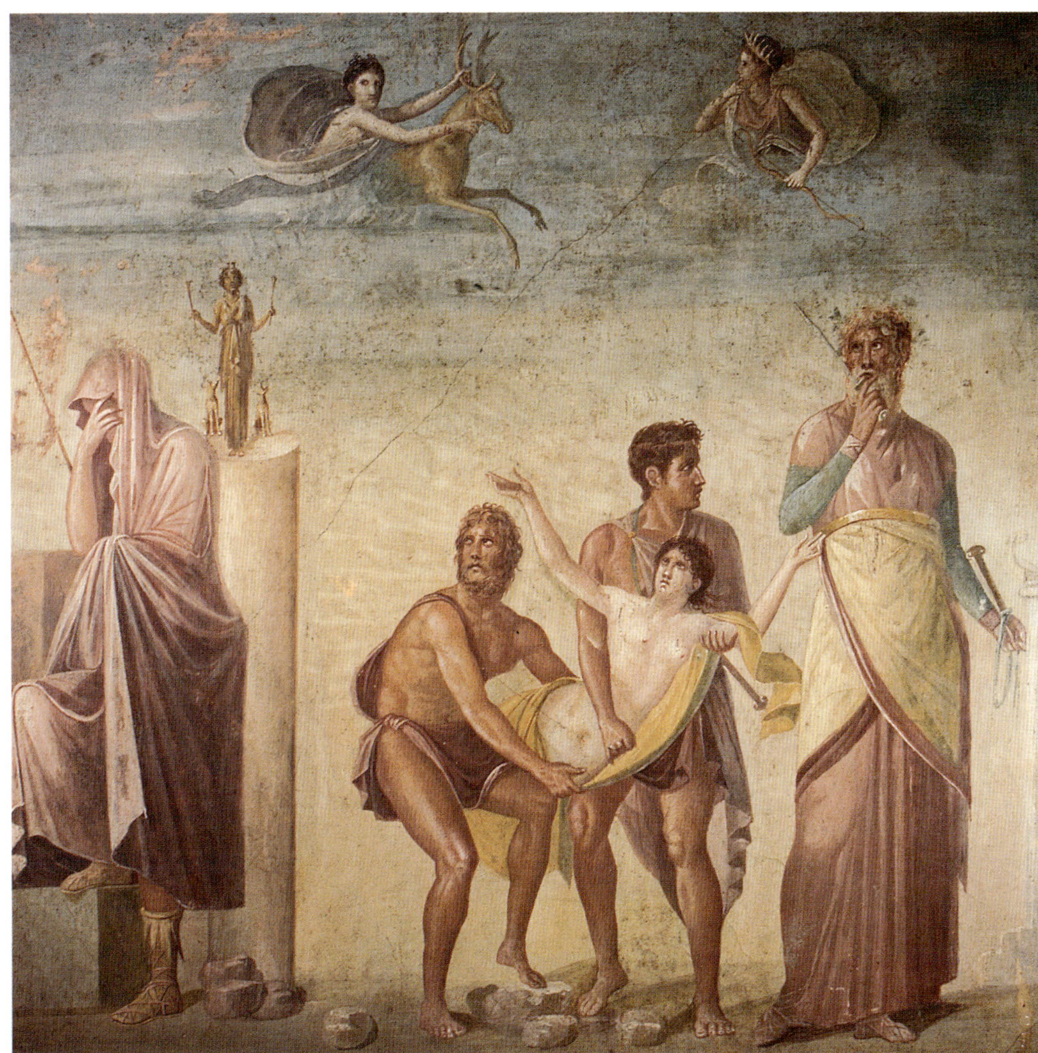

32 opposite
The Collector of Pictures in the Time of Augustus, 1867
Oil on wood, 71 × 46·4 cm (28 × 18¼ in)
Private collection

33
The Sacrifice of Iphigenia, Roman, 1st century AD
Wall painting from Pompeii (House of the Tragic Poet), H 1·26 m (49⅝ in)
Archaeological Museum, Naples

painting, then a reproduction of a painting from Herculaneum thought to be a copy of *Medea* by the Greek painter Timomachus. To the right we see another Pompeian painting associated with a Greek original, the *Sacrifice of Iphigenia* (Pl.33) by Timanthes; the first letters of the name are clearly visible on the frame. Ignoring these acclaimed works, a group of standing clients are inspecting a painting of a lion. Another seated group look at a painting on an easel, invisible to Alma-Tadema's viewers; the inscription on its back links it to Apelles, known to the Roman public as the most famous of all Greek painters.[63] While the other paintings are based on Pompeian mosaics and frescoes, the works of Apelles survive only in descriptions by ancient authors.

In 1868 Alma-Tadema embarked on a series of paintings depicting wealthy Romans giving a private viewing of choice pieces from their own collections. Ancient collectors, according to Pliny, were anxious to display their art works.[64] *A Roman Art Lover* (Pl.34) depicts a splendid *atrium* (courtyard at the centre of the house) in which a seated man displays a statuette of a well-known ancient statue-type, the *Venus Anadyomene* (Venus binding her hair) to an admiring circle of guests.[65] The most striking aspect of the statuette is its material: it is the attractive and expensive gold and lapis lazuli which are arousing so much attention. To the right of the group a marble statue of the Dancing Faun (Uffizi Gallery, Florence), a high-status piece known from the Renaissance, acts as a mere fountain decoration. The collector here, like the clients in the sculpture-gallery paintings, is more interested in expensive materials than in artistic worth, and recalls Pliny's tart comments on Roman collectors: 'to me the majority of these collectors seem only to make a pretence of being connoisseurs, so as to separate themselves from the multitude, rather than to have any exceptionally refined insight in this matter.'[66]

Alma-Tadema's vast library included works by ancient moralists, satirists and love poets – Cicero, Seneca, Juvenal, Persius, Martial, Horace, Ovid, Tibullus and Propertius – who all dwell on Roman luxury.[67] Another text included in the library is Petronius' risqué masterpiece, the *Satyricon*,[68] which offers a dry critique of the pretensions of the nouveaux riches. In Alma-Tadema's wealthy connoisseurs we can discern something of Petronius' 'Dinner of Trimalchio', at which Trimalchio, a boorish freedman, tries to impress his dinner guests with his wealth and extravagance. Like Alma-Tadema's hosts, Trimalchio displays wealth through expensive materials: his silver plate is inscribed with its weight in silver;[69] the chef is presented with an expensive drinking cup on a tray of Corinthian bronze; bronze figures decorate his lamps; tables are solid silver and pottery inlaid with gold.[70] If the artist's aim is to imply a link between the pretensions of Roman art collectors and those of his own contemporaries, then he is playing a sophisticated but dangerous game: it is his own patrons who are the target of his satire. Paradoxically, though, it is this very evocation of a decadent Rome which appealed to popular constructions of antiquity and, evidently, to the buyers of Alma-

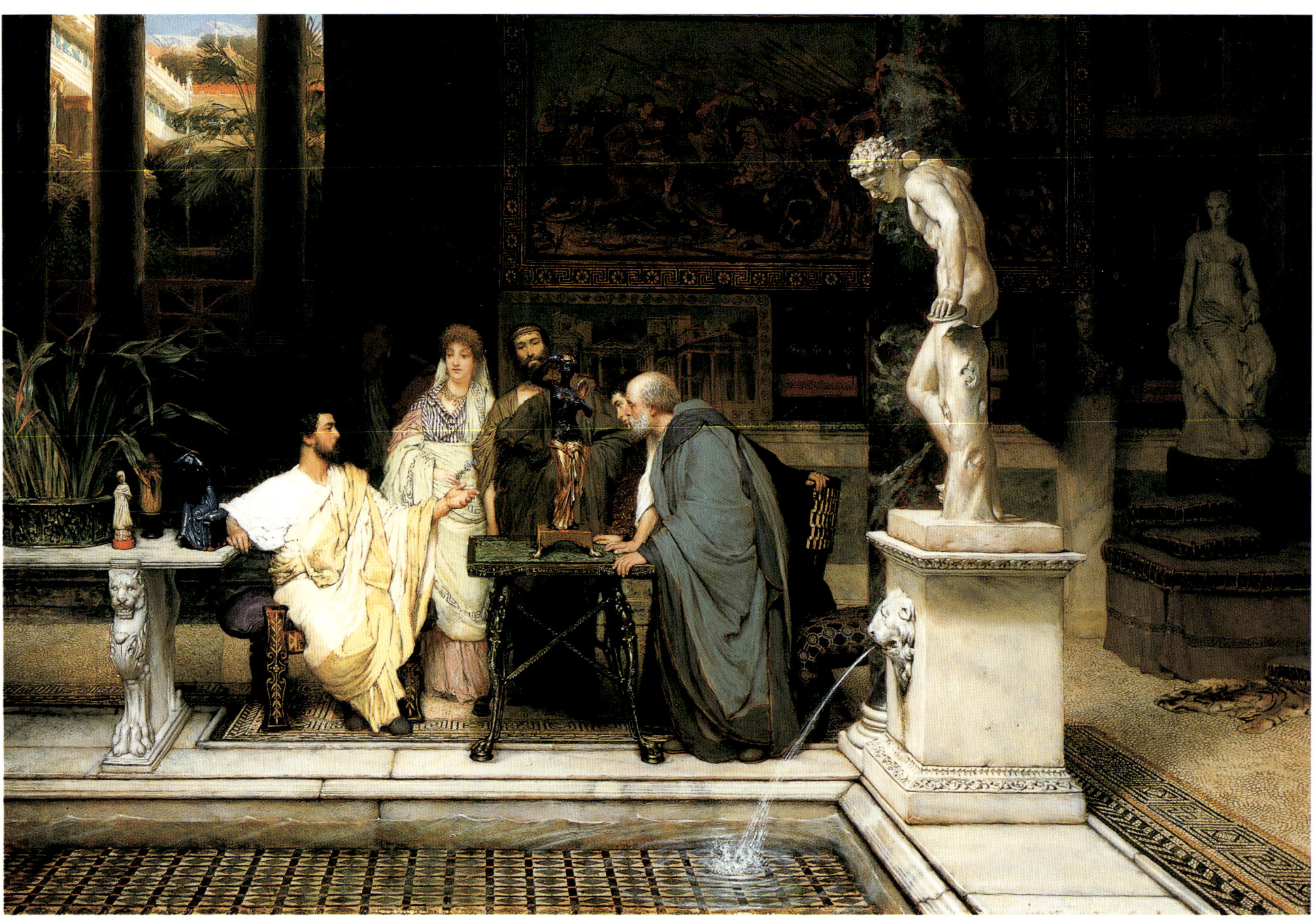

34
A Roman Art Lover, 1868
Oil on wood, 53·3 × 80 cm (21 × 31½ in)
Yale University Art Gallery, New Haven,
Mary Gertrude Abbey Fund

35 opposite
The Flower Market, 1868
Oil on wood, 42·12 × 58 cm (16⅝ × 22⅞ in)
Manchester City Art Galleries

Tadema's pictures, whether they recognized themselves in the role of the ancient idle rich or not. We may wonder whether Alma-Tadema's detached irony conceals a calculated attempt to humiliate patrons unfamiliar with Pliny's discussions of Roman social life; we must assume not.

Despite his preoccupation with wealth and leisure, Alma-Tadema also endeavours to show scenes from everyday life. Pompeian excavations under Fiorelli, which concentrated on many of the hitherto neglected poorer areas, uncovered evidence for the life of ordinary people. *The Armourer's Shop* (1866) depicts three men examining a sword in the interior of a small shop, *The Flower Market* (Pl.35), a corner of a busy market place with wine shop and flower stall, and *Wine and Gossip* (1869), the interior of a wine shop. *The Flower Market*, in particular, makes use of many Pompeian features, including distinctive oval stepping stones in the street, a reconstructed shop front as found in François Mazois's *Les Ruines de Pompei*,[71] a portable stove from Herculaneum (Archaeological Museum, Naples) and inscriptions with elongated red lettering. The inscription on the wall of the shop front has been identified as an election poster: the candidate, Marcus Epidius Sabinus, and his supporter, Suedius Clemens, are familiar names found in surviving Pompeian inscriptions.[72]

It took Alma-Tadema three-and-a half years to fulfil the terms of Gambart's contract; the commission was completed in 1868 and thirty-four paintings were produced during the period. Gambart was attracting buyers in Britain and America as well as Europe. Among early patrons were José de Murrieta, the Marques de Santurce, a merchant banker of Spanish descent living in London who owned *Lesbia Weeping over her Sparrow*, *Proclaiming Claudius Emperor* and the two paintings entitled *A Roman Art Lover*. By the 1870s, Murrieta had acquired twenty of Alma-Tadema's works. The American collector,

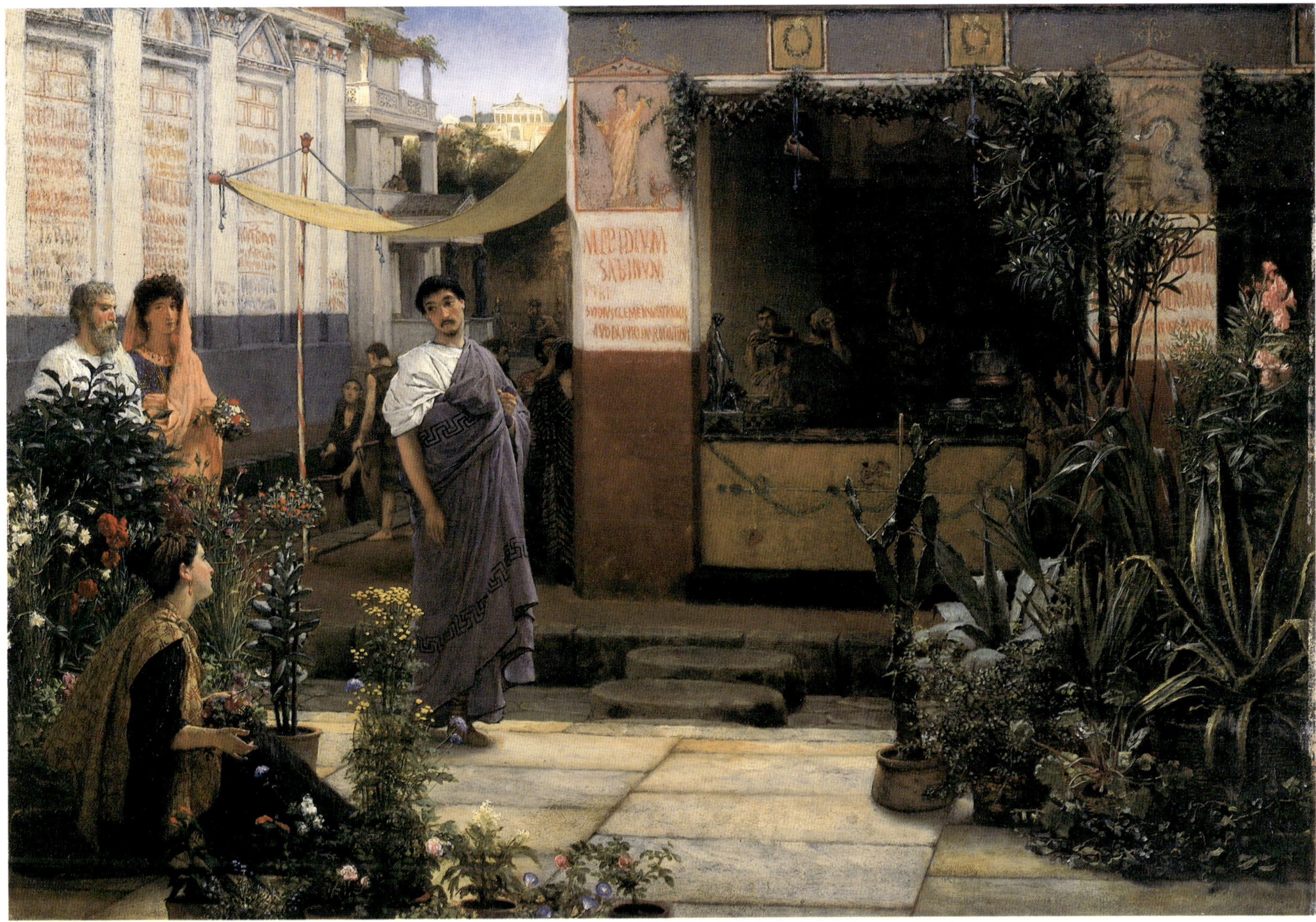

W Prescot Hunt, bought *In the Peristylum* (1866) and *Tibullus at Delia's*. Gambart offered Alma-Tadema a second contract for forty-eight more pictures. Paintings were divided into three classes, the first at the same rate as the previous pictures, *c*.£80, the second rising to £100 and the third to £120. With the demands of a growing family, Alma-Tadema accepted a contract which ensured financial security but also demanded a continued high level of productivity.

In 1869, after years of ill heath, Pauline Alma-Tadema died of smallpox, leaving her husband with two young daughters. She remains a shadowy figure as no independent testimony survives about her personality and Alma-Tadema's only recorded comment on their relationship – 'I married, in September 1863'[73] – is less than revealing. His sister, Artje, took over the role of housekeeper and remained with the family until 1873 when she married a German lithographer.[74] Alma-Tadema gave up painting for four months, and his first painting after his wife's death, *The Convalescent* (1869), may well have been inspired by her illness. Suffering from ill health himself, Alma-Tadema arrived in London in the winter of 1869-70 to consult the physician, Sir Henry Thompson, on Gambart's advice. In London he was introduced to members of various artistic circles, and it was during this trip that he first met his future second wife, Laura Epps.

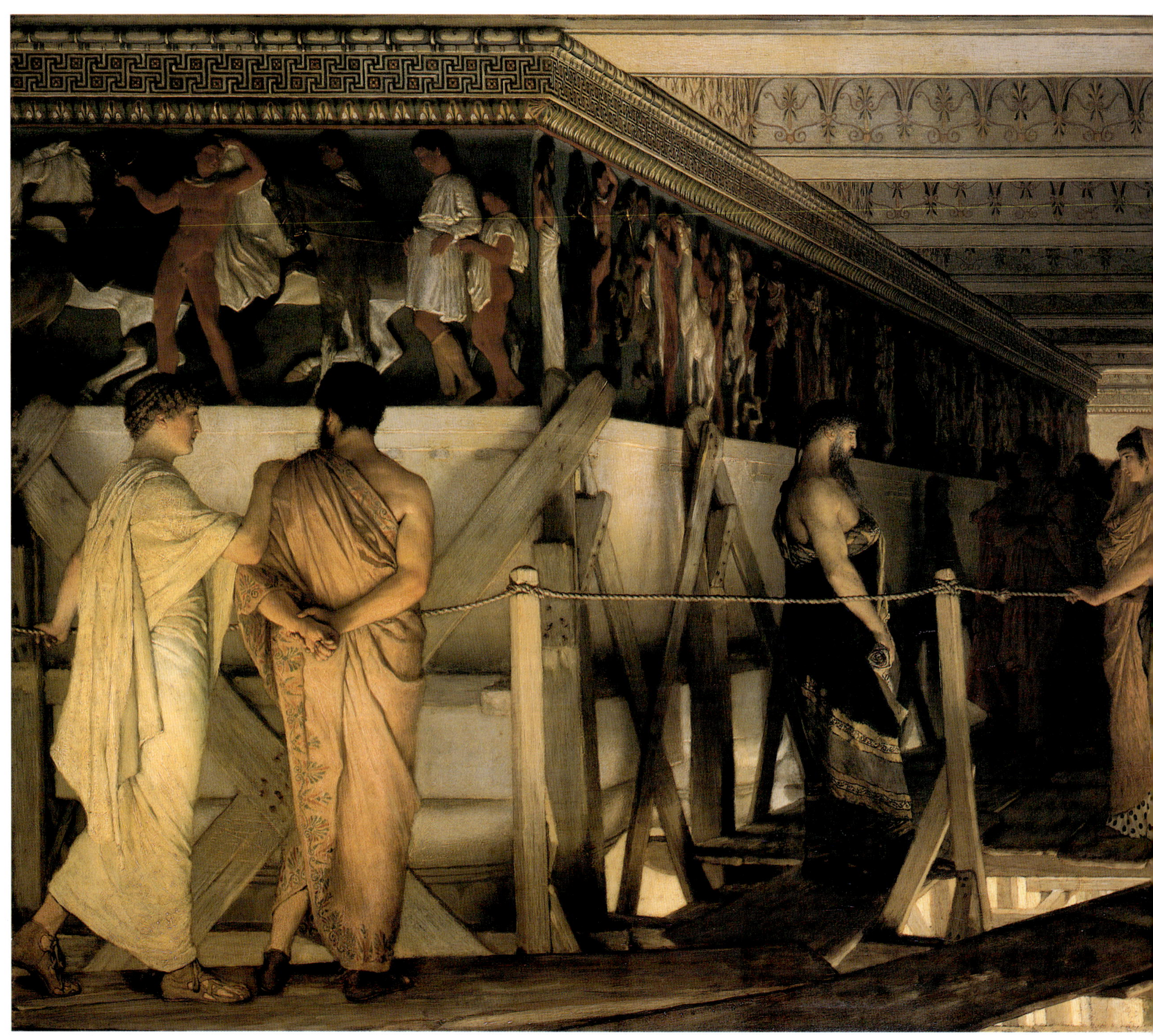

I/4

GREECE AND ROME

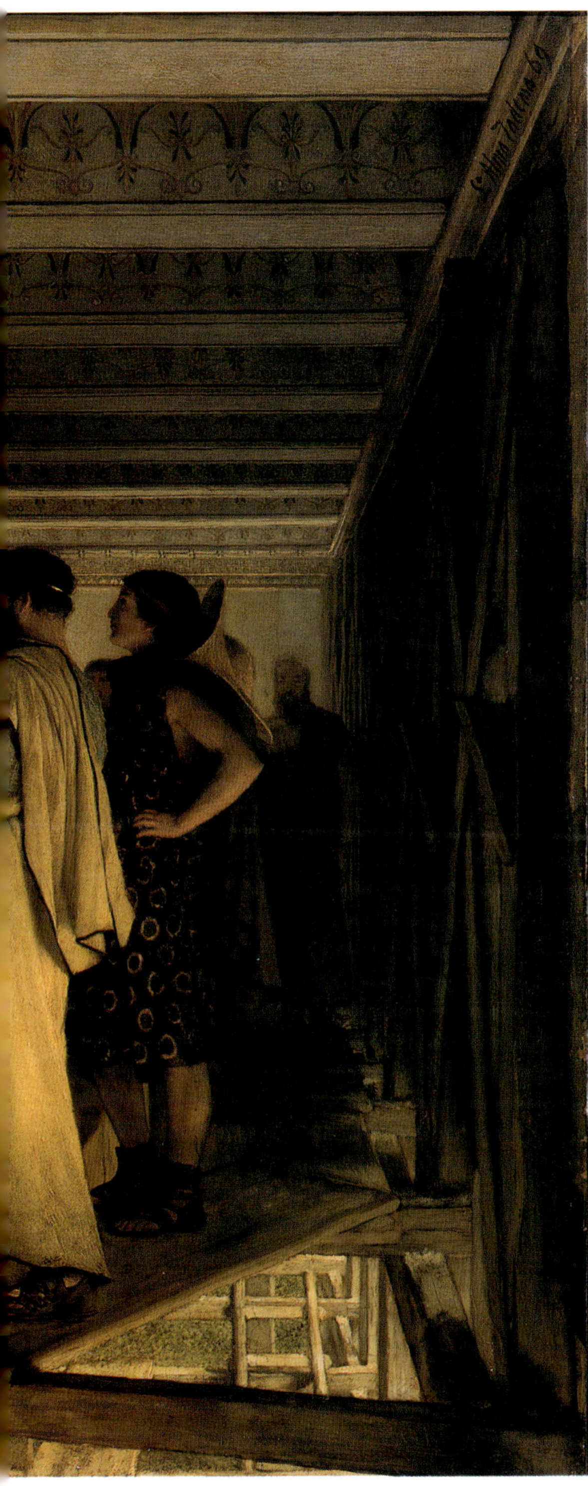

While Alma-Tadema's reputation rests on his paintings of Roman life, among his early classical paintings are a small number of Greek subjects. At the beginning of his career, the artist completed one mythological painting (the watercolour, *The Death of Hippolytus*), but the mature artist, eschewing mythological themes, instead chose Greek genre, literary and historical scenes. Mid-nineteenth-century mythological paintings followed a Renaissance tradition of large canvases depicting the nude, but Alma-Tadema's painting style was more suited to smaller canvases which concentrated on material detail. The first major Greek painting, *Phidias Showing the Frieze of the Parthenon to his Friends* (Pl.36), illustrates the most admired architectural monument to have survived from antiquity. The Parthenon sculptures (consisting of many of the pedimental sculptures, metopes and frieze), had been brought from the Acropolis in Athens to London by Lord Elgin and acquired by the British Museum in 1816. They were widely seen as the pinnacle of artistic achievement.

Alma-Tadema's Phidias is a dignified and grand figure set apart from his admiring audience of Athenian notables. The depiction of the frieze is more surprising: it is not shown at eye-level as in its well-lit display in the British Museum galleries, but placed in its original position, inside the temple, high up on the dark *cella* walls above the inner porch at the west end of the building. Spectators stand on wooden scaffolding, unexpectedly reminding us that the creative process involved hard labour in difficult and even dangerous conditions.

Phidias Showing the Frieze of the Parthenon to his Friends reproduces slab XLII (Pl.37) and part of slab XLI of the north frieze, together with the full sequence of the west frieze. The artist could have studied the frieze on his visit to London in 1862, as the British Museum display included both the north-side originals and casts of the west frieze (which remained in situ in Athens). The most surprising aspect of the painting is the depiction of this frieze in colour. The question of ancient polychromy was a controversial topic. Nineteenth-century archaeological finds at Pompeii and Herculaneum and in Greek Asia Minor disclosed traces of paint on architecture and sculpture and thus suggested not a familiar white marble antiquity, but an ancient world emblazoned with colour.

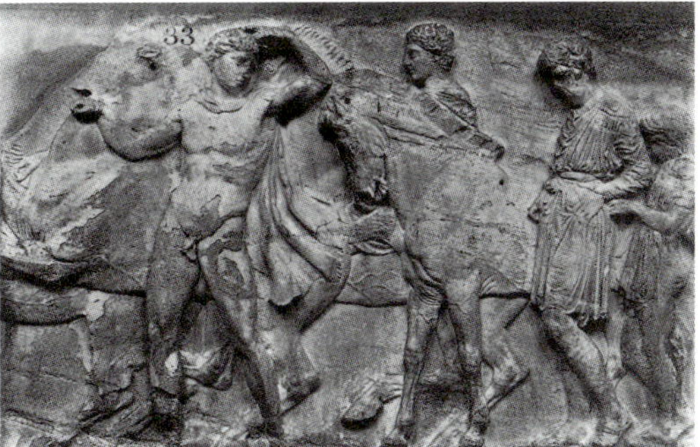

36 opposite
Phidias Showing the Frieze of the Parthenon to his Friends, 1868
Oil on wood, 72 × 110·5 cm (28⅜ × 43½ in)
Birmingham Museums and Art Gallery

37
North Frieze, Parthenon Sculptures, slab XLII, 5th century BC
Marble, British Museum, London: University of Birmingham

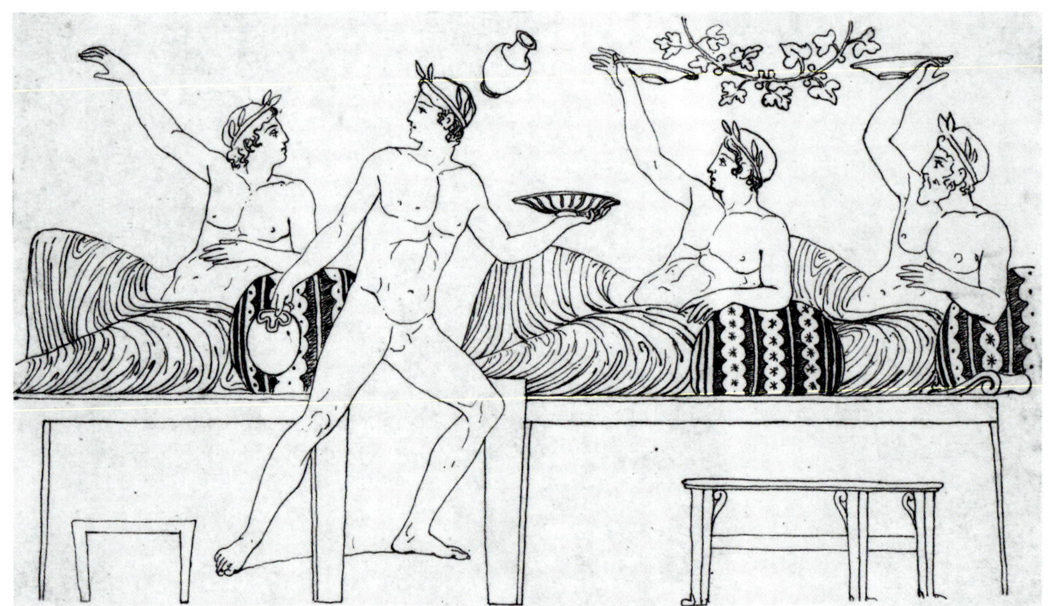

38
Sketch of a Symposium Scene from a Red-figure Vase, 1860s
Pencil on paper, 13.9 × 24.1 cm (5½ × 9½ in)
University of Birmingham

39
The Siesta, 1868
Oil on canvas, 130 × 360 cm (51⅛ × 141¾ in)
Prado, Madrid

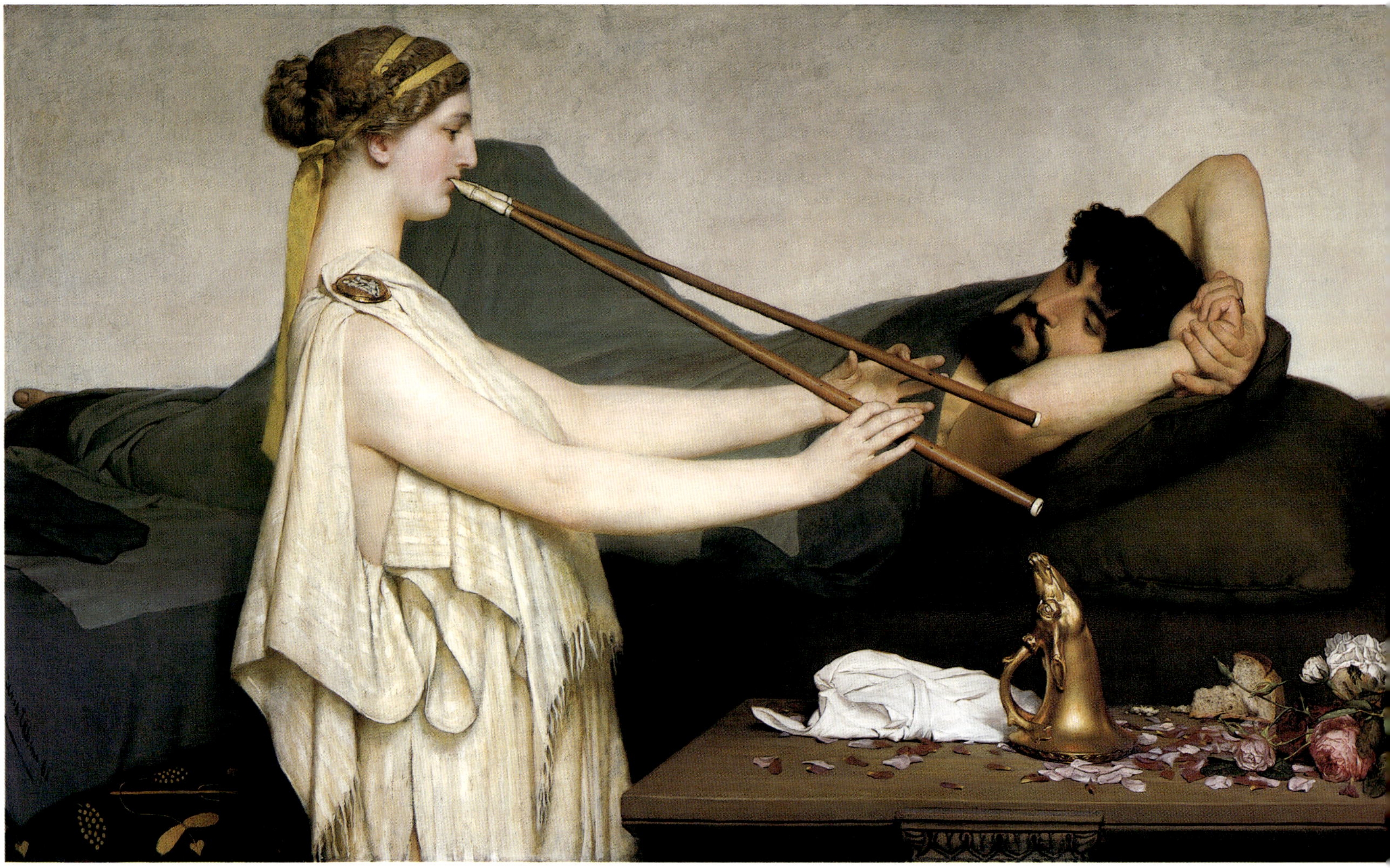

Modern artists and architects were increasingly to experiment with polychromy in their own works.[75] John Gibson's sculpture, *Tinted Venus,* received a controversial response when exhibited in Rome in 1854 and at the International Exhibition, London, in 1862 and archaeologists and public alike found it difficult to conceive of the Parthenon sculptures, long revered in their unpainted state, in bright colours. In 1836 the Trustees of the British Museum appointed a committee to investigate the possibility of polychromy on the Elgin marbles, but it failed to find any traces of colour.[76] Owen Jones, a convinced advocate of polychromy, brought the possibility of a coloured Parthenon to the British public's attention with the creation of a multi-coloured Greek court for the reopening of the Crystal Palace in 1854. Painted casts of the Elgin marbles formed his central display. The exhibition was preceded by public debates on polychromy at the Royal Institute of British Architects in London and by the publication of a series of articles and Jones's own 'An Apology for the Colouring of the Greek Court', as part of a series entitled, *The Fine Arts Court in the Crystal Palace, First Series.*[77] Alma-Tadema would have seen Jones's court on his first visit to London, and perhaps it was this reconstruction which inspired his own coloured version of the Parthenon frieze. *Phidias Showing the Frieze of the Parthenon to his Friends* was bought by the wealthy British wool merchant, David Price. Price acquired an important collection of works by modern artists, including a number of Orientalist and classical subjects, which he housed in a gallery at his London town house. Price refused to let *Phidias* be publicly exhibited and it was not shown until 1877. When it was exhibited again in London in 1882, critics, uneasy about the polychromy, were cautious in their praise.[78]

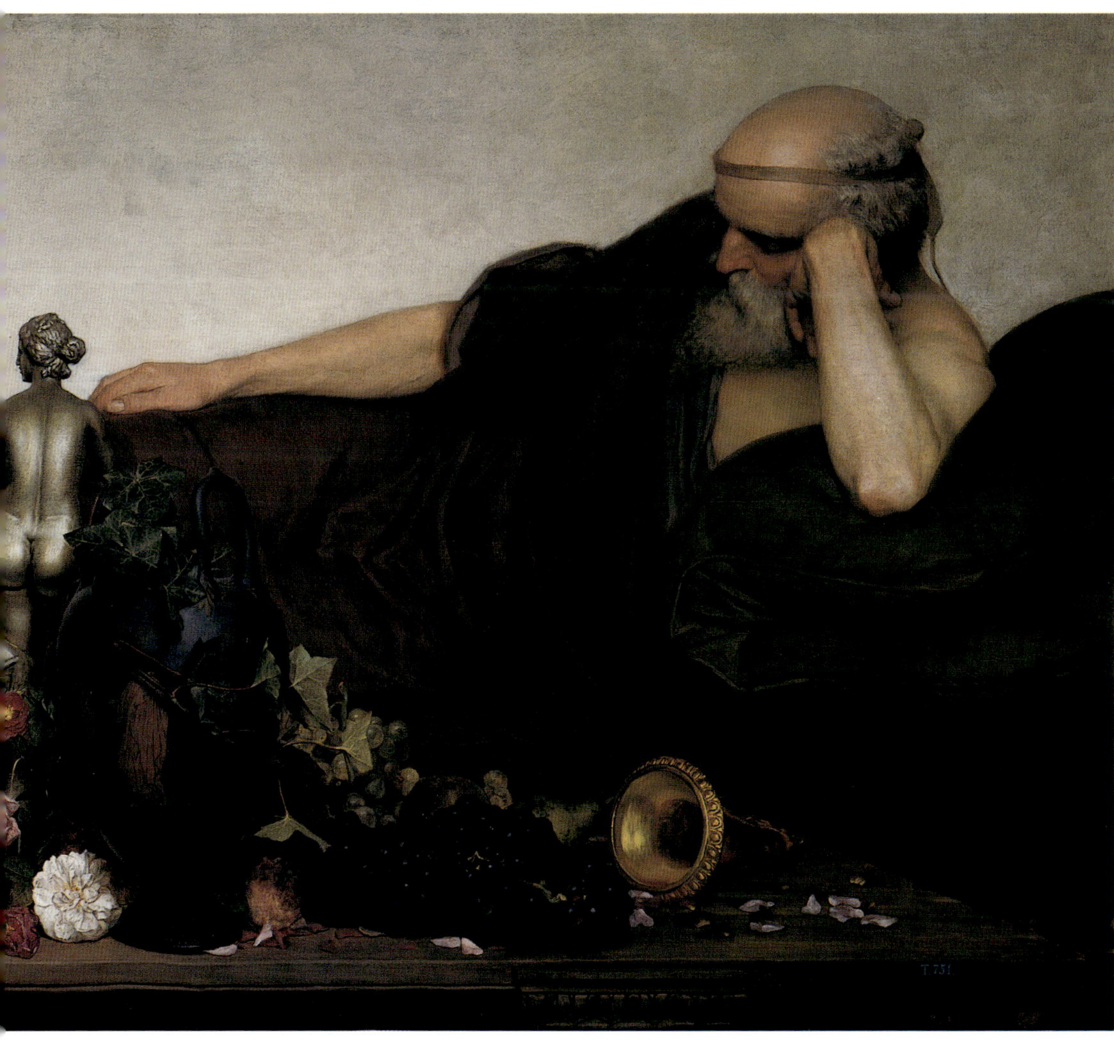

Alma-Tadema also embarked on a series of canvases depicting Greek dining customs. These paintings present new and surprising readings of Greek life by rejecting the normal visual representation of Greece – an idyllic vision based on myth or Homer – in favour of a hedonistic world of leisure and indulgence akin to the Roman connoisseur paintings around the same date. Two paintings were completed in 1868, both entitled *The Siesta*. Inspired by the numerous *symposium* or 'drinking-party' scenes which decorate red-figure vases, the paintings are frieze-like compositions of a horizontal, elongated format. The artist was clearly interested in Greek vase paintings as source material as shown by a number of pencil sketches reproducing vase decorations (Pl.38). The larger of the two siesta paintings (Pl.39) was intended as one of a series of three

40
A Pyrrhic Dance, 1869
Oil on wood, 40·6 × 81·3 cm (16 × 32 in)
Guildhall Art Gallery, London

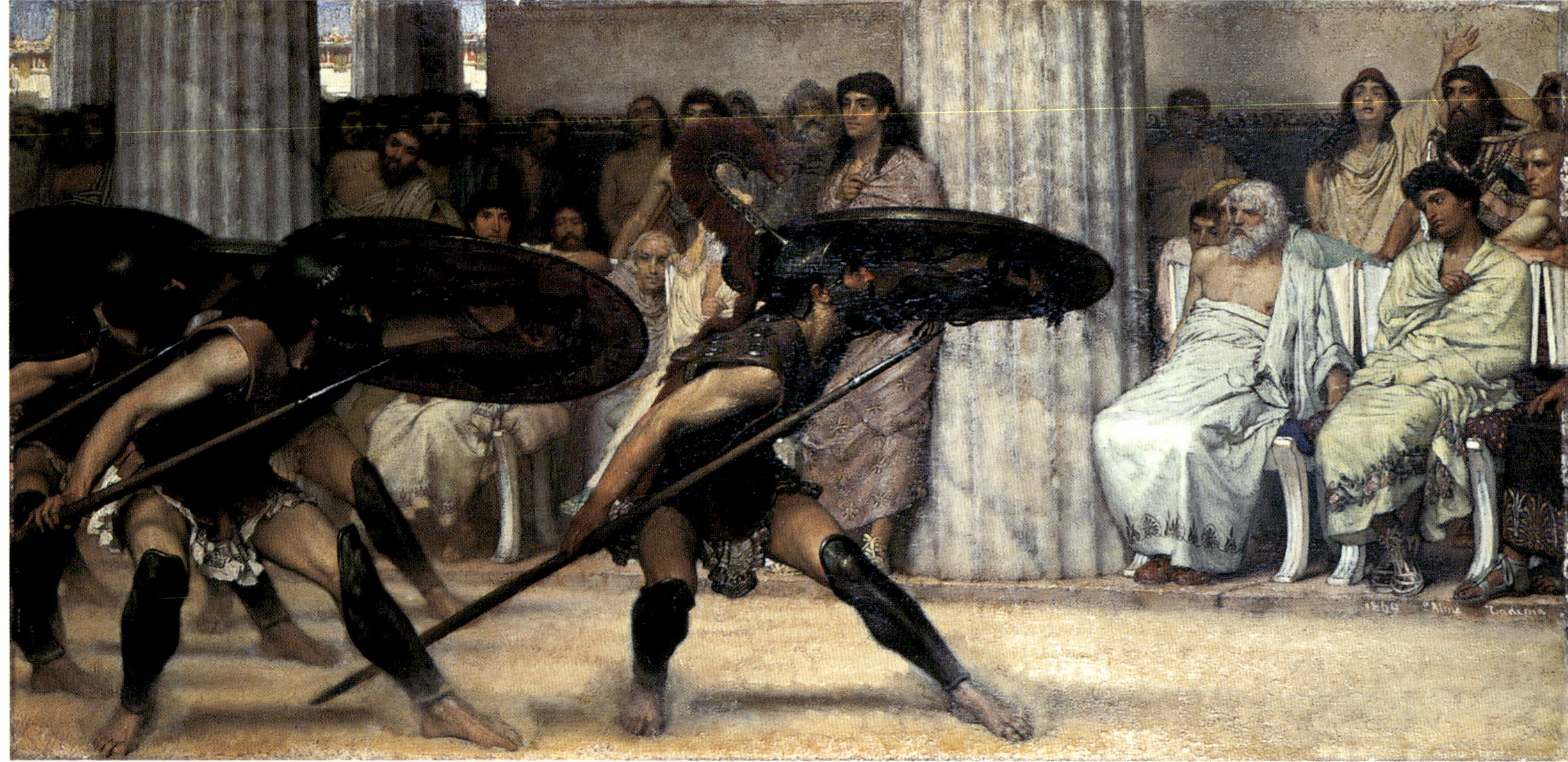

large compositions for a dining room, but, as a buyer could not be found, the series was never completed. Two reclining men, one older and the other younger, doze after dinner to the sound of a flute girl playing the *diaulos* (double flute). On the table before them, amidst scattered roses and grapes, rest two empty drinking cups, a red-figure vase entwined with ivy and a silver statuette of the Medici Venus (Uffizi Gallery, Florence). The much smaller *Siesta* shows a similar composition, only this time reversed. Once again two men recline and listen to a flute-girl while on a table before them rests a red-figure vase, drinking cup, perfume phial and silver statuette of the Farnese Hercules. In these two paintings, the artist toys with the viewer's certainty in the look of the ancient world by changing the size, material and function of well-known classical sculptures: the Venus and Hercules, both over life-size marble statues, are transformed into miniature silver table decorations.

Pictures which already confound traditional visual preconceptions about antiquity also hint at another (and to a contemporary audience, arguably, less acceptable) side of Greek life through lines of verse inscribed on the frame of the larger painting:

In the cool shade rest thee now,
Fair Bathyllus, in this tree;
Through its foliage to and fro,
Zephyr wanders dreamily.

The verses form part of *Anacreontea* 18, in which the poet seeks to ward off the heat of love. The *Anacreontea* is a collection of Greek poems long attributed to the early classical poet, Anacreon, but by the nineteenth century recognized as later and of unknown authorship. The poems of both Anacreon and the *Anacreontea* take as their subject wine, love and beautiful boys. And while Anacreontean verses set a voluptuous mood for the painting, the choice of lines which include Bathyllus – the beautiful youth and sometime lover of the poet – draws our attention to the homoeroticism of a *symposium* setting. An all-male preserve, the Greek *symposium* admitted women only as semi-professional *hetairae* (high-class prostitutes) or hired entertainers. The presence of an older and a younger man (although bearded) suggests a familiar relationship between the adult lover (*erastes*) and his beloved youth (*eromenos*). Such a reading is even suggested by Georg Ebers, who describes the painting in the following terms: 'a youth and an old man, like Anacreon and his favourite, have sat down together in friendly companionship, surrounded by an atmosphere of sweet repose; they listen, under the protection of Aphrodite, the bestower of happiness, amid flowers, wine, and fruit, to the dulcet tones of a flute.'[79] Through the use of archaeological and literary references,

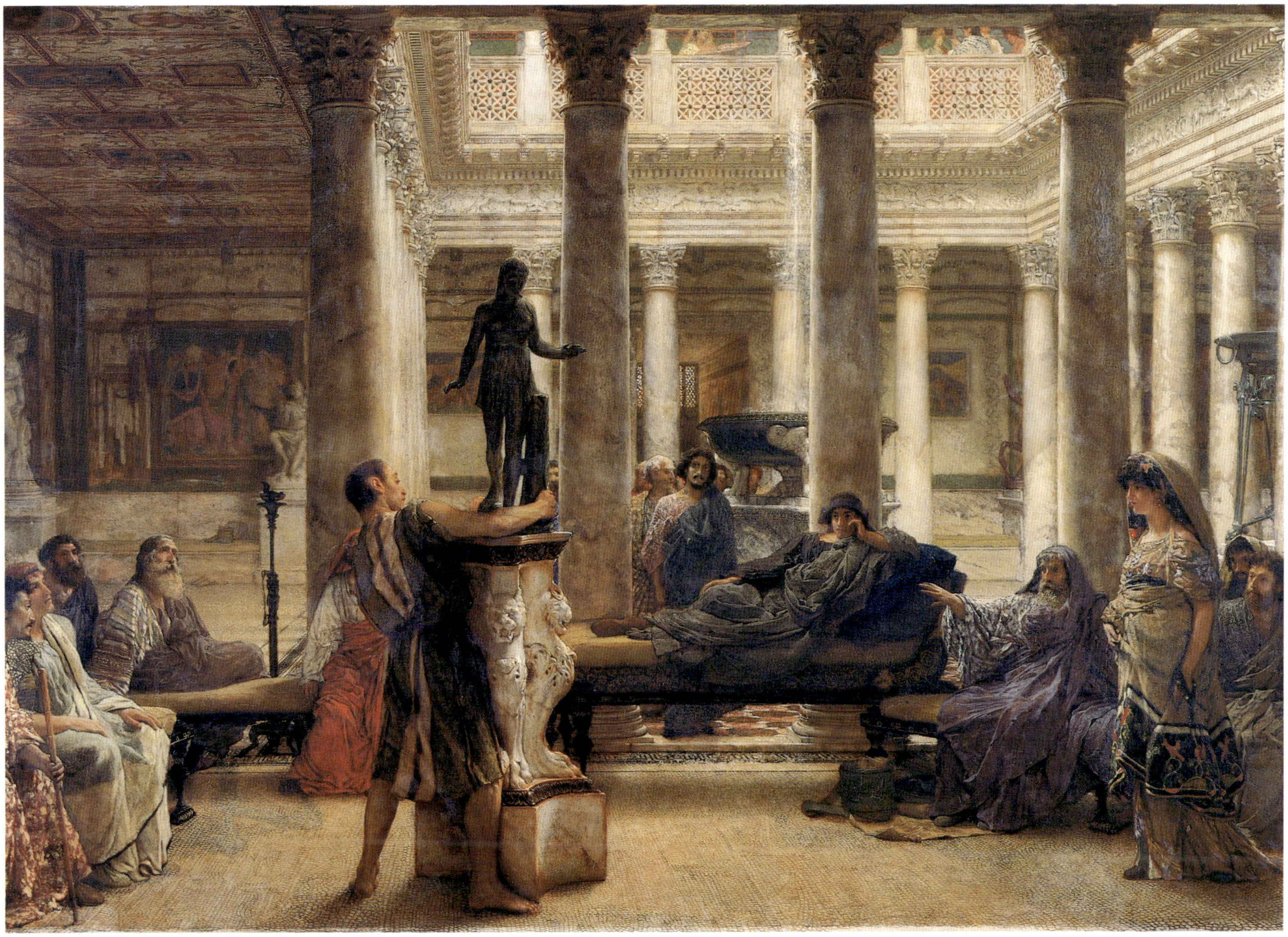

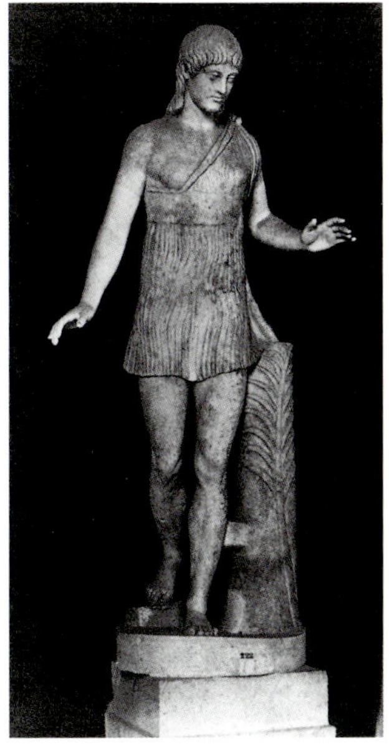

41
A Roman Art Lover, 1870
Oil on wood, 73·5 × 101·6 cm (29 × 40 in)
Milwaukee Art Museum, Layton Art Collection

42
Spartan Girl Athlete, Roman, 2nd century AD
Marble, Vatican Museum, Rome:
University of Birmingham

Alma-Tadema charges the educated viewer to rethink traditional constructions of ancient Greece.

Another allusion (although less unmistakeable) to the homoerotic nature of Greek culture is a feature of *A Pyrrhic Dance* (Pl.40), in which mature bearded men and clean-shaven and effeminate youths watch the performance of a military dance side by side.[80] Homoerotic allusions, even within a seemingly distant context, were potentially highly controversial given that a homosexual lifestyle in nineteenth-century Europe was relegated to the status of illegal subculture.

The Pyrrhic dance, whose origin remains obscure, was, by the Classical period, performed annually at the public Attic festival, the *Panathenaea*. In the Roman world performances took place in the arena. Alma-Tadema's dancers wear the armour of classical Greek soldiers (*hoplites*) – a large bronze shield (*hoplon*), helmet, corselet, leg greaves and javelin. As in *Phidias Showing the Frieze of the Parthenon to his Friends*, the artist has included polychromatic architectural decoration, although here we only glimpse the painted outer frieze of a Doric temple.

In 1869 the painting received favourable reviews, but its exhibition at the Grosvenor Gallery in 1882–3 prompted John Ruskin to offer a notorious critique in which he compared it to 'a microscopic view of a small detachment of black-beetles, in search of a dead rat.'[81] The painting clearly offended Ruskin because of its unconventional treatment of a revered subject. For him, Greek warfare should be as the splendid heroism and individual quest for glory he associated with Homer. In the same lecture Ruskin cites the passage from Homer's *Iliad* (18. 203–9) where Achilles routs the enemy by showing himself in triumph on the Greek ramparts.[82] In effect, Alma-Tadema challenges the Victorian equation of ancient warfare with a single named hero competing on the battlefield, and instead depicts a theatrical display of a ritualistic military dance by anonymous performers.

While Frederic Leighton and many other classical-subject painters saw the Hellenic world in terms of an idealized heroic and mythological past, Alma-Tadema's attitude to Greece, as to Rome, was refreshingly irreverent. The Greek dining series evokes a leisured world akin to imperial Rome, and even his treatment of Phidias and the Parthenon sculptures brings a tangibility to the most elevated symbol of Hellenism in the visual sphere. Ruskin offers an intelligent, if hostile, response to Alma-Tadema's achievement. By contrast, most critics writing in the late 1860s and 1870s were content to describe rather than analyse his paintings. Given their silence about his controversialities, his challenging construction of Greece has all the hallmarks of a private joke with a knowledgeable few among his viewing public.

Returning to Roman subjects, Alma-Tadema's next connoisseur painting, *A Roman Art Lover* (Pl.41), shows, in a characteristically splendid interior, a slave turning a statue so that it can be admired from all angles. The statue is the Spartan Girl Athlete (Pl.42) from the Vatican Museum, a piece included in the artist's photographic collection. Here it is reduced in size and transformed from its original marble to bronze, although the artist has curiously not removed the struts, needed to support marble, but unnecessary for bronze. The circle of admirers in previous paintings has expanded to an eager crowd. Cut off and obscured behind pillars we see glimpses of famous marble statues: the Medici Venus and the younger of a pair of Centaurs (Capitoline Museum, Rome), like the Venus, greatly admired since their discovery at Hadrian's villa in the eighteenth century. These highly regarded statues, hidden in corners, serve as an ironic contrast with the piece which the 'Roman art lover' values most highly.

By 1870, small, dark interiors had changed to accommodate more decorative detail and ornament. We find the single mosaic fountain in the background of *Catullus at Lesbia's* (Pl.22), painted in 1865, elaborated to the astonishing architectural structure of *A Roman Art Lover*, five years later. Rooms also appear less enclosed and more spacious. Instead of abruptly cutting off ceilings as in *Catullus at Lesbia's*, the painter ensures that the full height of a room is displayed as expansive and lofty, while in *Catullus Reading his Poems at Lesbia's House* (Pl.26), one side of the room is open, disclosing a townscape beyond.

A corner of the vast room of *A Roman Art Lover* provides the setting for *A Juggler* (Pl.43), painted one month earlier, in which we see richly painted walls and ceiling within an elaborate architectural structure of unfluted green Cipollino columns and elaborate Corinthian capitals and frieze. Once more the idle rich amuse themselves, but instead of admiring a collector's treasure, they watch an entertainer juggle eggs. The Egyptian identity of the juggler is highlighted by his dark skin and elaborate head scarf, also by the shabti box next to him; originally used for storing funerary statuettes, it is here irreverently transformed into a box for a juggler's equipment.

A similarly elaborate room appears in *The Vintage Festival* (Pl.44), depicting a Roman religious festival in honour of Bacchus, god of wine. Bacchic subjects had a special appeal for nineteenth-century artists, particularly the represen-

43
A Juggler, 1870
Oil on canvas, mounted on wood,
78·7 × 49·5 cm (31 × 19½ in)
Private collection

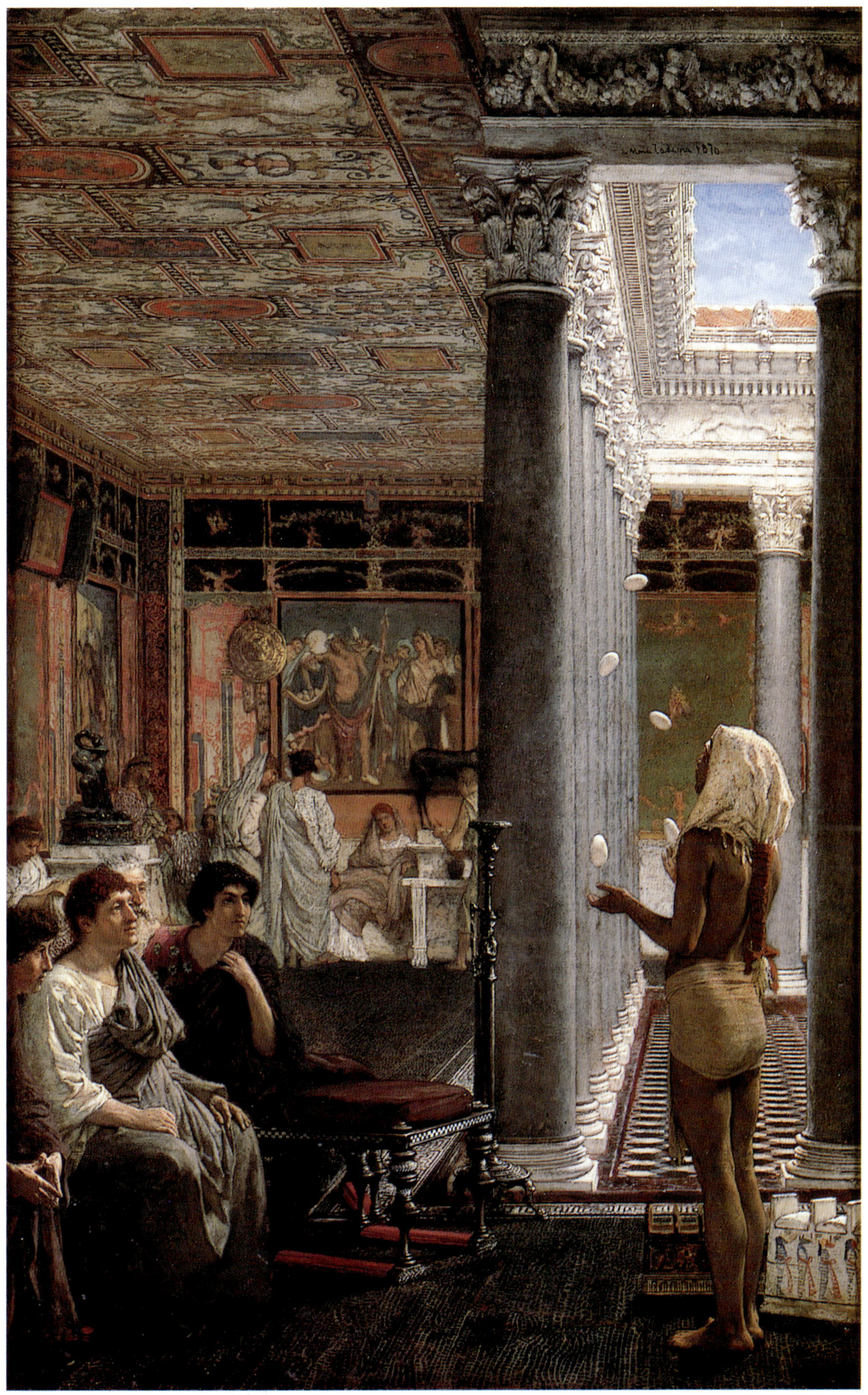

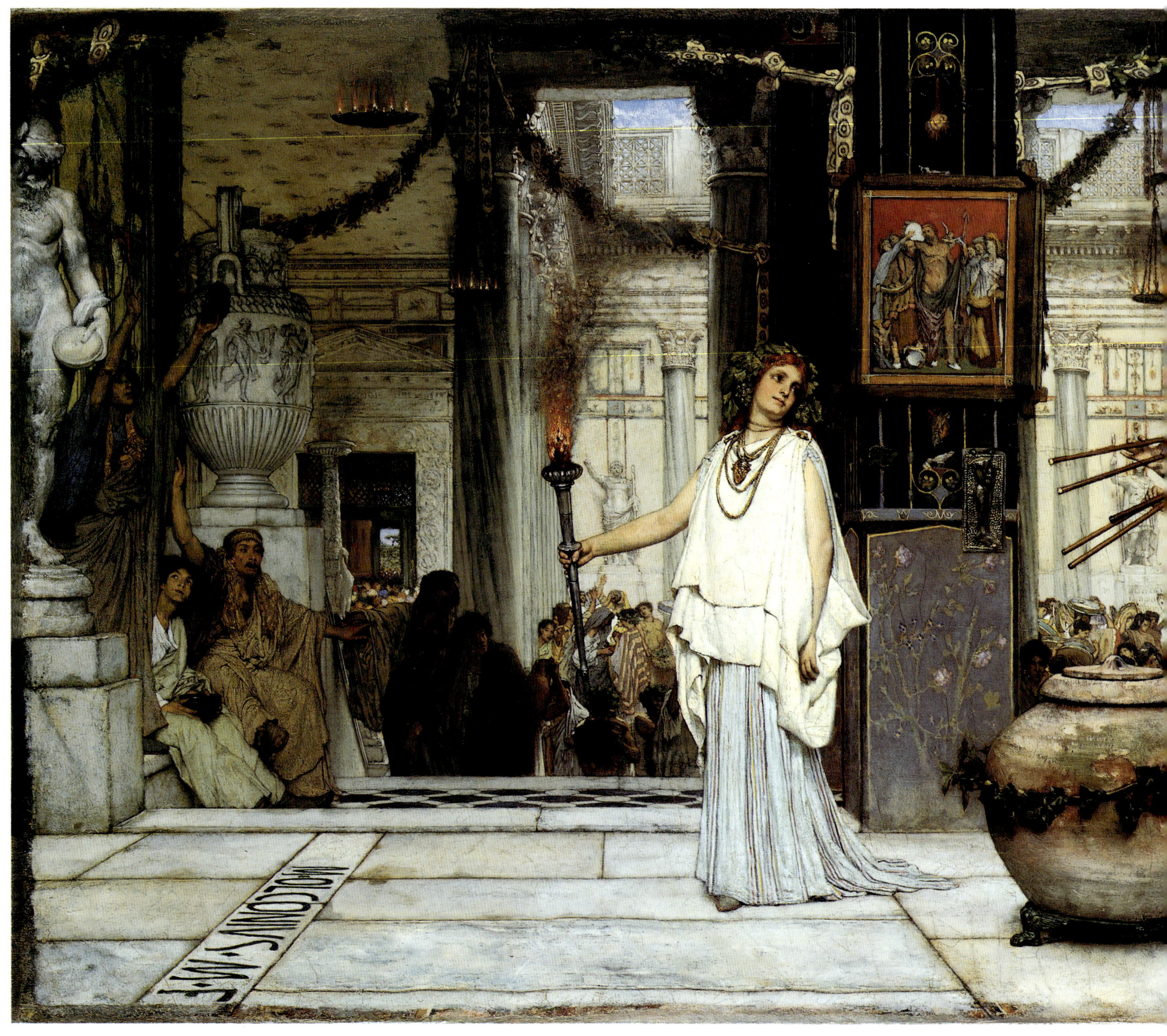

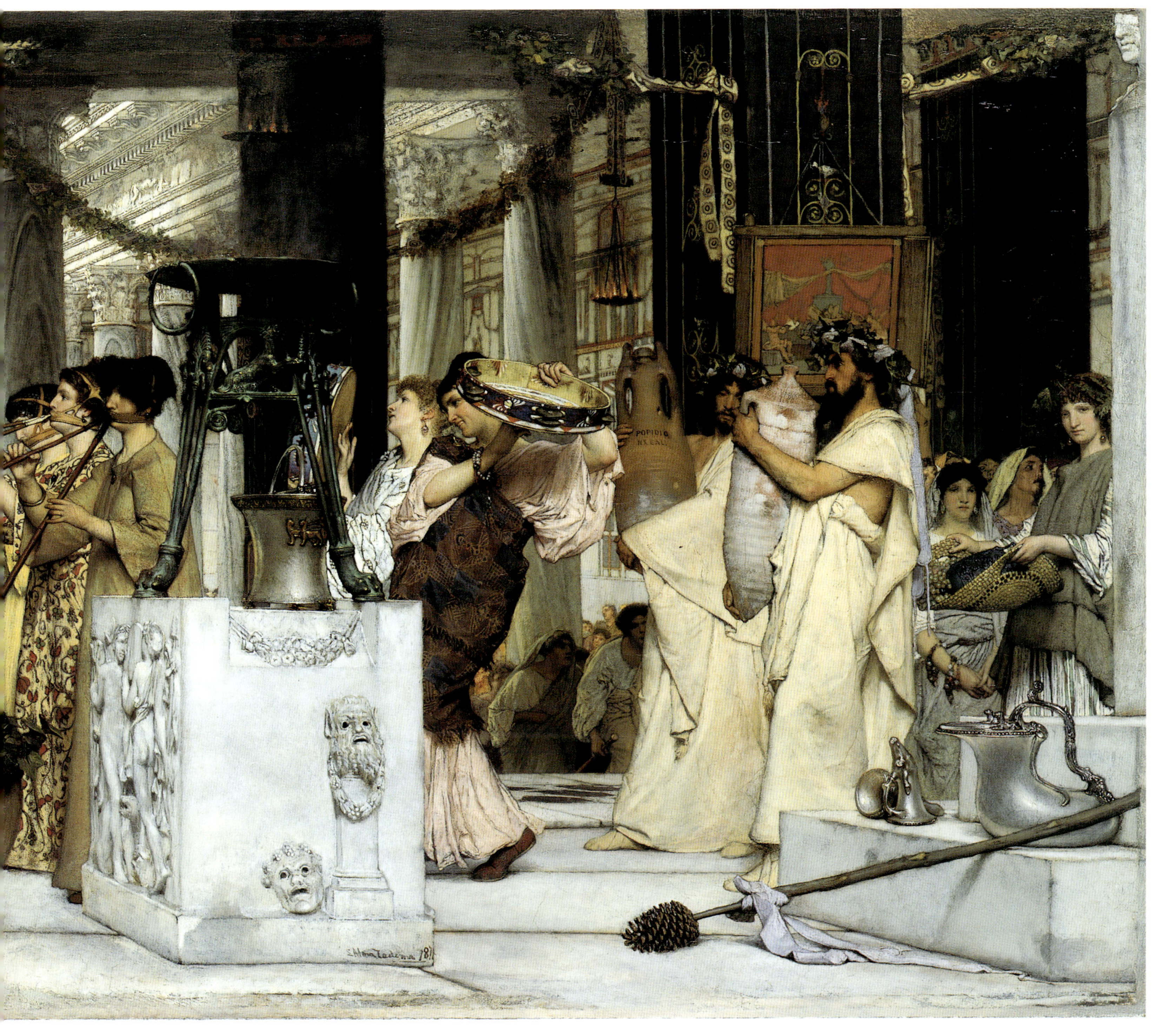

44
The Vintage Festival, 1870
Oil on canvas, 77 × 177 cm (30⅜ × 69⅝ in)
Hamburger Kunsthalle, Hamburg

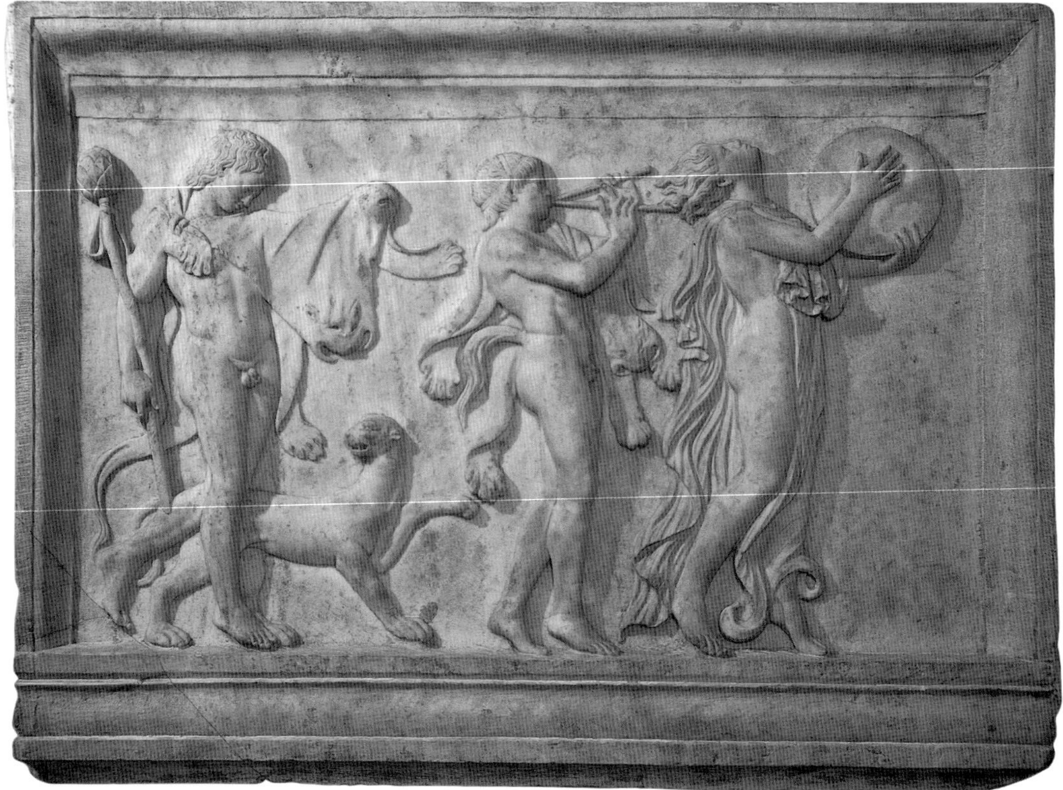

45
Dionysiac Relief, Roman, 1st–2nd century AD
Marble
British Museum, London

46
Marcus Holconius Rufus, Roman,
late 1st century BC–early 1st century AD
Marble, H 2·02 m (79½in)
Archaeological Museum, Naples

47
Temple of Bacchus at Baalbek, 2nd century AD
University of Birmingham

tation of scantily-clad and cavorting women worshippers, bacchants or maenads. The cult of Bacchus was officially welcomed to Rome from Greece, but in 186 BC Bacchanalia were prohibited after a scandalous exposé of 'debauchery and murders'.[83] Nevertheless, archaeological and iconographic evidence attests to continued worship within the private sphere. Greco-Roman relief sculptures of the Dionysus-Bacchus *thiasus* (band of followers) (Pl.45) show wild processions of cavorting maenads-bacchants, nymphs, satyrs and sileni, while free-standing sculptures of nymphs, satyrs, hermaphrodites and Pans exude a playful and erotic mood. Alma-Tadema had earlier employed members of the *thiasus* – a satyr and goat – to add an extra sexual frisson to *Catullus at Lesbia's*.[84]

The Vintage Festival appropriates many elements from ancient Bacchic iconography. A priestess adorned with ivy leaves and grapes, familiar attributes in statues of the god, leads the celebrants. Worshippers follow playing the *tibia* (double flutes) and *tympana* (tambourines); a *thyrsus* (staff topped with a pine cone) rests against the altar; and finally attendants carry a *liknon* (basket) of the vintage grapes. This ordered procession is only a part of the worship; in the background wilder figures dance and wave tympana in evocation of the more riotous behaviour described by Livy.

On the far left, the artist includes a floor inscription relating to Marcus Holconius Rufus, a member of the prominent Pompeian family (owners of the slave in *An Exedra*),[85] and yet the actual house of Marcus Holconius, situated on the Via dell'Abbondanza, could not have sported such magnificent architecture and decoration. Pompeii, after all, was a provincial town inhabited by the middle and lower classes. In place of the dark red walls which characterize his earlier Pompeian scenes, the artist has substituted a greater use of marble. The painting combines artefacts from Pompeii and from Rome, including a fresco depicting Hercules and Omphale from the House of Marcus Lucretius in Pompeii (also represented in *A Juggler*) and, in the background left, the famous statue of the Prima Porta Augustus (Pl.76), found at the villa of Livia just outside Rome. The companion statue on the far right is inscribed with the name Julius Caesar; a military portrait, it can be compared with a statue of Marcus Holconius himself, dressed in the uniform of a military tribune, originally situated at the cross-roads of Via Stabiana and Via dell'Abbondanza in Pompeii (Pl.46).

The impressive interior found in *A Roman Art Lover*, *A Juggler* and *The Vintage Festival* shows an ornate two-storied Corinthian atrium. The elaborate order with sculpted frieze is based on grand temple, rather than domestic, architecture. Indeed, the Corinthian capitals are surely an imitation of those from the portico of the second-century AD temple of Bacchus at Baalbek in Syria, one of the most extravagant of all surviving Roman structures and far removed from comparatively modest Pompeian domestic dwellings. Alma-Tadema's interest in the temple is confirmed by his possession of a selection of photographs showing some of its architectural detail, including the ceiling of the portico, frieze and capitals (Pl.47). While archaeological detail in earlier paintings such as *Catullus at Lesbia's* conformed to the notional date of the painting, here eclectic sources combine to create an impression of splendour and luxury while references to Pompeii function as authenticating signals but do not promise an accurate portrayal of high living in a provincial town.

Gambart paid a sum in excess of that arranged for *The Vintage Festival*. During a dinner hosted by the dealer for the artists of Brussels, Alma-Tadema found tucked into his table napkin an additional cheque for £100. *The Vintage Festival* was bought by the international financier and proprietor of a London banking firm, Baron Henry Schröder, for £1850. Prices for Alma-Tadema's paintings were beginning to soar, and Gambart's generosity in no way exceeded his profit. Schröder bought pictures by a number of continental artists, including Alma-Tadema's former teacher, Leys, and was eventually to own ten paintings by Alma-Tadema himself.[86]

During his five years in Brussels, Alma-Tadema was at the height of his productivity and had, at the same time, developed his own artistic style. He was also beginning to accrue honours

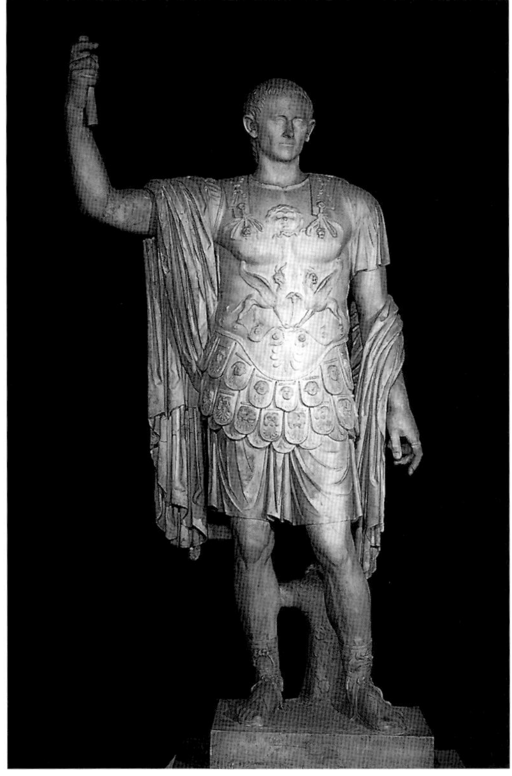

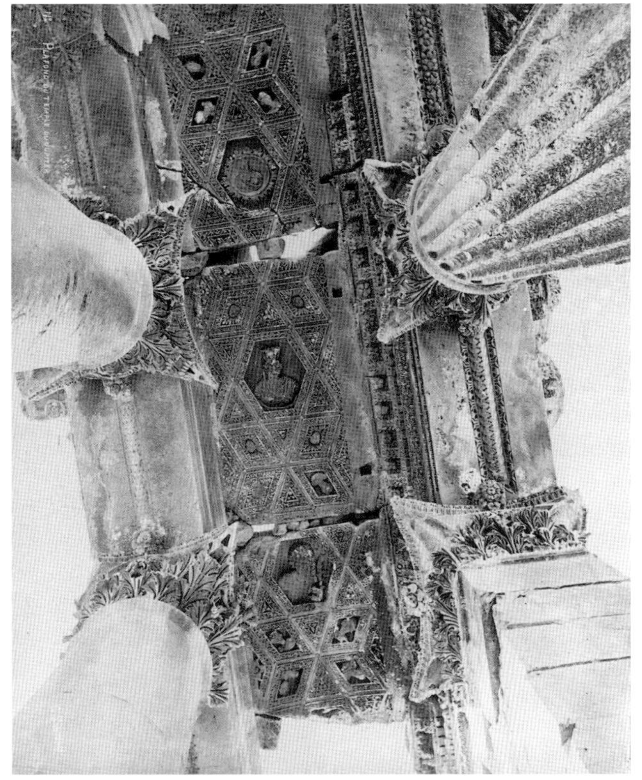

and medals across the continent: he was awarded the small gold medal at the Paris Salon in 1864 and the second-class medal at the 1867 Paris Exposition; in 1866 he was made Knight of the Order of Leopold by Leopold II of Belgium, and two years later he was knighted by King William of Holland. The artist, eager to consolidate his European reputation, was keen to leave Brussels. In 1868 he wrote a letter to his cousin and pupil, Hendrik Willem Mesdag (later to become a successful maritime painter): 'One thing is certain: my reputation in Paris is greater than in Holland and Belgium. Everyone knows me there. I have even met a gentleman who has offered to build me a house on his land to suit my wishes.'[87] The decision not to settle in Paris may have been prompted by the outbreak of the Franco-Prussian war in 1870, after which a number of continental artists (including Claude Monet, Camille Pissarro, Aimé-Jules Dalou, Gustave Doré, Henri Fantin-Latour, Alphonse Legros, Alfred Sisley and Jean-Léon Gérôme) stayed temporarily in London. In the same year the Alma-Tadema family moved to London where they were to make a permanent home.

Alma-Tadema left Brussels having distinguished himself as an artist who employed the traditions of European painting in pursuit of a very individual style. His early Merovingian subjects present a surprising vision of late antiquity which centres on Gaul rather than Rome, while the Egyptian pictures reject an eroticized East in favour of meticulous archaeological reconstruction. By 1870, however, he was best-known for his classical subjects in which he combines the historicizing of the Dutch-Belgian tradition and the classicism of the French Néo-Grecs with a unique, and uniquely subversive, vision all of his own.

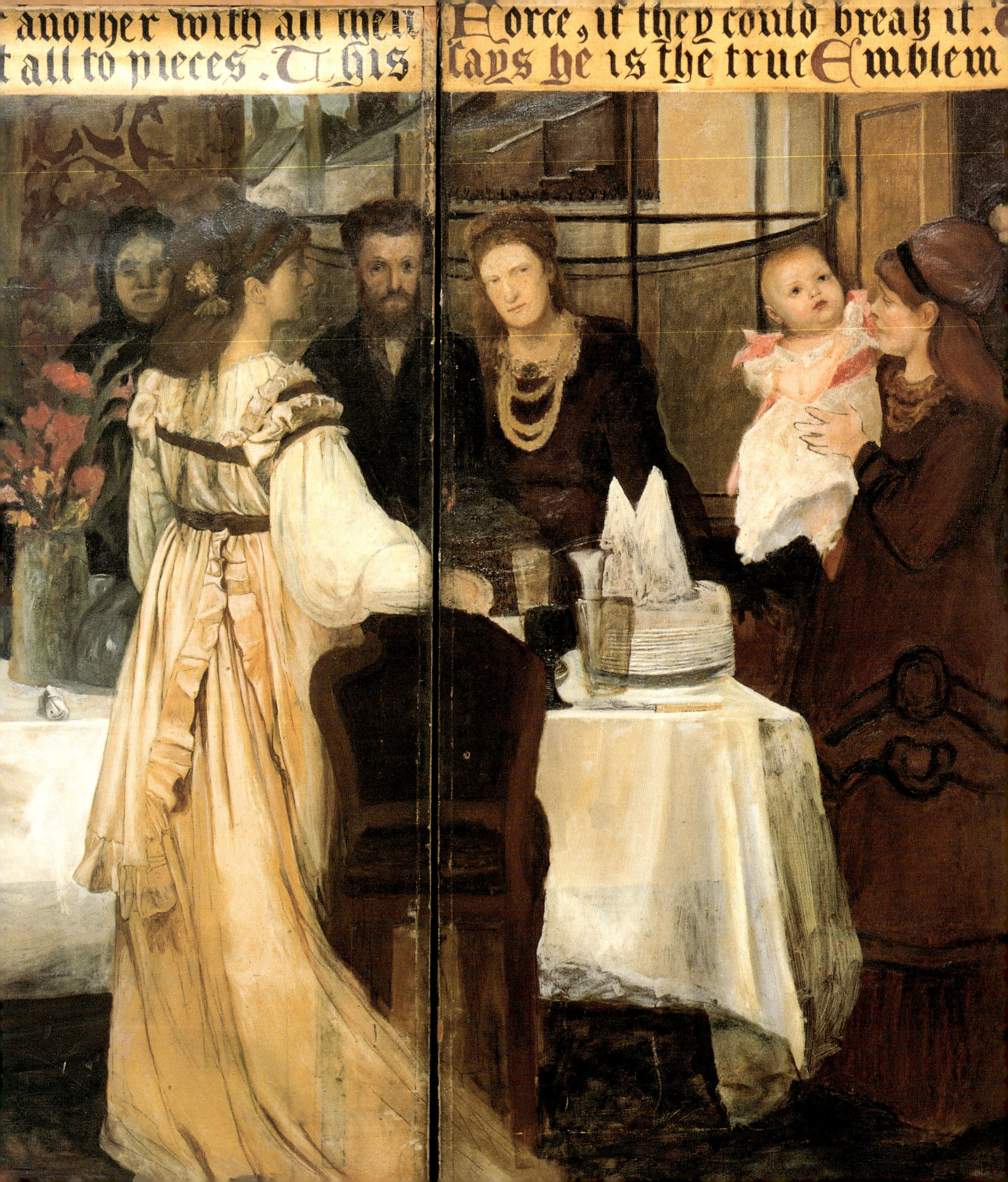

r another with all their Force, if they could break it.
t all to pieces. This says he is the true Emblem

1870–1887 ESTABLISHMENT AND SUCCESS

II/1
A DUTCH PAINTER IN LONDON

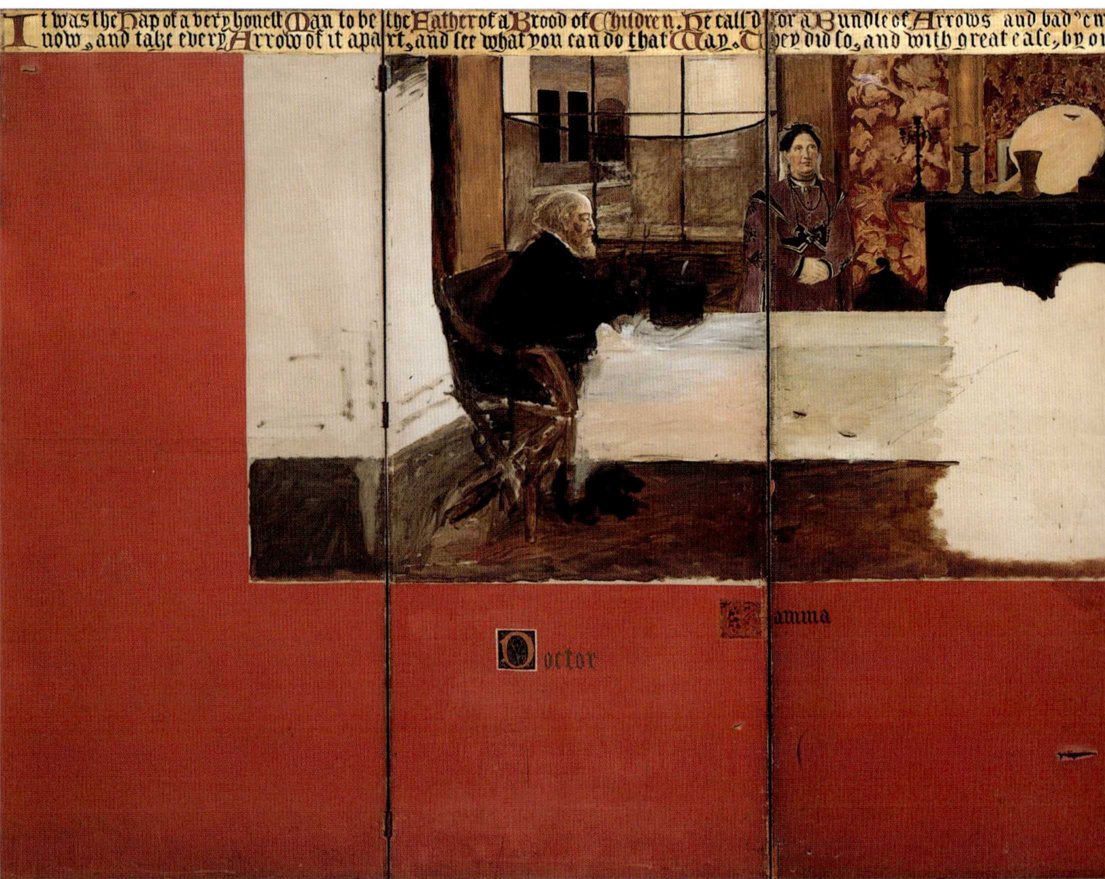

48 previous page
The Epps Family Screen (detail of Pl.49)

49
The Epps Family Screen, 1870–1
Oil on canvas, six hinged panels each 182·9 × 78·7 cm (72 × 31 in)
Victoria and Albert Museum, London

Alma-Tadema's decision to leave Brussels may well have involved commercial reasons. Despite the national honours conferred upon him, critical responses by the Dutch and Belgian press were muted and he did not receive the kind of glittering reviews which attracted wealthy patrons.[88] Alma-Tadema did find a defender in Carel Vosmaer, who from the 1870s began cataloguing the artist's work. As co-editor of *De Nederlandsche Spectator*, Vosmaer was able to promote Alma-Tadema in the press, but, for the most part, his type of classical-subject genre painting was very much out of vogue with current Dutch and Belgian art and attracted little positive critical coverage.

A Dutch critic in the *Kunstkronijk* complained: 'less attuned to the national movement in art, and not at all recalling Dutch everyday life in subject matter, is Alma-Tadema … who has chosen his theme from Greek or Roman antiquity.'[89] By the late 1860s, Dutch and Flemish history painting was still nationalist in character, while, at the same time, low-life genre subjects and landscapes were becoming increasingly popular. Alma-Tadema's Egyptian and classical paintings must have seemed remote from current art trends. By contrast, classical subjects were fashionable in other parts of Europe including France and Britain. In Britain from the mid-1860s, artists such as G. F. Watts (1817–1904), Frederic Leighton (1830–96), Edward Poynter (1836–1918) and Albert Moore (1841–93) were united by their common interest in representing the ancient world on the modern canvas. One of the first public displays of classical subjects by young British artists was the Royal Academy exhibition of 1865, which included, among painters of quite different orientation and allegiance, such varied

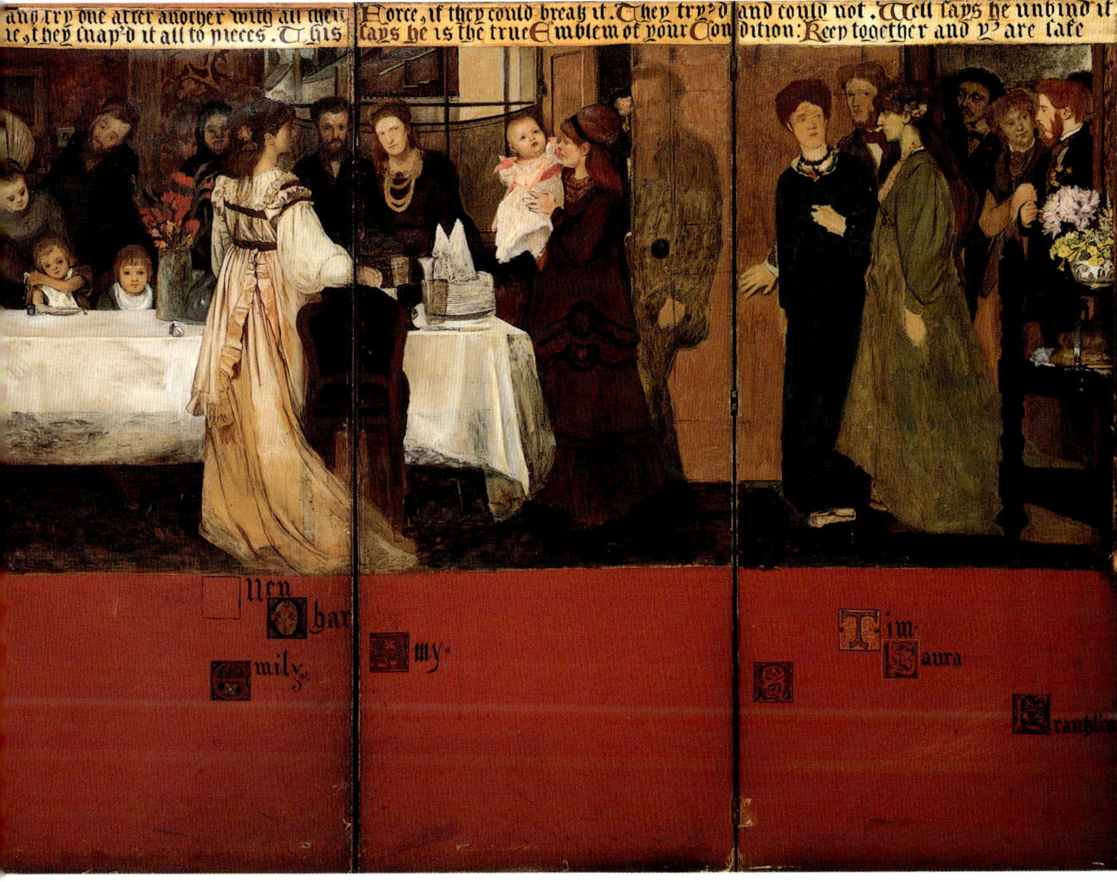

works as Frederic Leighton's *Helen of Troy*, John Everett Millais's *Romans Leaving Britain*, Simeon Solomon's *Habet!* and Edward Poynter's *Faithful unto Death*. By 1868 Frederic Leighton, as new Academician and member of the Hanging Committee of the Royal Academy of Arts, was in a position to ensure that classical subjects were well represented on the Academy walls and, from then on, many classical-subject painters progressed through the Academy ranks as a guaranteed route to success.

Alma-Tadema's archaeologically accurate genre painting offered no direct challenge to the British classical-subject painters, who each worked within the boundaries of their own distinct styles. Watts concentrated on large allegorical and mythological canvases which drew on Greek art as a primary source, while Leighton's graceful and idealized visions of a Hellenic past looked to Greek art, myth and literature for subject, drapery and figure-type. Moore was a unique creative talent who used classical-type motifs as embellishment of aesthetic paintings without subject. Poynter embraced a more eclective œuvre which included works of a historical, mythological and archaeological cast, and only turned to archaeological genre subjects in the 1880s, arguably influenced by Alma-Tadema's example. The novelty of Alma-Tadema's approach was proclaimed in a review of *The Juggler* (exhibited at the Royal Academy in 1870): 'Alma-Tadema is difficult of classification: be belongs to no school, or, in other words, he himself is a school.'[90] Classical (and Egyptian) themes were well-used by his contemporaries, but Alma-Tadema's originality lies in a striving to present traditional subjects in a fresh manner.

Critical coverage of Alma-Tadema by the British press was generally enthusiastic. *Roman Lady Returning Home from Market*, exhibited at the French Gallery in 1866, received a long description accompanied by an engraving in the *Illustrated London News*.[91] Alma-Tadema exhibited his first works at the Royal Academy in 1869. *A Roman Art Lover* and *A Pyrrhic Dance* (Pl.40) received a fair measure of critical attention. Although the critic of the *Illustrated London News* detected 'a too obvious straining for archaeological originality',[92] it is significant that the pictures merited discussion, while F G Stephens, writing in the *Athenaeum*, attributed to them 'a great deal of spirit and originality'.[93]

Critics were keen to acknowledge Alma-Tadema's originality, but they concentrated on archaeological exactitude and aesthetic appeal, at the expense of ironic or subversive content.[94] Even F.G. Stephens, who was to become a per-

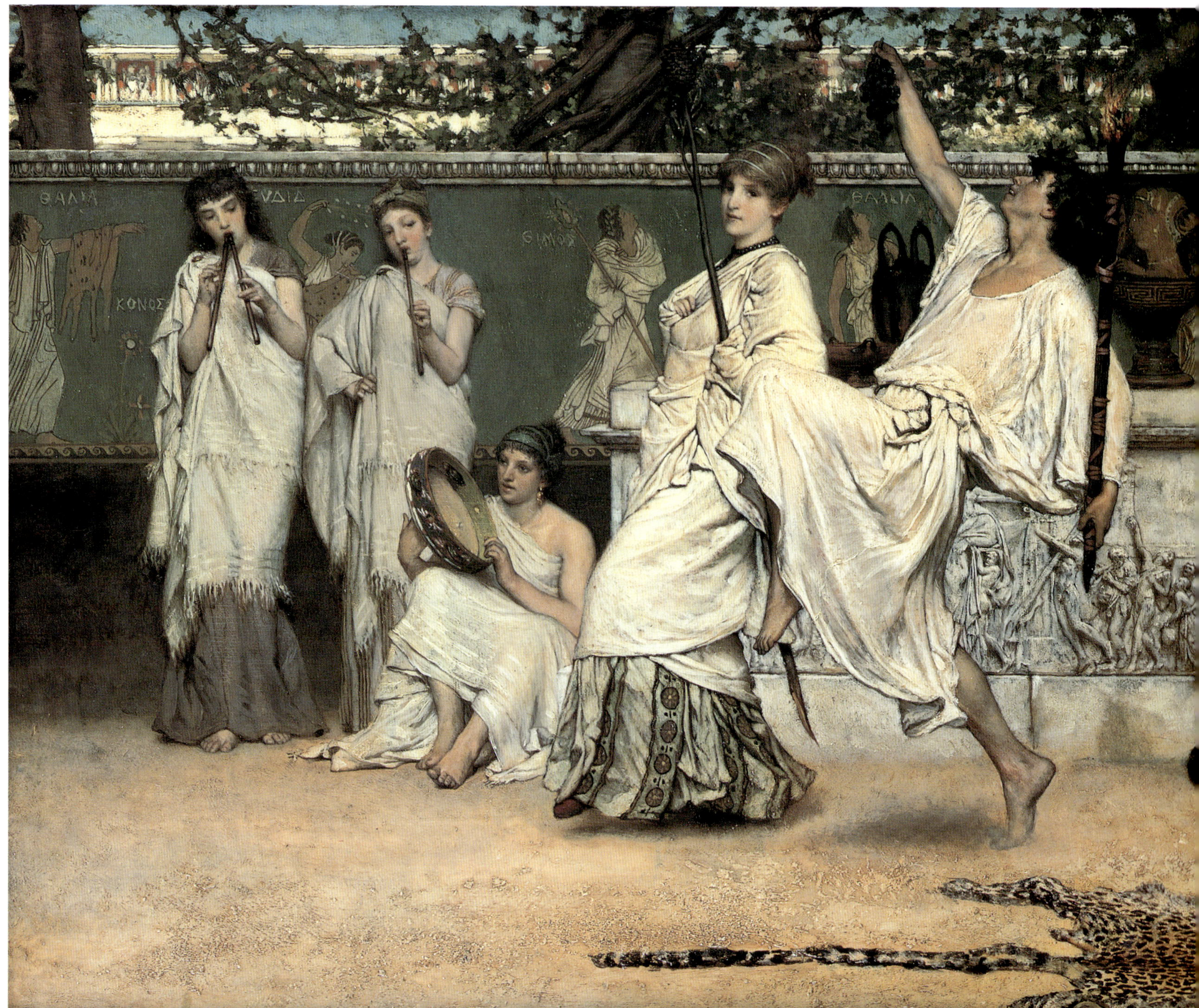

50
A Private Celebration, 1871
Oil on wood, 42·1 × 82·5 cm ($16\frac{5}{8} \times 32\frac{1}{2}$ in)
Private collection

51
Sketch of a Red-figure Vase by the Dinos Painter in the Archaeological Museum, Naples, 1860s
Pencil on paper, 13.9 × 42.5 cm ($5\frac{1}{2} \times 16\frac{3}{4}$ in)
University of Birmingham

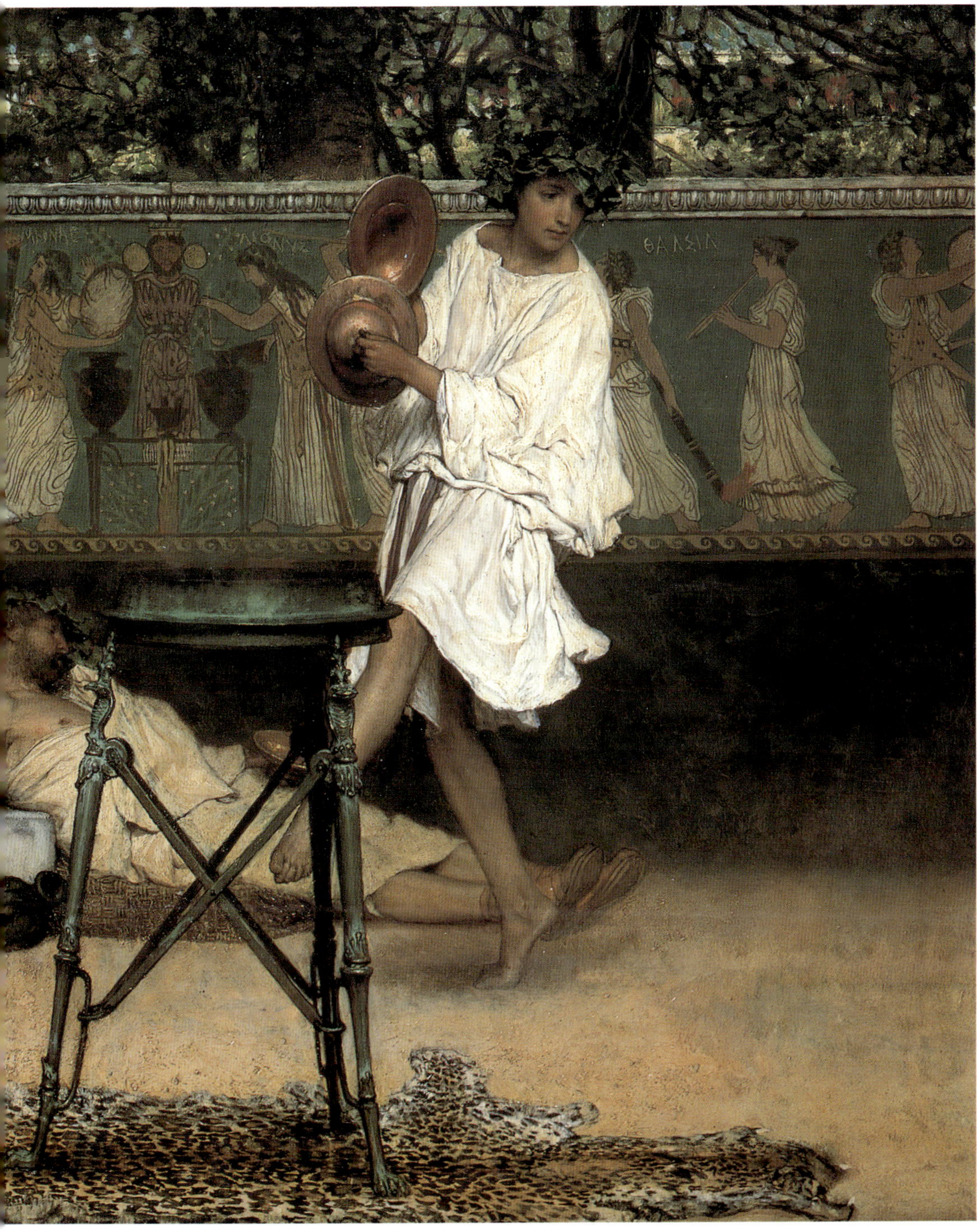

sonal friend of the artist, aims to identify sources rather than uncover additional meanings. In his own lifetime, Alma-Tadema went without any thorough-going critical scrutiny, at least in the public domain, and only now is critical debate beginning to engage with the range of meanings in his canvases.

The artist's first London residence was 4 Camden Square, the home of Frederick Goodall. Goodall was an Orientalizing painter who, after his first trip to Egypt in 1858, produced mostly biblical and historical genre scenes as well as modern genre scenes of contemporary Egypt. Alma-Tadema, who was probably introduced to Goodall by Gambart, was renting the house for six months while Goodall was away on a second trip to Egypt. On Goodall's return he prepared to move to the outskirts of London, while Alma-Tadema continued to occupy his house. Alma-Tadema's first painting completed in London was *The First Whisper of Love* (1870), which can be counted as one of the first of many courtship scenes in ancient settings which were to become characteristic of his later career.[95] It is also the first painting to have a sentimental anecdotal title, perhaps in a calculated attempt to appeal to English taste.

Alma-Tadema was to remain in London for the rest of his life but he, nonetheless, remained reluctant to part with his Dutch lineage. Philip Carr recalls:

> He never became anything like an Englishman, either in his appearance – short and stocky, with a large face and an untidy small beard – or in his speech. His mastery of our language remained elementary to the end of his long life, and, with his Dutch accent to add to the confusion, he was sometimes incomprehensible, especially when he roared with laughter at his own, usually rather childish, funny stories, and became suddenly furious if you did not laugh too.[96]

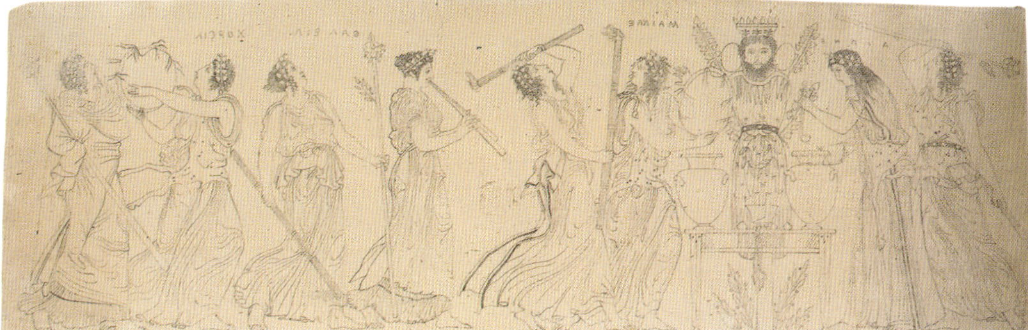

From the time of his move to London, a picture of the man emerges in numerous anecdotes by his contemporaries. The playful and humorous side of his personality is in keeping with his pictorial irony but his raucous and, at times, unruly manner is at odds with the sophistications present in many of his paintings.

On his visit to Britain in 1869 Alma-Tadema had been introduced to Laura Epps (1852–1909), the seventeen-year old daughter of George Napoleon Epps and Anne Bacon Epps. George Napoleon Epps was a respected physician who attracted well-known and wealthy patients. In the late 1840s he had treated Emily Brontë before her

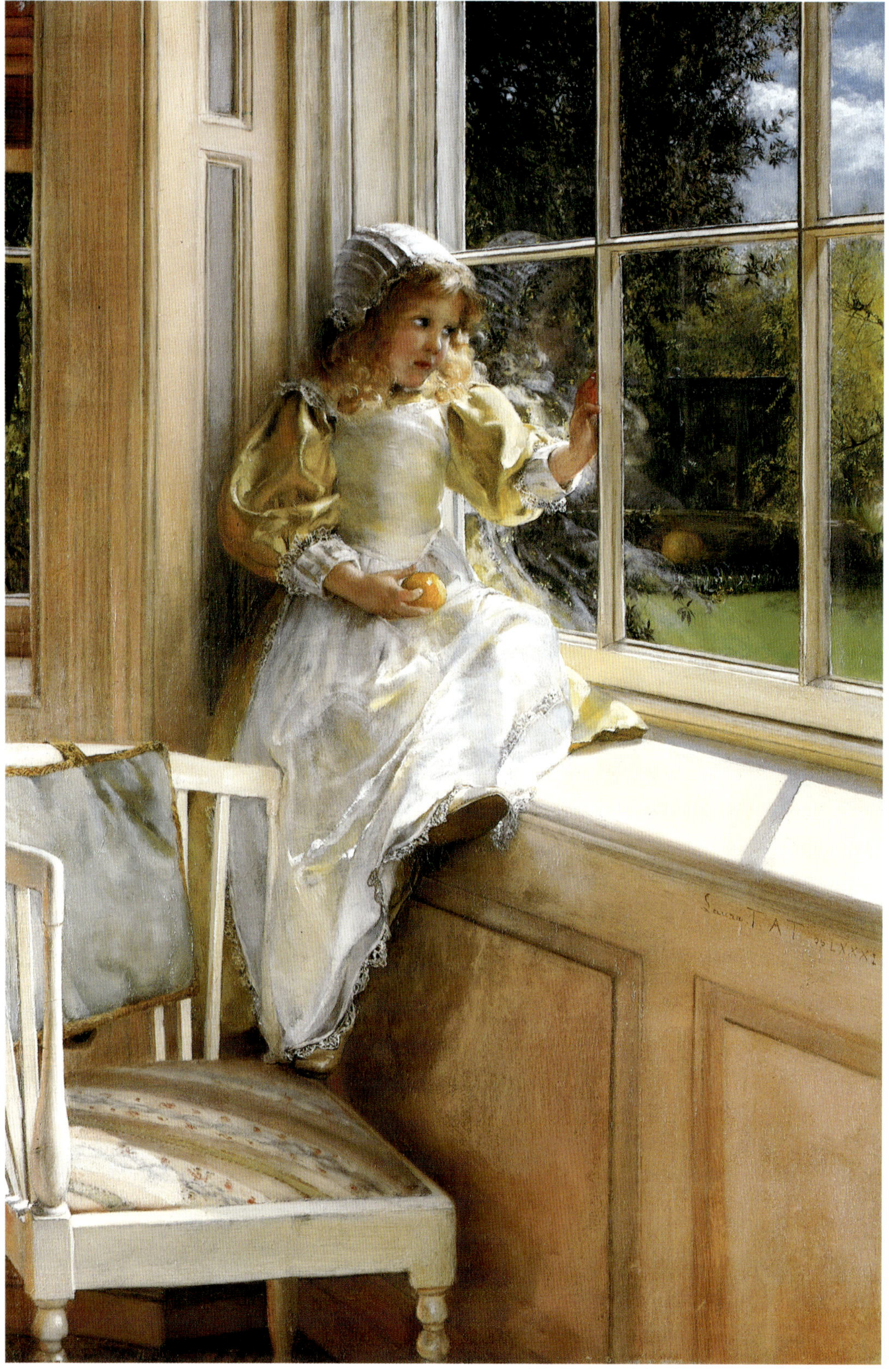

52
Laura Alma-Tadema, *Sunshine*, n.d.
Oil on canvas, 61·5 × 39·5 cm (24¼ × 15½ in)
Private collection

death from consumption.[97] Laura, like many upper-middle-class Victorian girls, was given painting lessons and Alma-Tadema, now in London, was engaged as her tutor. *The Epps Family Screen* (Pl.49), six canvas panels in the form of a folding screen, was begun, though not completed, as an aid to Laura Epps's tuition. It shows three generations of the Epps family in their dining room including George Napoleon Epps seated at the head of the table, Laura, the figure in green on the far right, and Alma-Tadema himself behind her in the doorway. The border is painted in bright red with the names of the figures above. Along the top of the screen is a gold border with an inscription in Gothic lettering appealing to family unity.

One contemporary of Laura Epps described her as 'one of the London beauties, of good stature, auburn-haired, with the warm body of a milkmaid, and a gentle, Greek face'.[98] Alma-Tadema did not usually take on the role of teacher,[99] and the exception he made for Laura Epps can be explained by the fact that the two soon became engaged and, in July 1871, married. Gambart had initial misgivings about the relationship: 'Tadema went last boxing day to a dance at Madox Brown's, fell in love at first sight with Miss Epps, the surgeon's daughter, & is going to marry as soon as she names the day – it plays havoc with his painting; he cannot turn to work since.'[100] Gambart's fears were misplaced and the courtship did not hinder the progress of his work. According to a letter to Carel Vosmaer, Alma-Tadema worked on *A Private Celebration* and a copy of *Queen Fredegonda at the Death-Bed of Bishop Praetextatus* from 4 am until 9·30 am before getting married at 10 am.[101]

Laura Alma-Tadema was to become a painter in her own right. (Pl.52) She painted domestic genre scenes, often in historical Dutch settings. Her choice of subjects in no way competed with her husband's, while her Dutch settings paid homage to his background. In the shadow of her husband's success, it must have been difficult for her to assert her own artistic identity, but the marriage provided her with opportunities to engage with artistic circles, an advantage generally denied to aspiring women artists.

The couple painted their self-portraits at the time of their marriage (Pl.53). Two portraits are contained in a single frame and encircled by an inscription in Latin giving the name, age, date and place of birth of each. Both portraits are painted in the same sketchy style. The couple travelled to Belgium and Holland on their honeymoon and on their return moved from Camden Square to the more fashionable area of Regent's Park and Townshend House, 17 Tichfield Terrace, Park Road.

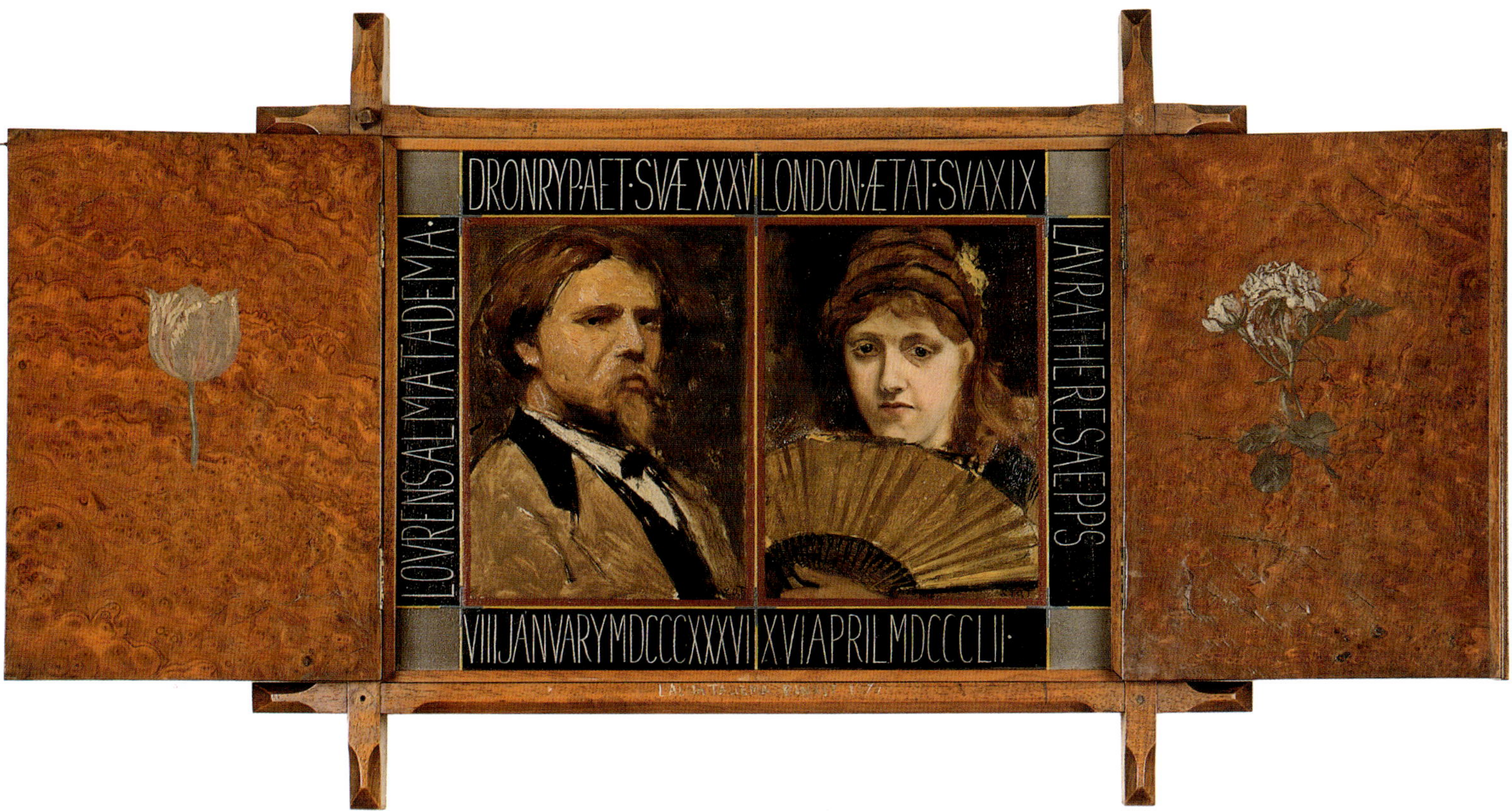

53
Self-Portraits of Lawrence Alma-Tadema and Laura Theresa Epps, 1871
Oil on wood, 27·5 × 37·5 cm (10⅞ × 14¾ in)
Fries Museum, Leeuwarden

Laura Alma-Tadema now also acted as a model for her husband. *A Private Celebration* (Pl.50) includes a portrait of Laura as the foreground female celebrant in a procession in honour of Bacchus. Her fair hair and complexion conformed to a type he was to include in many paintings, usually juxtaposed with a model who was, by contrast, distinctly dark. The figures in *A Private Celebration* are represented in a frieze-like composition reminiscent of Leighton's processional paintings, *Syracusan Bride* (1866) and *The Daphnephoria* (1876). Alma-Tadema's figures echo the wall painting behind, which itself ingeniously copies a vase painting from a red-figure vase by the Dinos painter in the Archaeological Museum, Naples, which was sketched by the artist either during a trip to Italy or from a published illustration (Pl.51).

Domestic life did not interrupt Alma-Tadema's work, and the year after his marriage he produced one of his most interesting, and subversive, readings of Roman history. *A Roman Emperor AD 41* (Pl.54) was described by F. G. Stephens as 'an illustration of one of the most significant events in the decadence of Rome'.[102] The artist repeats the subject of *Proclaiming Claudius Emperor*, painted four years earlier, and looks to the death of the emperor Caligula and the accession of his uncle, Claudius. The title, *A Roman Emperor AD 41*, is both ambiguous and ironic: the scene contains not one, but two emperors, both of them unedifying specimens. We have Claudius, an unlikely candidate, plagued by a congenital abnormality and for most of his life treated as an imbecile by the imperial circle, here a terrified coward, and Gaius Caligula, known to posterity as an insane tyrant and here an almost indistinguishable corpse amongst a heap of bodies. Alma-Tadema follows the account of the Roman historian, Suetonius:

> When the assassins of Gaius shut out the crowd under the pretence that the emperor wished to be alone, Claudius was ousted with the rest and withdrew to an apartment called the Hermaeum; and a little later, in great terror at the news of the murder, he stole away to a balcony hard by and hid among the curtains which hung before the door. As he cowered there, a common soldier, who was prowling about at random, saw his feet, and intending to ask who he was, pulled him out and recognized him; and when Claudius fell at his feet in terror, he hailed him as emperor.[103]

Alma-Tadema, like Suetonius, sets the scene in the 'Hermaeum' (House of Hermes), as shown by the *herm* (pedestal surmounted by portrait bust) of Augustus, now ominously blood-stained.

Furthermore, by painting Claudius' slippers a prominent red, he unmistakably alludes to Suetonius' anecdote of Claudius' discovery because of his protruding feet. Their colour has an added significance: only patricians were allowed to wear high-heeled red shoes, and thus our attention is drawn to the discrepancy between Claudius' status and his cringing position. Caligula, too, can be recognized by his feet. He is surely the owner of the green boots amongst the corpses; a witty reference to Caligula's name, meaning 'little boots', coined when as a child he wore the costume of a soldier, military boots and all.[104]

Indeed, the whole painting is full of witty references which juxtapose the ignoble present with a more heroic past. A wall painting of the battle of Actium is cut off at the top of the canvas, the battle which in 31 BC saw the triumph of Augustus (or Octavian, as he was known before assuming the grander name) over Mark Antony and Cleopatra. The inclusion of domestic altar, snake mosaic and inscription relating to the Genius of the imperial family on the right of the canvas highlights the fact that Caligula is murdered before the very altar of his more noble ancestors. Alma-Tadema follows the anecdotal style of his Latin source and, like Suetonius, he invites us to view this inglorious moment in imperial history with an amused irreverence and irony.

In 1872 Alma-Tadema organized his paintings into an identification system by including an opus number under his signature and assigning his earlier pictures numbers as well. *Portrait of my Sister, Artje*, painted in 1851, is numbered opus I, while two months before his death he completed *Preparations in the Coliseum*, opus CCCVIII. Such a system would make it difficult for fakes to be passed off as originals, together with the extra advantage that Gambart (who usually requested that all paintings delivered to him after July should be dated for the following season) could present each consecutive painting as the artist's very latest work.

Influenced, perhaps, by his stay in Goodall's house, which contained an Egyptian library as well as Orientalizing artefacts and studio props, Alma-Tadema now produced two Egyptian paintings. In April 1872 he completed *An Egyptian Widow at the Time of Diocletian* (Pl.55). A reworking of *The Mummy in the Roman Period*, it shows Egyptian funerary rites as a group of mourners gather around a mummy in an interior derived from Ptolemaic (Romano-Egyptian) temple architecture. Musicians attached to the priestly order lament the dead while the widow leans weeping over the mummy case. A preparatory pencil sketch, like the sketch for *Egyptian Chess Players* (Pl.17), concentrates on figure

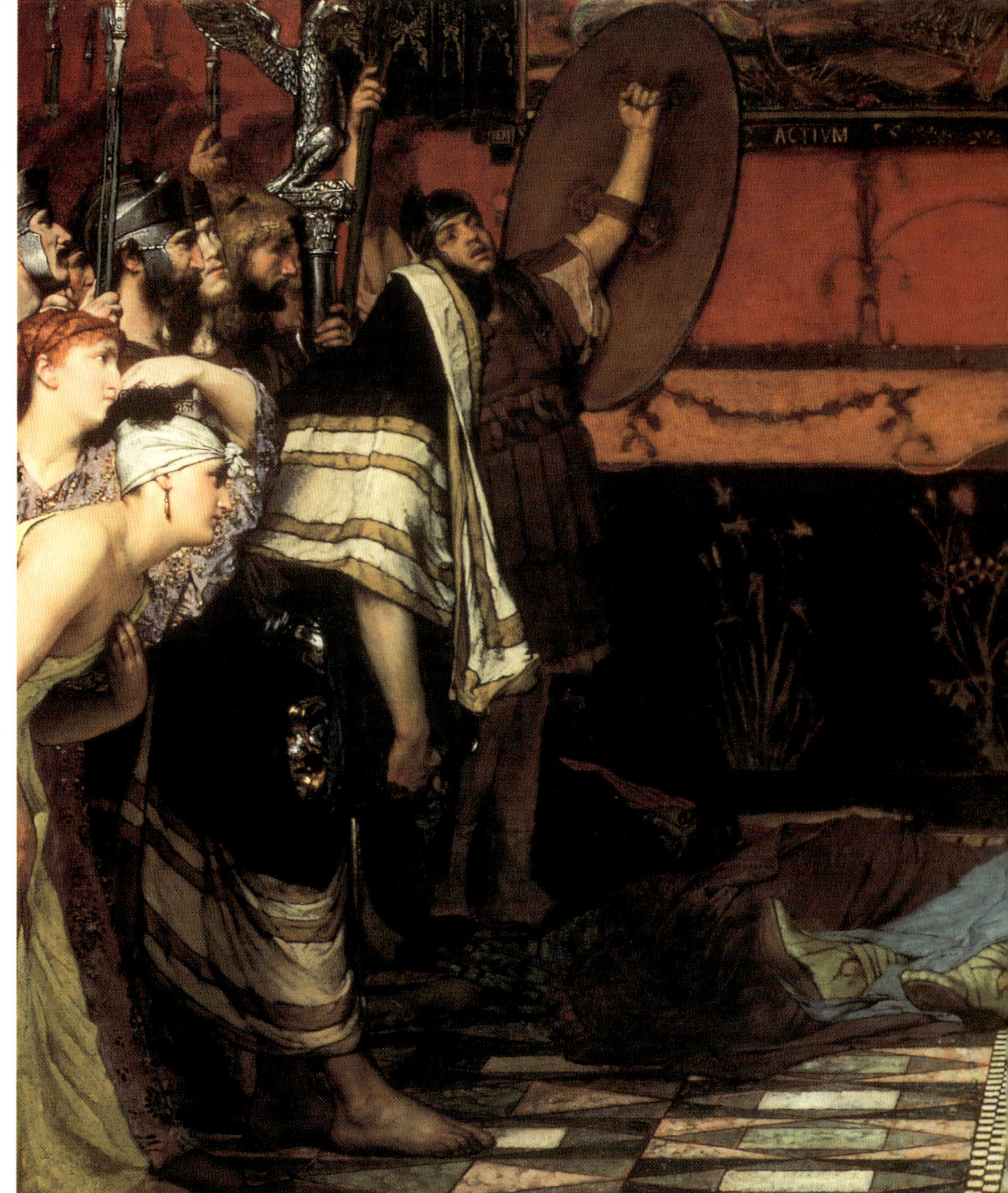

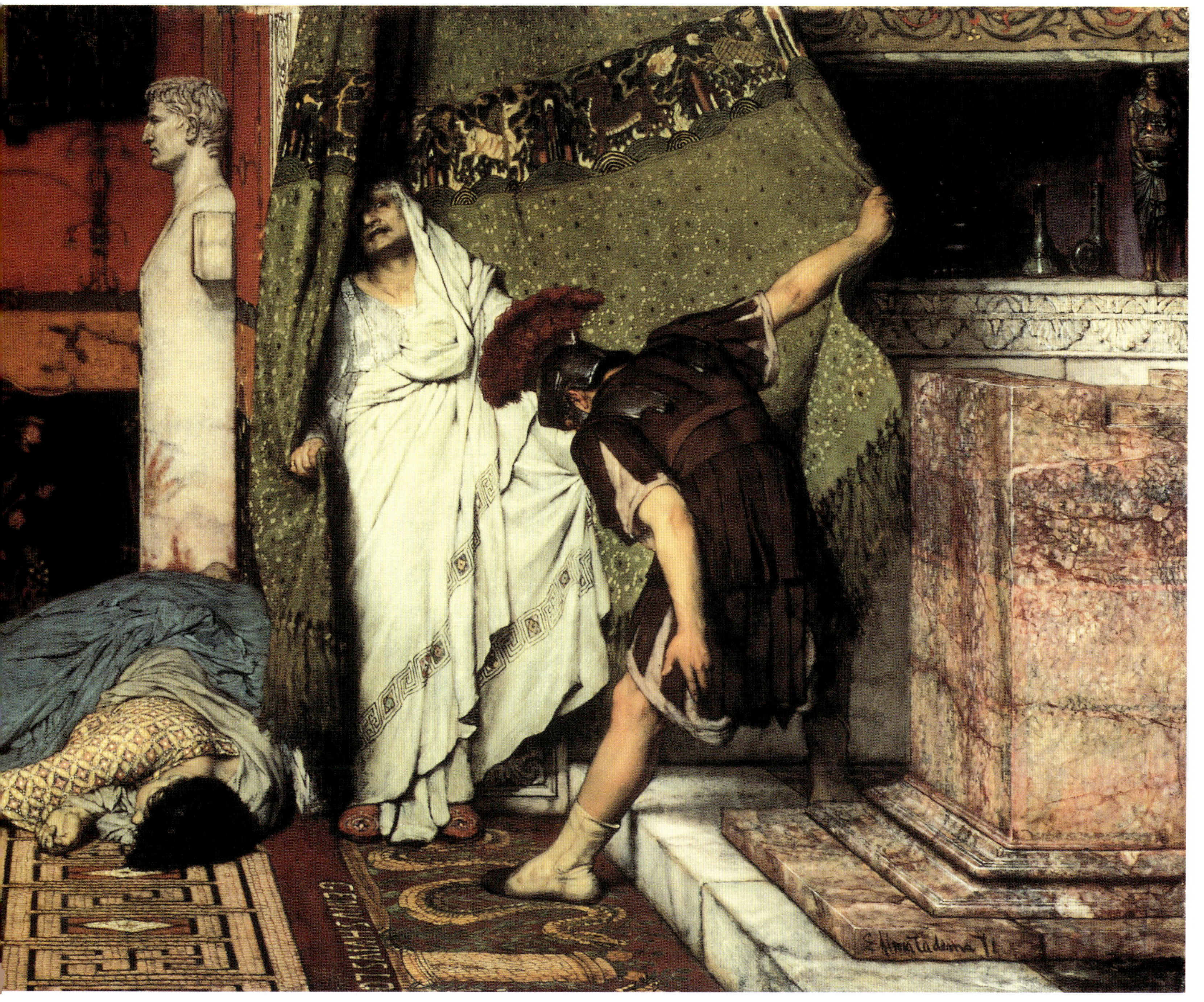

54
A Roman Emperor AD 41, 1872
Oil on canvas, 83·8 × 174·2 cm (33 × 68⅝ in)
Walters Art Gallery, Baltimore

55 overleaf
An Egyptian Widow in the Time of Diocletian, 1872
Oil on wood, 74·9 × 99·1 cm (29½ × 39 in)
Rijksmuseum, Amsterdam

drawing rather than archaeologically detailed background and reveals that the artist was anxious to capture the pathos of the mourning widow.

The painting was exhibited at the Royal Academy in 1873 as *The Mummy: Roman Period* and at the Grosvenor Gallery in 1882–3 as *The Widow*. In 1880 Alma-Tadema referred to it himself as *The Widow or The Mummy from the Time of Diocletian*,[105] and it is now generally known as *An Egyptian Widow at the Time of Diocletian*. The addition of a historically specific title is significant: the reign of Diocletian (AD 84–305) witnessed a revolt in Alexandria against Roman rule; the city was besieged for eight months and a large part of it destroyed, after which Egypt sank into submission. A scene of mourning is thus appropriate to mark such a turbulent period in Romano-Egyptian history. Conversely, the Egyptian widow mourning her dead husband can then also be read as symbolizing the death of paganism. Diocletian can, after all, be claimed as the last important pagan emperor. His reign saw the last major Christian persecutions, as the Emperor Constantine (AD 306–37) granted Christians legal recognition only six years after the end of Diocletian's reign. Whatever the artist's intention, the painting is unusual in its emotional timbre.

Once again Alma-Tadema has set his scene in an archaeologically detailed interior. The columns with floral capitals are similar to those from the Ptolemaic-Roman temple of Isis at Philae (Pl.12). To the right is a painted *cartonnage* or mummy case, behind which sits a richly painted coffin. The coffin is based on a wooden vaulted sarcophagus from the grave of the Theban *archon*, Soter, in the British Museum (dated to c.AD 110), although the artist excludes the gilded figure of a hawk on top of the lid of the original. The decoration on the low rear wall is inspired by the papyrus *Djedhor Book of the Dead* also in the British Museum. Egyptian sources, like classical sources, are transformed to suit the artist's purpose and present a challenge for the audience to recognize and relocate. The harp is based on an illustration from J. G. Wilkinson's *Manners and Customs of the Ancient Egyptians*,[106] while the harpist, a recurrent figure in nineteenth-century paintings of ancient Egypt and indeed in Egyptianizing visual culture in general, derives from Egyptian tomb paintings. In the background right we see a lion-headed statue of the goddess Sakhmet, one of a group of granite statues from Thebes in the British Museum. The statue dates from the reign of Amenophis III (c.1417–1379 BC) in the Eighteenth Dynasty and is the only Pharaonic artefact in a largely Romano-Ptolemaic scene.

The same combination of archaeological accuracy and high emotion is present in *The Death of the First-Born* (Pl.56), painted in July of the same year. It is a reworking of *The Sad Father*, and takes its subject from Exodus 12:29–31 and the tenth plague of Egypt sent by God to deliver the Israelites from bondage:

> And it came to pass, that at midnight the Lord smote all the firstborn in the land of Egypt, from the firstborn of Pharaoh that sat on his throne unto the firstborn of the captive that was in the dungeon ... And Pharaoh rose up in the night, he, and all his servants, and all the Egyptians; and there was a great cry in Egypt ... And he called for Moses and Aaron by night, and said: 'Rise up, and get you forth from among my people, both ye and the children of Israel.'

The painting shows Pharaoh holding the dead child in his lap while his wife leans over the body in lamentation. The foreground figures make gestures of mourning and musicians in the background play in a ritual for the dead. A physician sits on the left with eyes downcast, his bottles of medicines in a basket beside him having failed. On the far right Moses and Aaron enter the room. The family group present a scene of almost unbearable pathos: the bent figure of the mother, convulsed in mourning, juxtaposes with the dignified and restrained Pharaoh whose grief confronts the viewer through his handsome young face.

Georg Ebers, in his biography of the artist, points out that the walls recall the halls of Rameses III and the china dish covered with flowers is from Tell el-Yetoudiya. For the extraordinary face of the Pharaoh, the artist must have studied Egyptian portrait sculpture. And most astonishingly, 'as if the master had foreseen what was not discovered until ten years after the completion of his work, he laid at the feet of the corpse a garland of flowers deceptively like those which have been found in the royal coffins at Dēr el-Bachri.'[107] One of the most significant Egyptological finds of the nineteenth century was the excavation of Royal mummies in the 1880s at Deir el-Bahri, on the left bank of the Nile opposite Karnak, by the French Egyptologist, Gaston Maspero. While flower garlands had been excavated at other sites, Ebers uses the Deir el-Bahri example to highlight Alma-Tadema's understanding of Egyptian archaeology, so extensive that he is in a position to anticipate a find before it has come to light.

Other archaeological details include a stone ear stele in the British Museum, a votive gift for the gods requesting that prayers be 'heard'. Pharaoh's son wears a gold chain with green scarab mounted in gold, based on an exhibit in

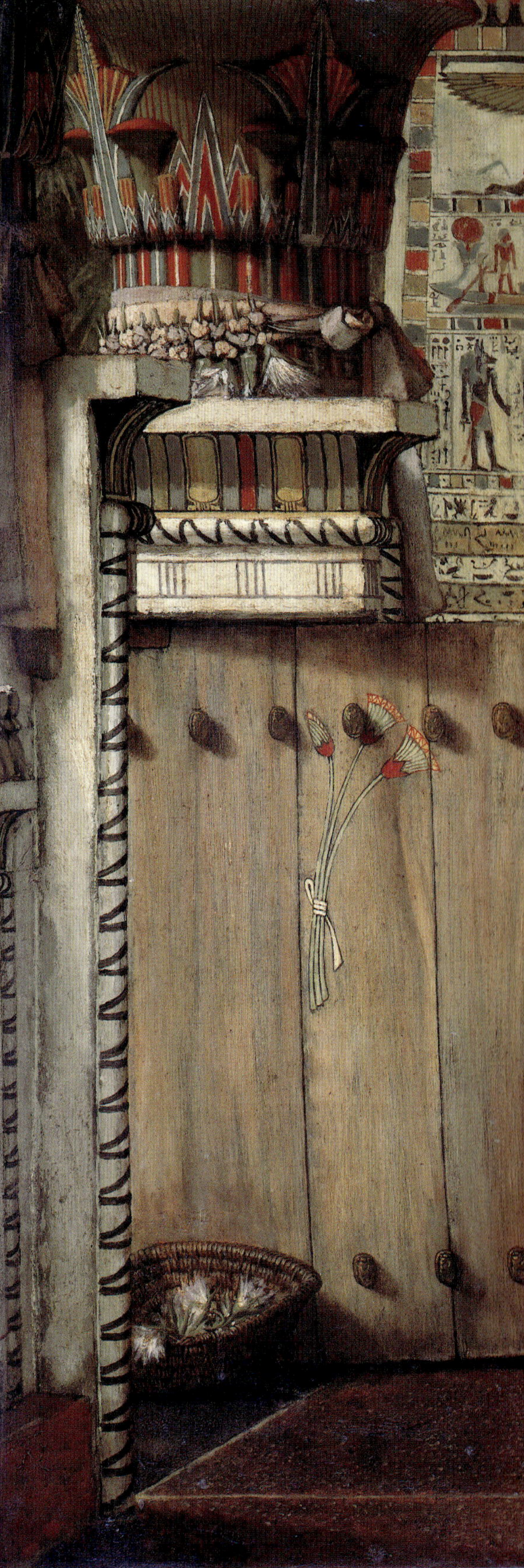

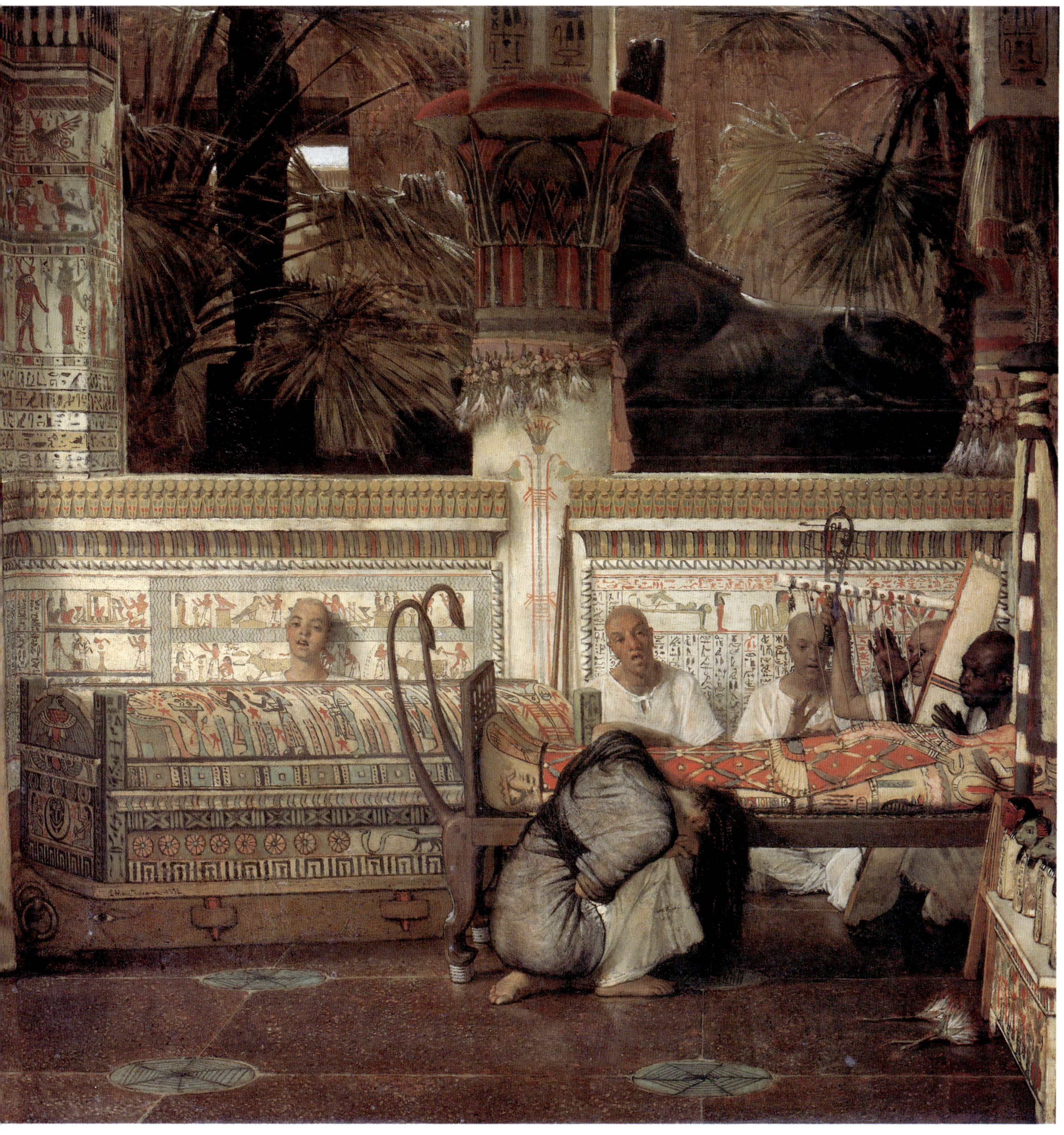

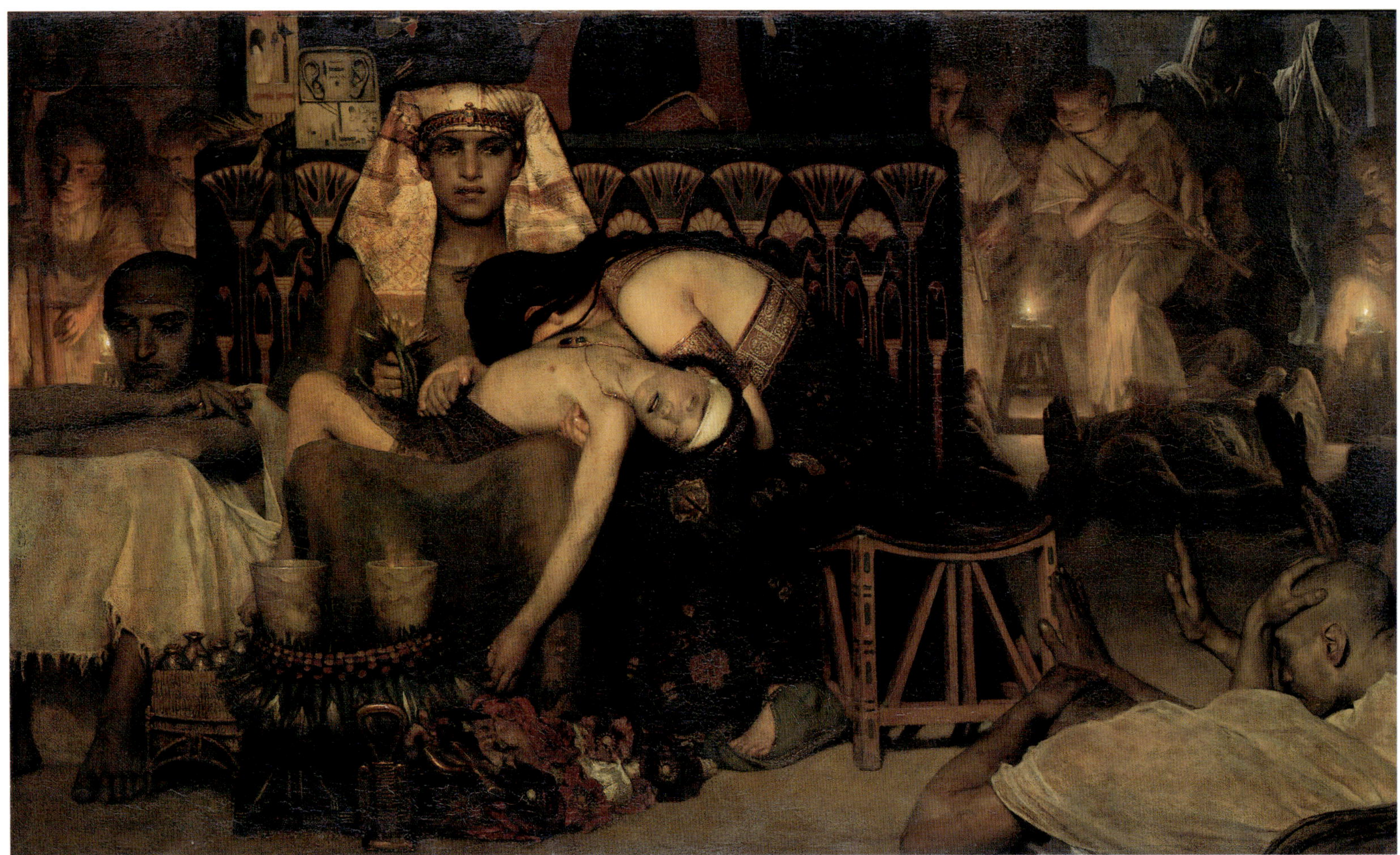

the Rijksmusem van Oudhenden in Leiden which is also represented in *The Sad Father*. Raven points out that a cartouche on the left of the ear stele dates to the reign of Rameses II (*c*.1304–1237 BC) in the Nineteenth Dynasty, the period in which Moses was generally placed by nineteenth-century scholars.[108] Antiquarian detail in the classical-subject paintings often points to an ironic subtext, but in the Egyptian pictures – often of a highly emotional rather than ironic timbre – it tends to confirm the proficiency of the artist as Egyptologist and also takes on an authenticating role. Whereas many biblical scenes were set in indefinable landscape settings, Alma-Tadema recasts the biblical world in a recognizable Egyptian time and place.

The Death of the First-Born was awarded a gold medal at the Berlin Royal Academy in 1872, as well as the gold medal at the Paris Exposition Universelle. It was sold to Gambart as part of his second commission, but bought back by the artist in 1879 at double the price. Alma-Tadema later tried to sell it to the museum in Dresden when he needed money for the renovation of his new house. He was unable to make a sale as the price demanded was too high, and the artist did not attempt to sell it again but kept it in his studio until his death, after which it was bequeathed to the Rijksmusem, Amsterdam. It can be counted as one of his most striking works. Ebers remarked of the painting: 'had Tadema finished nothing except this picture, he would still be entitled to number himself among the foremost artists of his age.'[109] Alma-Tadema may have felt a personal connection with his subject: his own first born, a son, Eugène, had died as an infant in 1864.

Joseph, Overseer of Pharaoh's Granaries (Pl.57), completed two years later, is another biblical subject, this time from Genesis 41. Sold into slavery in Egypt by his jealous half-brothers, Joseph enters the house of Potiphar. Although his master respects him, Potiphar's wife makes advances to Joseph, which he refuses. She avenges herself with allegations against Joseph and he is sent to prison. He is subsequently released to interpret Pharaoh's two dreams, and in gratitude Pharaoh makes him overseer of the food supply and the land. The imposing bewigged figure of Joseph sits on a throne while a scribe works seated on the floor beside him. The elaborate wig is based on one preserved in a tomb in Thebes of which the artist owned a photograph (Pl.58). Dating from roughly the Eighteenth Dynasty, it is consistent with the notional date of the scene, but the wig was believed to have been originally worn by a woman and not a man. As in his classical paintings, the artist is willing to manipulate visual sources to suit his purpose.

For the wall painting of men and geese in the background, Alma-Tadema has, once again, clearly turned to the tomb paintings of 'Nebamun' in the British Museum, transformed into 'real' women in *Pastimes in Ancient Egypt*, and reproduced by the artist in a series of watercolour studies (Pl.59). The whole tomb painting shows a scribe recording a census of geese on Nebamun's estate and is quite in keeping with this scene of a scribe recording Pharaoh's grain supply. Dating from the Eighteenth Dynasty, it is, furthermore, roughly compatible with nineteenth-century notions of biblical Egypt.[110] The cartouche on the throne belongs to Tuthmosis III, once again a ruler of the Eighteenth Dynasty (*c*.1504–1450 BC).

Joseph, Overseer of Pharaoh's Granaries was Alma-Tadema's last Egyptian picture for thirty years. His interest in Egypt did not, however, wane, as illustrated by the impressive array of Egyptological-archaeological publications in his

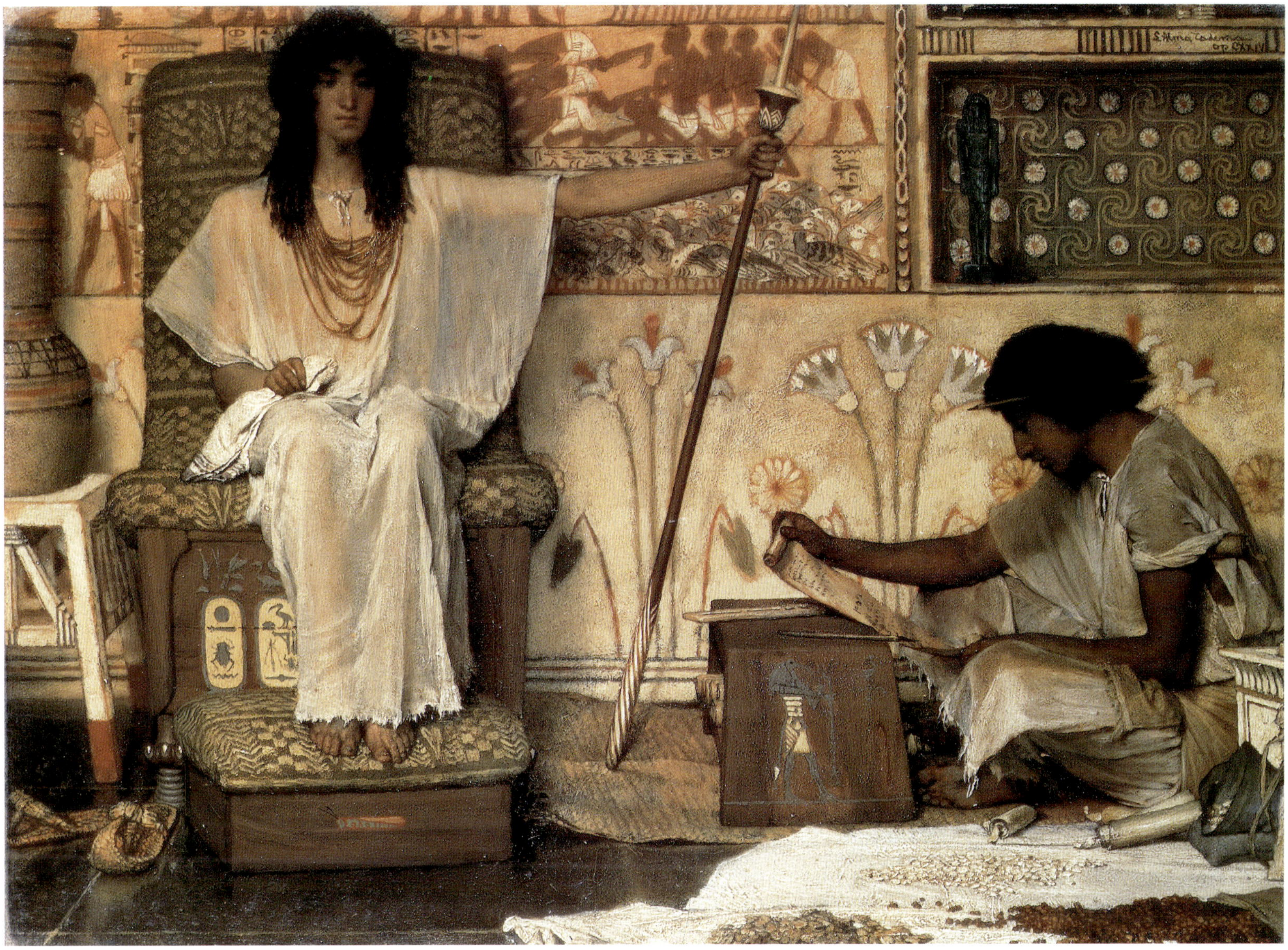

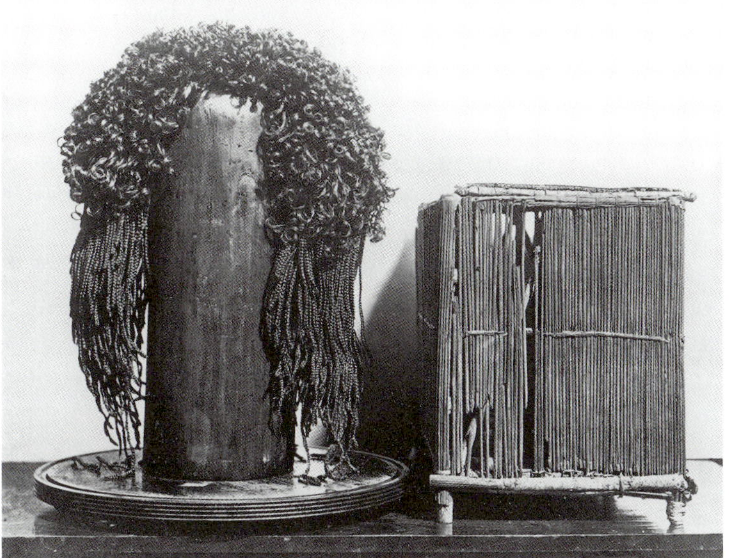

56 opposite
The Death of the First-Born, 1872
Oil on canvas, 79·9 × 124·5 cm (31½ × 49 in)
Rijksmuseum, Amsterdam

57
Joseph, Overseer of Pharaoh's Granaries, 1874
Oil on canvas, 33 × 43·1 cm (13 × 17 in)
Private collection

58
Egyptian Wig and Wig Box, 18th Dynasty
University of Birmingham

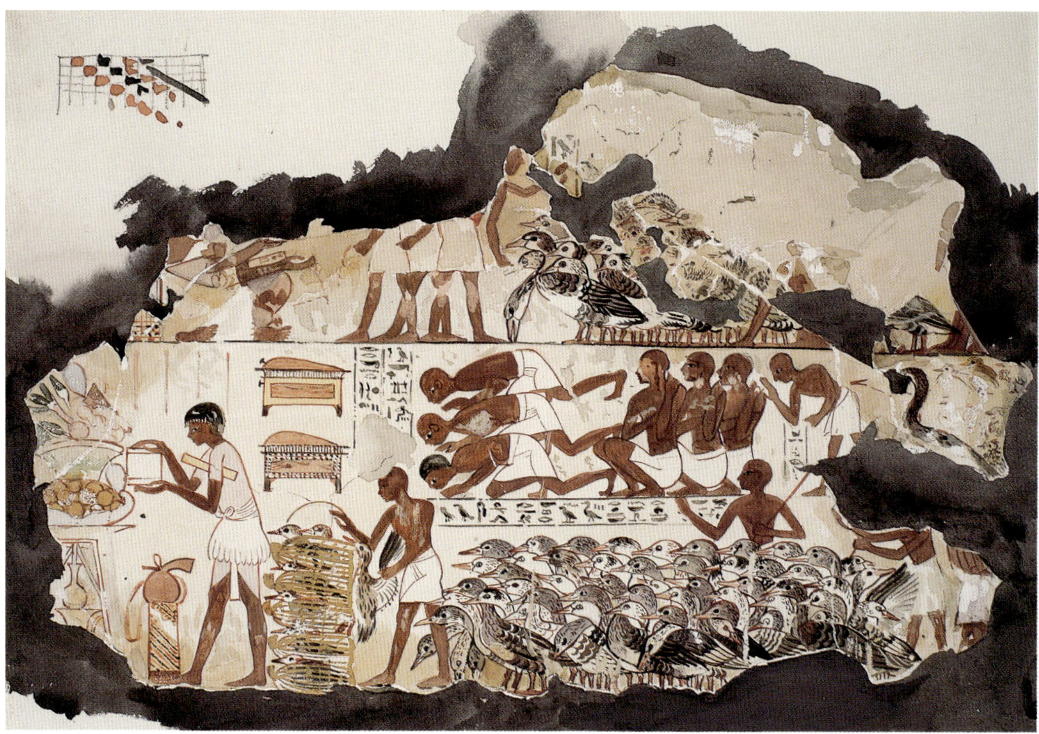

59
Copy of wall painting from the tomb of Nebamun in the British Museum, London, 1860s
Watercolour, 19.7 × 28.6 cm (7¾ × 11¼ in)
University of Birmingham

library ranging in date from the 1850s until his death in 1912. The decision to concentrate on classical subjects may have been prompted by critical responses. Although the Egyptian pictures were noted by British critics, the tone of their reviews is respectful rather than enthusiastic. For example, the critic of the *Art Journal* saw *An Egyptian Widow* as 'sombre', 'sad' and 'strange'.[111] The association of Egypt and solemnity was indeed given historical currency by contemporary discussions of ancient Egypt, and yet this is not the usual language of art criticism. The *Illustrated London News* similarly described *The Death of the First-Born* as a 'sombre but highly original Egyptian temple scene', whereas the three small paintings comprising a Greek dining series – *The Dinner*, *The Wine* and *The Siesta* – shown at the same exhibition, were, by contrast, seen to be 'gemlike in their colour and finish'.[112] Likewise, F. G. Stephens gave a sober account of *The Death of the First-Born*, while saving his enthusiasm for the Greek paintings and their detail: 'the woven fabrics, the marble, the lucent ivory carvings of the couch, the solidity of the bronze, the brilliancy of the flesh, and the manifold tints of the marbles'.[113] *Joseph, Overseer of Pharaoh's Granaries* was exhibited at the same Academy exhibition as the large and important painting, *The Picture Gallery*, and as a consequence received far less critical coverage.

Egypt, nonetheless, continued to fuel the British imagination. In 1878 Cleopatra's Needle (presented to the British nation by the Viceroy of Egypt in 1820) was erected on the Embankment along with Egyptianizing base and a series of benches. In 1882 Egypt became a British protectorate after an internal rebellion to end foreign control, while in 1895 British forces under Kitchener invaded Sudan, thus ensuring that modern Egypt was headline news. As far as archaeology was concerned, the Egypt Exploration Fund was founded in 1882 for the purpose of fieldwork and scholarly research. Alma-Tadema himself donated money to the Fund in the 1880s.[114] With its support, the excavations of William Flinders Petrie made significant discoveries, including mummy portraits from the Fayum, while the 1890s saw extensive finds of papyri in the same area. On a more popular level, Liberty and Company marketed Egyptianizing furniture based on examples in the British Museum, and E.W. Godwin produced his own Egyptianizing furniture marketed at the Art Furnishers Alliance in the 1870s and 1880s.[115]

Although Alma-Tadema no longer painted Egyptian subjects, other British artists – Frederick Goodall and Edwin Long in particular – were making careers out of mainly doing so. Edwin Long (1820–91) made his first tour of Egypt and

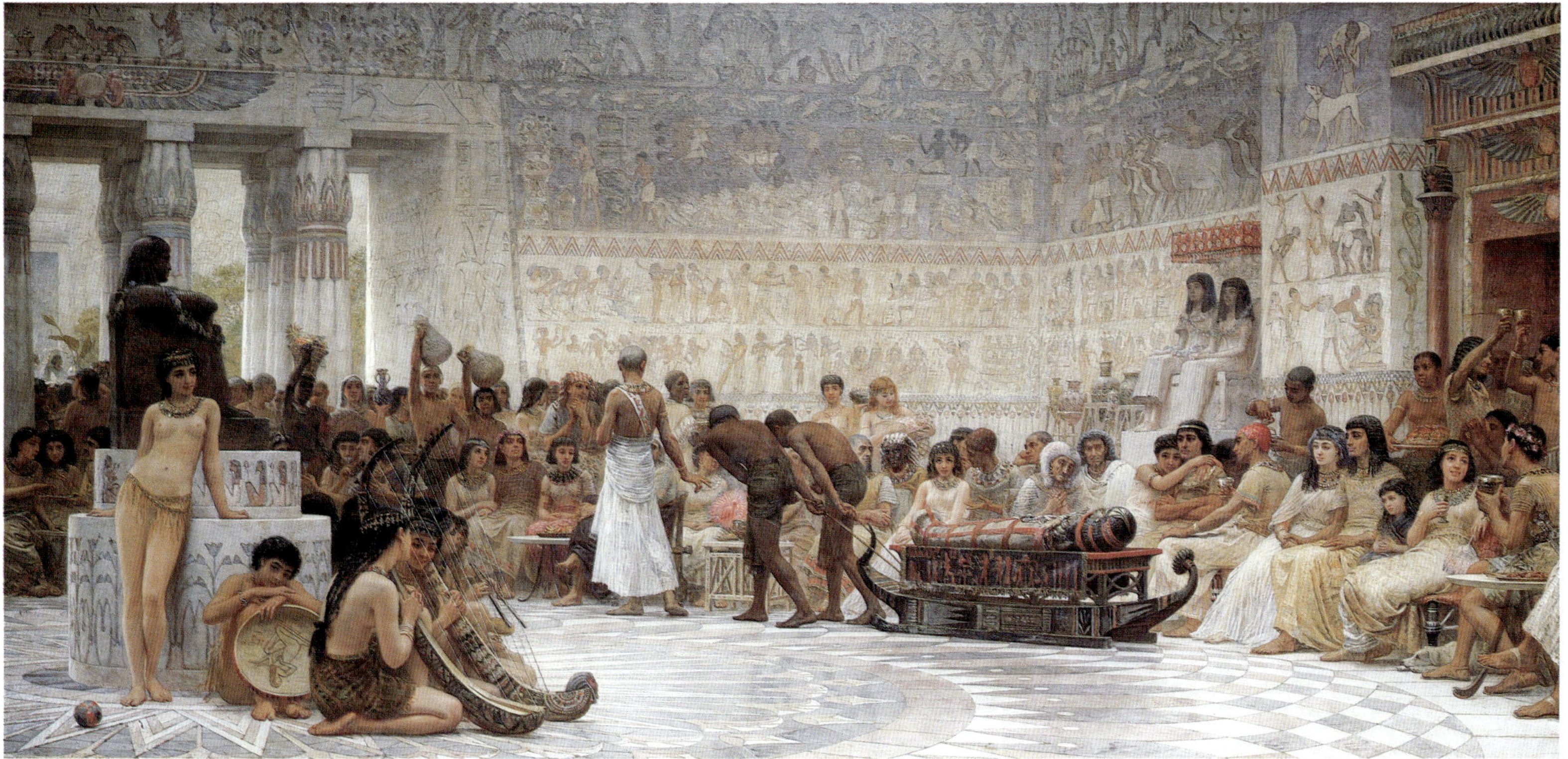

Syria in 1874, after which he produced genre and biblical subjects in archaeological settings. Long's *An Egyptian Feast* (Pl.60), in fact, recalls *Pastimes in Ancient Egypt* in both setting and subject. Based on a story from the Greek historian, Herodotus, it depicts the display of a mummy at a feast to remind the guests of human mortality and is set within a grand architectural interior that includes painted walls and mosaic floor. Unlike Alma-Tadema, though, Goodall and Long consistently appealed to notions of an exotic East with their numerous depictions of female flesh.[116]

Alma-Tadema evidently held his small number of Egyptian paintings in high regard. We have seen that he was only willing to part with *The Death of the First-Born* to a public collection, and then at a high price. In a letter to Vosmaer, Alma-Tadema states that he and his friends pressed the Rijksmuseum in Amsterdam to acquire *An Egyptian Widow* in 1880, as he was keen to have a good representation of his work in such a major Dutch gallery, but once again the price asked was considered too high.[117] These two paintings, in particular, have a special place in his œuvre as they contain an emotionality not present elsewhere. Although he discontinued Egyptian paintings between the mid-1870s and his last Egyptian picture, *The Finding of Moses* (1904),[118] Alma-Tadema still incorporated occasional Egyptian details in classical paintings throughout his career.[119]

After his move to London, Alma-Tadema soon anglicized his name to Lawrence and in 1873 was granted letters of denization from the Queen.[120] This new national identity created difficulties with his participation in the Dutch group of artists in the Vienna Internationale as there were some who felt that he should not be allowed to participate in Vienna as an expatriate. Under mounting pressure, Alma-Tadema eventually withdrew his entries. Gambart had been showing Alma-Tadema's works in London at the French Gallery's exhibitions of French and Flemish art from 1865, but, no longer belonging to either category, he stopped exhibiting there after 1871. He was, accordingly, now determined to forge a role for himself within the traditions of British painting.

Pictures were selling well, and Alma-Tadema's first British honour was election as Associate member of the Royal Society of Painters in Water-Colours after exhibiting *The Picture* at its 1873 summer exhibition. The artist was determined to live in a suitable style, and the family's first permanent London residence, Townshend House, was a showpiece designed, like many Victorian artists' houses, for entertaining guests and patrons and for displaying pictures. Situated on the fringes of St John's Wood, a popular artists' residential area, it was decorated in an eclectic style incorporating Pompeian, Dutch, Japanese and Byzantine motifs.[121]

The family consisted of Alma-Tadema, Laura,

60
Edwin Long, *An Egyptian Feast*, 1877
Oil on canvas, 189·2 × 381 cm (74½ × 150 in)
Cartwright Hall Art Gallery, Bradford

61
This is our Corner (Portrait of Laurense and Anna Alma-Tadema), 1873
Oil on wood, 56·5 × 47 cm (22¼ × 18½ in)
Van Gogh Museum, Amsterdam

62 opposite
Anna Alma-Tadema, *The Drawing Room at Townshend House*, 1885
Watercolour, 26 × 17·5 cm (10¼ × 6⅞ in)
Royal Academy of Arts, London

63
Joe Parkin Maynall, *Alma-Tadema in his Studio at Townshend House*, 1884
Photo-engraving
National Portrait Gallery, London

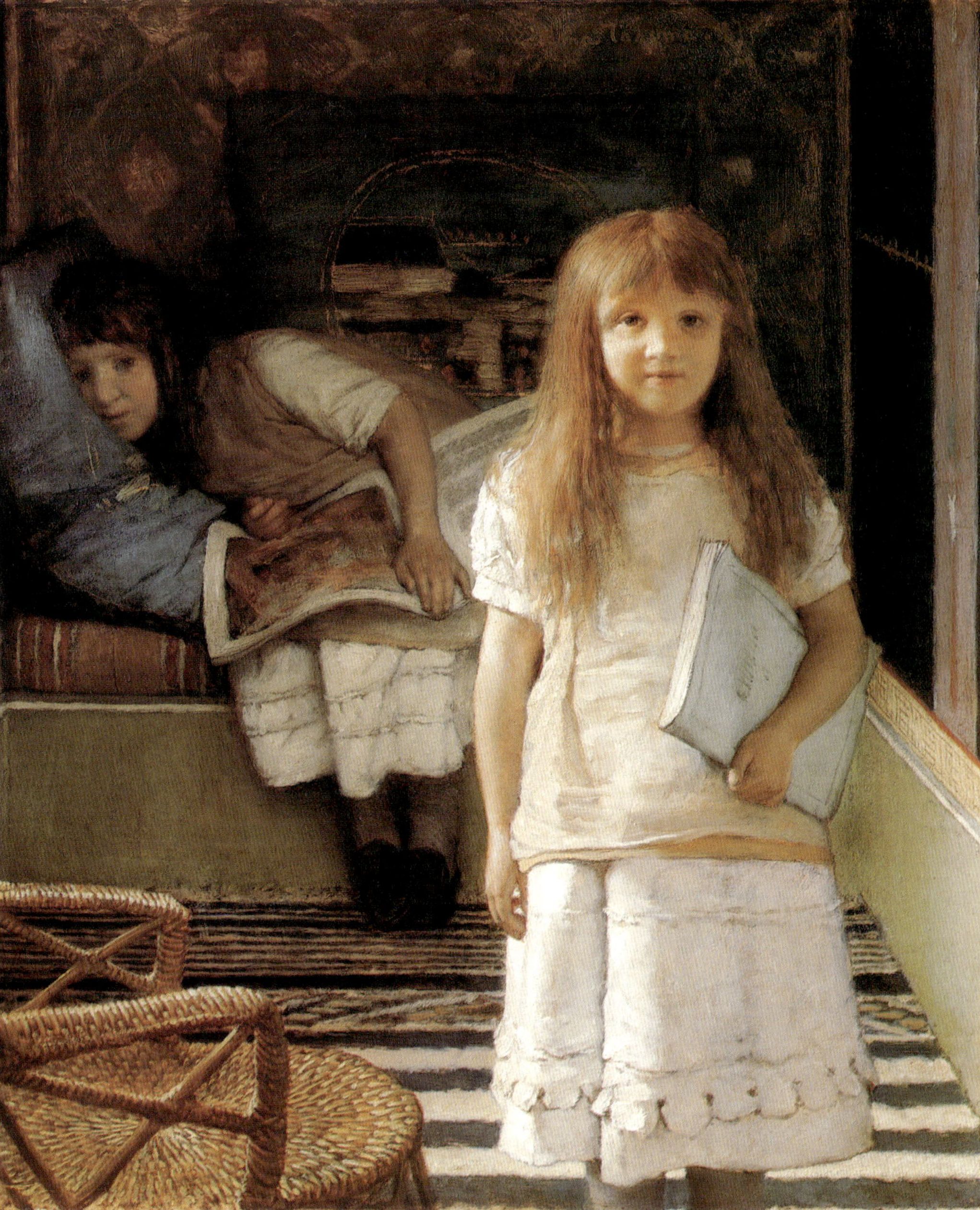

his two daughters from his previous marriage and his sister Artje. *This is Our Corner* (Pl.61) is an informal portrait of his two daughters, Laurense (born 1865), standing in the foreground and Anna (born 1867), seated on the couch behind. The setting, Townshend House, displays characteristically eclectic decorative details. Blue cushions are enlivened with Chinese or Japanese designs, and the wall on the right has a classicizing border, while the cool colours and black and white striped rug recall aesthetic interiors.[122]

In October 1874 Alma-Tadema and his wife were at Penkill Castle, Ayrshire, Scotland, visiting the poet and artist, William Bell Scott. Alma-Tadema was working on illustrations for a volume of Scott's poetry, published in 1875. Scott recalls Alma-Tadema's strength of personality as regards both work and leisure. He was the 'loudest and most overpowering of housemates. It was of little use to protest against his robustness as to advise him about his designs; his vigour became boundless, and his good humour endless.'[123]

Back in London, an explosion on a barge on Regent's Canal resulted in casualties and severe damage to houses in the vicinity. Anna and Laurense were at home and they were awoken in the early hours of the morning to find a window-sash blown onto their bed and the room covered in hazelnuts, part of the cargo of the barge. No one was hurt and none of the paintings were dam-

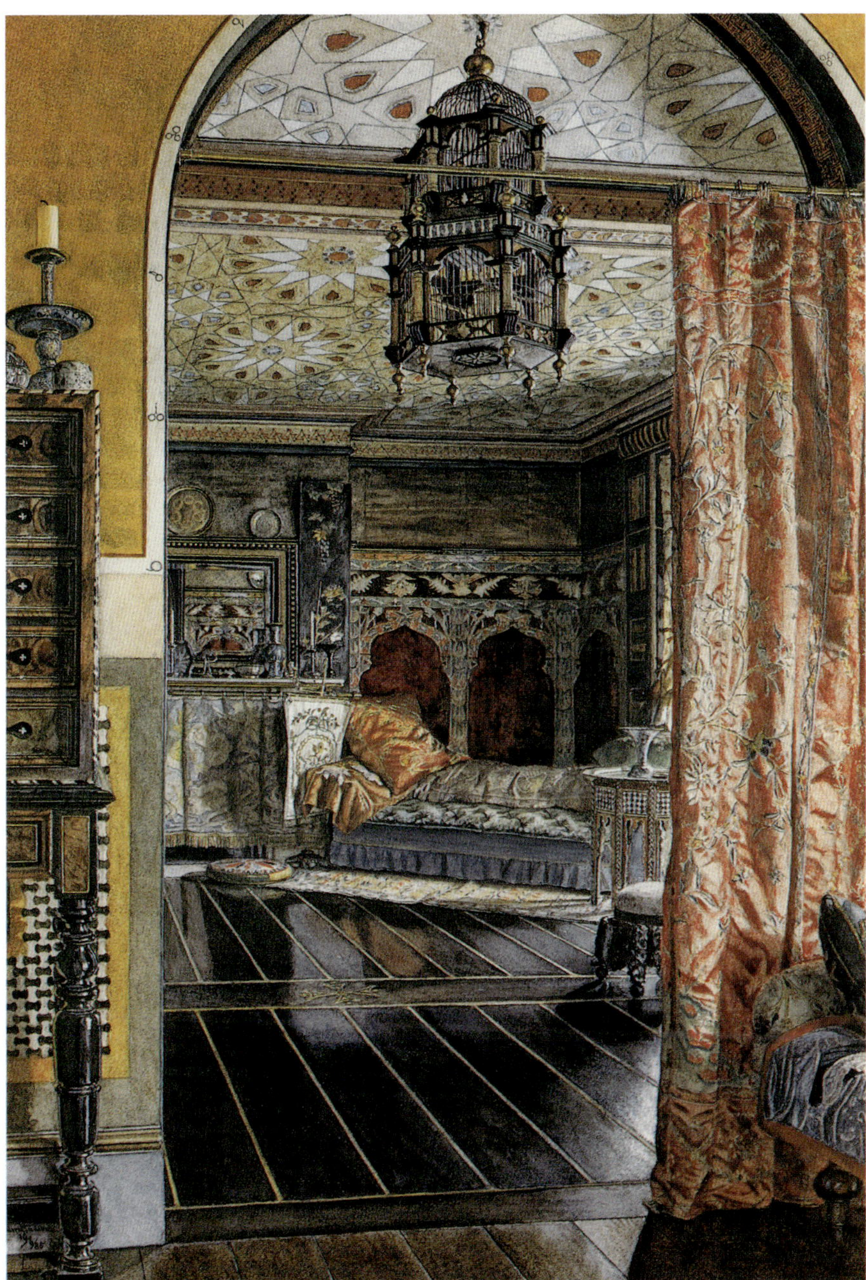

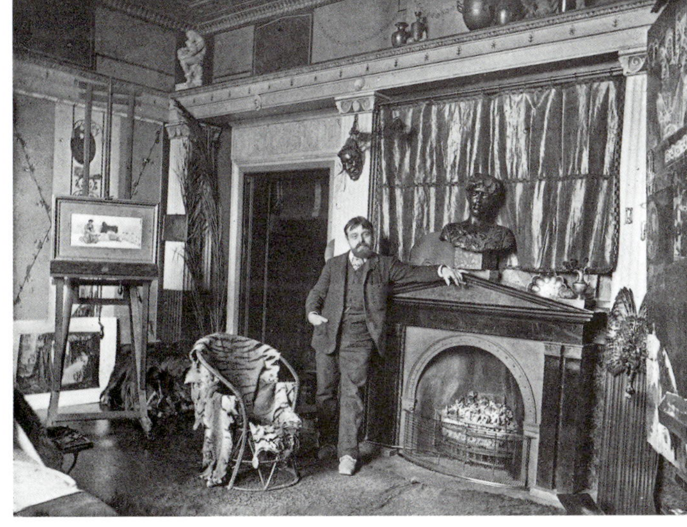

aged, but the house needed considerable work. Alma-Tadema wasted no time in having it repaired and redecorated with the help of the architects George Aitchison and William Burges. Both men were high-profile figures: Burges was known for his work in Gothic revival architecture and Aitchison for aesthetic interior design. Aitchison had designed a house for Frederic Leighton in 1865 (arguably the most famous of London artists' houses) and was later to add the Arab hall, the centre-piece of the house and a prime example of a fashionable Moorish-style interior.

Alma-Tadema's refurbished house was described and illustrated in the press.[124] Like many other artists, keen to consolidate a growing reputation, he used a conspicuous display of wealth to signify success and a fashionable style of interior decoration to denote artistic taste. The gold room, so-called after unvarnished gold leaf on walls and ceiling, sported a Byzantine-style dado supporting ornaments and a miniature copy of the Parthenon frieze in ebony and ivory. An alcove covered with a curtain and lit by a window of translucent Mexican onyx hosted an ornate grand piano. Leading from the gold room, and separated from it by a curtain of embroidered Chinese silk, was an Orientalizing drawing room with a Moorish ceiling and Persian-style divan, materials and cushions. A view of the drawing room from the gold room was later painted by the artist's elder daughter, Anna (Pl.62). In typical eclectic style, the conservatory housed a water tank in the form of an *impluvium* in a Roman *atrium* alongside a hammock, palm leaves and Chinese lanterns. One room re-created a Dutch seventeenth-century interior with panels of oak and rosewood, latticed windows and blue and white china and glassware. The couple's initials, LAT, were incorporated into the decoration of several rooms. The studio (Pl.63) is described in one contemporary account as 'Pompeian red, with many-coloured arabesques ... panels and medallions of light blue etc., on which the gods and goddesses

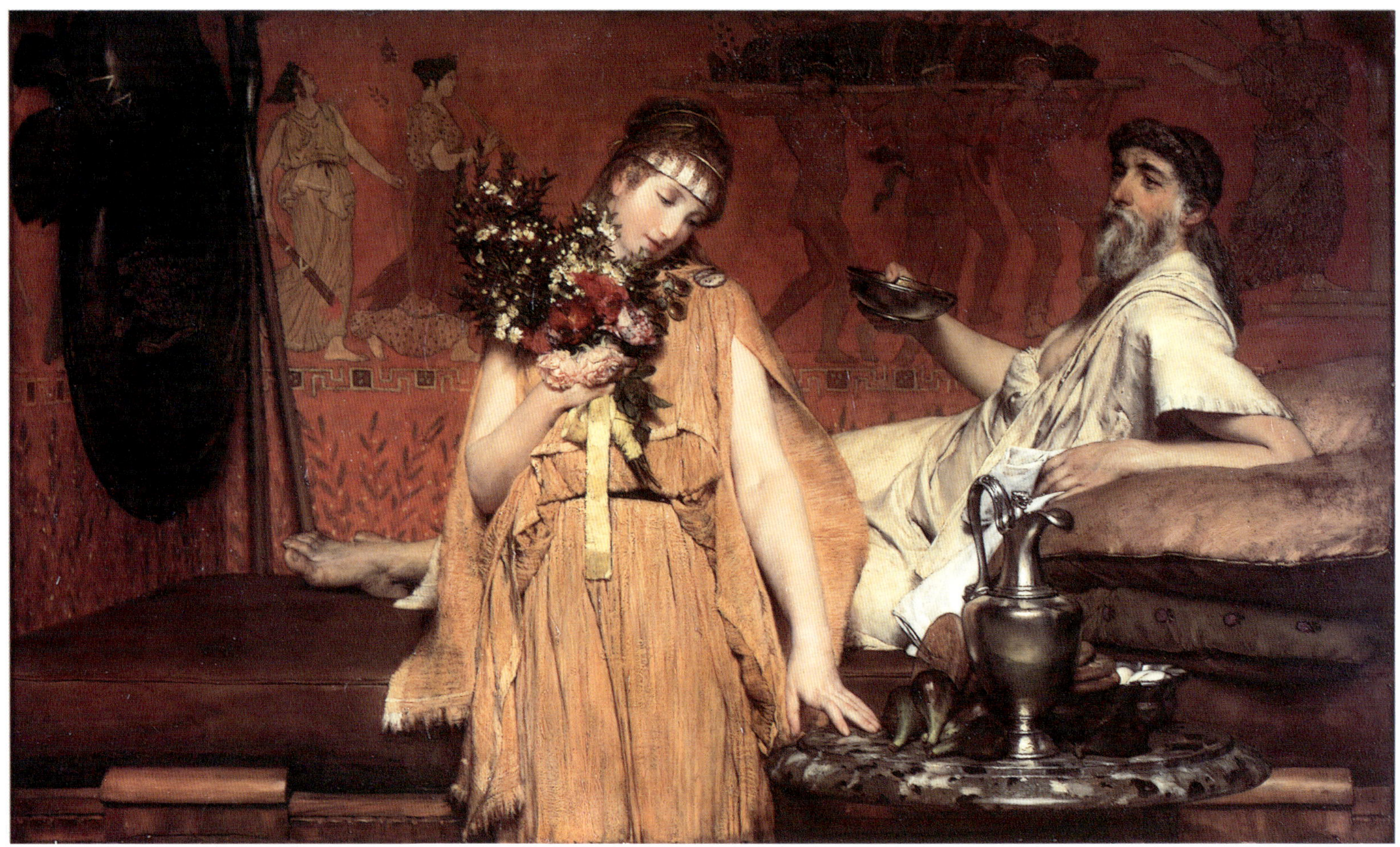

disport',[125] while another report informs us that the tints are 'somewhat expressionless'.[126] From these two descriptions it is clear that the artist had chosen Pompeian colours, though not only the usual red, but also pastel shades of whites, blues and greens.

Alma-Tadema himself records that the decoration of his studio had a pronounced effect on his work:

> When I found that the black Pompeian decorations of my early Antwerp studio made me paint my pictures too heavy, I had my next studio painted red. There they go too hot. So moving to Brussels, I painted my studio light green: and when I arrived in London, my first studio was blue green. The influence was such that you could classify my pictures according to the influence produced upon them by the surroundings.[127]

From the early 1870s his works are indeed characterized by a greater use of open space, lighter colours and more use of marble. At the same time, he continued his exploration of familiar themes and repeated the format of earlier paintings.

A second Greek dining series, comprising *The Dinner* (1872), *Greek Wine* (1872) and *The Siesta* (1873), was commissioned by Frederick Turner via Gambart. The paintings follow the horizontal format of the earlier series and all show reclining men accompanied by slave boys or flute girls. Another dining painting, *The Service* (1875), draws our attention to the homoerotic side of the *symposium*. Four handsome youths carry a table and wine amphorae; they are all nude, except for wreathes of ivy decorating their hair. Alma-Tadema had already hinted at the homoerotic side of Greek culture in *The Siesta* and *A Pyrrhic Dance*; such a decision is surprising given the stigma attached to a homosexual lifestyle in nineteenth-century Europe.[128] The Pre-Raphaelite painter Simeon Solomon was arrested on a charge of committing homosexual acts in 1873 and his career more or less ruined as a consequence. However, the veiled allusions here may be targeted at a select audience: *The Service* was not sold through Gambart and was instead traded for a picture with a friend, Alfred Verwee, a Flemish painter working in Paris.

Alma-Tadema's own photographic collection includes a number of photographs of nude

64
Between Hope and Fear, 1876
Oil on canvas, 78·1 × 128·2 cm (30¾ × 50½ in)
Private collection

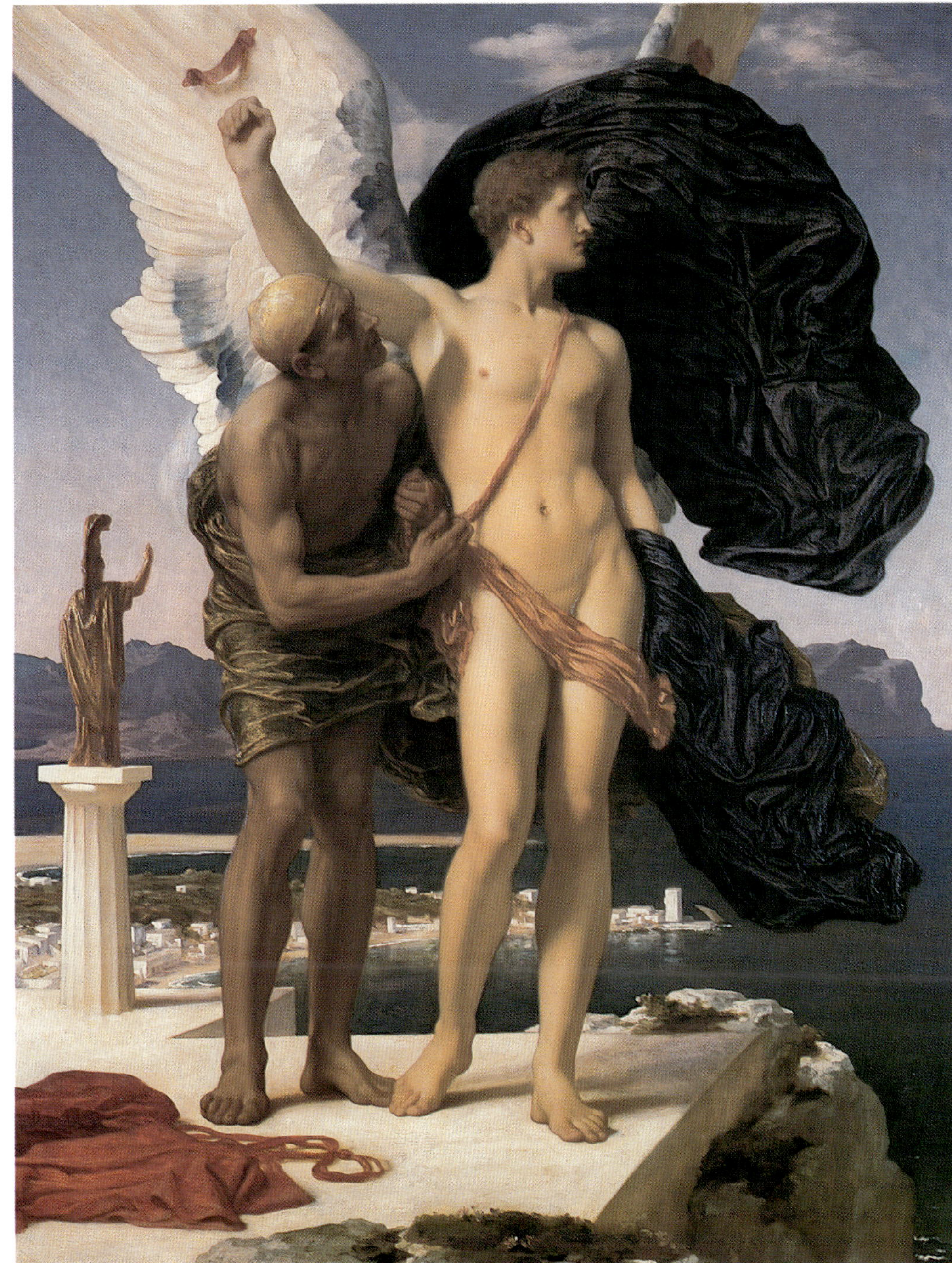

65
Frederic Leighton, *Daedalus and Icarus*, c. 1869
Oil on canvas, 138·2 × 106·5 cm (54⅜ × 41⅞ in)
The Faringdon Collection Trust,
Buscot Park, Oxfordshire

youths by Baron von Gloeden and Guglielmo Plüschow, all taken at ancient sites in southern Italy.[129] In the 1880s Gloeden and Plüschow settled at Taormina in Sicily to make a lucrative living out of photographing the local boys; the resulting photographs are arguably a form of soft pornography which exploits the poverty of the area and its residents. However, in 1890 Gloeden's photographs were published in the first issue of the respectable art magazine, *The Studio*, and both he and Plüschow were accepted as serious photographers. They were even praised by the German archaeologist, Rudolf Hauser, for attempting to reconstruct ancient life.[130] Alma-Tadema's interest in their work, likewise, appears to have been archaeological rather than prurient. The photographs in his collection are interspersed alongside others of architecture, statuary and artefacts, and his own labels indicate archaeological location and ignore the boys altogether.

The final dining painting, *Between Hope and Fear* (Pl.64), once again evokes the risqué nature of *symposium* in the form of an older man and a younger woman. Although a conventional reading of the painting might point to the identification of the two figures as a daughter and father (asking his permission to marry?), the background wall painting – of satyrs carrying a giant phallus – lends a suitably erotic frisson to the scene and suggests that the couple may well be prostitute and client.

Alma-Tadema, like other classical-subject painters, looked to Greco-Roman sculpture for the representation of drapery, figure-types and poses. Most sought inspiration from well-known

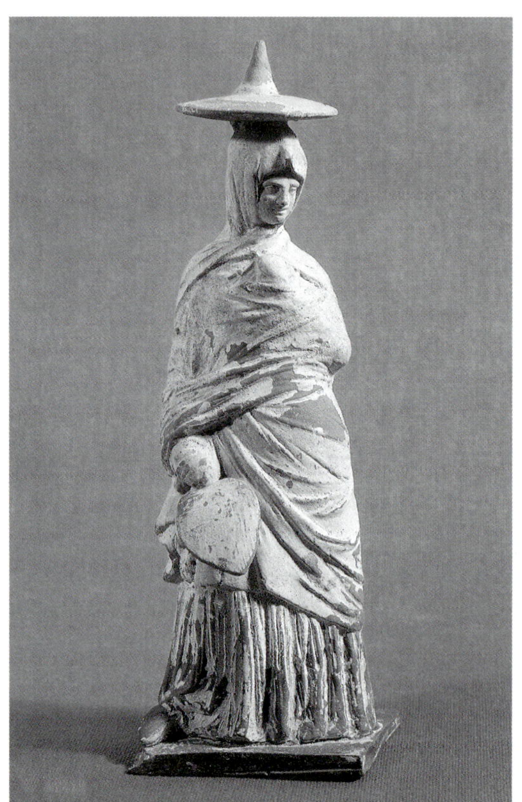

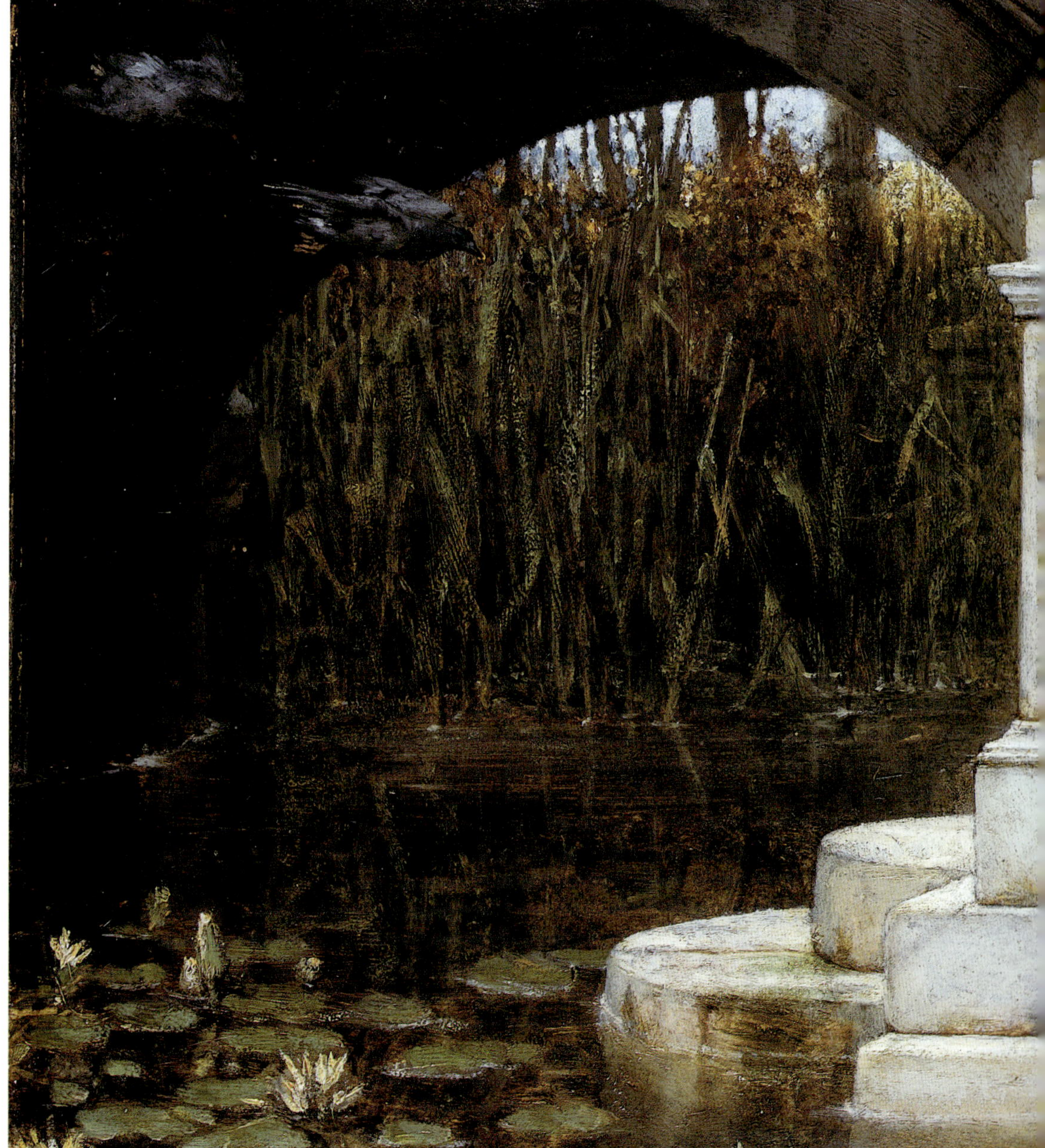

66 above left
Tanagra statuette, Greek, 3rd century BC
Terracotta, H 20 cm (7⅞ in)
British Museum, London

67
Fishing, 1873
Oil on wood, 19 × 40·6 cm (7½ × 16 in)
Hamburger Kunsthalle, Hamburg

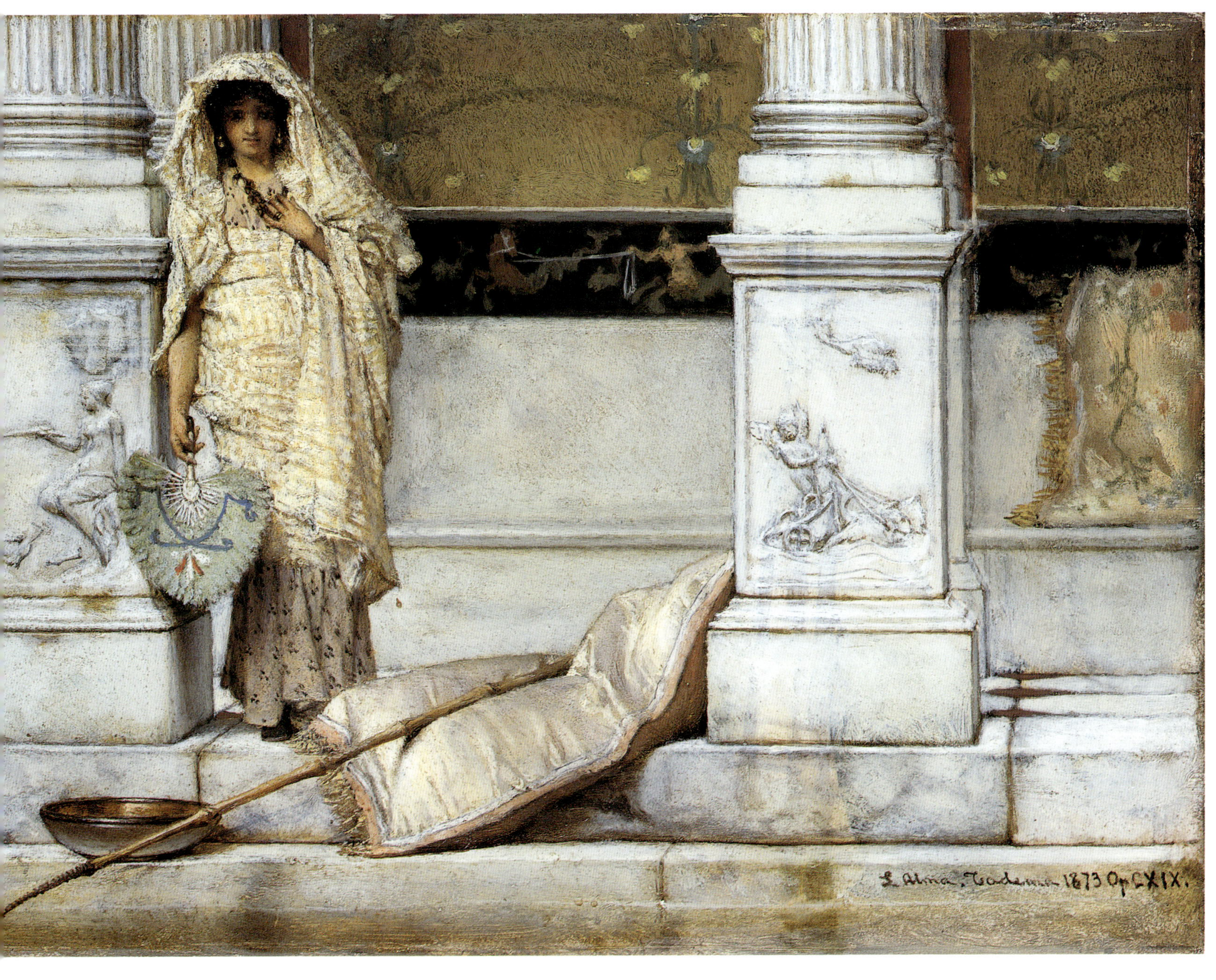
L. Alma Tadema 1873 Op CXIX.

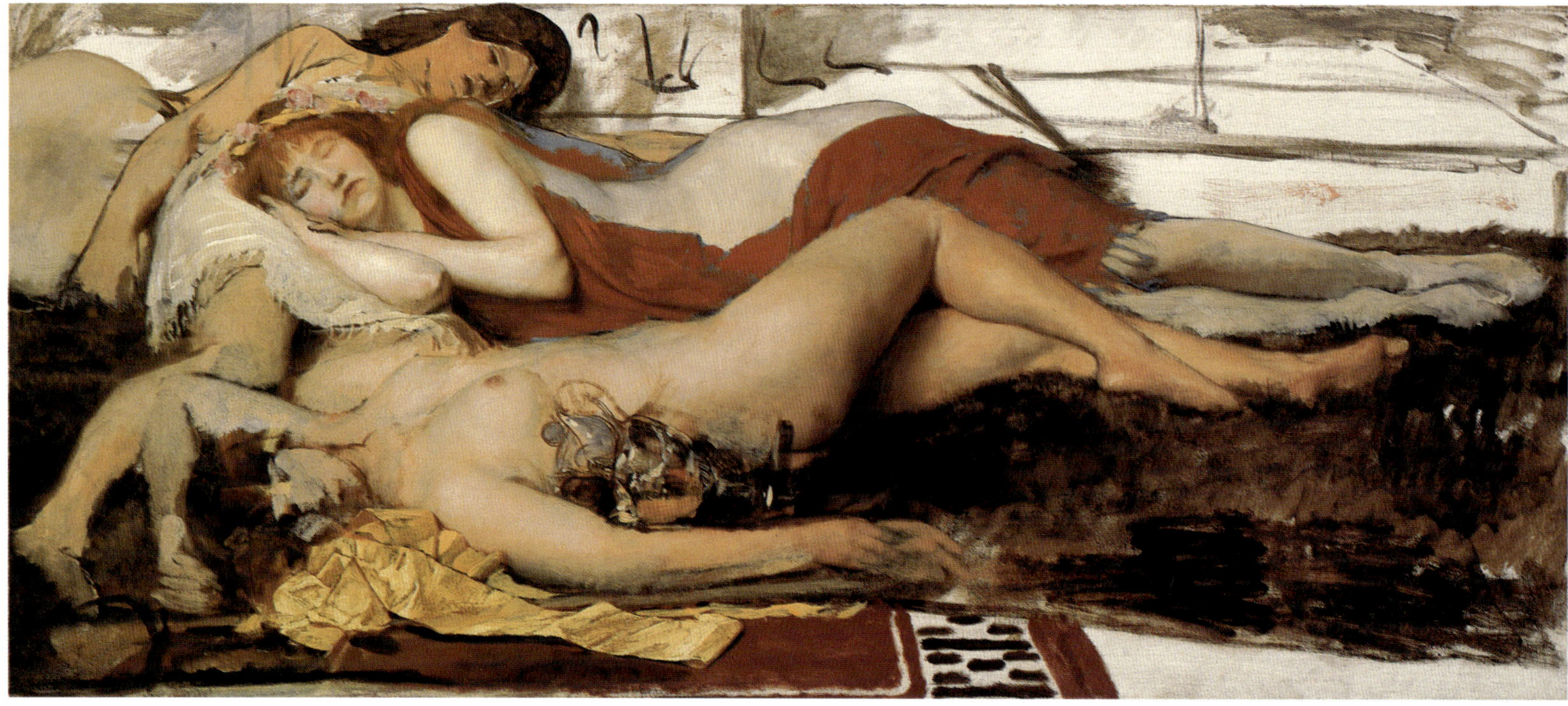

classical works, usually Greek sculpture of the fifth and fourth centuries BC. Frederic Leighton's *Daedalus and Icarus* (Pl.65) is inspired by celebrated sculptures of the ideal male nude,[131] and G. F. Watts' *Ariadne on Naxos* (1875) by the 'Fates', figures K, L and M from the east pediment of the Parthenon. Alma-Tadema's use of sculptural prototypes differs in that instead of high-status statues, he looks to lesser-known sources which often exploit the latest archaeological discoveries. The standing female figure in *Fishing* (Pl.67) follows the standard format of a Greek terracotta figurine known as a Tanagra statuette (Pl.66) – pose, drapery, head-covering, fan and jewellery – just after the first discoveries of such artefacts.[132] Although Greek terracotta statuettes had survived in both private and public collections, in 1870 Tanagra, a city of ancient Boeotia, yielded a wealth of statuettes plundered from grave sites in the area. By 1873 Tanagra statuettes (and also a number of forgeries) were widely available on the Athenian antiquities market. They quickly became sought after and found their way into a number of European private and public collections.[133]

The first public exhibition of Tanagras was mounted in 1878 at the Trocadéro, Paris, and ten years later the first major exhibition was held in London at the Burlington Fine Arts Club. By 1891 Tanagras were so in vogue that in Oscar Wilde's *The Picture of Dorian Gray*, Dorian could exclaim of the beauty of Sibyl Vane: 'she had all the delicate grace of that Tanagra figurine that you have in your studio, Basil.'[134] Alma-Tadema himself owned a number of Tanagra fragments and copies. In many later paintings, female dress of *himation* (cloak) pulled across *chiton* (tunic) in cross axis recalls fourth- and third-century BC Tanagra statuettes as well as sculptural drapery, while here the Tanagra reference affirms the artist's up-to-date archaeological knowledge. The practice of citing classical sculpture as the prototypes for figures was used by painters from the Renaissance, but Alma-Tadema contributes a new approach to an old tradition by looking to small-scale domestic art rather than to high-status, life-size statues.

The first years in London also saw the artist experimenting with a new subject. The unfinished *Exhausted Maenides* [sic] (Pl.68), showing three women sleeping off a Bacchanalian revel, is his first major exercise in the depiction of the nude. The female nude was an important component of the work of other artists who exhibited classical subjects, and this large canvas showing three female nudes follows a conventional pattern. *Exhausted Maenides*, given to Carel Vosmaer during a visit to London, was left unfinished. Nonetheless, Alma-Tadema did exhibit a similar picture at the Royal Academy in 1876, *After the Dance* (1875), a single reclining female nude, based on the foreground figure from the previous painting. The decision to branch out from his usual archaeological genre paintings may have been prompted by a desire to extend his range; furthermore, as figure painting was traditionally accorded the highest place in the hierarchy of artistic forms, it was important for the

68
Exhausted Maenides, *c.*1873-4
Oil on canvas (unfinished), 59·1 × 132 cm (23½ × 52 in)
Van Gogh Museum, Amsterdam

69
The Picture Gallery, 1874
Oil on canvas, 219·7 × 166 cm (86½ × 65⅜ in)
Towneley Hall Art Gallery and Museum, Burnley

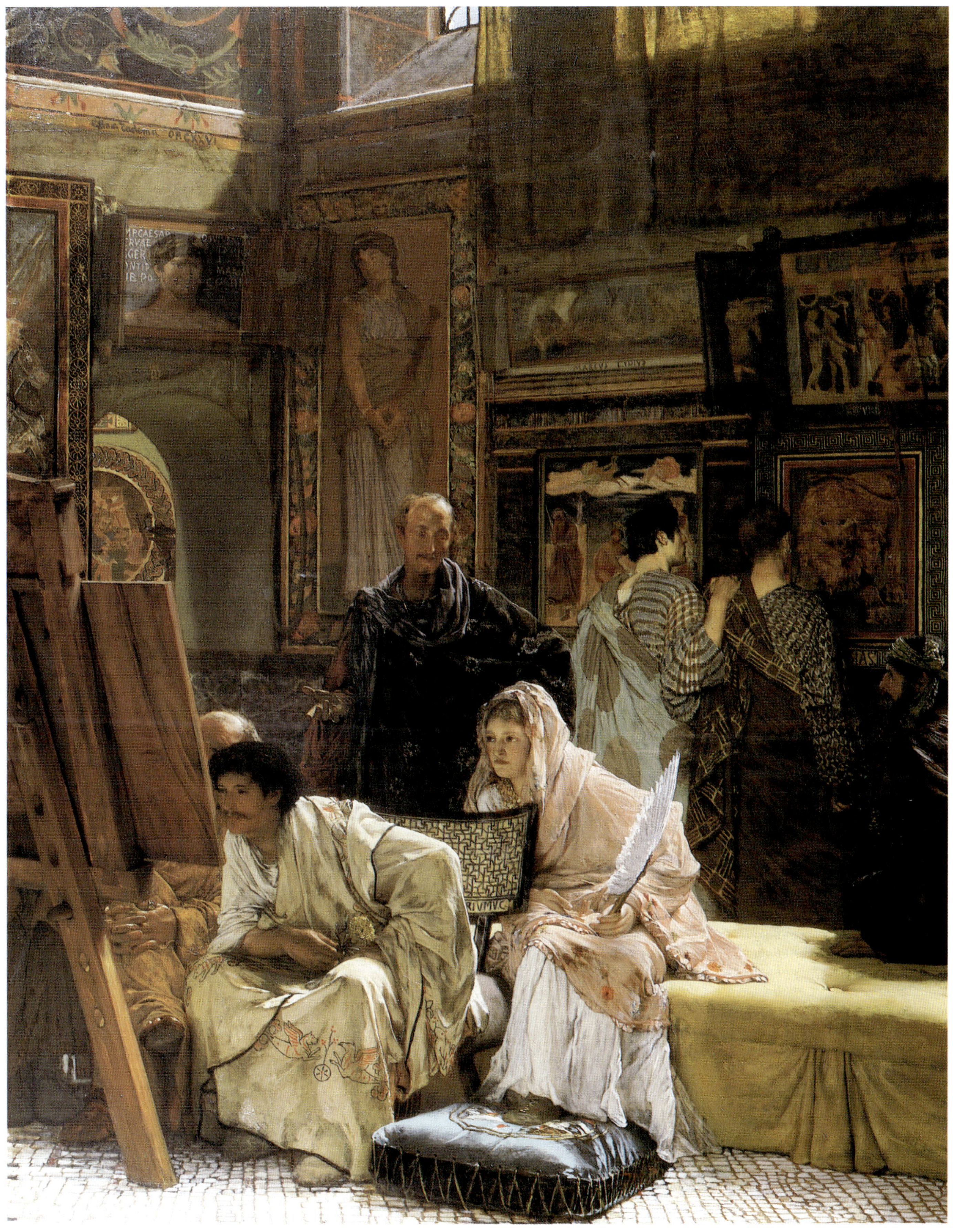

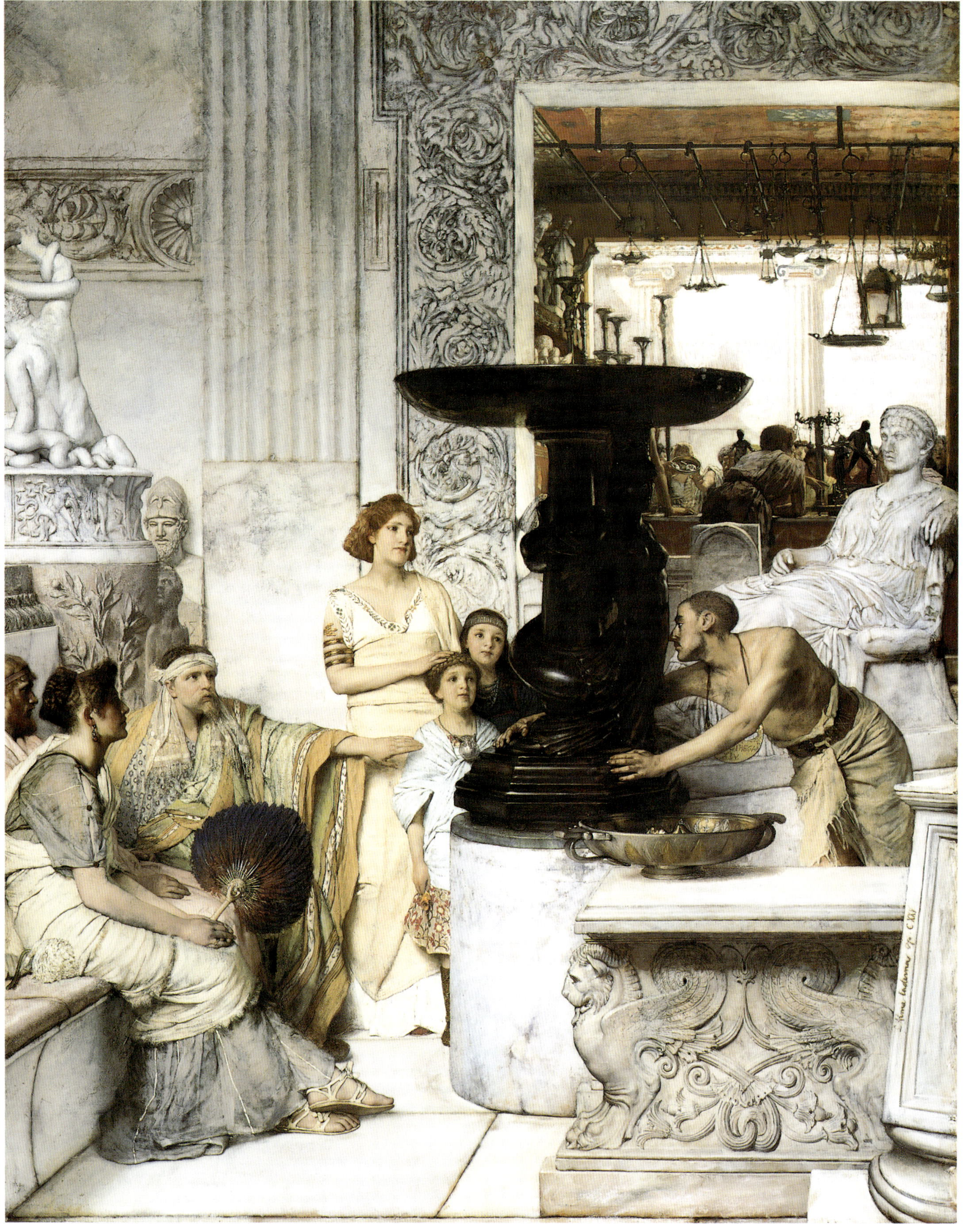

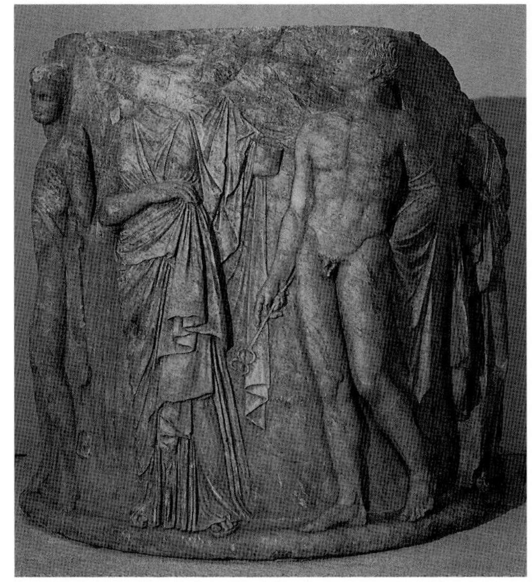

70 opposite
The Sculpture Gallery, 1874
Oil on canvas, 223·4 × 171·5 cm (87¾ × 67½ in)
Hood Museum of Art, Dartmouth College, Hanover NH, Gift of Arthur M. Loew

71
Column Drum from the Temple of Artemis at Ephesus, Greek, 4th century BC
Marble, H 1·64 m (64½ in)
British Museum, London

artist to consider presenting himself as a painter of the nude. Alma-Tadema, however, was clearly more comfortable with material objects than with expanses of human flesh, and he rarely returned to large-scale nudes.

In its unfinished state, *Exhausted Maenides* reveals something of the artist's technique. Dark outlines of underdrawing are clearly visible as the artist had begun to work with broad strokes of colour. He focused on finishing the figures while leaving the background and accessories until later. His painting method involved working directly on the canvas, from a quick initial sketch up to the final version; consequently very few preparatory sketches survive.

Returning to familiar ground Alma-Tadema produced another series of paintings on Roman picture and sculpture galleries. The subject and content of these pictures is similar to the earlier series on the same theme, but stylistic development is evident in the artist's increased technical skill in the depiction of material objects: fabrics, bronze, silver and marble. *The Picture Gallery* (Pl.69) repeats the same four paintings from *The Collector of Pictures at the Time of Augustus*:[135] the *Battle of Issus*, *Medea* by Timomachus, *The Sacrifice of Iphigenia* by Timanthes (Pl.33) and a picture of a lion. The frame of the lion now has an inscription which identifies the painter as Pausias, praised in antiquity as an animal painter. The architectural scene is replaced by a portrait of the emperor Nerva, while three more paintings are added including a painting inscribed with the name of the Roman painter, Marcus Ludius (mentioned by Pliny as a landscape painter working in the time of Augustus[136]) and, on the far left, another reproduction of a Pompeian mosaic, 'Rehearsal in the House of the Tragic Poet'. Both clients and dealer are contemporary portraits. The standing male figure in the centre is Gambart. Seated at the easel are the painter and dealer, Henry Wallis, and Gambart's nephew, the dealer Charles Deschamps. The two figures standing examining pictures in the background are P.J. Pilgeram and Léon Lefèvre, the successors to Gambart's London business. The seated man on the right may be identified as the French art dealer Paul Durand-Ruel, and the seated woman as Gambart's mistress, Madame Angelée.[137]

Antistius Labeon: AD 75 (1874) portrays a more intimate private viewing in the house of an amateur Roman artist. Pliny tells us that 'Titedius Labeo, a former praetor who died recently in extreme old age and who once even served as the proconsul of the province of Gallia Narbonensis, used to take great pride in his own miniature paintings.'[138] Painting, however, was not seen as an entirely suitable pastime for the upper classes, and Pliny continues, 'but the ridicule directed at him [Labeo] for this bordered on invective.' The ridiculed Labeo evidently appealed to the artist's sense of humour, but beyond that, the painting hints at a double focus that is a familiar feature of his work: on the one hand, an overtly impartial or admiring image of the ancient (especially the Roman) world; on the other, a subversive implication situated, above all, in the background knowledge which an informed reader of the painting might hope to have. Once again the connoisseurs are represented in the form of the artist's family with Washington Epps (the artist's brother-in-law), George Napoleon Epps (the artist's father-in-law, who had died four months before the painting was completed) and Laura Alma-Tadema. The artist, Labeo, is based on Alma-Tadema himself.

In *The Sculpture Gallery* (Pl.70), as in *A Sculpture Gallery in Rome at the Time of Augustus*, clients are clearly more concerned with material than with artistic merit. The bronze they are eyeing is an ornamental statue of the mythological sea monster, Scylla (Archaeological Museum, Naples). By contrast, the background statues are all recognizable marble sculptures, which include a bust of Pericles, known from a number of Roman copies, and, as in the earlier sculpture gallery painting, the seated Agrippina. The statue of the infant Hercules wrestling with serpents is a marble version of a sixteenth-century bronze now attributed to the Italian sculptor Guglielmo della Porta (Capodimonte Museum, Naples).[139] It is incongruously placed on top of a fourth-century BC column drum from the temple of Artemis at Ephesus (Pl.71). The column drum, as the only Greek original in the gallery, should, by both modern and ancient standards, be the most highly valued object, but here it is merely used as a statue base. Ruskin objected to Alma-Tadema's meddling with the hierarchy of ancient art and noted: 'the artistic skill has succeeded with all its objects in the degree of their unimportance. The piece of silver plate is painted best; the griffin bas-relief it stands on, second best; the statue of the empress worse than the griffins, and the living personages worse than the statue.'[140] Ruskin's artistic judgements are sound, in so far as Alma-Tadema did excel in painting material objects rather than the living model, but he totally misses the ironic commentary: in a culture which valued silver above most things except gold, the plate becomes the most important item.

All the figures (except for the slave) are contemporary portraits: Washington Epps is seated on the far left next to his sister, Ellen Gosse (wife of the literary figure, Edmund Gosse), then Alma-Tadema with outstretched arm and a standing Laura, Anna and Laurense. Including portraits of family, friends and business connections would seem to be a flattering gesture and yet, given that the paintings view Romans collectors in terms of acquisition rather than discernment, an amusing irony becomes apparent as the artist points to his own dealer and even himself in the ridiculous role of ignorant connoisseur.

In the 1870s, Gambart, who had bought a villa, Les Palmiers in Nice, was rarely in London. Having virtually retired, he concentrated on beautifying his villa and entertaining on a lavish scale. *The Picture Gallery* and *The Sculpture Gallery*, commissioned for Gambart's villa, remained in his collection of prized pictures until his death in 1903. Some artists, such as Rosa Bonheur, continued to rely on Gambart; Frederick Goodall's fortunes even declined after Gambart moved to Nice and he eventually died bankrupt. Alma-Tadema, however, continued to prosper; he worked with Gambart's successors, Pilgeram and Lefèvre, and even maintained connections with Charles Deschamps, who dealt mainly in Impressionist and other modernist European art.

The Sculpture Gallery is the artist's first major painting to depict what was to become his trademark: a bravura display of white marble. Alma-Tadema remembers his first contact with polished marble as an art student:

> I was first attracted to the artistic possibilities of marble when visiting Ghent in 1858. A friend happened to take me into a certain clubhouse ... which had a marble smoking-room. I don't suppose the room was of any exceptional magnificence, but it was the finest marble room I had then seen, and its wonderful whiteness and atmosphere made an extraordinary impression upon me.[141]

From the 1870s the representation of marble was to assume a major role in his works, and painted decoration, in particular, is gradually replaced by marble as the artist's interest moves from Pompeii to the city of Rome itself.[142] While excavations at Pompeii continued throughout the century, work at high-profile sites in Rome revealed many new finds. In 1863 the site of the villa of Livia outside Rome had yielded the famous statue of the Prima Porta Augustus. Excavations commenced at the Palatine and the House of Livia in the 1860s, and ten years later archaeologists began work on the Forum, the Capitoline Hill and the Colosseum. In 1875 Giuseppe Fiorelli, who had previously been Director of Excavations at Pompeii, took the position of Director of Museums and Excavations at Rome. One of Alma-Tadema's first representations of the city is a painting entitled *On the Steps of the Capitol* (1874). The title places the scene in Rome, although the setting is of indistinct steps near an unidentifiable arch. The artist challenges the viewer's preconceptions by suggesting a well-known location and then depicting an unknown corner. Although Alma-Tadema abandoned Pompeian-style interiors in the 1870s, he still made use of Pompeian discoveries until the end of his career. Imitations of wall paintings from the House of the Dioscuri and the House of the Vettii appear in *Spring* of 1894, while *A Favourite Custom* of 1909 reconstructs the Stabian and Forum baths.[143]

72
Spring in the Gardens of the Villa Borghese, 1877
Watercolour, 29·9 × 20·3 cm (11¾ × 8 in)
Private collection

II/2
INTO THE ACADEMY

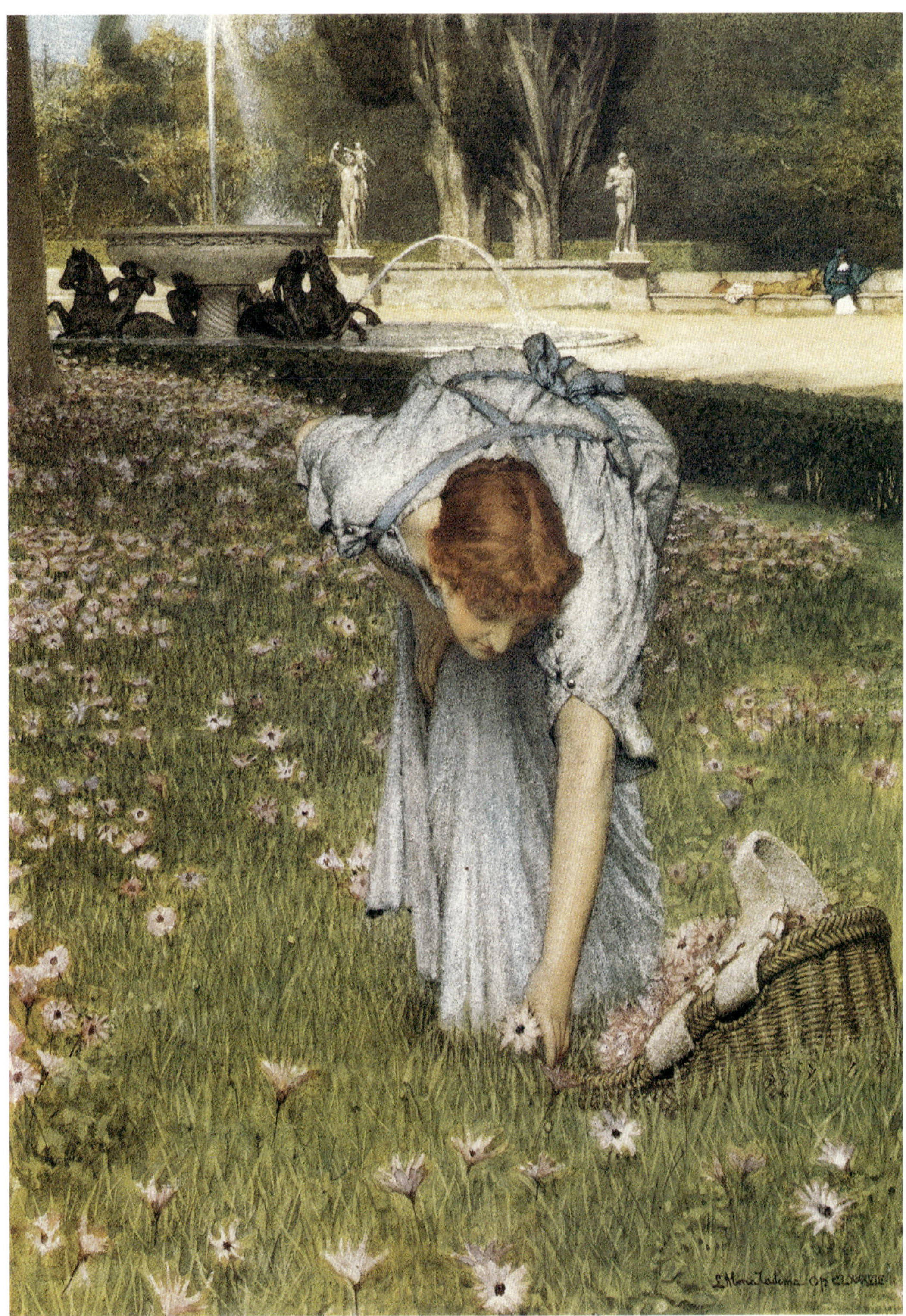

The Picture Gallery and *The Sculpture Gallery*, exhibited at the Royal Academy in 1874 and 1875 respectively, led to Alma-Tadema's election as Associate in 1876. The Victorian art world was dominated by the Royal Academy of Arts, and its annual Summer Exhibition (showing works by contemporary artists) was undoubtedly the high point of the artistic calendar as well as an established part of the London 'Season'. Writing in 1930, E. F. Benson recalled: 'Orthodox English artists, who had won for themselves a recognised position as Associates of the Royal Academy or as Academicians, enjoyed during the sixties and seventies and eighties a period of unique commercial prosperity: never before or since have they found it so easy to sell at high prices the works which were hung on the line in the annual exhibition at Burlington House.'[144] Successful Academicians were virtually guaranteed membership of a cultural and social élite. Many artists chose to live in fashionable areas where they built themselves lavish studio-houses. Studio visits on 'Picture Sundays', held just before the Academy sending-in day, were desirable social activities. Interested in expanding social connections, Alma-Tadema acquired useful allies, not least the leading art critic F. G. Stephens. A portrait of Stephens's wife was given to the couple in 1873. The Alma-Tadema home regularly hosted Tuesday musical evenings, and the grand piano received the autographs of the musicians who played and attended the soirées. These names form a glittering list of the most famous international musical celebrities of the day including the French composer, Camille Saint-Saens; German pianist, Clara Schumann; Russian composer and pianist, Anton Rubinstein; Spanish violinist, Pablo Sarasate; Viennese conductor, Hans Richter; Austro-Hungarian violinist, Joseph Joachim, Polish-born pianist and singer, George Henschel; Dutch violinist, Maurice Sons. He was to paint portraits of Henschel (1879), Richter (1881) Joachim (1893) and Sons (Pl.126), all informal studies which were presented to the musicians as gifts.

Laura Alma-Tadema's development as an artist may have benefited from her husband's social connections, but as a woman she was excluded from the Academy's ranks as nineteenth-century Academicians never elected women members. Women's works were admitted to the Summer Exhibition and she began exhibiting at the Academy in 1873. Her paintings, like her hus-

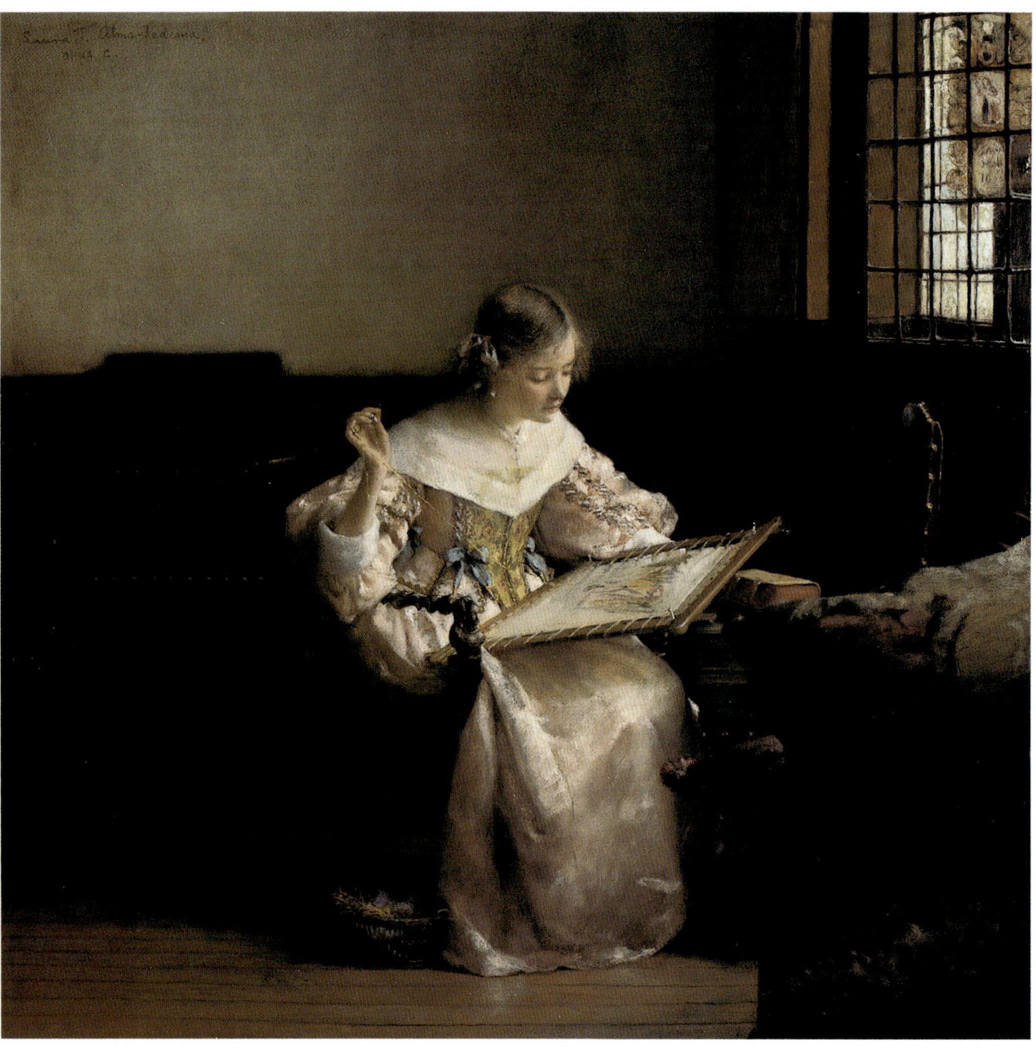

band's, were distinguished by delicate brush work and fine finish, but in contrast to her husband, her forte was the domestic and the sentimental. A typical example is *Sweet Industry* (Pl.73), showing a woman absorbed in work on a tapestry and set in a historical interior. For all the obvious differences between Lawrence's work and her own, Laura was unable to achieve much independent recognition. W. P. Frith assigns a chapter of his autobiography to 'Lady artists', where he describes Laura in only one sentence: 'The exhibited works of Mrs Alma-Tadema afford proofs of original power developed under the eye of her distinguished husband.'[145]

As a result of the rebuilding work in Townshand House, in 1875 the family left London for a tour of Europe which lasted five and a half months. Alma-Tadema obtained a studio in Rome where the eighteenth-century Borghese gardens were to form the setting for *A Corner of the Gardens of the Villa Borghese* (1876), *Spring in the Gardens of the Villa Borghese* and a watercolour of the same title (Pl.72). *Spring*, showing a woman picking flowers, is particularly unusual in that it transposes a figure in classical drapery to a modern setting. Rome was also the inspiration for *An Audience at Agrippa's* (Pl.74), a *tour de force* of white on white with marble statue set against marble architecture, the direct influence of a studio which was decorated all white. Marcus Vipsanius Agrippa, the powerful political ally and son-in-law of the Emperor Augustus, descends the steps of a sumptuous marble building followed by a retinue of clients. A small group of petitioners wait at the entrance with a tray of gold and silver plate. The palatial grandeur of blue-veined Carrara and green Cipollino marble confirms Agrippa's high status. Vitruvius, writing in the late Republic, confirms the necessity of a show of luxury in private dwellings belonging to men of rank and official importance.[146] In a later article entitled 'Marbles: their Ancient and Modern Application', Alma-Tadema discusses the extravagant marble buildings of Rome in the late Republic. He cites the example of Scarus, whose ostentatious atrium, according to Pliny, was supported by 38-foot high columns of black Lucullian marble.[147] In a reaction against such displays of wealth, Augustus attempted to curb the lavish use of marble in domestic architecture and instead encouraged a public building programme. The scheme was so successful that Suetonius writes that Augustus 'could justly boast that he found it [Rome] built of brick and left it in marble'.[148] Agrippa was the most conspicuous financier of Augustus' rebuilding programme; his projects included a Pantheon, the Basilica of Neptune, the baths of Agrippa, and a host of aqueducts and sewers. Here the dome of the sur-

73
Laura Alma-Tadema, *Sweet Industry*, *c*.1904
Oil on canvas, 36 × 35·6 cm (14⅛ × 14 in)
Manchester City Art Galleries

74 opposite
An Audience at Agrippa's, 1875
Oil on wood, 90·8 × 62·8 cm (35¾ × 24¾ in)
Dick Institute, Kilmarnock

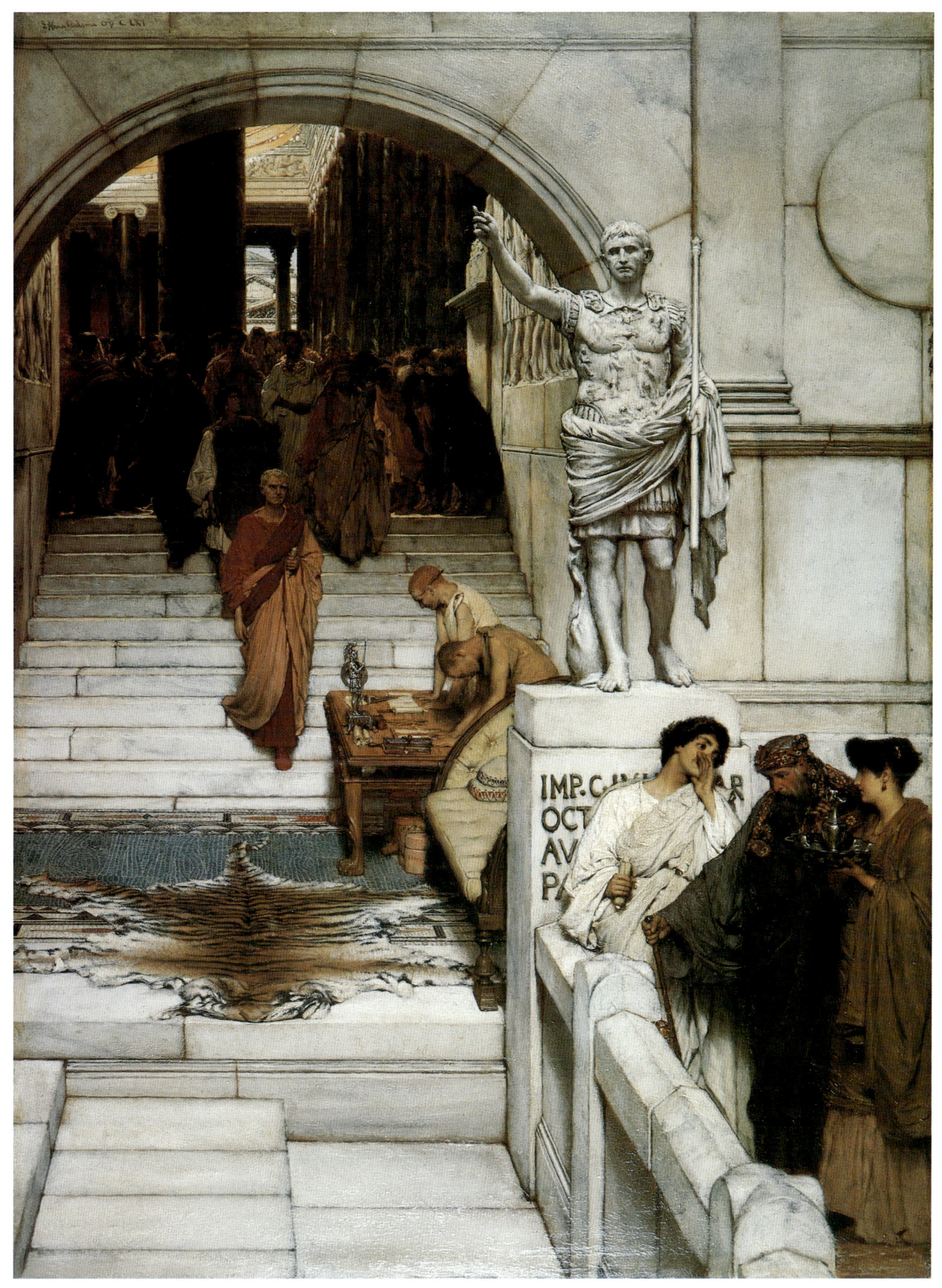
IMP.C.IN AR
OCT
AV
PA

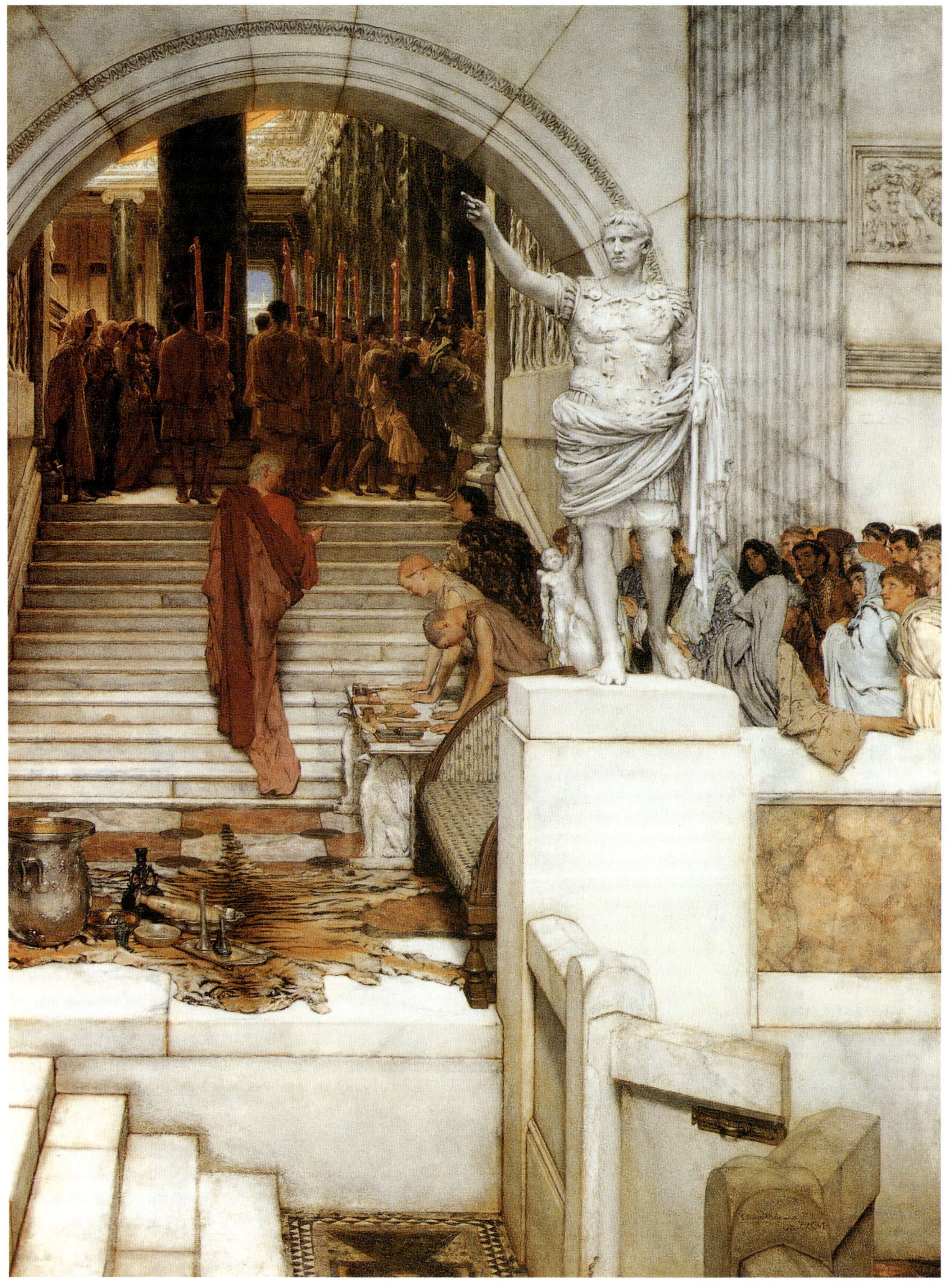

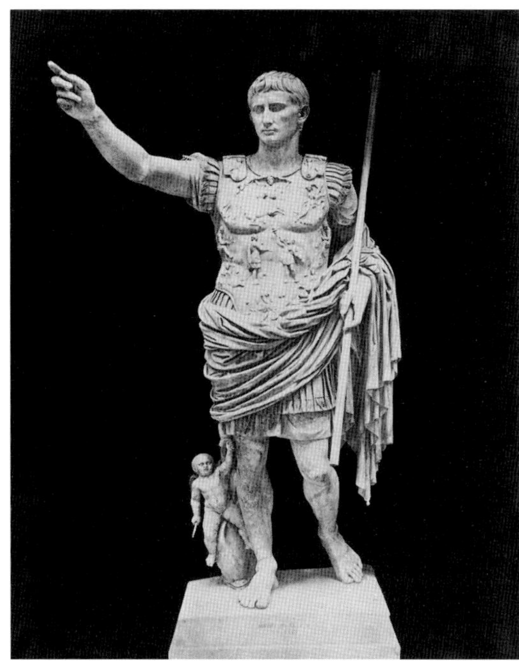

viving Pantheon, at the time of the painting credited as Agrippa's building, but later found to be Hadrianic, is glimpsed in the distance. Alma-Tadema perhaps hints at a degree of political hypocrisy on Agrippa's part: despite Augustus' clear views on extravagant private dwellings, Agrippa's house (even allowing for a reasonable show of wealth) is quite as spectacular as his public buildings.

Agrippa's costume and pose are reminiscent of standard Roman *togatus* (toga-clad) statues, while his distinctive features are modelled on surviving portraits. The figure of Agrippa appears diminutive compared with the huge statue, the Prima Porta Augustus (Pl.76), in the foreground. Discovered intact in 1863 at the villa of Livia, in Prima Porta outside Rome, it is a Tiberian copy (*c.* 15 AD) of an original statue erected to celebrate Augustus' military victory over the Parthians in 20 BC. Augustus is presented as a youthful military hero in contrast to the much older Agrippa who is preoccupied with civil matters. Despite Agrippa's lavish pretensions and, indeed, the allusion to his grand public buildings, he is completely overshadowed by the statue of Augustus. The real power in Rome, we are reminded, is held only by the Emperor himself.

The painting received stunning reviews when exhibited at the Royal Academy in 1876. The critic of the *Illustrated London News* summed up the enthusiasm with the statement: 'By general consent this picture is regarded as the most perfect work that Mr Alma-Tadema has submitted to the London public.'[149] Many critics concentrated on the quality of the painted marble, and yet, as often, the picture can be read on two different levels. *An Audience at Agrippa's* does indeed claim our attention for its striking display of light, colour and texture and yet, at the same time, it also offers a revealing glimpse of ancient political life.

Four years later, the composition was reversed in *After the Audience* (Pl.75), as Agrippa retraces his steps back to the palace after his day's work is completed. The painting was prompted by a commission from the Newcastle armaments manufacturer and art collector, Sir William Armstrong. Armstrong had seen *An Audience at Agrippa's* and asked for a similar picture. Alma-Tadema originally offered him *Between Hope and Fear* (Pl.64), which Armstrong refused on the grounds that it did not contain enough marble.[150] The artist's retort was a playful imitation of an earlier painting: 'Well if he wants to have marble, and that is dearer to him than figures then I will reverse the Audience and make the same thing, *After the Audience!* If all the people go away then he'll see their backs and marble will remain the main subject!'[151]

After the Audience duly disposed of the petitioners on the right and removed the dedication on the plinth of Augustus' statue, to reveal further expanses of plain marble. Armstrong rejected the painting and wanted nothing more to do with the artist. Alma-Tadema was indeed in a fortunate position, if he was able to alienate important patrons. *Between Hope and Fear*, meanwhile, was successfully exhibited at the Royal Academy in 1877 and soon found a buyer. There is no other example of Alma-Tadema treating his patrons in such a cavalier manner, and in general his keen business sense took precedence over the assertion of artistic integrity. On a commercial level, his success depended on satisfying the public demand for a recognizable and aesthetically pleasing Roman world, and his paintings seem to have been praised (and sold) on the basis of surface appeal rather than sophisticated allusion. There is little doubt, too, that many of his later pictures take on a formulaic quality, as the artist may be seen to repeat the representation of marble, sea and sky to satisfy his clients' requirements.

In 1876 Alma-Tadema completed one of the first of many courtship scenes, a type of picture which was to prove particularly popular. *Pleading* (Pl.77), an exquisite painting on a tiny scale, depicts a man lying on a marble bench, looking up imploringly at the woman seated next to him. It was used as the frontispiece for Georg Ebers's novella, *A Question*, although Ebers states that the novella was inspired by another work by the artist, itself entitled *A Question* (1877). The two paintings are very similar, the main difference being an inscription from the tomb of Porcius outside Pompeii, which is featured only in *A Question*. Alma-Tadema later returned Ebers's compliment with yet another very similar painting, a watercolour entitled *Xanthe and Phaon* (Pl.78), which uses the names of Ebers's protagonists. It was used as the frontispiece of the fourth edition of Ebers's *A Question* and included in *The Ebers Gallery*. All three paintings juxtapose swarthy male and pale-skinned female on a marble terrace overlooking the sea, a setting which comes to be Alma-Tadema's most familiar.

From the time of his election as Associate of the Royal Academy, the annual Summer Exhibition provided Alma-Tadema with his main source of public exposure. May 1877 saw the opening of the Grosvenor Gallery, a private gallery set up by Sir Coutts Lindsay as an alternative to the Royal Academy. In contrast to the Academy's selection process (where official connections with the Academy ensured that works submitted to the Hanging Committee would be chosen for the Summer exhibition), the Grosvenor Gallery instead invited artists to exhibit with the only

75 opposite
After the Audience, 1879
Oil on wood, 91·4 × 66 cm (36 × 26 in)
Private collection

76
Prima Porta Augustus, Roman, 1st century AD
Marble, Vatican Museum, Rome:
University of Birmingham

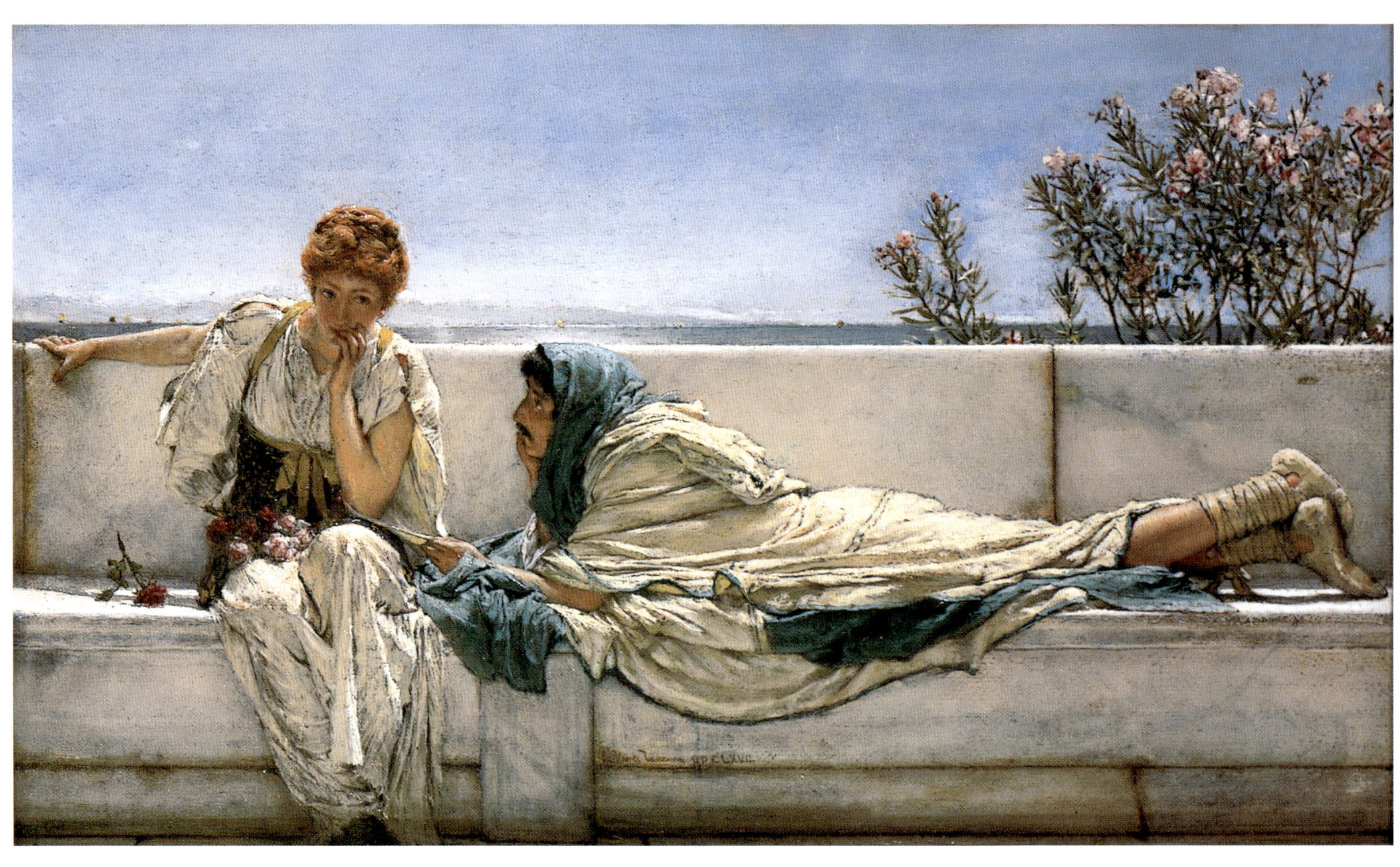

77
Pleading, 1876
Oil on canvas, 21·5 × 33·5 cm (8½ × 13¼ in)
Guildhall Art Gallery, London

78
Xanthe and Phaon, 1883
Watercolour, 45·1 × 32·4 cm (17¾ × 12¾ in)
Walters Art Gallery, Baltimore

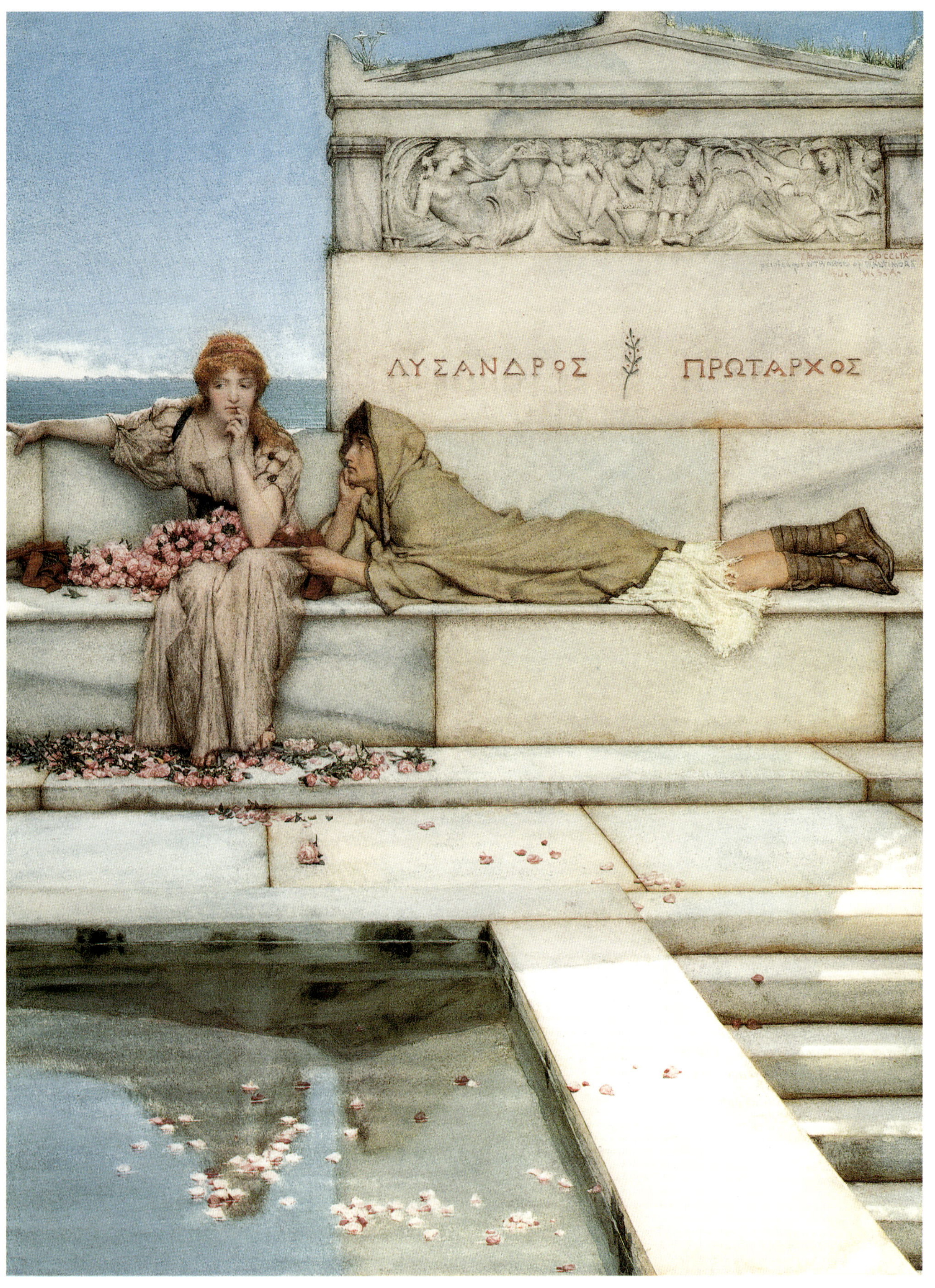
ΛΥΣΑΝΔΡΟΣ
ΠΡΩΤΑΡΧΟΣ

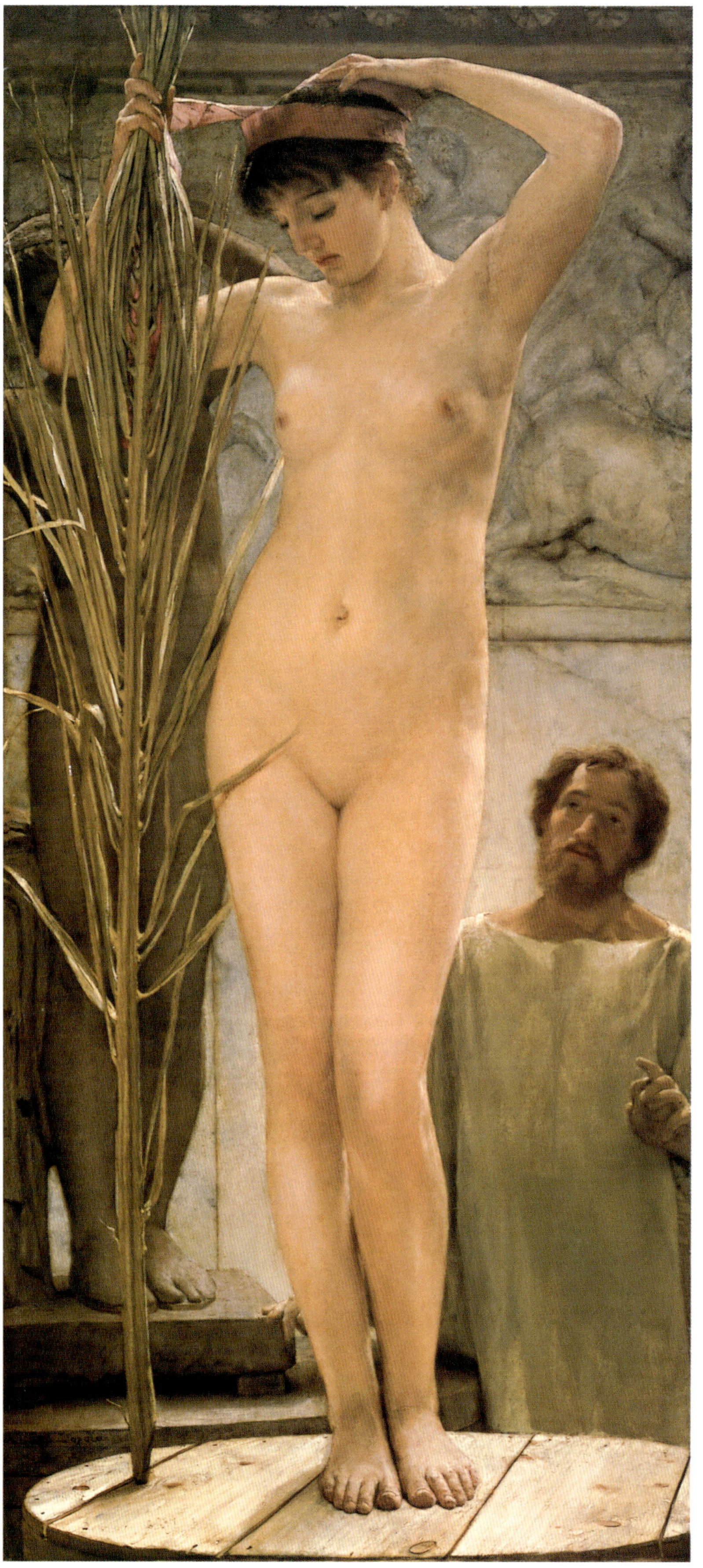

stipulation that the gallery would not show works which had been refused by the Academy. Exhibition was in lavish surroundings which imitated a private house rather than the cramped exhibition space at the Academy. The first exhibition included eight works by Alma-Tadema,[152] as well as Edward Burne-Jones, James McNeill Whistler, Albert Moore, Walter Crane and G. F. Watts. While some of these other artists had always remained aloof from the Academy, Alma-Tadema was an establishment figure who was also willing to ally himself with the aesthetic avant-garde. Indeed, Alma-Tadema's public and personal connections covered a wide sphere. The young Oscar Wilde wrote a review of the Grosvenor opening for the *Dublin University Magazine*. In a letter to the editor, he declared: 'I and Lord Ronald Gower and Mr Ruskin, and all artists of my acquaintance, hold that Alma-Tadema's drawing of men and women is disgraceful.'[153] Nevertheless, shortly afterwards Wilde was noticed (oddly, refusing to wear a disguise) at a masked ball at the Alma-Tadema's.[154] Furthermore, Alma-Tadema's library included a presentation copy of Wilde's 1881 edition of poems and a finely bound copy of Longus' *Daphnis and Chloe* with an inscription, 'To Alma-Tadema in admiration of the Great Beauty of his Art from Oscar Wilde'. Differences in approach and taste evidently did not signal social exclusiveness. In a world where even anti-establishment figures such as Rossetti and Whistler commanded high prices for their paintings, artists and writers of different allegiances enjoyed equal status in society and became familiar with each other through participation in the same social events.

Laura Alma-Tadema also exhibited works at the Grosvenor Gallery. The seven works which she showed between 1880 and 1887 all have anecdotal titles – *Hunt the Slipper*, *Sisters*, *Granny's Needle*, *May I Come In?*, *A Birthday*, *A Mother's Pride*, *Always Welcome* – indicating the type of sentimental genre subjects which she favoured. Alma-Tadema was willing to support the Grosvenor exhibition with a selection of works every year, but continued to reserve his major paintings for the Academy. The 1878 Academy exhibition showed *A Sculptor's Model* (Pl.79), his second and last full-scale depiction of the nude. As in *Exhausted Maenides* and *After the Dance*, archaeological detail has been replaced by the female form. Wilde's assertion that Alma-Tadema's 'drawing of men and women is disgraceful' is an overblown display of verbal histrionics, but it is true that more measured critics tended to acknowledge his depiction of material objects rather than the human body. He may, perhaps, have been eager to assert himself in an area where his reputation was less sure.

A Sculptor's Model was painted as an instructive work for John Collier, whose father, Sir Robert Collier (Lord Monkswell) had asked Alma-Tadema to take his son as a pupil. The artist refused, but agreed to paint a picture with the young student as observer, while Collier's father bought the finished painting in return.[155] As a mature artist Alma-Tadema employed studio assistants, chiefly engaged in architectural and perspective drawings, but did not take on any students. John Collier, who was to become a successful painter of genre and classical subjects, must have shown artistic promise while Lord Monkswell could have proved a useful patron, but Alma-Tadema was determined to maintain his position as working artist and not teacher.

It is apt that *A Sculptor's Model* should explore the creative process, with a sculptor working from the living model. Alma-Tadema also produced a series of oils on copperplate on the workings of ancient art – *Painters*, *Sculpture*, *Architecture* – exhibited together at the Grosvenor Gallery in 1878. All three were tiny canvases (31·1 × 31·7 cm) in contrast to the much larger *A Sculptor's Model*. Edward Burne-Jones summed up Alma-Tadema's work in one sentence: 'he paints little pictures as big as one's hand, full of beautiful marble and mosaic pavements.'[156] His smaller canvases are often his most distinctive, crowded with minuscule detail visible only through a magnifying glass.

Scenes of ancient artists at work serve to demystify what were, and are, often regarded as unchallengeable masterpieces of ancient art by concentrating on artistic endeavour and not on the end result. The focus of *A Sculptor's Model*, however, is not artistic creativity but the life-size female nude. It elicited a famous response from the Bishop of Carlisle: 'for a living artist to exhibit a life-sized almost photographic representation of a beautiful naked woman strikes my inartistic mind as somewhat if not very mischievous.'[157] Other British artists regularly exhibited paintings of the classicizing nude, but their nymphs and goddesses, distanced from the realities of a naked model in an artist's studio, were less problematic. Nudes attracted no adverse critical reaction as long as, veiled in the respectability of the classical tradition, they purported to represent a pagan deity and not a 'real' woman.[158]

The painting was censured for its depiction of a 'realistic' nude, but, ironically enough, Alma-Tadema's sculptor's model is based, in fact, on the Venus Esquilina, a statue excavated on the Esquiline Hill, Rome in 1874. It was undoubtedly seen by Alma-Tadema on his visit there in the winter of 1875–6, where he must have purchased a photograph (Pl.80). After its discovery, the

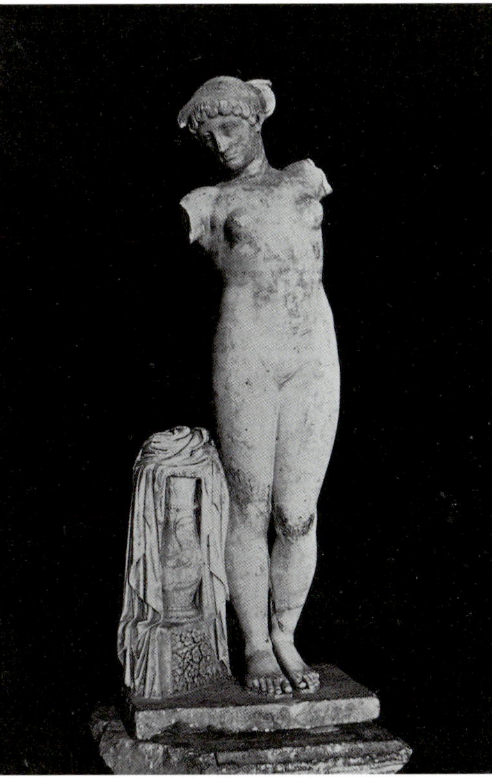

79 opposite
A Sculpture's Model, 1877
Oil on canvas, 195·5 × 86 cm (77 × 33⅞ in)
Private collection

80
Venus Esquilina, Greco-Roman, 1st century BC
Marble, Conservatori Museum, Rome:
University of Birmingham

81
Edward Poynter, *Diadumenē*, 1884
Oil on canvas, 51 × 50·9 cm (20⅛ × 20 in)
Royal Albert Memorial Museum, Exeter

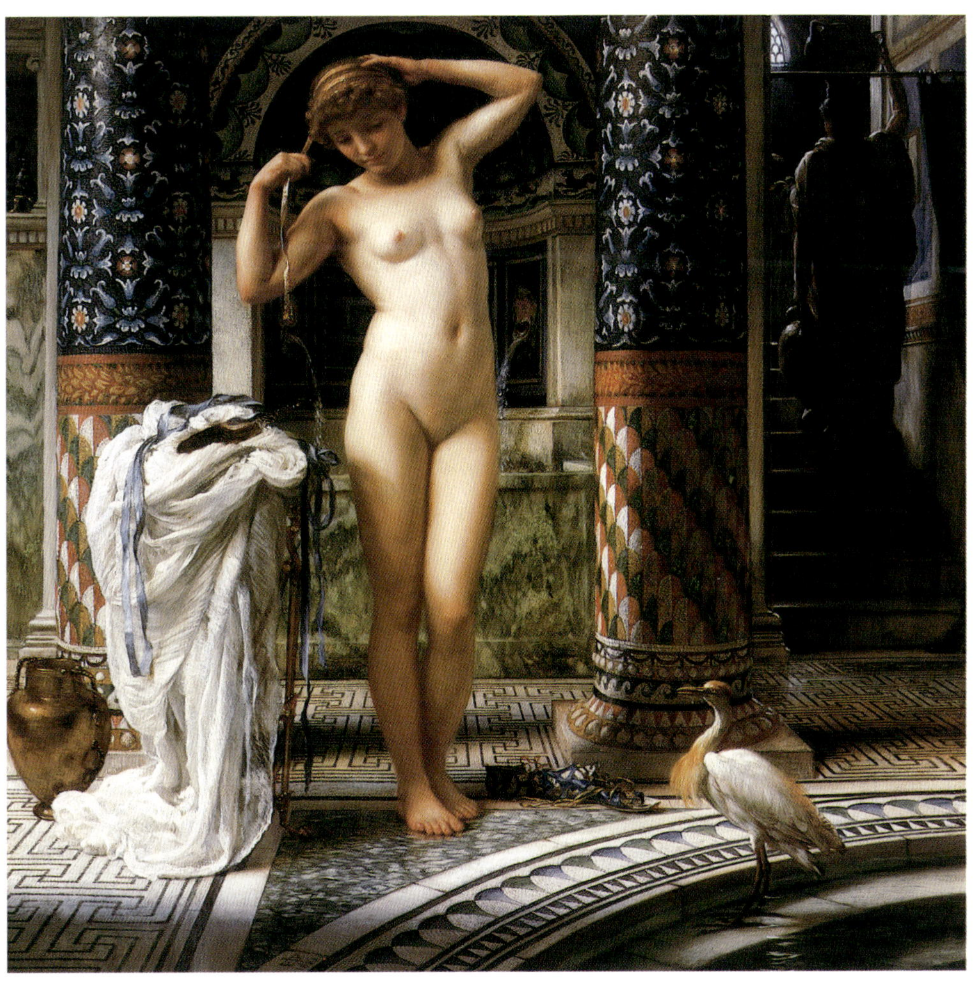

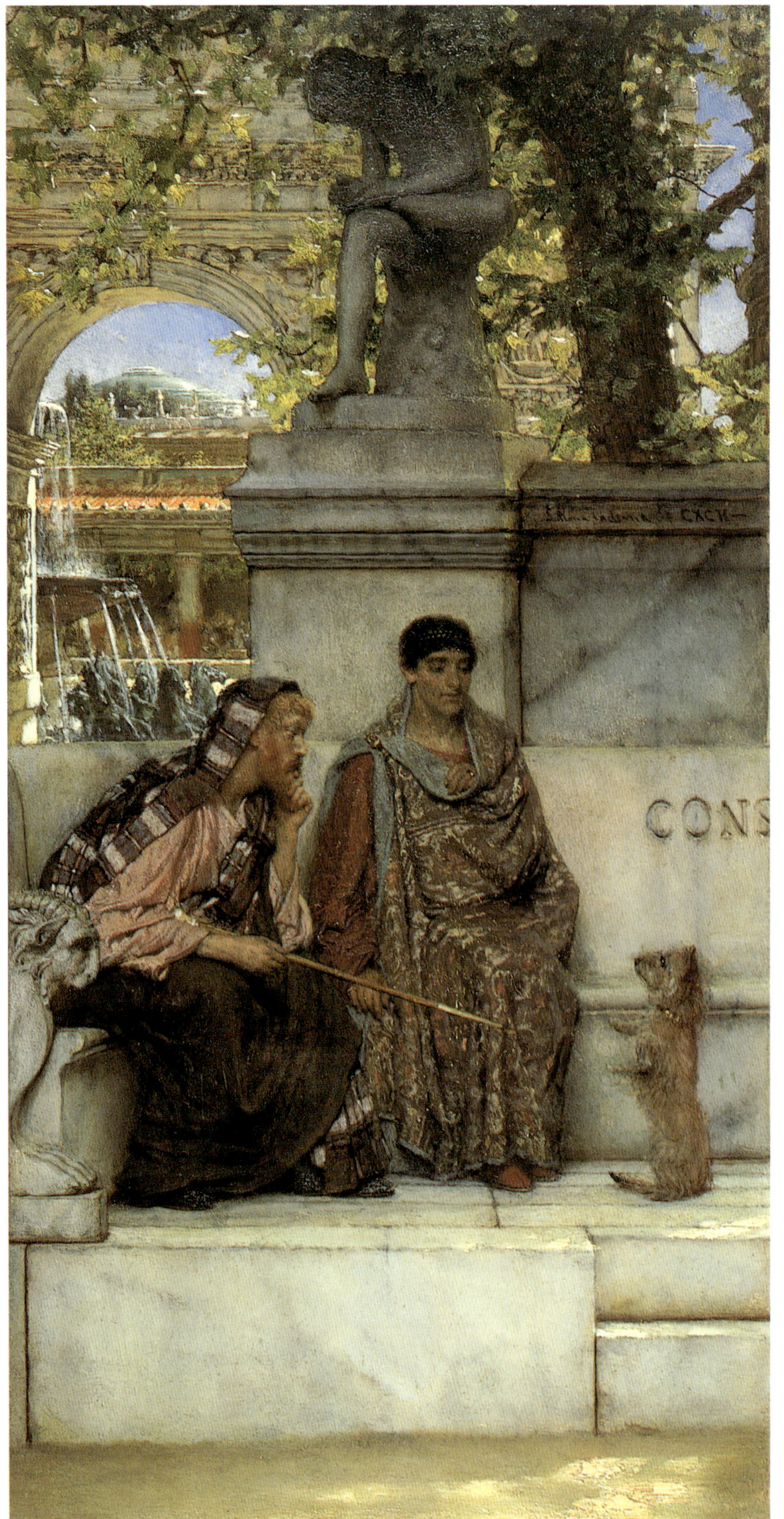

82
In the Time of Constantine, 1878
Oil on wood, 32·2 × 16 cm (12⅝ × 16¼ in)
William Morris Gallery, Walthamstow, London

83 opposite
Spinario, Roman copy of a 3rd-century BC original
Bronze, Conservatori Museum, Rome:
University of Birmingham

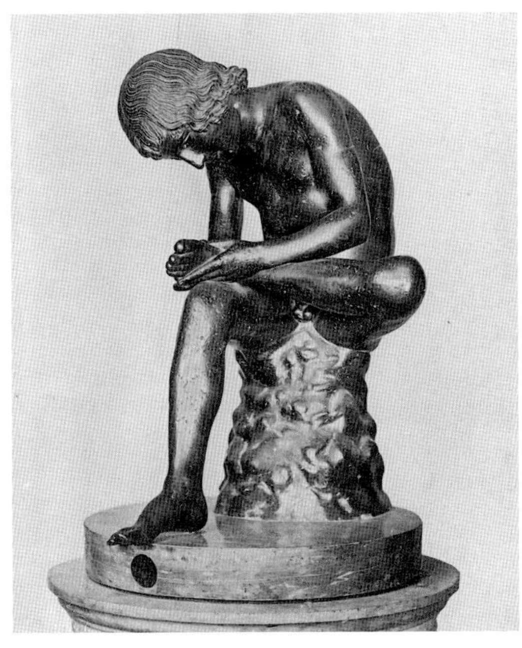

statue was hailed as a Greek original, but soon proved to be a Roman copy.[159] Although the figure was discovered without arms, the remains of the left hand on the top of her head suggest that her arms were raised and binding a fillet. Carlo Visconti's engravings of the statue restored the arms in the pose of a fillet binder,[160] and, accordingly, Alma-Tadema shows his model binding a fillet. The prototype was acknowledged by art critics at the time and four years later the accuracy of his representation was noted by the classical archaeologist W. C. Perry who, in a discussion of the statue, directs his readers' attention to Alma-Tadema's painting: 'The figure is familiar to the English public in the very beautiful picture called *The Painter's Model* [sic] by Mr Alma-Tadema, in which the painter has improved on the sculptor.'[161]

Edward Poynter was later to use the same statue as prototype for the standing female nude in *Diadumenē* (Pl.81). Like Alma-Tadema's sculptor's model, Poynter's nude is binding a fillet around her head. Poynter draws further attention to the fillet-binding pose by providing his painting with a title which is the female version of 'Diadumenos', the name given to a male athlete binding a fillet around his head by the Greek sculptor, Polyclitus and known in a number of Roman copies.[162]

Poynter, who began his career with historical and mythological paintings, had, by the 1880s, developed his own brand of historical genre painting. Undoubtedly influenced by Alma-Tadema, Poynter represents Romans at leisure in archaeologically accurate settings. The work of the two men differs in their choice of domestic architecture: Poynter eschews marble – Alma-Tadema's trademark – in favour of polychromatic mosaic settings. *Diadumenē*, which is a characteristic work, represents brightly-coloured mosaic and marble floor and walls, and mosaic columns and fountain, all based on Roman examples.

In 1878 Alma-Tadema and his wife spent three months travelling on the continent. In a letter to F. G. Stephens, the artist describes the Romantic appeal of Italy: 'Oranges and lemons, olives and springflowers, brown sunkissed mankind young and old, graceful and strong, sometimes very beautiful. Fine art and antiquity.' In the same letter, he writes that at Pompeii, 'the director of excavations had a room or two dug out for our benefit.'[163] His paintings of the time, nevertheless, reflect an interest in the city of Rome rather than Pompeii. *In the Time of Constantine* (Pl.82) is placed in a momentous period of Roman history; it was during the reign of the Emperor Constantine (AD 306–37) that Christianity was proclaimed the religion of the Empire. In ironic contrast, we see two richly dressed individuals merely teaching a dog tricks. The pleasures of the rich had changed little since men amused themselves by watching an entertainer in the early imperial Pompeii of *A Juggler*.[164]

The statue placed above the two men shows a boy pulling a thorn from his foot entitled the *Spinario* and known in bronze and marble Roman copies of a Greek original. Alma-Tadema owned a photograph of a bronze version (Pl.83), and while it is represented in marble here, it also appears as a bronze, cut off on the right of *Goldfish* (1900) and in the background of *Love's Jewelled Fetter* (Pl.158). The same statues often appear more than once, but they are never exactly the same. His one consistency is that they are always restored to pristine condition: missing detail is added and the surface presented as flawless and polished.

The architectural background once again emphasizes the splendour of Rome in contrast to the activity of the two men. We see the Arch of Constantine in the foreground, a small section of the Colosseum glimpsed on the far right, and the dome of the Pantheon seen through the arch. Although none of these monuments are placed in their actual relation to one another, they form a recognizable group comprising the most significant monuments in the city of Rome; furthermore, they are also precisely the sites around which recent archaeological activity had been centred. The fountain directly behind the arch is similar to an eighteenth-century structure from the Borghese Gardens.[165] The precision of the painting's title is at odds with his rather free representation of the topography of the city of Rome.

1878 also saw the election of Frederic Leighton as President of the Royal Academy, following the death of Sir Francis Grant. Leighton's presidency ensured that classicism, now firmly allied with traditional modes of representation, flourished along with the Academy. That year Alma-Tadema had sent ten entries to the British section of the Exposition Universelle, Paris, where *An Audience at Agrippa's* was awarded a second-class medal, but he was resentful at having won a second-class medal while Hubert Herkomer's *Last Muster* was awarded the gold. In a letter to Gambart, he complained: 'It's a little hard to see a Bavarian who has only known how to paint one picture which was worthwhile, carry off this great honour for England. Also I abstained from coming to look for my little reward, for I scarcely wanted to go up on the platform after Herkomer to receive less than him.'[166]

It is interesting to note that Alma-Tadema is doubly affronted by the fact that Herkomer, 'a Bavarian', is honoured in the British section of the exhibition in wilful disregard of his own Dutch origins. It must have been a compensation to receive a gold medal for *The Death of the First-Born* and a diploma as Officer of the Legion of Honour at the end of the Paris exhibition. Whatever his commercial success, Alma-Tadema was always sensitive to criticism and keenly aware of other artists. He once told Philip Carr: 'dey tell me I cannot draw. Dey say I am form blind. One ting I know, Leighton, 'e is colour blind.'[167]

In 1879 Alma-Tadema was elected a full Academician of the Royal Academy of Arts. Some time later, Edward Burne-Jones was reported to have said: 'Until Tadema's arrival Greek and Roman scenes were shocking things in the hands of the Academy.'[168] Before the mid-1860s British paintings of antiquity took the the form of titillating nudes in the style of William Etty and W. E. Frost or moralizing history painting in the style of Benjamin Haydon. Alma-Tadema was one of a number of young artists working in Britian who brought new approaches to the representation of the classical world, but it is his unique type of historical genre painting which Burne-Jones singles out as being the defining force of the new classical-subject movement.

At the same time he heard that the wealthy American collector William Walters wished to have a painting by him on the subject of Sappho and wrote to Charles Deschamps with his good news: '"Sappho", Walters, America, painting pictures, money, work, friendship, existence ... hang it all, it is too delightful!!!'[169] For his Diploma picture (a work presented to the Academy by all newly elected members), he intended to produce a painting showing the priests of Apollo, but as this was never completed, he offered *The Way to the Temple* (Pl.84) instead, three years later. This religious subject shows a woman seated at the entrance of a temple selling votive statuettes. The viewer's eye is drawn to the background where we are given an intriguing glimpse of a Bacchic procession and the sea far beyond. Critical reviews compared *The Way to the Temple* unfavourably with *An Oleander* (Pl.85),[170] a sumptuous interior showing a woman next to an oleander plant, also exhibited at the 1883 Academy exhibition. While *The Way to the Temple* demonstrates a clever perspective and an intriguing glimpse of ancient social life, it lacks the stunning colour scheme displayed in the other painting. Furthermore, the heavily draped woman in the foreground does not form a striking or appealing figure and there is, all in all, something irredeemably stolid about the whole conception. *The Way to the Temple* raises an intractable question: how far was Alma-Tadema's antiquity constructed to satisfy popular taste, and how far was it a personal vision? Given that

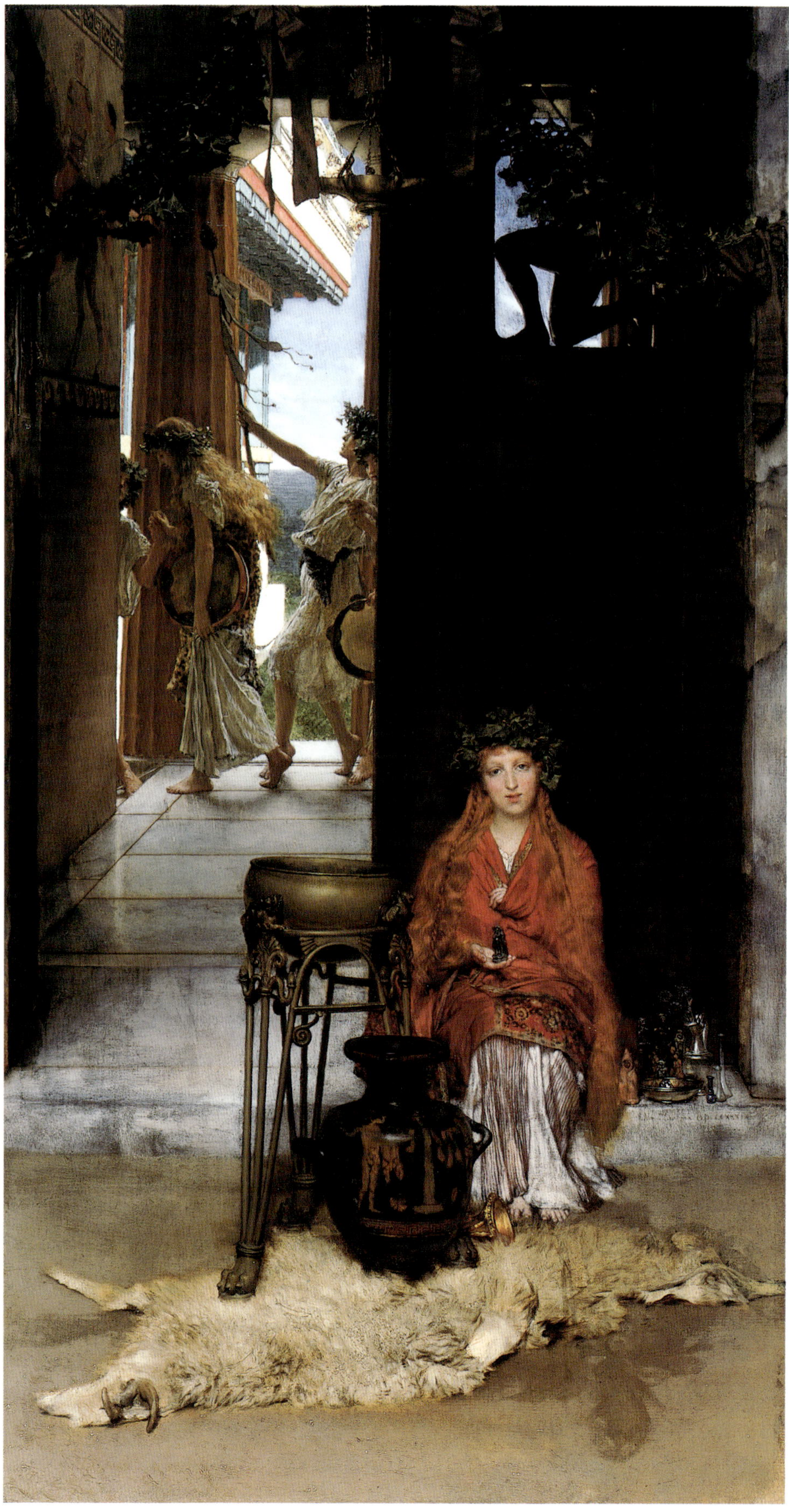

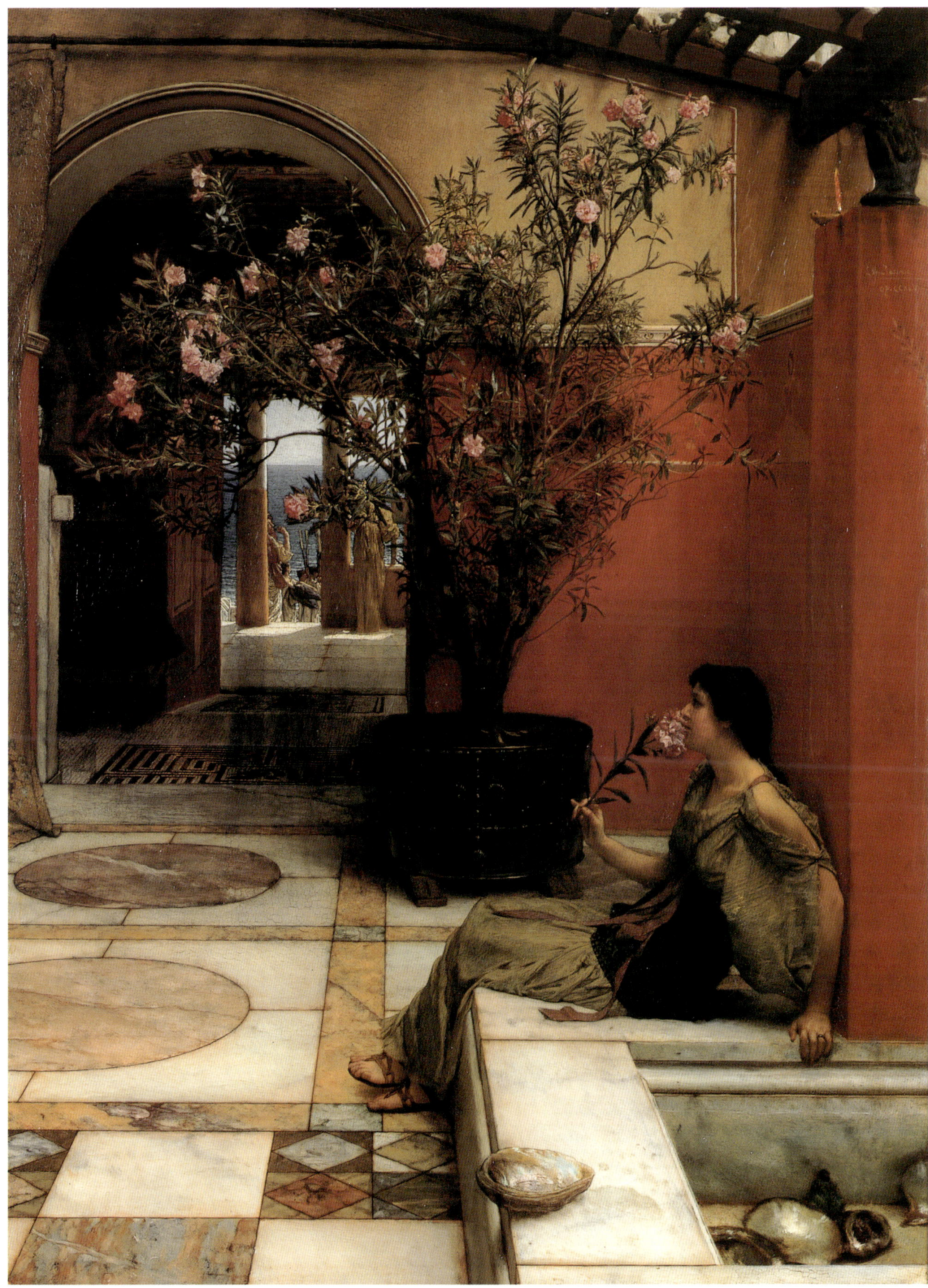

84 opposite
The Way to the Temple, 1882
Oil on canvas,
101·5 × 53·5 cm (40 × 21 in)
Royal Academy of Arts,
London

85
An Oleander, 1882
Oil on wood,
92·8 × 64·7 ($36\frac{1}{2} \times 25\frac{1}{2}$ in)
Private collection

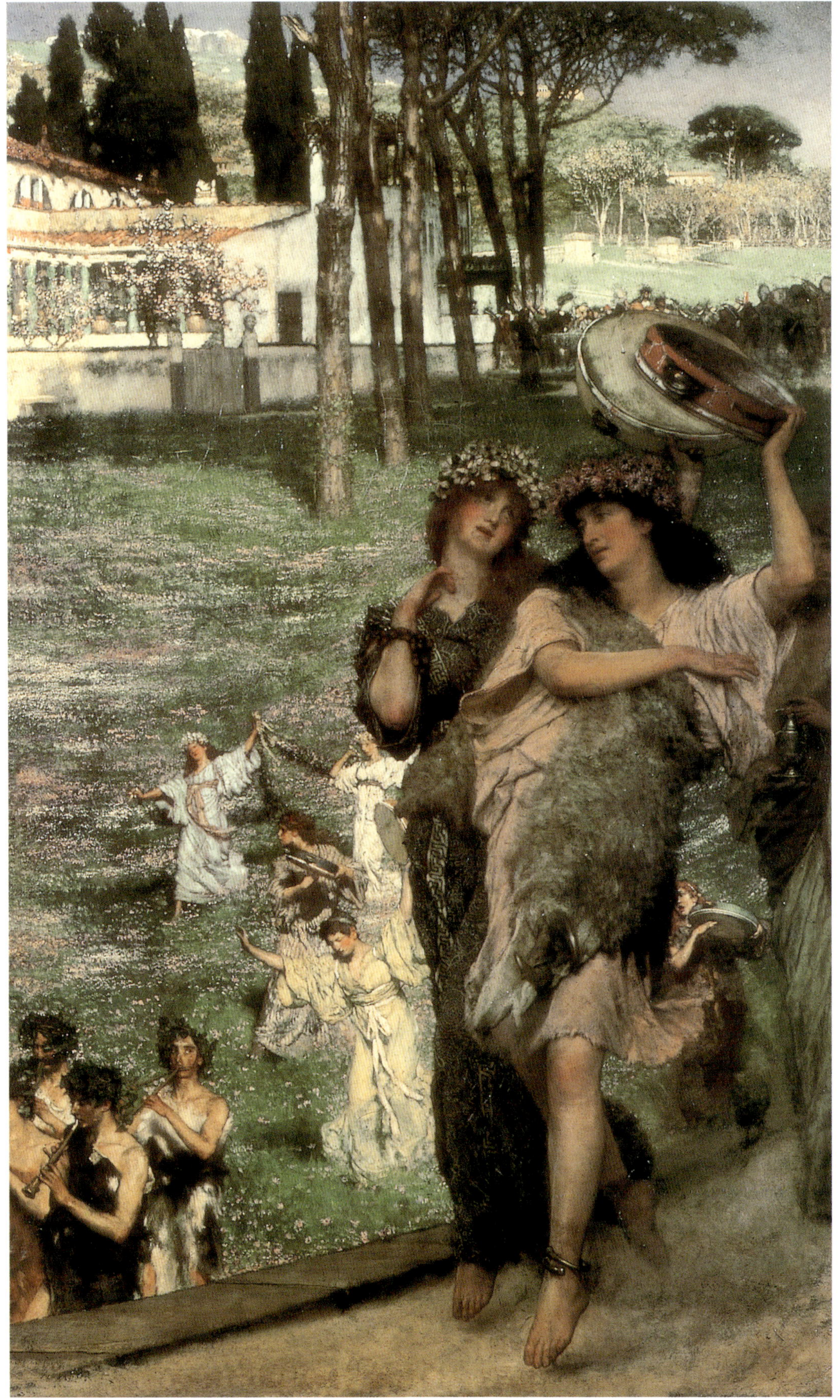

86
On the Road to the Temple of Ceres, 1879
Oil on canvas, 89 × 53·1 (35 × 20⅞ in)
Forbes Magazine collection, New York

this painting, devoid of compelling colour harmonies, grandiose display of marble, or even risqué or subversive allusion, was not commissioned by a private patron or sold through a dealer, we can, at least, assume that, in general, it is his instinct for the popular assessment of antiquity that dictates his choices of theme.

The Diploma painting illustrates the artist's interest in ancient religious ritual around this time. He had previously explored Roman religious practices with *The Vintage Festival* (Pl.44), *In the Temple* (1871), *A Private Celebration* (Pl.50), *A Bacchante* (1875) and *Autumn* (1877), all placed in urban settings. He now turned to rustic celebrations with *On the Road to the Temple of Ceres* (1879) (Pl.86) and *A Harvest Festival* (1880). The earlier painting depicts worshippers in an informal procession winding across the fields, while the second shows a smaller group assembled around an open fire. Ceres (the Roman goddess of the crops, who had been assimilated to the Greek goddess, Demeter) is associated with human fertility as well as a productive harvest. Both paintings include the same dancing woman, dressed in an animal skin, her hair flying loose.

On the Road to the Temple of Ceres is accompanied by lines of verse from John Dryden's translation of Virgil's *Georgics*, which are printed on the frame:

When winter's rage abates,
  when cheerful hours
Awake the spring,
  and spring awakes the flow'rs,
On the green turf,
  thy fearless limbs display,
And celebrate the mighty mother's day,
For then the hills with pleasing shades
  are crown'd
And sleeps are sweeter on the silken
  ground:
With milder beams the sun securely
  shines.
Fat are the lambs and luscious are the
  wines.
Let ev'ry swain adore her pow'r divine,
And milk and honey mix with sparkling
  wine:
Let all the choir of clowns attend the
  show
In long procession, shouting as they go,
Invoking her to bless their yearly stores,
Inviting plenty to their crowded floors.
Thus in Spring and thus in Summer's
  heat,
Before the sickles touch the ripening
  wheat,
On Ceres call, and let the lab'ring hind
With oaken wreaths his hollow temples
  bind.
On Ceres let him call and Ceres praise,
With uncouth dances,
  and with country lays.

The lines, from Virgil's *Georgics* I (335–50 = Dryden I.463–82), form a well-known passage alluding to not one but three festivals: the Cerealia in April (339), the Ambarvalia in late May (341–7) and the beginning of the harvest (347–50). These lines are not merely incidental to the painting but constitute an immediate and central inspiration. Modern critics have observed that the female dancer displays unusual vibrancy;[171] after all, most of his paintings show static figures who are either sitting or reclining. There is, however, a connection between this surprising animation and the verse inscription. The crucial phrase is in line 350, 'uncouth dances' – 'motus incompositos'. The very sound and rhythm of the words conveys a clumsy movement, which Alma-Tadema has interpreted as a country girl dressed in a rough animal skin dancing with bare feet to the beat of a *tympanum*.[172]

In 1881 the picture commissioned by Walters, simply entitled *Sappho* (Pl.87), was completed. In a letter dated around 1880 Oscar Wilde offered the artist any advice he may want on ancient Greece: 'It is always a pleasure for me to work at any Greek subject, and a double pleasure to do so for anyone whose work mirrors so exquisitely and rightly, as does yours, that beautiful old Greek world.'[173] Despite Wilde's enthusiasm, Alma-Tadema had, for the most part, given up painting Greek subjects by the 1880s but it was Walters himself who dictated the subject of the seventh-century BC Greek poet of Lesbos.

Sappho was a popular subject in nineteenth-century art and literature. Two traditions exist surrounding her life: in one, Sappho was a possible lover of fellow poet and compatriot, Alcaeus, and threw herself off a cliff for the love of another man, Phaon; while in the other she is acclaimed as the prototypical lover of women.[174] In 1864 Simeon Solomon painted an erotic female embrace in the watercolour, *Sappho and Erinna in a Garden in Mytilene*.

Alma-Tadema's *Sappho* shows her gazing over a lecturn at fellow poet, Alcaeus, who is reading out his own poetry. Notwithstanding this cross-gender alignment, Sappho herself is accompanied by young women who sit on the benches behind her while one girl gently rests an arm on her back. They were coyly described by the critic of the *Magazine of Art* as Sappho's 'school of girls',[175] but the artist links his painting with the lesbian Sappho by inscribing the names of some of the lovers familiar from her poems on marble benches: Gongyla of Kolophon, Mnasidika, Atthis, Erinna of Teos, Anaktoria of Miletos.

87 overleaf
Sappho, 1881
Oil on canvas, 66·1 × 122 cm (26 × 48 in)
Walters Art Gallery, Baltimore

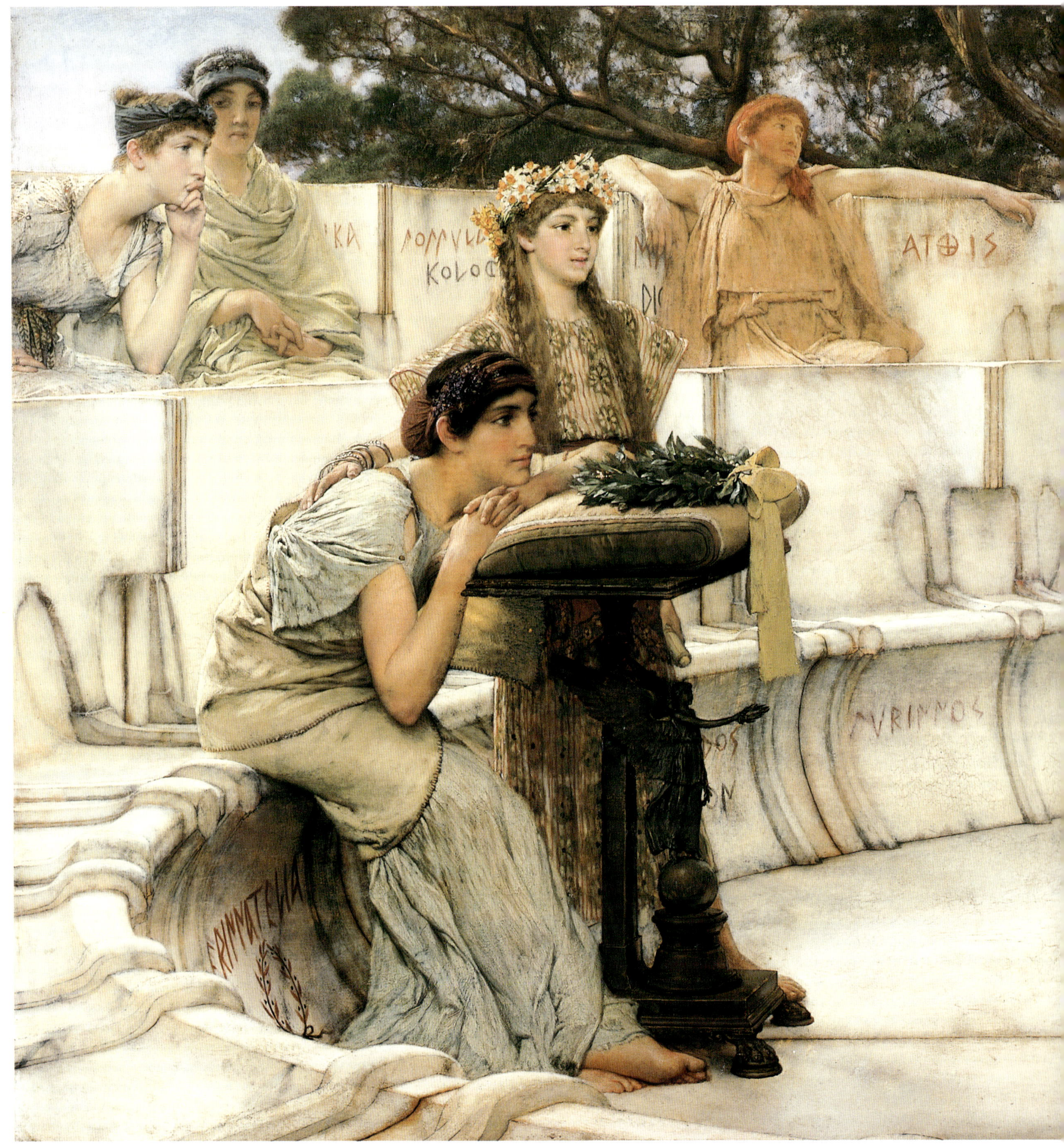

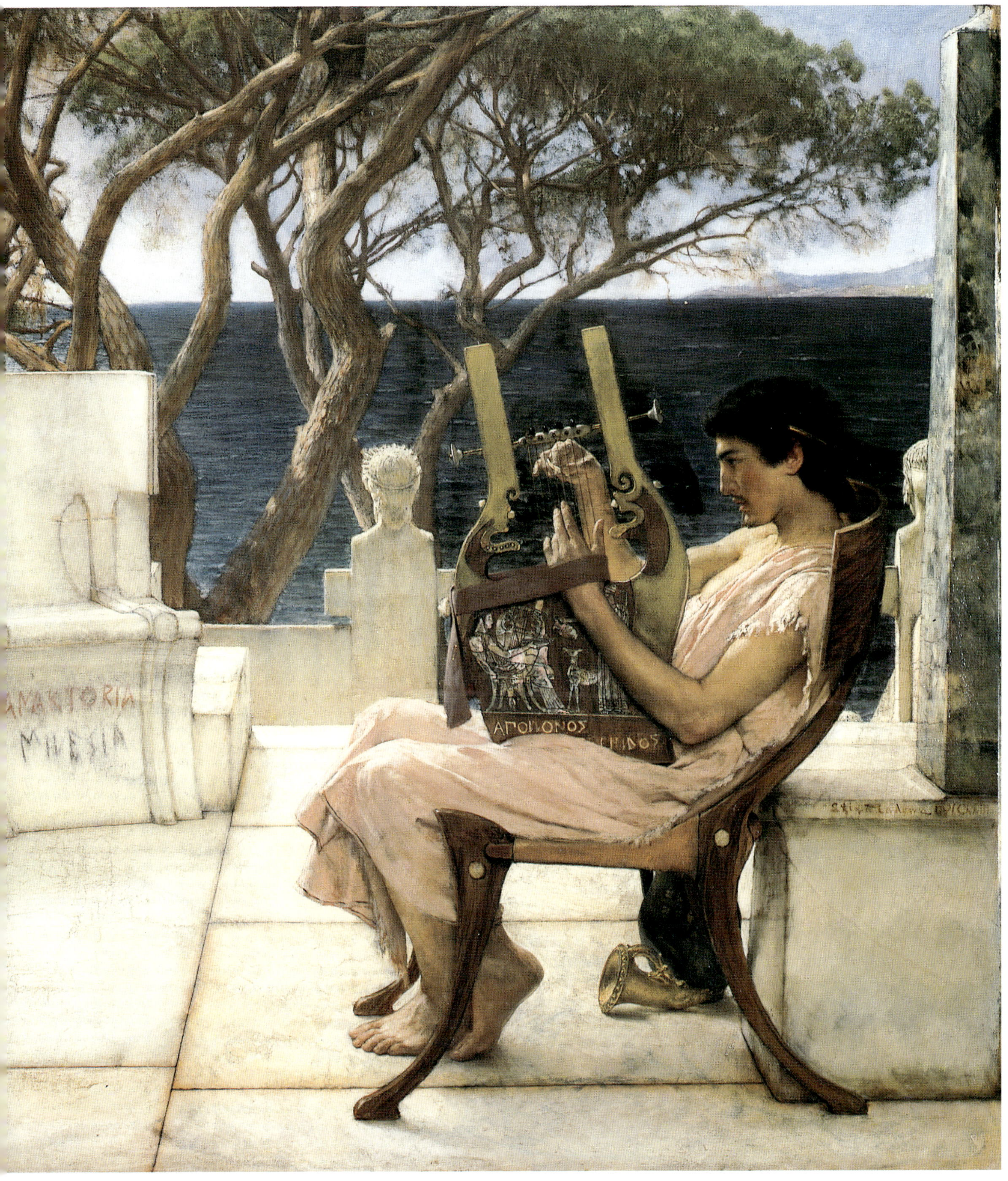

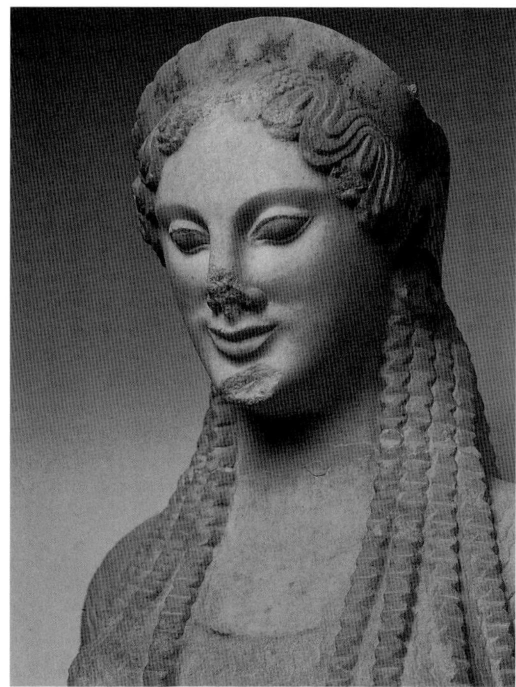

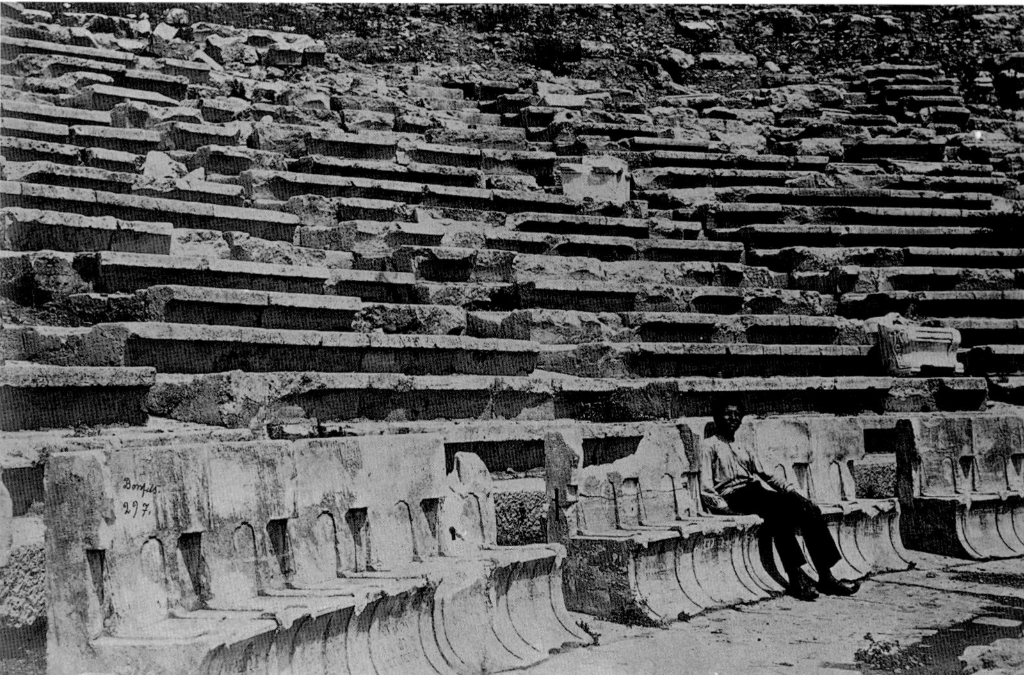

The reference to Erinna, furthermore, evokes Solomon's more risqué painting.[176] Yet Alma-Tadema forgoes the explicit visual possibilities that his subject affords by merely hinting at the lesbian Sapphic tradition. His interest in the ancient world, ultimately, is vested in its corruption, luxury and sexuality and yet his access to all of this is essentially intellectual and conceptual. Here it is the half-hidden inscriptions alone which point to the other side of Greece.

Covert suggestions of lesbianism went unnoticed by critics who received the painting enthusiastically as an idealized vision of antiquity. Most praised the painting's technical skill and colouring; for example, Joseph Comyns Carr, writing in the *Academy*, admired 'the brilliant fairness of white marble, the intense blue of a sapphire sea or a southern sky'.[177] The one unfavourable response was from the *New York Nation* which took an unusual stance in criticizing the archaeological detail and pedantically claiming that the inscribed letter forms are impossible as Lesbian characters of the notional date of the painting.[178] In fact, the letter forms, if not in this sense authentic, are certainly appropriately archaic (seventh-sixth century BC) rather than classical (fifth century BC). Another archaizing feature is the figure of the standing girl. Her stiff position, long braided hair, slight smile and crinkled drapery evoke archaic *korai* (Pl.88), many of which were excavated on the Acropolis in Athens in the 1880s.

As in many paintings, Alma-Tadema draws on a wide variety of archaeological sources. The benches imitate those from the Hellenistic Theatre of Dionysus at Athens (excavated in 1861) (Pl.89), Alcaeus' *cithara* is decorated with a scene from a fifth-century BC red figure vase in the British Museum, and the bronze lectern derives from a Pompeian table. The head of Sappho herself, particularly her characteristic hairstyle, is copied from Roman portrait busts of the poet (Pl.90). The combination of widely differing archaeological details and the transformation of sources from one medium to another displays both meticulous research and a lively ingenuity. *Sappho* presents no faithful archaeological reconstruction but a suggestion of antiquity based on an imaginative combination of sources.

Alma-Tadema's manipulation of visual sources is both playful and provocative. Our certainty in the look of antiquity is challenged with surprising juxtapositions: recognizable statues and artefacts are often presented in an unusual scale and material or placed behind pillars and cut off at the edge of the canvas. One is not surprised to hear that he owned a *herm* sculpted with his own image, seen crowned with a laurel wreath in a photograph of his studio (Pl.91). In an uncharacteristic example of unambiguous humour, as opposed to veiled irony, the same herm is represented in *The Departure* (Pl.92), as if it were a Roman bust, though dryly inscribed with the artist's own name.

A painting with more overtly risqué suggestions than *Sappho* was the much smaller *Tepidarium* (Pl.93), completed in the same year. In the setting of the luke-warm room of the Roman bath house, a languorous nude reclines on an animal skin. Her flushed face and exhausted attitude would be more suited to the hot bath (*caldarium*). So great is her lassitude that the ostrich feather fan has almost slipped from her hand. It is (we may think) the tiny dimensions of the canvas that diminish what would be an overwhelming eroticism, had she been a life-size figure. Alma-Tadema had previously explored Roman bathing customs with a series of small paintings showing groups of women engaged in the bathing ritual.[179] Archaeological reconstructions of actual baths sanctioned nudity and informed the viewer of the environment and social customs of the ancient Romans. However, here the only visible detail which confirms a Roman setting is the *strigil* (applied by slaves to scrape oil off the body) which the woman holds in her hand. The *strigil* acts as validating artefact and yet, at the same time, it is an unmistakable phallic image. Unnoticed by contemporary critics, the phallic *strigil* has an explicit quality for a modern audience, well-attuned to sexual imagery. With the exception of the unfinished *Exhausted Maenides* and *After the Dance* (and possibly *A Sculptor's Model*), *Tepidarium* is Alma-Tadema's only straightforward example of erotic art; more usually, eroticism is conveyed only through archaeological and literary allusion. Having abandoned large-scale studies of the nude after *A Sculptor's Model*, Alma-Tadema continued to produce nudes in his bath-house pictures. These are all placed in historically authentic settings, and where the nude in *Tepidarium* is powerfully erotic, those in other paintings may be seen as little more than titillating accessories to impressive architectural reconstructions.

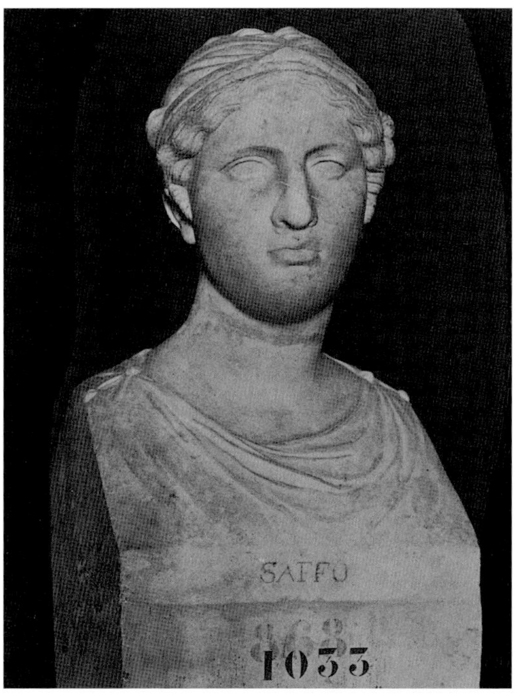

88 opposite
Archaic Kore, Greek, 6th century BC
Marble, H 1·15m
Acropolis Museum, Athens

89
Theatre of Dionysus, Athens:
University of Birmingham

90 above
Portrait Bust of Sappho, Roman, marble
Villa Albani, Rome:
University of Birmingham

The next bath picture, *An Apodyterium* (changing room) (Pl.94), showing female nudes in an archaeologically specific interior, was exhibited at the Academy in 1886. Background figures busy themselves in bath preparations; in the foreground a nude woman unties bindings on her legs; beside her, another woman, about to disrobe, gazes at the viewer with no trace of self-conscious reserve. In 1885 a controversy surrounding the exhibition of the nude at the Royal Academy Summer Exhibition had raged in the letter pages of *The Times* after 'a British Matron' wrote a letter of complaint calling the public's attention to an excessive display of nudity on the Academy walls.[180] A heated debate continued in a series of letters to the editor for the next month. Although Alma-Tadema was not cited, other painters of classical subjects were, and Poynter's *Diadumenè*, in particular, was singled out for much criticism. However, *An Apodyterium*, unlike other representations of the nude, presents an architectural setting as the focal point of the picture and the nudes as merely incidental. In any case, the controversy seems to have been largely forgotten as the 1886 exhibition also showed John Collier's *Maenads*, a riot of nudes revelling in a wood, and Solomon J. Solomon's *Cassandra*, one of the most audaciously erotic of all Victorian nudes, to excellent reviews.

An Apodyterium was voted 'Picture of the Year' by the *Pall Mall Gazette*. The decision, made by the magazine's readers, reflected public opinion and confirmed that Alma-Tadema was, by the mid-1880s, a favourite of art critics and art-going public alike. A few years later a companion picture, *The Frigidarium* (1890) (cold bath), was painted for the owner of the previous work, Sir Max Waechter. An earlier watercolour entitled *A Balneator* (bath attendant) (1877) (Pl.95) unusually displays a male semi-nude. The male nude, although not as controversial as the female nude, was not as popular a subject. Painters who did represent the male body imitated Greco-Roman sculpture in pursuit of a masculine ideal as found in the straining musculature of the soldier in Poynter's *The Catapult* (1868) and the slender youth in Leighton's *Daedalus and Icarus* (Pl.65). Alma-Tadema looks to neither type of idealization and instead his *balneator*, a black slave holding a sponge and a ring of strigils, is a frank depiction of slavery in the Roman world. While the *strigil* in *Tepidarium* acts as an explicit phallic symbol, the ring of strigils here, copied from sets excavated in bath houses around the Roman world, may hint at the type of homoeroticism found in the Greek dining pictures but it essentially serves as a mundane functional object.

Alma-Tadema was travelling on the Continent again in 1882. Travel had become a regular feature of the artist's life and while his extended trips are the only ones documented, he may have visited Europe as often as once a year. At times the whole family travelled, and at others Alma-Tadema went with Laura or on his own. Roman Italy was, after all, his prime source of inspiration and visiting sites and museums was essential to his work. Vosmaer records that during a trip to Pompeii in 1883 the artist was working daily from 9am to 6pm, measuring and drawing houses.[181]

In London Alma-Tadema was preoccupied

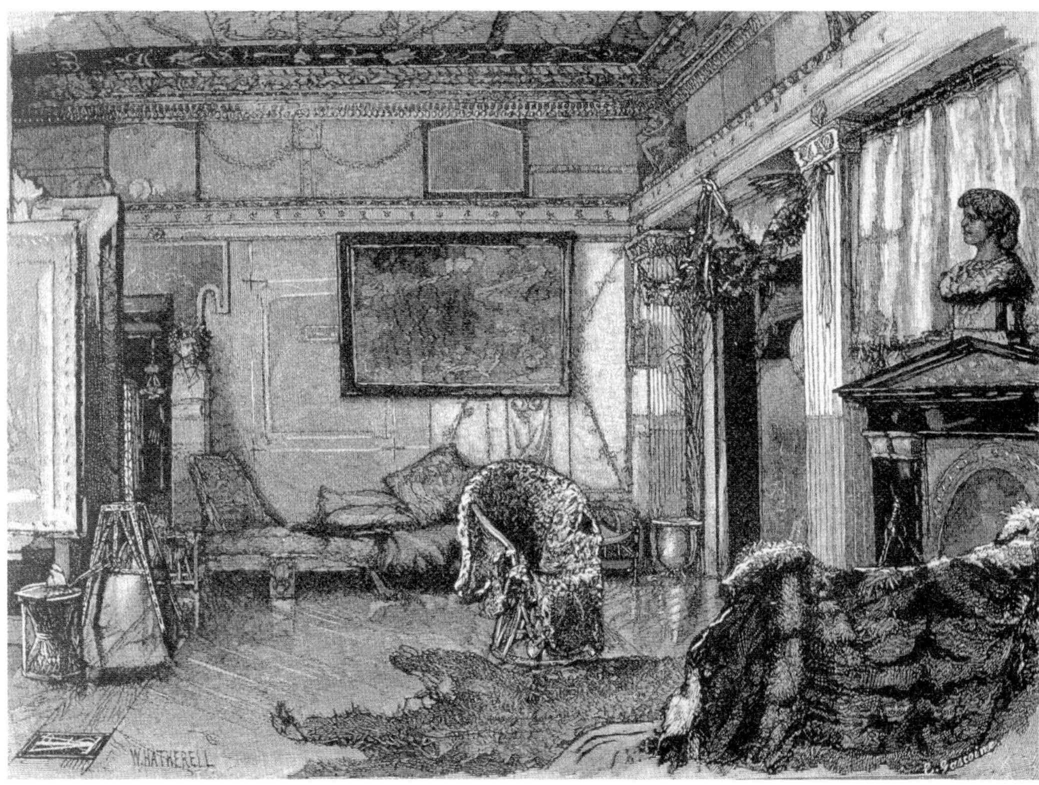

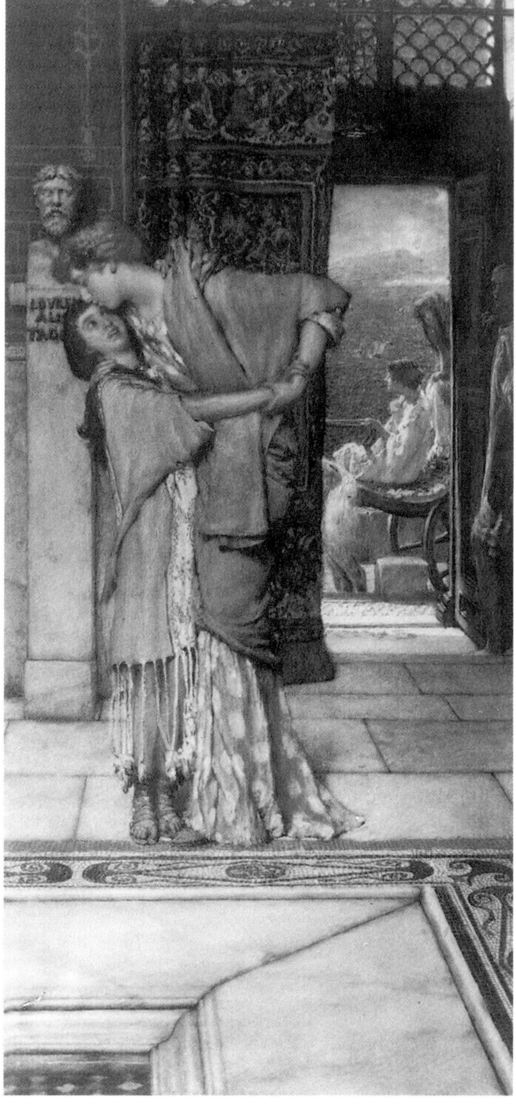

91 left
Alma-Tadema's studio in Townshend House
Magazine of Art, 1882, p.185

92 right
The Departure, 1880
Oil on wood, 30·5 × 14 cm (12 × 5½ in)
Location unknown

with the organization of a retrospective exhibition of his work hosted by the Grosvenor Gallery in the autumn and winter of 1882–3, alongside the works of the recently deceased landscape painter, Cecil Lawson, and nine sculptures by Giovanni Battista Amendola (including his portrait of Laura[182]). This was a notable mark of distinction as the gallery had initiated the practice of exhibiting retrospectives of living painters only the previous year with an exhibition of the long-established artist, G. F. Watts. Alma-Tadema was, however, a close personal friend of Joseph Comyns Carr, co-assistant of the gallery along with Charles Hallé. The exhibition showed 130 oils, and 54 drawings and watercolours, from the 1852 self-portrait to his very latest works. Unfortunately, it did not include all major pieces, an American tariff making it impossible for the pictures in American collections to appear. Nonetheless, by including portraits, landscapes and watercolours, as well as subject oils, it succeeded in presenting the artist's versatility and range. Reviews were, on the whole, positive. An article on the artist and his work published in the *Art Journal* to coincide with the exhibition began: 'The bright painter whom everybody admires – the public for his triumphs of technique, and the brothers for the legitimate means by which those triumphs are compassed.'[183]

By the 1880s, the locations of paintings had changed as settings of cluttered Pompeian interiors with dark rich tones gave way to exteriors with fewer archaeological accessories framed by glistening marble and Mediterranean sea and sky. We now see ancient life played out in the sumptuous palaces of Rome or the holiday villas along the coastline of the Bay of Naples. While Néo-Grec artists such as Gustave Boulanger continued to produce Pompeian-influenced scenes into the 1880s, Alma-Tadema had formulated his own type of historical genre painting which he now located in a very distinct setting.

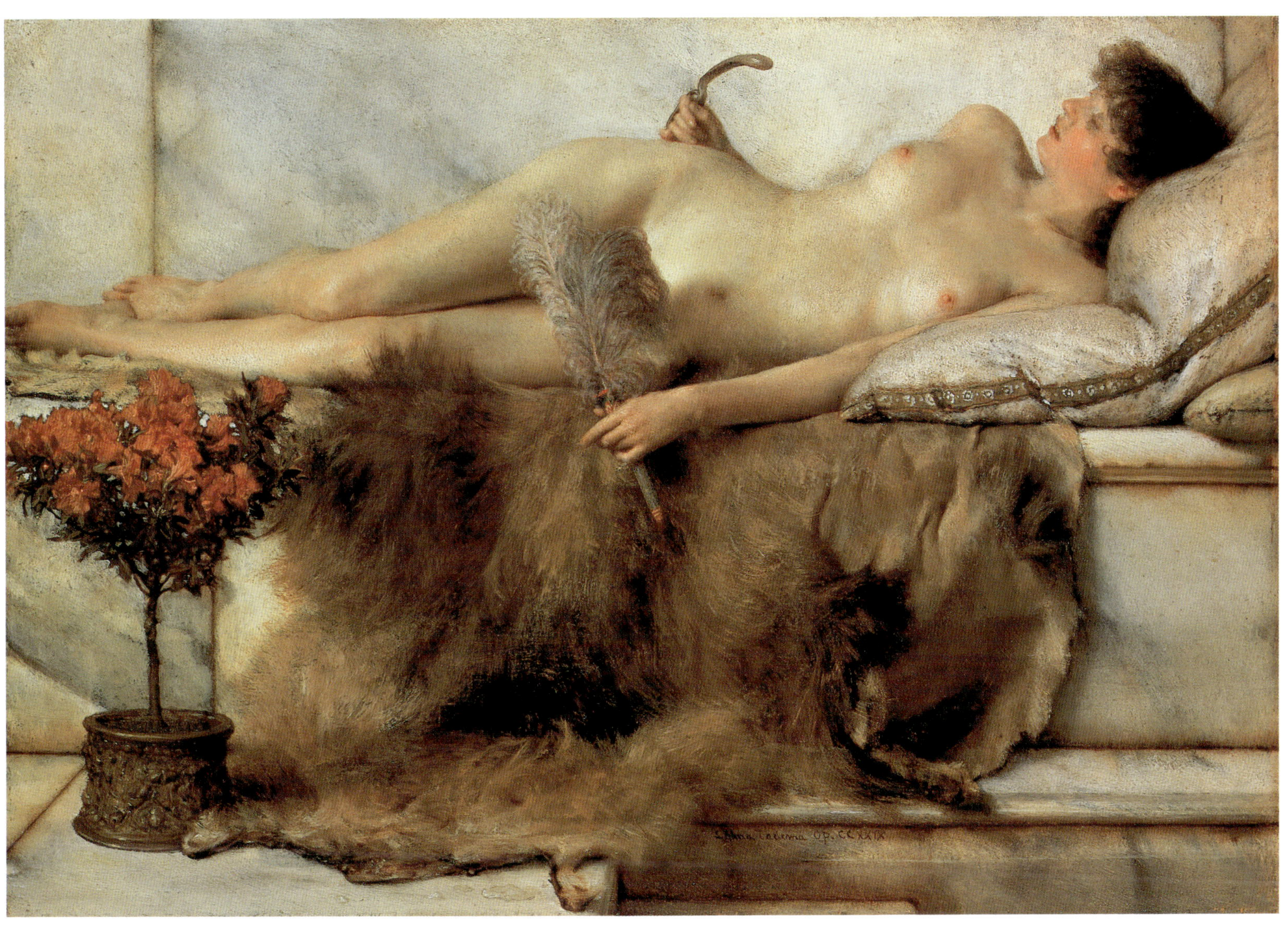

93
Tepidarium, 1881
Oil on wood, 24·2 × 33 cm ($9\frac{1}{2}$ × 13 in)
Lady Lever Art Gallery, Port Sunlight, Liverpool

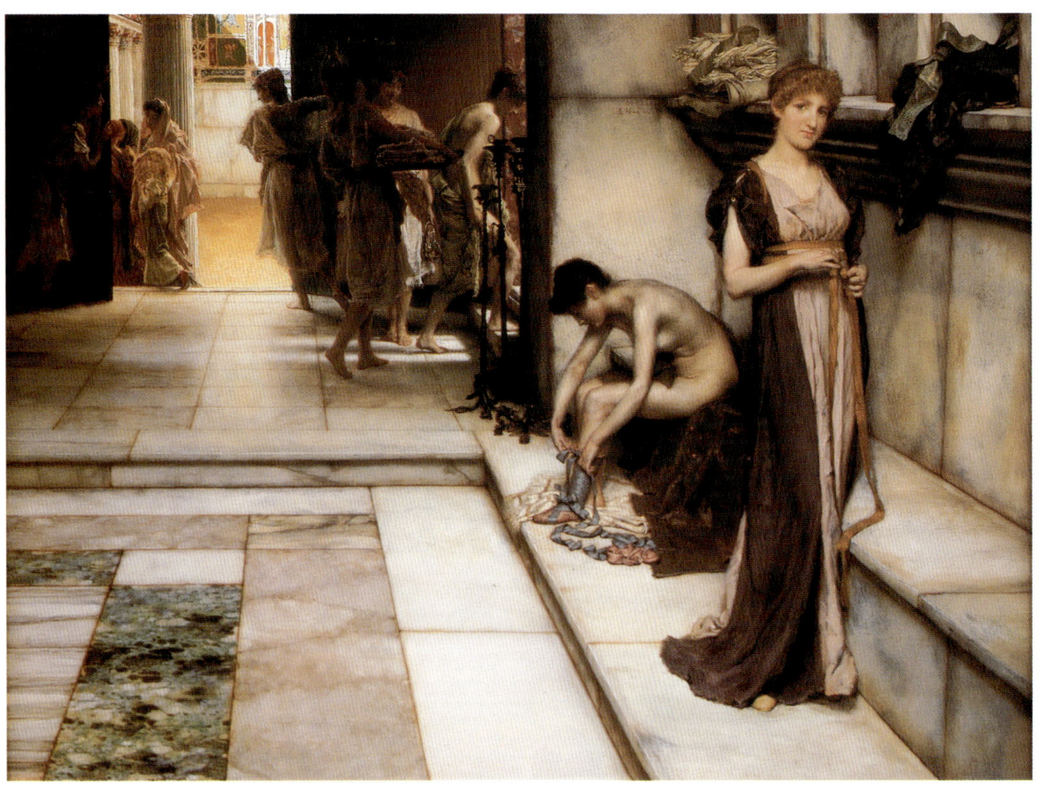

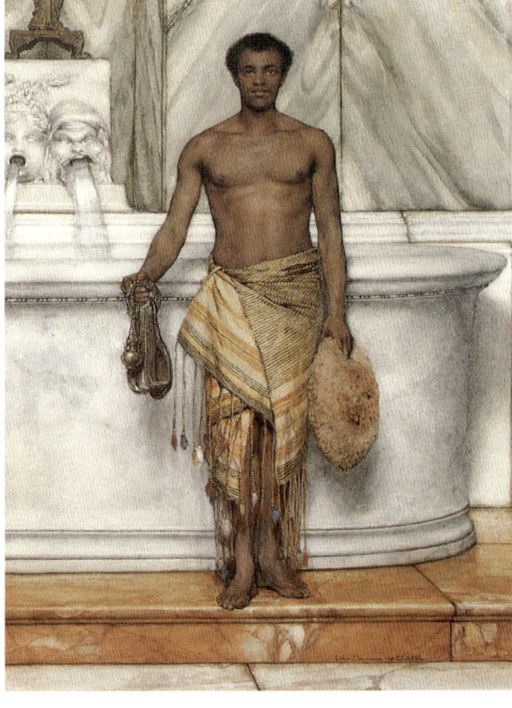

94
An Apodyterium, 1886
Oil on wood, 44·5 × 59·5 cm (17½ × 23⅜ in)
Private collection

95
A Balneator, 1877
Watercolour, 36·5 × 26·5 cm (14⅜ × 10⅜ in)
Private collection

He soon turned his attention to courtship pictures.[184] These paintings, though often interpreted in terms of middle- and upper-class Victorian social customs, surely look back to Latin love poetry, and behind it, to the attested world of Roman law and practice. In the early Roman Empire, women of high birth were often married when young for the purpose of political alliance and social advantage; marriages were frequently dissolved and new marriages entered into for much the same reasons. Love interests, then, seem to have developed through the illicit acquisition of lovers after marriage. Augustus' marriage laws promoted the sanctity of marriage and made adultery a public offence against the state, but only for women. Nevertheless, many chose to ignore these laws including Augustus' own daughter, Julia. Julia was notorious for her infidelity during a series of unhappy political marriages; according to Seneca her behaviour was 'shameless beyond the indictment of shamelessness, and made public the scandals of the imperial house.'[185] The unfortunate Julia was eventually convicted of adultery and exiled.

The women of Latin love poetry emerge as individuals who, although often married, lead liberated lives with few constraints. For instance, Catullus' Lesbia and Tibullus' Delia are not respectable Roman matrons, but fashionable women who prefer their lovers to be numerous and rich. Poems describe all manner of ruses to deceive a husband. These are summed up by Tibullus, who proposes that Venus favours those who love by stealth:

> You too, Delia: be bold and trick the
>   guard.
> You must do and dare,
>   for Venus helps the brave.
> She favours the young man who
>   reconnoitres a new threshold,

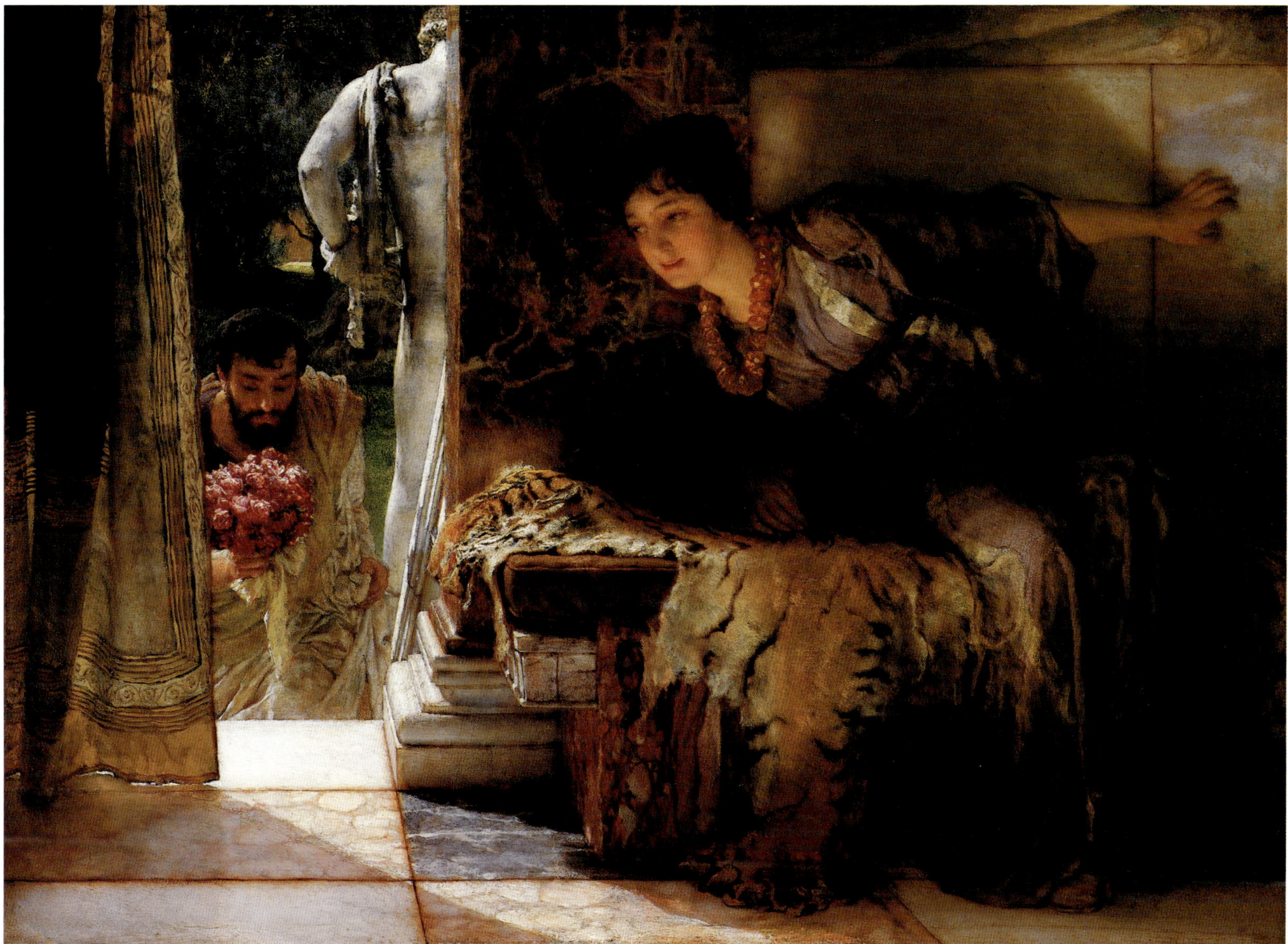

96
Welcome Footsteps, 1883
Oil on wood, 41·9 × 54·8 cm ($16\frac{1}{2} \times 21\frac{5}{8}$ in)
Private collection

and the girl who opens a door
with home-made key.
She teaches the withdrawal by stealth
from the soft bed,
the inaudible positioning of feet,
the conference by nod,
in the presence of a husband,
concealment of sweet words in signals
pre-arranged.[186]

If, accordingly, we read any courtship painting in a Roman rather than a Victorian context, the meaning is immediately subverted. For example, *Welcome Footsteps* (Pl.96) appears to show a typical courtship scene of a woman waiting indoors for her suitor to arrive. She listens impatiently for footsteps while a man climbs the steps holding a bunch of flowers. On closer inspection, we find that this is no sentimental love scene. An enclosed setting and the expectant, even anxious attitude of the woman implies a context of secrecy; is she waiting for her lover to arrive while her husband is away? Dramatically cropped, yet still visible behind the curtain, a nude male statue serves as a reminder of masculine potency, and we may conclude that the footsteps belong not to a respectable sweetheart but an illicit lover.

Such paintings cannot be read as conventional courtship scenes in which contemporary dress had been replaced with toga and stola and the drawing room with a marble terrace. Given the subversive subtext, Alma-Tadema's courtship paintings may shed an intriguing light on Victorian etiquette: does the artist suggest that Victorian women who, like Julia, Lesbia and Delia, were expected to conform to particular ideals of behaviour, did not conform as readily as might be expected?

II/3
LANDSCAPES, PORTRAITS, WATERCOLOURS

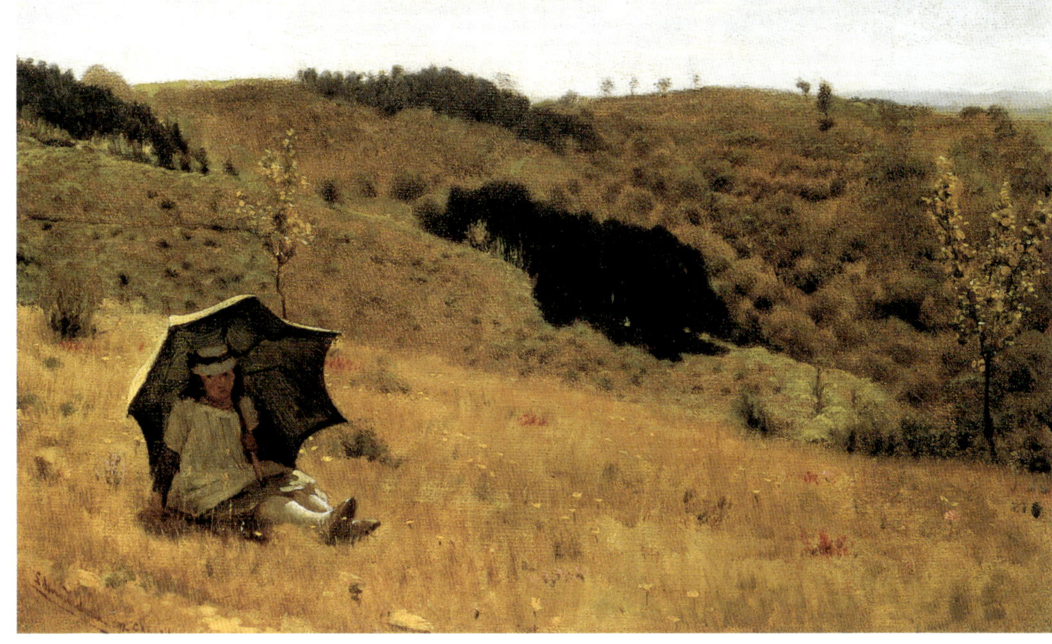

97
Sunny Days, 1874
Oil on canvas, 21·5 × 34·2 cm (8½ × 13½ in)
Yale University Art Gallery, New Haven

During the 1870s Alma-Tadema turned, perhaps surprisingly, to landscape painting. Although exhibited, many landscapes were given as gifts to friends. Usually completed on holiday, they were evidently considered as private works in contrast to his commercial subject pictures. Alma-Tadema's priority was the production of classical pictures which quickly found buyers, but with no commercial pressure he chose a very different type of style and subject. A holiday in Germany in 1874 resulted in *Landscape Near Munster* and *Munster Cathedral*, both exhibited at the Society of French Artists. In the same year the family were holidaying in Surrey where Alma-Tadema produced *Sunny Days* (Pl.97), showing a portrait of the artist's daughter, Anna, seated on a hillside and shading herself from the sun under a parasol. Exhibited at the Dudley Gallery, the painting was given to the young artist, John Collier.

While on holiday at Penkill Castle, Scotland, in 1875, the artist produced *Carriage Drive at Penkill Castle* and *A Peep Through the Trees*. In the same year, *Haystacks*, exhibited at the Society of French Artists, is particularly unusual in that it shows a rural agricultural scene of labourers at work in a hayfield. *Venice, Grand Canal* (Pl.98) is the artist's only urban landscape of this period. It was given as a gift to Georg Ebers. For the rest of the decade Alma-Tadema continued to produce landscape oils during each family holiday, including *From the Firehills of Fairlight, Hastings* (1877), given to the painter Felix Moscheles, *View from the Neckar River* (*c*.1874–7), given to the engraver Leopold Lowenstam and *A Landscape near Haslemere, Surrey* (1878), a wedding gift to the sculptor George Blackall Simmonds. Rather than finely detailed studio paintings, Alma-Tadema's landscapes are canvases executed in the open air. From the 1850s French landscape paintings by Millet, Corot and artists of the Barbizon school were exhibited at the French Gallery in London. Later to influence a whole generation of British landscape painters, such works had more of an effect on Alma-

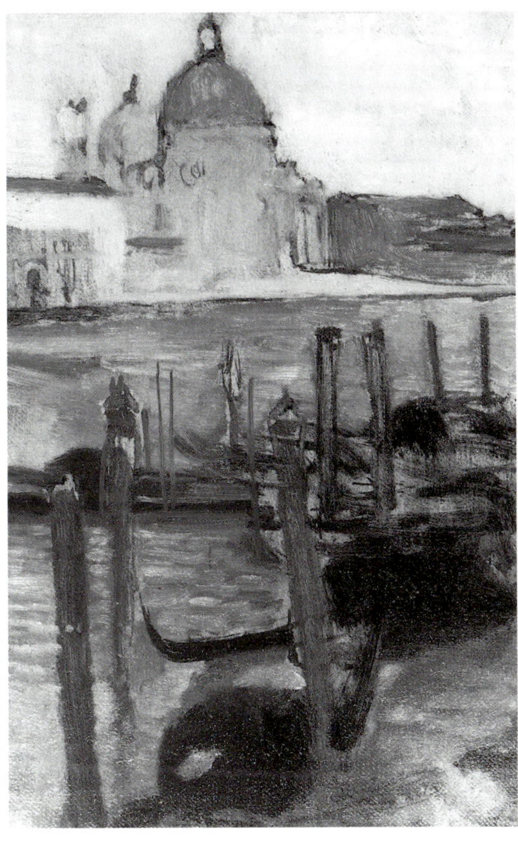

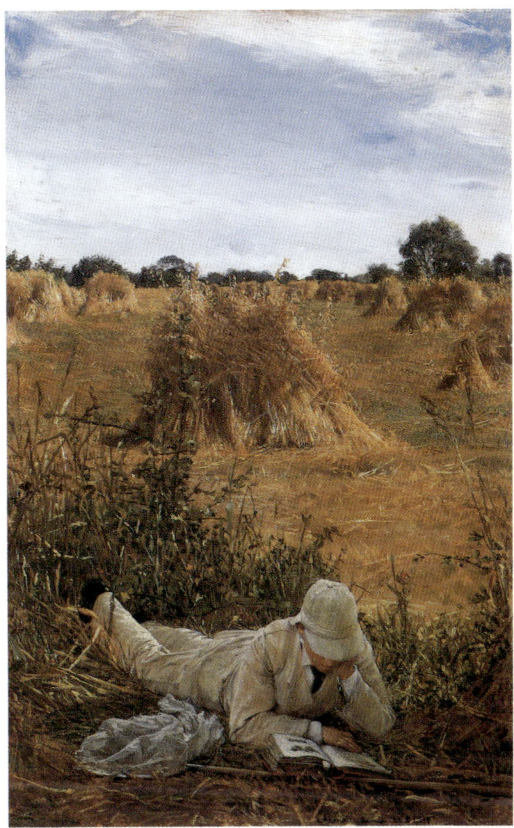

98
Venice, Grand Canal, 1875
Oil on canvas (mounted on board),
34 × 22·5 cm (13⅜ × 8⅞ in)
Location unknown

99
94 Degrees in the Shade, 1876
Oil on canvas (mounted on wood),
35·5 × 21·6 cm (14 × 8½ in)
Fitzwilliam Museum, Cambridge

Tadema than traditional Academic landscapes. In June 1879 Alma-Tadema met the influential French plein-air landscape painter Jules Bastien-Lepage, who was visiting Britain for the first time. They formed a lasting friendship and Bastion-Lepage stayed at Alma-Tadema's house on subsequent visits to London and painted a portrait of Laura as a gift for the couple.

Like Alma-Tadema, his contemporary Frederic Leighton painted various landscapes in the form of rapid oil sketches on trips to Italy, Greece and North Africa. Both artists considered their landscapes as private works executed for enjoyment rather than for the commercial market. 1880 saw an end to Alma-Tadema's interest in this kind of work. *A Pastorale*, painted in that year, transposes a landscape to an ancient setting and shows a Roman herdsman leading yoked oxen.

During the 1870s and 1880s, Alma-Tadema was also to prove himself as a portrait painter. Avoiding the usual formal society commissions, however, he choose to concentrate on intimate depictions of family and friends. *94 Degrees in the Shade* (Pl.99) is a portrait of Herbert Thompson, the seventeen-year-old son of Alma-Tadema's friend and doctor, Sir Henry Thompson. It evokes the balmy heat of a summer afternoon as a boy reads, absorbed in a book on butterflies, his net on the ground before him, in the shaded corner of a hayfield. Alma-Tadema was to paint the young Herbert Thompson again as a handsome youth wearing a red smoking hat with tassel (Pl.100). A label on the back of the panel reads: 'A sketch of Herbert, made on board the *Gipsey*, on the cabin door, by Alma-Tadema, when he stayed with us for a sketching visit in the year 1877 – Henry Thompson.' The artist also produced a companion portrait of Henry Thompson (Pl.101), once again an informal depiction of a family friend. In 1873 he had completed a portrait of Kate Thompson, the family's eldest daughter and in 1883 he produced a portrait of Thompson's wife, Lady Kate Fanny Thompson. Thompson eventually acquired eight paintings by Alma-Tadema, either bought through Gambart or presented as gifts.

Portrait of Aimé-Jules Dalou, His Wife and Daughter (Pl.102) is once again a depiction of the artist's friends. It shows the French sculptor, Dalou, cigarette in hand, in an informal, even bohemian, family group. Dalou lived in exile in England after his involvement with events in the Paris Commune in 1870–1 and returned after the amnesty of 1879. The portrait was painted in exchange for a terracotta bust of Laura (accidentally destroyed in Alma-Tadema's house around 1905).

From the 1880s portraits played a more important part of his output. 'People generally', Alma-Tadema plaintively remarked in an interview with Frederick Dolman, 'always seem to forget that I paint portraits.'[187] Opposed to portraiture which showed an individual against a dark and indistinguishable background, he instead favoured settings which recalled personal connections: 'if I were to order the portrait of somebody dear to me, I should certainly like to have that person painted surrounded by accessories

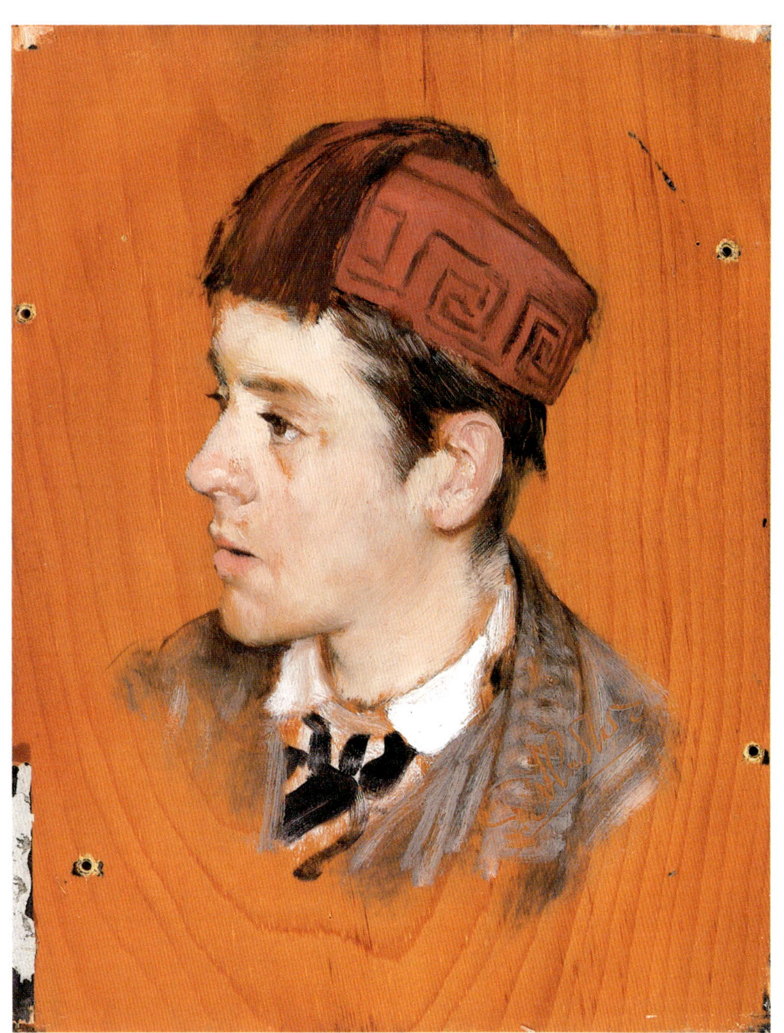

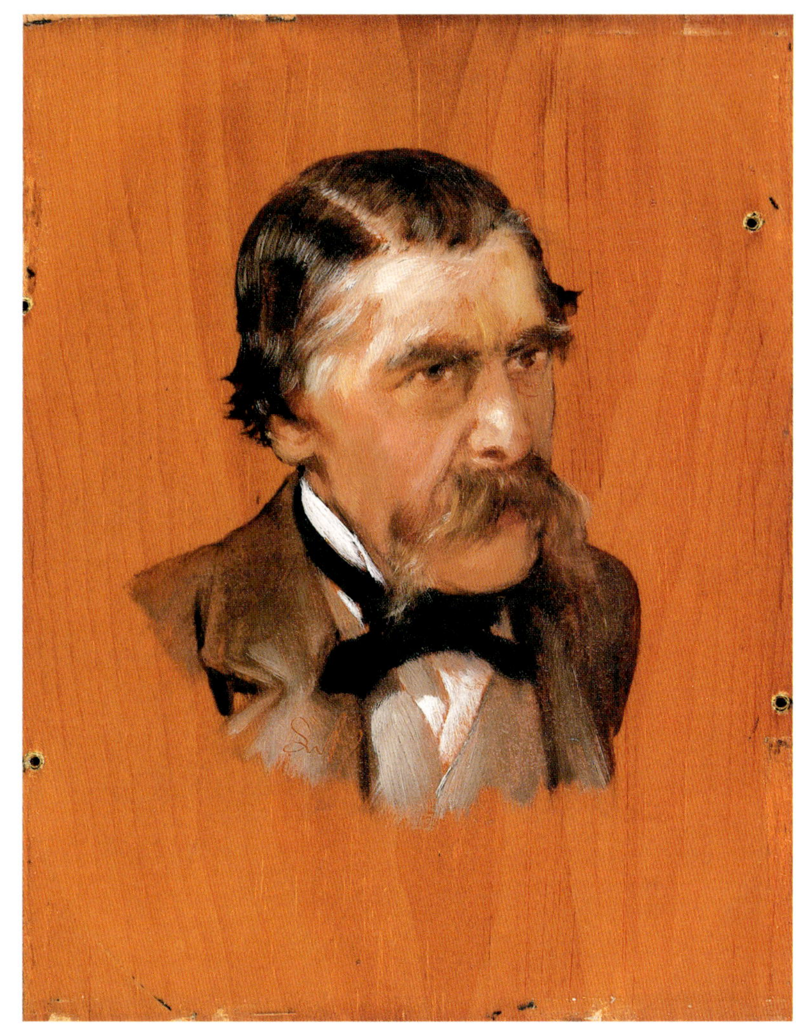

100
Portrait of Herbert Thompson, 1877
Oil on wood, 28·3 × 22·6 cm (11⅛ × 8⅞ in)
Fitzwilliam Museum, Cambridge

101
Portrait of Sir Henry Thompson, 1878
Oil on wood, 28·1 × 20·9 cm (11 × 8¼ in)
Fitzwilliam Museum, Cambridge

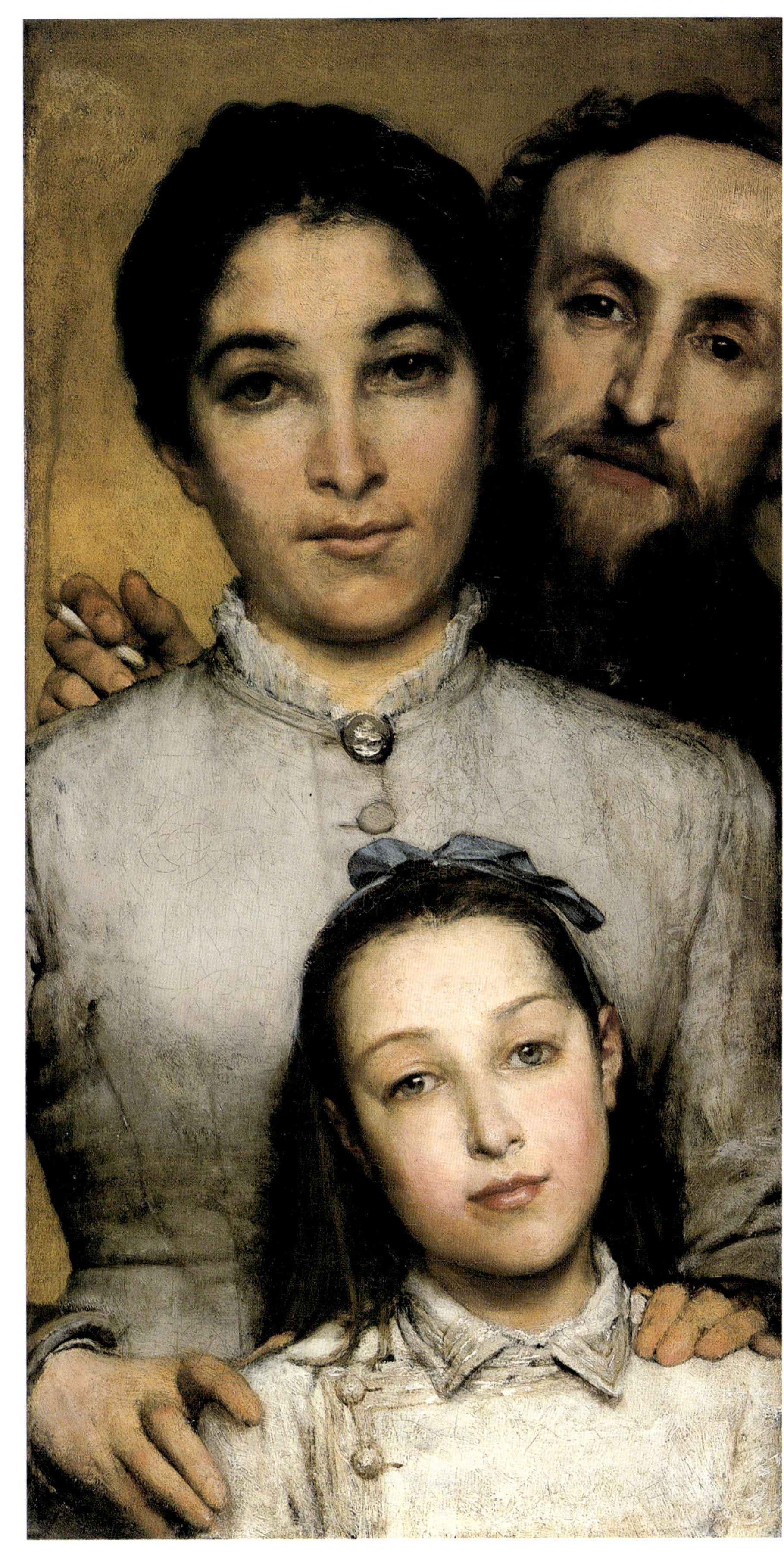

102
Portrait of Aimé-Jules Dalou, his Wife and Daughter,
1876
Oil on canvas, 84 × 30·5 cm (33⅛ × 12 in)
Musée d'Orsay, Paris

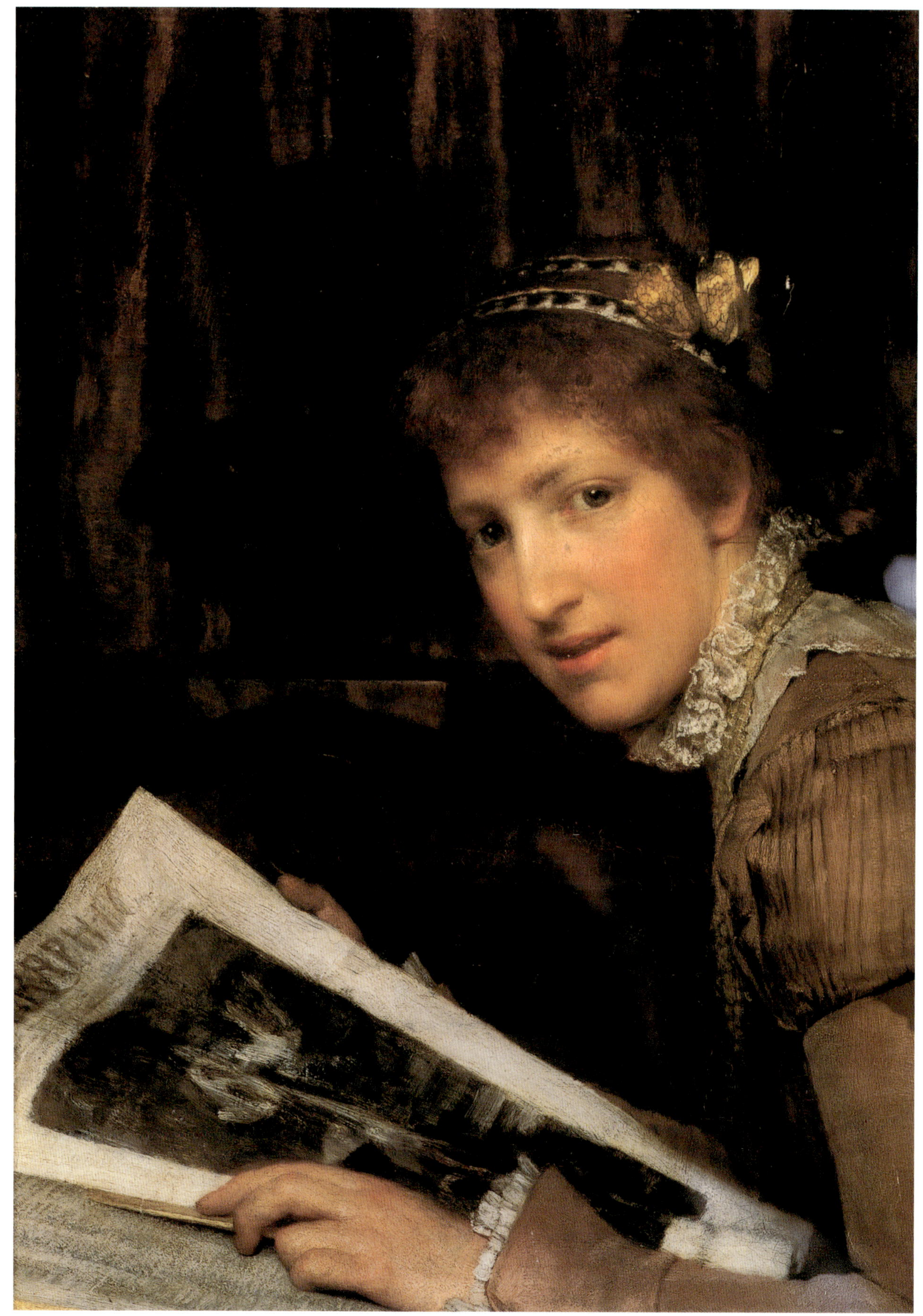

LAWRENCE ALMA-TADEMA 108

which awakened in my memory (say) a pleasant meeting, or pleasant hours.'[188]

A portrait of Laura entitled *Interrupted* (Pl.103) was commissioned by the magazine *The Graphic* for an exhibition on types of female beauty. Whatever Laura's claims to be a 'London beauty' in her early youth,[189] the portrait is hardly calculated to provide corroborative evidence from her more mature years. The fact is, though, that in contrast to the female figures by many artists, the women in Alma-Tadema's paintings are rarely eroticized creations designed to appeal to contemporary notions of the beautiful woman. In 1904 the *Strand Magazine* carried an article which complained that 'the re-creator of ancient Rome has never drawn a really pretty woman.'[190] For all the intriguing variety of their settings, his women display an ordinariness that is far removed from (say) the compelling looks of Leighton's models: Anna Risi, Lily Langtree, Dorothy Dene. It is no accident that his access to the erotic side of ancient life should be through suggestion and allusion; depiction of striking human beauty, in any conventional Victorian sense, is not a priority. For this exhibition, other artists selected literary and historical heroines, but he chose his own wife, at home and next to the portrait bust by Dalou, while wryly placed beside her is a copy of *The Graphic*.

More formal portraits are seen with his representations of three Presidents of the Royal Institute of British Architects: *Portrait of John F Whichcord FSA, PRIBA* (1882), *Portrait of Alfred Waterhouse RA, PRIBA* (1891) and *Portrait of George Aitchison RA, PRIBA* (1900) (Pl.104). One of his few society portraits is *Portrait of Catherine, Duchess of Cleveland* (1883). Vosmaer remarked on seeing the final stages of the picture, 'a good portrait in spite of her ... horse's head ... salva reverentia.'[191]

Informal subjects include depictions of Alma-Tadema's friends, most of whom belong to cosmopolitan artistic circles. Many of the musicians who played at Alma-Tadema's musical soirees were rewarded with portraits including the pianist George Henschel (1879), the Portuguese singer and violinist Jules Diaz de Soris (1888), the Polish pianist Ignacy Paderewski (Pl.127), the German violinist Joseph Joachim (1893) and the Dutch violinist Maurice Sons (Pl.126). Portraits of fellow artists were exchanged for other art works: a portrait of the Italian sculptor, Giovanni Battista Amendola (1883) shows him working on a bronze and silver statuette of Laura which was given to the artist in return for the portrait. Likewise, a portrait of the sculptor George Simmonds (1895) was painted in exchange for a sculpted silver shield. These portraits give us an indication of Alma-Tadema's social circle and suggest that while he was eager to assume a position in British society he was also determined to maintain European connections. Portraits of Count von Bylandt (Dutch Envoy Extraordinary) (1883) and the Reverend Adama van Scheltema, minister of the Dutch Church of Austin Friars, London (1888) also illustrate his involvement with the Dutch community in London. The refusal of society commissions (often the mainstay of an artist's income), in favour of works which generated little or no profit, is testament to Alma-Tadema's financial security. A prolific painter, he completed enough saleable subject pictures every year to be able to indulge himself in landscapes and portraits produced for pleasure.

His attitude to work which did not generate enough profit is indicated in a letter to Georg Ebers. After contributing an illustration to *The Ebers Gallery* in 1883, Alma-Tadema voiced his reluctance to produce another: 'These things cost me as much trouble as an oil painting would ... to earn one hundred pounds for a month of work is not enough. I know that will seem very strange to you but when I tell you that in order to master oil painting I gave up everything else in 1859 and have but seldom touched a pencil or pen or a water-colour.'[192] Alma-Tadema maintains a hard-headed attitude to business even at the risk of offending a personal friend. If landscapes and portraits were categorized as leisure rather than work, watercolours, on the other hand, seem to be reluctantly considered an essential part of an artist's œuvre.

In 1881 Alma-Tadema was elected a full member of the Royal Water-Colour Society although he only produced a small number of watercolours throughout his career, fifty-one of which were assigned opus numbers (the earliest of them being *Faust and Marguerite*[193]). Oil painting was indeed a far more lucrative trade than working in watercolour, and Alma-Tadema was determined to work at an acceptable profit by relating his watercolours to oils. *An Exedra* (1869) is repeated in watercolour as *An Exedra* (1871), *Fishing* (1873) as *Fishing* (1875) and *On the Steps of the Capitol* (1874) as *The Garland Seller* (1874). The watercolour *Attracted* (1899) is repeated as the oil *Under the Roof of Blue Ionian Weather* (1901), and *A Kiss Welcome* (1881) as *A Parting Kiss* (1882). The watercolour *Ask Me No More* (Pl.105) is repeated with only a few changes in detail twenty years later as an oil of the same title (Pl.106). *Resting* (1882) is reproduced in reverse in the watercolour *Dolce Far Niente* (1882), while the female figure in both watercolour and oil derives from the seated woman in the upper background of *Sappho*. Merely repeating the composition in a different medium meant a saleable product with relatively little effort.

The diploma picture for the Royal Water-

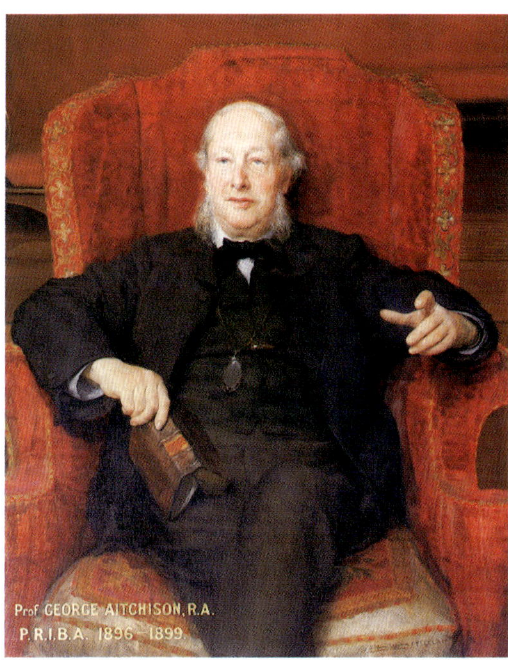

103 opposite
Interrupted, 1880
Oil on wood, 43·2 × 30·5 cm (17 × 12 in)
Fulham Public Library, London

104
Portrait of George Aitchison PRIBA, RA, 1900
Oil on canvas, 116 × 91·5 cm (45⅝ × 36 in)
RIBA, London

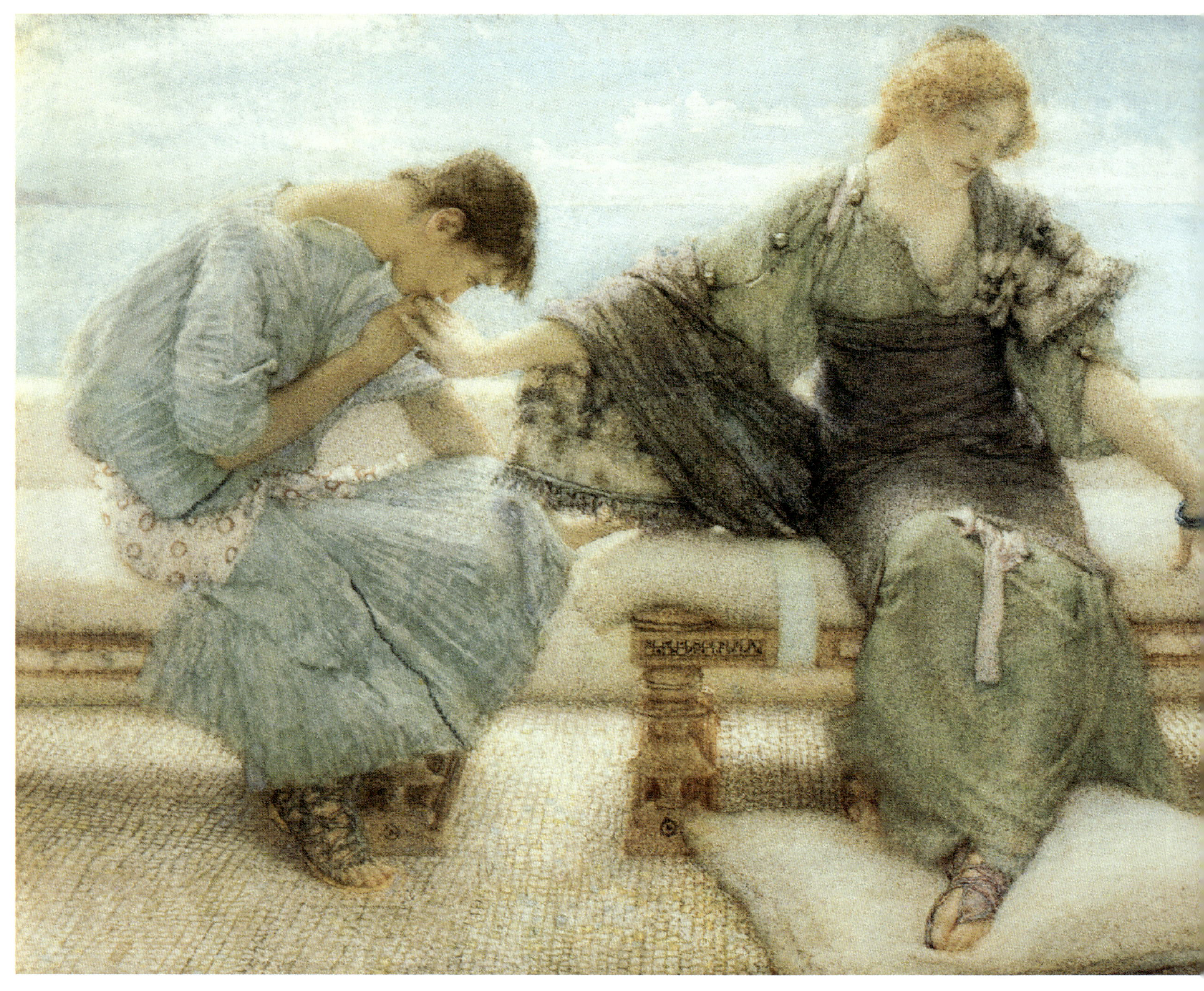

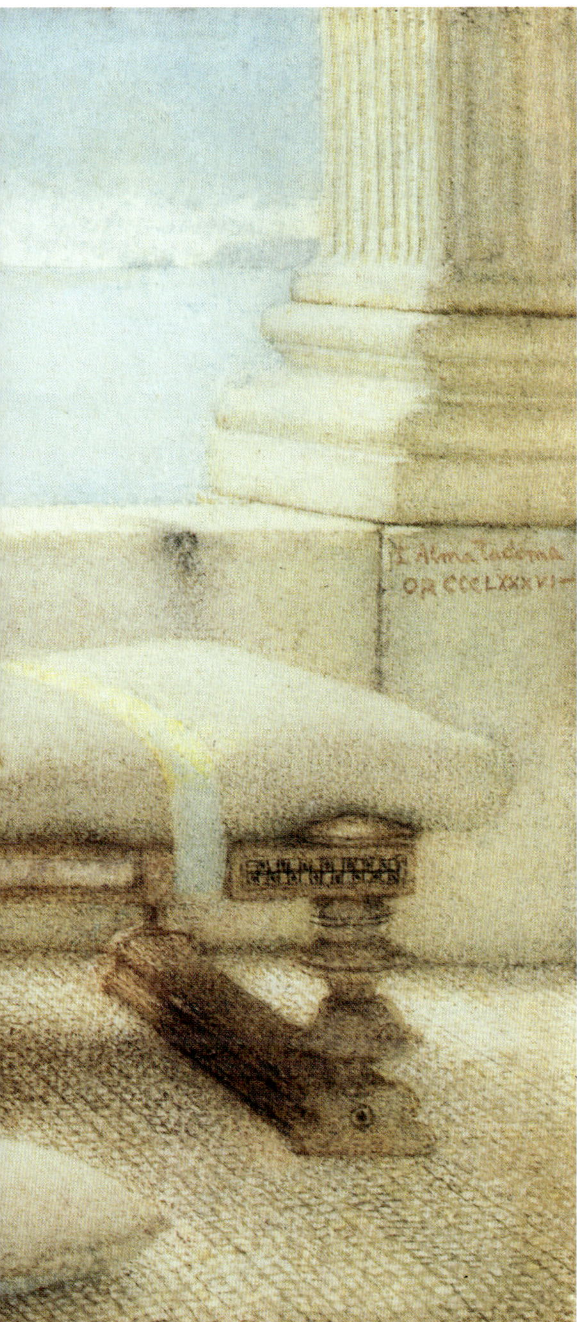

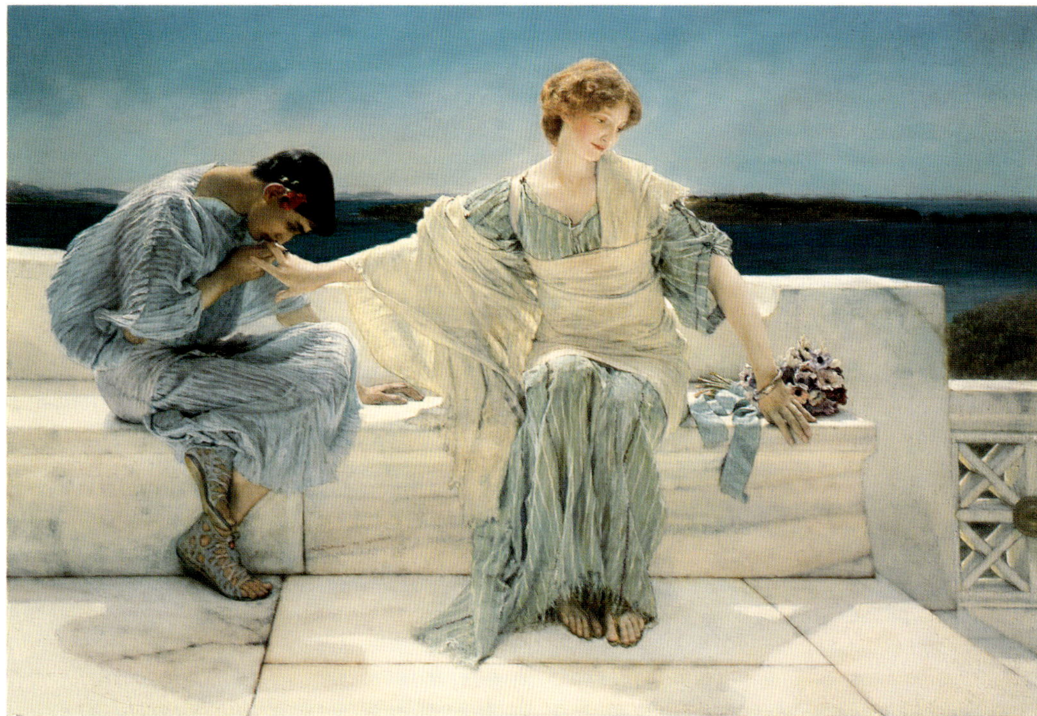

105
Ask Me No More, 1886
Watercolour
Private collection

106
Ask Me No More, 1906
Oil on canvas, 80·1 × 115·7 cm (31½ × 45½ in)
Private collection

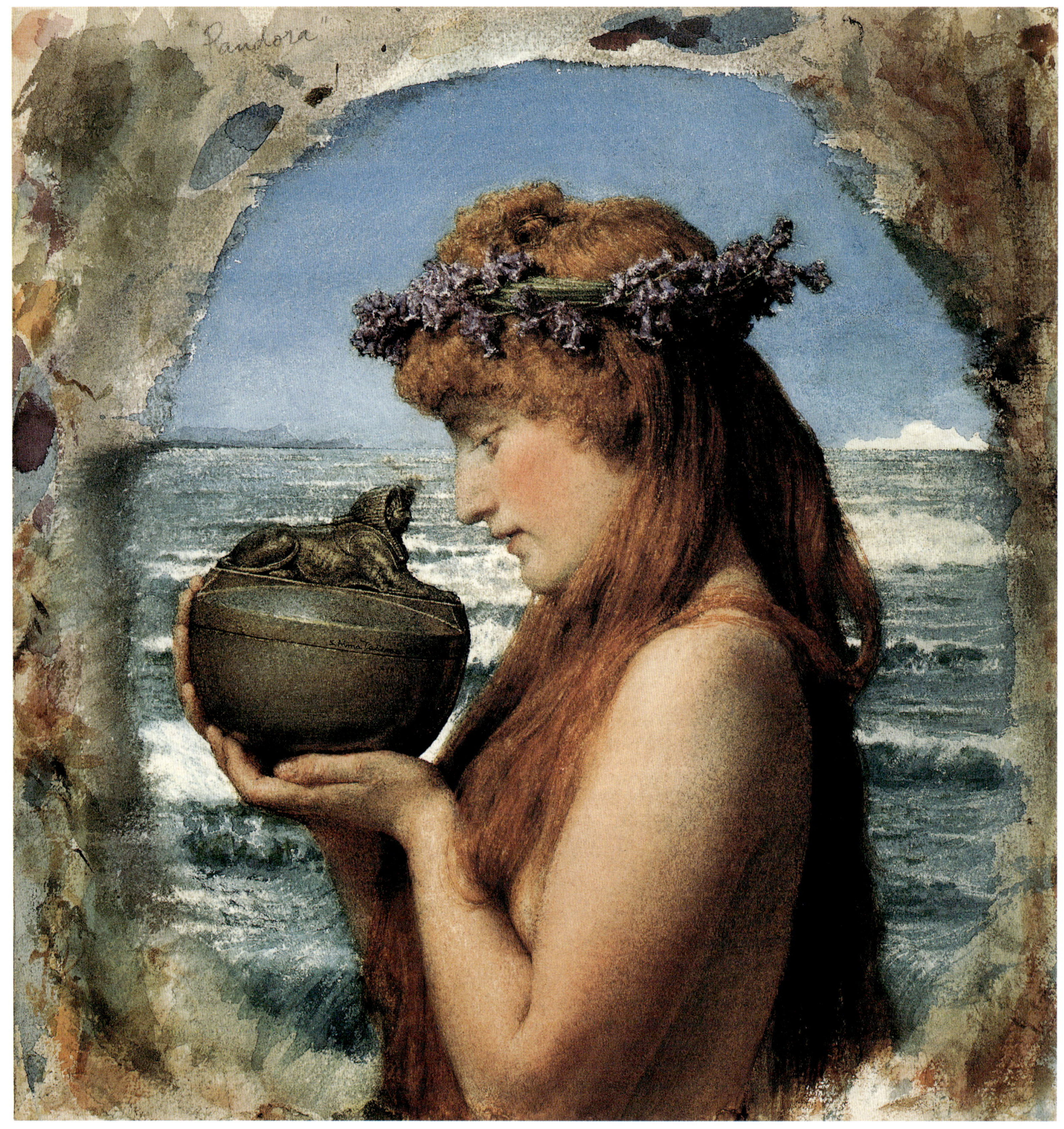
"Pandora"

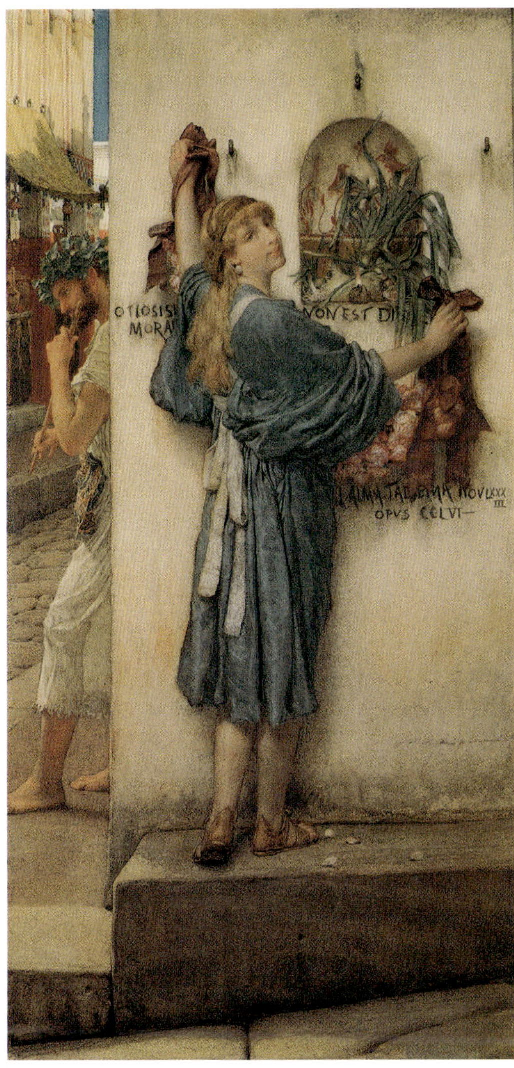

107 opposite
Pandora, 1881
Watercolour, 26 × 24·3 cm (10¼ × 9⅝ in)
Royal Watercolour Society, London

108
A Street Altar, 1883
Watercolour, 34·7 × 17·3 cm (13⅝ × 6¾ in)
Cecil Higgins Art Gallery, Bedford

colour Society, *Pandora* (Pl.107), is unrelated to any oil. The only Greek mythological painting produced by the mature artist, it depicts the archetypal *femme fatale*, a subject favoured by other artists including Dante Gabriel Rossetti and John William Waterhouse. The early Greek poet Hesiod tells us that Pandora was given to the world as a punishment for Prometheus' trickery in inducing Zeus to take the fat and bones from sacrificial offerings and leave the flesh for humankind.[194] She was made from wet clay by Hephaestus, given life by Athena, charm and beauty by Aphrodite, dressed and wreathed in flowers by the Seasons, but lastly 'the quicksilver messenger [Hermes] put in her breast/ Lies and wheedling words and a cheating heart'.[195] Pandora opened the jar which contained all the world's evils, leaving only hope inside. Alma-Tadema's Pandora clutches the fateful jar in her hands. She gazes at the sphinx decoration on the lid, and sphinx and *femme fatale* become symbolic of all the terrors of the predatory female.

Another watercolour, *A Street Altar* (Pl.108), painted three years later, is also unconnected with any oil. A very different subject, which seemingly depicts Roman religious customs, like *Pandora* it assumes a disquieting construction of gender roles in the ancient world. A woman hangs a garland around a painted wall niche already filled with offerings. She looks over her shoulder, flashing the viewer an enigmatic smile, while a flute player loiters mysteriously in the background. Behind the standing woman a partly obscured inscription reads:

> Otiosis locus hic non est.
> Discede Morator

which translates as:

> There is no place here for the idle:
> procrastinator, depart !

This is surely an ironic message to the flute player idling on the street corner. Yet the full meaning of the scene only becomes apparent when we realize that the lines form an actual inscription found at Pompeii and significantly situated on a wall along the 'Street of the Brothels'. The woman's smile can immediately be interpreted as a 'come hither' look, and the flute player as perhaps a prospective, though not very promising, client.

Although this was not his preferred medium, Alma-Tadema was a competent watercolourist who occasionally incorporated into his watercolours the lively irony found in his oils. His style, however, was much more suited to oil painting, which allowed the display of an impressive technique in the depiction of material objects.

11/4

THE ARTIST AT HOME

In 1883 Alma-Tadema bought a new house, 17 Grove End Road, at the centre of the fashionable artists' district of St John's Wood. The house formerly belonged to Jean-Jacques Tissot and had additions including a studio-salon, a gardener's lodge and a formal pond ringed by an Ionic colonnade shown in several of Tissot's works. After Tissot left London in 1882, the house remained empty until bought by Alma-Tadema. It was extensively remodelled to Alma-Tadema's own design with four-fifths of Tissot's house being demolished. As architect, Alma-Tadema employed Alfred Calderon, the son of his friend and neighbour, the painter Philip Calderon. Contract drawings were signed by the contractor William Downs in August 1885. The first task was to convert the gardener's lodge into an interim studio where the artist continued to work until the house was completed.

Renovations meant considerable expense, and between 1883 and 1888 Alma-Tadema concentrated on large canvases which could be sold at high prices. He chose historical themes for most of these works as history painting, formerly the subject of public commissions, was traditionally executed on a grand scale. In 1883 he completed *The Meeting of Antony and Cleopatra* (Pl.109) which, although a Romano-Egyptian history painting, does not look to an ancient source but illustrates Antony's first meeting with Cleopatra as described by Shakespeare's Enobarbus (*Antony and Cleopatra* II. ii):

The barge she sat in, like a burnish'd throne,
Burn'd on the water: the poop was beaten gold;
Purple the sails, and so perfumed that
The winds were love-sick with them; the oars were silver,
Which to the tune of flutes kept stroke, and made
The water which they beat to follow faster,
As amorous of their strokes. For her own person,
It beggar'd all description: she did lie
In her pavilion, – cloth-of-gold, of tissue –
O'er-picturing that Venus where we see

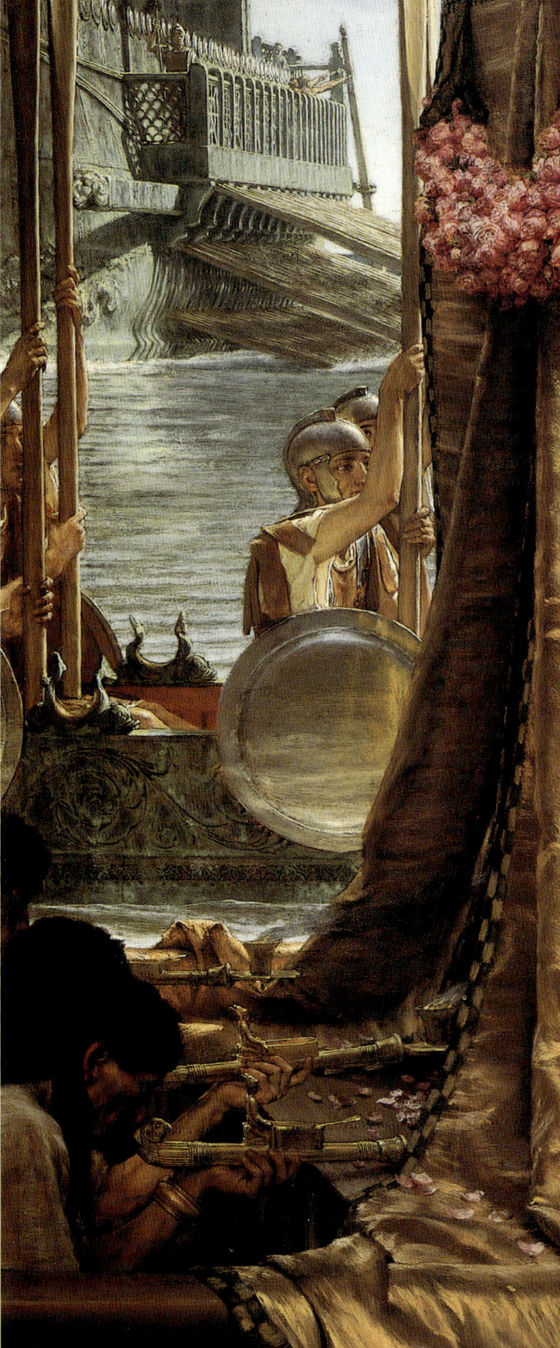

109
The Meeting of Antony and Cleopatra, 1883
Oil on wood, 65·5 × 92·3 cm (25¾ × 36⅜ in)
Private collection

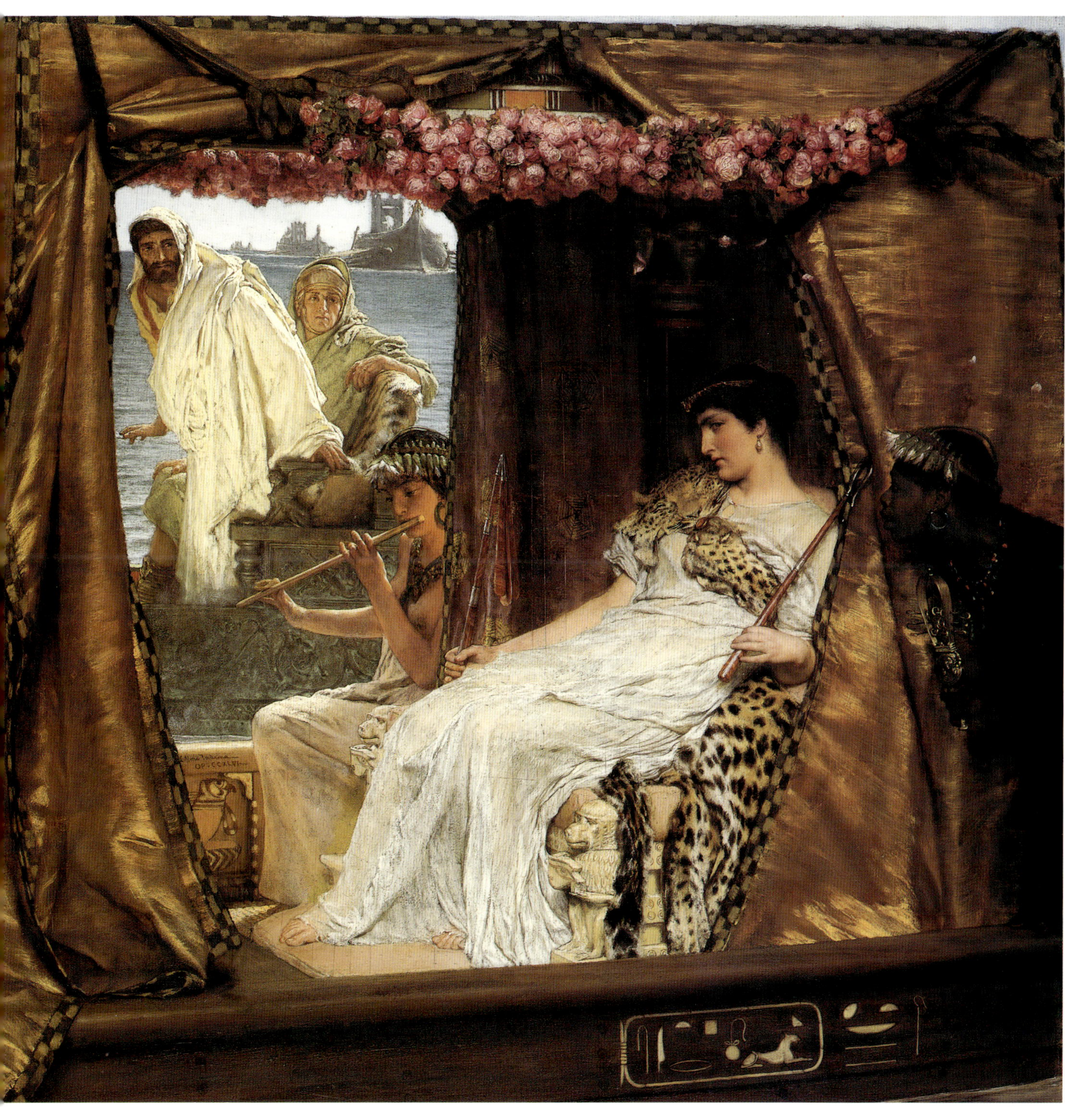

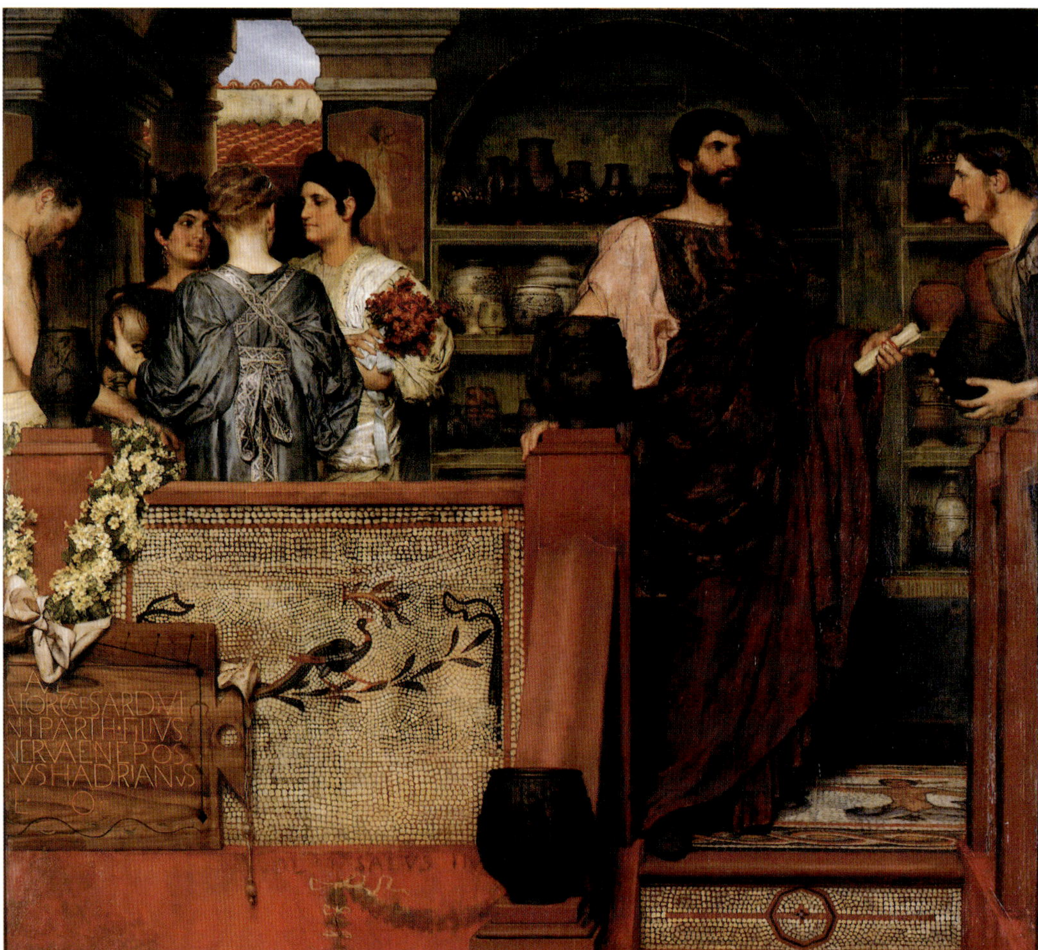

110 top left
Hadrian Visiting a Romano-British Pottery, 1884
Oil on canvas (cut and repainted),
159 × 171 cm (62⅝ × 67⅜ in)
Stedelijk Museum, Amsterdam

111
The Roman Potters in Britain, 1884
Oil on canvas (cut and repainted),
76·2 × 119·4 cm (30 × 47 in)
Royal Collections, The Hague

112 far right
A Romano-British Potter, 1884
Oil on canvas (cut and repainted),
152·5 × 80 cm (60 × 31½ in)
Musée d'Orsay, Paris

> The fancy out-work nature: On each side her
> Stood pretty dimpled boys, like smiling Cupids,
> With divers-colour'd fans, whose wind did seem
> To glow the delicate cheeks which they did cool,
> And what they undid did.

The details of Cleopatra's gilded barge, the music of flutes and perfumed breezes (depicted as incense blown through pipes) are all derived from the play. Between 1850 and 1912, *Antony and Cleopatra* was regularly staged at London's theatres,[196] ensuring that Shakespeare's Cleopatra – tragic heroine and doomed lover – remained at the forefront of the popular imagination. At the same time, she was typically cast in one of a number of roles: the Oriental queen (although Macedonian Greek by descent), the exotic voluptuary, and most often the *femme fatale*. Cleopatra becomes Algernon Swinburne's beautiful but deathly queen in a poem entitled 'Cleopatra',[197] in his description of a Michelangelo drawing,[198] and as one of the procession of notorious women in 'The Masque of Queen Bersabe.'[199] Théophile Gautier's short story, *One of Cleopatra's Nights* (1845), describes the queen, exhausted by ennui, choosing a young lover who is willing to be executed after tasting just one night of pleasure with her. The same Cleopatra is painted by Alexandre Cabanel in *Cleopatra Testing Poisons on Condemned Prisoners* (1887). In Jean-Léon Gérôme's *Cleopatra Before Caesar* (1866), she has acquired the lineaments of an Orientalist fantasy, standing displaying herself semi-naked to Julius Caesar like a slave in a seraglio. Likewise, in Gustave Moreau's *Cleopatra* (1887), though more *femme fatale* than harem slave, Cleopatra is still a product of the mysterious and exotic East. The very name Cleopatra is drawn inexorably into lists with Nero, Heliogabalus and assorted Eastern potentates, all resonant with connotations of luxury, sensuality and decadent excess. Gautier laments not having been a 'contemporary of Sardanapalus; of Teglath Phalazar; of Cleopatra, queen of Egypt; or even of Heliogabalus, emperor of Rome and priest of the Sun'.[200]

Alma-Tadema's Cleopatra is stately queen, exotic lover and *femme fatale*, all in one. Regal status is signified by the Pharaonic crook and flail which she carries, while the erotic languor of her pose and sumptuous diaphanous dress exude voluptuousness. Cleopatra herself is based on an earlier picture, *Cleopatra* (1875), which shows a profile portrait of the queen. Here she appears unconcerned at Antony's arrival; he peers at her in awe while she, with sensually lowered lids, keeps her gaze fixed on the spectator. Quite unlike Alma-Tadema's earlier Egyptian paintings, *The Meeting of Antony and Cleopatra* assumes an eroticized construction of the East.

The following year in 1884, another Roman history painting was completed, although of a very different stamp. In *Hadrian in England: Visiting a Romano-British Pottery*, the Emperor is shown taking an interest in ordinary life. Hadrian spent much of his reign in provincial travels; Georg Ebers's novel *The Emperor* (1881) describes his visit to Egypt. Alma-Tadema's scene recalls Dio Cassius' report on the Emperor's inspection of garrisons and forts: 'he personally viewed and investigated absolutely everything.'[201] Hadrian stands on an upper tier, while below him a workman carries pots on his head;

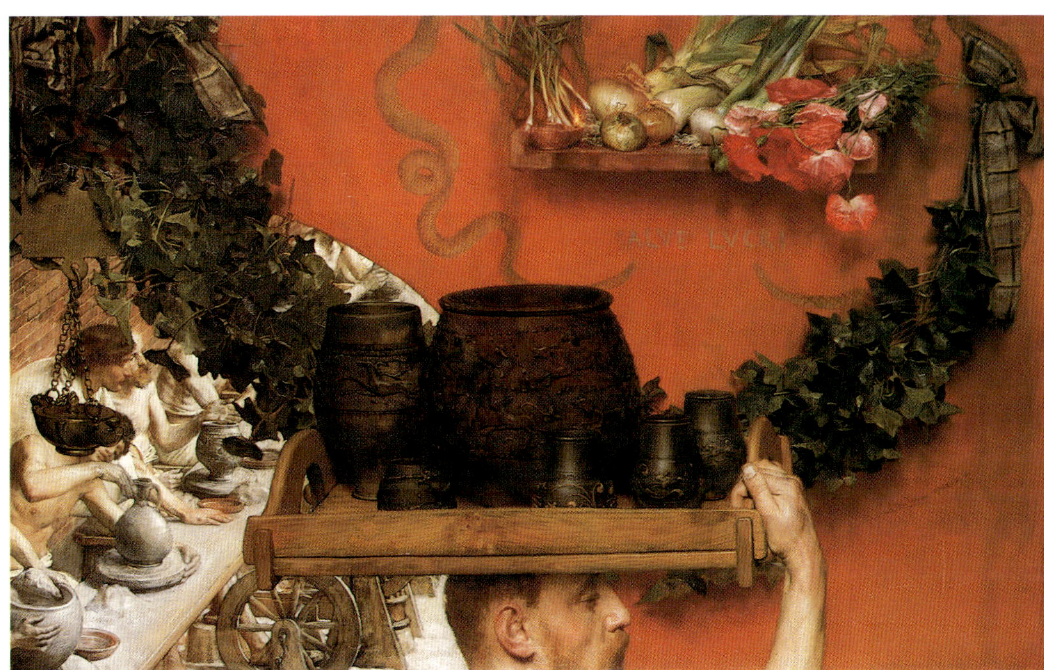

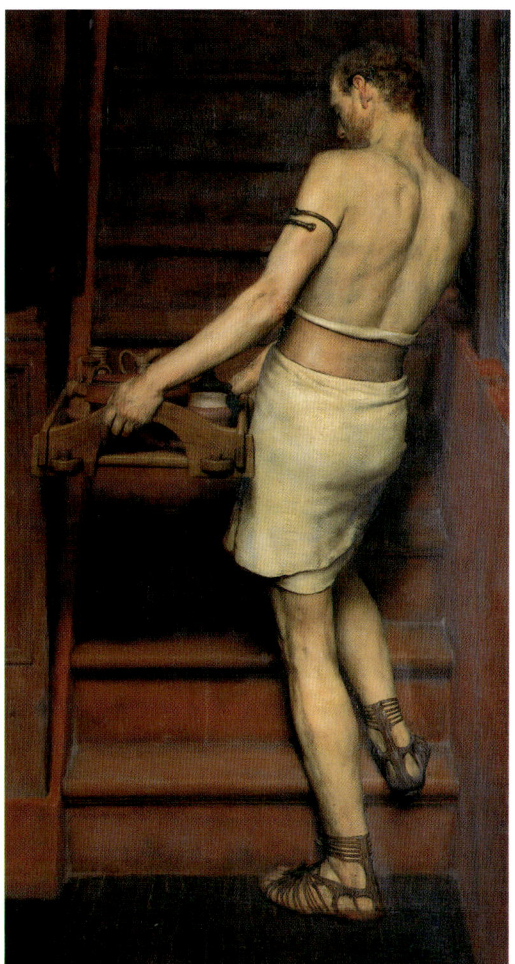

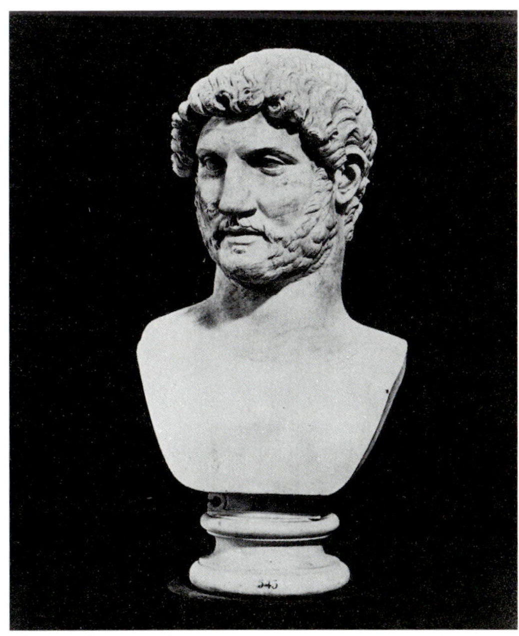

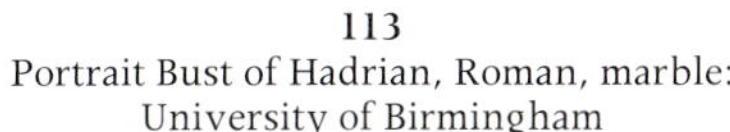

113
Portrait Bust of Hadrian, Roman, marble:
University of Birmingham

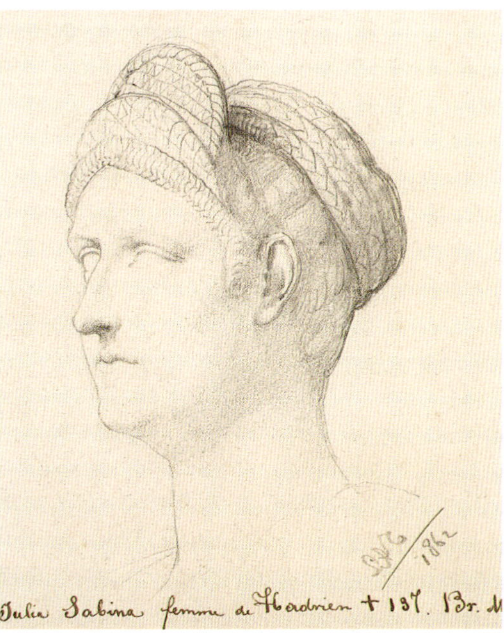

114
Julia Sabina, 1862
Pencil on paper, 10.1 × 12.7 cm (4 × 5 in):
University of Birmingham

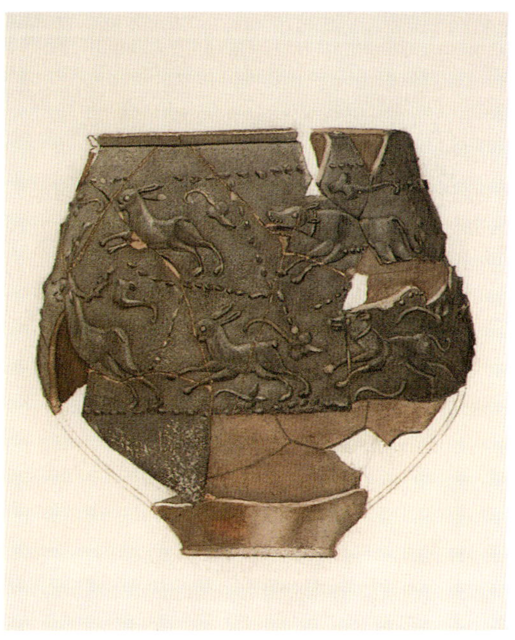

115
J J Gaul, Romano-British pot, 1880s
Watercolour, 13 × 12.7 cm ($5\frac{1}{8}$ × 5 in):
University of Birmingham

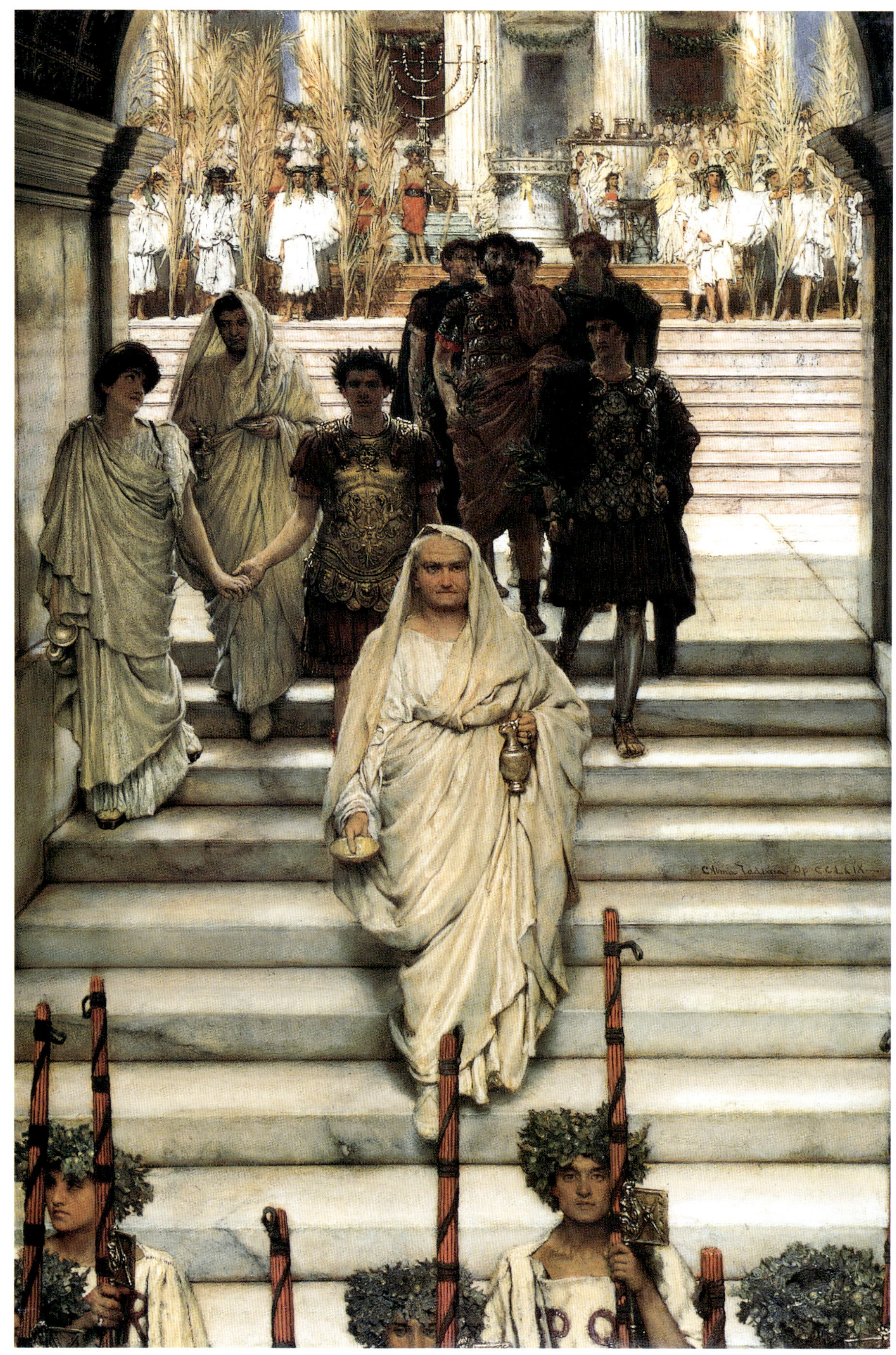

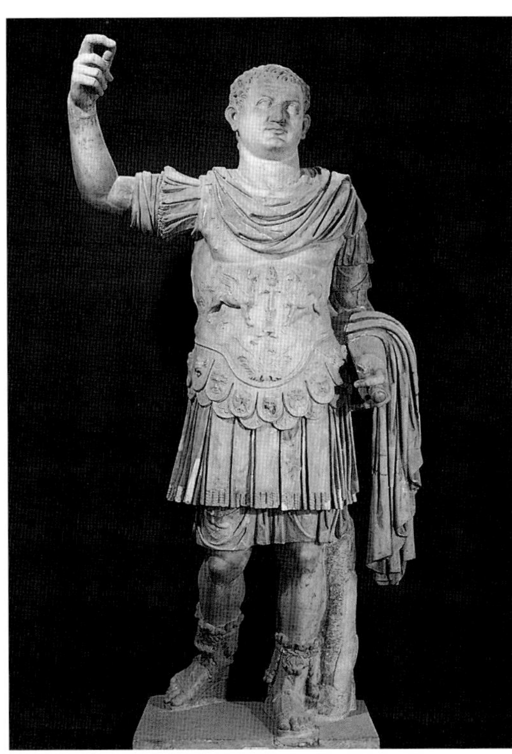

116 opposite
The Triumph of Titus: AD 71, 1885
Oil on wood, 44·3 × 29·1 cm (17½ × 11½ in)
Walters Art Gallery, Baltimore

117
Cuirassed Statue of Titus from Herculaneum, 1st century AD
Marble
Archaeological Museum, Naples

behind him a production line of workmen fashion clay; and to the side, another workman climbs the stairs. After exhibition, the painting was divided by the artist into three sections showing the Emperor and his circle (Pl.110), potters at work (Pl.111) and a slave or workman ascending the stairs (Pl.112).[202] The third section displays fine figure drawing unrivalled in his other works; it remained unsold and in the artist's possession until his death, when it was bequeathed to a public collection. The reasons for the division remain unclear although the artist may have been dissatisfied with the complicated composition which juxtaposed the workings of the pottery and the imperial circle on two separate tiers.

Hadrian and his wife, Julia Sabina, are based on portrait busts of the imperial couple like those included in Alma-Tadema's photographic collection (Pl.113, Pl.114). The pots imitate actual Romano-British pots, sketches of which the artist kept for reference. The central pot is based on a drawing by J. J. Gaul (an assistant used by Alma-Tadema and other artists, including William Blake Richmond) (Pl.115). In an incomplete state, it has been skilfully restored by the artist. However, archaeological interest aside, *Hadrian in England* lacks the dynamic realization of ancient political life found in, for example, *A Roman Emperor AD 41* (Pl.54). The pairing of imperial circle with the everyday workings of a provincial pottery is incongruous and Alma-Tadema is at his best when making clear distinctions between the two categories of historical and historical genre painting. Furthermore, the provincial travels of a 'good' emperor lack the subversive edge which makes his exploration of the less salubrious side of imperial history so compelling.

After *Hadrian in England* Alma-Tadema continued his exploration of the other side of Roman history with *The Triumph of Titus AD 71* (Pl.116). The artist returns to an outdoor setting and displays fine marble painting in the form of a grand architectural vista. It depicts part of the triumphal procession celebrating Titus' famous sack of Jerusalem, under the reign of the Emperor Vespasian. The old Vespasian, wearing a toga, heads the imperial party, followed by his son, Titus, in golden armour, Titus' daughter, Julia, and his brother and successor, Domitian. Vespasian's unmistakable face with broad forehead, hooked nose and tight, thin lips, is copied from portrait busts of the ageing Emperor. Titus, with his similarly broad face, carries the family resemblance, while his distinctive breastplate is based on a cuirassed statue from Herculaneum (Pl.117). The representation of Domitian once again imitates portraits of the young prince.

Alma-Tadema was particularly concerned to justify the authenticity of his scene. A letter to the commissioner of the painting, William Walters, reveals meticulous research: 'some writers speak of Vespasian having accompanied Titus in the Triumphal Cart.[203] I disbelieve this, on account of no plastic monuments agreeing with that position. In the bas-relief on the Arch of Titus, Titus is certainly alone.'[204] Nevertheless, another letter confesses that, in one respect at least, artistic considerations override historical accuracy. Although Julia was only a child at the time of the triumph, Alma-Tadema chose to represent her as a grown woman for the sake of a balanced composition.[205] From the first Roman subjects in the mid-1860s, Alma-Tadema chooses particular archaeological artefacts which play an authenticating, intellectual role, and yet, ultimately, all of these particular choices are governed by the aesthetic logic of each composition as an individual work of art.

The main literary source for the painting was, no doubt, the Greco-Roman historian Josephus, who describes the triumph and details the savage sack of Jerusalem and the destruction of the Temple.[206] Alma-Tadema reminds the viewer of these cruel events with a display of spoils laid out in the background – golden menorah, table of shew-bread, incense cups and trumpets – all described by Josephus,[207] and depicted in one of the two central bays of the Arch of Titus. Imperial procession coupled with magnificent public architecture points to a celebration of the Roman Empire but, at the same time, archaeological artefacts signify the death and destruction which accompany military victory. While many modern scholars assume that Victorian depictions of imperial Rome serve as positive analogies for British imperialism in the nineteenth century, *The Triumph of Titus* suggests that such a reading is problematic. Whether or not Alma-Tadema was consciously making a modern political point, his is a painting which ostensibly presents the grandeur of an imperial triumph but also lingers on the destructions and spoliations of imperialism.[208]

The Triumph of Titus was sold for $20,000, making it one of the most expensive pictures in the world of nineteenth-century art. The extravagance of the price can be gauged when compared with Edwin Long's *The Babylonian Marriage Market* (1875), which achieved an auction house record for any work by a living British artist sold in a British sale room, when sold at Christie's in 1882 for £6,625.

As he was now concentrating much of his artistic energy on large history paintings, during the 1880s Alma-Tadema's annual output dropped from around twelve to five. The drop was partly due also to his participation in a number of new

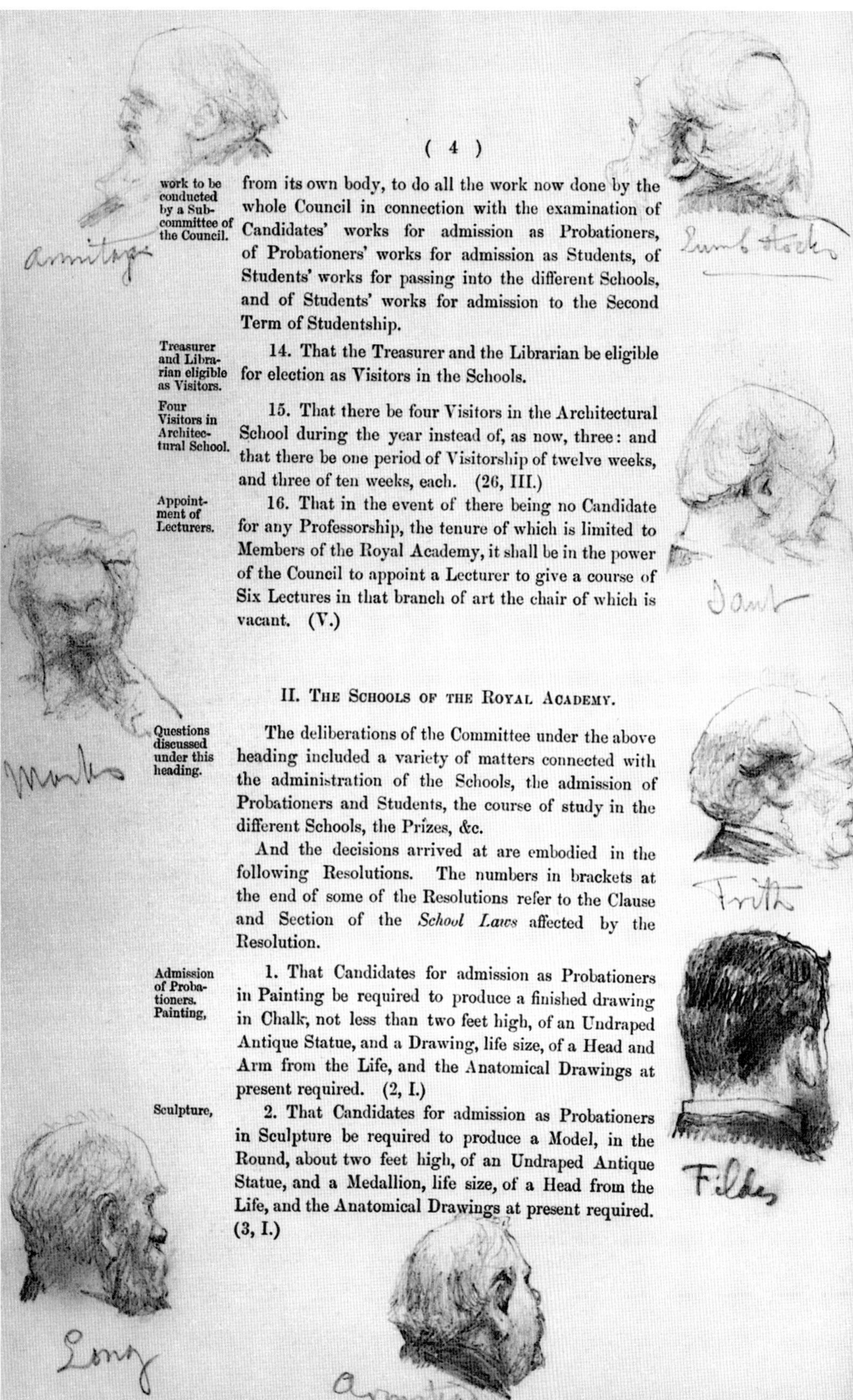

(4)

work to be conducted by a Sub-committee of the Council. from its own body, to do all the work now done by the whole Council in connection with the examination of Candidates' works for admission as Probationers, of Probationers' works for admission as Students, of Students' works for passing into the different Schools, and of Students' works for admission to the Second Term of Studentship.

Treasurer and Librarian eligible as Visitors. 14. That the Treasurer and the Librarian be eligible for election as Visitors in the Schools.

Four Visitors in Architectural School. 15. That there be four Visitors in the Architectural School during the year instead of, as now, three: and that there be one period of Visitorship of twelve weeks, and three of ten weeks, each. (26, III.)

Appointment of Lecturers. 16. That in the event of there being no Candidate for any Professorship, the tenure of which is limited to Members of the Royal Academy, it shall be in the power of the Council to appoint a Lecturer to give a course of Six Lectures in that branch of art the chair of which is vacant. (V.)

II. The Schools of the Royal Academy.

Questions discussed under this heading. The deliberations of the Committee under the above heading included a variety of matters connected with the administration of the Schools, the admission of Probationers and Students, the course of study in the different Schools, the Prizes, &c.

And the decisions arrived at are embodied in the following Resolutions. The numbers in brackets at the end of some of the Resolutions refer to the Clause and Section of the *School Laws* affected by the Resolution.

Admission of Probationers. Painting, 1. That Candidates for admission as Probationers in Painting be required to produce a finished drawing in Chalk, not less than two feet high, of an Undraped Antique Statue, and a Drawing, life size, of a Head and Arm from the Life, and the Anatomical Drawings at present required. (2, I.)

Sculpture, 2. That Candidates for admission as Probationers in Sculpture be required to produce a Model, in the Round, about two feet high, of an Undraped Antique Statue, and a Medallion, life size, of a Head from the Life, and the Anatomical Drawings at present required. (3, I.)

projects aside from painting. As a Royal Academician, he was expected to undertake teaching duties. The young artist Herbert Schmalz was said to have rushed back to London from Antwerp on learning that Alma-Tadema was to be a Visiting Professor at the Academy schools.[209] Alma-Tadema's own attitude to such official responsibilities can be gauged from pencil sketches drawn in the margins of a *Royal Academy of Arts Special Committee Report* (Pl.118). During a meeting the artist amused himself by sketching the portraits of Academicians present: from right to left Lumb Stocks, James Sant, W P Frith, Luke Fildes, Henry Hugh Armstead, Edwin Long, Henry Stacy Marks and Edward Armitage. On another page, his doodles comment on the contents of the report. Next to motion 14 – 'That the Treasurer and the Librarian be eligible for election as Visitors in the Schools' – he has drawn two jubilant dancing figures and three exclamation marks, surely a characteristic shot of irony at the expense of himself and his fellow Academicians, and their reluctance to undertake teaching duties (Pl.119). No Academicians ever enthused about teaching in the Royal Academy Schools, but for Alma-Tadema, who rarely accepted private pupils into his studio, the responsibility may have been especially onerous. Another Academic duty was to serve on the Hanging Committee for the annual Summer Exhibition. Alma-Tadema was put in the awkward position of having to witness his wife's works come under the scrutiny of the committee. Frederick Goodall related that one year a nervous Alma-Tadema watched one of Laura's pictures being handed around to each member and breathed a sigh of relief when, after the picture was passed unanimously, he admitted his connection with the artist.[210]

To escape from official duties the Alma-Tadema family regularly visited the home of Frank Millet and his wife and Edwin Austin Abbey, at Broadway in the Cotswolds. Millet and Abbey, both landscape painters, established a retreat in the country which attracted artists and writers such as John Singer Sargent and Henry James. Visitors indulged in work and relaxation including regular games of tennis in which Alma-Tadema distinguished himself as being 'comically awful, roaring with laughter at his mistakes'.[211]

From the mid-1880s Alma Tadema was busy with renovations on his new house. He was said to have spent the fantastic sum of £70,000 (equivalent to a couple of million pounds at today's prices) on remodelling the house to his own specifications. The money spent on the house illustrates Alma-Tadema's very substantial wealth at the height of his career. Alma-Tadema relates in his reminiscences that the number seventeen was his lucky number: he met Laura when she was seventeen; Townshend House was no. 17 Tichfield Terrace; the new house was 17 Grove End Road; renovations began on 17 August; and the family took up residence on 17 November, three years later.[212]

The remodelled house had a total of sixty-six rooms, including three studios of diminishing size for Alma-Tadema, his wife, Laura, and elder daughter, Anna. As in Townshend House, the decorative scheme incorporated eclectic motifs including the mixture of Chinese, Japanese and Moorish details found in fashionable aesthetic interiors. Alma-Tadema owned a collection of Chinese and Japanese porcelain and pottery; in 1892 he became a charter member of the Japan Society, founded to promote Japanese art and culture, and three years later accepted the position of Vice President. This interest was evidently a social activity and, as such, separate from his professional life. He also possessed a number of Egyptian and Roman antiquities, mostly pottery and small bronze decorative items. Although the collection featured casts and copies of well-known works such as the Hermes of Praxiteles, a bust of Septimius Severus and numerous reproductions of Roman silverware, the inclusion of Roman stucco work, terracotta antefixes, weighing scales, arrow heads and samples of Pompeian grating illustrates the artist's serious interest in archaeology.

The finished building differed from other artists' houses in that it completely transformed an existing house (rather than being newly built or merely redecorated) and used not only an eclectic mix of materials and details, but surprising juxtapositions. The entrance was decorated with an imitation of the Eumachia door frame from Pompeii (represented in *The Sculpture Gallery*) and the door decorated with a knocker in the shape of an ancient mask with 'Salve' ('Welcome') inscribed on the lintel. The entrance hall consisted of narrow wall panels which over the years were filled with pictures by the artist's friends and which eventually comprised 45 narrow oil paintings placed around an *exedra*-shaped bench (Pl.120). Most of the major players in the world of late Victorian art world were represented in a variety of styles and subjects, including Briton Riviere's *Lions*, Alfred East's *Valley of Sweet Waters*, Val Prinsep's *An Indian Girl*, Frederic Leighton's *Bath of Psyche*, Alfred Parsons's *Apple Blossom*, Marcus Stone's *In the Garden*, Henry Stacy Marks's *At the Anchor Inn* and John Singer Sargent's *A Javanese Girl*.[213]

Sargent is reported to have once commented disparagingly of Alma-Tadema's work: 'Of course it is clever ... but of course it's not art in any sense whatever.'[214] This tongue-in-cheek remark is far more revealing than much positive art criticism of Alma-Tadema. While most critics concentrated on describing and not analysing his works, Sargent acknowledges, if negatively, their intellectual content. Sargent's own work, largely concerned with texture, light and colour, appeals to the senses and not the intellect, and he fails to admit that Alma-Tadema's purpose is to appeal to both simultaneously. Nevertheless, despite professional differences, prominent artists maintained a cohesive social group, while the range of names present here illustrates Alma-Tadema's personal popularity. An inscription above the fireplace in the hall read: 'I count myself in nothing else so happy, As in a soul remembering my good friends.' The motto expresses the importance of friendships, artistic and otherwise, and yet its sentimental timbre seems at odds with the general lack of sentimentality in Alma-Tadema's paintings.

Leading from the hall way was a copper staircase which the artist referred to as his 'scala d'onore' ('stairs of honour'). The atrium at the back of the house was not open to the sky (as in a Roman house), but borrowed light from a glass roof over a marble basin in the corner. Columns around the basin supported an upper walkway which led to the studio. The antique theme extended into the smoking room, while a dining room beyond was executed in a variety of woods. Anna's rooms on the first floor occupied half the area of Laura's below. For Laura's studio, a team of craftsmen was brought in from Holland to re-create a Dutch sixteenth-century oak-beamed ceiling, wall panelling and chimney piece, with adjoining bedroom of accompanying Dutch woodwork and Delft tileware. The rooms were in keeping with her work of historical genre scenes in Dutch sixteenth- and seventeeth-century settings.

Laura's studio paled into insignificance beside that of the master of the house (Pls. 121, 122). Alma-Tadema's studio was a lofty room with a semi-domed apse at the south end. To the left was a raised gallery decorated with a copper frieze by William Reynolds Stephens based on the artist's own *The Women of Amphissa*.[215] In the apse was the inscription 'Ars longa, vita brevis' ('Art is long, life is short') and above the door, the motto 'As the sun colours flowers, so art colours life.' A huge north window was designed to beam a light to the back of the apse, while the apse itself, or possibly the whole ceiling, was coated with aluminium leaf. This cast a silvery light, allowing the artist to simulate a Mediterranean-type sunlight even in the winter months.

In My Studio (1893) depicts a female model in classical-type dress smelling roses in a vase. The

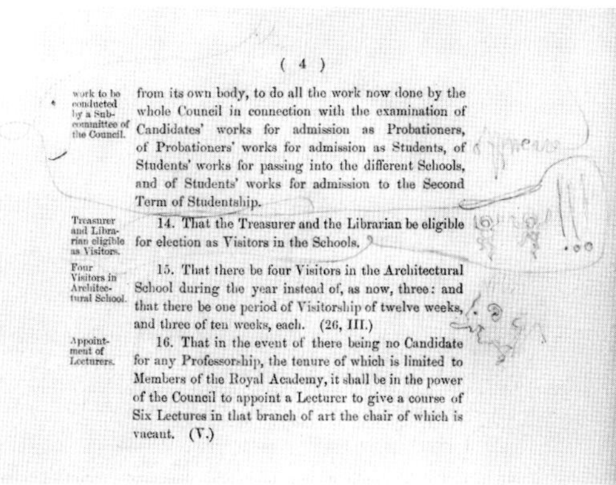

(4)

Work to be conducted by a Sub-committee of the Council. from its own body, to do all the work now done by the whole Council in connection with the examination of Candidates' works for admission as Probationers, of Probationers' works for admission as Students, of Students' works for passing into the different Schools, and of Students' works for admission to the Second Term of Studentship.

Treasurer and Librarian eligible as Visitors. 14. That the Treasurer and the Librarian be eligible for election as Visitors in the Schools.

Four Visitors in Architectural School. 15. That there be four Visitors in the Architectural School during the year instead of, as now, three: and that there be one period of Visitorship of twelve weeks, and three of ten weeks, each. (26, III.)

Appointment of Lecturers. 16. That in the event of there being no Candidate for any Professorship, the tenure of which is limited to Members of the Royal Academy, it shall be in the power of the Council to appoint a Lecturer to give a course of Six Lectures in that branch of art the chair of which is vacant. (V.)

118 & 119
Drawings in the margin of Royal Academy Report of the Special Committee, 1888
Forbes Magazine collection, New York

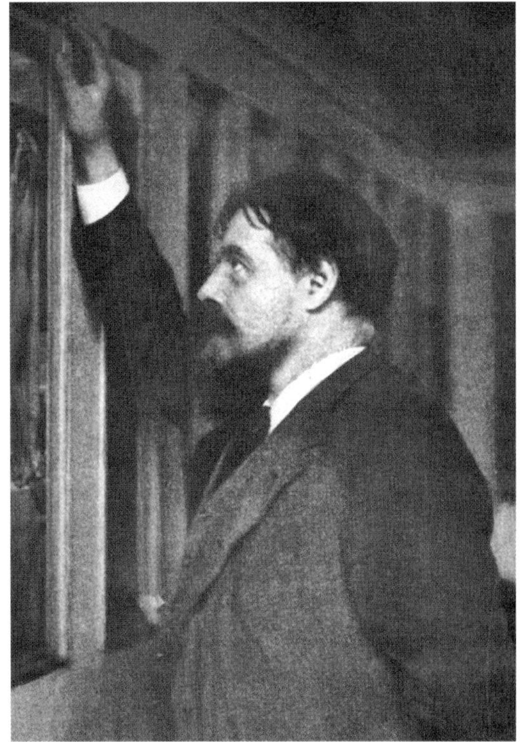

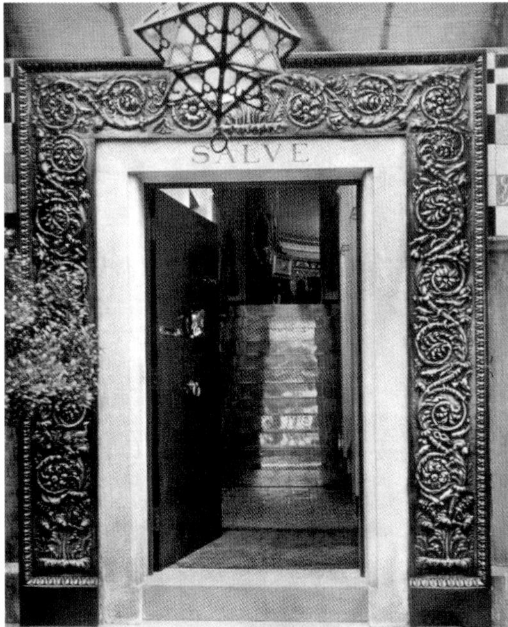

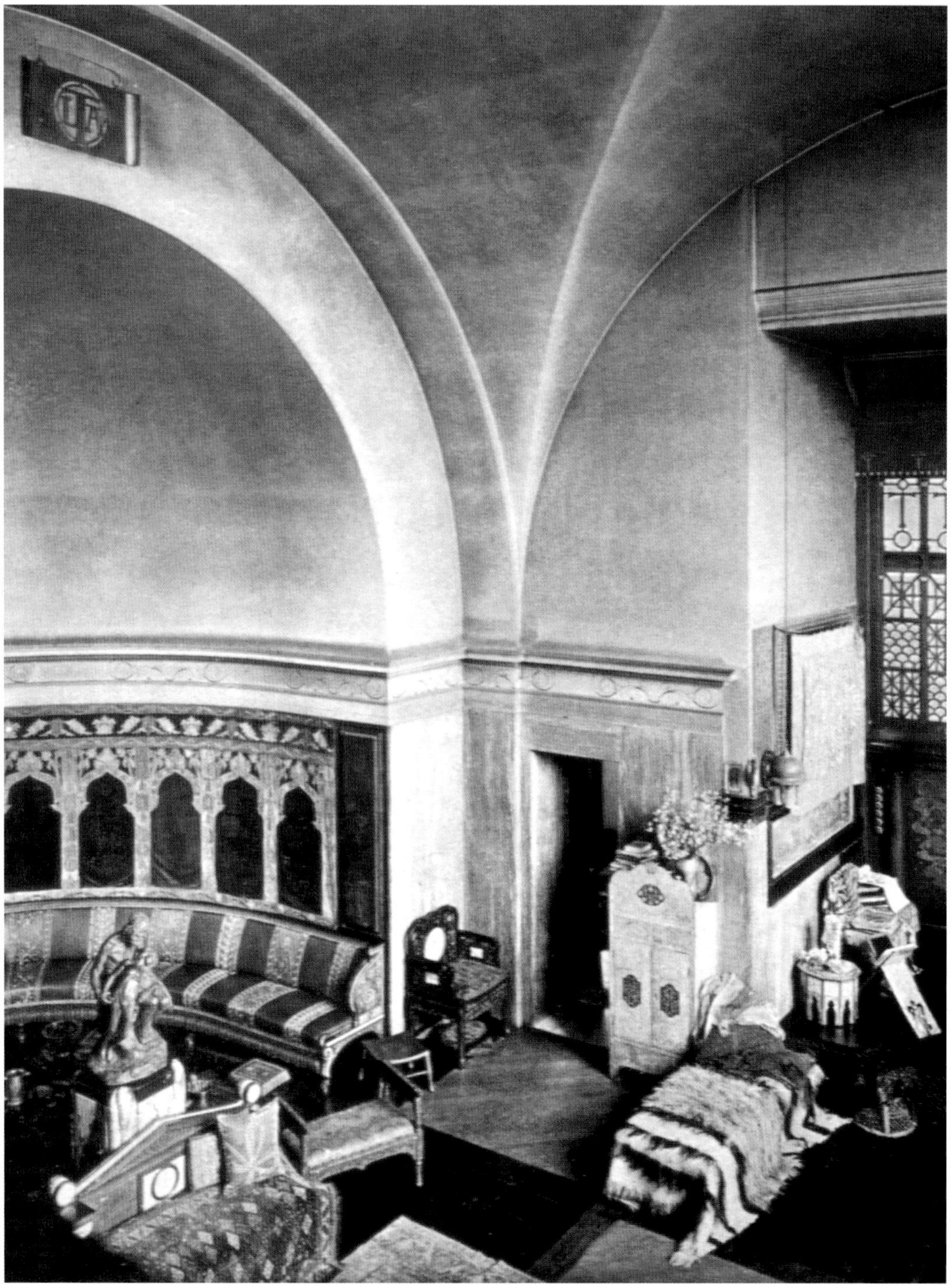

120
Alma-Tadema in the Hall of Panels, Grove End Road
Magazine of Art, Nov. 1896-Oct. 1897, p.42

121
View into Alma-Tadema's Studio through the Entrance Door
Art Journal, Christmas Number, 1910, p.28

122
View of the Studio from the Balcony
Art Journal, Christmas Number, 1910, p.29

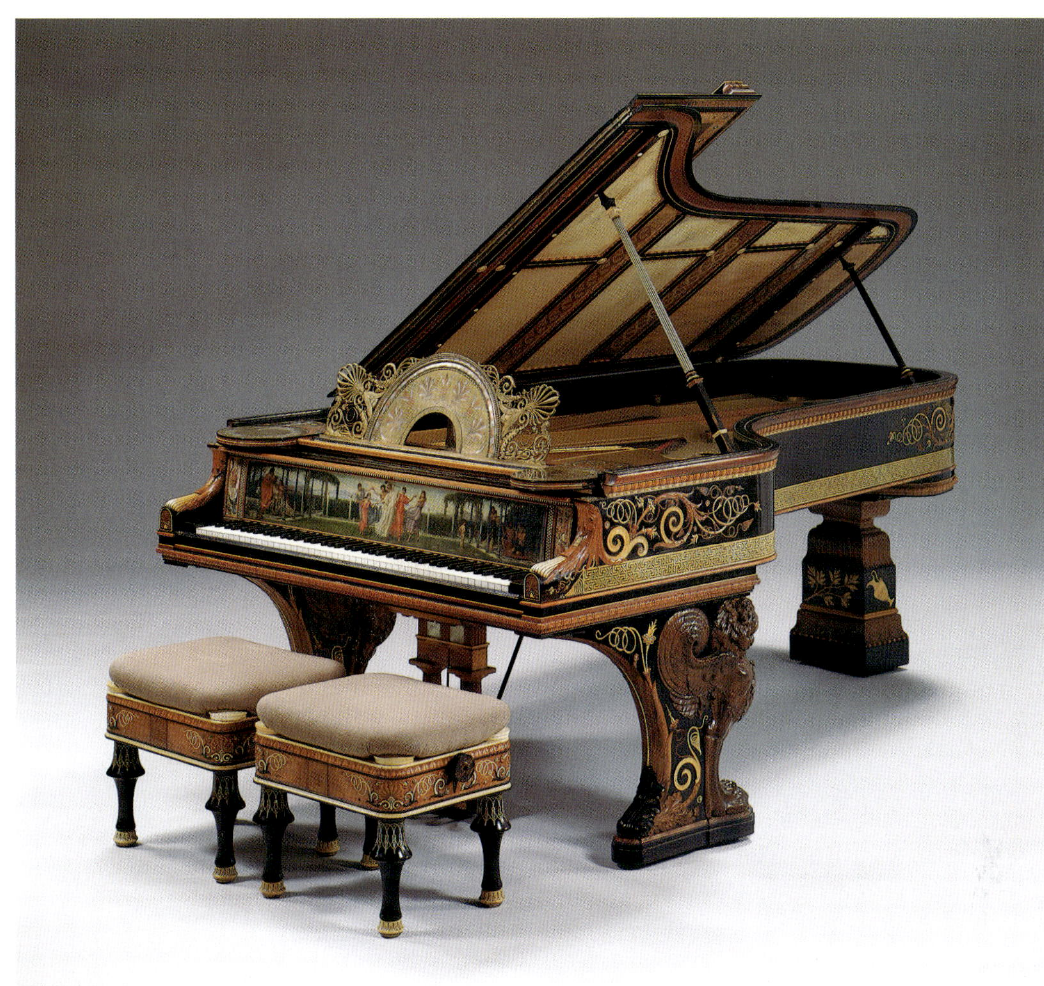

123
The Marquand Grand Piano
Private collection

setting is the studio alcove, with onyx window in the background, in front of which is a fourteenth-century Chinese temple screen. A red and gold embroidered Indian tablecloth covers the piano while a tiger skin in the background is a familiar studio prop found in a number of paintings. *In My Studio* was presented to Leighton in exchange for the *Bath of Psyche*, one of the many paintings in the 'Hall of Panels'.

The house did not grow larger but the artist continued to add features such as a Pompeian-style entrance loggia with mosaic flooring. As in Townshend House, personalized features adorned the interior, including the initials LAT interwoven into decorative detail. Angela Thirkell, the granddaughter of Burne-Jones, recalls childhood memories of the house and its owner: 'Grove End Road, with Tadema's stories which were so difficult to understand until his own infectious laugh warned you that he had reached the point, the agate windows and the brazen stairs.'[216] Thirkell goes on to describe her embarrassment on being unable to understand Alma-Tadema's Dutch accent. After laughing at what she took to be an amusing anecdote from her host, she was confronted with an outraged Alma-Tadema who exclaimed: 'What for do you laugh when I tell you that Alfred Parsons's mother is dead?'[217] Although a sense of humour is apparent in both the man and his work, it is impossible not to be struck by the disparity between the sophisticated ironies of Alma-Tadema's paintings and the quaintness of his social persona. Not all of Alma-Tadema's acquaintances were able to reconcile the artist with the man. Lodewijk van Deyssel described a studio visit in 1898: 'I am full of praise concerning the studio, but found the master however a disappointment. I had imagined him to be more refined, but he's fairly vulgar.'[218] The house, often referred to as 'Casa Tadema', was well publicized in magazines and journals. Descriptions affirmed Alma-Tadema's role as architect and interior designer as well as established artist, and yet many readers, and visitors, may, like van Deyssel, have been disappointed by what could be seen as a pretentious and vulgar display of wealth.

Alma-Tadema was involved in other interior design projects as well as that of his own house. Between 1884 and 1887 he was working on the design of the music room of Henry Marquand's New York mansion. Marquand (1819–1902), who made his fortune in banking and investment, was a connoisseur and one of the creators and directors of the Metropolitan Museum of Art. The rooms of Marquand's house were themed: an English Renaissance dining room hung with late sixteenth-century Flemish tapestries, a Japanese room to house Marquand's collection of Asian art, and a Moorish smoking room. The music room was to be classical, and Alma-Tadema was assigned a limitless budget. This was, then, a lucrative project which, along with the large and expensive canvases sold around the same time, allowed him to spend lavish amounts of money on his own house.

He designed for Marquand a suite of furniture consisting of twenty-nine items including, as the centre-piece of the room, a grand piano executed by Johnstone, Norman & Co. of New Bond Street (Pl.123). An ebony and sandalwood case is decorated with ivory, coral and mother-of-pearl, inlaid with cedar and boxwood decorations. The lid is inlaid with the names of Apollo and the nine

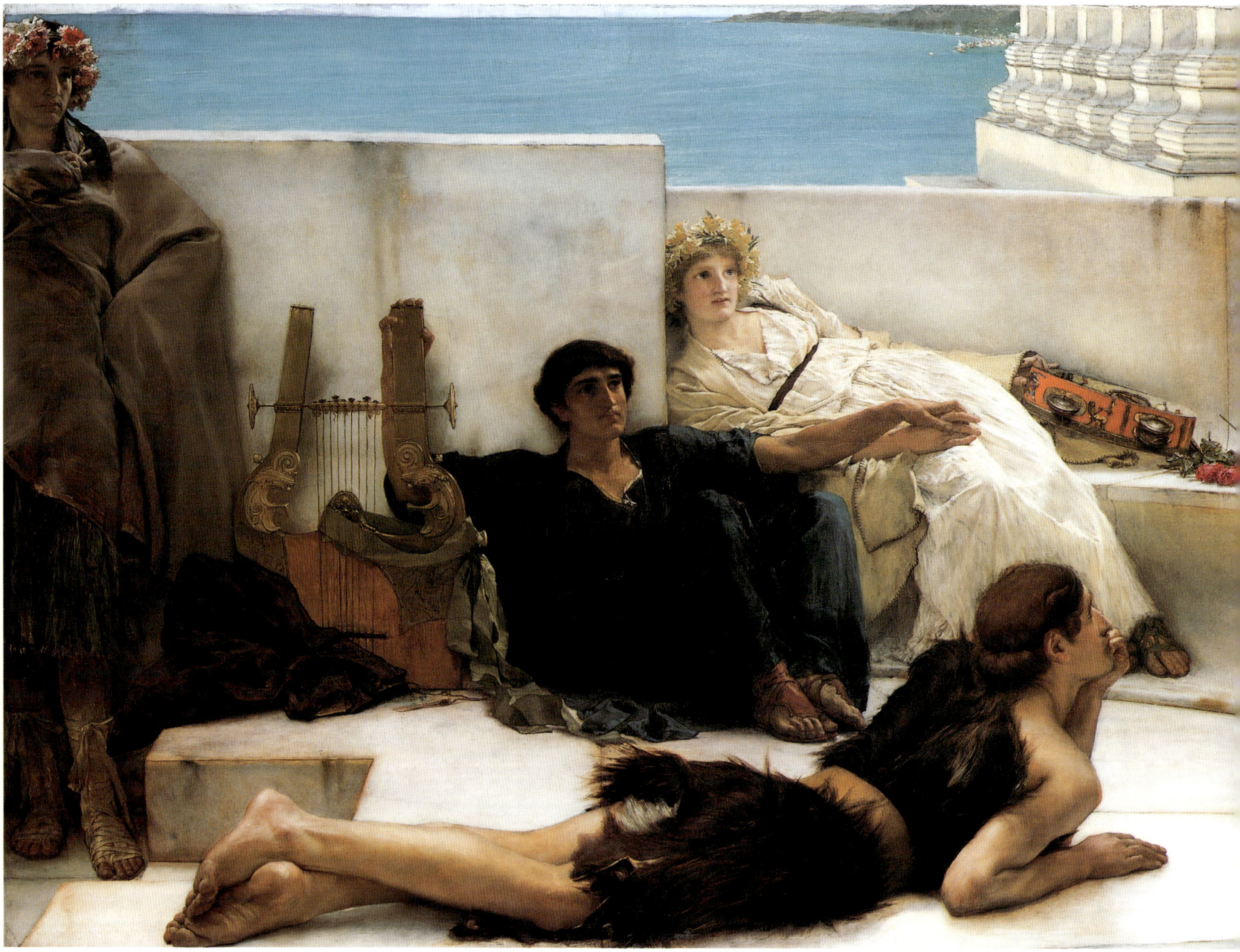

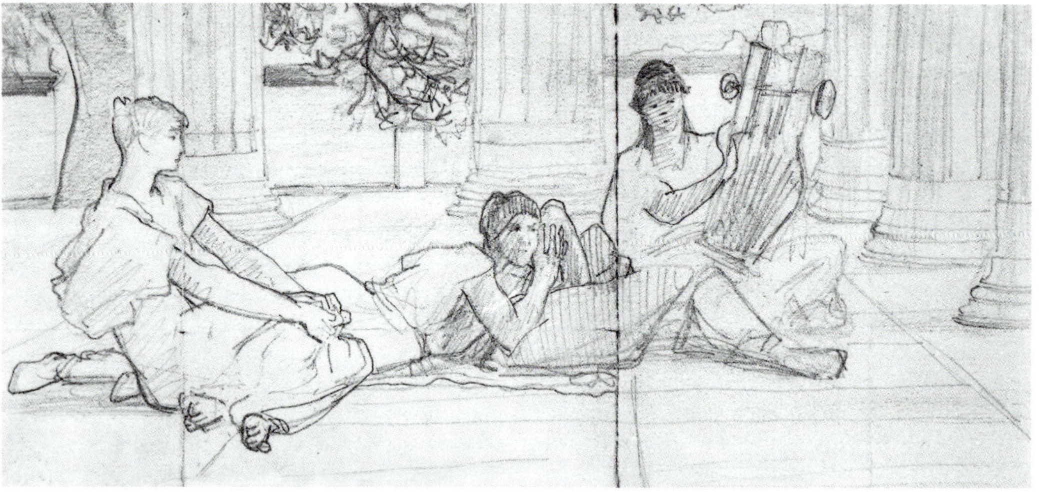

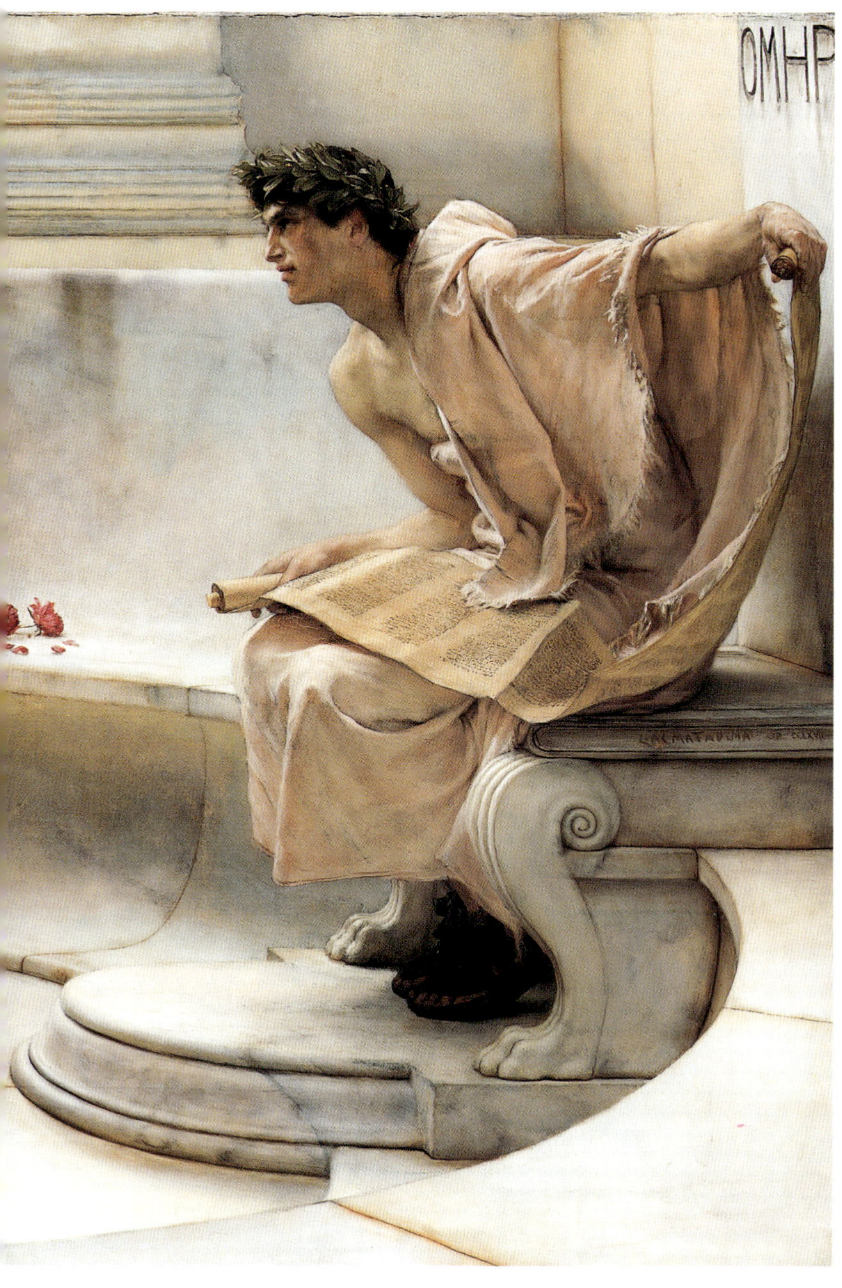

124
A Reading from Homer, 1885
Oil on canvas, 91·4 × 183·8 cm (36 × 72⅜ in)
Philadelphia Museum of Art,
George W. Elkins Collection

125
Study for *A Reading from Homer*, 1884–5
Pencil on paper, 11·4 × 22·9 cm (4½ × 9 in)
Private collection

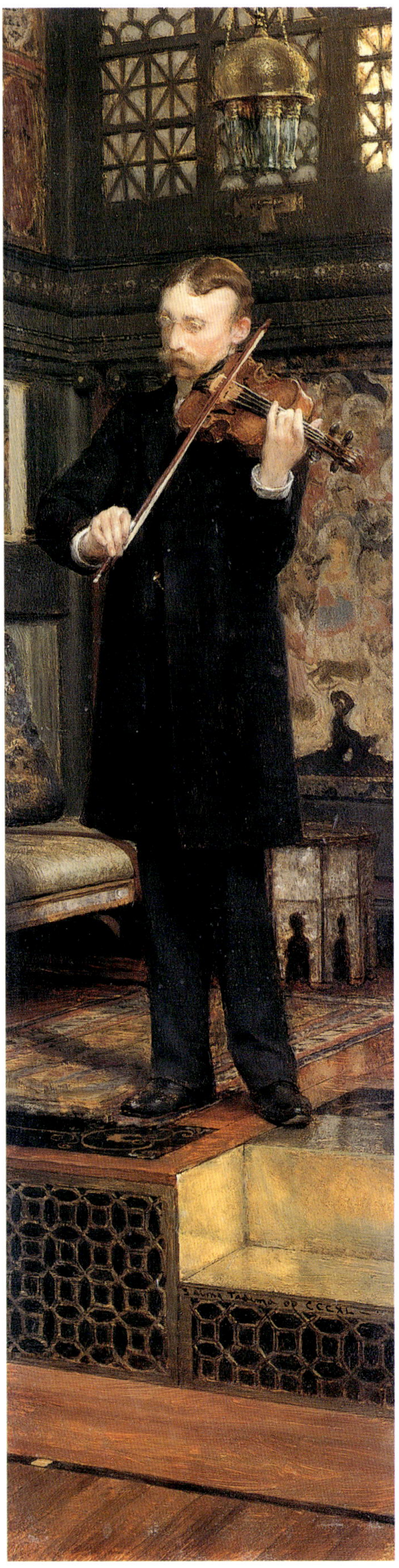

Muses associated with the arts, each encircled by flower wreaths.[219] The inside of the keyboard cover is decorated with a signed painting by Edward Poynter of a garden peristyle in which celebrants dance in a circle. Poynter painted a larger version of the subject which was exhibited at the Royal Academy in 1894, entitled *Horae Serenae*.[220] The piano was accompanied by two stools, once again elaborately inlaid and with columnar legs based on Pompeian examples.

Ceiling decoration was by Leighton with paintings of the Muses showing Melpomene and Thalia; between them is seated Mnemosyne, mother of the Muses. Also shown are a bacchante and faun and a female personification of the poetry of love crowned with irises. Edward Onslow Ford executed in bronze Alma-Tadema's design for a pair of andirons and fenders, based on the herm of a satyr playing the flute in the Archaeological Museum, Naples. Actual Greek vases, antique busts and copies of bronzes adorned the room.

Two paintings by Alma-Tadema, *Amo Te, Ama Me* (1881) and *A Reading from Homer* (Pl.124), were hung in prominent positions in the room. *Amo Te, Ama Me* is a courtship scene of two lovers on a marble terrace overlooking the sea. The sentimental title (love me, as I love you) derives from Carel Vosmaer's novel, *The Amazon* (1880) in which the words are inscribed on a ring which Aisma (a Dutch artist based on Alma-Tadema himself) gives to his love, Marciana. *A Reading from Homer* is one of Alma-Tadema's few 'Greek' subjects. However, given its setting on a familiar marble terrace overlooking the sea and the diversity of the audience listening to the recitation, nothing in the setting identifies it as Greek except for the inscription in the top right of the canvas – OMHP – four Greek capital letters whimsically cut off to read 'Homer' rather than the Greek name, 'Homeros'. The tambourine and lyre may well refer to the placement of the picture in a music room.

The usual nineteenth-century representation of the world of Homer was either in the form of an illustration of the *Iliad* or *Odyssey* or a portrayal of the poet himself as a noble and dignified old man. Here, as in *Phidias Showing the Frieze of the Parthenon to his Friends*, the artist attempts to bring some tangibility to one of the most highly regarded and seemingly distant aspects of antiquity. Nonetheless, some critics objected to such treatment. Claude Phillips of the *Academy* complained that the faces were of a 'low order' and asked: 'not so, surely, looked Greeks, even when fallen from their high estate, as they listened to the soul-stirring verses of their revered bard!'[221]

A preparatory pencil sketch for this painting (Pl.125) was rejected by Henry Marquand and was finally used as the basis for *Love's Votaries*, six years later.[222] Alma-Tadema replaced the all-female group found in the sketch with a male reader and almost exclusively male audience. Perhaps Marquand considered Homer too 'manly' a subject to be interpreted in terms of languorous females.

Alma-Tadema continued to work as an interior designer when in 1890 a Decoration Sub-Committee was formed of himself, Poynter and the businessman Arthur Lucas to redecorate the interior of the Athenaeum Club in London. The work was completed in 1893. Much of the decoration no longer survives, but plans of the decorative scheme illustrate variegated marble cladding, gilded capitals and mosaic floors, much as seen in Alma-Tadema's own paintings.[223]

Meanwhile Casa Tadema, now refurbished and lavishly decorated, was set up as a showpiece which brought much publicity and allowed the artist to entertain in style. The grand piano – played by many illustrious guests – was housed in the studio, which was a public space as much as a work place. The raised recess in which the piano stood forms the background for a portrait of violinist, Maurice Sons (Pl.126). A fellow native of Holland, Sons was leader of the Scottish Orchestra from the 1880s and in 1904 became leader of the Queen's Hall Orchestra in London.

One of the regular family guests was the Polish pianist Paderewski, a musical celebrity in 1890s London, whose flamboyant personality and distinctive looks attracted much attention. Burne-Jones wrote to his friend, Lady Horner: 'There's a beautiful fellow in London named Paderewski and I want to have a face like him, and look like him and can't ... He looks so like Swinburne looked at twenty that I could cry over past things, and the pretty ways of him ... and a face like Sir Galahad, and the Archangel Gabriel.'[224] With his shock of red hair and delicate features, Paderewski was a distinctive presence who did indeed resemble the young Swinburne. He was sketched by Burne-Jones, sculpted by Alfred Gilbert and painted by Alma-Tadema (Pl.127). When Queen Victoria's daughter, Princess Louise, Duchess of Argyll, learned that Alma-Tadema was to paint the pianist's portrait, she asked to be allowed to paint him too. Eventually Paderewski sat in Alma-Tadema's studio for the artist and the Duchess of Argyll, as well as for Alma-Tadema's wife and daughter, Anna. The family's social circle was wide and included bohemian groups of artists, writers and musicians as well as society figures and members of the aristocracy.

Joseph Comyns Carr remembered the Tuesday receptions at both Townshend House and Grove End Road, which brought together around thirty

126 opposite
Portrait of Maurice Sons, 1896
Oil on canvas, 50·8 × 12·7 cm (20 × 5 in)
Private collection

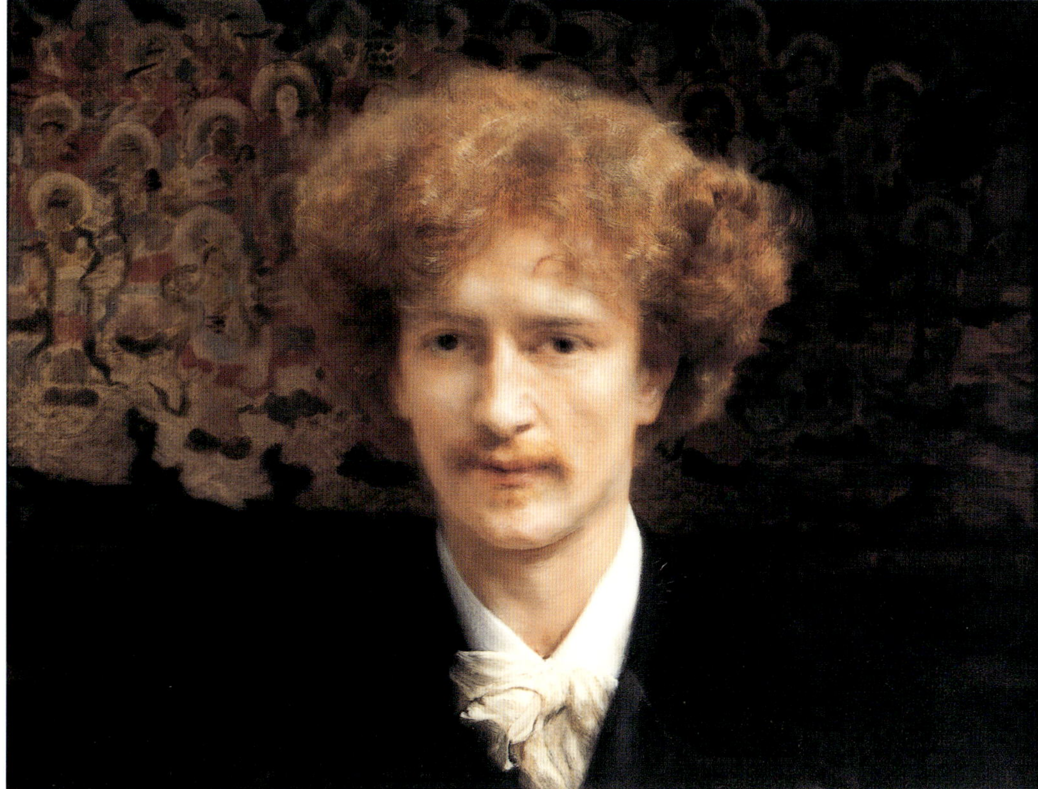

127
Portrait of Ignacy Jan Paderewski, 1891
Oil on canvas, 45·7 × 58·4 cm (18 × 23 in)
National Museum, Warsaw

people and included 'an excellent supper' and music. He was struck by the ease and informality with which the host treated his guests. Alma-Tadema's birthday parties were especially lively, and Carr recalled that one year someone gave him a clockwork tiger:

> Tadema was absolutely fascinated by the antics of this mimic beast, remaining under the spell of its enchantment during the whole of the evening, and whenever a pause in the music permitted it, I could hear the whirr of the wheels of the clock as the delighted owner of this new plaything prepared to start it again upon an excursion round the room.[225]

Despite anecdotes of a humorous man preoccupied with childish pleasures, Alma-Tadema's character is defined by his keen business sense. He is recorded as saying (in his inimitable broken English): 'So long I paint my picture, I work 'ard, I work slow to get 'im right. If 'e is not right, I paint 'im out, once, twice. But when 'e is finished, I am not an artist no more. I am a tradesman.'[226]

Little sense of the personality of Laura Alma-Tadema emerges from anecdotes relating to social activities in Grove End Road, and little is recorded about her life or her relationship with her husband. The fact that she was married to a public figure with such a strong character, as well as a striking artistic presence, ensured that Laura, like her predecessor, Pauline, remains a shadowy figure as far as personal reminiscences of the period are concerned. One revealing glimpse is to be found in her attitude to the suffrage movement. In 1889 the *Nineteenth Century* published a statement entitled 'An Appeal against Female Suffrage', which was signed by a number of prominent women, including 'Mrs Alma-Tadema'. Despite her twofold identity as working artist as well as artist's wife, Laura is seen here to ally herself publicly with traditional female roles. Something of this attitude, perhaps, is reflected in her paintings, in which women are invariably depicted in a domestic space.

Alma-Tadema, meanwhile, ventured to establish a public persona defined by wealth, taste and celebrity. His well-publicized show house did much to enhance such a profile. Casa Tadema, moreover, also had an effect on his working practice. Sun-lit outdoor scenes of glistening marble and bright sea and sky, favoured from the 1880s, were accomplished with the help of the studio's aluminium dome. The interior of the house was designed to produce a series of vistas, several of which looked towards the onyx screen from Townshend House. Many paintings from the 1890s onwards show not only a Mediterranean coastline but spectacular vistas and daring perspective, perhaps influenced by the space and vantage points of the house.

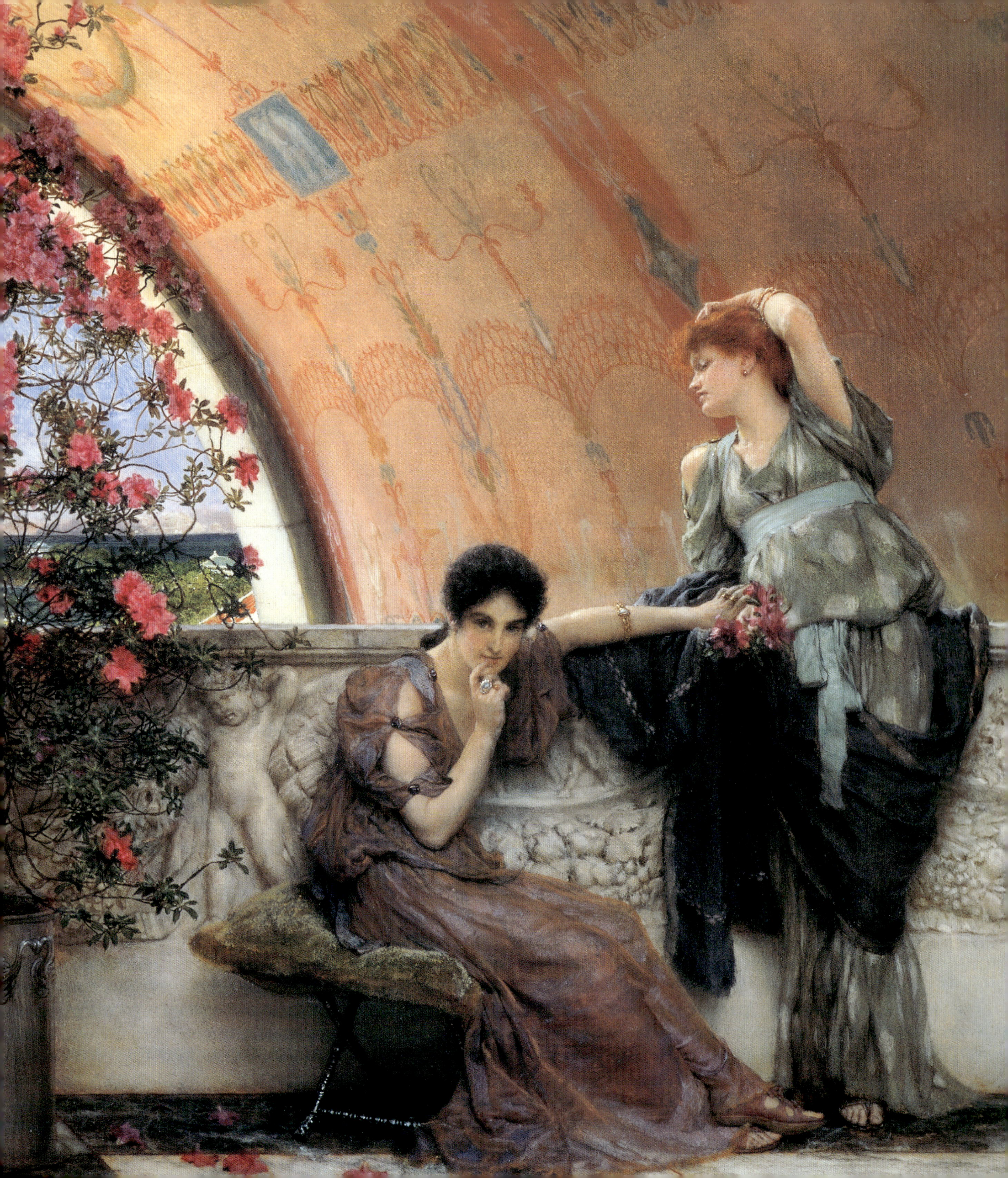

1887–1912
FINAL HONOURS AND THE END OF A CAREER

III/1

VIEWS OF ANTIQUITY

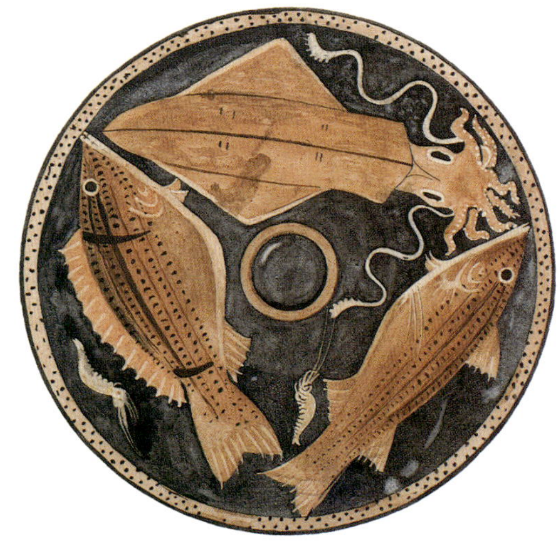

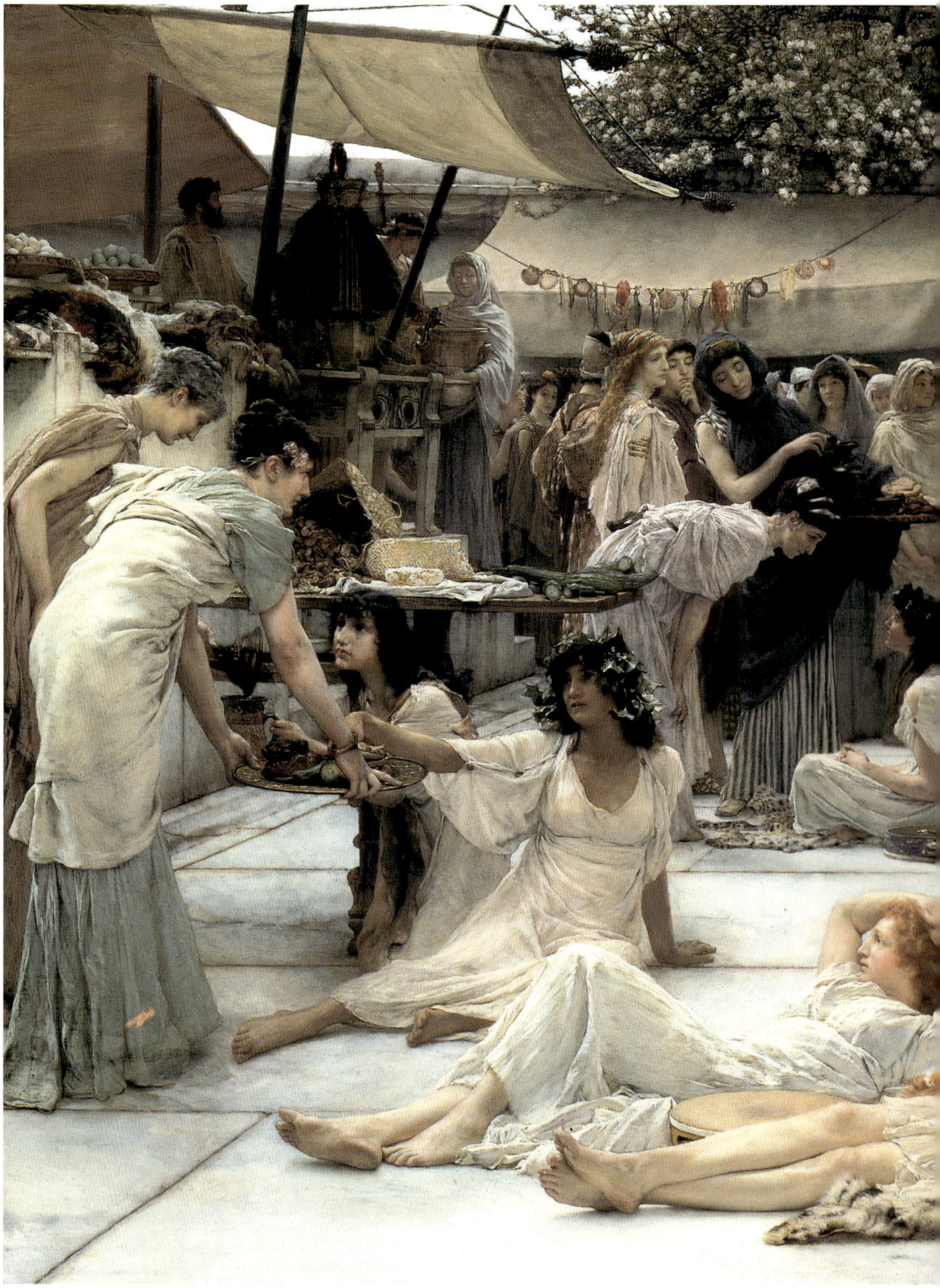

128 previous page
Unconscious Rivals (detail of Pl.146)

129
Sicilian Fish-Plate, 1880s
Watercolour, 25.4 × 35.5 cm (10 × 14 in):
University of Birmingham

130 right
The Women of Amphissa, 1887
Oil on canvas, 121·8 × 182·8 cm (48 × 72 in)
Sterling and Francine Clark Institute, Williamstown MA

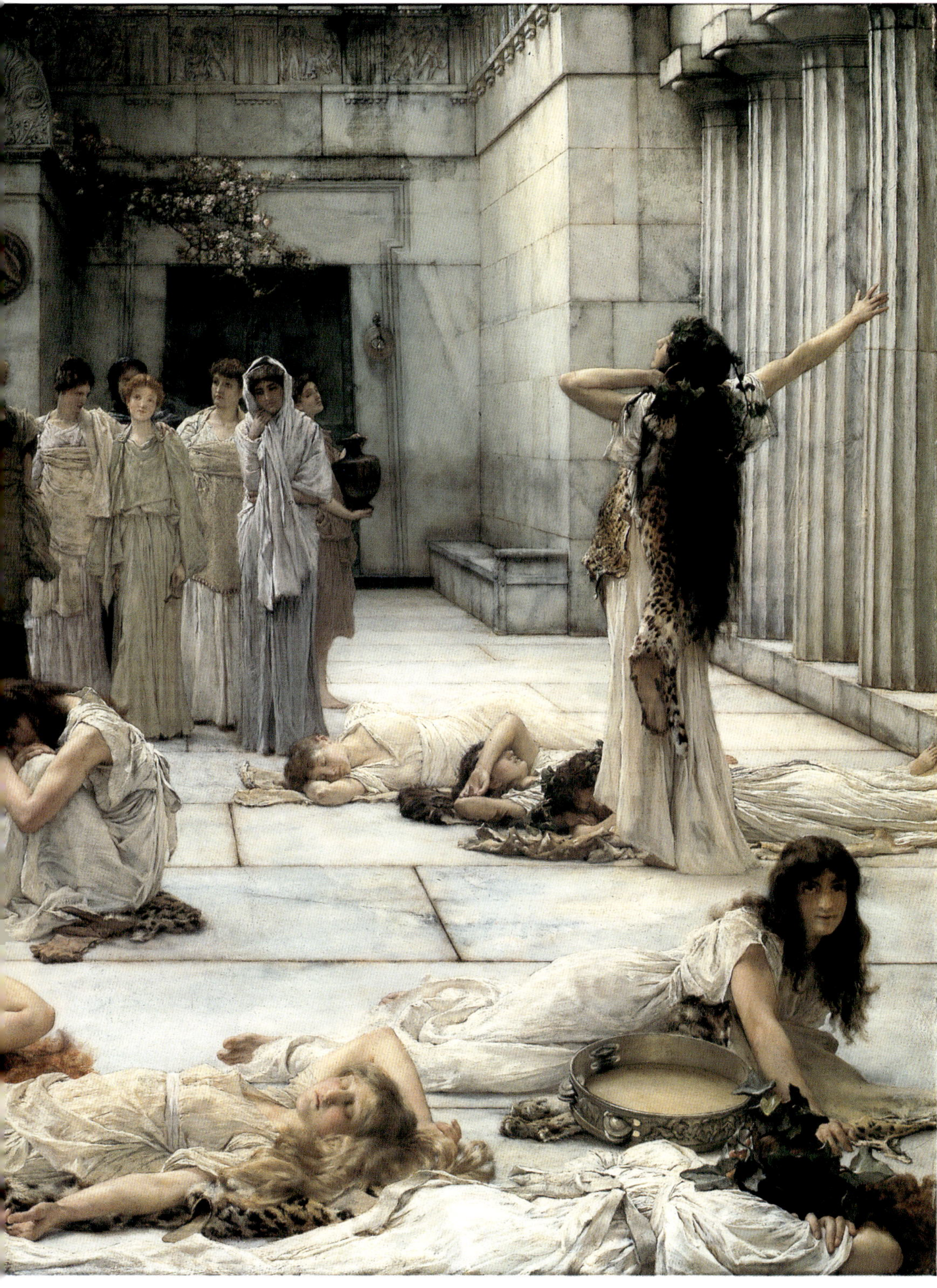

1887 marked Queen Victoria's fiftieth year on the throne. Alma-Tadema's work shown at Jubilee exhibitions commemorating the event included thirteen oil paintings at the Royal Manchester Institution's Jubilee Exhibition and two watercolours at the Royal Society of Painters in Water-Colours. In the same year Charles Hallé and Joseph Comyns Carr left the Grosvenor Gallery to open the New Gallery. Although Alma-Tadema continued to exhibit at the Grosvenor until its closure in 1890, he had no difficulty in extending his allegiance and participated in the New Gallery's opening in May with five works.[227] He exhibited works at the New Gallery for twelve years and also served on its consultative committee, but still continued to reserve large subject pictures for the Academy.

The painting shown at the Academy that year was Alma-Tadema's last major Greek subject, a large canvas entitled *The Women of Amphissa* (Pl.130). The scene depicted purports to be set in northern Greece during the fourth century BC. The source is Plutarch's *Moralia* (249–50), which was quoted without ascription in the Royal Academy exhibition catalogue:

> During the holy war that followed the taking of Delphi by the Phocians, it chanced that the Thyades, women sacred to Dionysos, were seized with religious frenzy, and, wandering aimlessly, came at night to the city of Amphissa, which was in league with Phocis, and their enemy. But, being weary, and unconscious of danger, they lay down in the market-place and slept. When the wives of Amphissa heard this, they hastened to the spot, fearing lest the Thyades should suffer insult or injury; and standing round the sleepers, waited till they had awakened, then tended them and gave them food. After which, having asked leave of their husbands, they led the wanderers from the city, safe unto the boundaries of their own land.

Plutarch's story is part of a series primarily concerned to demonstrate the bravery of women. But though the painting's title suggests that Alma-Tadema also intends to present a study of female compassion and courage, it is not the women of Amphissa but the more striking *thyades* or maenads who engage the viewer's attention. Unlike the heavily draped townswomen

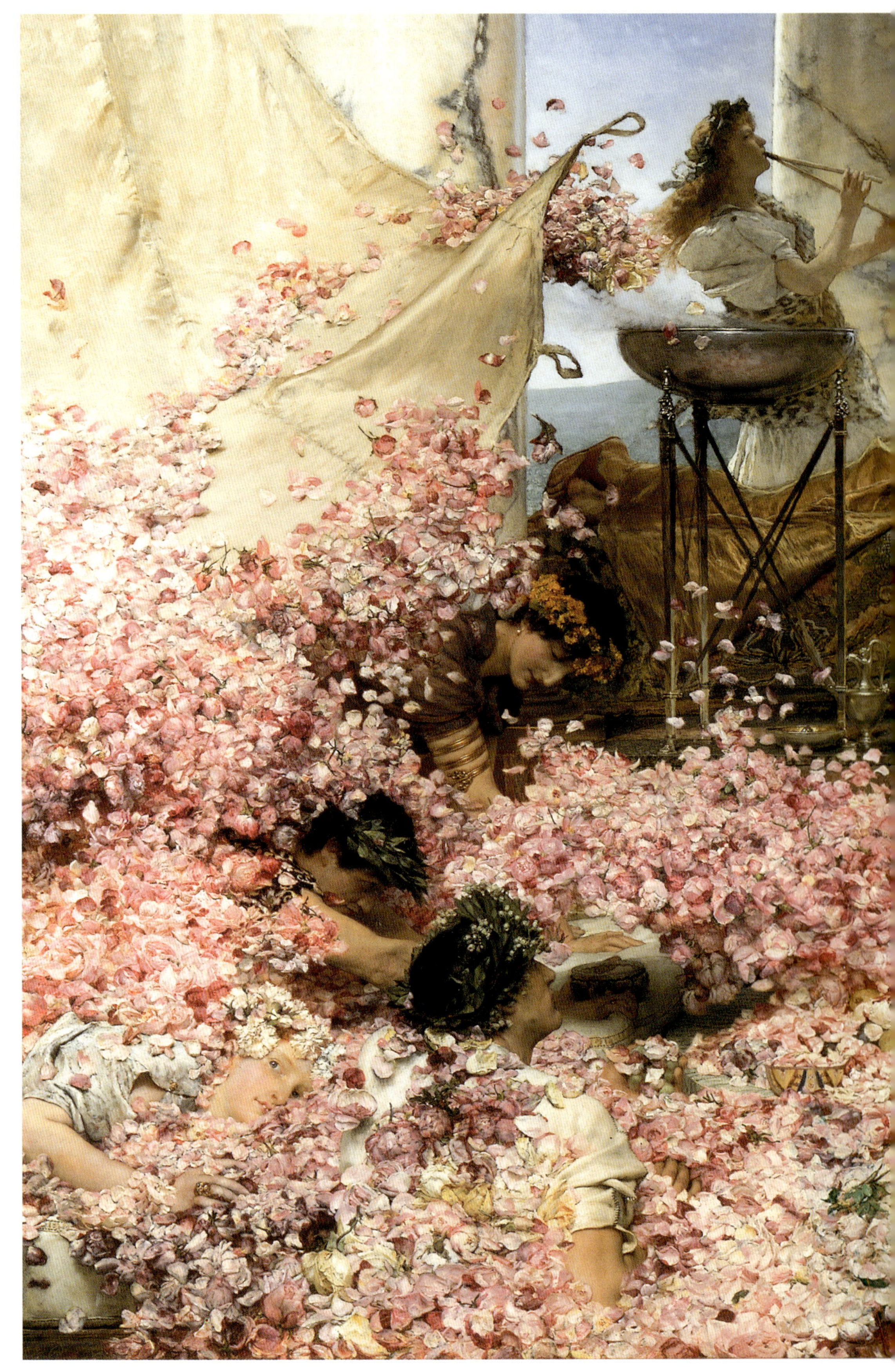

131
The Roses of Heliogabalus, 1888
Oil on canvas, 132·1 × 213·9 cm (52 × 84¼ in)
Private collection

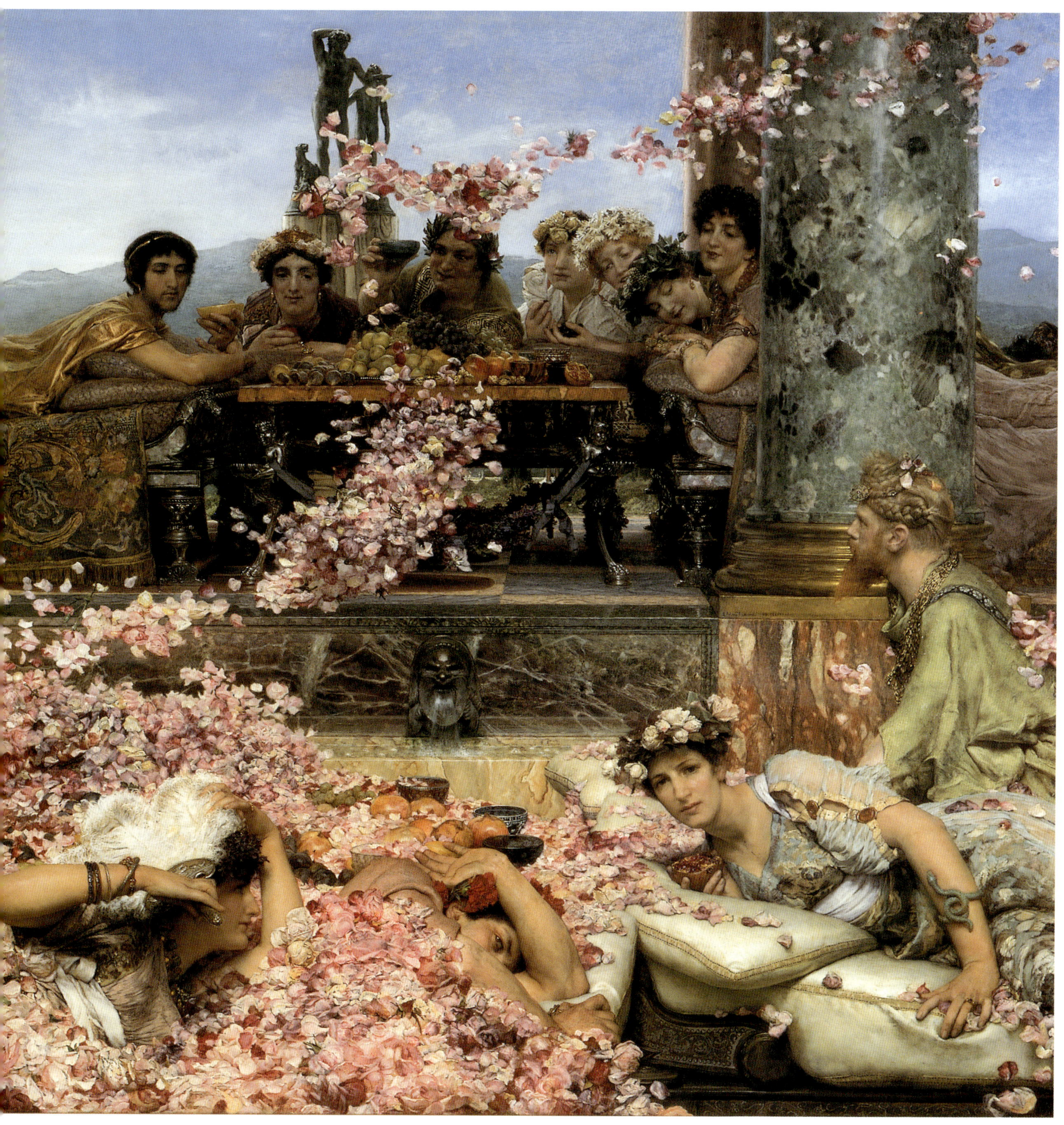

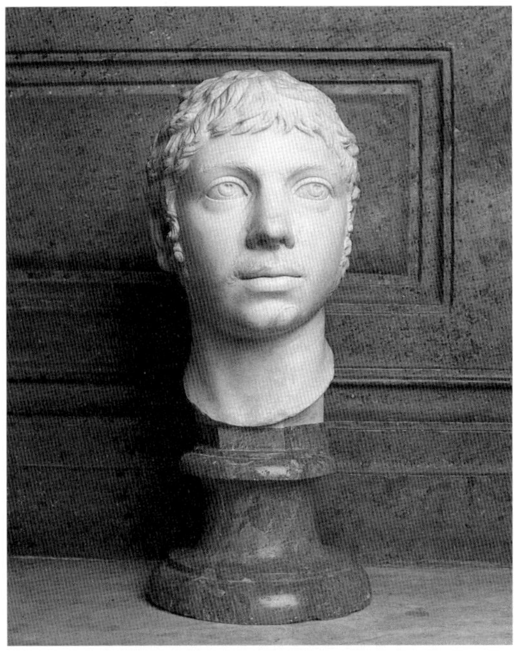

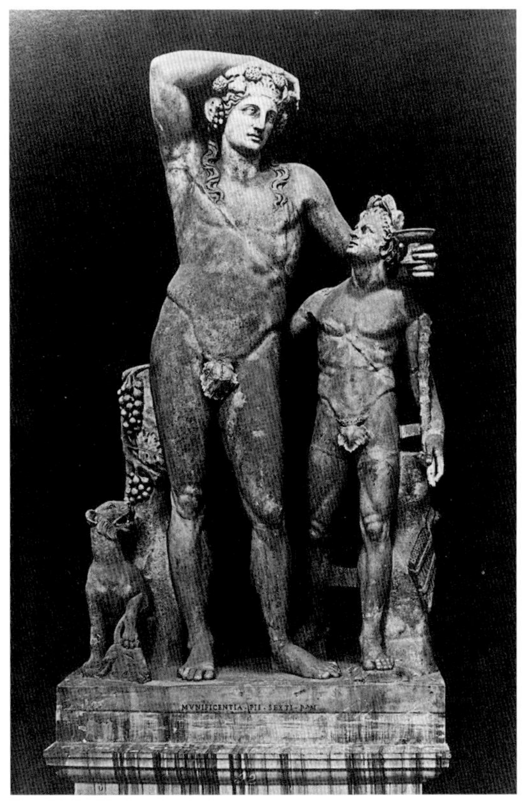

132 far left
Portrait Bust of Heliogabalus, Roman, 3rd century AD
Capitoline Museum, Rome

133 left
Bacchus and Ampelus, Roman
Marble, Vatican Museum, Rome:
University of Birmingham

134
In a Rose Garden, 1889
Oil on canvas, 37·5 × 49·5 cm (14¾ × 19½ in)
Private collection

135 far right
The back drawing room, 14 Hyde Park Terrace, London,
residence of Mr (later Sir) John Aird
Art Journal, May 1891, p.138

on the periphery, the maenads slowly awakening after the night's revel lie centre stage, in abandoned positions, their hair loose, their clothing in disarray. The sleeping maenads evoke earlier paintings, *Exhausted Maenides*, *After the Dance*, and *Tepidarium*,[228] in which sleeping or reclining nudes exude a powerful eroticism.

Stalls laden with refreshments – eggs, poultry, wine, honeycombs and cucumbers – stand in the corner of the market place. The market place itself is equipped with an array of classical accessories while archaeological details are drawn from a variety of sources including, appropriately, the fourth-century Greek world. Artefacts are combined ingeniously to produce novel, even whimsical, effects, albeit in pursuance of the theme of the painting. A fourth-century funeral stele is used as a column capital. Below the capital hangs a fourth-century Sicilian fish-plate, outdoors and near a string of real fish. The artist produced a number of watercolour studies of ancient fish-plates (Pl.129). The maenads sport their usual ivy wreaths, animal skins and *tympana*. *Thyrsoi*, although usually carried by maenads, here support an awning covering the food. Architectural detail includes metopes copied from the temple of Hera at Selinus in Sicily, discovered in 1877. They depict Heracles fighting the Amazons, and Actaeon attacked by his own hounds for spying on Artemis bathing. The metopes not only illustrate the artist's knowledge of recent archaeological discoveries but are especially significant in this setting as both myths portray female subjects, who, like the maenads, are outside the traditional perimeters of society. The painting was to win the Medal of Honour at the Paris Exposition Universelle two years later.

The 1888 Academy exhibition showed what was to become one of Alma-Tadema's best-known works, *The Roses of Heliogabalus* (Pl.131).[229] The short reign of the young Roman Emperor, Marcus Aurelius Antoninus, better known as Elagabalus or Heliogabalus, is documented by several late-antique historians, including the *Scriptores Historiae Augustae* ('Writers of Augustan History'), from which Alma-Tadema has selected the following episode:

> In a banqueting-room with a reversible ceiling he once overwhelmed his parasites with violets and other flowers, so that some of them were actually smothered to death being unable to crawl out to the top.[230]

Although Alma-Tadema may not have expected his audience to be familiar with the text,[231] he would have been certain that they would have a notion of Heliogabalus as a mad, lurid and excessive tyrant. This popular nineteenth-century view of the young Emperor, was, however, largely based on the responses of scholars and writers to the catalogue of scandals – political corruption, cruelty, licentiousness and extravagance – contained in the *Scriptores Historiae Augustae*, a largely anecdotal and sensational text. The overall impression of his inglorious reign was sufficiently enshrined in the popular consciousness for Heliogabalus to have found his way into Gilbert and Sullivan's *The Pirates of Penzance*.[232] In asserting that he is 'the very model of a modern Major-General', the General can claim: 'I quote in elegiacs all the crimes of Heliogabalus.'[233]

A complementary notion of Heliogabalus, as consummate voluptuary, was acknowledged from the mid-nineteenth century by writers across Europe. We have already seen how Gautier looked back regretfully to the reigns of rulers Sardanapalus, Teglath Phalazar, Cleopatra and Heliogabalus.[234] J. K. Huysmans describes the young Emperor in the most appealing terms: 'treading in silver dust and sand of gold, his head crowned with a tiara and his clothes studded with jewels'.[235] Indeed, Alma-Tadema's Heliogabalus, reclining on a couch towards the centre of the painting, could easily have emerged from the pages of Huysmans's *Against Nature*. He appears to be suffering from that nineteenth-century malady – *ennui* – and like Huysmans's hero, Des Esseintes, he seeks to alleviate his boredom with the most extreme of diversions.

Alma-Tadema depicts the emperor as a young man with delicate features, large eyes and a slight moustache. This face is not imaginary, but based on the only securely identified portrait of Heliogabalus in the Capitoline Museum, Rome (Pl.132).

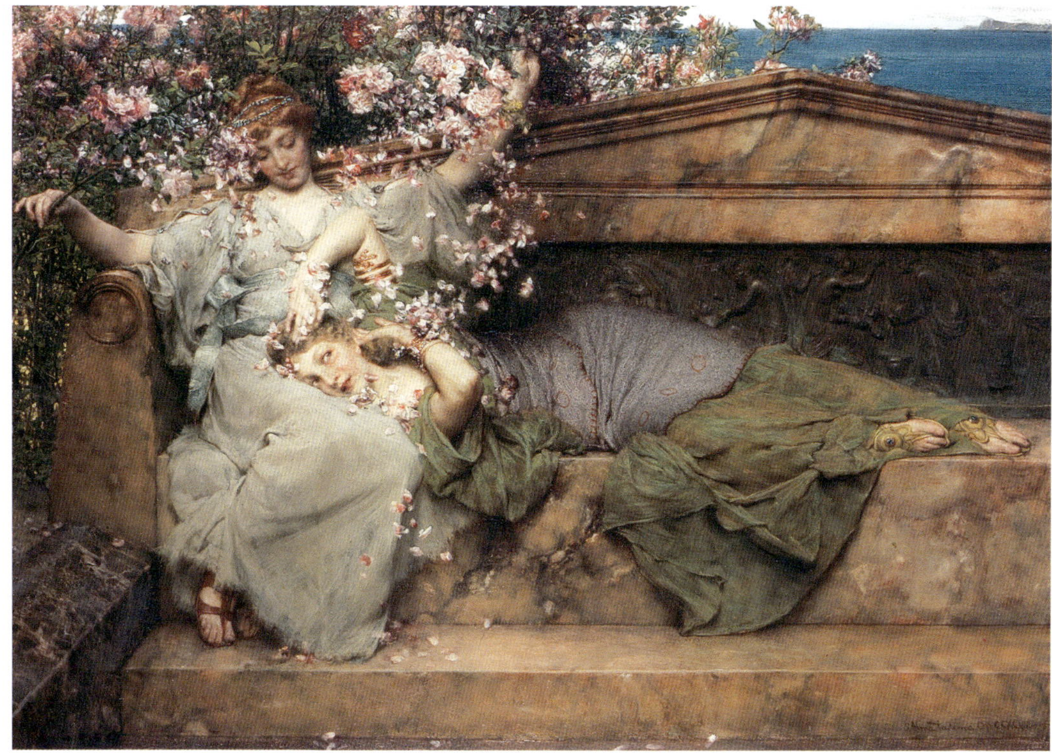

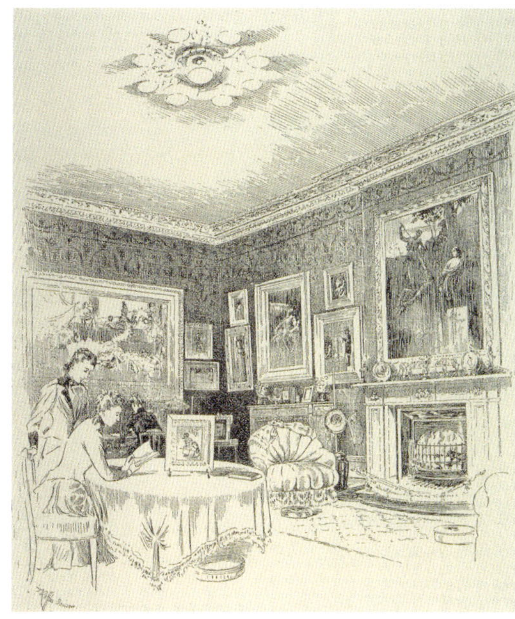

Oscar Wilde, in a letter from Italy to the publisher Leonard Smithers, even describes this very same portrait bust in terms of fin-de-siècle fashions of youthful beauty:

> I saw the other day in the museum here the bust of a young man of grave, somewhat severe beauty, and the most delicate refinement of type, rather like a young Oxonian of a very charming kind, the expression of pride and *ennui*. On referring to the catalogue I found that it was the Emperor *Heliogabalus*; it was most curious and has filled me with a desire to write his life.[236]

The voluptuous atmosphere of Alma-Tadema's painting draws on the same notion of Heliogabalus as found in Gautier, Huysmans and Wilde. At the same time he imitates details from his Latin textual source. Like the Heliogabalus of the *Scriptores Historiae Augustae*, Alma-Tadema's emperor wears a tunic of silk and gold thread and adorns himself with jewels and a diadem. Following the text, dining couches are inlaid with silver and mother-of-pearl and the palace embellished with expensive variegated marbles of red porphyry and green Laconian marble. Other details are based on archaeological artefacts and, as usual, Alma-Tadema's use of archaeology is not arbitrary, but instead contributes some meaning to the scene. In the background stands a bronze statue of Bacchus, faun and panther, copied from an actual marble group in the Vatican Museum and included in Alma-Tadema's photographic collection (Pl.133). While a Bacchic motif is appropriate to a scene of revelry, the statue can also be identified as Bacchus and Ampelus, the god and his youthful lover, and here surely alludes to homosexual pleasures favoured by the Emperor. The abundance of rich accessories also serves to distance the potentially horrifying subject, so much so that we have to remind ourselves that the emperor is, after all, murdering his guests.

Significantly, Alma-Tadema deviates from the *Scriptores Historiae Augustae* in one crucial detail. Rather than 'violets and other flowers', it is only roses that now fall from a silken canopy. In terms of Victorian flower imagery, roses are most commonly associated with beauty and with sensuous love. Later in the century, the rose appears, perfumed with more than a hint of decadence. The opening sentence of Oscar Wilde's *The Picture of Dorian Gray* begins: 'The studio was filled with the rich odour of roses.'

In the ancient world, roses likewise appear as emblems of love, but they also carry with them a distinctive aura of imperial excess. It was Athenaeus' Cleopatra who once gave a banquet at which the guests were knee-deep in rose petals,[237] Suetonius' Nero who once demanded that a courtier spend over four million sesterces on roses for a dinner party in his honour,[238] and Tacitus' Vitellius who visited a grizzly battlefield after his path was strewn with rose petals.[239] Intensely aware of the resonances of roses (both ancient and modern), Alma-Tadema has used them to displace the 'violets and other flowers', and thereby he has, in effect, outdone his source in subverting the official face of Rome. The following year, *In a Rose Garden* (Pl.134), once again by way of showing the rich at their leisure, depicts a cascade of rose petals, yet instead of a mad emperor suffocating his dinner guests, one woman shakes the petals of a rose bush down on her delighted companion.

Contemporary critics who discussed *The Roses of Heliogabalus* were ambivalent about its lack of moral content: they greatly admired execution and detail, but were less than reconciled to the sumptuous treatment of its cruel subject.[240] The Victorian public were invited to enjoy the same corrupt Rome in historical novels and toga plays,[241] but both novelists and playwrights were assiduous in cultivating a moral agenda whereby 'good' characters (often Christians) were set up to be admired and 'bad' characters (often Roman emperors) to be abhorred. Alma-Tadema abstains from such moralizing and, instead, simply invites his audience to enjoy the show.

The Roses of Heliogabalus was commissioned by the wealthy engineer, Mr (later Sir) John Aird, for the large sum of £4,000. J. F. Boyes, in an article on Aird's collection for the *Art Journal* of 1891, writes that it was considered the collection's prize picture.[242] An illustration in the same article shows the painting hanging in Aird's back

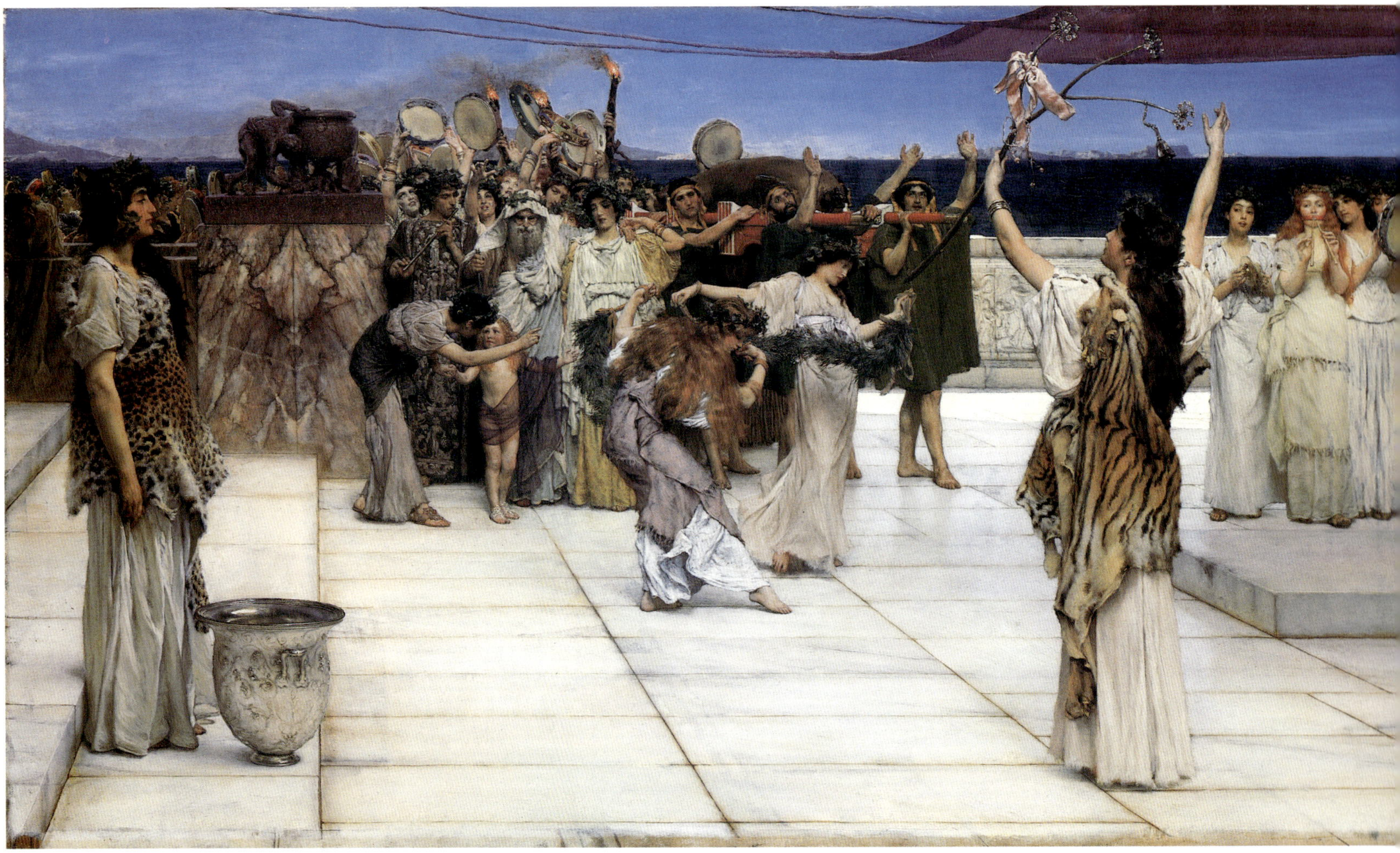

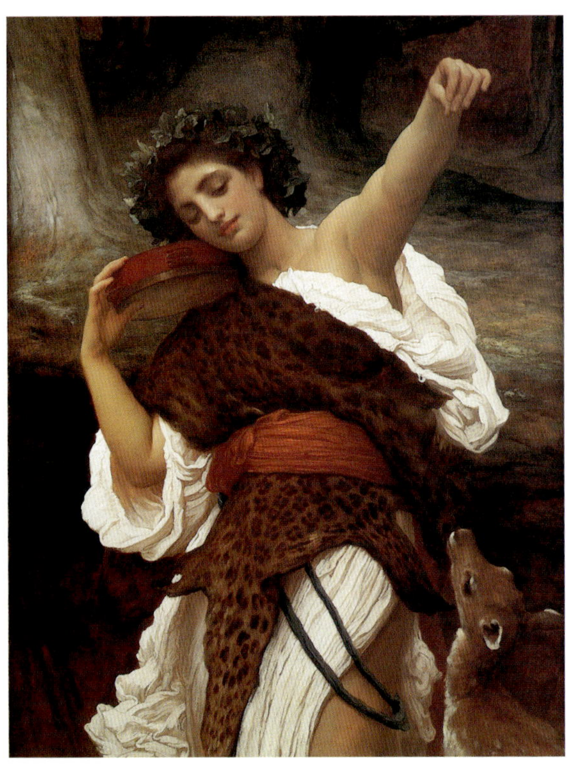

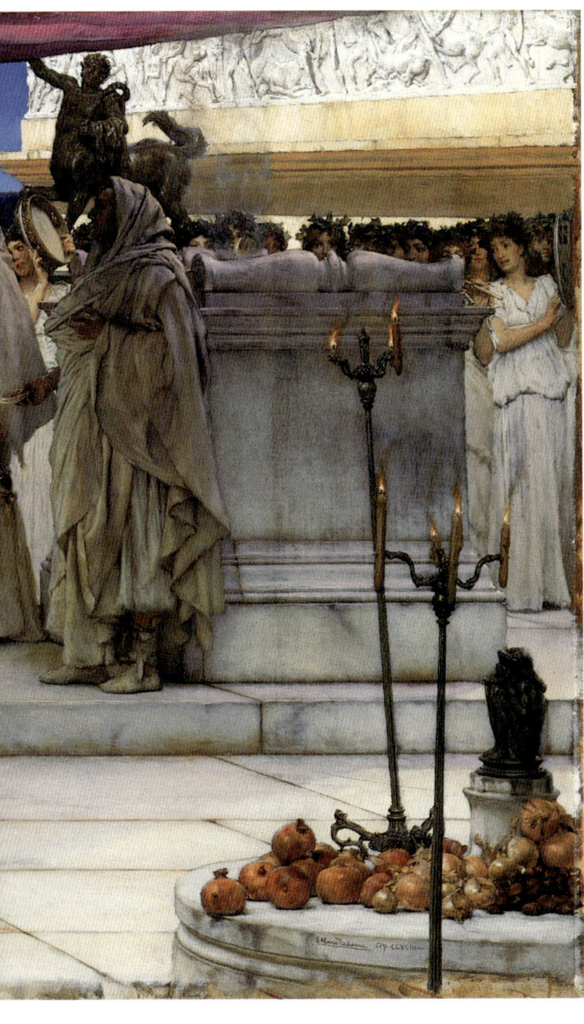

drawing room behind Mrs Aird and two of her daughters (Pl.135). Sublimely incongruous in its domestic setting, Aird's display of *The Roses* raises the question of how he and his family viewed the painting. Frank Dicksee's *Chivalry* was also hung in Aird's back drawing room, a painting described by Boyes as a 'distressed maiden ... bound to a tree, from which she is about to be delivered by an armed knight.'[243] Today's audience reacts to *Chivalry* with unease: it is a picture founded on gender stereotypes which invites the viewer to take a sado-erotic pleasure in the image of a bound woman. The Aird family probably raised no such objections. And similarly, what today can be read as both a complicated construction of Roman history and an amoral revel in Roman decadence may well have been appreciated by its owner, first and foremost, as a splendid illustration of artistic technique.

A perfectionist, Alma-Tadema is known to have made alterations to paintings on the eve of exhibition and even after a work had already found a buyer. *The Roses of Heliogabalus* was completed on Varnishing Day, 'while the picture was hanging on the wall, and the artist, pipe in mouth, and without model or study of any kind, was keeping up a lively conversation with a little ring of men around him.'[244] G. D. Leslie recalls that it was not uncommon for Alma-Tadema to retouch a picture on Varnishing Day at the Royal Academy:

> By permission of the council he would have the one on which he wished to work taken to the empty classroom, which was used for the Life School in the evenings. There seated comfortably with the picture on an easel before him, with a big cigar in his mouth, and a number of sketches and studies around him, he did wonderful work on it, even at times making extensive alterations with extraordinary swiftness and dexterity. He always joined the others, however, at the four o'clock tea, when he immediately became one of the most lively and amusing of the lighter-hearted set.[245]

Although many painters made adjustments on Varnishing Day, these anecdotes provide ample evidence of the ease and informality, combined with consummate professionalism, with which Alma-Tadema approached his working practice.

Another major painting, *A Dedication to Bacchus* (Pl.136), was exhibited the following year. An exhibition at the Lefèvre Gallery, London was dedicated solely to this large picture, which was commissioned for the collection of Baron Schröder as a companion piece to *The Vintage Festival*.[246] The occasion is the initiation of a Roman child into the cult of Bacchus. Sunlight shines through a canopy, casting a violet shadow on the solemn figures of a veiled priest and priestess who await the child in front of a marble altar. Beside them a group of musicians play the cymbals, *tibia* and *tympana*. To the left of the altar the child waits with a crowd of worshippers including four men carrying a huge wineskin to be offered as a libation to the god. F. G. Stephens, in a pamphlet accompanying the painting's exhibition, stresses that *A Dedication to Bacchus* has no connection with what he calls 'the beastly orgies' described in Livy's account of the Bacchanalian scandal in 186 BC.[247] In the initiation scene religiosity is certainly more apparent than Bacchanalian fervour. However, as if disposed to try to sanitize the subject, Stephens has chosen to ignore the crowd of ivy-wreathed celebrants waving *tympana* cut off at the edge of the canvas. As in *The Vintage Festival*, the behaviour of these background figures indicates the wild revelry described by Livy and suggests that beyond the immediate scene a more riotous Bacchanalia is being enjoyed.

A bacchant dressed in a leopard skin stands by a silver *crater*, used for mixing the dedicatory wine with water, based on a famous piece from the Hildesheim treasure, discovered in 1868. Another bacchant in a tiger skin waves a branch decorated with silver flowers, a bell and ribbon. The setting is the peristyle of a temple overlooking the sea. A frieze in the upper right corner, depicting the battle between Lapiths and centaurs, is copied from the frieze of the fifth-century BC temple of Apollo at Bassae (acquired by the British Museum in 1818). Below the frieze stands another centaur, known through a number of Roman marble copies of a pair of Hellenistic bronze originals. As in *The Sculpture Gallery*, the artist plays with the notion of copies and represents either the Hellenistic original or an imagined bronze Roman copy. Either way, he has managed to eliminate an ugly support at the statue's stomach, an integral part of the marble copies, by obscuring this part of the figure behind the priest's head. In ancient art, centaurs were traditionally depicted in mythological representations as members of Dionysus-Bacchus' *thiasus* (band of followers). Such a *thiasus* of satyrs and bacchants can be glimpsed on the balustrade's frieze.

The porphyry statue on the left of the canvas is of a kneeling man lighting a fire beneath a brazier. Similar ancient sculptural groups exist of fire-lighters preparing a brazier while the sacrificial animal is slaughtered. Along with the battle frieze, this image reminds us of the violent nature of certain aspects of the ancient world. On

136 top
A Dedication to Bacchus, 1889
Oil on canvas, 77·5 × 177·5 cm (30½ × 69⅞ in)
Hamburger Kunsthalle, Hamburg

137
Frederic Leighton, *Bacchante*, c.1892
Oil on canvas, 131·5 × 96·5 cm (51¾ × 38 in)
Forbes Magazine Collection, New York

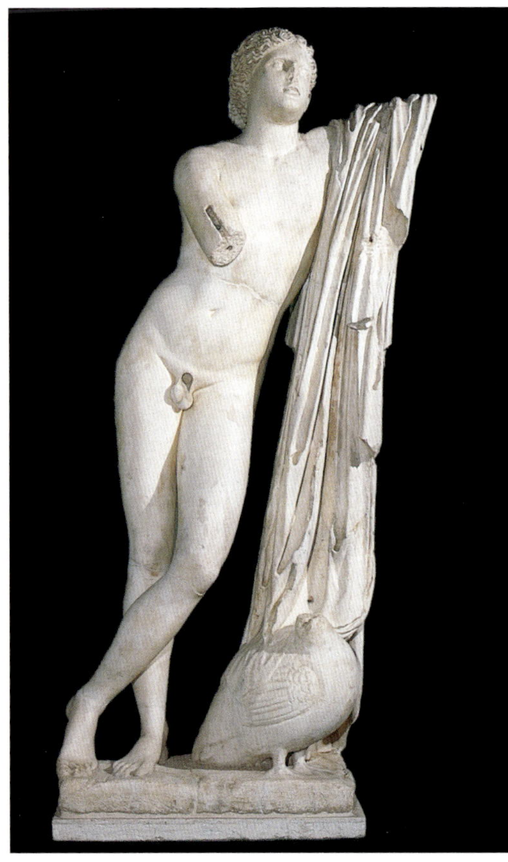

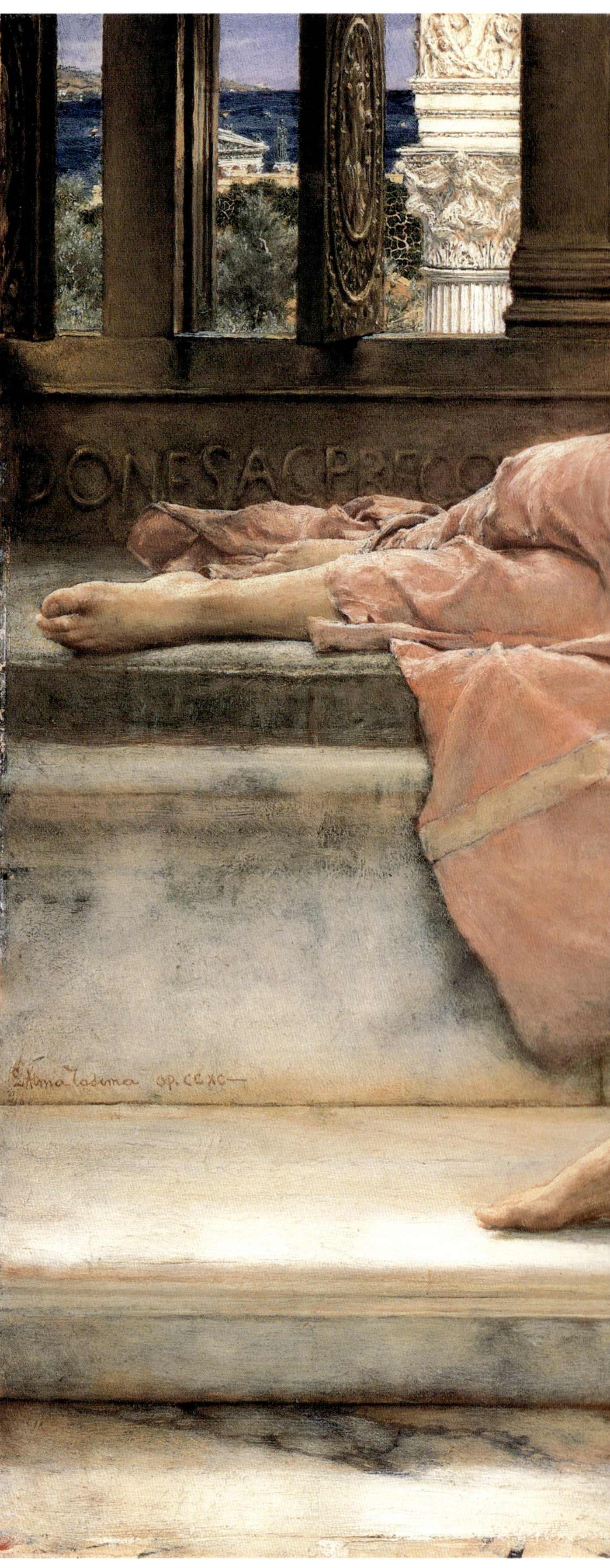

138
Pothos, Roman copy of 4th-century BC Greek original
Marble, H 1·80m
Capitoline Museum, Rome

139 right
A Favourite Poet, 1889
Oil on wood, 36·9 × 49·6 cm (14½ × 19½in)
Lady Lever Art Gallery, Port Sunlight, Liverpool

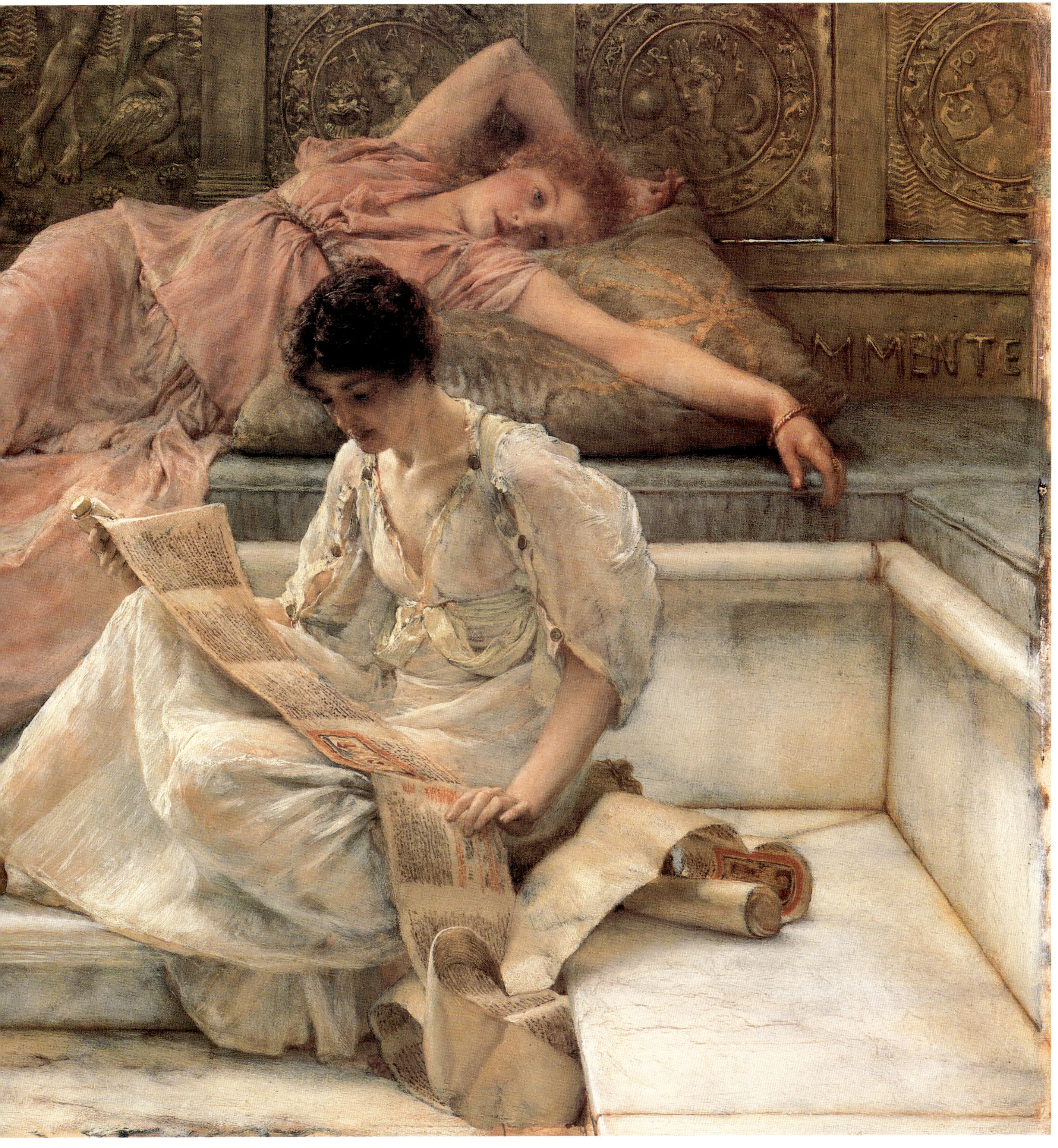
MMENTE

an initial reading *A Dedication to Bacchus* appears as a respectable and ordered representation of ancient religious ritual, but on closer inspection imagery of sexuality, Bacchanalian revelry and cruelty reveals a more violent and orgiastic side of Roman life.

While Alma-Tadema maintains an interest in an unofficial side of Roman life, the hinting here at the wilder nature of Bacchic worship may have been prompted by the owner of the painting. Schröder eventually possessed ten paintings by Alma-Tadema, a number of which were either of Bacchic or bath house subjects, while many other paintings in his collection illustrated more overtly erotic themes including Jean-Léon Gérôme's *Phryne Before the Tribunal* (1861), showing the notorious Greek prostitute displayed nude before a public court.

From ostentatious public processions to modest domestic rites, Alma-Tadema reveals a wide-ranging interest in the rich diversity which constitutes Roman religion. The majority of his religious paintings show Bacchanalia. While Dionysiac-Bacchic subjects were popular with other painters, they rarely involved the irrational or savage face of religious ritual – presented most vividly in Euripides' *Bacchae*, where maenads tear Pentheus' body limb from limb – and British classical-subject painting, on the whole, had little interest in the darker side of ancient myth and religion. Leighton's *Bacchante* (Pl.137) shows a sweet-faced girl who plays the tambourine and clicks her fingers at an inquisitive fawn. Alma-Tadema, like Leighton, presents, on the surface, a sanitized version of the Bacchanalia, but at the same time he also hints at the more savage aspect of ancient myth and ritual. In Continental Europe, Dionysiac paintings are often infused with a wilder and more sexual mood as women, endowed with atavistic desire, frolic with the half-human followers of Dionysus.[248] Even William Bouguereau, best known for his coy nymphs and cupids, represents four nude beauties assaulting a satyr in *Nymphs and Satyr* (1873).

In the same year that *A Dedication to Bacchus* was shown at the Lefèvre Gallery, a very different but equally intriguing work, *A Favourite Poet* (Pl.139), was exhibited at the New Gallery. Set in a sumptuous interior with a glimpse of sea through an open window, *A Favourite Poet* shows a woman reading from a papyrus roll to her reclining companion. As often, one woman has a dark complexion and the other is distinctly fair. Partly obscured behind the reclining figure, a bronze wall panel is inscribed with a short passage from the Roman poet, Horace. It is no surprise that the favourite poet here is Horace: he was perhaps the best-known of all ancient poets in nineteenth-century England.[249] Victorian classicist, W. Y. Sellar, wrote of the *Odes*, 'scarcely any work in any literature has been so widely and so familiarly known';[250] while for Andrew Lang, Horace was 'of mortals the most human, the friend of my friends and of so many generations of men'.[251] Horace was also cited in the works of creative writers of the period. For example, the poet Ernest Dowson uses lines from the *Odes* as titles of two of his poems,[252] while many more Horatian allusions are scattered throughout his works.[253] Alma-Tadema had already completed *A Difficult Line from Horace* (1881), a depiction of a man puzzling over a line of verse, which was even used as the frontispiece for an edition of Horace's works.[254]

For this painter of Roman life, Horace's *Odes* epitomize a light-hearted and carefree urbanity, often associated with some love interest, and played out at a luxurious Rome or a resort on the Bay of Naples. Indeed, even when no inscription or quotation cites a Horatian source, the mood, setting and subject are often sufficient to reveal it. In 1883 the critic of the *Art Journal* proclaimed of the men and women from Alma-Tadema's paintings: 'we name [them] from the *Odes* of Horace.'[255]

The partly obscured inscription in *A Favourite Poet* forms lines 18-19 from *Odes* 1.31. Lines 18-20 run as follows:

> Latoe, dones et, precor, integra
> cum mente, nec turpem senectam
> degere nec cithara carentem.

and translate as:

> Grant, son of Latona, that I may enjoy what I have
> with good health and, I pray, with sound mind,
> and that my old age may not be squalid
> and not without the lyre.[256]

The subject of the ode is the poet's prayer to Apollo on the occasion of Augustus' dedication of the temple of Apollo on the Palatine in 28 BC. Horace asks that he may not be without the lyre – that is, the 'poetry' or joys of love – in his old age. The two beautiful women, one of whom is a reclining figure with flushed cheeks, point us to the erotic pleasures for which the poet hopes, and perhaps the women hope too.[257] Furthermore, one of the wall panels shows the lower legs of a statue; cut-off at the knees and transformed from a marble sculpture to a bronze relief, it is still recognizable as a statue known as *Pothos* or desire (Pl.138).[258] Textual inscription and archaeological detail here have no subversive significance, but instead a softly erotic mood is suggested in the form of the women, which is confirmed, as often, through erudite allusion.

140 top
Love's Votaries, 1891
Oil on canvas, 87·6 × 165·7 cm (34½ × 65¼ in)
Laing Art Gallery, Newcastle-upon-Tyne

141
Albert Moore, *Dreamers*, 1879–82
Oil on canvas, 68·5 × 119·2 cm (27 × 46⅞ in)
Birmingham Museums and Art Gallery

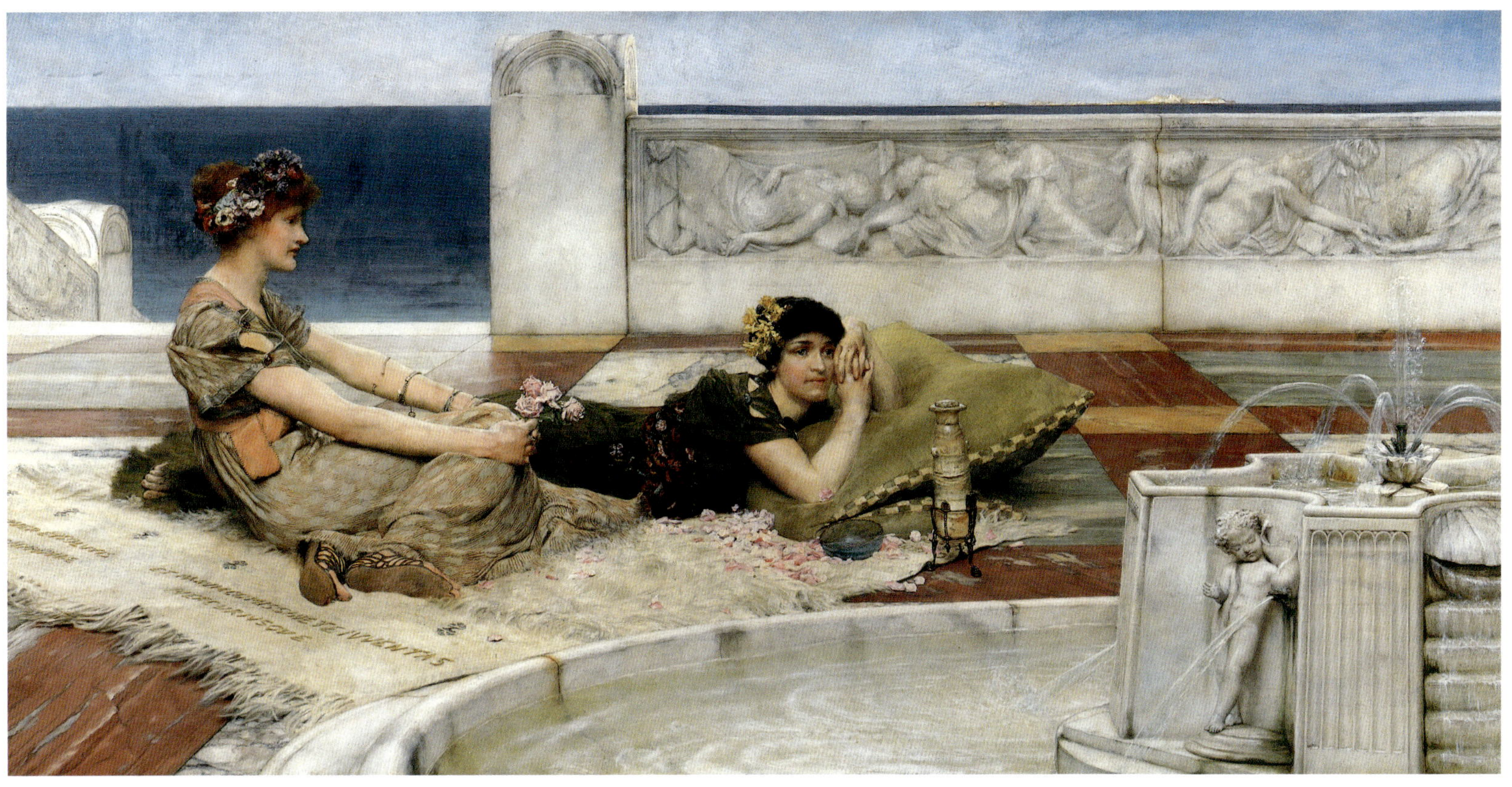

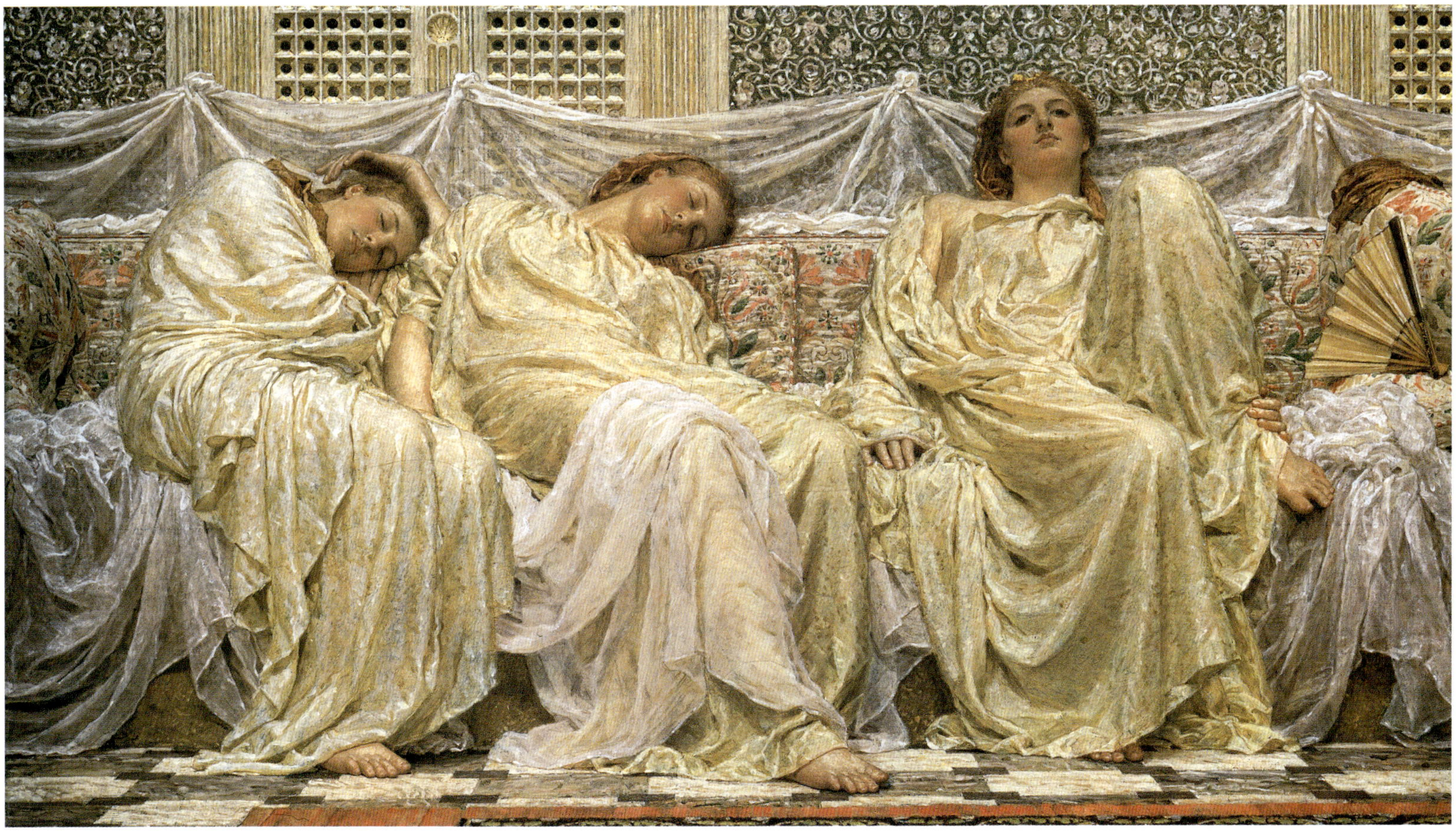

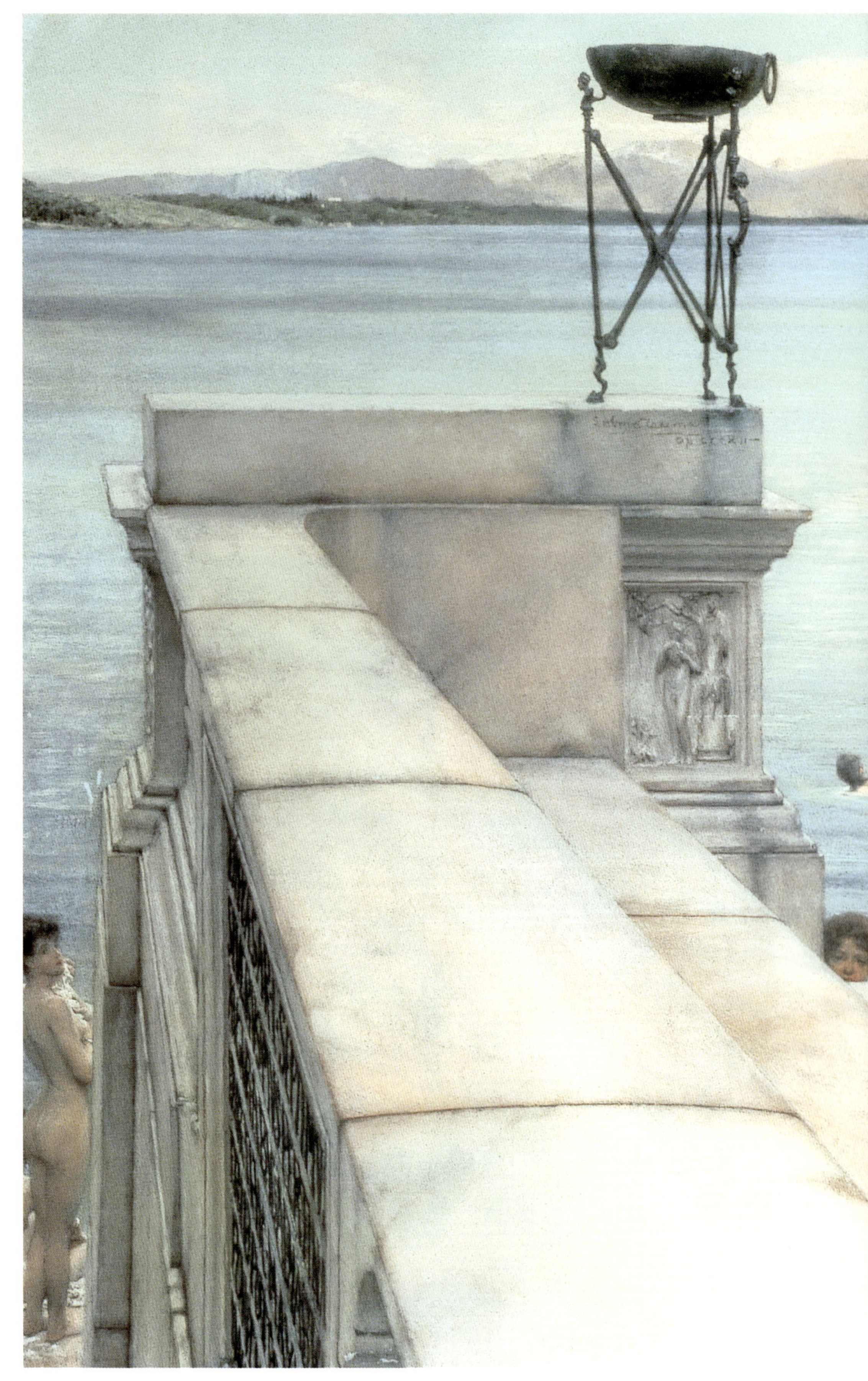

142
The Kiss, 1891
Oil on wood, 45·7 × 62·7 cm (18 × 24⅝ in)
Private collection

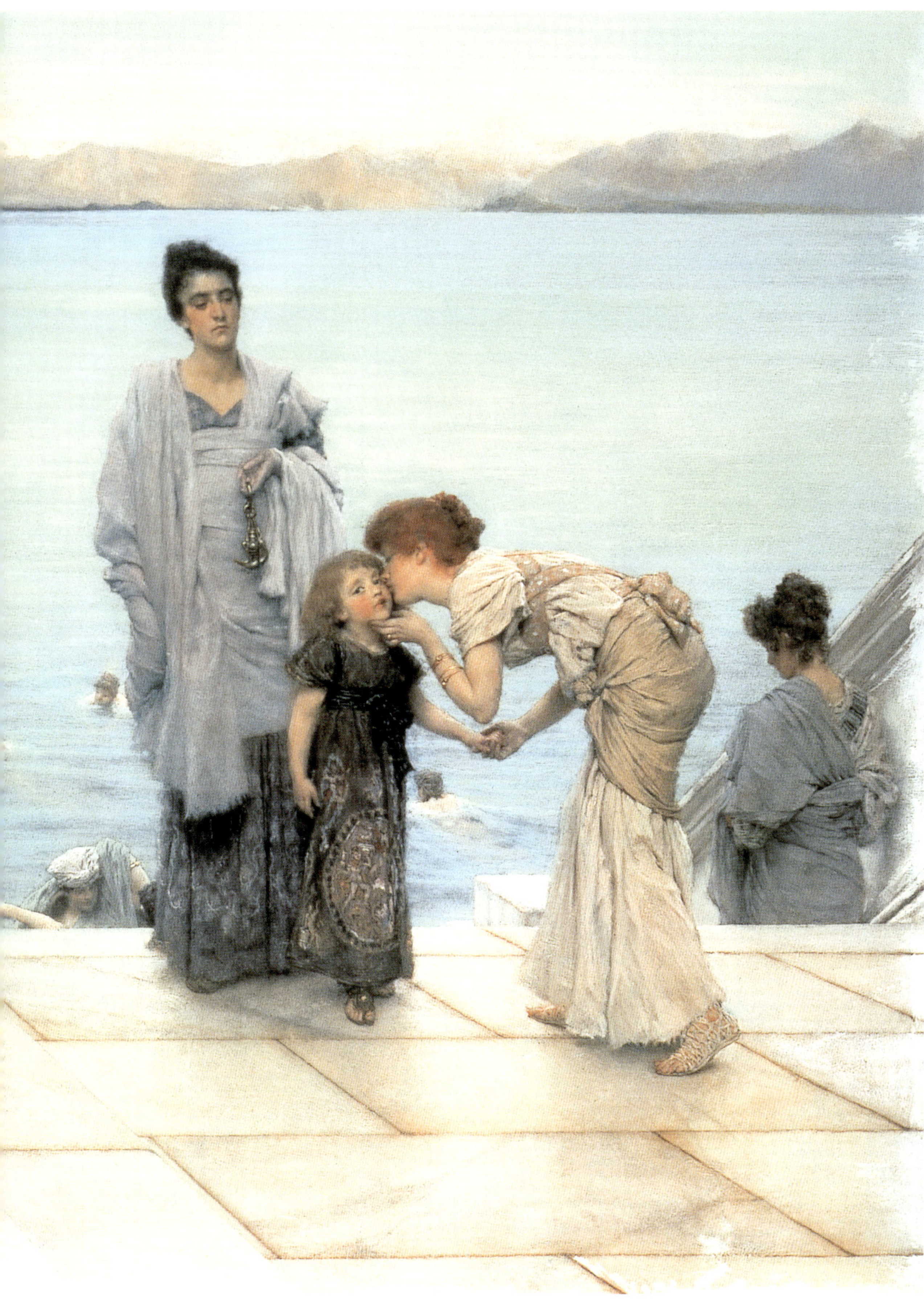

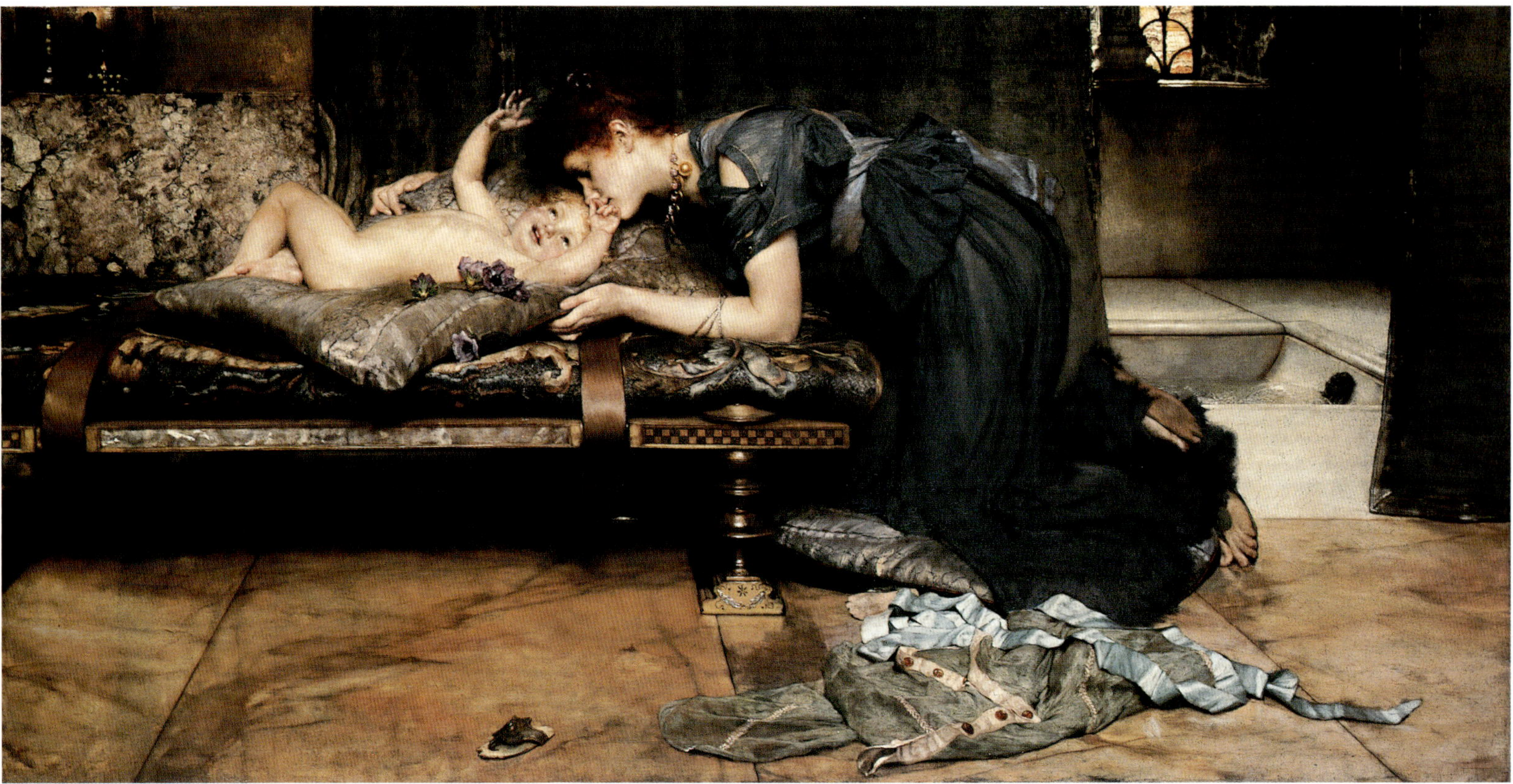

Two years later, lines from Horace's *Odes* have a similar function. In *Love's Votaries* (Pl.140) Horatian verses appear as embroidered letters edging a rug. These form lines 5-8 of *Odes* 1.30, a prayer to Venus, urging the goddess to leave Cyprus and hurry to Glycera who summons her:

> Your ardent boy must hurry along with you
> and Nymphs and Graces with their girdles loose
> and Youth, so uncongenial without you,
> and Mercury.[259]

Love's Votaries shows two women on a marble terrace leading down to the sea. Once again, one woman is reclining and the other seated. Like the listener in *A Favourite Poet*, they have flushed cheeks and gaze dreamily into the distance. Behind them, a balustrade is decorated with a frieze of female figures echoing their own positions, while in the foreground, water gently runs from a fountain decorated with a statuette of Cupid.

A Favourite Poet and *Love's Votaries* amply illustrate the scope of Alma-Tadema's appeal. Representations of languorous women had been popularized in the works of Albert Moore (Pl.141), and, in echoing the type, so Alma-Tadema draws on a recognizable vision of an idyllic pseudo-classical world. The paintings also offer pleasing composition and surface, while, at the same time, learned references to Latin texts provide a challenge for the educated viewer. Over Alma-Tadema's whole career, this is a characteristic prescription: the aesthetic delight and the reassurance of a recognizably familiar construct of antiquity – from mad emperors to leisured women – and the stimulus of the unexpected.

In 1890 the family were on the continent staying at Georg Ebers's summer home at Tutzing in Bavaria. There Alma-Tadema produced an oil sketch, *A Lake in Bavaria*, painted from Ebers's garden. The setting was to provide the background for *The Kiss* (Pl.142), a bathing scene, commissioned by Max Waechter to accompany *An Apodyterium* and *The Frigidarium*.[260] This scene of sparkling marble balcony leading down to the sea is a world away from the modern realities of Kaiser Wilhelm's Europe and can be compared with later paintings set in the Bay of Naples.

More unusually, in one painting, *An Earthly Paradise* (Pl.143), Victorian sentiment is transposed into an ancient setting. A familiar Victorian genre subject of mother and child, the composition is reminiscent of William Quiller Orchardson's *Master Baby* (Pl.144). Alma-Tadema has replaced the modern couch with a Roman disc-legged bench and dressed the mother in classical drapery.[261] A catalogue quotation from Algernon Swinburne's 'Olive' accompanied the painting: 'All the heaven of heavens in one/ Little child'. From *Poems and Ballads: Third Series* (1889), this sentimental poem, far removed from the heady sensuality of Swinburne's earlier verse, complements the mood of the painting. An unusually large canvas for Alma-Tadema (although not as large as Orchardson's), it leaves us to wonder why he should have chosen to paint such a slight subject on so grand a scale. Mother and baby pictures were a speciality of Laura Alma-Tadema and it may be that she had some influence on her husband's choice of subject here.

In May 1892 the Alma-Tademas were staying with Edwin Austin Abbey at Morgan Hall in Gloucestershire. At the time Abbey shared a studio with John Singer Sargent. Sargent's negative comments on Alma-Tadema's work have already been noted,[262] and yet all three men were able to enter into profitable artistic debate: 'Tadema was always a very welcome guest for he had the rare faculty ... of immediately perceiving what an artist was driving at and could discuss it from the artist's point of view even when that differed from his own.'[263] Although Alma-Tadema worked in a very particular style, he maintained a lively interest in the work of other artists and was aware of current art trends across Europe. His own landscape paintings, which make use of a technique very different to his

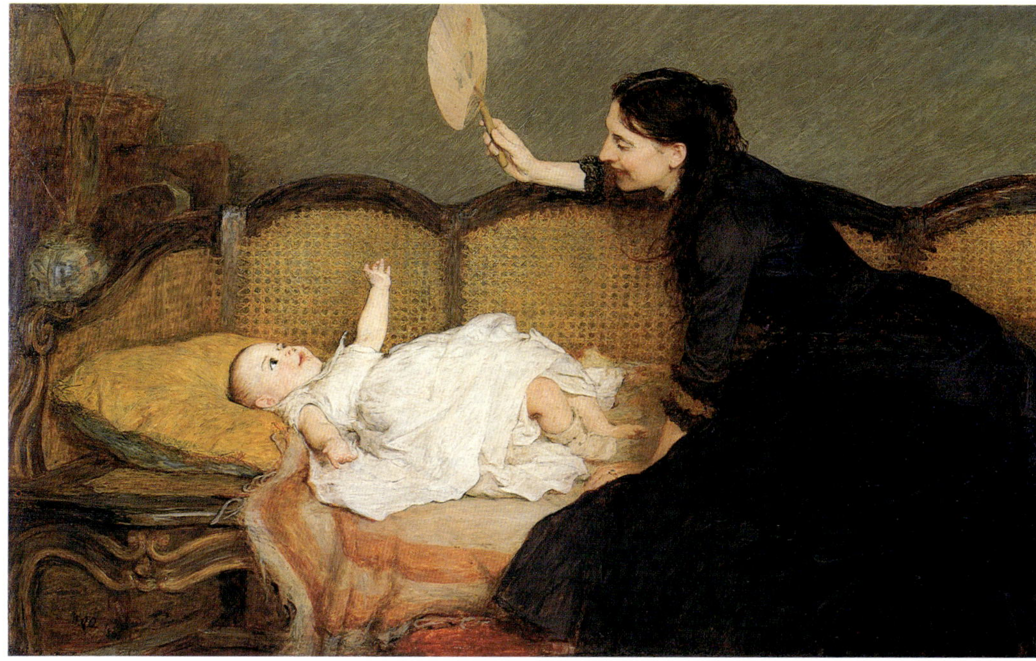

143 opposite
An Earthly Paradise, 1891
Oil on canvas, 86·5 × 165 cm (34 × 65 in)
Private collection

144
William Quiller Orchardson, *Master Baby*, 1886
Oil on canvas, 108 × 166 cm (42½ × 65⅜ in)
National Gallery of Scotland, Edinburgh

usual working methods, are testament to his open-minded approach to painting.

Alma-Tadema returned to Latin poetry with *The Poet Gallus Dreaming* (Pl.145), shown at the New Gallery in 1892. Whereas the paintings which include Horatian verses induce the viewer to decipher and recognize familiar lines hidden within the canvas, this work offers a very different challenge. Did the artist expect his audience to recognize a Latin poet who is, to the modern world, an obscure figure of whose work virtually nothing survives? C Cornelius Gallus was born in Gaul in 66 BC; after moving to Rome as a young man he secured the patronage of Augustus and became one of a circle of successful poets which included Virgil, Ovid, Horace and Tibullus. Gallus was rewarded for his support of Augustus during the civil war with the prefecture of Egypt, but he later offended the Emperor and was condemned to exile.[264] Rather than endure exile, Gallus killed himself in 26 BC.

Alma-Tadema seems to depict the unfortunate Gallus in exile, looking out over the sea and dreaming of home. Ovid was similarly exiled; his experiences are recorded in the Tristia, in which he too contemplates suicide. Like many of Alma-Tadema's paintings of the 1880s and 1890s, *The Poet Gallus Dreaming* shows a clear Mediterranean sea and sky. This was not as unlikely an exile destination as it may seem; although Ovid was banished to Tomis, a town near the Danube on the outer limits of the Empire, both the daughter and granddaughter of Augustus were exiled to the island of Pandataria, off the coast of Campania, and Agrippina, wife of Germanicus, to Tremerus off the coast of Apulia.

Although virtually nothing of Gallus' work survives,[265] an interest in the poet was fostered by W. A. Becker's imaginative description of his downfall in *Gallus: Roman Scenes of the Time of Augustus*. Published in Leipzig in 1838, Becker's work was soon translated into English and reprinted many times throughout the Victorian period.[266] Becker portrays Gallus' lifestyle as a pampered and leisured existence. He owns a town house and a villa in Campania, both of which are sumptuously decorated and adorned with Greek statuary and silver plate. Although *The Poet Gallus Dreaming* is itself not based on Becker's fictional Gallus (who, like the historical Gallus, never reaches exile, but kills himself before leaving Rome), Alma-Tadema's paintings elsewhere certainly use either Becker or the same classical literary sources as the novel. In Becker, Gallus' friend, Lentulus, invites guests to dinner, not merely for the oysters 'but for the purpose of admiring a work of art of surpassing grace and beauty'.[267] Similar scenes are depicted in Alma-Tadema's connoisseur paintings in which (we recall) the artist takes his customary wry look at rich collectors.

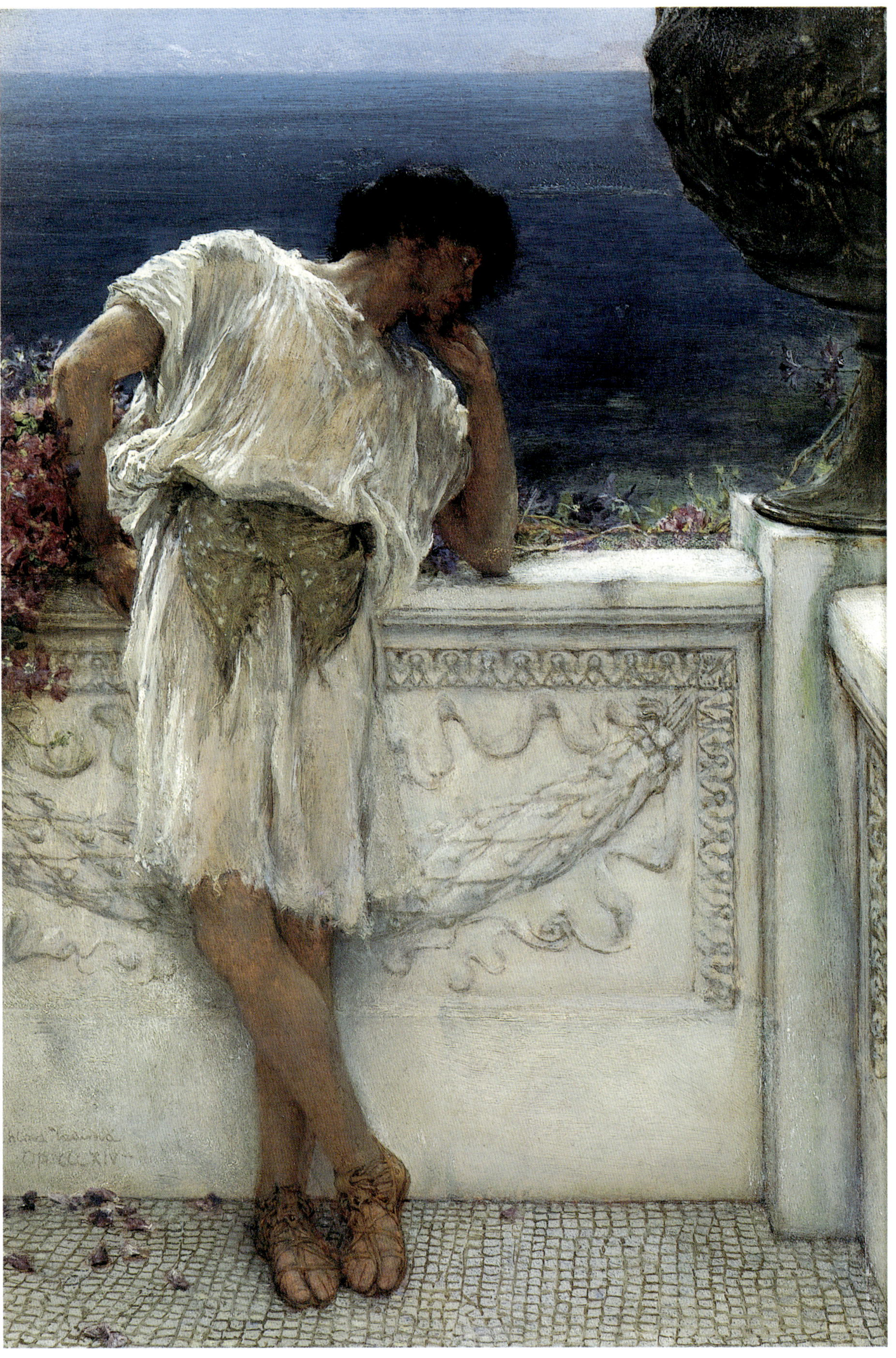

In Becker, again, Gallus visits Baiae, where, much as in Alma-Tadema's paintings of the Bay of Naples, couples enjoy sailing parties, make love and idle away the hours overlooking a Mediterranean sea.[268] One episode has a more overt connection with an individual painting. As Gallus and his party make their way through the streets of Rome, they see 'an Egyptian juggler' performing to a crowd.[269] Alma-Tadema's *A Juggler* (Pl.43) shows the same performer transposed to an indoor setting where he amuses a more select audience.

Whether or not the viewer picks up Alma-Tadema's references to Becker or indeed identifies the poet himself, the painting, of a wistful young man looking out over a brilliant blue sea, commands our attention in itself. How much interest Alma-Tadema's patrons took in his classical references, we cannot know. Many of his British clients were self-made businessmen – David Price, wool merchant; Jacob Burnett, manufacturing chemist; Holbrook Gaskell, newspaper owner; James Hall, ship owner; William Hesketh Lever, soap manufacturer; John Aird, engineer – who would hardly have had the leisure to familiarize themselves with Latin texts or the biography of an obscure Roman poet. It was essential to Alma-Tadema's success that, however felicitous his hidden references, his paintings maintain a compelling harmony of composition, colour and form.

Throughout the 1890s Alma-Tadema's favourite subject remains wealthy Rome at play, and while the earlier paintings display an incisive wit at the expense of, for instance, boorish art collectors, in later works we are invited to take a quieter delight in groups of indolent women and pairs of lovers who face each other or gaze out across a clear blue sea. Female hairstyles now become more flattering and less unmistakably Flavian; individuals no longer wear elaborate clothes of gaudy colours. Wealth and status are not illustrated by a clutter of archaeological artefacts but are implicit in location and leisurely employment.

As early as 1869, the setting of *An Exedra* (Pl.29) shows the outskirts of Pompeii, with coastline behind. The attitude of the two men looking at sailing boats in the distance anticipates a number of later paintings which depict individuals gazing out towards a clear blue sea. From the 1880s, Alma-Tadema's most characteristic paintings are now those of groups of women, couples and lovers sitting on their marble terraces with the sea and distant coastline behind. Even paintings set within marbled and painted interiors, such as *A Favourite Poet* (Pl.138), and *Unconscious Rivals* (Pl.146), are so constructed as to allow a glimpse of sea in the background.

145
The Poet Gallus Dreaming, 1892
Oil on wood, 23·5 × 16·3 cm (9¼ × 6⅜ in)
Private collection

A number of Alma-Tadema's pictures were shown at the British section of the Worlds Columbian Exposition, Chicago, in 1893. Alongside his British clients, he was beginning to attract American patrons. In the 1880s he had been commissioned to decorate Henry Marquand's music room. Between 1877 and 1897 American millionaire William Henry Vanderbilt bought five works, and *Coign of Vantage* was acquired by the American collector, Lilia Babbitt Hyde. Many later works were sold by Arthur Tooth and Sons, London, and Knoedler and Company, New York. In the enviable position of being able to attract buyers throughout Britain, Europe and America, Alma-Tadema was not short of dealers wanting to sell his works. In 1889 the Lefèvre Gallery mounted an exhibition, complete with catalogue, solely for *A Dedication to Bacchus*; Tooth and Sons were to do the same for *The Coliseum* in 1907. An anecdote by Walter Sickert helps define Alma-Tadema's status in the late Victorian art world:

> I remember a distinguished member of the New English Art Club coming to see me in a state of tragi-comic indignation, which, though it was only half-serious, contained a legitimate grievance: 'I am going down to Whitechapel: Aitken has given Tadema's picture a rope in front and palms. Palms in pots! I am going to insist on a rope and palms in front of mine.'[270]

Although potted palms were hardly a conventional measure of success, here they indicate Alma-Tadema's value to a dealer as a saleable commodity.

Courtship paintings continue, although the favourite configuration is now pairs or small groups of women. Albert Moore's paintings of languorous women in an enclosed space (Pl.141) proclaimed an association between a classical-type setting and female indolence, and Alma-Tadema's paintings of women on marble terraces certainly assume this association as a familiar image. However, while Moore combines classicism with japonaiserie, ancient with modern, to convey a peculiar timelessness, Alma-Tadema sites his scenes in a recognizable Roman world. Many of Alma-Tadema's paintings of women around this date, like the works of Moore, have no ostensible narrative, and yet title and visual imagery within the scene often hint at a specific meaning. *Unconscious Rivals*, exhibited at the New Gallery in 1893, shows two women in a spectacular setting of painted barrel vault and dazzling white marble. The gorgeous painted ceiling is of central importance. The artist recalled:

> The painting of the picture *Unconscious*

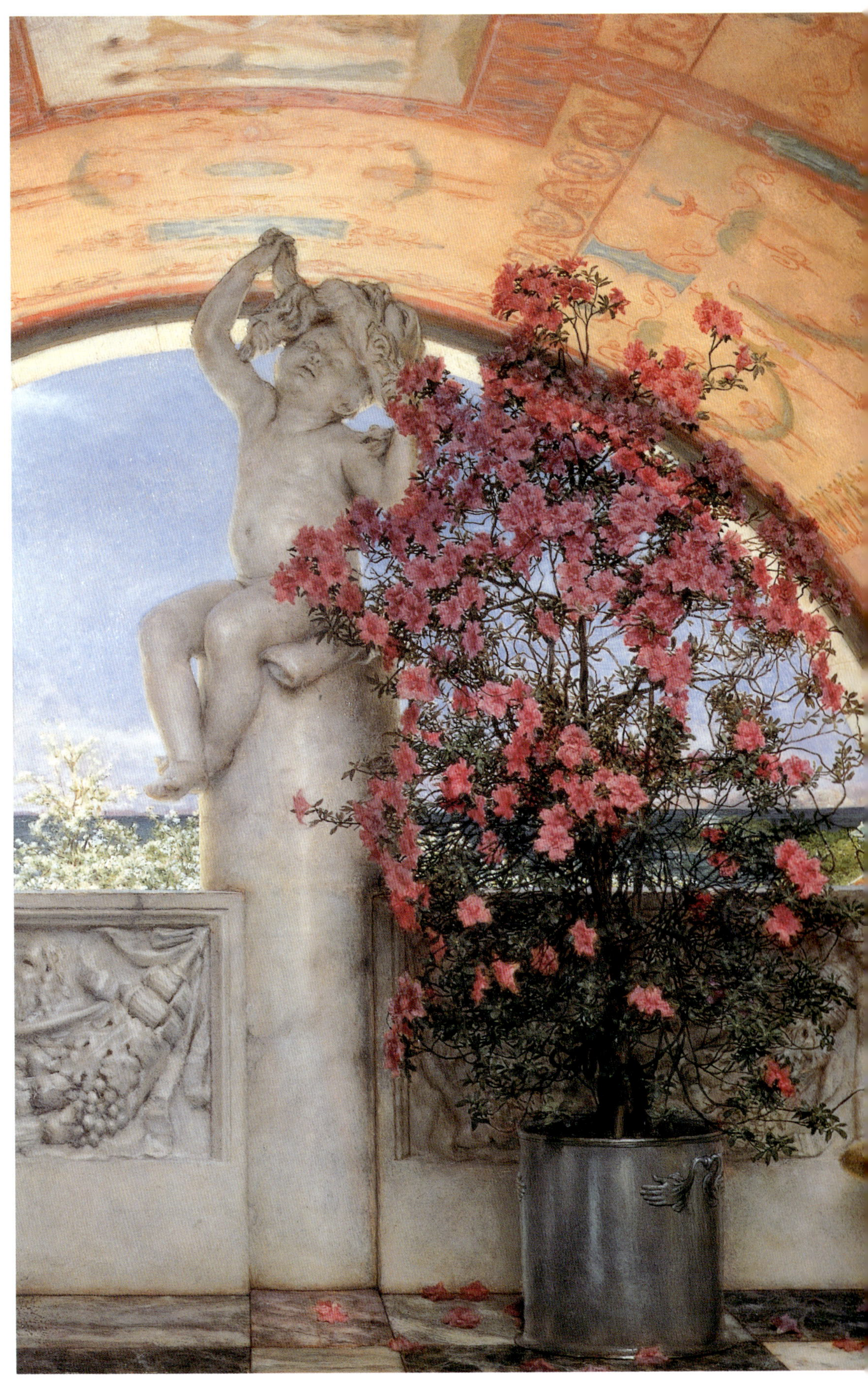

146
Unconscious Rivals, 1893
Oil on canvas, 45·1 × 62·8 cm (17¾ × 24¾ in)
Bristol City Museum and Art Gallery

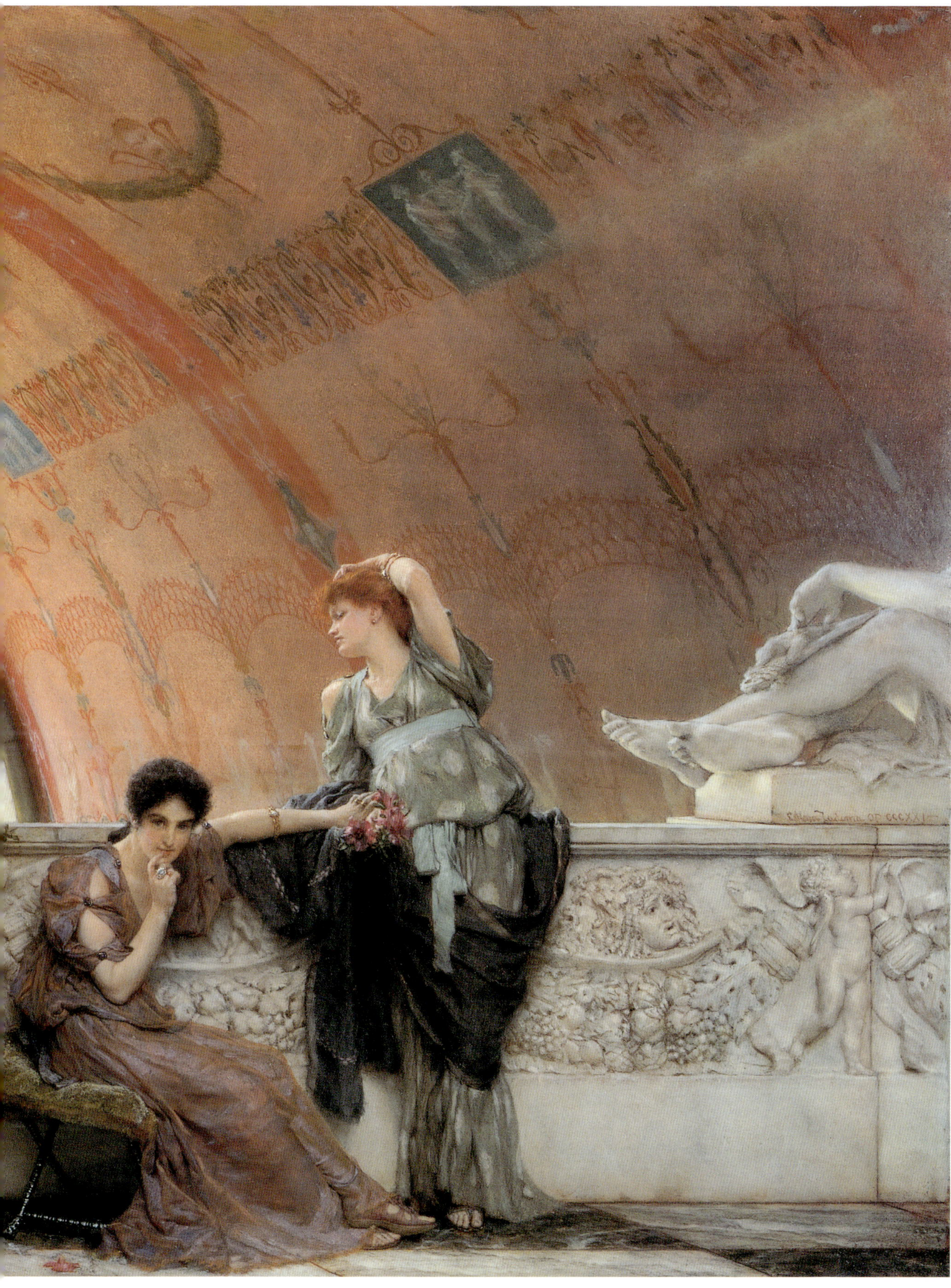

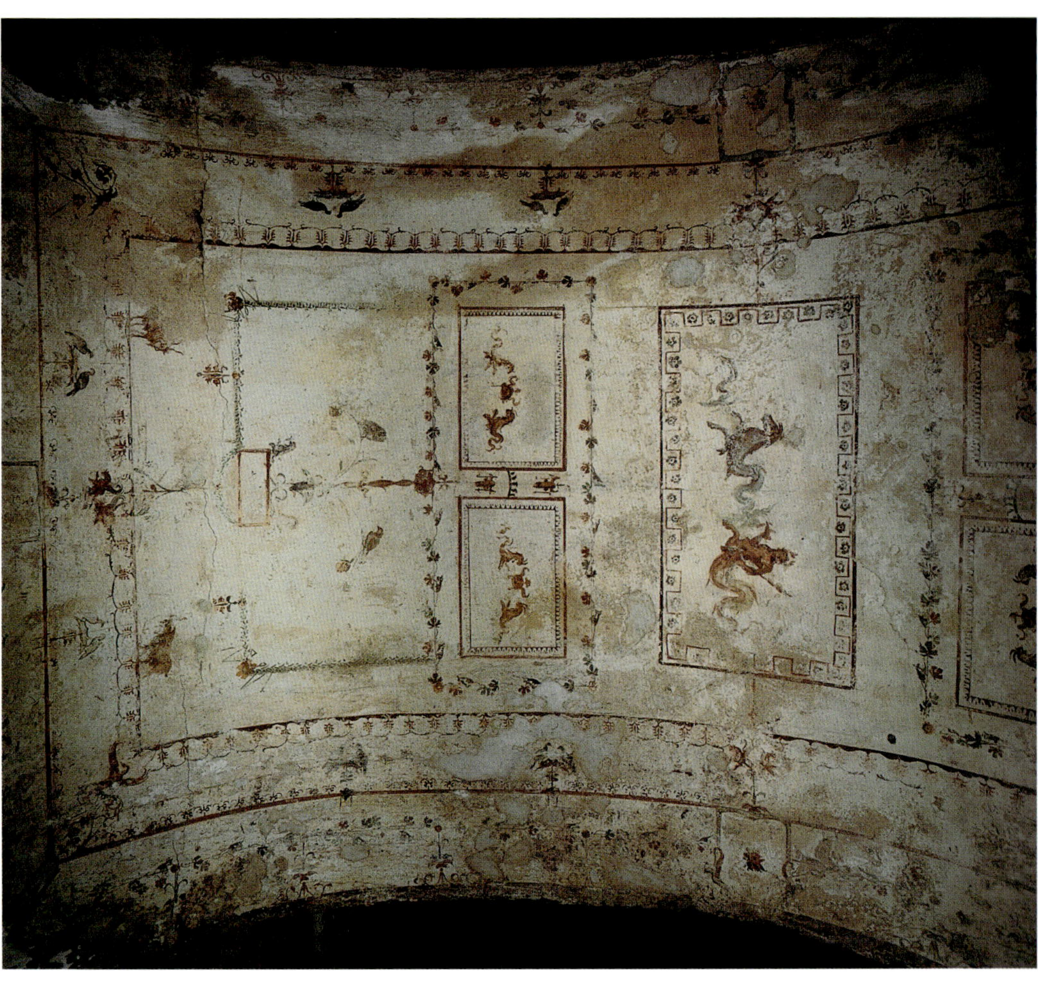

147
Ceiling painting from Nero's Golden House, Rome
c.AD 65

148 opposite
Seated Gladiator, Roman
Marble, Palazzo Altemps, Rome:
University of Birmingham

> *Rivals* in some sense had its origin in the destruction by myself of a painted ceiling which I had put into another picture (*The Spring*) and which failed to satisfy me. Friends who had seen that ceiling expostulated with me for rubbing it out, so when I came to paint *Unconscious Rivals* I reinserted it. To express it more aptly, I painted the picture in order to use that ceiling![271]

The ceiling itself can have no ancient prototype as no known decorated ceiling on such a scale remains intact. The closest equivalents are the vaulted ceilings from Nero's Golden House in Rome which were discovered in the sixteenth century (Pl.147).

In this painting archaeological detail does not have a decorative function or even an authenticating role alone, but also acts as a signifier. The title, *Unconscious Rivals*, sets up some elusive expectation of flirtations, or hopes, or actual love affairs involving the two women represented and some unspecified man, but it is only archaeological imagery that allows us to read anything more of their situation. The women rest against a balcony wall which is embellished with a relief of swags and masks supported by Cupids based on an original in the Archaeological Museum, Naples. Cupids are obviously emblems of love, while masks betoken dissemblance or deceit. The idea of disguise is enforced by the huge statue of a Cupid trying on a mask of Silenus from the Capitoline Museum, Rome. The sculpture at the right of the picture is a Greco-Roman statue of a seated gladiator from the Palazzo Altemps, Rome, and included in Alma-Tadema's photographic collection (Pl.148); cut off at the knees, it is also disguised and obscured. The gladiator brings with it suggestive hints of notorious associations between gladiators and imperial Roman women. Even respectable matrons were notorious for their passionate support of favourite combatants and for affairs with gladiators outside the ring. The Roman satirist Juvenal records the example of Eppia, a senator's wife who runs away with a gladiator:

> What did Eppia see in him to make her put up
> With being labelled 'The Gladiatress'?
> Her poppet, her Sergius
> Was no chicken, forty at least, with a dud

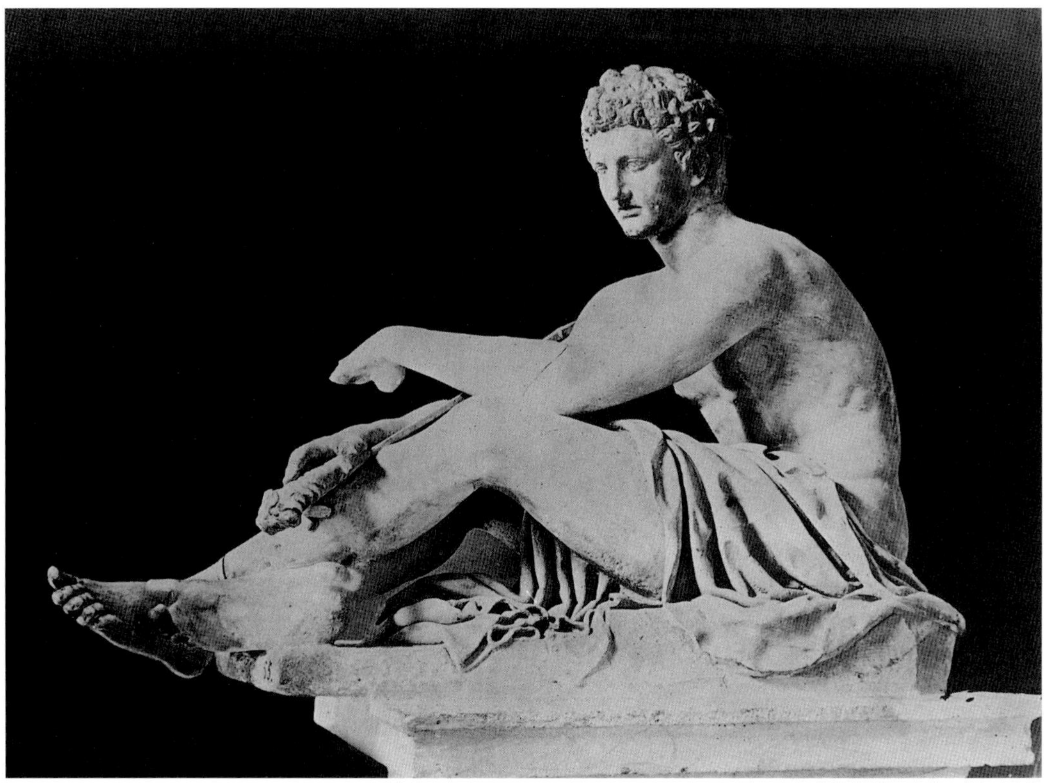

arm that held promise
Of early retirement. Besides, his face
looked a proper mess –
Helmet-scarred, a great wen on his nose,
an unpleasant
Discharge from one constantly weeping
eye. What of it?
He was a gladiator.[272]

Risqué associations between women and gladiators had already featured in Simeon Solomon's *Habet!* (Pl.157), with its depiction of an all-female audience captivated by a gladiatorial contest. Alma-Tadema's painting is not a depiction of gladiatorial combat or even of an admiring female audience and instead he only hints at associations between the two through his use of archaeological detail. The gladiator is even cut off abruptly at the edge of the canvas, thus making the coded imagery even more difficult to decipher. His work can be compared with that of European symbolist artists such as Gustave Moreau, Gustav Klimt and Fernand Khnopff who likewise employ a complicated system of imagery which directs the viewer to extract meaning from paintings which, on an initial reading, appear deliberately recondite.[273]

Another picture whose meaning depends upon the decoding of imagery is *Spring* (Pl.149).[274] It took fours years to complete this large canvas which was bought, along with *Fortune's Favourite*, by a German collector, Robert Mendelssohn-Bartholdy (a relative of the composer). The painting shows a colourful procession, headed by angelic flower girls, winding its way through the marble-lined streets of imperial Rome. The occasion is the April Floralia, sacred to Flora, the ancient Italian goddess of flowers, vegetation and fertility.[275] This gorgeous depiction of marble, flowers, pretty girls and Mediterranean sunlight is a seemingly innocent and joyous scene, and yet, hidden amongst the crowd, is a standard bearing a Latin inscription (Pl.150), which is in fact a fragmentary verse addressed to the fertility god Priapus, once ascribed to the Latin poet Catullus.[276] A modern translation reads:

I dedicate, I consecrate this grove to thee,
Priapus, whose home and woodlands are
at Lampsacus;
there, among the coastal cities of the
Hellespont,
they chiefly worship thee: their shores are

149 overleaf
Spring, 1894
Oil on canvas, 179·2 × 80·3 cm ($70\frac{1}{2} \times 31\frac{5}{8}$ in)
J. Paul Getty Museum, Malibu

150 overleaf
Spring (detail)

rich in oysters![277]

The presence of a Priapic dedication suggests that the scene is not as ingenuous as it at first appears and prompts us to reconsider other details within the painting. Attached to the frame are lines from Swinburne's poem 'Dedication', written in 1865:

In a land of clear colours and stories,
In a region of shadowless hours,
Where earth has a garment of glories
And a murmur of musical flowers.

These lines too seem innocent enough until we read the rest of the stanza:

In woods where the spring half uncovers
The flush of her amorous face,
By the waters that listen for lovers,
For these is there place.

These unquoted lines associate the emergence of Spring with the budding of sexual love. By the 1890s Swinburne's verse was characterized by the sentimental 'Olive', but twenty years earlier the author of 'Dedication' had been a fiery and subversive spirit, linked with Dante Gabriel Rossetti and the 'fleshly school of poetry', and known for both his reckless lifestyle and his extravagant, erotic-masochistic verse. The choice of Catullus and Swinburne is well calculated: not only is the temper of both poets far removed from innocent pleasures, but the two are specifically connected through Swinburne's Catullan allusions in his own poetry. This very address to Priapus is cited by Swinburne in two poems published together with 'Dedication'. Swinburne's Dolores, in the poem of the same name, is the offspring of Priapus and Libitina. She is hailed as a 'goddess anew' even though 'the old world is broken' and 'the oyster-bed teems out of reach'. A similar reference to Priapus and Lampsacus is found in 'Faustine'.[278]

Archaeological details in the painting also hint at the subversive and the risqué. The roundels of the banner and *tympana* carried by the celebrants are decorated with paintings of semi-nude frolicking couples. The roundel figures imitate nymphs and satyrs from wall paintings in the House of the Dioscuri at Pompeii (Pls. 151, 152), while the *tympana* paintings imitate those from the House of the Vetii at Pompeii, excavated in 1894, the very year the painting was completed. Also hidden amongst the crowd are two silver herms of satyrs, each carrying a baby Dionysus, which are based on marble originals in the Archaeological Museum, Naples (Pl.153). Satyrs have an infamous reputation as the most sexually active, or at least sexually aroused, followers of Dionysus. Further allusion to Bacchanalia is found in the form of ivy wreaths worn by members of the procession. The artist had

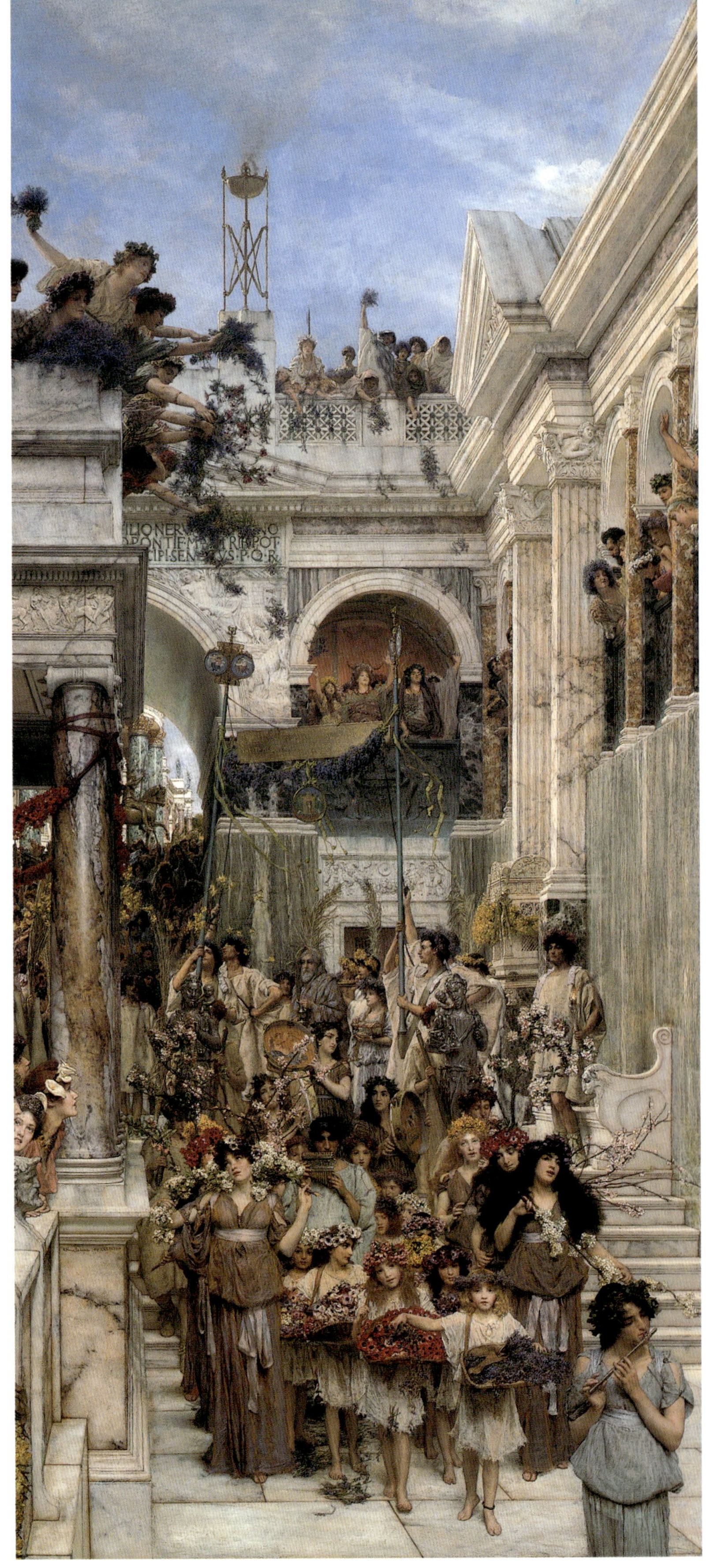

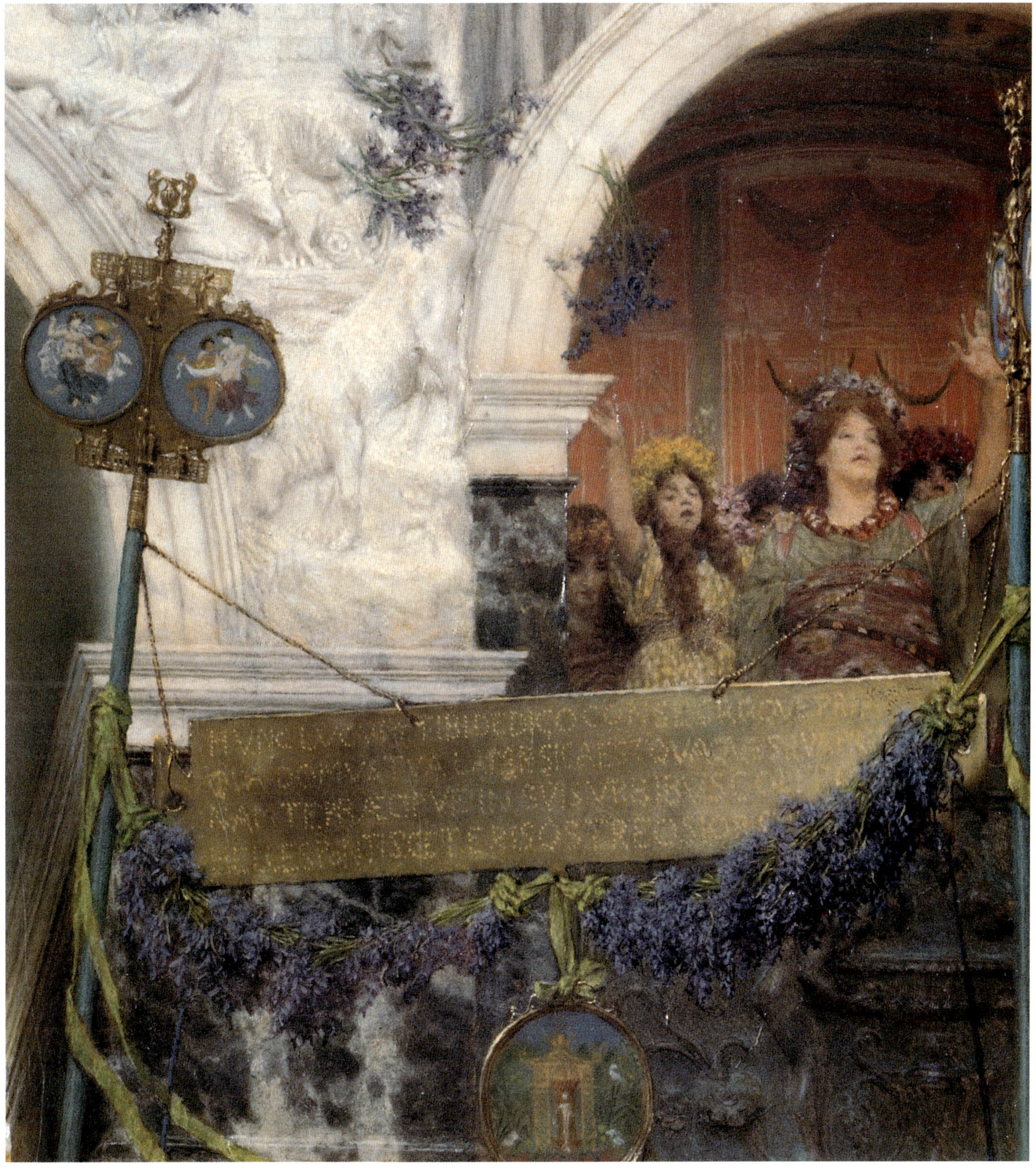

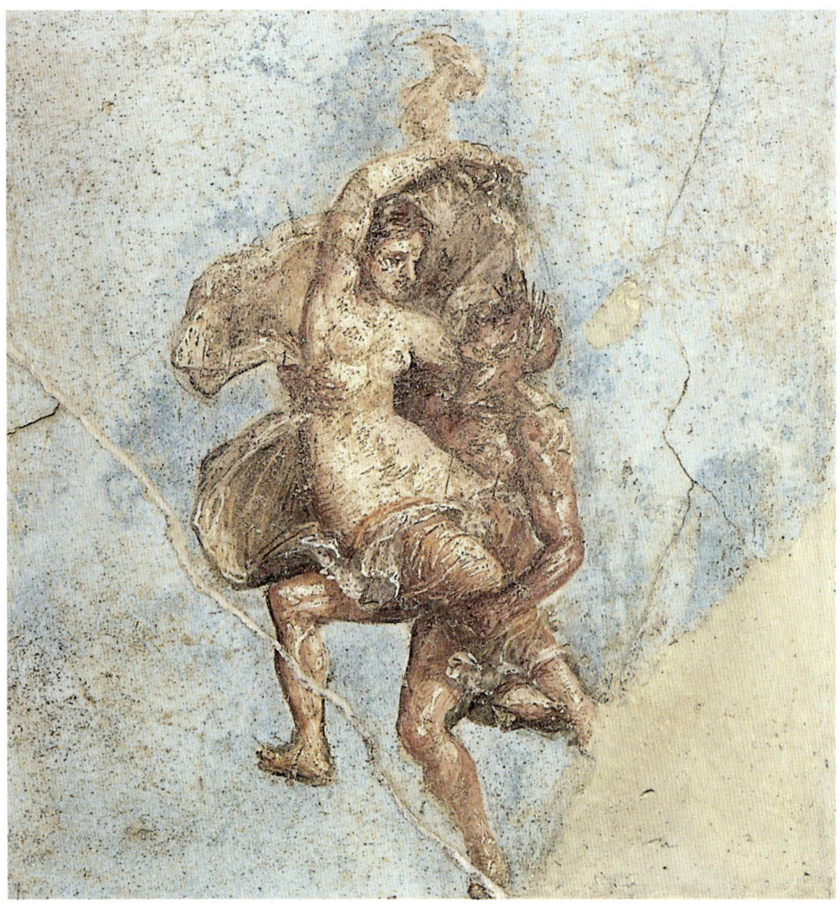

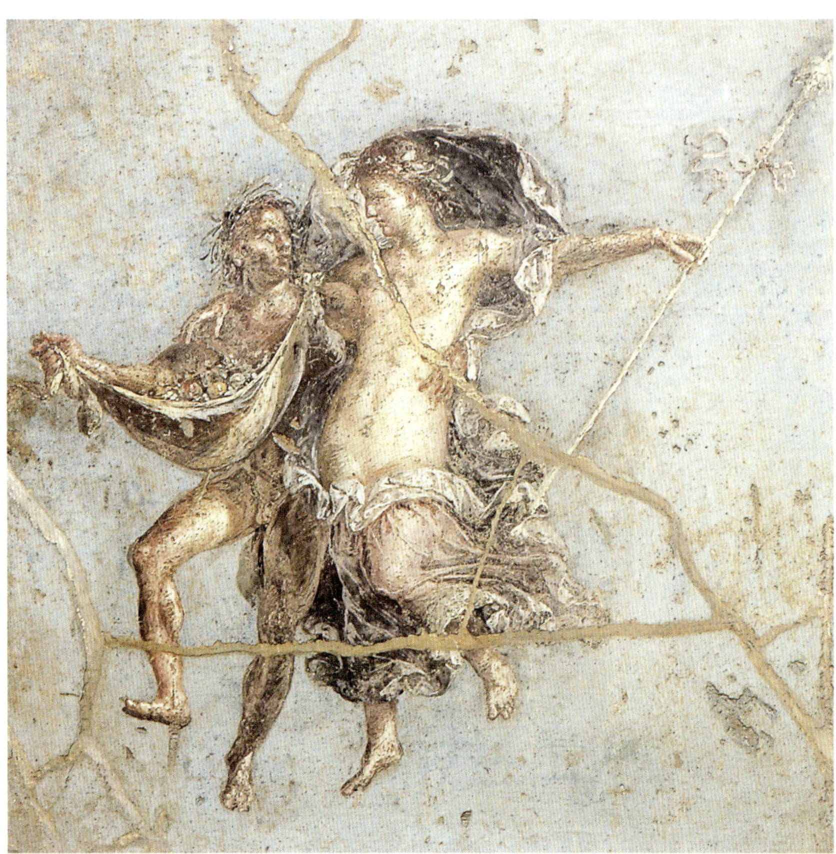

151
Faun and Bacchant, Roman Wall Painting from the House of the Dioscuri, Pompeii, 1st century AD
Archaeological Museum, Naples

152
Faun and Bacchant, Roman Wall Painting from the House of the Dioscuri, Pompeii, 1st century AD
Archaeological Museum, Naples

153 opposite
Herm of Satyr with Baby Dionysus, Roman Marble, Archaeological Museum, Naples:
University of Birmingham

already used Dionysiac-Bacchic imagery – the wall painting of satyr and goat in *Catullus at Lesbia's*; the statue of Bacchus and Ampelus in *The Roses of Heliogabalus* – for the purpose of sexual suggestion.

A very different type of image to those playful nymphs and satyrs is provided by a frieze of the savage battle of Lapiths and Centaurs from the Greek temple of Apollo at Bassae (also represented in *A Dedication to Bacchus*). Although originally decorating the interior of the main room of the temple, it now appears on the exterior of a building. This fifth-century BC frieze seems doubly out of place in an imperial Roman setting (an inscription from the arch of Trajan at Benevento places the scene in or after the Hadrianic period in the second century AD). The artist is inviting us to think – but of what? Is it perhaps that the savage aspect of the frieze is to suggest the wild and irrational emotionalism beneath the surface of Roman state religion?

These Dionysiac, erotic and disturbing resonances evoke a less than salubrious element within the Roman spring festival, a notion which is indeed not purely the artist's invention, for the Floralia emerges from ancient texts – Ovid's *Fasti* and Juvenal[279] – as a promiscuous and drunken occasion. Perhaps most significantly, the Floralia is credited with similar associations in the *Scriptores Historiae Augustae*, the text that Alma-Tadema had used for *The Roses of Heliogabalus*. Heliogabalus had a penchant for a particular charioteer whom, the author says, 'he loved to such an extent that he used to kiss him in the groin, which it is indecent to mention, claiming that he was celebrating the festival of Flora.'[280]

The pageant is framed by stunning architectural structures of variegated marble. Although the detail derives from attested works of widely differing periods, the Hadrianic inscription suggests that Alma-Tadema is pointing to a representation of imperial Rome. Nevertheless, the fanciful arched façades topped by pediments and parapets have no ancient parallel. Colourful procession, rich and even disturbing symbolism, magnificent architecture: all this is calculated to create an exciting and imaginative vision of the splendour, but also the hidden depths, of Rome.

A more realistic evocation of the architectural splendour of the city of Rome is provided in *The Coliseum* (Pl.154). Women on a marble balcony are presented with a lofty view of the Colosseum, the huge amphitheatre begun by Vespasian, completed by his successors Titus and Domitian and officially opened in 80 AD. A large marble vase in the foreground is decorated with a scene of a hunting relief, a reminder of bloody combat in the arena behind and a sharp contrast with the richly dressed women watching the crowd. The Colosseum itself (Pl.155) is meticulously restored and even decorated with statues placed in niches in three tiers around the building. Statues in the second tier, although conscripted to the background and painted in miniature form, can still be identified as well-known pieces: a four-horse chariot group, possibly the four bronze horses from San Marco, Venice; the Prima Porta Augustus; the seated boxer (Terme Museum, Rome); Uffizi Wrestlers (Uffizi Gallery, Florence); the Discobolus (Pl.156); Cincinnatus (Louvre, Paris); Aristogeiton's outstretched arm from the Tyrannicides (Archaeological Museum, Naples). These statues are not chosen at random but are all linked with athletic or military triumph where, as in gladiatorial combat, victory is of the essence. The chariot group, the boxer, the Discobolos and the Wrestlers are all athletic champions; the Tyrannicides is a sculptural group which depicts two aristocrats who attempted to kill an Athenian tyrant; the Prima Porta Augustus was erected to commemorate a military triumph over the Parthians; Lucius Quinctius Cincinnatus was a dictator of ancient Rome who won a victory over the Sabines.

Amphitheatre scenes were among stock images of nineteenth-century classical-subject painting, and many artists concentrated on the gruesome details of the games. Gérôme's *Ave Caesar, Morituri Te Salutant* (1859) and *Pollice Verso* (1874) depict combat in the arena, while Simeon Solomon's *Habet!* (Pl.157) portrays a bloodthirsty female audience. Christian persecution is the subject of Herbert Schmalz's *Faithful unto Death: Christianae ad Leones* (1888) which shows semi-nude female martyrs bound to stakes in the amphitheatre. Gérôme's *The Christian Martyr's Last Prayer* (1863–83) and Henryk Siemiradzi's *Nero's Torches* (1876) and *The Christian Dirce* (1897) all dwell on the aftermath of carnage. Alma-Tadema's *The Coliseum*, by contrast, invites no such voyeuristic, sadistic, pseudo-erotic pleasure, and instead only hints at the savagery of the setting through archaeological imagery.

A painting which contrasts the cruelty of the games with the pampered existence of wealthy Rome, at the same time hints at a more familiar theme: love in the ancient world. The three figures may be mother and two daughters, one of whom is of marriageable age. As the elder daughter leans over the balcony, is she doing more than merely surveying the scene? Is she perhaps looking for a suitor? The hunting imagery then takes on a new significance as the woman seeking to win a husband or lover becomes contender and predator. The love motif is highlighted by the presence of a bronze statue of a crouching Aphrodite. Love interest in a gladiatorial setting

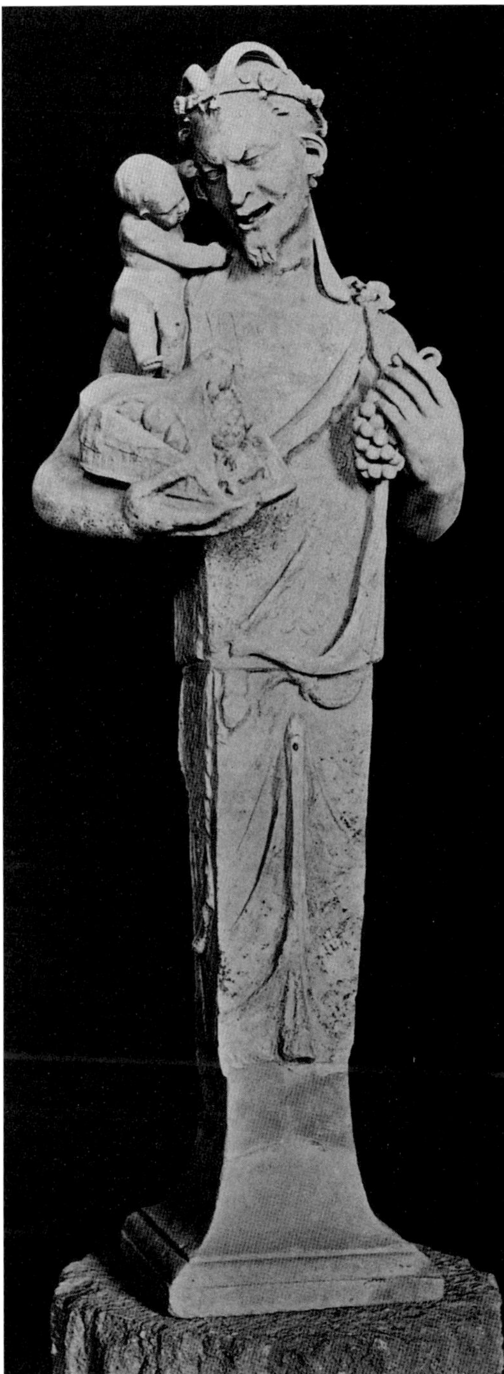

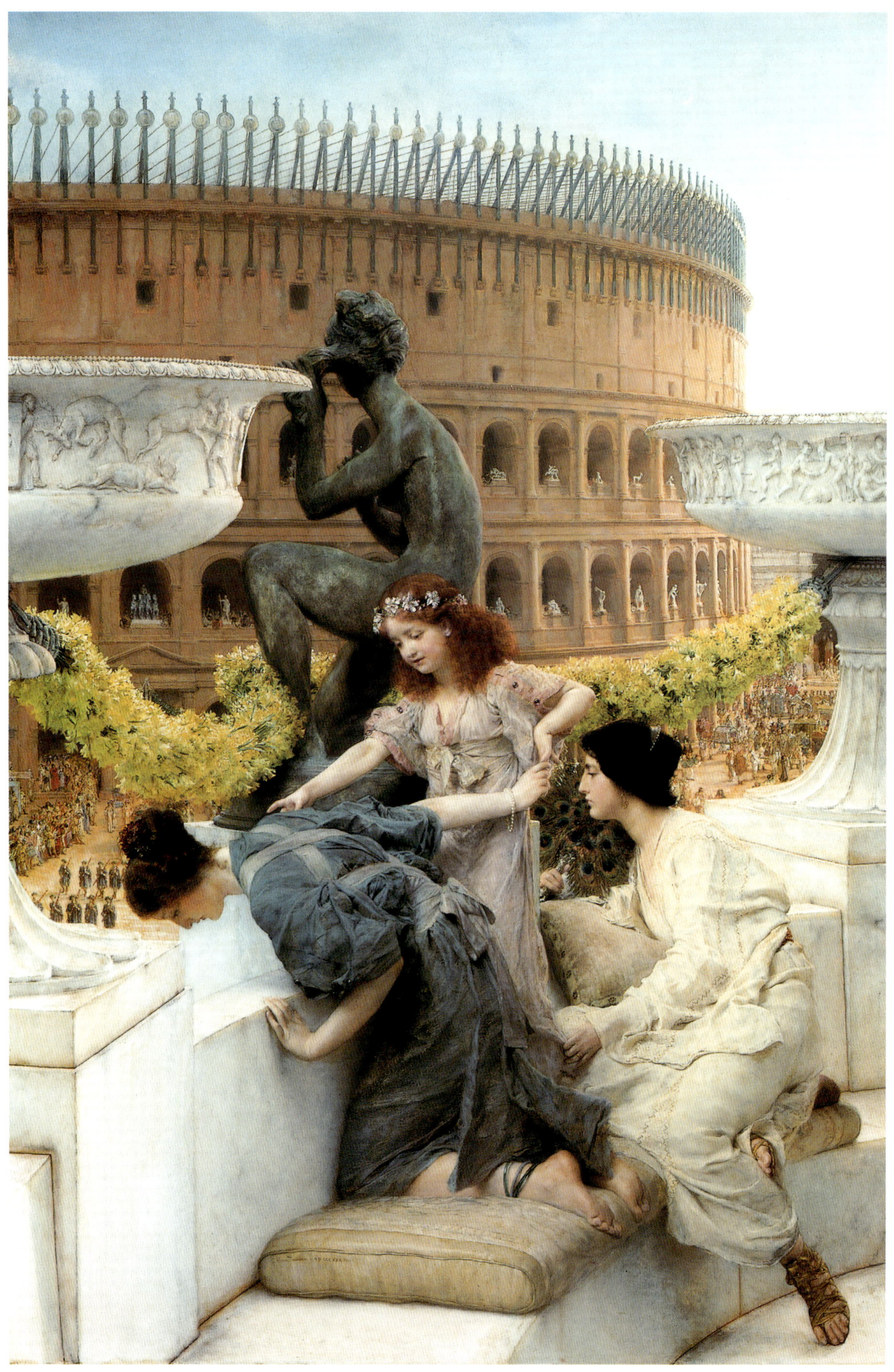

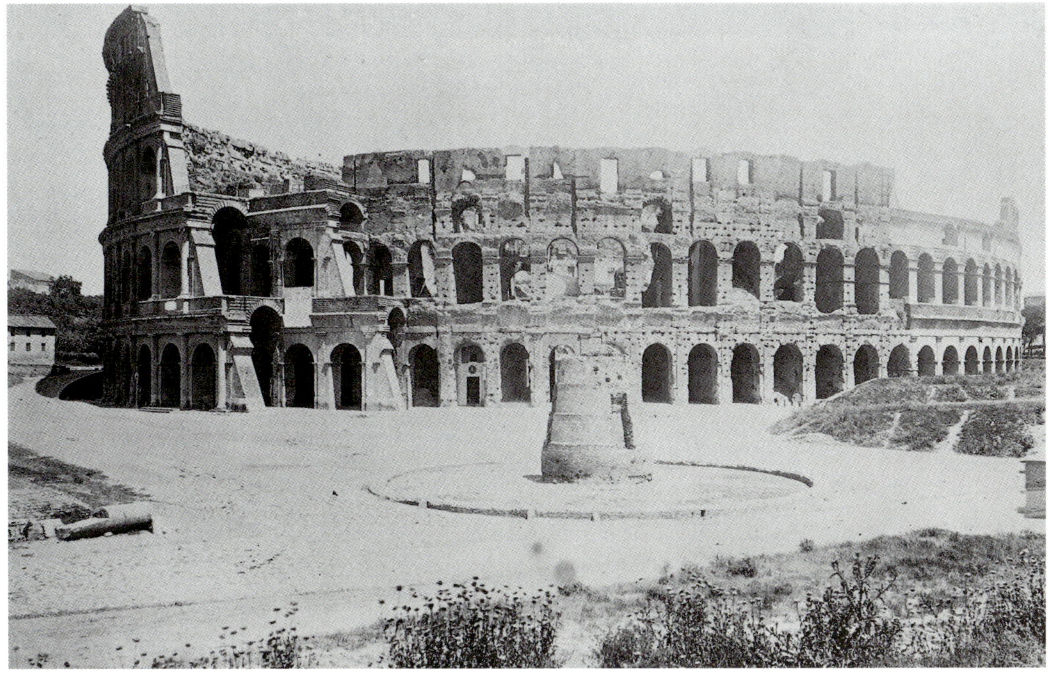

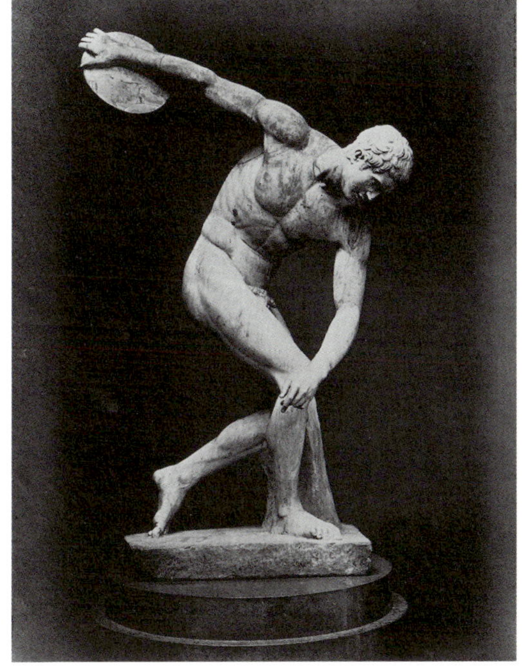

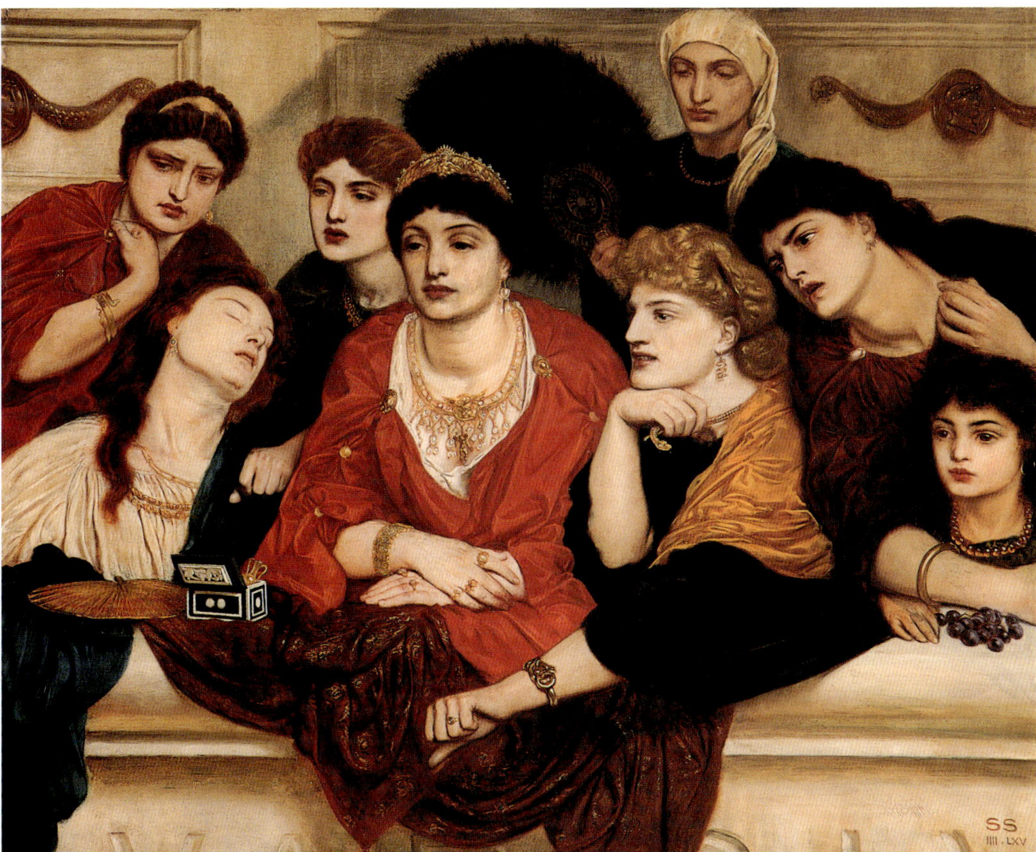

154 opposite
The Coliseum, 1896
Oil on wood, 112 × 73·6 cm (44⅛ × 29 in)
Private collection

155 top left
The Colosseum, Rome:
University of Birmingham

156 top right
Discobolos, Roman copy of a 5th-century BC original
Marble, British Museum, London:
University of Birmingham

157
Simeon Solomon, *Habet!*, 1865
Oil on canvas, 122 × 101·5 cm (48 × 40 in)
Private collection

has, as we have seen in *Unconscious Rivals*, additional risqué undertones.

Alongside such ambitious reconstructions of the city of Rome, Alma-Tadema continued to produce small paintings showing couples or groups of women, all set on marble balconies overlooking the sea. Such paintings always found buyers and were also well received by critics, but only in terms of the repetition of a successful formula. For example, M H Spielmann wrote, in a review of the 1894 Royal Academy Summer Exhibition, 'Mr Tadema is much the same as usual in a deft and tender little canvas in which the marble-painting is again the chief attraction.'[281] Spielmann gives no further description, attempts no reading of the scene nor does he even identify the painting by its title. Such criticism misrepresents pictures which have a significance beyond their admirable depiction of marble, particularly when considered within their Roman context.

Paintings such as *A Foregone Conclusion* (1885) and *Love's Jewelled Fetter* (Pl.158) have generally been taken to portray episodes involving engagement or betrothal ceremonies in a modern sense, for all the Roman accoutrements. In a Roman context, however, the presentation of a ring lacks its habitual modern significance, and the most seemingly straightforward depictions of betrothals are open to alternative interpretations. For instance, the ring that one woman displays to her friend in *Love's Jewelled Fetter* may or may not be an engagement ring. Perhaps it is an expensive love gift. The inclusion of the word 'fetter' in the title, after all, hardly suggests romance, and as the woman is dressed in all her finery, the painting could easily be read as a depiction of a mistress who values her lover for his wealth, rather than as an image of conjugal fidelity. Hanging from a marble pillar in the background is an Egyptian Mummy portrait of a young man. From Roman Egypt, many such portraits were excavated in the 1880s at the Fayum, an oasis close to the Nile valley.[282] Placed at the centre of Alma-Tadema's canvas, this portrait confirms that the female space is dominated by a male presence.

In *Fortune's Favourite* (1895), one woman on a marble *exedra* displays the contents of a jewellery box to her companions. The statue in the background, the Uffizi Wrestlers, once again alludes to masculinity and perhaps to the absent male figure who has bestowed such costly gifts. In *Whispering Noon* (Pl.159), two women sit on a marble bench. In front of them, water from a fountain runs into a marble pond, and, behind them, gorgeous colour harmonies combine in sea, sky and blue and purple delphiniums. Despite the soothing setting, the mood is disquieting: one woman whispers to another and both gaze,

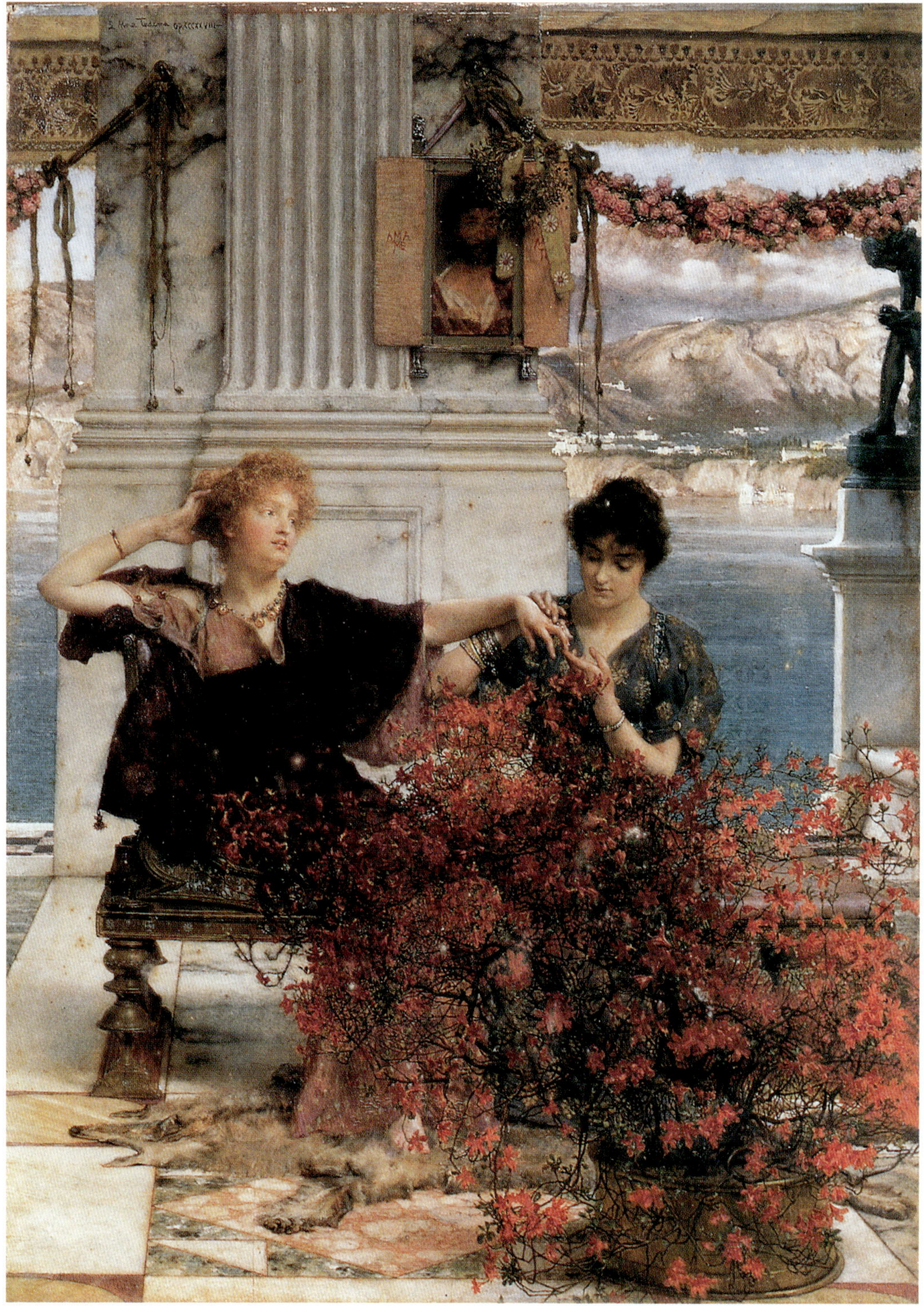

158
Love's Jewelled Fetter, 1895
Oil on canvas, 63·5 × 46·1 cm (25 × 18⅛ in)
Private collection

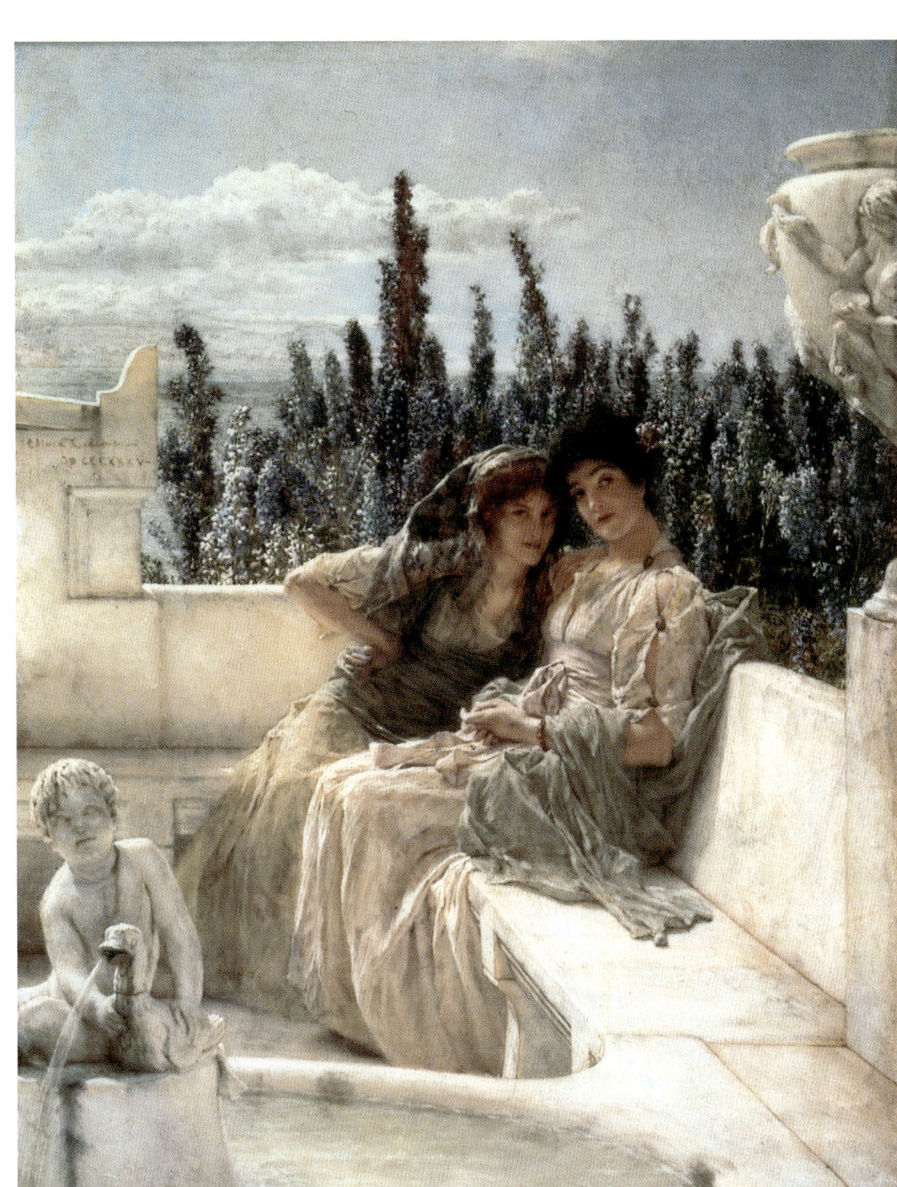

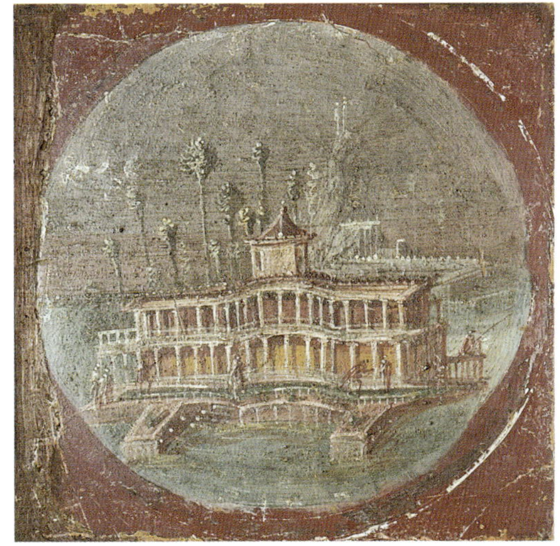

159
Whispering Noon, 1896
Oil on canvas, 56 × 39·3 cm (22 × 15½ in)
Private collection

160
Roman Wall Painting from Stabiae, 1st century AD
Archaeological Museum, Naples

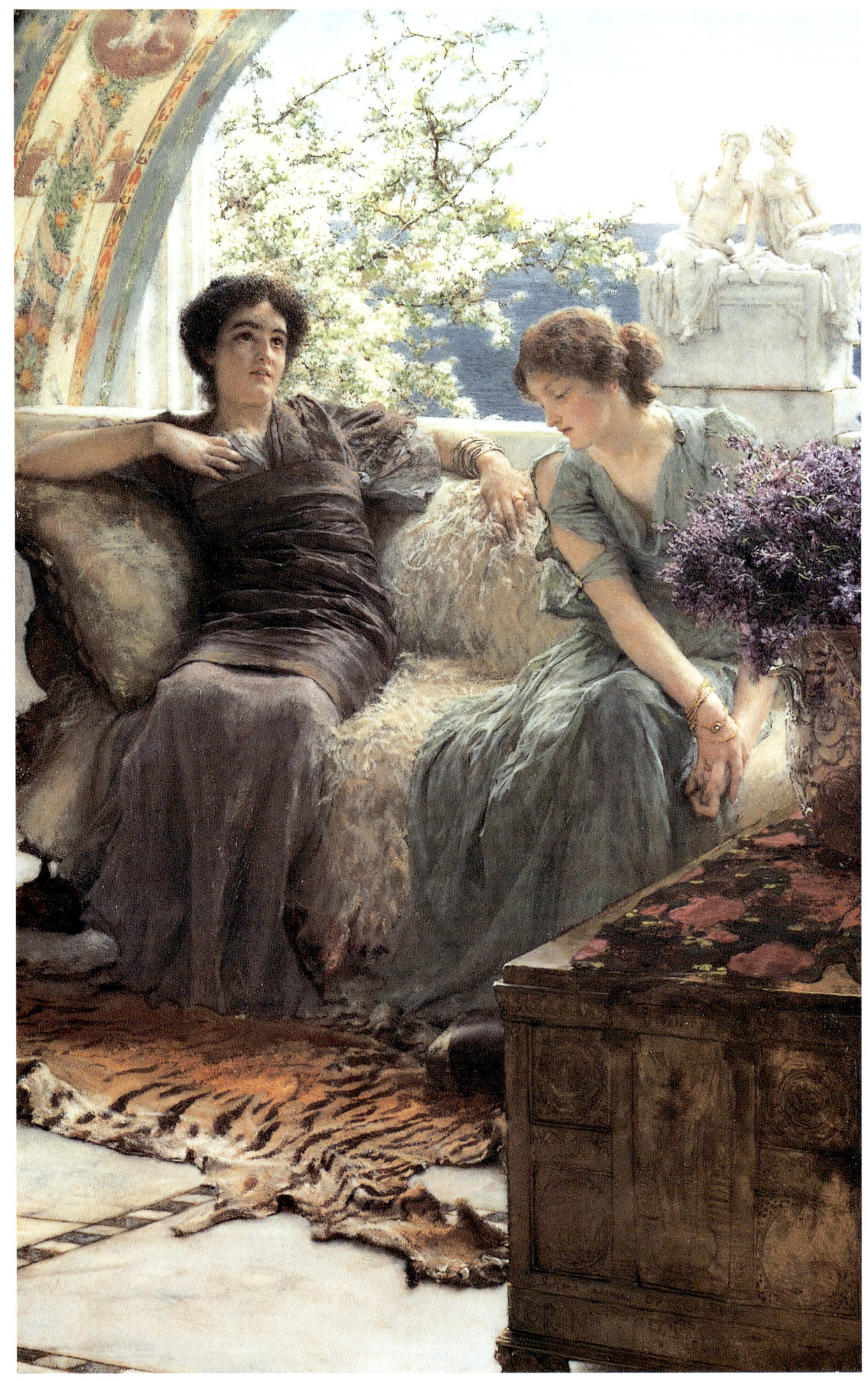

LAWRENCE ALMA-TADEMA 160

almost accusingly, at the viewer. Even paintings of male and female couples are not straightforward courtship scenes: the titles alone – *Unwelcome Confidence* (Pl.161), *The First Reproach* (1872), *My Sister Is Not In* (1879), *A Difference of Opinion* (Pl.162), *Vain Courtship* (1900) – suggest some problematizing of a love relationship.

Further significance is added to the reading of this group of paintings through the identification of their location, undoubtedly the Bay of Naples, a playground for the rich and famous from the early Empire.[283] The wealthy built spectacular seaside villas (*villae maritimae*), which they daringly placed on the edges of cliffs. The most glamorous of the *villae maritimae* was Tiberius' palace, the Villa Iovis, the remains of which still stand on the eastern clifftop of Capri. From the Latin poet Statius we have a vivid description of the sumptuous villa of Pollius Felix overlooking the bay of Puteoli;[284] and Roman wall paintings, such as a roundel from Stabiae (Pl.160) showing a sumptuous two-storied mansion, provide some visual record of palatial splendour; but only traces of these fabulous villas remain. In the nineteenth century, as today, grand hotels replaced the seaside villas, many of them built on the same sites.

Alma-Tadema usually displays nothing but small corners of his *villae maritimae*. Only a few paintings – *Your Carriage Stops the Way* (1880) and *Resting* (Pl.163) – re-create a coastline dotted with magnificent marble buildings. In *Resting* a woman sits on a marble *exedra*; behind her, a large marble structure on the edge of a cliff is enlivened with red and blue polychromatic colouring. The painting, sold through a Parisian dealer, was accompanied by lines of verse in French addressed to a woman named as Lais.[285] As Lais was the name of a famous Greek *hetaera* or courtesan, we are to think not only of a leisured life along the Bay of Naples but of high-class prostitution.

Certain resorts along the coast, in particular the popular seaside town of Baiae, had an unmistakably risqué reputation. The Roman moralist Seneca makes sure he leaves the day after he reaches town,[286] while the poet Propertius is insistent on the advice he gives his lover, Cynthia:

> But you must quickly leave degenerate Baiae:
> Those beaches bring divorce to many,
> Beaches for long the enemy of decent girls.
> A curse on Baiae's waters, love's disgrace![287]

Once we recognize the connotations of the district, the meaning and mood of paintings set in the Bay of Naples assume an extra frisson. *Coign of Vantage* (Pl.164) depicts three women high up

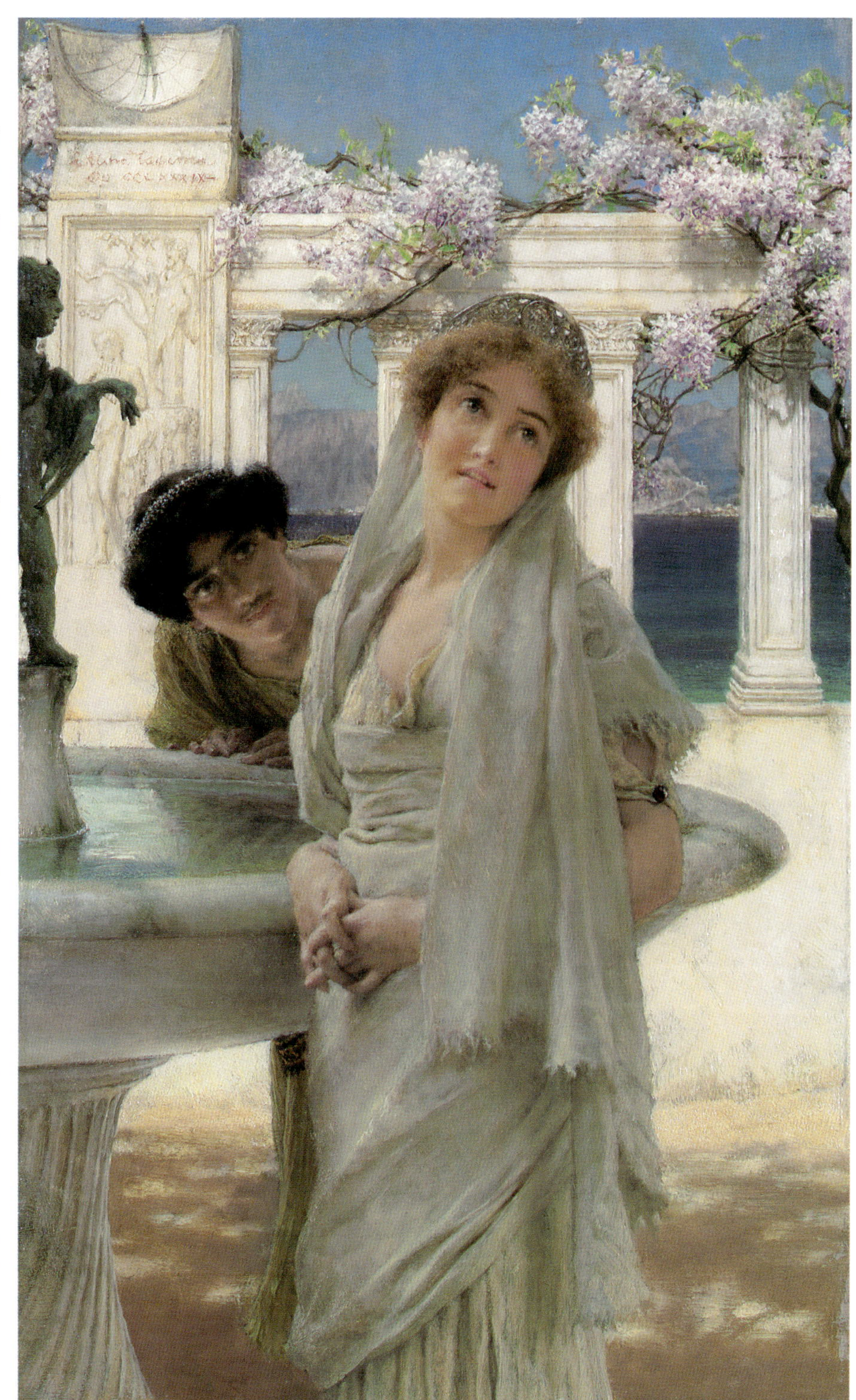

161 opposite
Unwelcome Confidence, 1895
Oil on wood, 47·5 × 28·5 cm (18 × 11¼ in)
Private collection

162
A Difference of Opinion, 1896
Oil on wood, 38·1 × 22·3 cm (15 × 8¾ in)
Private collection

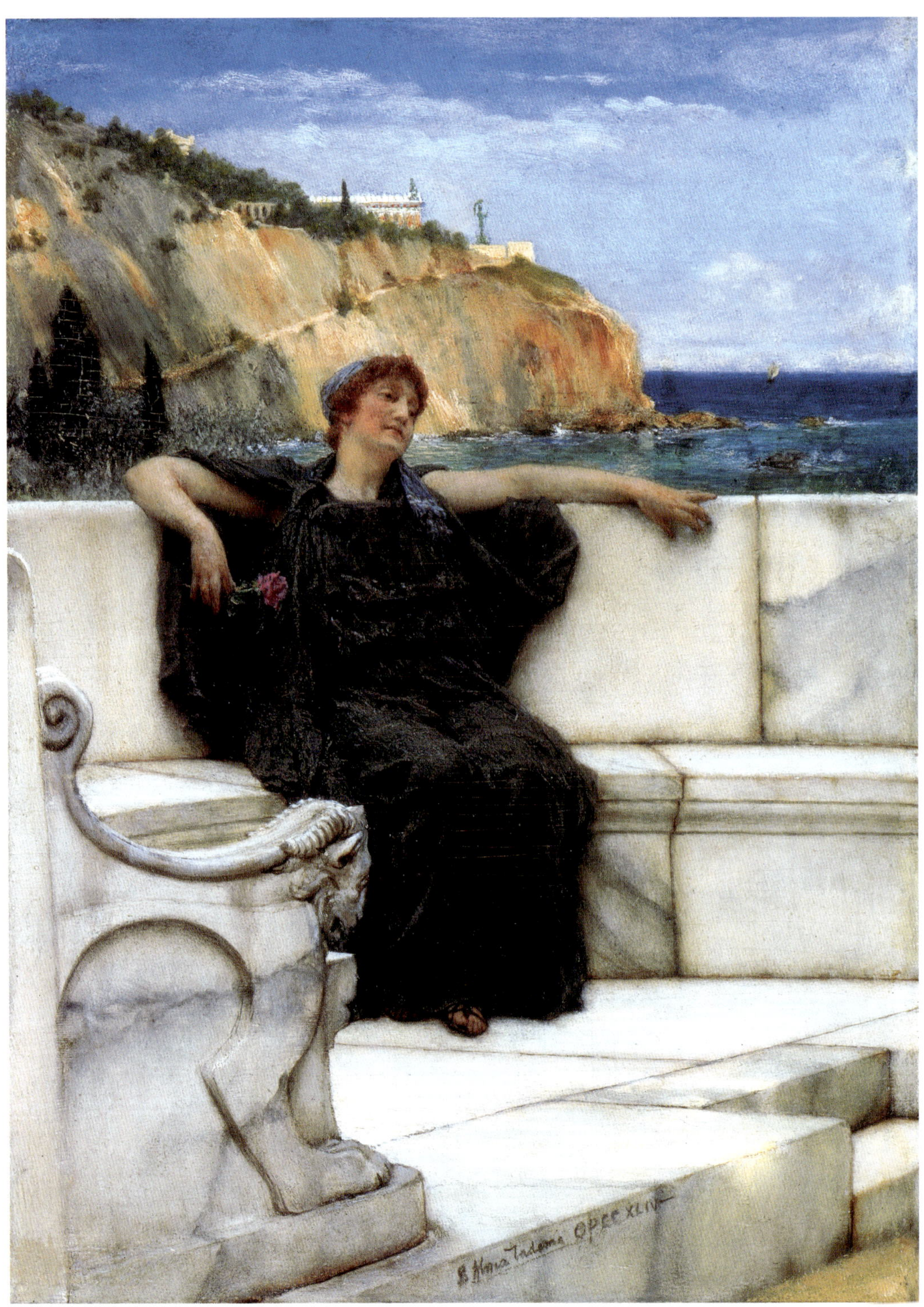

on a lofty marble terrace gazing down on ships sailing in the sea far below. The artist displays a spectacular perspective as our eye follows those of the woman leaning over the parapet to a dizzying drop and the sea far below.

The bronze animal in this painting has been identified as a free copy of a red granite Egyptian sphinx from the Villa San Michele at Capri, the home of Swedish writer and physician, Axel Munthe, built in the 1890s on the site of an ancient Roman house.[288] It is likely that Alma-Tadema may have been a house guest of Munthe. In any case, Alma-Tadema's choice of Capri, site of the most ostentatious *villa maritima*, that of the Emperor Tiberius, clearly indicates that his intention is to evoke the world of the imperial Bay of Naples at its most leisured and luxurious. The setting also recalls Ebers's house on the shores of the Starnberger See, complete with sculpted lions flanking steps leading down to the water's edge, and the artist may well have been struck by the similarities between this nineteenth-century holiday home and Roman *villae maritimae*.

The three women are represented as fashionable and rich aristocrats on holiday. Dressed in fine silks and adorned with jewels and fresh flowers, these women may not be the respectable Roman matrons one might assume, but pleasure-loving girls in search of the frivolous enjoyments of the Bay. From their elevated position the women watch the ships sailing into the Bay, surely pleasure boats: Seneca mentions exuberant sailing parties in his disapproving description of riotous living that he encountered on a visit to Baiae.[289] Similarly, Cicero's vivid account of the scandalous life of the aristocratic Clodia Metelli (the real woman identified as Catullus' Lesbia), lists, amongst her indulgences, trips to Baiae, beach-parties and boating picnics.[290]

Subject-matter and style change as pictures of wealthy Pompeians in archaeologically specific settings make way for couples or small groups of women on terraces overlooking the Mediterranean sea. Dark interiors are replaced by sun-lit exteriors and Roman Italy becomes one eternal sunny afternoon. Themes of luxury and leisure, nevertheless, remain constant and *Coign of Vantage* points to the same construction of Roman life found in *Catullus at Lesbia's*, painted thirty years earlier.

163
Resting, 1882
Oil on wood, 23·5 × 16·6 cm (9¼ × 6½in)
Private collection

164 opposite
Coign of Vantage, 1895
Oil on wood, 64 × 44·5 cm (25¼ × 17½in)
J. Paul Getty Museum, Malibu

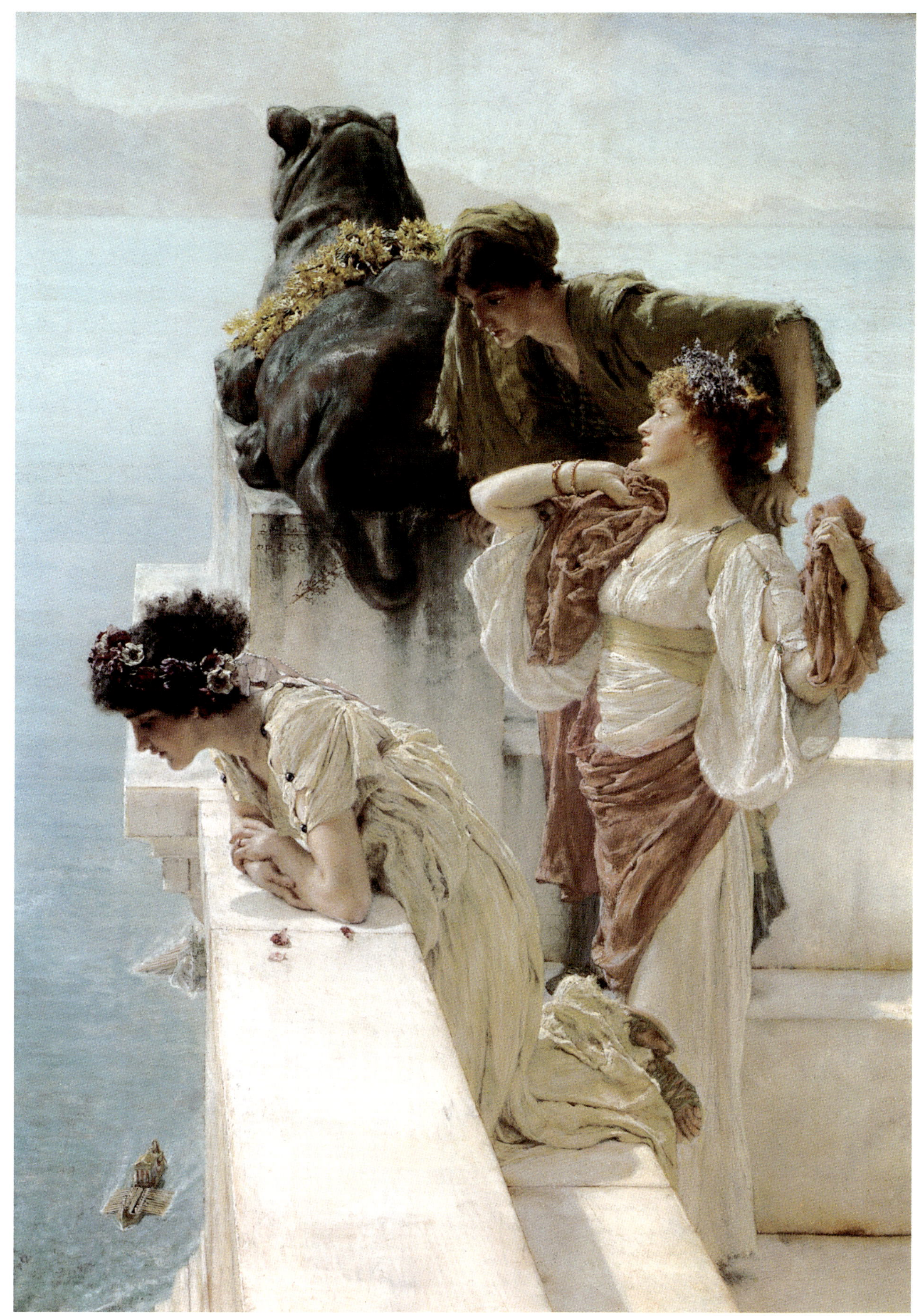

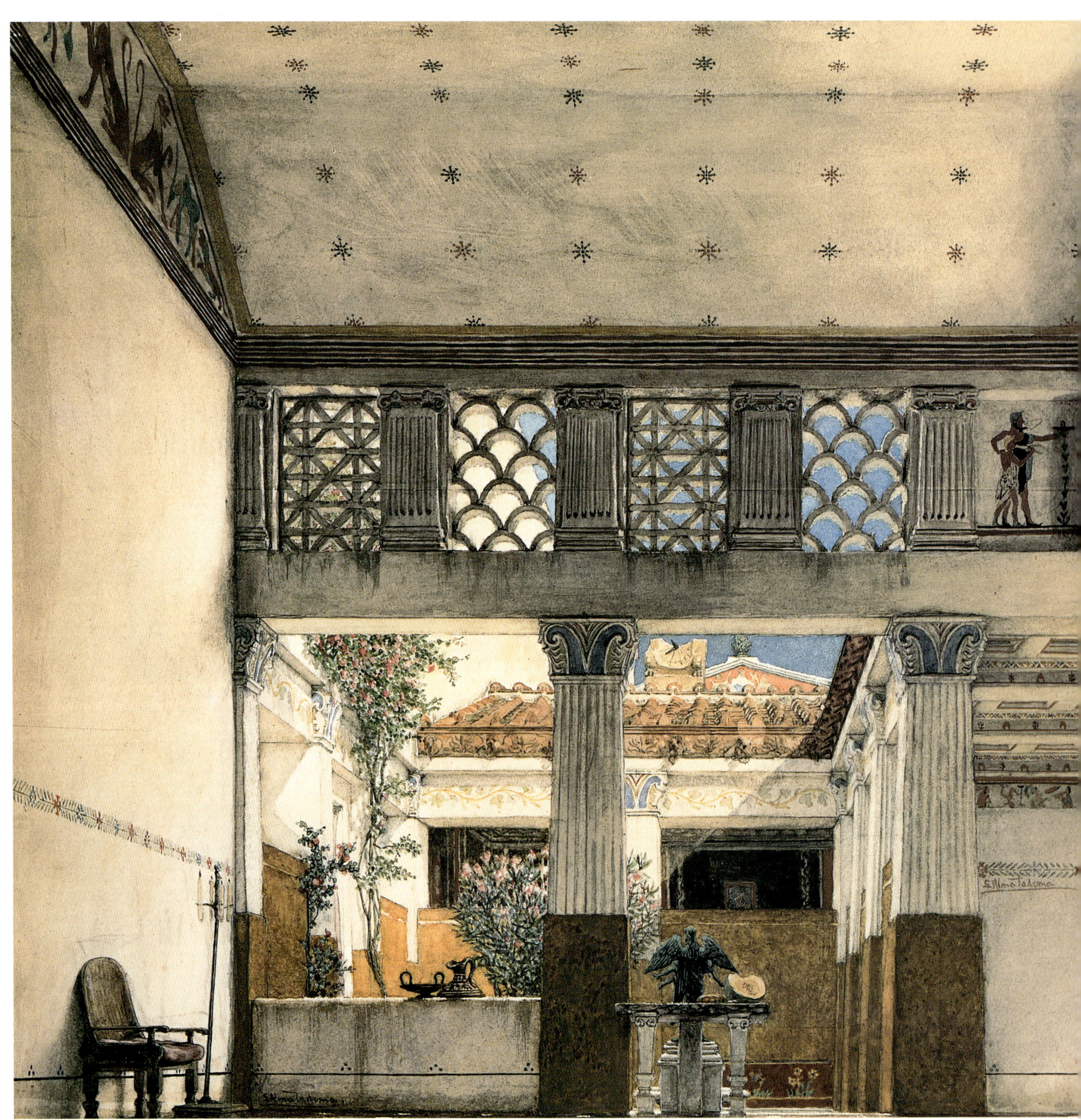

III/2
THE THEATRE

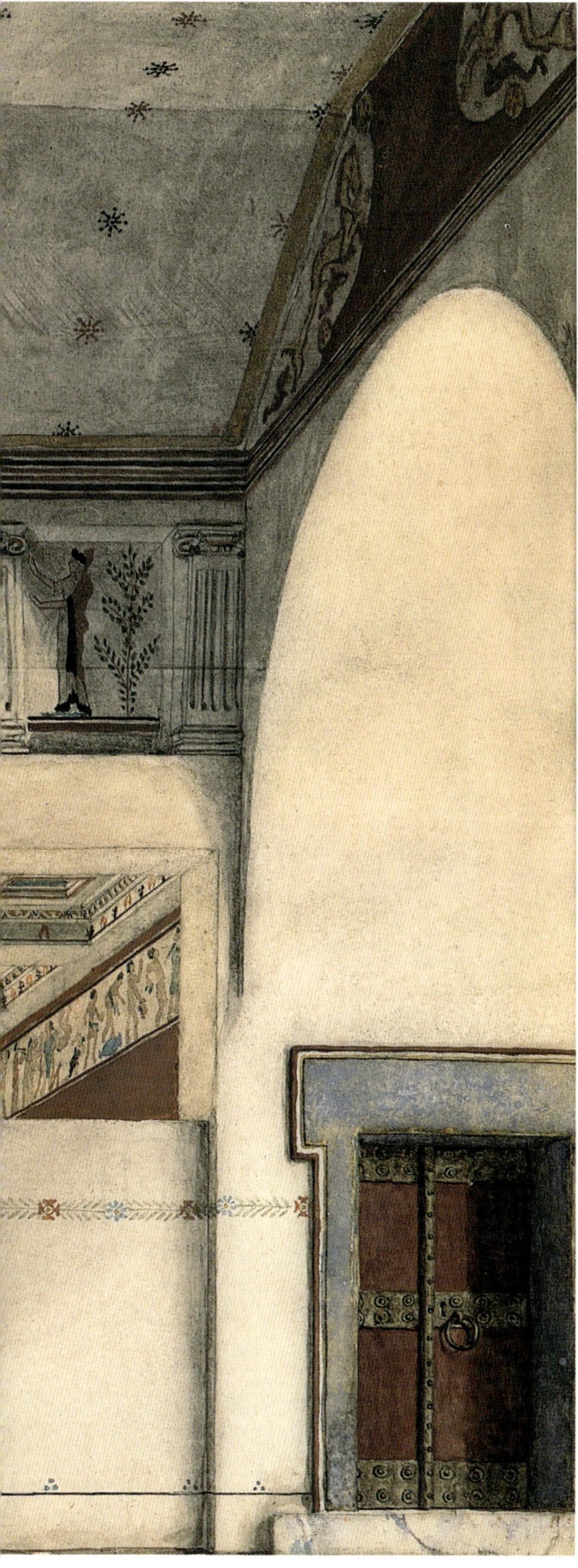

During the 1890s Alma-Tadema played an important role in the visualization of the ancient world on the Victorian stage. He designed stage sets and costumes for major Shakespearean and modern dramatic productions. His involvement with the theatre began in 1880 with Frank Benson's amateur production of Aeschylus' *Agamemnon* performed in the original Greek at Balliol College, Oxford. Benson sought the advice of classical scholars and eminent artists to ensure an authentic production. He reports in his memoirs: 'Many scholars rallied round. Professor Newton, of the British Museum, gave most helpful advice. Burne-Jones, Alma-Tadema, Leighton, by letter, and ocular demonstration of Bolton sheeting and fine linen and twisted muslin, gave me my first initiation into the mysteries of Greek drapery.'[291]

In an attempt to emulate the historical validity and cultural élitism associated with the high-art traditions of classical painting, amateur productions in London sought advice from the same authorities. In 1883 a charity performance of Professor George Warr's *The Tale of Troy: or Scenes and Tableaux from Homer* was staged at a private theatre with advice from the archaeologist, Charles Newton, and help from Leighton, Poynter and G. F. Watts regarding the arrangement of tableaux. In 1886 Warr's *The Story of Orestes* was performed with tableaux arranged by Poynter, Watts and Walter Crane. In the same year, John Todhunter's verse drama *Helena in Troas* was staged with advice from Alexander Murray of the British Museum and theatre designs by E. W. Godwin.[292] To judge from contemporary critical responses to these productions, aesthetic appeal and archaeological accuracy were valued above the dramatic quality of text and performance. Many artists offered support to these and other amateur productions, but Alma-Tadema alone went on to work in the professional theatre. His first semi-professional engagement was *Romeo and Juliet*, put on by Frank Benson with most of the amateur cast of the *Agamemnon* in 1881 at the Imperial Theatre, London, for which he (along with William Blake Richmond) acted as scenery and costume designer.

As early as 1879, Alma-Tadema had been commissioned by the celebrated actor-manager, Henry Irving, to design sets for a production of Shakespeare's *Coriolanus*. After the initial designs, the production was postponed and even-

165
Interior of Caius Martius' House, 1901
Watercolour with pencil and bodycolour, 36·3 × 50·7 cm ($14\frac{1}{4}$ × 20 in)
Manchester City Art Galleries

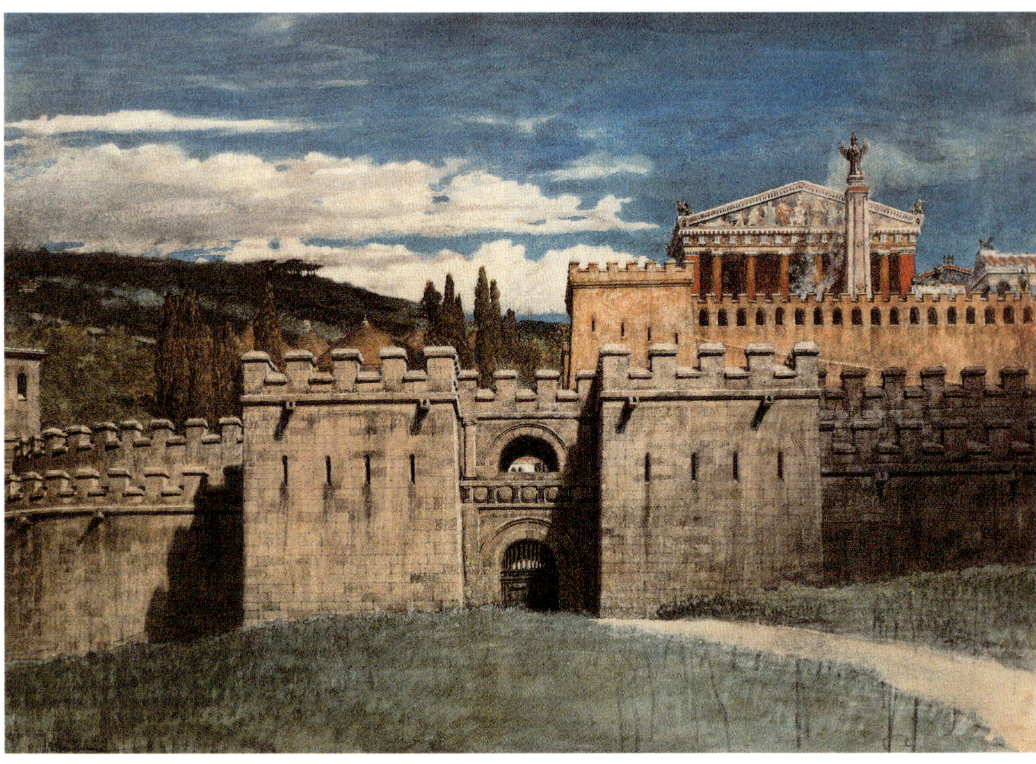

166
Antium seen from outside the City Walls: Design for Coriolanus, 1880s
Watercolour, 38·9 × 51·6 cm (15⅜ × 20¼ in)
Private collection

167 opposite left
Julia Neilson as Hypatia
The Sketch 1 March 1893, p.30

168 opposite right
Evelyn Millard as Portia
Magazine of Art, 1900, p.33

tually staged in 1901. Set in the Etruscan period, the production called for a highly original scenic design.[293] Alma-Tadema's method was to make a small model of the proscenium and the stage of the Lyceum theatre for his designs. Both model and designs were displayed at the Scenic Artists' Exhibition in 1905. He also produced watercolours based on the designs, for instance, *The Interior of Caius Martius' House* (Pl.165). With so little Etruscan architecture remaining, the artist looked to Vitruvius and Etruscan tomb decoration. The interior of Aufidius' house imitates tombs at Corneto, and an early fourth-century BC bronze chimera in Florence Archaeological Museum appears in a scene outside Aufidius' house. A pencil sketch of *Antium seen from outside the City Walls* (Pl.166) shows solid battlements with a more elegant classicizing temple in the background. The most significant aspect of the designs was the absence of marble, which, although now familiarly associated with images of Rome, was not present in the fifth and sixth centuries BC. The originality of his designs was stressed in the theatre programme which refers to a rejection of Neo-classicism in favour of archaeological authenticity. Meanwhile, in 1892 Alma-Tadema turned to Tudor England for Irving's *Henry VIII*. In 1896–7 he also worked on Irving's *Cymbeline*, where once again novel and ingenious sets and costumes were devised. Irving noted that the artist was dealing with 'a period almost new in art – the carved and ornamented wood, stone, and metal work of the early Britons.'[294]

During the 1890s the classical world was brought to the popular stage in the form of the Roman subject drama or toga play.[295] Toga plays were either adaptations of popular Roman historical novels such as Charles Kingsley's *Hypatia* (1854), Lew Wallace's *Ben-Hur* (1880) and Henryk Sienkiewicz's *Quo Vadis?* (1895) or original scripts following the basic formula of the standard historical novel. Paintings illustrating scenes from novels set a useful precedent for stage interpretation. David Mayer points out that the chariot race, the main attraction of *Ben-Hur* staged at the Theatre Royal, Drury Lane, in 1902 and again in 1912, was based on a painting of 1893, *The Chariot-Race* by Alexander von Wagner.[296] One of the first toga plays was Tennyson's verse drama, *The Cup*, set in the late Roman Empire and produced by Henry Irving in 1881, with himself and Ellen Terry in the leading roles. The subject is taken from Plutarch's discourses on the bravery of women, a text which Alma-Tadema turned to himself in *The Women of Amphissa*.[297] Sets and costumes were designed by E. W. Godwin, and while the play was a success, the authenticity of the sets was awarded special praise. The actor-manager, Wilson Barrett, produced a series of successful melodramas on classical themes including *Claudian* (1883), *Clito* (1886) and his most successful production, *The Sign of the Cross* (1895).

Alma-Tadema too turned to the popular theatre with Herbert Beerbohm Tree's 1893 toga play, an adaptation of Charles Kingsley's

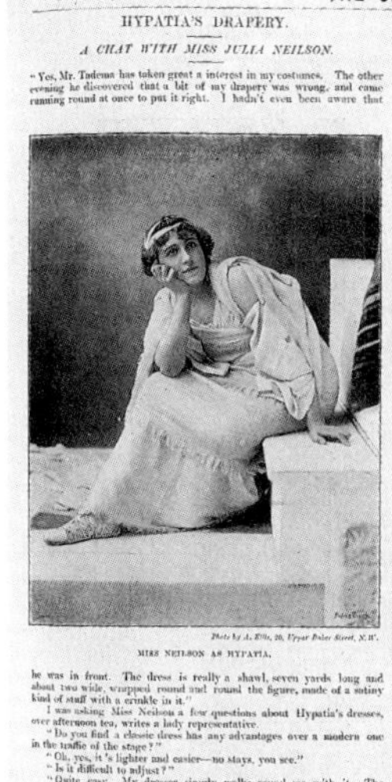

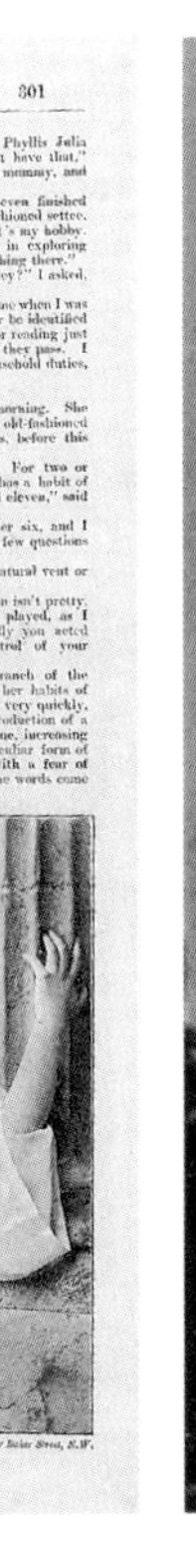

March 1, 1893 THE SKETCH. 301

HYPATIA'S DRAPERY.

A CHAT WITH MISS JULIA NEILSON.

"Yes, Mr. Tadema has taken great a interest in my costumes. The other evening he discovered that a bit of my drapery was wrong, and came running round at once to put it right. I hadn't even been aware that he was in front. The dress is really a shawl, seven yards long and about two wide, wrapped round and round the figure, made of a satiny kind of stuff with a crinkle in it."

Photo by A. Ellis, 20, Upper Baker Street, N.W.

MISS NEILSON AS HYPATIA.

I was asking Miss Neilson a few questions about Hypatia's dresses, over afternoon tea, writes a lady representative.

"Do you find a classic dress has any advantages over a modern one in the traffic of the stage?"

"Oh, yes, it's lighter and easier—no stays, you see."

"Is it difficult to adjust?"

"Quite easy. My dresser simply walks round me with it. The sleeve drapery is caught up with turquoises and ruby buttons."

"Yet I know one dressmaker who spent hours with a piece of stuff and a model trying to copy it. We fully expect to see something Grecian among the spring novelties. Stage dress seems to have such an influence on fashion."

"Well, if they copy my dress," laughs Miss Neilson, "they can't wear stays. Wouldn't that be a serious obstacle? I believe my gowns in 'The Dancing Girl' were copied."

"What about that wonderful coiffure you wear in the first act. Do you consider it becoming?"

"Rather. Mr. Tadema says it's pure Greek. Some of the other ladies' head-dresses are rather pretty, don't you think? I wear my own hair, though, of course, the loose curls at the back are artificial. It would be a rather inconvenient head-dress to die in—I have two falls—so my hair is done less elaborately for the last act."

Then I asked Miss Neilson—or Mrs. Terry, as one calls her at home—to tell me something about her taste in dress off the stage. She was wearing a neat black serge gown, and had her hair arranged—not in the horrid "bun," or chignon style—in a pretty, loose knot. I thought she looked handsomer off the stage than on.

"Oh! I love old clothes. When I get a dress that I like I stick to it. Colours I seldom wear, because I'm so tall. I prefer neutral tints, and I am very fond of black."

"Have I any pets? Yes, one who is all the world to me. You shall see her."

"Why, I didn't know you had a baby."

"Well, I have you see, and she rules the house. Phyllis Julia Neilson Terry. She's four months old. No, no, we can't have that," as the little mouth puckered ominously. "Come to your mummy, and be quiet."

"We've only been here a little while, and haven't even finished furnishing yet," she goes on, sitting down on an old-fashioned settee, with baby on her lap. "I am so fond of old furniture. It's my hobby. Not old oak—Chippendale and marqueterie. We delight in exploring out-of-the-way streets, and picking up a thing here and a thing there."

"Do your literary tastes make you an admirer of Kingsley?" I asked, presently.

"I love the book. I remember reading it for the first time when I was at school in Germany. Little did I think that I should ever be identified with such a work. No, I don't get a great deal of time for reading just now. The days seem to pass without one's knowing how they pass. I always have a walk or a drive, and then there are my household duties, and friends to see."

"Do you see much of Miss Terry?"

"Nell? Oh yes, I have been calling upon her this morning. She gave me this," picking up a silver rattle with a bit of old-fashioned ribbon fastened to it. "It was a present one Christmas, before this young lady was born or thought of."

The young lady alluded to became very lively now. For two or three minutes one could scarcely get a word in. "She has a habit of waking every day about six, and she won't go to sleep till eleven," said the mother. "I'll ring the bell and let nurse take her."

The grandfather's clock pointed to the half hour after six, and I knew that I had only a few minutes more to stay, so I put a few questions on an old matter which has lately been discussed.

"Do you think good acting is allowing your feelings natural vent or having them under complete control?"

"Real grief is often not effective on the stage. It often isn't pretty. Sometimes, when I have felt my part very deeply, and played, as I thought, better than usual, a friend has said: 'How badly you acted to-night.' No, I think you must have complete control of your emotions."

This fairly emphatic opinion seemed to close that branch of the subject; so my next questions were designed to get at her habits of study and her feelings on the stage. "I learn my parts very quickly, and mostly while I pace the room. A week before the production of a piece a feeling of nervous anxiety begins to grow upon me, increasing till the first night is over. After that, I suffer from a peculiar form of stage-fright. While playing, I am suddenly stricken with a fear of forgetting my words, but when the time comes for them the words come

Photo by A. Ellis, 20, Upper Baker Street, N.W.

MISS NEILSON AS HYPATIA.

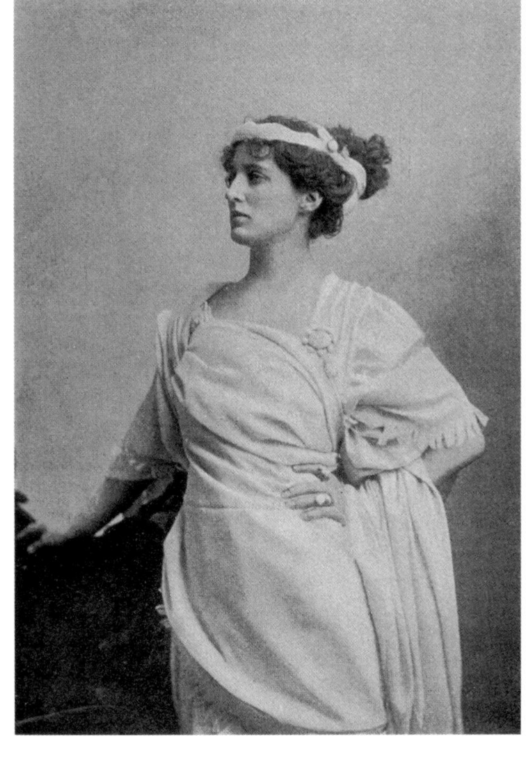

Hypatia, staged at the Theatre Royal, Haymarket. Although the adaptation by G. Stuart Ogilvie was not judged a success, critics praised Tree's acting, the loveliness of Julia Neilson as Hypatia, and, above all, the sets and costumes.[298] Tree remembered: 'notably beautiful was the scene in which Hypatia addressed the school, which was like a painting by Tadema himself.'[299] For the representation of fourth-century AD Alexandria, Alma-Tadema turned to Ebers's publications on Egypt: 'One reason why I especially appreciated your book was because I am since Christmas busy with reconstructing Alexandria for a play which will be reproduced here of *Hypatia* ... There is wretchedly little known of that once brilliant city.'[300] The actress Julia Neilson (Pl.167) recalls Alma-Tadema's concern over the costumes: 'Mr Alma-Tadema has taken a great interest in my costumes. The other evening he discovered that a bit of my drapery was wrong, and came running around at once to put it right.'[301] Her costume – head binding and himation wrapped around *chiton* – is clearly based on the characteristic female dress in Alma-Tadema's own paintings.[302]

Alma-Tadema's theatrical excursions also expanded his social connections. Frank Benson's wife, Constance, recalled the musical evenings in Grove End Road: 'many were the delightful entertainments we went to at Alma-Tadema's beautiful house in St John's Wood. There we met all the artists of the day, and had the privilege of seeing his beautiful pictures. He used to show me through a magnifying glass, the marvellous delicacy of his flower painting.'[303]

In 1898 Alma-Tadema was working with Tree again on a production of *Julius Caesar*,[304] in which he advised on costume, scenery and other practicalities, including the form of the Roman handshake.[305] Alma-Tadema himself recounted problems with authenticity: 'I had no end of difficulty in persuading them to be truly Roman in appearance. Portia would wear jewels and so on.'[306] Nonetheless, an illustration of Evelyn Millard as Portia (Pl.168) reveals that he was successful in persuading her to appear without jewellery. Other difficulties arose as Tree requested that Alma-Tadema incorporate the work of the French artist Jean-Léon Gérôme into his designs. Edwin Booth's 1871 production of *Julius Caesar* in New York had based the assassination of Caesar on Gérôme's famous painting, *The Death of Caesar* (Pl.169), in which the dead body of Caesar lies in front of Pompey's statue. Eventually Tree rejected Gérôme's configuration: an illustration of the staging of the death scene (Pl.170) shows Pompey's statue to the left, while Caesar's body lies to the centre of the stage.

The production was a success and, once again, sets and costumes were singled out for particular praise. George Bernard Shaw hailed Alma-Tadema as 'the real hero of the revival', and suggested that 'the scenery and stage colouring deserve everything that has been said of them'.[307] Criticism, however, was voiced against Eastern-style architecture in the forum:

> All the pomp and majesty of a highly-civilised and cultured Empire, all these garlands and roses and rich Eastern hangings, suit rather the time when we speak of Roman emperors than that archaic city which had all the virtues, steadfast courage, and patient endurance of the older Latin stock.[308]

Accuracy of stage design was evidently taken very seriously. The theatre issued an official apologia stating that, although the forum scene was anachronistic in date, it was not so in spirit and quite in keeping with the pleasure-seeking society of late Republican Rome. The fact was that as in many of Alma-Tadema's works, archaeological details were taken from different periods. Alma-Tadema delighted in challenging the viewer's preconceptions and certainties about the look of the ancient world by changing the size, material and function of statuary and by combining artefacts of widely differing dates in the same composition. At the same time, these artefacts were chosen to add meaning and significance to any given scene.

One of his most striking innovations in the theatre was the introduction of a new style of toga, replacing a 'thin linen robe of somewhat scanty proportions ... something like a voluminous night-shirt' with 'a huge garment of heavy cloth which would allow infinite varieties of wearing, and which would preserve the body

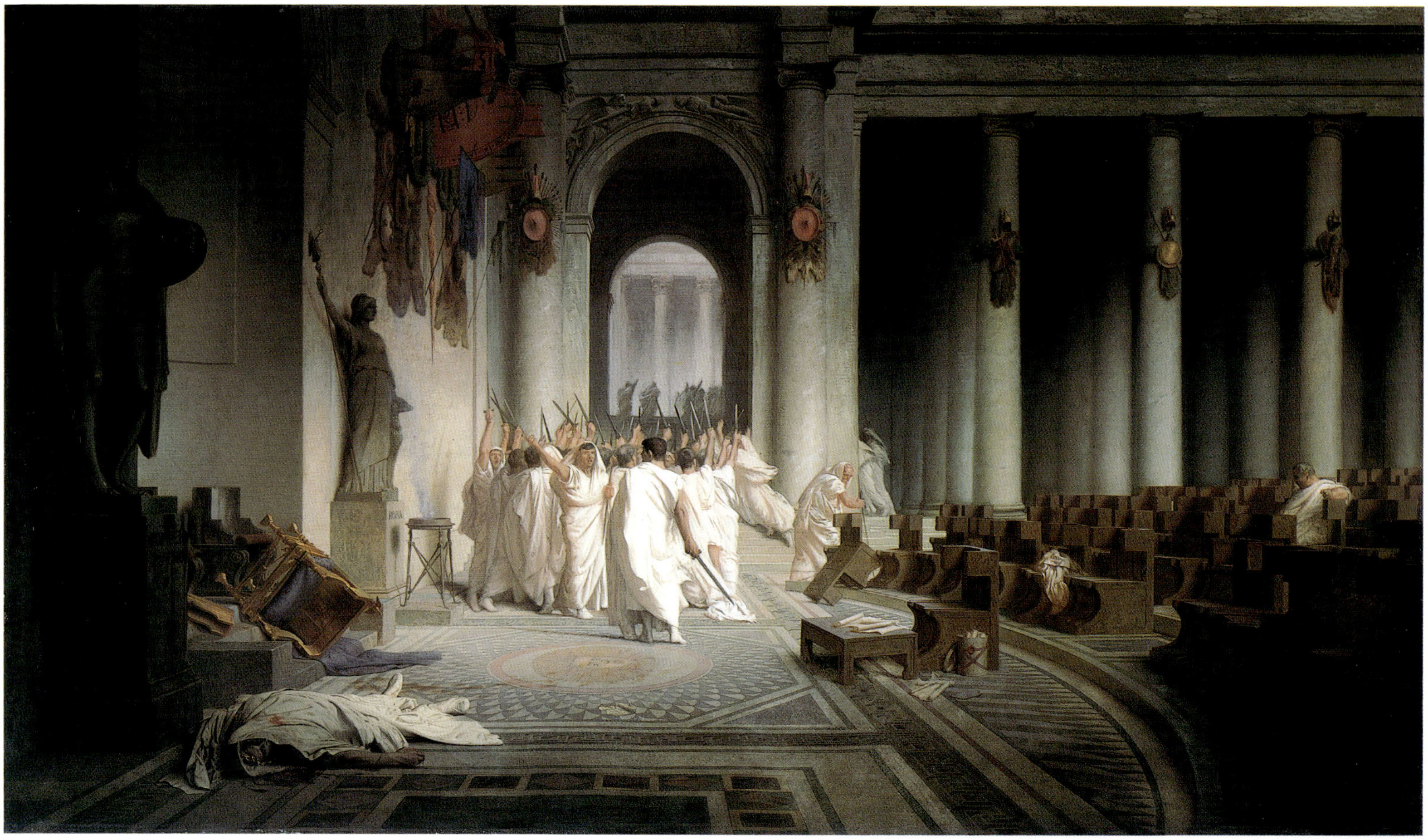

169 top
Jean-Léon Gérôme, *The Death of Caesar*, 1867
Oil on canvas, $85\cdot5\times145\cdot2$ cm ($33\frac{5}{8}\times57\frac{1}{8}$ in)
Walters Art Gallery, Baltimore

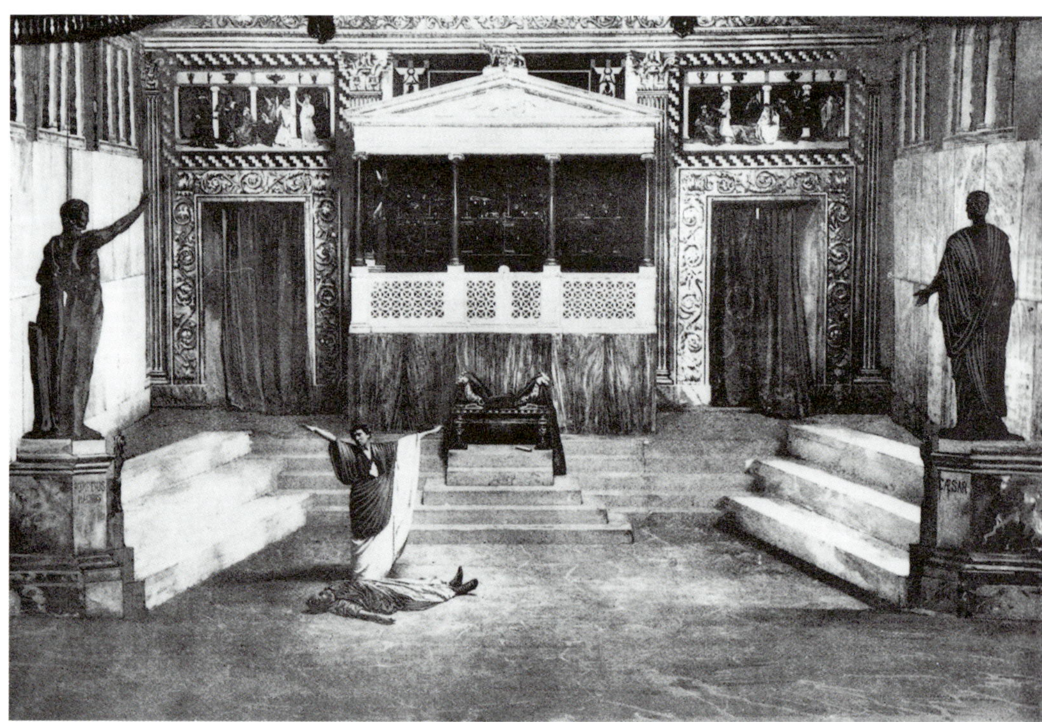

170
The Death of Caesar from Herbert Beerbohm Tree's production of *Julius Caesar*
The Sketch 9 February 1898, p.91

from the burning heat of the day and the reacting chills of night.'[309] Alma-Tadema's work in the Victorian theatre set a precedent for future classical-subject productions and attention (although not strict adherence) to archaeological detail became commonplace from the 1890s to the second decade of the twentieth century. The scene painter Joseph Harker, who worked with Alma-Tadema on *Hypatia*, *Julius Caesar* and *Coriolanus*, recalls a more direct inspiration in describing his method for painting a scene for Shaw's *Caesar and Cleopatra*, staged in 1907:

> I had been given only the vaguest details about the scene that was needed and acting on my own initiative had modelled a country house on the banks of the river Nile, with a garden full of blue flowers fringing the river, my source of inspiration being a beautiful picture by Alma-Tadema.[310]

In a similar spirit, Percy Macquoid, who designed the costumes for Stephen Phillips's *Nero*, staged in 1906, undoubtedly imitates Alma-Tadema's Roman paintings. Macquoid's drawing for the costume of Lalage the maid (Pl.171) shows a blue *himation* worn over a violet *chiton* as worn by the standing woman in *Silver Favourites* (Pl.181).

It has been suggested that Alma-Tadema's work even had an influence on cinematic representations of antiquity. Certainly, the tradition of archaeological authenticity, initiated by Alma-Tadema and others in nineteenth-century stage productions, was inherited by early films and carried on to the heyday of Hollywood and beyond. The panoramic views and crowd scenes in Alma-Tadema's paintings are, furthermore, alleged to have directly inspired the Hollywood epics of Cecil B. Demille.[311]

Alma-Tadema's work for the stage illustrates the diversity of his achievements: he excelled in painting, interior design and theatrical design. His productions went some way to revolutionizing the representation of antiquity in the Victorian and Edwardian theatre and even looked forward to the way the classical world would appear in the cinema. Given his involvement in the theatrical world, it is not surprising that one of his own paintings, *The Meeting of Antony and Cleopatra* (Pl.109), is based on a scene from Shakespeare's play.

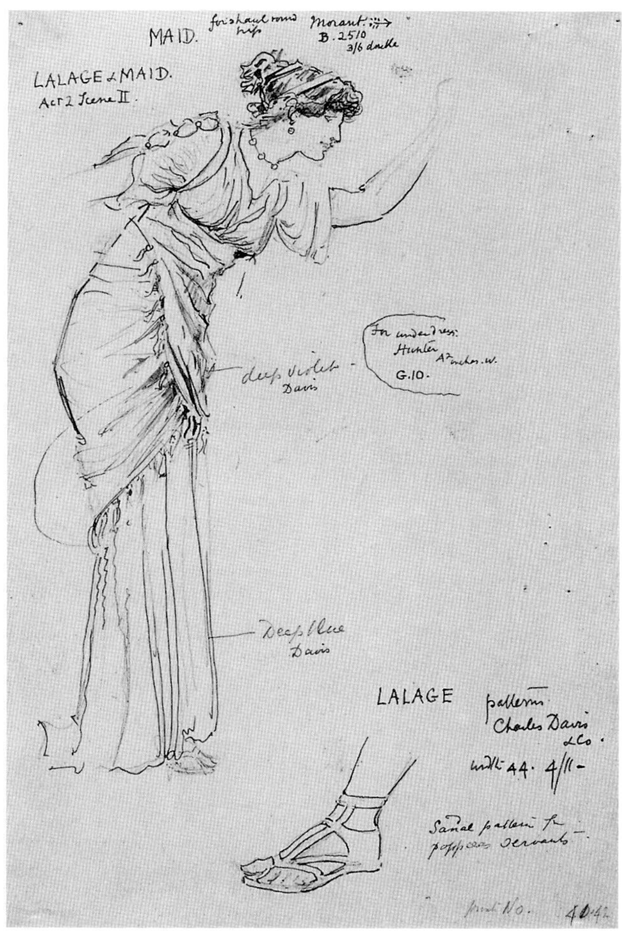

171
Percy Macquoid, drawing for costume of Lalage the maid in Stephen Phillips's *Nero*, 1905-6
Pencil on paper, 25·5 × 17 cm (10 × 6¾ in)
University of Bristol

III/3

THE FINAL YEARS

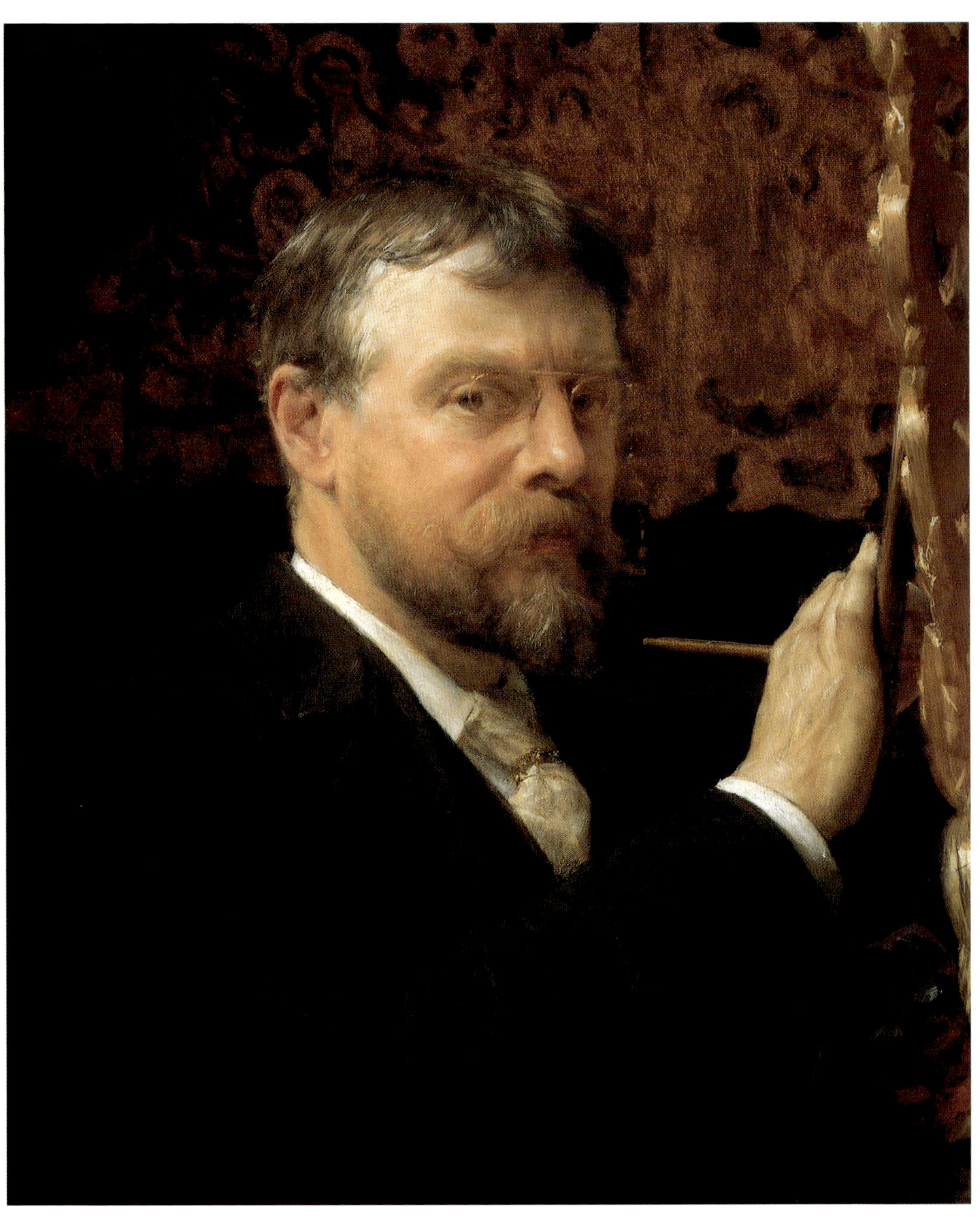

172
Self-Portrait, 1896
Oil on canvas, 65·7 × 52·8 cm (25⅞ × 20¾ in)
Uffizi, Florence

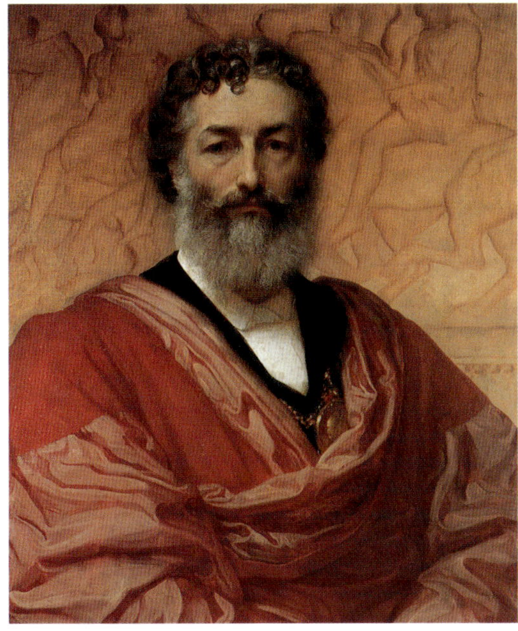

173
Frederic Leighton, *Self-Portrait*, 1880
Oil on canvas, 76·5 × 64·1 cm (30⅛ × 25¼ in)
Uffizi, Florence

By the end of the nineteenth century the reputation of the Royal Academy as the guardian of excellence in British art was gradually being undermined. As early as 1880, Joseph Comyns Carr judged that the Academy would need 'some vigorous measure of re-organisation in order to bring it into sympathy with the greatly increased demands of the time',[312] and, as the opening years of the new century unfolded the attack intensified. New artistic trends from the continent – Impressionism, Post-Impressionism, Fauvism, Cubism – were beginning to shape the future of modern art, but the Academy and its members remained resolute in their determination to maintain traditional art forms. Independent exhibition societies were formed to show the works of young artists excluded from the Academy. Around the same time, the Slade School of Art, established as an alternative to the Academy Schools, produced a succession of remarkable young artists – Augustus John, William Orpen, David Bomberg, Stanley Spencer – who were to play a leading role in challenging the old traditions of British art.

From 1890 D. S. MacColl, art critic for the *Spectator*, and George Moore, for the *Speaker*, launched a new movement in art criticism which championed progressive young artists but also sought to discredit the Academy and prominent Academicians at every opportunity.[313] Moore attacked archaeological exactitude in art, and singled out Alma-Tadema's *Sappho* for special condemnation, judging it to be 'as interesting as a page of Smith's *Classical Dictionary*'.[314] Over a century of privilege and prestige could, however, not be so easily undermined, and for the general public the Royal Academy continued to stand as the summit of British artistic achievement, and its members continued to enjoy wealth and status.

In 1896 Alma-Tadema was honoured with a commission for a self-portrait (Pl.172) for the celebrated gallery of painters' self-portraits at the Uffizi Gallery in Florence. It was a mark of some achievement to be present in a collection which began in the seventeenth century and included many of the Old Masters. Frederic Leighton had been commissioned for a portrait in 1880, and here is a conspicuous contrast between the likenesses of the two men. Leighton (Pl.173) shows himself dressed in the robes of his honorary doctorate from Oxford University, wearing the gold medal of his Presidency and posed before the equestrian frieze of the Parthenon sculptures. By contrast, Alma-Tadema's image is far less pretentious; it shows the artist dressed in an ordinary dark suit with a backdrop of embroidered cloth. Paintbrush in hand, as in his very first self-portrait, he presents himself as a working artist. It is curious that the robust sense of humour evident in his personality does not manifest itself in his self-portrait.

In the same year, 51 of his pictures were shown at the Royal Society of Artists spring exhibition in Birmingham. He was to finish his term as president in the autumn, and hence it was appropriate that as principal exhibitor he was granted special privileges. Invited to make any required alterations to the exhibition, he ousted the members' entries from most of the large gallery to hang his own in a single line. During a dinner given in his honour, when the members expressed a certain dissatisfaction, 'Alma-Tadema himself was serenely unconscious of anything wrong, but all through the evening told stories in quaint broken English.'[315]

Queen Victoria's Diamond Jubilee in 1897 meant that Alma-Tadema was obliged to fulfil his duties as Academician and be present at the many attendant events. A letter from Laura to Georg Ebers, apologizing for not being able to visit Tutzing, accounts for Alma-Tadema's time during this period: 'The fact is that so much of Tadema's time is taken up officially, what with all the exhibitions and different societies to which my husband belongs, he is always having to go to "meetings" and with the social life too throughout the Winter, Spring and early Summer, his time for work is very much swallowed up and broken.'[316] Social life seems to have

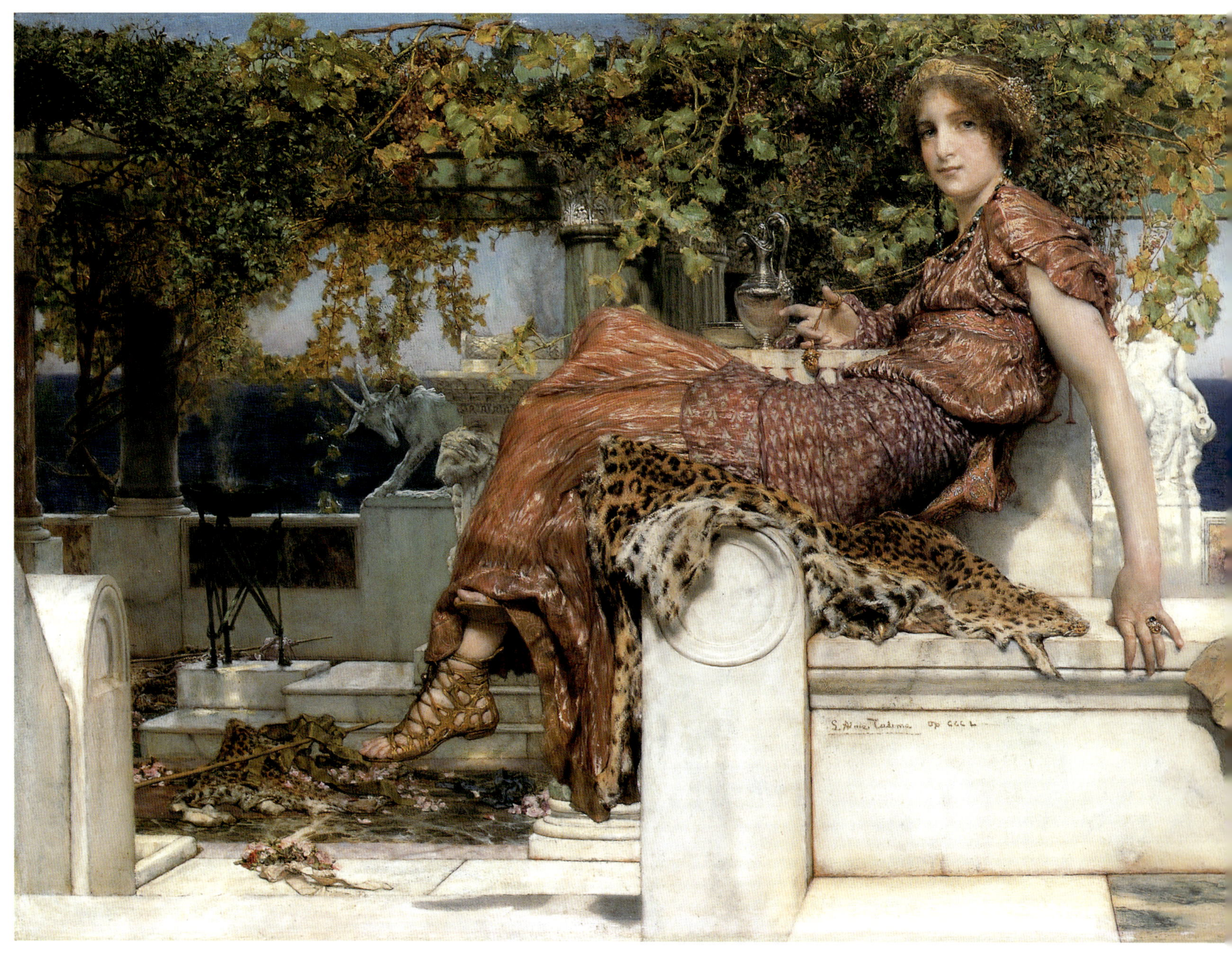

174
The Conversion of Paula by Saint Jerome, 1898
Oil on wood, 53·5 × 111·8 cm (21 × 44 in)
Private collection

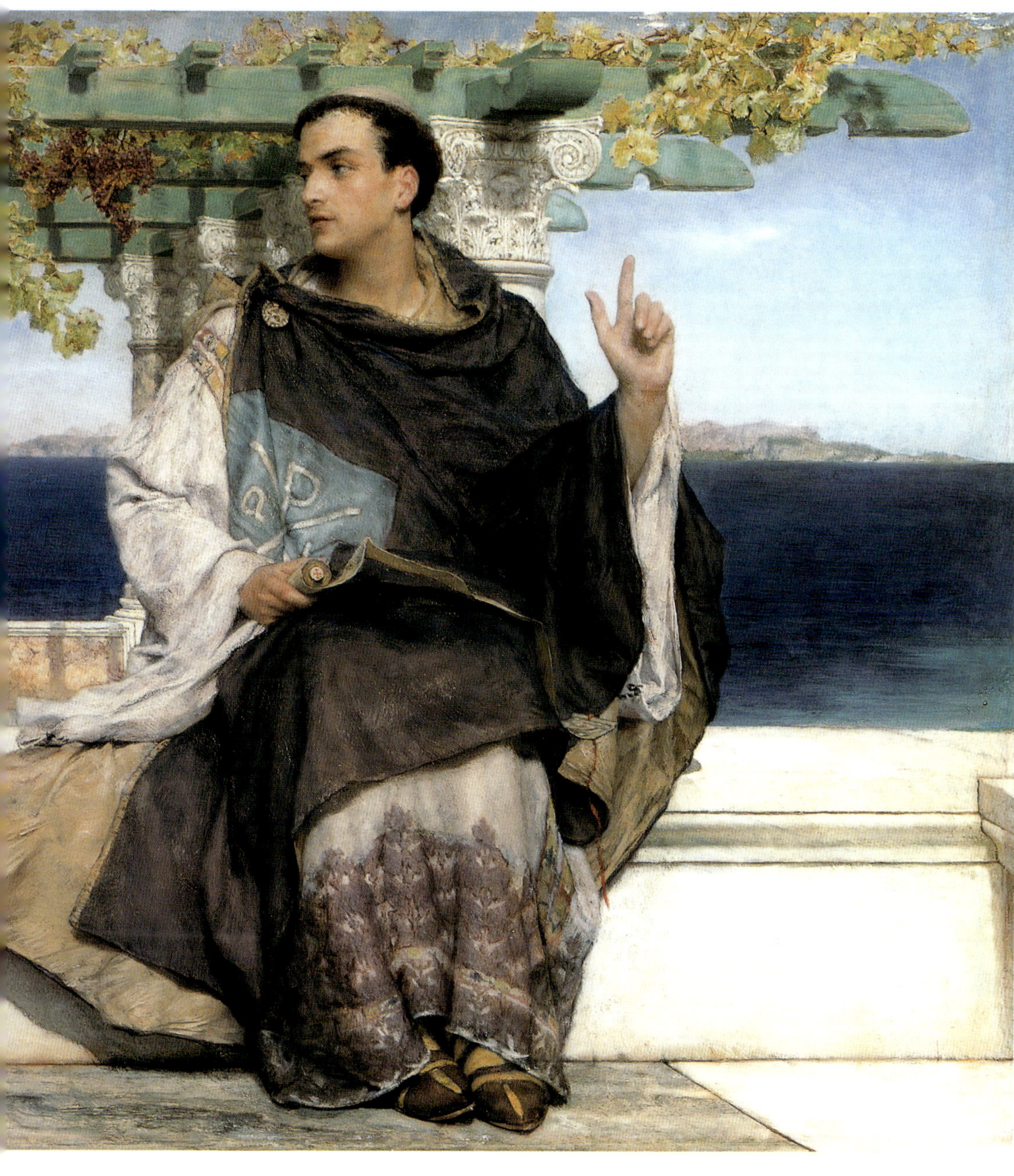

been of prime importance to the artist. Invitations to functions and events as well as hosting his own gatherings confirmed Alma-Tadema's position in society. However, he obviously did not view such occasions as tedious obligations and entered into festivities with relish. A theatrical production of classical tableaux at the home of the Ionides family found Alma-Tadema in attendance 'in toga and eye-glasses crowned with flowers'.[317]

For his next major painting Alma-Tadema turned to Christianity in the Roman world with *The Conversion of Paula by Saint Jerome* (Pl.174). While his early Merovingian scenes depict a Christianized late antiquity, all of the other classical-religious paintings look at pagan rites. Victorian representations of Christians in the Roman world tend to dwell on scenes of persecution in which the spectator is torn between outraged sympathy and voyeuristic enjoyment.[318] Toleration and conversion in the later Empire was evidently perceived as a far less compelling subject.

The Conversion of Paula by Saint Jerome shows the celebrated churchman, Jerome, discoursing to Paula, a high-born Roman lady, and presupposes a familiar narrative: Jerome (AD 347–420) begins his career as a monk in Palestine, and later withdraws to the Arabian desert to lead a completely ascetic life; on his return he goes to Rome where he becomes confessor to various patrician women. Paula we know as one of a group of Christian women who, on the death of her husband, gave herself up completely to a religious life. Alma-Tadema's painting is a fanciful representation of the young Paula as a wealthy and pleasure-loving aristocrat.[319]

Paula and Jerome sit on a marble terrace beneath a vine-covered pergola. The artist presents the cleric as a youthful and attractive figure, quite unlike usual representations of a tormented and ascetic hermit (such as Leighton's Diploma picture, *Saint Jerome* (1869)). Paula perches on the end of a marble bench with her back to Jerome and appears completely uninterested in his conversation. She sits on a leopard skin, while the accoutrements of Bacchic worship – *thyrsus* and scattered flowers – rest beside her. The statues in the background, although half-obscured, can also be seen to have a connection with the Bacchic cult. Both the goat and seated nymph (traditional members of the *thiasus*) are probably halves of playfully erotic sculptural groups. Favoured decorative items appear in more than one painting and a jug here, much changed from the weathered bronze original in Naples Museum, also appears in *An Audience at Agrippa's* (Pl.74), *A Bath* (1876), *The Way to the Temple* (Pl.84), *A Dedication to Bacchus* (Pl.135), *The Triumph of Titus AD 71* (Pl.116), *A*

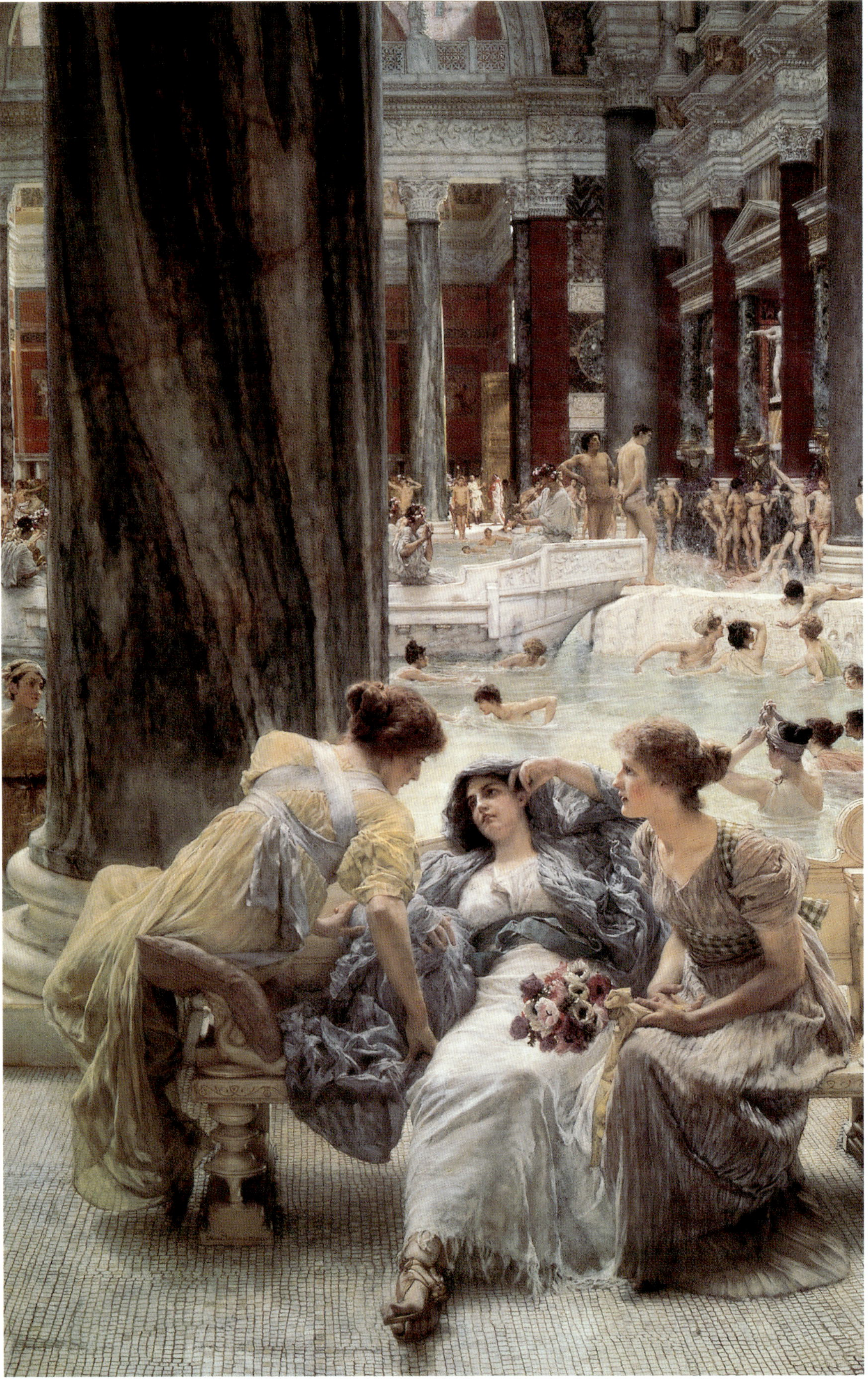

LAWRENCE ALMA-TADEMA 174

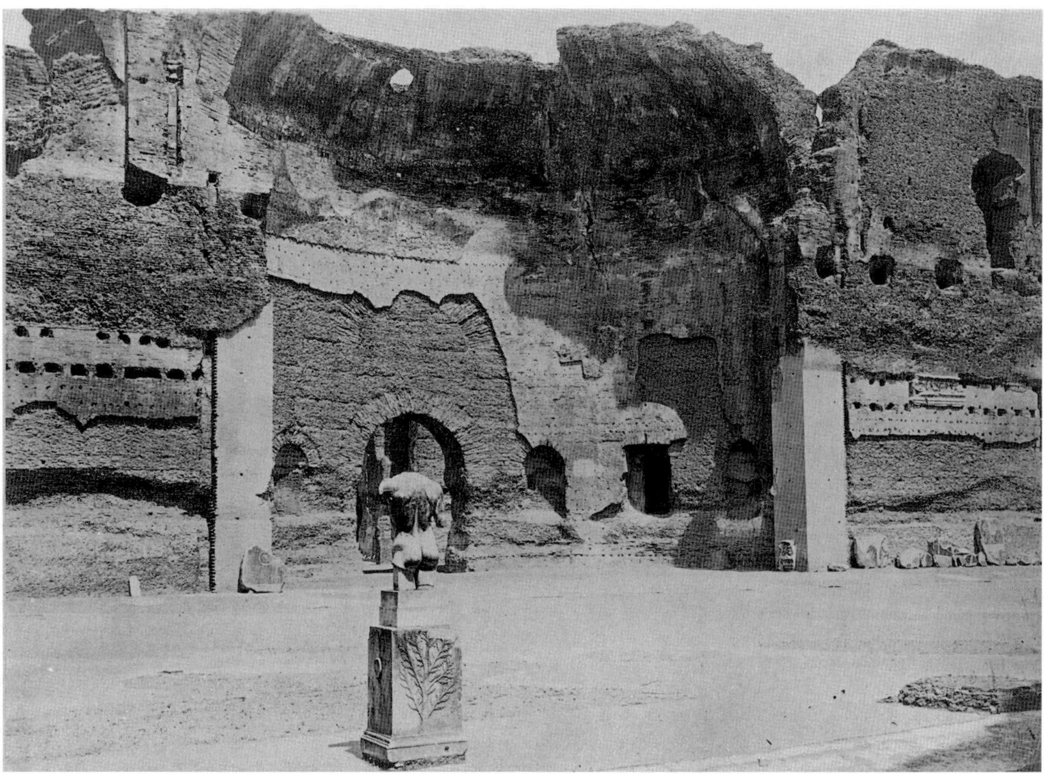

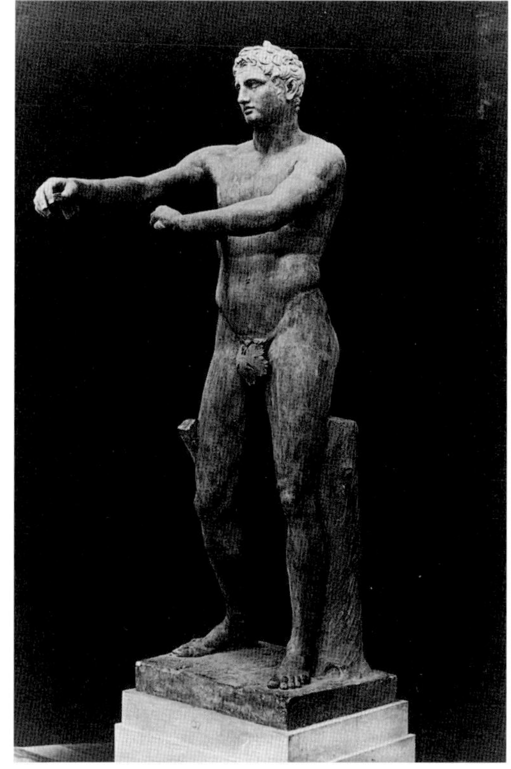

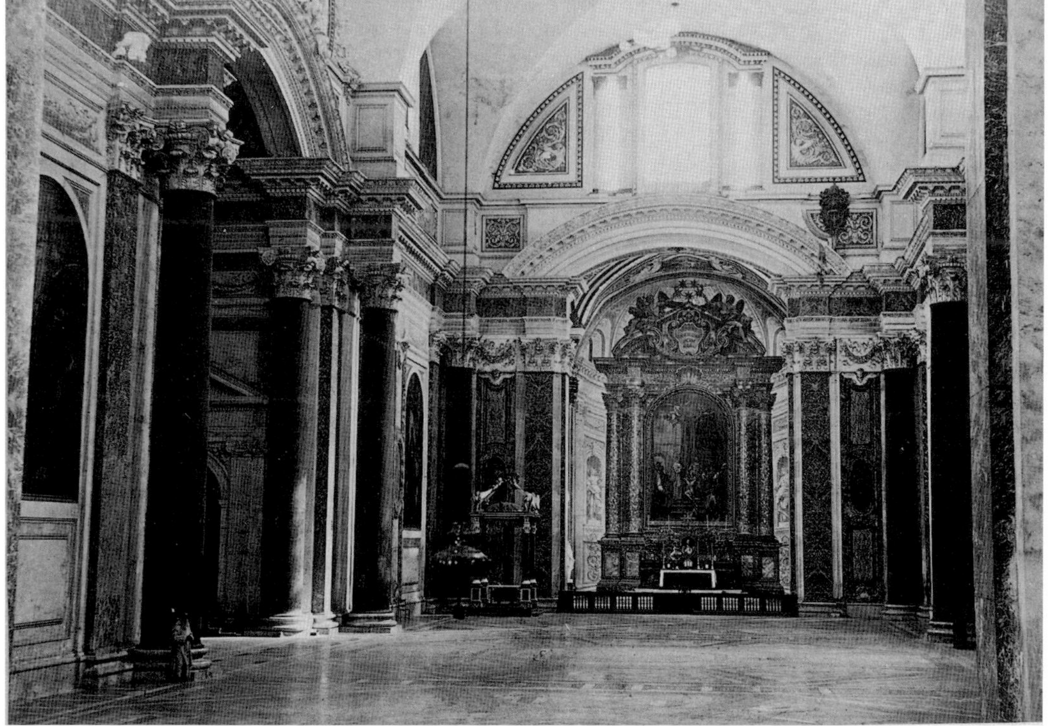

175 opposite
Thermae Antoninianae, 1899
Oil on canvas, 152·5 × 95 cm (60 × 37⅜ in)
Private collection

176 top left
The Baths of Caracalla, Rome:
University of Birmingham

177 top right
Apoxyomenos, Roman copy of a 4th-century original
Marble, Vatican Museum, Rome:
University of Birmingham

178 bottom
The Baths of Diocletian (Church of S. Maria degli Angeli), Rome:
University of Birmingham

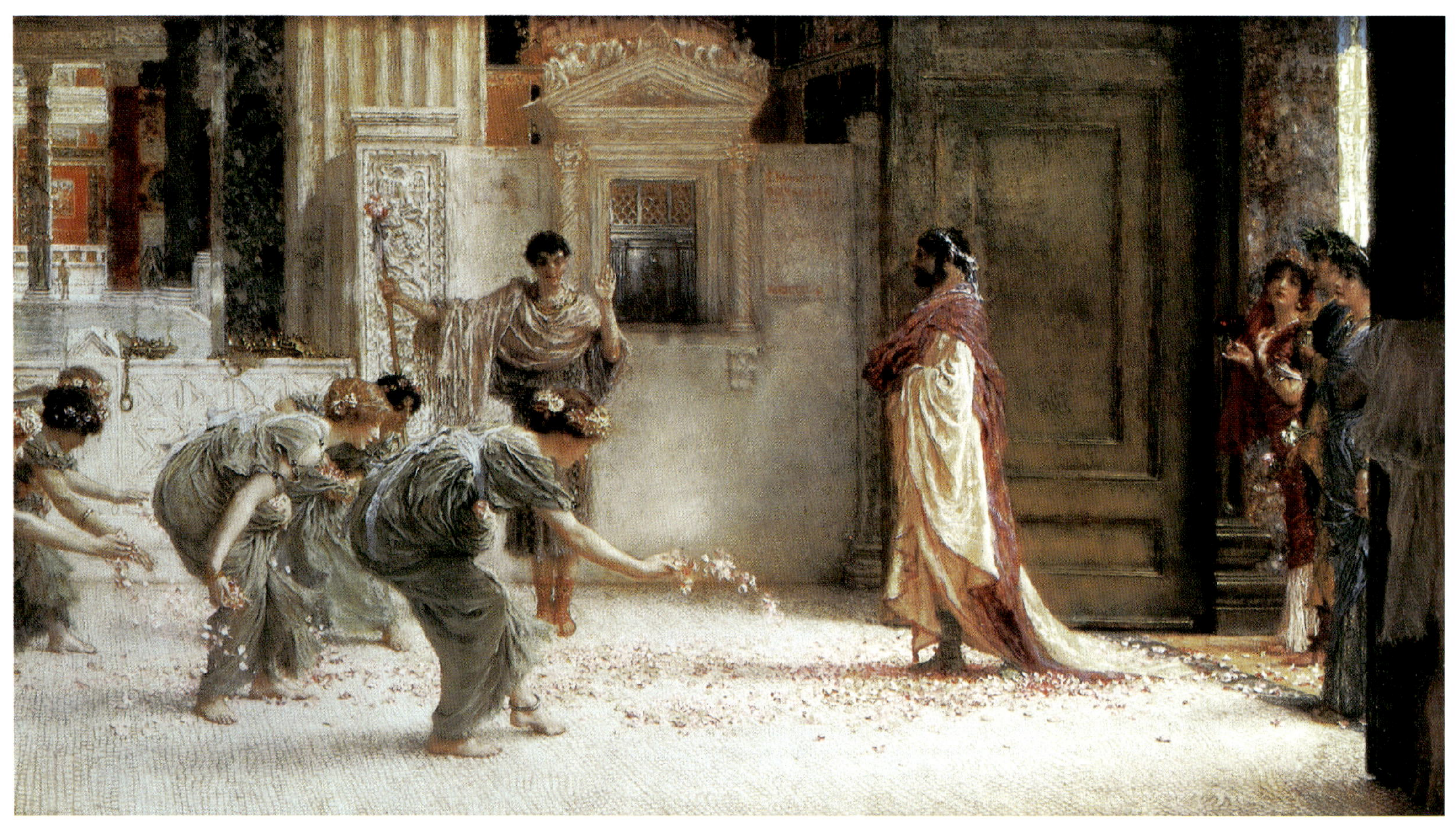

179
Caracalla, 1902
Oil on wood, 23·5 × 39·5 cm (9¼ × 15½ in)
Private collection

Silent Greeting (1889), and *The Roses of Heliogabalus* (Pl.131), and, on an enlarged scale, in *Between Hope and Fear* (Pl.64).

The gorgeous setting, the Bacchic accessories, the beautiful Paula in her fine dress and jewellery, combine to provide such a strongly attractive vision of paganism that the painting could easily be retitled 'The Temptation of Saint Jerome'. It is only because we are assumed to know that the historical Paula followed Jerome from Rome to Palestine that we are assured of ultimate Christian success. Contemporary critics were uneasy about this tongue-in-cheek portrayal of the triumph of Christianity. The critic of the *Magazine of Art* concluded that: 'it is difficult to believe that the artist was quite serious in his realisation of the weak missionary before whose apparently limp and uninspiring exhortations the imperious beauty yields up her pagan faith.'[320]

It could be argued that many of Alma-Tadema's representations of ancient Rome court controversy in that he consistently looks to the corrupt and the risqué. And yet in general it is only the half-hidden archaeological imagery and obscured allusions to textual sources which lead us to such a Rome. By contrast, in *The Conversion of Paula by Saint Jerome*, it is not veiled imagery but the 'weak missionary' and the 'imperious beauty' themselves who subversively proclaim the attractions of pagan over Christian. If this was an experiment, by way of sounding out public taste, Alma-Tadema was evidently not disposed to repeat it. He returned to his methods, his usual marble, flowers and Mediterranean sunlight and his usual subversive imagery. His reviewers rewarded him by returning to their usual terms of praise and raised no more moral objections.

Marble terraces set against sparkling Mediterranean sea and sky had now become Alma-Tadema's trademark. In an interview in 1899, the artist was asked: 'And yet your work, Sir Lawrence, is mostly of the same kind – the public won't let you paint much without blue sky and white marble in it.' He replied: 'That is true, but it only increases, I think, the strain upon the artist. I have attained – at least, people think I have attained – to excellence in a certain groove of art. I must continue to work in that groove, but at the same time I must not merely repeat myself.'[321]

Marble, once again, was to prove the focal point of his next major work, *Thermae Antoninianae* (Pl.175). The spectacular Thermae Antoninianae or Baths of Caracalla were initiated by Septimius Severus and completed by Caracalla at the beginning of the third century AD. Originally encompassing a vast area, the baths and exercise and leisure spaces were lavishly decorated with stunning variegated marbles, exotic stones and mosaics. Alma-Tadema owned a number of photographs of the well-preserved site situated on the outskirts of Rome (Pl.176). The first modern study of the site was undertaken with Abel Blouet's 1828 publication,[322] followed by drawings by the Russian architect, S. A. Ivanoff, of the restored baths in 1847 and 1848. Ivanoff's drawings were published in 1898, along with a commentary by the archaeologist C. Huelsen.[323] Alma-Tadema's painting, completed a year after Huelsen's publication, must surely have been influenced by Ivanoff's lavish and imaginative reconstructions of the baths.

Another possible source is the slightly later, larger and equally lavish bath complex of the Baths of Diocletian in Rome, of which Alma-Tadema also owned a number of photographs (Pl.178).[324] Excavations did not begin at the site until 1889 with a major publication the following year.[325] However, in 1563 the *frigidarium* had been converted into the church of Santa Maria degli Angeli by Michelangelo. Eight colossal red granite columns became the nave of the church and perpetuated something of the luxuriant magnificence of the original baths. Although Alma-Tadema's painting does not follow the exact format of the Baths of Diocletian, he may well have used Michelangelo's conversion as a guide for both architectural detail and imaginative use of space.

The painting encapsulates not only the magnificence of the bath house but the social nature of the Roman bath ritual. Beginning after lunch and lasting for several hours, it involved not only washing and bathing, but exercise, socializing and relaxation. In the foreground, a group of women are absorbed in conversation, while behind them figures of both sexes bathe, swim and frolic. Among the crowd, garlanded flute players contribute to the leisurely ambience. The heady combination of indolent women, bathers and opulent surroundings led F. G. Stephens to declare that 'the frivolous society of the decaying Empire lives again in this picture.'[326] The same atmosphere of extravagance and *ennui* is found in *The Roses of Heliogabalus*,[327] and in both paintings one is captivated by a scene of indulgence and in no way provoked to make a moral judgement on the perceived idleness of ancient Rome, or indeed any moral judgement at all.

In the background right, the outstretched arm of a statue is visible in a niche. This sculpture is a well-known Greco-Roman statue, the Apoxyomenos (Pl.177), an athlete scraping oil from his body with a strigil. Interestingly, the artist has not included actual statues found in the baths, the Farnese Hercules or Dirce and the bull. The Greek athlete cleaning his body after exercise makes a pointed comparison with the attitude of the indolent Roman bathers, while further light on Alma-Tadema's choice of the Apoxyomenos is shed by Pliny, who mentions the statue as a favourite statue of the Emperor Tiberius:

> Although at the beginning of his principate he kept control of himself, he was unable to do so in this case, and had the statue removed to his bedroom, substituting another in its place. But the Roman people became so indignant at this that they raised an outcry at the theatre shouting 'Give us back our Apoxyomenos!' So despite his admiration for it, the emperor returned it.[328]

This tacit association injects an extra element of eroticism into the scene.

After *Thermae Antoninianae* was exhibited at the Academy and returned to the artist, small details were altered.[329] A perfectionist himself, Alma-Tadema demanded the same kind of commitment from those he worked with. Millie Lowestam, the daughter of the engraver Leopold Lowenstam, stated that working with Alma-Tadema was difficult and almost impossible for her father, the artist never being satisfied and always demanding changes and corrections.[330]

Two years after the painting was exhibited, Alma-Tadema cited it as his favourite picture in an interview in the *Strand Magazine*,[331] while he also chose to reproduce a section of it for another painting, *Caracalla* (Pl.179). *Thermae Antoninianae*, a painting of women and bathers, also includes a portrait of the Emperor Caracalla, although miniaturized and relegated to the back of the canvas. In *Caracalla*, the Emperor, a beautifully dressed young man walking on a carpet of rose petals, makes his entrance to the fabulous baths dedicated in his honour.

Alma-Tadema's standing in the British art world was acknowledged with a knighthood in 1899. He could now be counted among the list of illustrious Dutch-Flemish artists who were knighted by British monarchs: Rubens, Van Dyck, Lely, Kneller. The Royal Academy of Arts held a large banquet in his honour at the Hotel Metropole. The celebration was postponed owing to Laura's ill health but on 4 November 160 guests assembled, including all the major names in the world of contemporary British art. In 1896 Frederic Leighton had died: he was succeeded briefly, as President of the Royal Academy, by John Everett Millais and then by another classical-subject painter, Edward Poynter. For this occasion, as Poynter was away, Edward Onslow Ford acted as the Master of Ceremonies. Joseph Comyns Carr composed a poem

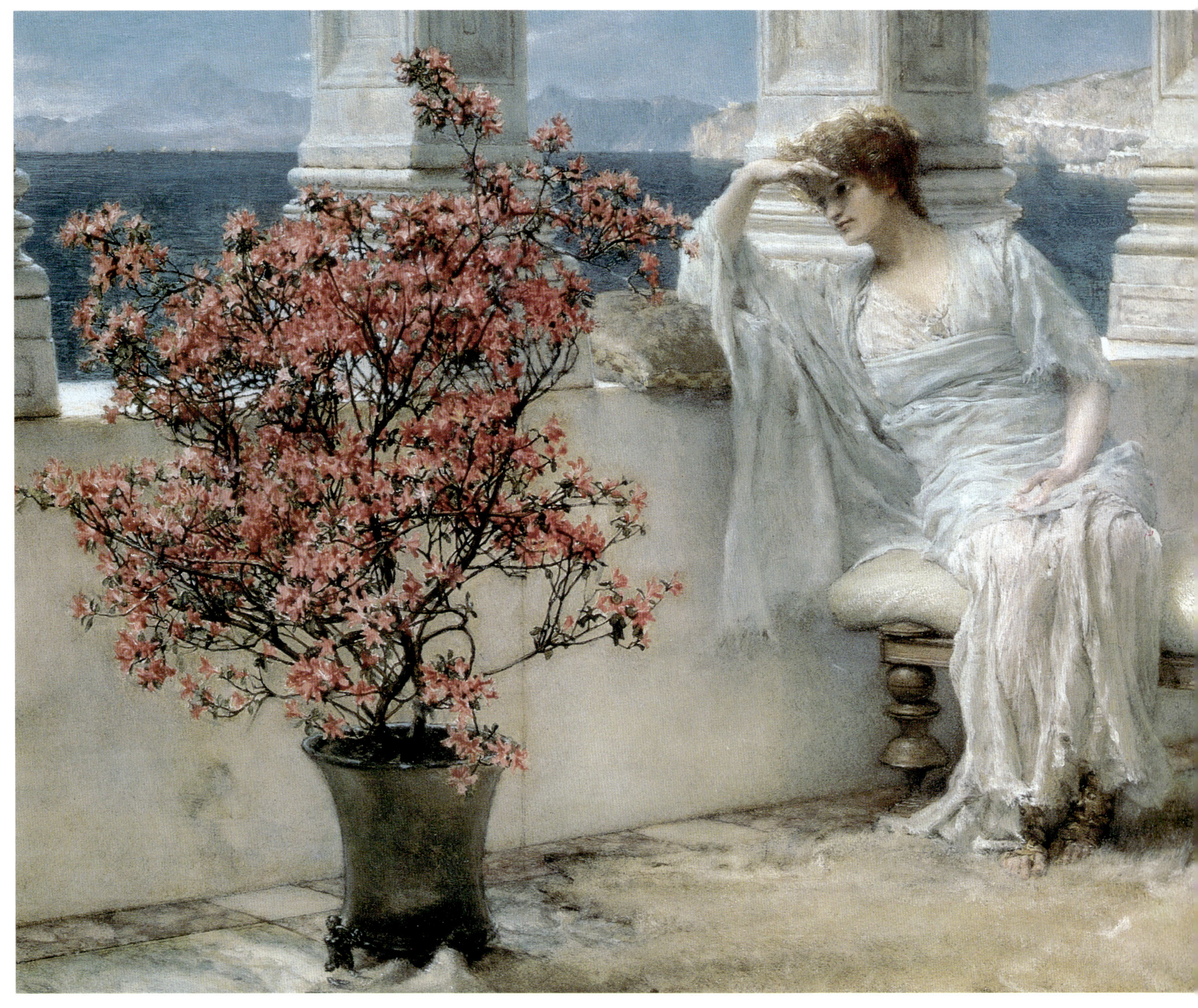

180
Her Eyes Are with her Thoughts and They Are Far Away, 1897
Oil on wood, 22·9 × 38·2 cm (9 × 15 in)
Private collection

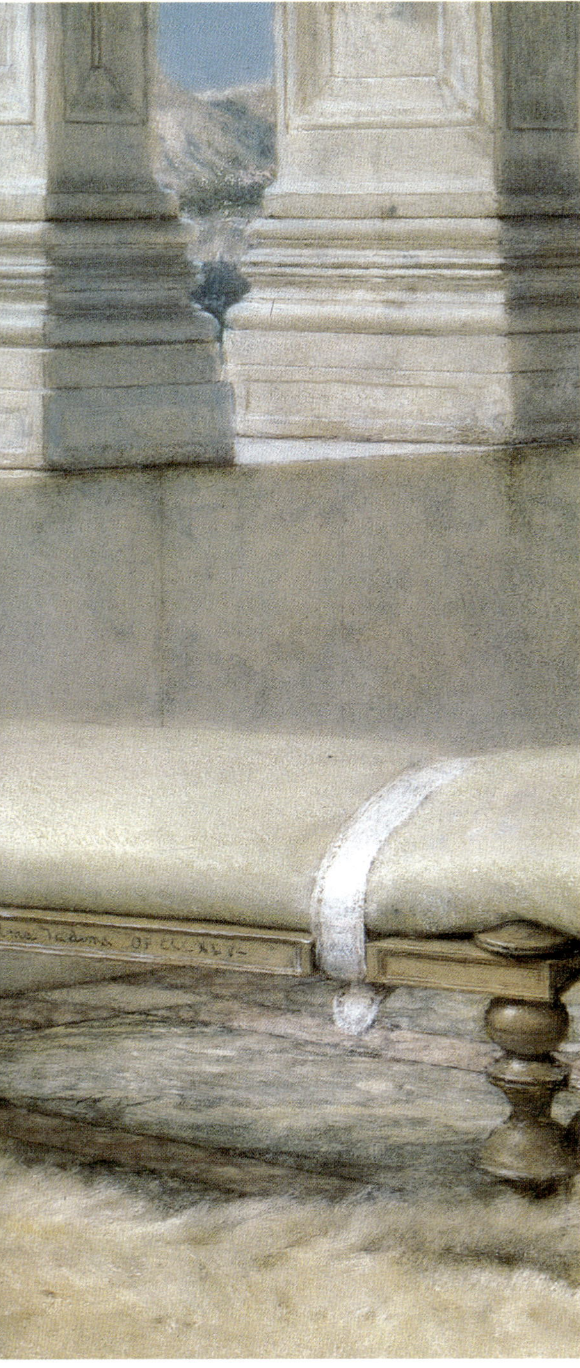

for the occasion entitled 'The Carmen Tademare',[332] which was set to music by George Henschel. The chorus runs:

Who knows him well he best can tell
That a stouter friend hath no man
Than this lusty knight, who for our delight
Hast painted Greek and Roman.
Then here let every citizen,
Who holds a brush or wields a pen,
Drink deep as his Zuyder Zee
To Alma-Tad
Of the Royal Acad.
Of the Royal Academee.[333]

The tone of the poem is in keeping with Alma-Tadema's own jocular humour and it is testimony to his engaging personality that an institution as relatively formal and conservative as the Royal Academy of Arts should choose to honour one of its members in such a warm and familiar manner.

Despite the self-congratulatory timbre of this celebration, by the turn of the century the Academy did not have much to be optimistic about. The tide of critical opinion was beginning to turn against traditional modes of representation as upheld by the Academy and its members. The 1900 Exposition Universelle in Paris was the largest international exhibition of contemporary art held to date and included a number of works by Alma-Tadema as well as other leading Academicians. But some critical responses to the British entries were muted at best, and one critic declared that the works on display amounted to 'something insipid, old-fashioned, verging on the puerile at time ... If England wants to remain worth its old glory, it must leave its museums, studios and pundits and look outside !'[334]

Back in London, D. S. MacColl even went as far as attacking classical-subject canvases on moral grounds. In a review of the 1900 Royal Academy exhibition he berated Alma-Tadema's *Vain Courtship*, along with Poynter's *Diana and Endymion*, for attempting to 'revive the manners of a corrupt and effete period to tickle an exhausted palate'. MacColl continued, 'the amours of a Diana, the intrigues of a Roman atrium have little that is ennobling in their suggestions.'[335] Ironically enough, traditional voices notoriously attacked Degas's *L' Absinthe* (1876), when exhibited in London in 1893, on exactly the same charge.

W. B. Yeats defined the end of one era and heralded the beginning of another with the famous words: 'In 1900 everybody got down off his stilts; henceforth nobody drank absinthe with his black coffee; nobody went mad; nobody committed suicide; nobody joined the Catholic church; or if they did I have forgotten.'[336] While literary Decadence, to which Yeats refers, may have given way, tidily, to a new century, Victorian artists still sought to uphold the old traditions of painting in a modern world and Alma-Tadema, who maintained his standing within the world of British art, went on to produce some of his most important and best-known paintings in the first decade of the twentieth century.

In 1902 he made his first visit to Egypt, accompanying the party of Sir John Aird for the dedication of the Assuit and Aswan dams, Aird's most spectacular engineering projects. He recalled his impressions in a letter to a friend:

> Egypt is funny. The first impression of the people at least for a day or two was that I was at Beerbohm Tree's theatre, and that they were all the 'supers' from one of his Oriental plays, say *Herod*. It was too funny, and it was funny never to see a woman in the streets of Cairo ... all men and then those magenta sunsets, so absurd![337]

This humorous response is quite unlike the typical travelogues of the time, in which Western travellers are both awed and seduced by the country and its people.[338]

Throughout this last period of creativity, Alma-Tadema continued to produce paintings which repeat the successful formula of women on marble terraces overlooking the sea. These include *Under the Roof of Blue Ionian Weather* (1901), *The Year's at the Spring, All's Right with the World* (1902) and *Ask Me No More* (Pl.106). An interesting aspect of these paintings is the use of English poetry as title. The practice of employing English poetry for titles and catalogue quotations seems to have begun around the 1840s and by the 1880s was adopted by many British artists. *The Year's at the Spring, All's Right with the World* combines the first and last lines from Pippa's song in Browning's 'Pippa Passes'; *Under the Roof of Blue Ionian Weather* uses a line from Shelley's 'Epipsychidion' (542); and *Ask Me No More* takes its title from Tennyson's 'The Princess: A Medley' (2834–8).

These paintings, having no connection with the narrative of the poems from which the lines are taken, use poetry to complement an invariably serene mood. Surface serenity is, furthermore, no longer subverted by ironic subtext. Shelley's lines form part of a description of a vision the poet has created to escape from the torment and desperation of his hopeless love, and Tennyson's 'Ask me no more ... for at a touch I yield' is Princess Ida's reluctant and tormented acceptance of marriage. Both paintings, by contrast, show idyllic scenes of lovers on marble terraces. The title of *Her Eyes Are with her Thoughts and They Are Far Away* (Pl.180) is not only taken out of context, but is a misquotation. The actual words, from Byron's *Childe Harold's Pilgrimage*,

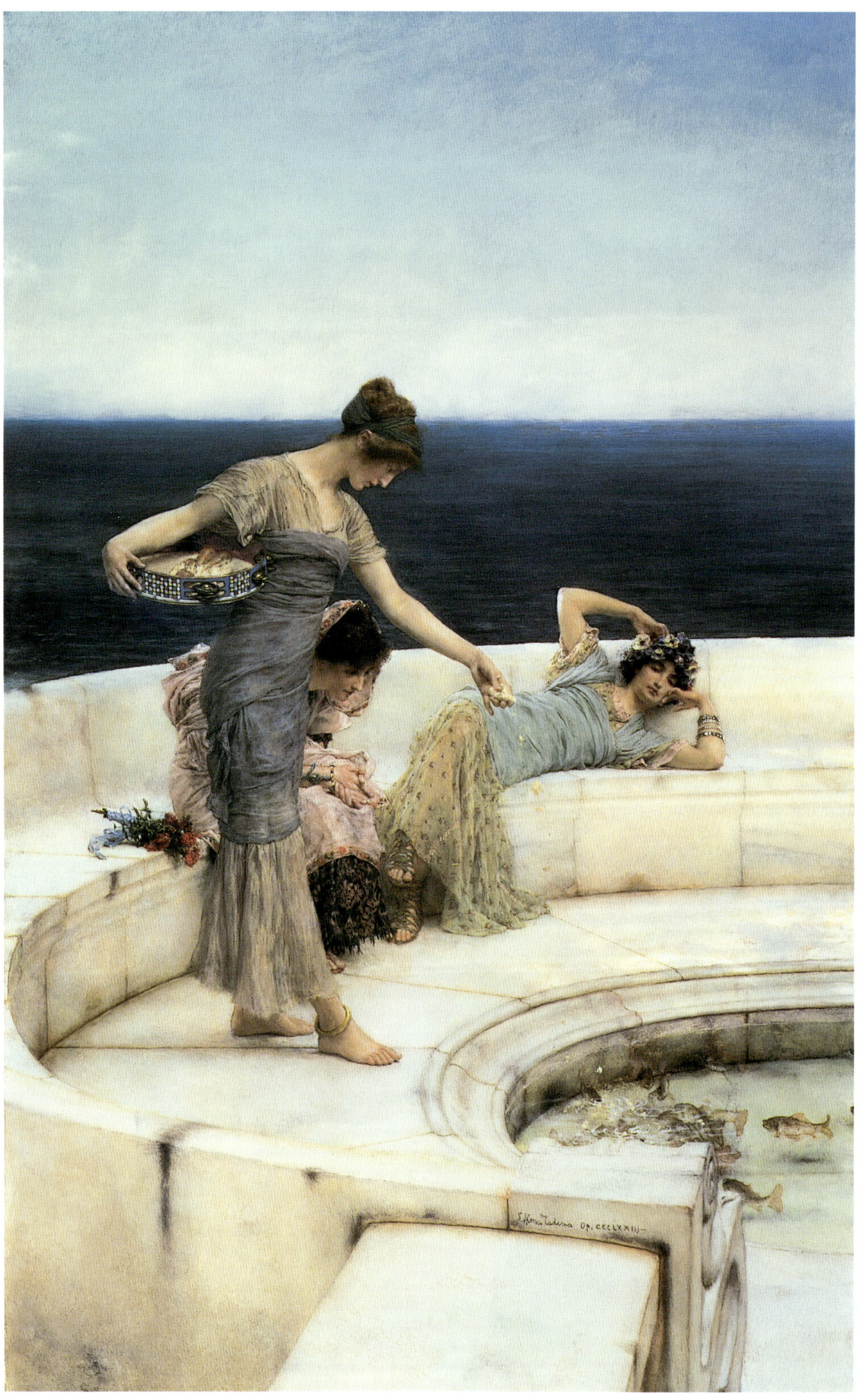

LAWRENCE ALMA-TADEMA 180

'His eyes were with his heart, and that was far away', are transformed to suit the painting of a contemplative woman on a marble terrace.[339] In these instances, certainly, the English poetic tradition is not identified as a suitable source of any ironic or subversive undertones, unlike its ancient counterpart.

Victorian literary and artistic figures were members of the same social milieu, attended the same functions, and joined the same clubs. The Rabelais Club, for example, included among its members Alma-Tadema, Thomas Hardy, Henry James and George Du Maurier. Du Maurier, who resembled Alma-Tadema in looks, was often mistaken for the artist. When admirers addressed Du Maurier with the words 'Oh, Mr Tadema! I really *must* tell you! I do so adore your pictures!', he would imitate the artist's Dutch accent and reply 'Gom to me on my Chewsdays', leaving a mystified Alma-Tadema to greet these uninvited guests.[340] Although Alma-Tadema was at home with the writers of his day, he often looked to the works of popular Romantic and Victorian poets associated with an earlier age. Just as he cites Horace, one of the best-known poets from the canon of ancient authors, in the form of verse inscriptions within paintings, so he finds in Horace's modern counterparts – Shelley, Byron, Tennyson, Swinburne – his titles and catalogue quotations.

Another painting to make use of English poetry is *Silver Favourites* (Pl.181), which includes lines from Wordsworth's 'Gold and Silver Fishes in a Vase' as a frame inscription:

Where, sensitive of every ray,
that smites this tiny sea,
Your scaly panoplies repay
the loan with usury.

Silver Favourites has little connection with the Wordsworthian lines, and instead presents a glorious scene of leisured life along the Bay of Naples much in the vein of *Coign of Vantage* (Pl.164). The 'silver favourites' of the title are the fish in the marble pond; a comparison can be made with the women, enclosed in a marble *exedra*, perhaps themselves the 'favourites' of wealthy male lovers. The curve of the *exedra* echoes the curve of the circular fishpond and both women and fish appear as decorative objects in a controlled space.

We are presented with an added frisson through the activity of the women: feeding fish. One glamorous feature of the *villa maritima* was its lavish and expensive fish pond. Especially popular in the late Republic and early Empire, fish ponds are to be found at the remains of villas along the Bay of Naples and in domestic settings at Pompeii and Herculaneum. The keeping of fish as pets became a fashionable extravagance mentioned by ancient writers: Cicero complains that men care more about their fish ponds than the affairs of state,[341] and Tacitus' Agrippina remarks that while she was planning Nero's rise, the wealthy aristocrat, Domitia, 'was beautifying her fish-ponds at her beloved Baiae'.[342] Pliny writes of even further indulgences:

Subsequently affection for individual

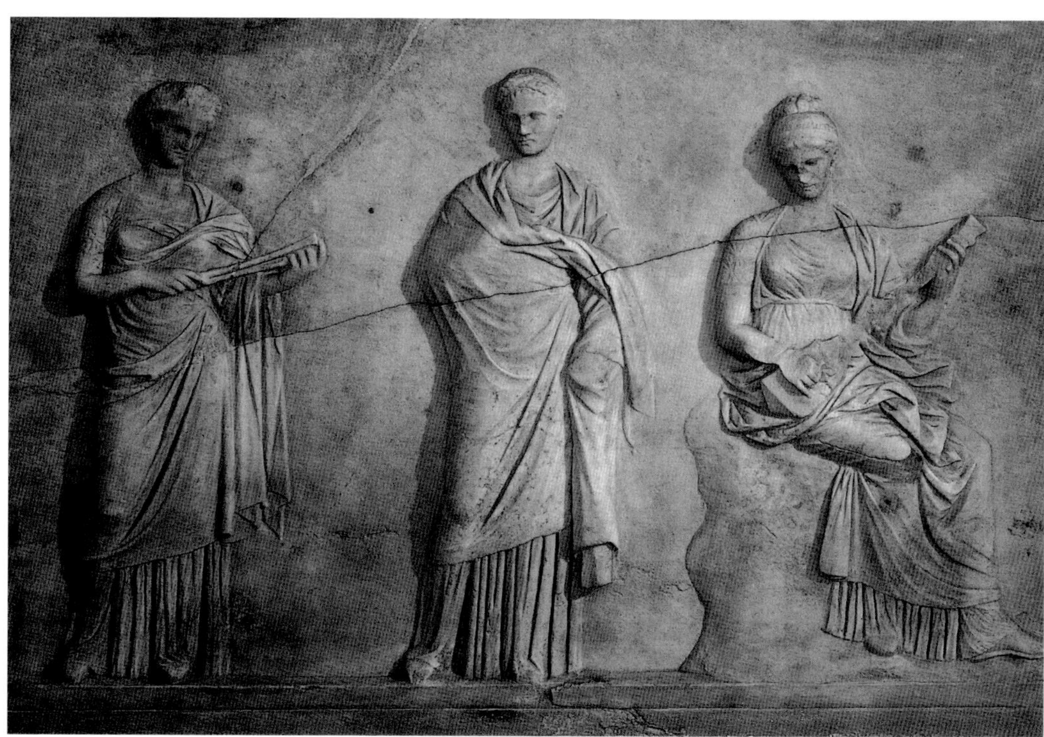

181 opposite
Silver Favourites, 1903
Oil on wood, 69·1 × 42·2 cm ($27\frac{1}{4} \times 16\frac{5}{8}$ in)
Manchester City Art Galleries

182
Three Muses, Statue Base from Mantinea, Greek, 4th century BC
Marble, H 98 cm, ($38\frac{1}{2}$ in)
National Archaeological Museum, Athens

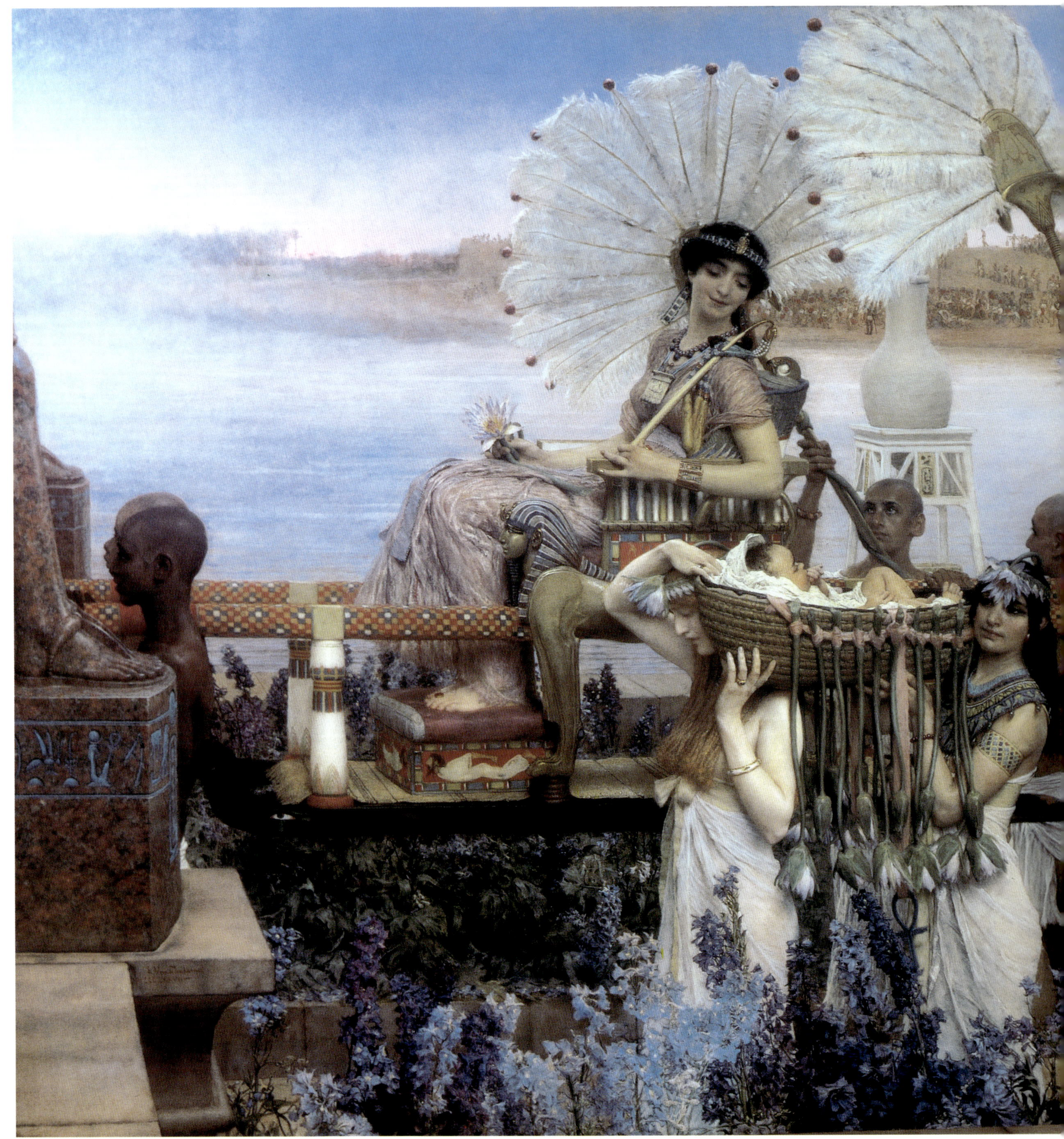

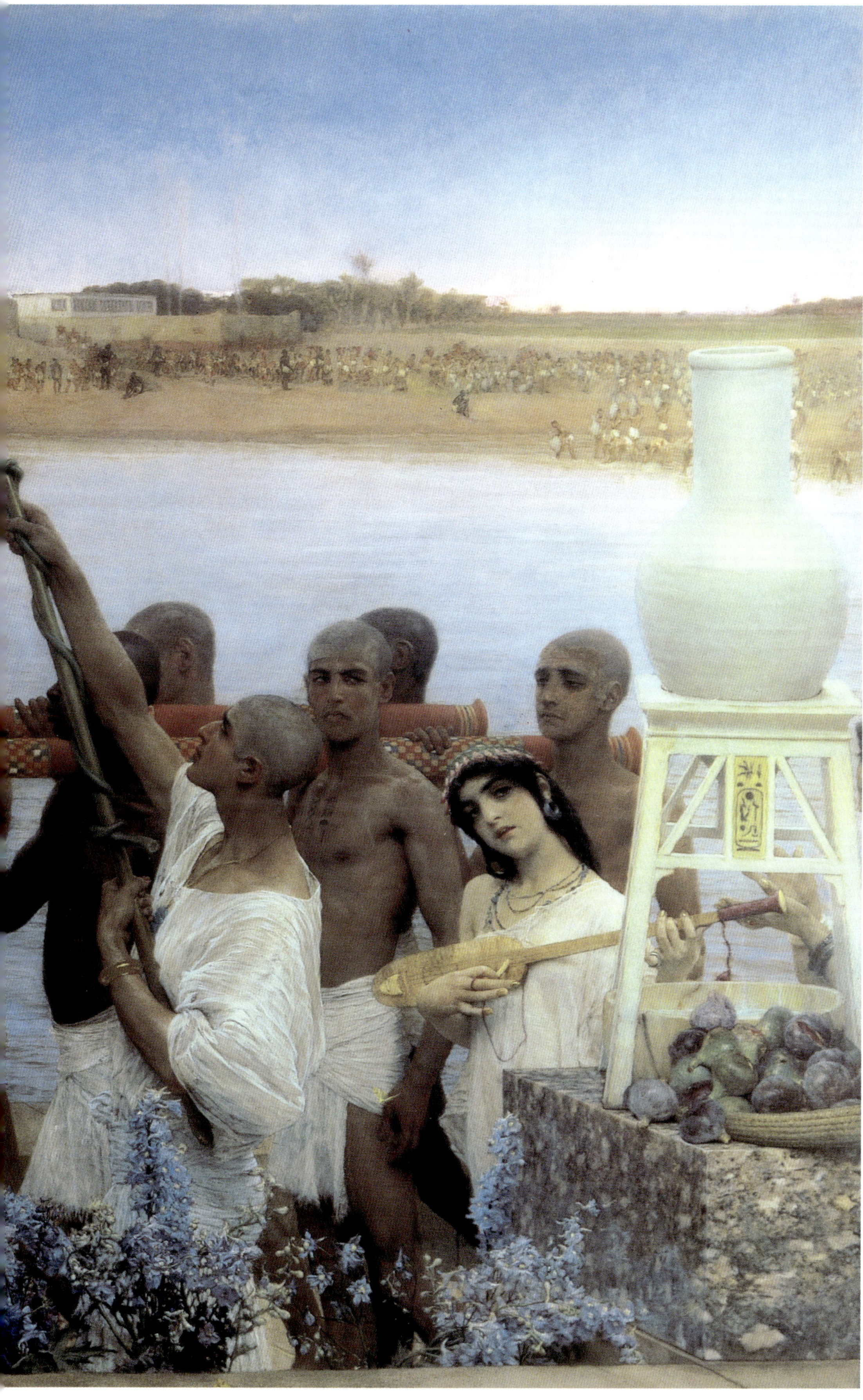

183
The Finding of Moses, 1904
Oil on canvas, 137·7 × 213·4 cm (54¼ × 84 in)
Private collection

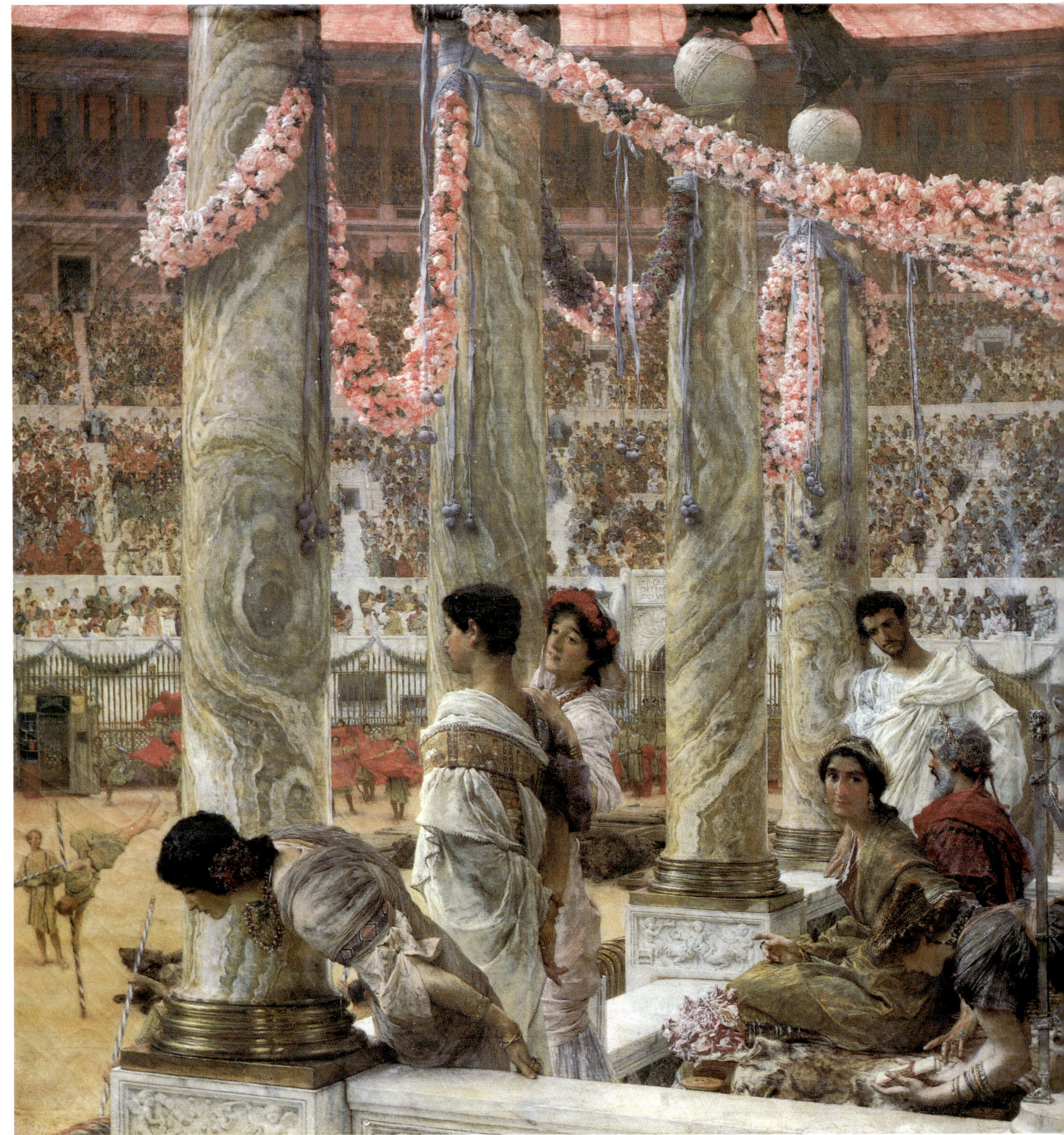

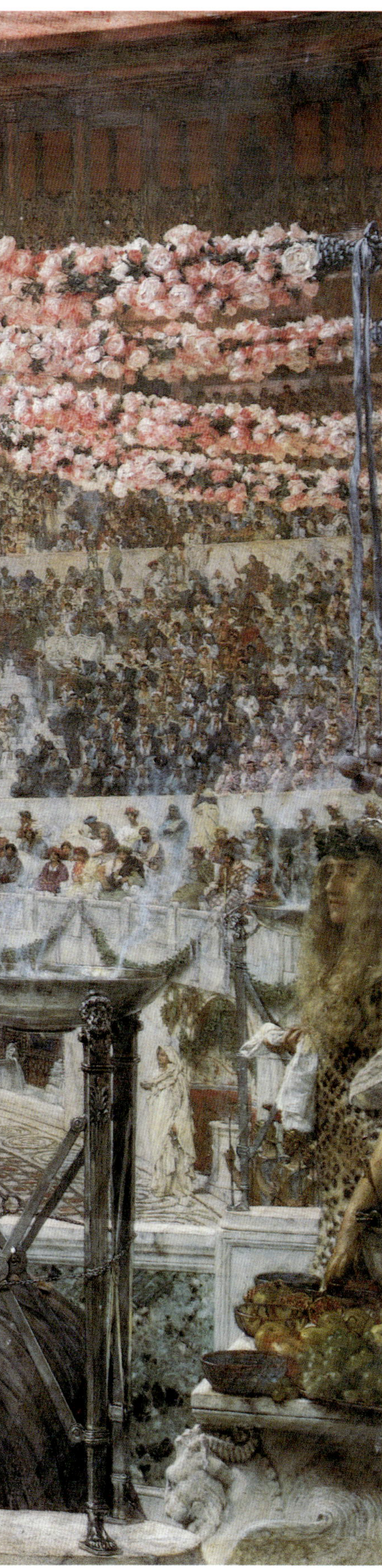

fishes came into fashion. At Baculo in the Baiae district the pleader Hortensius had a fishpond containing a lamprey which he fell so deeply in love with that he is believed to have wept when it expired. At the same country house Drusus' wife, Antonia, adorned her favourite lamprey with earrings, and its reputation made some people extremely eager to visit Baculo.[343]

Fishing (Pl.67) also recalls such fish pond anecdotes with its depiction of a woman resting against a marble pillar in front of steps leading down to a huge fish pond.[344] The drapery worn by the women in *Fishing* and *Silver Favourites* illustrates Alma-Tadema's use of sculptural prototypes for his typical female dress: particular sources are Tanagra statuettes and fourth-century BC sculpture such as the Mantinea base (Pl.182).

The Victorian age came to an end with the death of Queen Victoria in 1901, but British life carried on much as before and Victorian painters continued to thrive in the Edwardian world. Gambart died in 1903 and the collection of paintings he had kept in Les Palmiers, Nice, was put up for sale at Christie's. He had ordered a smaller version of *A Dedication to Bacchus*, painted for Baron Schröder in 1889, and now it proved to be the most valuable painting in his estate. It was bought by Agnew's for £5,880 and achieved a record sale-room price for a work by Alma-Tadema sold in Britain.

In June 1904 King Edward VII conferred on Alma-Tadema the newly instituted Order of Merit. It was presented to two other great names from the world of Victorian art, Holman Hunt and G. F. Watts, on the same day. There were some who objected and Roger Fry, the voice of the new critics, lamented in the *Nation*: 'How long will it take to disinfect the Order of Merit of Alma-Tadema's scented soap?'[345] Two years later Alma-Tadema was honoured with another award in the form of the Gold Medal of the Royal Institute of British Architects. An address by the president, John Belcher, during the award ceremony discussed Alma-Tadema's contribution to architecture with special mention of his own house, set designs for *Coriolanus*, and the paintings, *Architecture in Ancient Rome*, *Phidias Showing the Frieze of the Parthenon to his Friends*, *Thermae Antoninianae* and his Colosseum pictures.[346] It may seem strange that Alma-Tadema, a painter, was granted such a prestigious architectural award but he had always maintained strong connections with the Institute and had produced portraits of three of its presidents.[347] The representation of ancient buildings in his pictures together with his work

184
Caracalla and Geta, 1907
Oil on wood, 123·2 × 153·7 cm (48½ × 60½ in)
Private collection

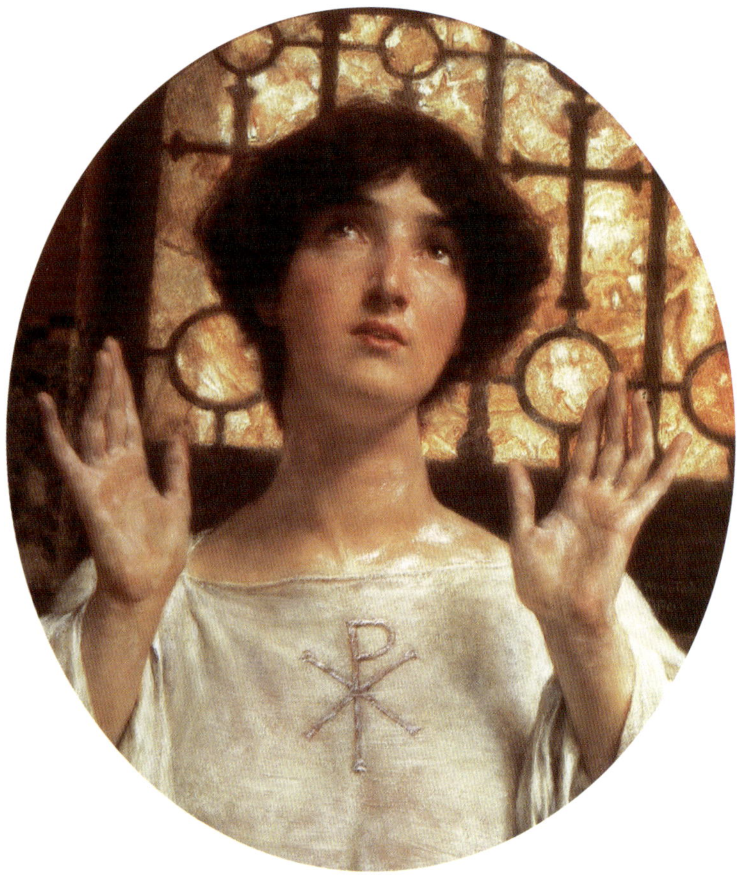

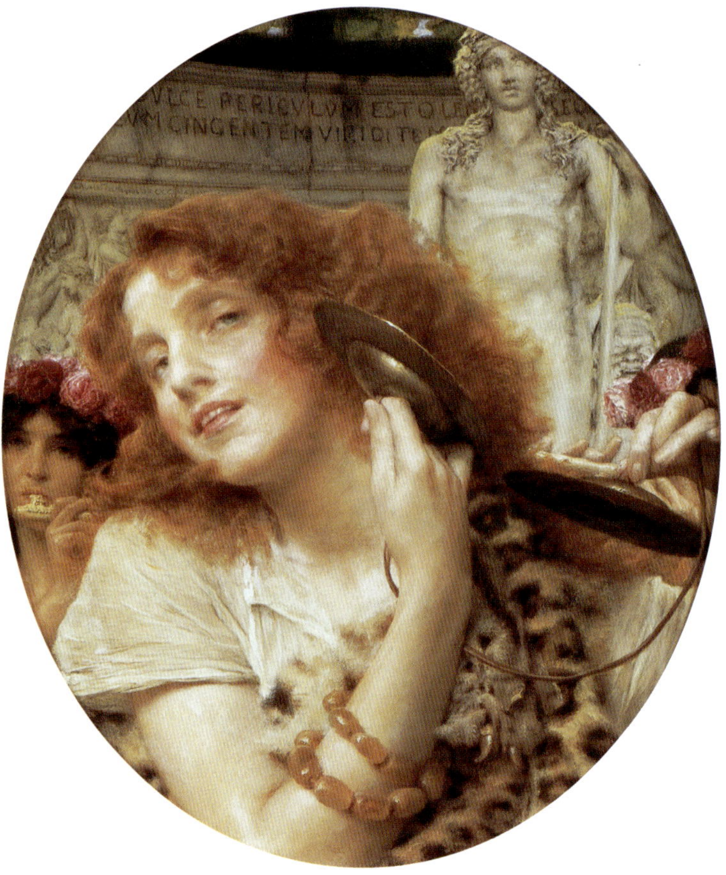

for the stage did much to promote a public awareness and admiration for architecture itself. Likewise, the house in Grove End Road was presented in the press as a marvel not only of interior design but of architectural construction.

Between 1906 and his death in 1912, production was comparatively small, but Alma-Tadema continued to produce ambitious paintings which matched the quality of earlier works. The Egyptian trip resulted in *The Finding of Moses* (Pl.183), a huge canvas commissioned by Sir John Aird for £5,250. The finding of Moses from Exodus 2:6 was a popular art-historical subject; Alma-Tadema's painting shows Moses carried in procession alongside Pharaoh's daughter. Cartouches of Rameses II are found on stands supporting the jars and, as in earlier paintings, serve to identify biblical Egypt with a recognizable and documented historical past. Pharoah's daughter is carried in a litter in imitation of Egyptian pictorial art showing the gods carried in procession by priests. Her footstool is decorated with images of vanquished enemies as often found on royal furniture. The painting includes the juxtaposition of Alma-Tadema's favourite types of model. One woman is distinctly fair and another dark, while Pharoah's daughter, with dark hair and pale skin, is some way between the two. The male attendants, like most of Alma-Tadema's men, have dark complexions, while their shaven heads identify them with the representation of Roman slaves in *An Exedra* (Pl.29) and *The Sculpture Gallery* (Pl.70).

As in *Whispering Noon* (Pl.159), delphiniums decorate the background, with a distant landscape beyond. Just as the Roman paintings of Pompeian interiors are succeeded by sunlit exterior scenes, so this painting, in a broad landscape setting, is quite distinct from the earlier Egyptian pictures, all placed in highly ornate interiors. Although part of the appeal of the picture is its display of the male and female body, Alma-Tadema, as often, goes some way to distance himself from an eroticized construct of the East: his procession of Pharaoh's daughter and attendants is far more decorous than the feast of female flesh found in paintings of the same subject by Frederick Goodall and Edwin Long.[348]

1907 saw the last important subject painting, *Caracalla and Geta* (Pl.184), which evokes a sumptuous vision of imperial intrigue in the third century AD.[349] Once again the Roman history that engages Alma-Tadema's interest looks to an underside of political and social life. *Caracalla and Geta* shows a family outing to the Colosseum – with the Emperor, Septimius Severus, his wife Julia Domna, and their two sons, Caracalla and Geta. The artist has studied surviving portraits of the imperial family to portray the group accurately. The apparently uneventful scene conceals a lurid potential for violence, and the amphitheatre is a fit setting to remind the viewer of the political intrigue, jealousy and death which will soon surround this family. On the death of Septimius Severus, Caracalla and Geta were jointly to administer the Empire. Yet their enmity towards each other was only thinly disguised, until, in a sham reconciliation, Caracalla met his brother at their mother's apartment and had him killed. Caracalla then went on a murdering spree, executing thousands who had any connection with his brother. Gibbon describes Caracalla as the worst of tyrants: 'the tyranny of Tiberius, Nero and Domitian, who resided almost constantly at Rome, or in the adjacent villas, was confined to the senatorial and equestrian orders. But Caracalla was the common enemy of mankind.'[350] Alma-Tadema's Caracalla lounges broodily against a pillar, in the background but at the right hand of Septimius Severus, while Geta shows himself to the crowd.[351]

The scene is set in a huge section of the interior of the Colosseum showing the arena, marble corridor and podium occupied by the imperial family, followed by three rows of seats for senior officials and vestal virgins. Above the podium the seating is divided into two tiers: one for knights and another for tribunes and citizens, above this is the portico within which the poor are crowded.[352] Alma-Tadema calculated that about 5,000 figures could be seen in the part of the Colosseum depicted and he meticulously painted the 2,500 who would be visible without being obscured behind columns or garlands.[353] He imaginatively interprets niches in the podium wall as fountains, recesses as altars, and openings in the second tier as shops.[354]

The Colosseum setting acts as an allusion to the future bloodshed in the lives of Caracalla and Geta, but the scene is treated in a most entrancing manner and the spectator is drawn, not to the bear-baiting just glimpsed in the arena, but to many sumptuous details: Cippolino marble columns decorated with golden capitals and bases, silver tripods wafting incense into the air and garlands of violets and full-blown roses. Paintings depicting Roman political history invariably show a corrupt and infamous world while, at the same time, the treatment of such scenes becomes increasingly sumptuous and captivating. The cruelty of ancient Rome is inseparable from an overriding vision of beauty, luxury and splendour. Thus a scene showing lovers on the Bay of Naples is painted with the same exquisite background and luxurious accessories as a scene of intrigue at court. Not completed in time for the Royal Academy Summer exhibition, *Caracalla and Geta* was exhibited by Arthur Tooth and Sons for whom it had been commissioned for the princely sum of £10,000.

In the same year he returned once more to ancient religion with two companion paintings, *Orante* (Pl.185) and *Bacchante* (Pl.186), both commissioned by Sir John Aird. In *Orante*, a female Christian devotee stands in front of a stained-glass window. She wears a plain, unbleached tunic embroidered with a Christian symbol. *Bacchante*, by contrast, shows a golden-haired bacchant, her lips parted and her cheeks flushed. In the background we see what appears to be a Bacchic frieze and, to the right, a Greco-Roman statue of Bacchus included in the artist's photographic collection (Pl.187). This softly moulded, slightly effeminate nude complements the heady sensuality of the scene. The bacchant herself, clashing cymbals, echoes a figure in a red-figure vase painting already used by Alma-Tadema in *A Private Celebration*.[355] While *Orante* raises her eyes to heaven, *Bacchante* gazes seductively at the viewer through heavy-lidded eyes. Her rich colouring, tousled golden locks, glowing amber necklace and diaphanous dress, along with the full-blown roses adorning the hair of some musicians in the background, leave the spectator in no doubt as to the appeal of the pagan world. Despite some critics' reservations about the moral message behind *The Conversion of Paula*, the artist once again makes an unfavourable contrast between an ascetic Christianity and a sensuous paganism.

An inscription running along the top of the canvas is intentionally obscured by the statue and abruptly cut off on either side. Nevertheless, it can be identified as a sequence of verse which reads:

> ... dulce periculum est,
> O Lenaee, sequi deum
> Cingentem viridi tempora pampino.

The verses translate as:

> Sweet is the danger, Lenaeus,
> in following the god, wreathing
> my forehead with the green tendrils of
> the vine.[356]

They form lines 18-20 of Horace's *Odes* 3.25 in which the poet compares poetic inspiration to Dionysiac frenzy. In this context, Horace's piquant summation of the pleasure and danger of Dionysiac worship appears as a warning. Does the artist use the lines to alert us to the irrationality of Dionysiac ritual or the threat of the *femme fatale*? It is surely the alluring bacchant who is the sweet danger ('dulce periculum') here.

Another portrait of a golden-haired woman forms the subject of *The Golden Hour* (Pl.188).

185 top left
Orante, 1907
Oil on wood, 41·5 × 33·5 cm (16⅜ × 13⅛ in)
Private collection

186 bottom left
Bacchante, 1907
Oil on wood, 41·5 × 33·5 cm (16⅜ × 13⅛ in)
Private collection

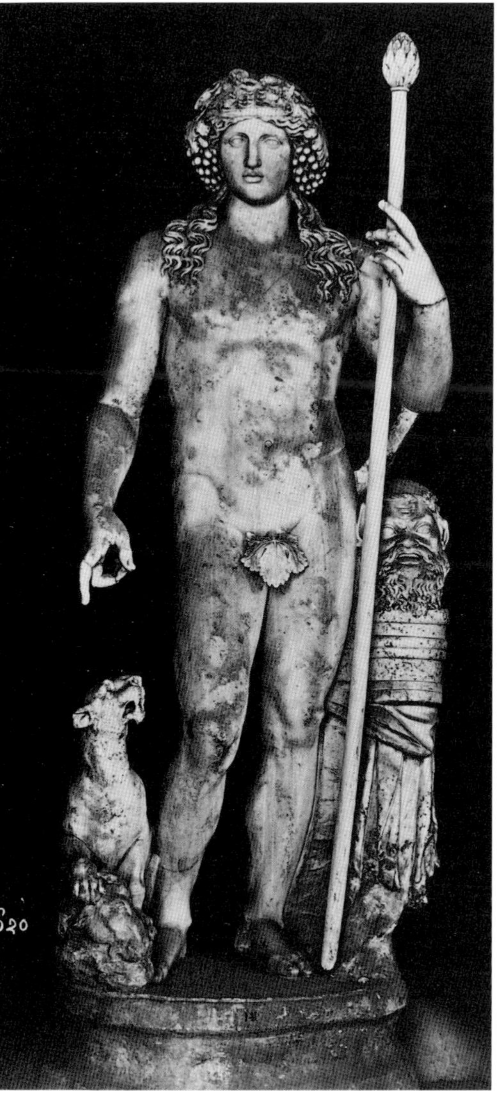

187
Bacchus, Roman
Marble, untraced:
University of Birmingham

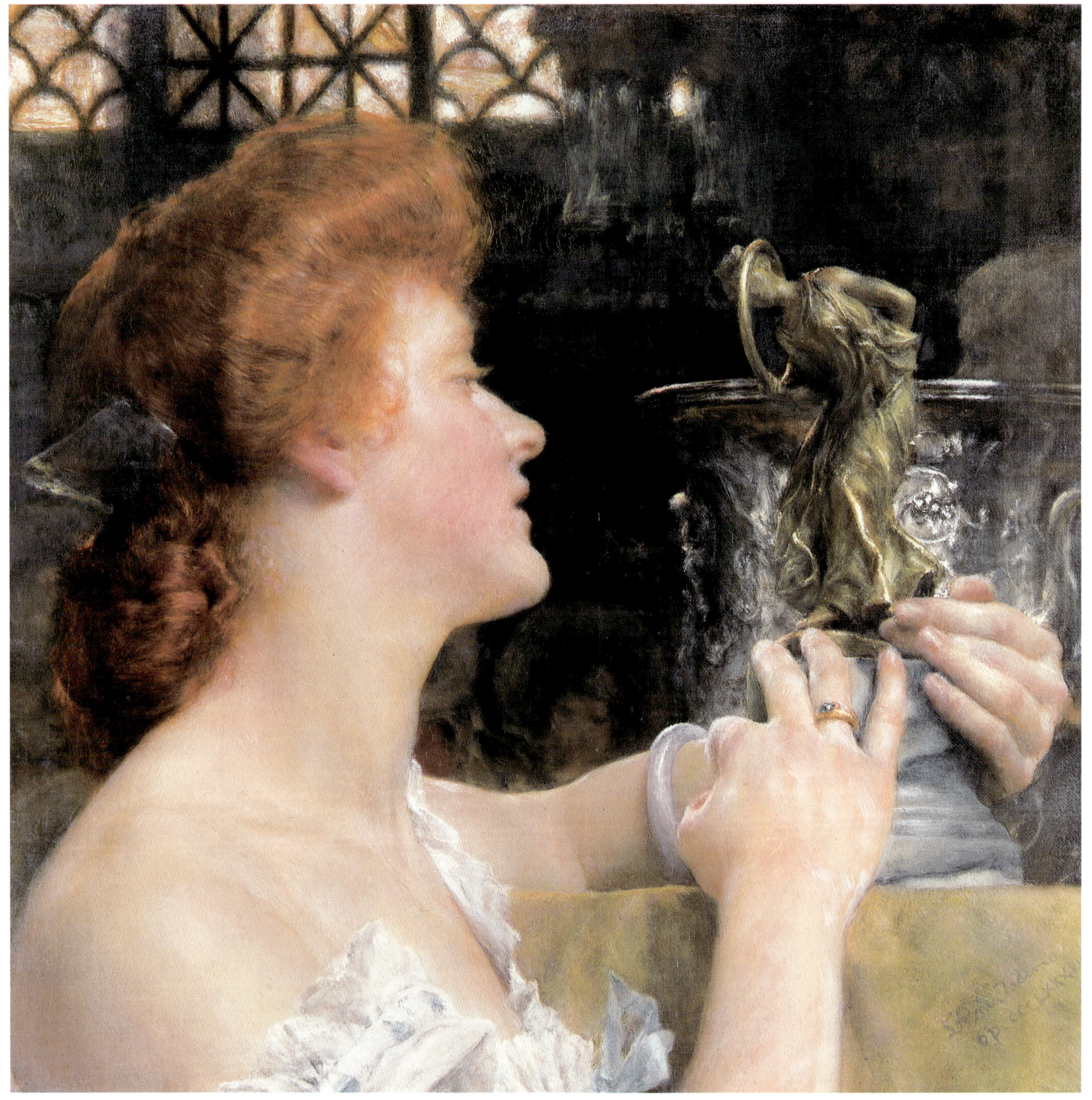

188
The Golden Hour, 1908
Oil on canvas, 35·5 × 35·5 cm (14 × 14 in)
Private collection

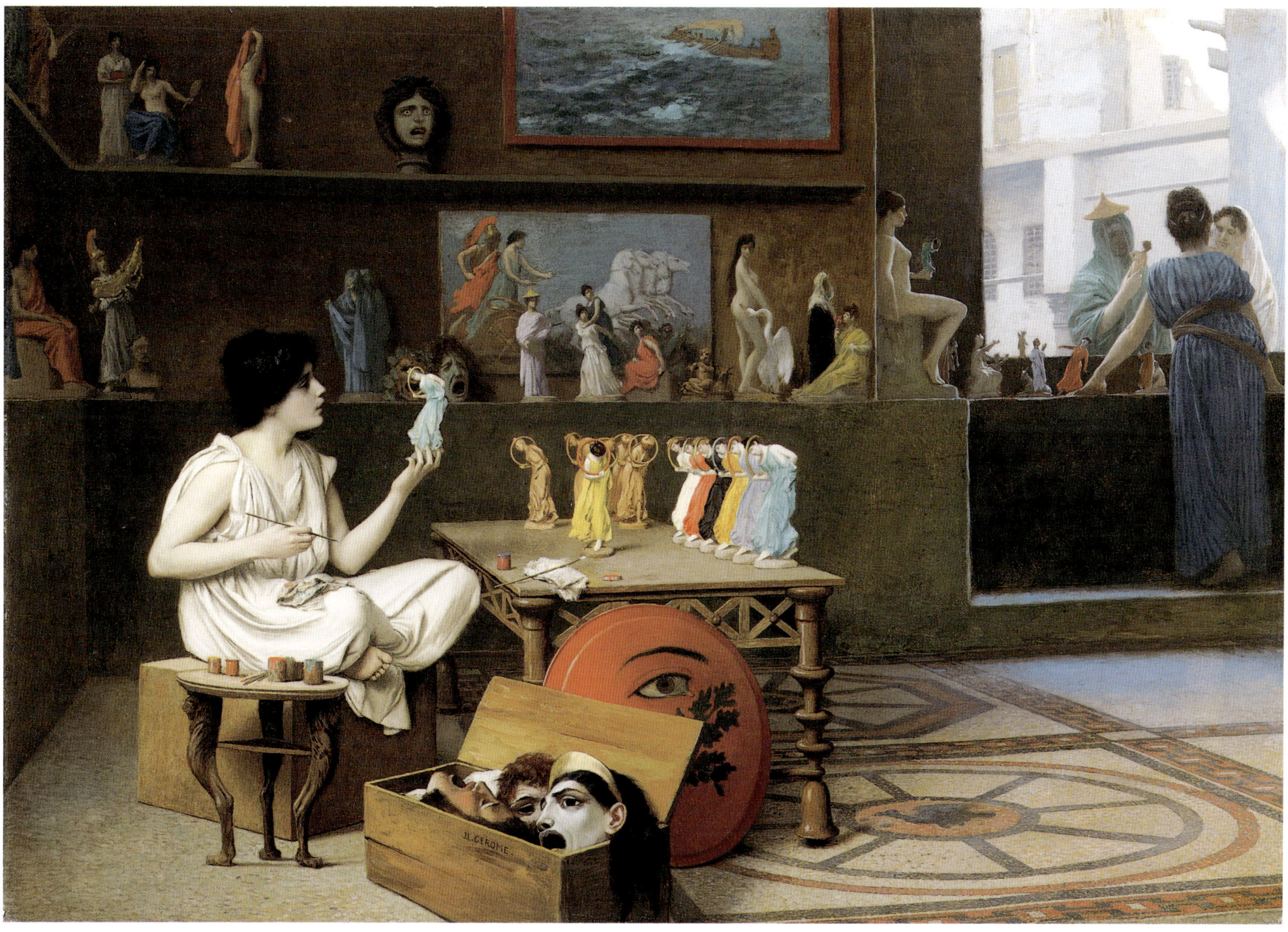

189
Jean-Léon Gérôme, *Painting Breathes Life into Sculpture*, 1893
Oil on canvas, 50·1 × 68·8 cm (19¾ × 27⅛ in)
Art Gallery of Ontario, Toronto

This woman here does not engage the viewer's gaze but admires a bronze statuette. The statuette is not an ancient work, but Jean-Léon Gérôme's hoop dancer. The hoop dancer was Gérôme's own version of a Tanagra statuette, executed in bronze and reproduced in polychromy in his paintings (Pl.189). Gérôme, who had died in 1904, had some influence on Alma-Tadema's work, particularly the Neo-Grèc-type Pompeian paintings, completed in the 1860s around the time when the two first met. Both artists had developed similar interests in antiquity, but while Gérôme went on to concentrate on straightforward depictions of eroticism (*Phryne Before the Tribunal*) and bloodshed (*Ave Caesar, Morituri Te Salutant*), Alma-Tadema's access to the same themes was a far more subtle combination of archaeological and literary reference and allusion. Alma-Tadema had refused to use Gérôme's *Death of Caesar* in the stage designs for Herbert Beerbohm Tree's *Julius Caesar* but in *The Golden Hour* he offers a posthumous tribute to the French artist. In the 1908 Royal Academy exhibition Alma-Tadema showed *The Golden Hour* and a self-portrait painted as Diploma picture for election to the Accademia Romana di San Luca, Rome. It was repainted in 1912 with the addition of a straw hat.

He sent a single entry to the 1909 Academy exhibition, *A Favourite Custom* (Pl.190), a final bath scene which combines impressive archaeological reconstruction with a cheerful eroticism. The building is an ingenious combination of the Stabian Baths (fourth century BC to first century AD) and the Forum Baths (first century BC to first century AD) at Pompeii. Stucco work above the door and niches around the walls are copied from the well-preserved men's *apodyterium* from the Stabian baths (Pl.191) while the fluted ceiling imitates the vaulted ceiling of the men's *caldarium* of the Forum baths.[357]

Unlike the much later baths of Caracalla, the

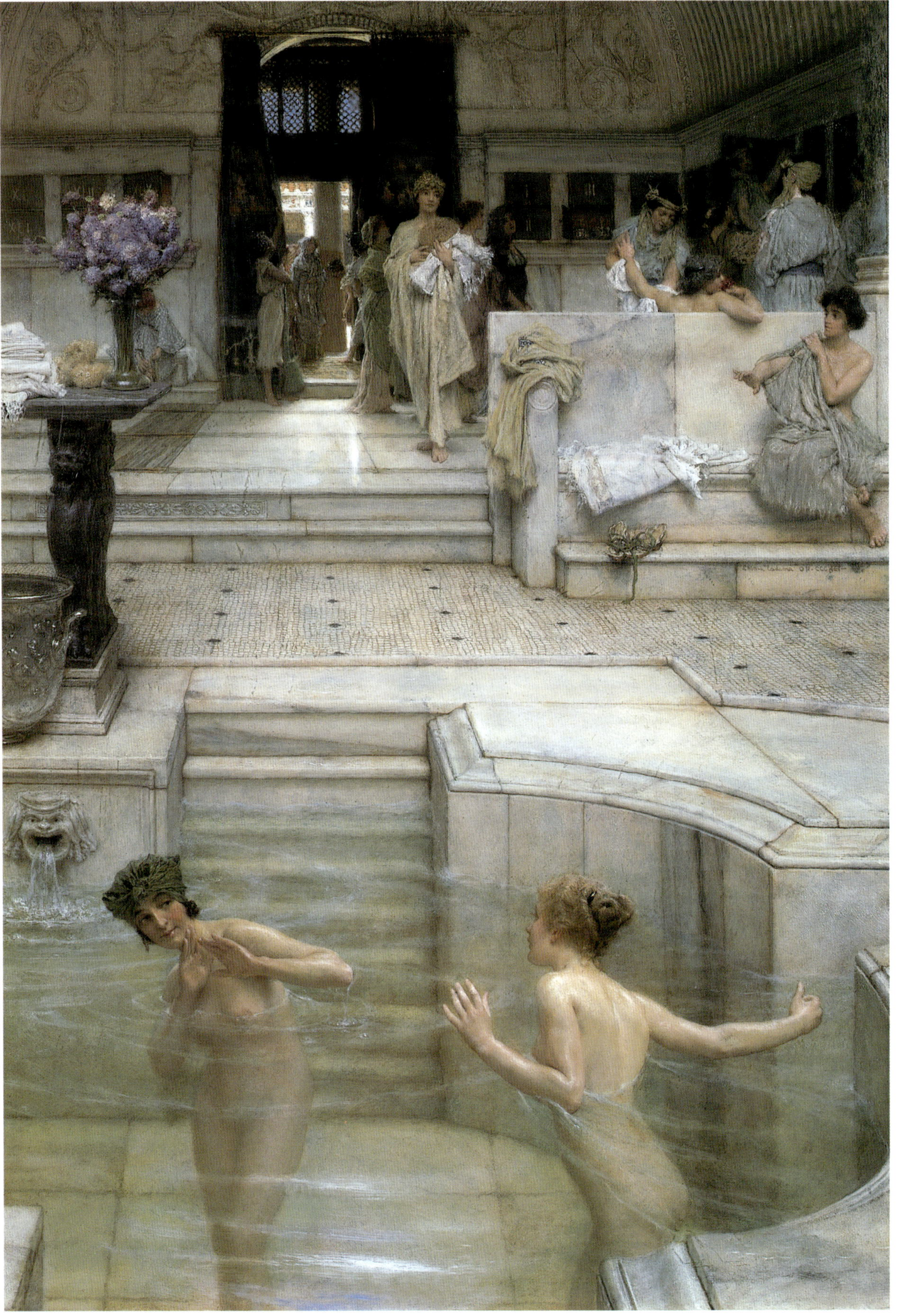

LAWRENCE ALMA-TADEMA

Stabian and Forum baths were not magnificent marble-lined structures but, as in a number of his Pompeian scenes, Alma-Tadema has elaborated on the original architecture for a much more sumptuous setting. Using a device derived from his Dutch heritage, the artist presents us with intriguing views as the eye is drawn through one space to another and we are led from one interior to another and ultimately to an exterior beyond. The Hildesheim *crater* appears in the middle ground. Alma-Tadema owned a copy of the original, and, as a recognizable studio prop, it also features in *A Dedication to Bacchus*, *After the Audience* and *The Golden Hour*. Despite the impressive archaeological reconstructions and artefacts, it is the two nudes, splashing each other in the foreground, which define this painting's playful mood.

The painting received the honour of being bought for the nation by the Chantrey Bequest, a sum of money bequeathed to the Royal Academy by Sir Francis Chantrey for the yearly purchase of paintings and sculpture by artists working in Britain. The distinction was, however, marred by attacks by D. S. MacColl on the Academy's management of the Chantrey Bequest. Through a series of letters and articles which he published in 1904 as a pamphlet entitled *The Maladministration of the Chantrey Bequest*, MacColl initiated a campaign against the Academy's choice and method of buying Chantrey pictures. He accused the Academy of flouting the terms of Chantrey's will by purchasing inferior paintings by its own members at the expense of superior work by those outside its ranks. In the same year a House of Lords Select Committee was appointed to investigate the matter, and a number of prominent Academicians were summoned to face questions.[358]

In spite of the controversy surrounding the Chantrey Bequest, it was no small honour for the artist, now aged 73, to have his work recognized in this way. *A Favourite Custom* illustrates Alma-Tadema's usual display of colour harmony, play of light, and, of course, exquisite rendition of marble. A description of Alma-Tadema's *A Bath* (1876) was included in Oscar Wilde's review of the opening of the Grosvenor Gallery in 1877; the same piece of writing could equally be applied to *A Favourite Custom*: 'There is a delightful sense of coolness about the picture, and one can almost imagine that one hears the splash of water, and the girls' chatter. It is wonderful what a world of atmosphere and reality may be condensed into a very small space.'[359]

On 15 August 1909 Laura Alma-Tadema died aged 57. She was buried in Kensal Green cemetery. Laura had maintained her career as an artist and exhibited at the Paris Salon, the Grosvenor

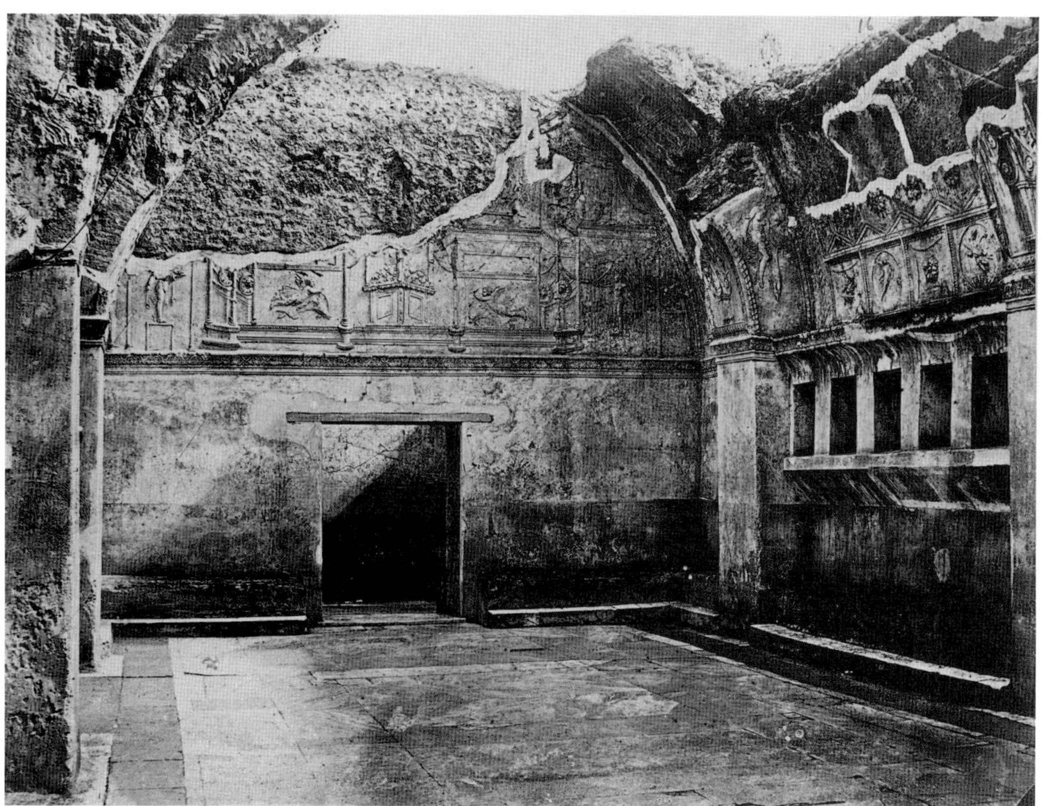

190 opposite
A Favourite Custom, 1909
Oil on wood, 66·1 × 45 cm (26 × 17¾ in)
Tate Gallery, London

191
Men's Apodyterium, Stabian baths, Pompeii:
University of Birmingham

and New Galleries and the Royal Academy. Like many female artists of her time, she concentrated on domestic scenes of women and children. Although she acted as a mother to Alma-Tadema's two daughters, Laura had no children herself, and we can only speculate on whether her paintings of mothers and babies derived from personal interest or merely conformed to Victorian notions of acceptable subjects for women artists. Alma-Tadema and his daughters helped organize a memorial exhibition in her honour, held at the Fine Art Society, London, in 1910. The critic of the *Athenaeum* was impressed by a few notable works: 'One swallow does not make a summer, but in the present state of art one or two fine pictures suffice to give importance to a show, the more so when, as in this instance, they display a side of an artist's talent hitherto unrevealed to a general public.'[360] In the same year King Edward VII died; to commemorate the coronation of George V in June 1911, Alma-Tadema painted a watercolour, *An Offering*, as a gift for Queen Mary and contributed seven works to a large coronation exhibition held in Shepherds Bush, a display which was to be the last important showing of his works in his lifetime.

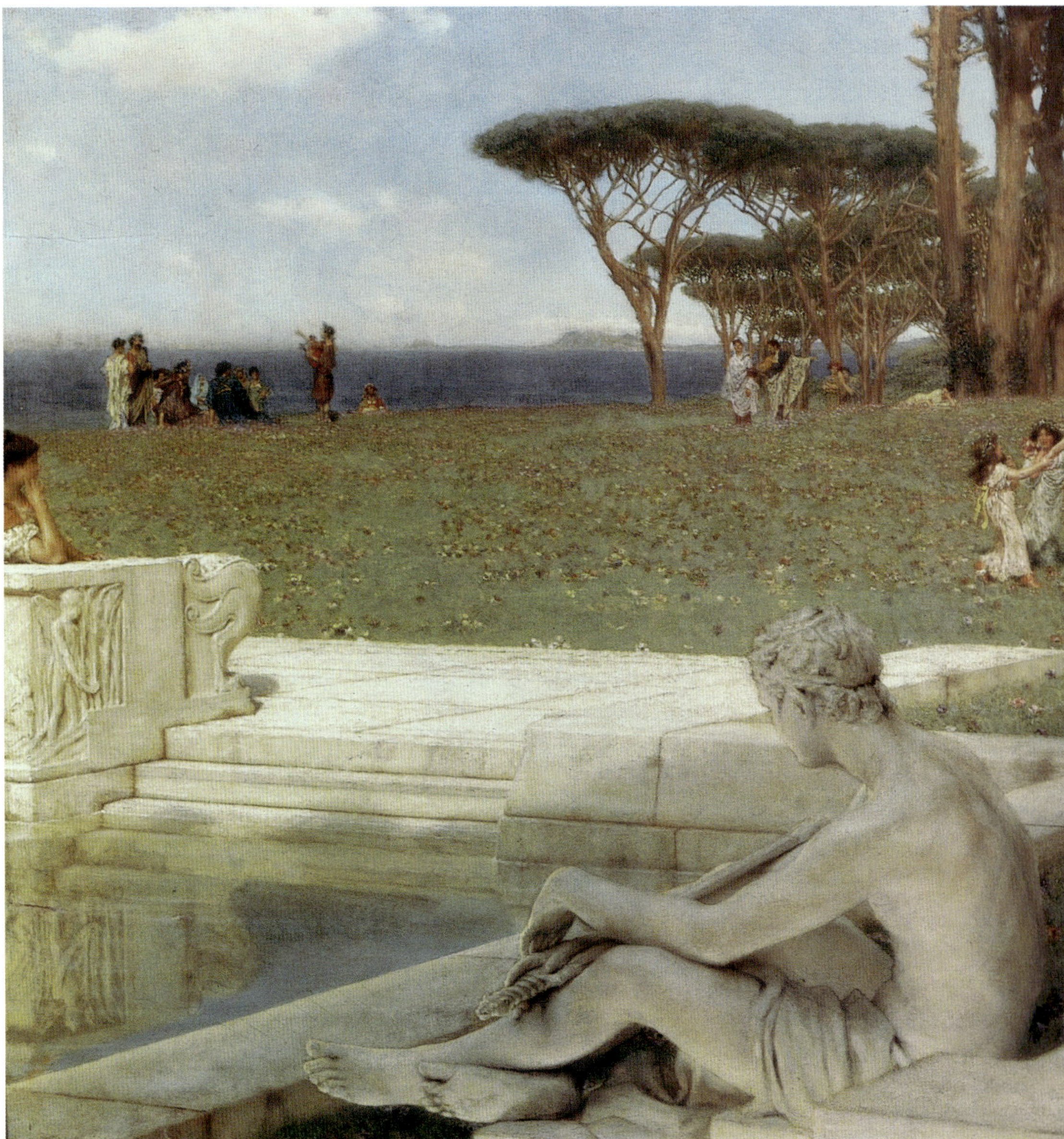

Alma-Tadema completed one of his last major works in 1910, and his only oil of the year: *The Voice of Spring* (Pl.192). As often, a woman sits on a marble *exedra*; before her is the statue of the seated gladiator (Pl.148) found in *Unconscious Rivals*,[361] here seemingly gazing at his own reflection in a marble pond. Unusually, the scene is placed within a landscape background, in which small groups of figures walk, sit, pick flowers, listen to a poet with lyre and dance. At the centre of the painting offerings burn on top of an altar, suggesting that this painting is another exploration of ancient religious ritual, but without archaeological or literary references the symbolism remains elusive. An uncharacteristic melancholy pervades the picture, and like Albert Moore's *The Loves of the Winds and the Seasons* (1893), painted just before Moore's death, it must surely be viewed as a presentiment of transience by an ageing artist.

Alma-Tadema's work has been linked with that of European Symbolist painters.[362] As an artist of international reputation, he can be cited as an influence on European figures such as the Austrian artist, Gustav Klimt and Belgian artist, Fernand Khnopff (Pl.193). Both incorporate classical motifs into their works and also use Alma-Tadema's unconventional compositional devices such as abrupt cut-offs at the edge of the canvas. They, like Alma-Tadema, also employ coded imagery to convey meaning to their canvases. *The Voice of Spring* conversely appears to be influenced by Symbolist painting as its imagery,

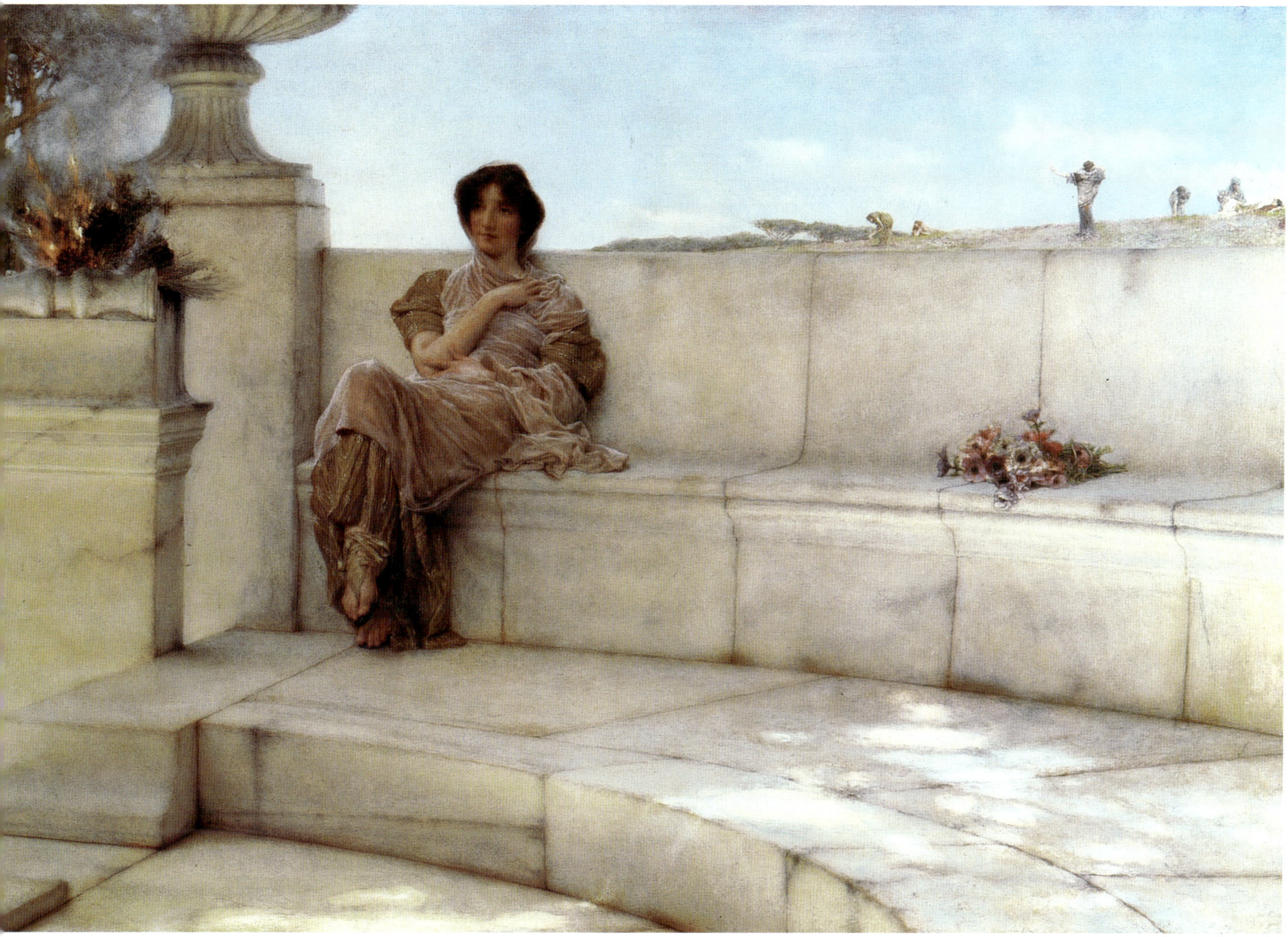

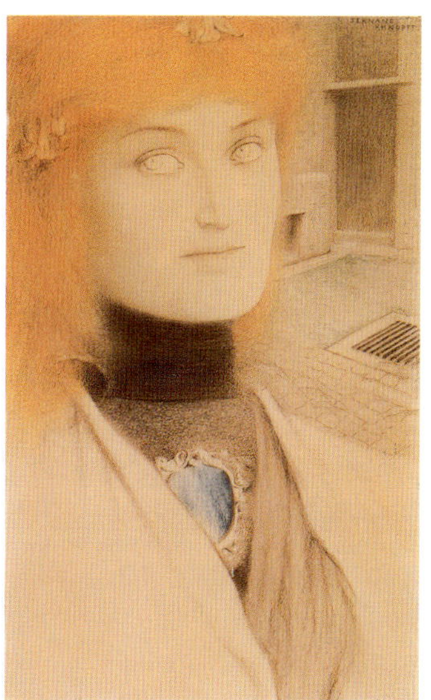

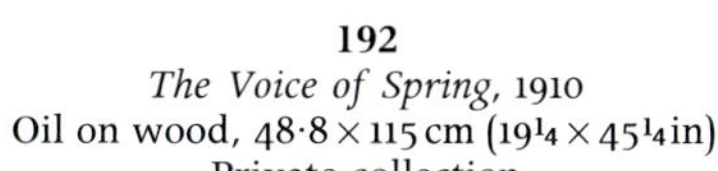

192
The Voice of Spring, 1910
Oil on wood, 48·8 × 115 cm (19¼ × 45¼in)
Private collection

193
Fernand Khnopff, *Who Shall Deliver Me?*, 1891
Coloured chalk on paper, 22·3 × 13 cm (8¾ × 5⅛in)
Private collection

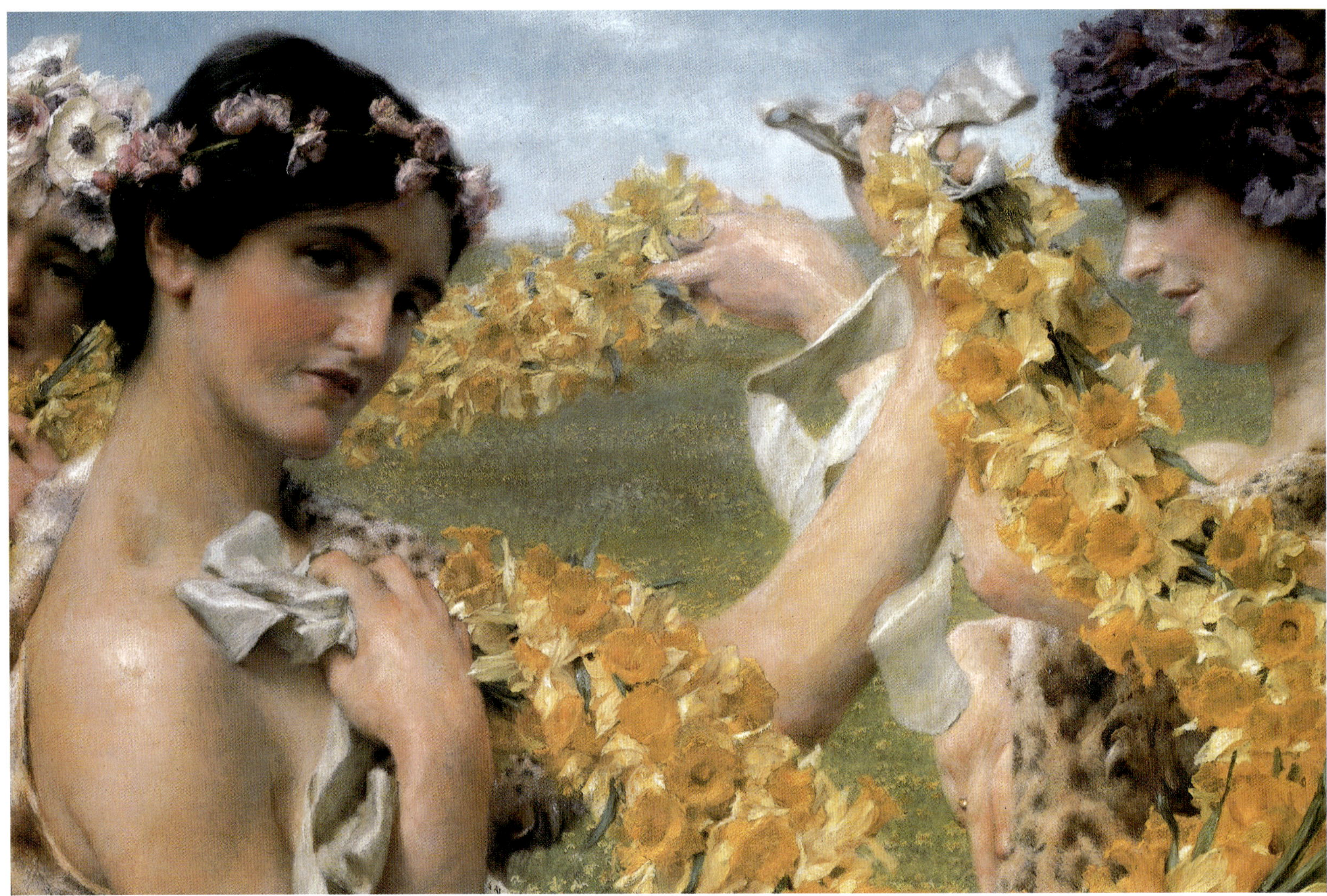

like that in the work of Klimt, Khnopff and others, is particularly obscure and difficult to decipher. Furthermore, the painting, a sad meditation on the changing seasons and the transience of life, explores themes familiar in the works of the Symbolists but new to Alma-Tadema. The background even recalls the unworldly landscapes of the French artist, Puvis de Chavannes. *A Summer Offering* (1911) and *When Flowers Return* (Pl.194), both showing women and flowers, are once again Symbolist-influenced paintings which, tinged with sadness, explore the theme of changing seasons.

At the very end of his career, the artist returned to more familiar themes and to Egypt with *Cleopatra at the Temple of Isis at Philae* (Pl.195), which remained unfinished at his death. During his visit to Egypt in 1902 Alma-Tadema had completed a *Study of the Columns in the Temple of Isis at Philae*. The choice of Philae as a setting is particularly poignant. It was an island surrounded by a ring of granite rock and covered in lush vegetation until the construction of Aird's dam (the Aswan dam), when Philae was flooded, and its buildings dismantled and re-erected on a nearby island above the water level.

Alma-Tadema resigned from the Royal Academy Council in 1911 after thirty-one years as Academician. His last major oil shown at the summer exhibition, *Preparations in the Coliseum* (Pl.196), is a large and ambitious painting which repeats and expands the right-hand corner of *Caracalla and Geta* (Pl.184). A female attendant stands next to a silver tripod and table laden with refreshments. The crowd has not yet arrived and we can admire the archaeological reconstruction of the Colosseum down to the minute detail of inscribed numbers on the back of the seats. Painted at the age of 76, the quality of detail, texture and colour clearly matches that in earlier works. Although the painting repeats the familiar prescription of archaeologically specific detail and setting, connections with Symbolism are once more apparent: the attendant's face is reminiscent of the stylized features of Khnopff's women,[363] while her expression and gaze appear significant but enigmatic.

In the summer of 1912 Alma-Tadema was accompanied by his daughter Anna to Kaiserhof Spa, Wiesbaden, Germany where he was undergoing treatment for ulceration of the stomach. There he died on 28 June. He was buried with full ceremony in St Paul's Cathedral at noon on 5 July. It was an honour to be buried alongside other notable Victorian artists – Leighton, Millais, Holman Hunt – as well as great names from the traditions of British painting – Turner, Landseer, Reynolds – and an even greater honour to rest beside Van Dyck, the Flemish painter who had so distinguished himself in the British tradition. The value of the estate was £58,834 gross. The Rijksmuseum, Amsterdam was bequeathed the *The Death of the First-Born* and the Luxembourg Museum, Paris, the *Romano-British Potter* (a section of *Hadrian in England*), while a number of small decorative items were given to the Fries Museum in Leeuwarden.

The house and its contents were put up for sale by Hampton and Sons, but the house re-

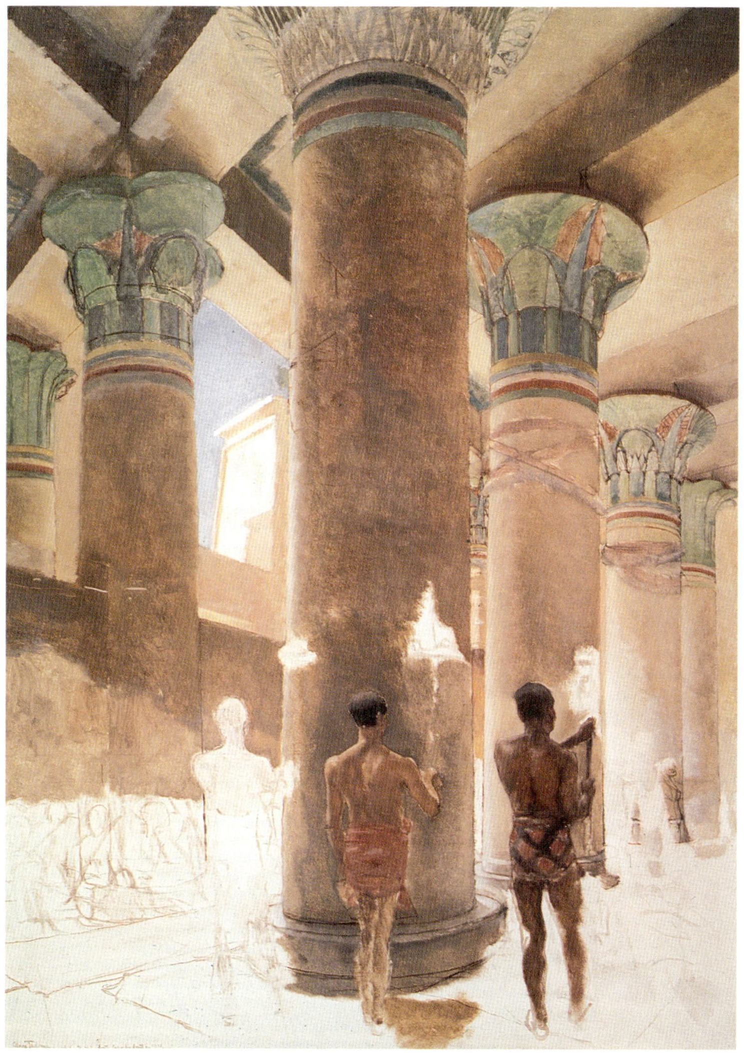

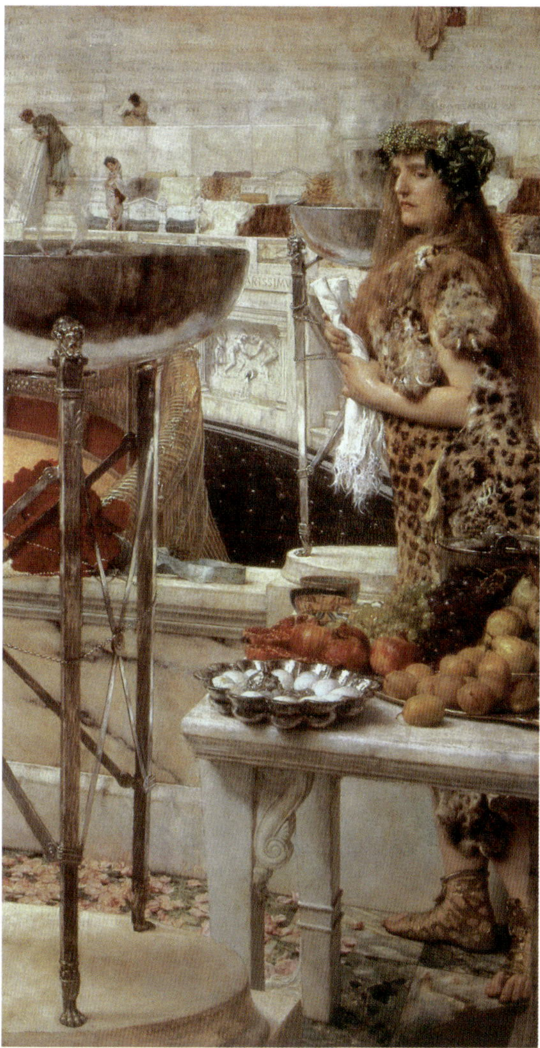

mained unsold until 1920.[364] Later converted into flats, the splendid interior was lost and today only the outer shell remains. A Memorial Fund was instituted after the artist's death, which donated his library (containing around four thousand books and five thousand photographs) to be housed at the Victoria and Albert Museum on behalf of the Nation.[365] His daughters received only £100 each, their furniture and personal belongings, and were granted a trust fund, the capital of which after their deaths was to go to the Royal Academy. Anna had begun a career as a painter and had had some success at exhibition, but stopped painting after her father's death. Laurense pursued a career as a writer. Neither married. Laurense died in 1940 and Anna in 1943.

194 opposite
When Flowers Return, 1911
Oil on wood, 35·5 × 52·1 cm (14 × 20½ in)
Private collection

195
Cleopatra at the Temple of Isis at Philae, 1912
Oil on canvas (unfinished), 150·2 × 106·7 cm (59⅛ × 42 in)
Victoria and Albert Museum, London

196
Preparations in the Coliseum, 1912
Oil on canvas, 154 × 80 cm (60⅝ × 31½ in)
Private collection

III/4
ALMA-TADEMA IN RETROSPECT

In the winter of 1912–13 the Royal Academy held a memorial exhibition of the works of Alma-Tadema including 213 oils, watercolours and drawings. Around the same time, Roger Fry held his second exhibition of Post-Impressionist art at the Grafton Galleries, London. Fry's first Post-Impressionist exhibition, held in 1910-11, was greeted with negative reviews but this new exhibition received a more favourable reception from critics and public alike. Most critics decried Alma-Tadema's works in favour of the Post-Impressionists.[366] The critic of the *Athenaeum*, who had little positive to say of the exhibition itself, explained the re-evaluation of Alma-Tadema in terms of incomprehension by new critics, who 'write of him, indeed, if they write sincerely, as though he belonged to another age and another country', and added, 'perhaps no collection of the works of a recently deceased artist could throw into stronger relief the change of outlook which art criticism has undergone in the last twenty years.'[367]

The British reception of modern European art brought the domestic battle between the conservative Royal Academy and its progressive opponents to a new and decisive phase. As a consequence, the whole world of modern art came out against Alma-Tadema, and his work became a symbol of the old order versus the new. The most scathing attack was by Roger Fry, writing in the *Nation*, who likened the artist's figures to 'highly-scented soap'.[368] Nevertheless, Alma-Tadema still had his defenders. The *Nation* published its quota of correspondence against Fry, including a letter from George Bernard Shaw, who, while maintaining a certain ironic detachment worthy of the artist himself, sums up something of Alma-Tadema's contribution:

> I think we are bound to admit that he was original and sincere, as well as astonishingly handy with his tools, and that, if there was a marked demand for his work, it was a demand that he created, and not one that he was faithless to himself in following. If all his contemporaries had had half his character, English painting would have been considerably the richer today.[369]

The correspondence columns of *The Times* became a forum for the old guard with Philip Burne-Jones, William Blake Richmond and others taking the critics to task.[370] Richmond also published an article entitled 'A Great Artist and his Little Critics' for the *National Review* in which he unashamedly proclaimed Alma-Tadema 'one of the greatest painters in modern Europe'.[371] John Collier likewise published an article in the *Nineteenth Century* which censured the critics and praised the artist,[372] and Poynter came to Alma-Tadema's defence in his annual Presidential Address.[373] Yet, at least as far as the educated public and the new critics were concerned, the cause of the Academy and traditional art forms was lost. By the second decade of the twentieth century, the heyday of Academic painting was over. At the same time, classical subjects had become outmoded and classicism, in the form of a high-art tradition in direct descent from the Renaissance, had effectively ceased.

Back in 1883 Oscar Wilde had advised art students: 'As regards archaeology, then, avoid it altogether: archaeology is merely the science of making excuses for bad art ... How worthless archaeology is in art you can estimate by the fact of its being so popular. Popularity is the crown of laurel which the world puts on bad art.'[374] Fry, MacColl and the others had inherited such antipathy to the popular, and, ironically, Alma-Tadema's unqualified success now counted against him. A number of imitators continued to reproduce the formula of classically draped women in Pompeian-style interiors or on marble terraces,[375] but this was no more than the homage of the second-rate to the master: it was Alma-Tadema who initiated and, uniquely, explored this popular and saleable genre of Roman-subject painting. To a new generation, such images were linked solely with commercial acceptibility, irrespective of their deeper resonances or indeed of the overall significance of Alma-Tadema and his work for British art as a whole.

From the 1920s to the 1960s, Alma-Tadema's reputation, along with Victorian painting in general, was in decline. The lowest point is suggested by the provenance of *The Finding of Moses* (Pl.183). An apocryphal story tells of it being stripped of its frame and left in an alleyway. What is attested fact is that, when it came up for sale in 1960 at M. Newman Ltd., London, a buyer could not be found. After six months it was put up for sale at Christie's, where once again a buyer could not be found. Newman's then tried to dispose of *The Finding of Moses and The Roses of Heliogabalus* (which also failed to sell) by giving both canvases away without charge to any museum or public building, but there were still no takers. Eventually both paintings went to New York where they finally found buyers.[376]

Over the last thirty years, Victorian painting has enjoyed a striking revival in public interest, and once again Alma-Tadema's paintings command high prices in the sale rooms. In 1954 *The Year's at the Spring, All's Right with the World* was sold by the Royal Albert Memorial Museum, Exeter, for £136; when the same painting came up for sale at Sotheby's, New York in 1990, it fetched £94,675. Only a few years later, in 1995, *The Finding of Moses* was sold for £1,562,500 at Christie's, New York. Today the paintings of Alma-Tadema, popularly reproduced on posters, calendars and greetings cards, are familiar to a wide audience. At the same time, his works are now the subject of serious revaluation.

Alma-Tadema, the man, confronts us as a great and greatly respected member of the high cultural and social élite of his day, yet also as someone of vivacious personality and irresistible sense of humour, who regaled his guests with stories and jokes often rendered unintelligible by his strong Dutch accent. And while contradictions seem to characterize his personality, dualities also define his work. His archaeological reconstructions and meticulous brush betoken a lifetime of intensive intellectual and artistic endeavour, while, at the same time, many of his paintings depend on a distinctive sense of irony and humour: one Roman emperor is portrayed as a terrified coward; chattering women upstage another emperor in the very baths which bear his name; erotic symbolism abounds in a seemingly innocent scene of a spring festival. The artist consistently confounds our expectations by suggesting one notion of antiquity and then challenging the viewer to seek another. Something of Alma-Tadema's spectacular success must be ascribed to the effortless ease with which he contrives to satisfy a popular and an élite taste at one and the same time. He assumes familiar constructions of a decadent Rome, but leads the knowledgeable viewer to a sophisticated re-reading of such a Rome through half-obscured references to ancient sources. Ultimately, as a painter (and a perfectionist), he seeks to create each work as a compelling harmony of composition, colour, light, form and texture.

We return finally to Alma-Tadema's famous claim: 'the old Romans were human flesh and blood like ourselves, moved by the same passions and emotions.'[377] What are these 'passions and emotions'? – cruelty, greed, indolence and erotic desires, as exposed and berated by Rome's own satirists and moralists ? If Alma-Tadema's covert intention is to read such disreputable aspects of Roman life into Victorian society, then the final irony is at his own audience's expense. The question, indeed, how Alma-Tadema's paintings were viewed by his patrons and the general art-going public, remains unanswered. Did subversive undercurrents remain undetected ? Were his paintings precisely calculated to appeal to a taste for the subversive and the risqué? Contemporary critics, certainly, did not usually discuss Alma-Tadema's choice of literary and archaeological sources in these terms, but were they, along with his viewers and patrons, nevertheless, complicit in constructing such an enticing vision of the ancient past?

The defining feature of Alma-Tadema's work is arguably challenging subversions beneath exquisite surfaces. This achievement points to a larger significance for his art than Fry or indeed his own conservative defenders allowed. Although Alma-Tadema belongs within the academic tradition, his innovations and his influence, nevertheless, transcend the confines of the academic. His compositional devices and use of coded imagery made an impact on progressive European art in the form of continental Symbolism. At the same time, he shares preoccupations with avant-garde literary movements and the work of J.K. Huysmans and Oscar Wilde. *The Roses of Heliogabalus* alone can claim to have helped shape the nineteenth-century construction of ancient Rome. In 1892 *Alagabal* was chosen as the title of a book of poems published by the German poet, Stefan George. Only four years after Alma-Tadema's painting, George chose the same episode from the *Scriptores Historiae Augustae* for the subject of a poem in his collection. Like Alma-Tadema, George represents the emperor's guests as subject to a cascade of falling roses:

> Open the sluices
> Floodgate looses
> Roses, flaunted...
> Drowning under.[378]

Nero, by the British playwright, Stephen Phillips, includes a similar tribute to the artist. A banquet scene at the end of Act 2 displays flowers falling upon Nero's guests and, as in *The Roses of Heliogabalus*, roses play an important part in the scene. The stage direction reads: 'At a sign from Nero, flowers descend from the ceiling. At first lilies, then of deeper and deeper colour. At last a tempest of roses ...'[379] At the same moment, the young prince Britannicus is called upon to sing and, having sipped from a poisoned cup, like the guests of Alma-Tadema's Heliogabalus, dies beneath a shower of roses.

Notable in a quite different area is Alma-Tadema's influence on modern cinematic design. His impact on Cecil B. DeMille has already been mentioned, while at the beginning of the twenty-first century, the designers of the Oscar-winning Roman epic, *Gladiator* (2001), cite the paintings of Alma-Tadema as a central source of inspiration.[380] His is a distinctive presence within the traditions of Victorian painting, and, at the same time, his work presents itself as significant in the context of nineteenth-century European art and literature and beyond it to modern popular culture in the form of Hollywood film.

As Shaw had stated, Alma-Tadema can be applauded for his originality: he approaches all his subjects with a striking individuality. The Merovingian paintings from his early career present a vivid portrayal of late antiquity which centres on Gaul rather than Rome; the Egyptian pictures reject the usual construction of an eroticized East and instead combine meticulous archaeological detail and serious emotion; landscapes executed in the open air contrast with his finely detailed studio paintings; portraits favour informal depictions of family and friends rather than society commissions.

Alma-Tadema is often ranked with Leighton and Poynter as one of the three major classical-subject painters in Victorian Britain. Contemporary commercial success and critical appreciation support this assessment of his position within British art. And yet while his name is linked with Leighton, Poynter and other painters of classical or classicizing pictures such as Watts and Moore, their work is only connected through a common interest in classical themes. Unlike the others, Alma-Tadema eschews a timeless and idyllic Hellenism in favour of a specific, historical and unidealized antiquity. Here tensions between sensual surface and intellectual content dazzle and intrigue as technical brilliance and aesthetic appeal are coupled with a playful but pointed irony. From the social and artistic life of the Greeks to the power struggles of imperial Rome and the *dolce vita* along the bay of Naples, a rich variety of ancient promises and admissions is subjected to the sharp revelation and the subversive commentary of an unfailingly elegant visual code.

NOTES

1 Georg Ebers, *Lorenz Alma Tadema: His Life and Works*, trans. Mary J. Safford (New York, 1886), Helen Zimmern, *Sir Lawrence Alma-Tadema* (London, 1902), Percy Cross Standing, *Sir Lawrence Alma-Tadema* (London, 1905).

2 Mostly uncovered by Vern Swanson, *The Biography and Catalogue Raisonné of the Paintings of Sir Lawrence Alma-Tadema* (London, 1990), an indispensable resource which lists all paintings and their provenance and offers the only modern biography of the artist. Among the primary sources of material concerning Alma-Tadema's life is an archive in the Heslop room, Main Library, University of Birmingham, which also contains the artist's photographic collection along with a number of pencil sketches and watercolours.

3 Frederick Dolman, 'Illustrated Interviews: LXVIII, Sir Lawrence Alma-Tadema', *Strand Magazine*, Dec. 1899, p.607.

4 Christopher Forbes, *Victorians in Togas: Paintings by Sir Lawrence Alma-Tadema from the Collection of Allen Funt* (Metropolitan Museum of Art, New York, 1973) and Richard Jenkyns, *The Victorians and Ancient Greece* (Oxford, 1980) and *Dignity and Decadence: Victorian Art and the Classical Inheritance* (London, 1996). For a direct challenge to this argument, see Elizabeth Prettejohn, 'Lawrence Alma-Tadema and the Modern City of Ancient Rome', in Andrew Hopkins, ed., *Responding to the Antique* (Cambridge, forthcoming).

5 1863, 1866–7, 1874–5, 1878, 1883, 1900.

6 Lawrence Alma-Tadema, 'My Reminiscences', *Strand Magazine*, 37 (1909), p.288.

7 Christened Lourens, he changed the spelling to Laurens while living in Antwerp and anglicized the name to Lawrence after he moved to Britain in 1870.

8 Ebers, p.3, adds that the name was chosen partly because of its 'euphonious sound'.

9 Fred Edmonds, 'The Boyhood of Alma-Tadema', *Boys Own Paper*, 1 March 1890, p.348.

10 Alma-Tadema (1909), p.287.

11 Edmund Gosse, 'Lawrence Alma-Tadema RA', F. G. Dumas, ed., *Illustrated Biographies of Modern Artists* (London, 1882), p.77, suggests that they did not want a Friesian pupil.

12 *An Old Staircase in Antwerp Exchange* (1854), *Staircase in the House of the Brewer's Guild, Antwerp* (1854–6) and *Study of a Staircase in the Old Museum at Antwerp* (1856).

13 Ebers, p.8.

14 Standing, p.14.

15 H. S. N. Van Wickevoort Crommelin, 'Laurens Alma-Tadema RA', Max Rooses, ed., *Dutch Painters of the Nineteenth Century* (London, 1898–1901), pp.160–1.

16 Swanson (1990), cat.43.

17 Standing, p.23.

18 Edward Gibbon, *The History of the Decline and Fall of the Roman Empire*, ed., J. B. Bury, 7 vols. (London, 1909), vol. 4, p.116.

19 Gregory of Tours, *The History of the Franks*, III.18, trans. Lewis Thorpe (Harmondsworth, 1974).

20 Alma-Tadema (1909), p.289.

21 The composition was repeated in a large chalk drawing (1861), a smaller drawing in charcoal and watercolour (1859) and another oil version (1868).

22 Lawrence Alma-Tadema, 'Laurens Alma-Tadema, RA', T. P. O'Conner ed., *In the Days of My Youth*, (London, 1901), p.204.

23 Alma-Tadema (1909), p.290.

24 *Journal of the RIBA*, 30 June 1906, p.441.

25 See pp.28–41.

26 Zimmern (1902), pp.9–10.

27 Zimmern, p.11, says that it was Leys himself who redirected the cab.

28 I am grateful to Dominic Montserrat for generously sharing his knowledge of the nineteenth-century reception of Egypt.

29 Standing, p.34.

30 Another section of the painting became *The Grand Chamberlain to King Sesostris the Great* (1869).

31 Maarten Raven, 'Alma-Tadema als Amateur-Egyptolog', *Bulletin van het Rijksmuseum* 27 (1980), pp.103–17.

32 Raven, p.104.

33 Jeremy Maas, *Gambart: Prince to the Victorian Art World* (London, 1975), p.196.

34 *Art Journal*, 1874, p.100.

35 'Nebamun' can be dated to the reign of Thutmose IV, *c*.1400 BC.

36 Raven, p.105.

37 Laura Alma-Tadema also contributed an illustration entitled *Dear Linachen You Will Not Die*.

38 S. L. Gilman and D. J. Parent, ed., *Conversations with Nietzsche: A Life in the Words of his Contemporaries* (Oxford, 1987), p.204.

39 Christopher Forbes, *Victorians in Togas: Paintings by Sir Lawrence Alma-Tadema* from the *Collection of Allen Funt* (Metropolitan Museum of Art, New York, 1973).

40 August Mau, *Geschichte der Decoration Wandmalerei in Pompeji* (Berlin, 1873), translated into English as *Pompeii: its Life and Art* (London, 1899).

41 House of the Vettii, excavated 1894–5; *Boscoreale*, 1894–6.

42 Standing, p.23.

43 See pp.34, 155, 189.

44 Elizabeth Prettejohn pinpoints the emergence of British historical genre painting to the 1865 Royal Academy Exhibition in which six Roman subject pictures appeared, *Imagining Rome: British Artists and Rome in the Nineteenth Century* (Bristol City Museum & Art Gallery, 1996), p.64.

45 Stored in the Heslop Room, Main Library, University of Birmingham.

46 Alma-Tadema Library: *Hand List of Books* (Heslop Room, Main Library, University of Birmingham).

47 See T. P. Wiseman, *Catullus and his World: A Reappraisal* (London, 1985).

48 Cicero, *Pro Caelio*, 15.35, trans. R. Gardner (Cambridge MA and London, 1987).

49 Catullus, 3.1–3, trans. Guy Lee (Oxford, 1991).

50 See pp.76, 88–9, 98.

51 Ovid, *Ars Amatoria*, 3.165–6, trans. A. D. Melville (Oxford, 1990).

52 Frederick Dolman, 'Illustrated Interviews: LXVIII, Sir Lawrence Alma-Tadema', *Strand Magazine*, Dec. 1899, p.607; see introduction and conclusion.

53 Cicero, *De Re Publica*, 2.24–5.

54 Livy, 1. 54.6–7, trans. B. O. Foster (Cambridge MA and London, 1982–8).

55 For a full list, see E. A. Baker, *A Guide to Historical Fiction* (New York, 1968).

56 See pp.61–2.

57 For example, Juvenal, 6.120–5; Persius, 2.52; Martial, 9.22.

58 See Elizabeth Prettejohn's discussion of the transformation of sculpture from one material to another in *The Sculpture Gallery* (1874) in *Sir Lawrence Alma-Tadema* (Van Gogh Museum, Amsterdam, Walker Art Gallery, Liverpool, 1996), cat 35.

59 Pliny, *Natural History*, 34.6.14, 34.18.48.

60 Ibid., 34.1.

61 Martial, 9.59.1.

62 See Prettejohn in *Sir Lawrence Alma-Tadema*, cat.36.

63 Pliny, *Natural History*, 35.79: 'it was Apelles of Cos who surpassed all the painters that preceded and all who were to come after him', trans. H. Rackham (Cambridge MA and London, 1989–91).

64 For example, Asinius Pollio, 'being an ardent enthusiast, was anxious for his collection to attract sightseers', *Natural History*, 36.33.

65 Alma-Tadema completed a similar painting of the same title later in the same year: *A Roman Art Lover* (1868, Glasgow Art Gallery & Museum)

66 Pliny, *Natural History*, 34.3.6.

67 Alma-Tadema Library: *Hand List of Books* (Heslop Room, Main Library, University of Birmingham).

68 Alma-Tadema's library included a French translation: *Oeuvres Complètes de Petrone*, trans. M. Méguin de Guerle (Paris, 1862).

69 Petronius, *Satyricon*, 15.3.

70 Ibid., 73.

71 François Mazois, *Les Ruines de Pompei* (Paris, 1824–38), vol.2. See Prettejohn, *Sir Lawrence Alma-Tadema*, cat.14.

72 See Prettejohn, *Imagining Rome*, cat.46.

73 See p.20.

74 She died in Puerto Rico two years later.

75 See Andreas Bluhm, 'In Living Colour', *The Colour of Sculpture 1840–1910* (Van Gogh Museum, Amsterdam, Henry Moore Institute, Leeds, 1996–7).

76 See Ian Jenkins and A. P. Middleton, 'Paint on the Parthenon Sculptures', *Annual of the British School at Athens*, 83 (1988), pp.183–207.

77 See Wolfgang Drost, 'Colour, Sculpture, Mimesis', *The Colour of Sculpture 1840–1910*.

78 See, for example, *Athenaeum*, 8 Dec. 1882, p.779.

79 Ebers, p.46.

80 See Barrow, *Sir Lawrence Alma-Tadema*, cat. 16.

81 Ruskin, 'Classic Schools of Painting: Sir F. Leighton and Alma-Tadema', in E. T. Cook and Alexander Wedderburn ed., *The Art Of England and the Pleasures of England, The Works of John Ruskin* (London 1903–12), vol. 33, p.321.

82 Ibid., p.320.

83 Livy, 39.8–18.

84 See p.32.

85 See p.34.

86 See *Sir Lawrence Alma-Tadema*, cat.21.

87 Quoted by Teio Meendendorp and Luuk Pijl, 'Alma-Tadema's Artistic Training' in *Sir Lawrence Alma-Tadema*, p.28.

88 See Meendendorp and Pijl, in *Sir Lawrence Alma-Tadema*.

89 Quoted by Meendendorp and Pijl in *Sir Lawrence Alma-Tadema*, p.29.

90 *Art Journal*, 1870, p.165.

91 *Illustrated London News*, 30 June 1866, p.627.

92 *Illustrated London News*, 12 June 1869, p.602.

93 *Athenaeum*, 15 April 1865, p.527.

94 For a full discussion of critical coverage in the British press, see Elizabeth Prettejohn, 'Art and Materialism; English Critical Responses to Alma-Tadema 1865-1913', in *Sir Lawrence Alma-Tadema*.

95 Preceeded by two paintings of newly-wed couples: *The Honeymoon* (1867) and *The Mirror* (1868). For later courtship paintings, see pp.85, 102–3, 126, 160–1.

96 Philip Carr, 'Alma-Tadema and his Friends', *The Listener*, 9 Dec. 1954, p.1013.

97 M. Smith, ed., *The Letters of Charlotte Brontë*, 2 vols, (Oxford, 2000), vol.2, pp.150–2.

98 Nathaniel Hawthorne's son, Julian, quoted in Maas, p.234.

99 In Brussels, he did take his cousin, Hendrik Willem Mesdag, as a pupil.

100 Letter to Holman Hunt, 6 Dec. 1870, quoted in Maas, p.226.

101 Letter to Vosmaer, 3 May 1882, quoted in Swanson (1990), p.39.

102 *Athenaeum*, 29 Apr. 1871, p.531.

103 Suetonius, 'Claudius', 10.1–2, trans. J. C. Rolfe (Cambridge MA and London, 1989).

104 Suetonius, 'Gaius', 9.1.

105 Letter to Vosmaer, June 1880, quoted in Swanson (1990), cat. 141.

106 Raven (p.108) points out that both Wilkinson and Alma-Tadema represent it upside-down.

107 Ebers, p.65.

108 Samuel Sharpe, *The History of Egypt* (London, 1866) places Moses in the reign of Amenophis II (*c*.1450–1425 BC) in the Eighteenth Dynasty. Georg Ebers, *Egypt: Descriptive, Historical, and Picturesque* (London, 1881) cites the reign of Merneptah (*c*.1236–1223 BC in the Nineteenth Dynasty. It is generally accepted today that the Exodus took place in the Nineteenth Dynasty, although no exact date can be confirmed.

109 Ebers, p.65.

110 Sharpe places Joseph around 1400 BC Joseph brings the Israelites to Egypt to share his good fortune, but their descendants were treated as slaves and eventually led out of Egypt by Moses.

111 *Art Journal*, 'Review of the Paris Salon', 1873, p.175.
112 *Illustrated London News*, 10 May 1873, p.447.
113 *Athenaeum*, 3 May 1873, p.570.
114 Dominic Montserrat, 'To Make Death Beautiful: The Other Life of the Fayum Portraits', *Apollo*, July 1999, p.22.
115 See James Stevens Curl, *Egyptomania: The Egypt Revival, a Recurring Theme in the History of Taste* (Manchester, 1994).
116 See Herman De Meulenaere, *Ancient Egypt in Nineteenth-Century Painting* (Berko, 1992).
117 Letter to Vosmaer, June 1880, Swanson (1990), cat. 141.
118 See p.186.
119 See p.158.
120 Alma-Tadema's Letters of Denization made it unneccessary to apply for Letters of Naturalization, although both daughters became naturalized citizens. See letters to the editor of *The Times* (27 June 1912, p.5; 28 June 1912, p.11) on the question of Alma-Tadema's nationality.
121 For a discussion of Alma-Tadema's houses, see Julian Treuherz, 'Alma-Tadema, Aesthete, Architect and Interior Designer' in *Sir Lawrence Alma-Tadema.*
122 See Prettejohn, *Sir Lawrence Alma-Tadema*, cat.31.
123 *Autobiographical Notes of the Life of William Bell Scott*, 2 vols. (London, 1892), vol. 2, p.204.
124 Mary Eliza Haweis, *Beautiful Homes* (London, 1882); Wilfred Meynell, 'Artist's Homes: Mr Alma-Tadema's at North Gate, Regent's Park', *Magazine of Art*, 1882, pp.184–8.
125 Haweis, p.30.
126 Meynell, p.186.
127 'Mr Alma-Tadema on Art Training', *Journal of the RIBA*, 25 July 1895, p.624.
128 For a discussion of these issues, see Linda Dowling, *Hellenism and Homosexuality in Victorian England* (London, 1994) and for a discussion of homosexual themes in Victorian classical-subject painting, see Rosemary Barrow, 'Mad about the boy: Mythological Models and Victorian Painting', *Dialogos: Hellenic Studies Review*, 7, 2000-1.
129 See Ulrich Pohlmann, 'Alma-Tadema and photography', in *Sir Lawrence Alma-Tadema*, pp.116–18.
130 Ibid.
131 See Rosemary Barrow, 'Drapery, Sculture and the Praxitelean Ideal', in Tim Barringer and Elizabeth Prettejohn, ed., *Frederic Leighton: Antiquity, Renaissance, Modernity* (New Haven and London, 1999).
132 Other artists later developed an interest in Tanagras. See, for example, Whistler's *Tanagra* (as the date attributed to the painting is 1869, and the first Tanagras were not excavated until 1870, the title must have been appended later) and Gérôme's *Painting Breathes Life into Art* (1893).
133 See Reynold Higgins, *Tanagra and the Figurines* (London, 1986), pp.29–30.
134 Oscar Wilde, *The Picture of Dorian Gray* (Harmondsworth, 1970), p.87 [first published 1891].
135 See p.39.
136 Pliny, *Natural History*, 35.10.37.
137 See Prettejohn, *Sir Lawrence Alma-Tadema*, cat. 36.
138 Pliny, *Natural History*, 35.20.
139 Although in the nineteenth century, many believed the piece to be ancient.
140 Ruskin, *Academy Notes 1875*, ed. Cook and Wedderburn, vol.33, p.321; vol.14, p.271.
141 Frederick Dolman, 'Illustrated Interviews', *Strand Magazine*, Dec. 1899, p.605.
142 For a discussion of Alma-Tadema and the city, see Elizabeth Prettejohn, 'Lawrence Alma-Tadema and the Modern City of Ancient Rome', in Andrew Hopkins, ed., *Responding to the Antique* (Cambridge, forthcoming).
143 See pp.189–91.
144 E. F. Benson, *As We Were* (London, 1930), p.249.
145 W. P. Frith, *My Autobiography and Reminiscences*, 2 vols. (London, 1887), vol.2, p.327.
146 Vitruvius, 6.5.1–2
147 Lawrence Alma-Tadema, 'Marbles: Their Ancient and Modern Application', *Journal of the RIBA*, 14 (1907), p.174.
148 Suetonius, 'Augustus', 28.
149 *Illustrated London News*, 10 June 1876, p.570.
150 See Swanson (1990), p.50.
151 Ibid.
152 *Sunday Morning, A Seat, A Mirror, A Bath, Phidias Showing the Frieze of the Parthenon to his Friends, Sunflowers, Tarquinius Superbus*, a portrait.
153 Rupert Hart-Davis, ed., *The Letters of Oscar Wilde* (London, 1962), p.39.
154 Richard Ellman, *Oscar Wilde* (Harmondsworth, 1987), p.209.
155 See Swanson (1990), p.52.
156 Mary Lago, ed., *Burne-Jones Talking: His Conversations 1895–1898 Preserved by His Studio Assistant Thomas Rooke* (London, 1982), p.31.
157 Quoted in Swanson (1990), p.52. For an interesting interpretation of the eroticism of the figure, see Jenkyns (1996), pp.127-9.
158 See Alison Smith, *The Victorian Nude: Sexuality, Morality and Art* (Manchester, 1996).
159 *Academy*, 22 May 1875, p.539, claims that the statue is Greek, but by 4 September (p.265) the same journal has decided that 'the figure is undoubtedly Roman'. It was confirmed as a sculpture from the school of Pasiteles dating from the first century BC: Charles Waldstein, 'Pasiteles and Arkesilaos: The Venus Genetrix and the Venus of the Esquiline', *American Journal of Archaeology*, 3 (1887), pp.1–13.
160 Carlo Visconti, 'Di una statua di Venere rivenuta sul Esquilino', *Bulletino della Commissione Archeologica Municipale*, 1 (1875), pp.16–28.
161 W. C. Perry, *Greek and Roman Sculpture* (London, 1882), p.623, note 3.
162 *Diadumenē* , like *A Sculptor's Model*, was censured for its depiction of nudity: see p.89.
163 18 April 1878, F. G. Stephens archive, Bodleian Library, Oxford.
164 See p.49.
165 See Prettejohn in Hopkins (see n.4).
166 Letter to Gambart, 8 July 1878, University of Birmingham Library.
167 Philip Carr, p.1014.
168 Mary Lago, ed., *Burne-Jones Talking: His Conversations 1895–1898 Preserved by His Studio Assistant Thomas Rooke* (London, 1982), p.165.
169 Letter to Charles Deschamps, 19 June 1879, quoted in Swanson (1990), p.55.
170 For example, see the *Magazine of Art*, 1883, p.433.
171 Swanson (1990), cat. 254; *Empires Restored, Elysium Revisited: The Art of Sir Lawrence Alma-Tadema* (Clark Institute, Williamstown MA, 1991), cat.21.
172 For a discussion of this painting in relation to other Virgilian subjects, see Rosemary Barrow, 'Painting Virgil: Victorian Choices', *Proceedings of the Virgil Society* (forthcoming, 2002).
173 Quoted in *The Wilde Years: Oscar Wilde and the Art of His Time* (Barbican Centre, London 2000), p.88.
174 See E. Greene, ed., *Re-Reading Sappho: Reception and Transmission* (Berkeley, 1996).
175 *Magazine of Art*, 1881, p.309.
176 *Sappho and Erinna in a Garden in Mytilene* was, however, not exhibited and was thus known to very few.
177 *Academy*, 7 May 1881, p.343.
178 *Nation*, 16 Sept. 1886, pp.237–8.
179 *A Nymphaeum* (1875), *A Bath* (1876) and *A Safe Confidant* (1876).
180 *The Times*, 20 May 1885, p.10; the letter was entitled 'A Woman's Plea'. See Alison Smith, 'The British Matron and the Body Beautiful: the Nude Debate of 1885', in Elizabeth Prettejohn, ed., *After the Pre-Raphaelites: Art and Aestheticism in Victorian England* (Manchester, 1999).
181 See Swanson (1990), p.61.
182 See p.109.
183 *Art Journal*, 1883, p.33.
184 *My Sister Is Not In* (1879), *Amo Te Ama Me* (1881), *Shy* (1883), *Welcome Footsteps* (1883), *Expectations* (1885), *A Foregone Conclusion* (1885), *He Loves Me, He Loves Me Not* (1887), *A Silent Greeting* (1889).
185 Seneca, *De beneficiis*, 6.31, trans. John W. Basore (Cambridge MA, and London, 1985).
186 Tibullus, 1.2.15–22, trans. Guy Lee (Leeds, 1990).
187 Frederick Dolman, 'Illustrated Interviews: LXVIII, Sir Lawrence Alma-Tadema', *Strand Magazine*, Dec. 1899, p.613.
188 Standing, pp.122–3.
189 See p.60.
190 *Strand Magazine*, vol.27, 1904, p.295.
191 Quoted in Swanson (1990), cat. 284.
192 Letter to Ebers, 27 Dec. 1883, Quoted in Swanson (1990), p.62.
193 See p.12.
194 Hesiod, *Theogony*, 573–600; *Works and Days*, 72–110.
195 Hesiod, *Works and Days*, 97–8, trans. S. Lombardo (Indianapolis, 1993).
196 See M. Lamb, *Antony and Cleopatra on the English Stage* (Toronto, 1980).
197 To accompany a drawing by Frederick Sandys entitled *Cleopatra Dissolving the Pearl* in *The Cornhill Magazine*, 1866.
198 *The Fortnightly Review*, July 1868.
199 Swinburne, *Poems and Ballads, First Series* (London, 1866).
200 Théophile Gautier, *Une Nuit de Cléopatre* (Paris, 1884), pp.70–1.
201 Dio Cassius, 69.9, trans. Earnest Cary (Cambridge MA, and London, 1970–82).
202 For a discussion of the division of the painting, see Prettejohn, *Sir Lawrence Alma-Tadema*, cats. 63–5.
203 Alma-Tadema must be referring to Dio Cassius, 65. 12.
204 Letter to Walters, 9 May 1886, quoted in Swanson (1990), cat.307.
205 Letter to Walters, 4 Oct. 1884, see Swanson, ibid.
206 Josephus, *The Jewish War*, 1.
207 Ibid., 7.148–53.
208 For a reconsideration of imperalism in relation to *Spring*, see Prettejohn in Hopkins (see n.4).
209 Trevor Blakemore, *The Art of Herbert Schmalz* (London, 1911), p.18.
210 Frederick Goodall, *The Reminiscences of Frederick Goodall RA* (London, 1902), pp.164–5.
211 Quoted in Swanson (1990), p.68.
212 Alma-Tadema (1909), p.293.
213 For a full list, see Rudolph de Cordova, 'The Panels in Sir Lawrence Alma-Tadema's Hall', *Strand Magazine*, Dec. 1902, pp.615–30. The hall alone was said to be insured for £25,000.
214 Quoted in Swanson (1990), p.68.
215 See p.130–1.
216 Angela Thirkell, *Three Houses* (Oxford, 1931), p.26.
217 Quoted in Swanson (1990), p.99.
218 Ibid., p.97.
219 Euterpe (lyric poetry), Thalia (comedy and pastoral poetry), Melpomene (tragedy), Polyhymnia (religious poetry), Terpsichore (dancing and song), Calliope (epic poetry), Erato (love poetry), Clio (history), Urania (astronomy).
220 See Prettejohn, *Imagining Rome: British Artists and Rome in the Nineteenth Century* (Bristol City Museum and Art Gallery, 1996), cat. 61.
221 *Academy*, 9 May 1885, p.335.
222 See p.144.
223 See Bruce Boucher, 'Lawrence Alma-Tadema, Edward Poynter and the Redecoration of the Athenaeum Club', *Apollo*, Oct. 1999, pp.21–9.
224 Rom Landau, *Paderewski* (London, 1934), p.43.
225 Joseph Comyns Carr, *Coasting Bohemia* (London, 1914), p.28.
226 Philip Carr, p.1014.
227 *Portrait of Lady Kate Fanny Thompson, He Loves Me, He Loves Me Not, Study for The Roses of Heliogabalus, Portrait of the Revd. Adama van Scheltma, Venus and Mars.*
228 See p.76.
229 For further discussion of the painting, see Rosemary Barrow, 'The Scent of Roses: Alma-Tadema and the Other Side of Rome', *Bulletin of the Institute of Classical Studies*, 42 (1998), pp.198–201 and Barrow, *Sir Lawrence Alma-Tadema*, cat. 69.
230 *Scriptores Historiae Augustae*, 'Elagabalus', 21.5, trans. David Magie (Cambridge MA, and London, 1991).
231 Few of the many contemporary

commentators on the painting identified the episode; one exception is *The Daily Telegraph*, 5 May 1888, p.3.

232 First performed in 1879.

233 W. S. Gilbert, *The Savoy Operas* (London, 1970), p.458.

234 See p.116.

235 J. K. Huysmans, *Against Nature*, trans. R. Baldick (Harmondsworth, 1966), p.45 [first published 1884].

236 27 Oct. 1897, quoted in Rupert Hart-Davis, ed., *The Letters of Oscar Wilde* (London, 1962)

237 Athenaeus, *The Deipnosophists* 4.147–8.

238 Suetonius, 'Nero', 27.3.

239 Tacitus, *The Histories*, 2.70.

240 For example, *Magazine of Art* , 1888, p.268, *Academy*, 12 May 1888, p.330, *Morning Post*, 5 May 1888, p.5; *Daily Telegraph*, 5 May 1888, p.5.

241 See p.37.

242 J. F. Boyes, 'The Private Art Collections of London: Mr John Aird's in Hyde Park Terrace', *Art Journal*, 1891, p.138.

243 Ibid., p.139.

244 M. H. Spielmann, 'Laurence Alma-Tadema, RA: A Sketch', *Magazine of Art*, 1896–7, p.48.

245 G. D. Leslie, *The Inner Life of the Royal Academy* (London, 1914), pp.196–7.

246 F. G. Stephens, *Lawrence Alma-Tadema, A Dedication to Bacchus, Companion to the Famous Picture The Vintage Festival* (Lefèvre Gallery, London, 1889), p.23.

247 See p.52.

248 See Bram Dijkstra, *Idols of Perversity: Fantasies of Feminine Evil in Fin-de-Siècle Culture* (New York and Oxford, 1986), pp.275–82.

249 See Norman Vance, *The Victorians and Ancient Rome* (Oxford, 1997), pp.175–93.

250 W. Y. Sellar, *The Roman Poets of the Augustan Age* (Oxford, 1891).

251 Andew Lang, *Letters to Dead Authors* (London, 1886), p.178.

252 'Vitae summa brevis spem nos vetat incohare longam' from *Odes* 1.4.15 and 'Non sum qualis eram bonae sub regno Cynarae' from *Odes*, 4.1.3–4.

253 See Rowena Fowler, 'Ernest Dowson and the Classics', *The Yearbook of English Studies*, 3 (1973), pp.243–52.

254 *Q Horati Flacci: Opera*, ed., F. W. Cornish (London, 1882).

255 'The Works of Lawrence Alma-Tadema,' *Art Journal*, 1883, p.66.

256 Horace: *The Complete Odes and Epodes*, trans. David West (Oxford, 1997).

257 I am indebted to David West's interpretation of this painting in 'Death by Roses', *Ad familiares*, 13, 1997.

258 For a fuller discussion, see Barrow, *Sir Lawrence Alma-Tadema*, cat.71.

259 Trans. West.

260 See p.99.

261 M. H. Spielmann (*Magazine of Art*, 1896–7, p.50) describes Orchardson's work as an imitation of Alma-Tadema's; however, *Master Baby* was exhibited at the Grosvenor Gallery in 1886 and *An Earthly Paradise* at the Royal Academy in 1891.

262 See p.121.

263 Quoted in Swanson (1990), p.76.

264 The reasons for his exile are unclear: either a deliberate affront to Augustus or the arrogance of having statues of himself erected in Egypt and inscribing his own exploits on the pyramids.

265 It was not until 1978 that nine lines of verse were discovered in a papyrus found in a fortress in Egyptian Nubia.

266 Alma-Tadema's library includes a third German edition (Leipzig, 1863).

267 We soon find out that the admired 'work of art' is merely a portrait of a lap-dog: W. A. Becker, *Gallus* or *Roman Scenes of the Time of Augustus*, trans. Frederick Metcalfe (London, 1866), p.25.

268 See pp.147, 158–63, 179–85.

269 Becker, *Gallus*, p.44.

270 W. R. Sickert, 'The Contemporary Art Society', *The New Age*, 4 Aug. 1910, in *A Free House! Or The Artist as Crafsman*, ed., Osbert Sitwell (London, 1947), p.88.

271 T. P. O'Conner, ed., *In the Days of My Youth* (London, 1901), p.206.

272 Juvenal, *Satire* 6. 110ff., trans. Peter Green (Harmondsworth, 1967).

273 See p.194.

274 For a full discussion of the painting, see Louise Lippincott, *Lawrence Alma-Tadema: Spring* (California, 1990).

275 M. H. Spielmann, *Royal Academy Pictures 1895*.

276 *C Valerii Catulli Carmina*, ed., R. A. B. Mynors (Oxford, 1958) Fragmenta I. For a discussion of the Catullan ascription of this verse fragment, see Barrow (1998), pp.192–6.

277 Swinburne, *Poems and Ballads, First Series* (London, 1866).

278 See T. P. Wiseman, *Catullus and his World: a Reappraisal* (Cambridge 1985), pp.214–16.

279 Ovid, *Fasti*. 5.183–378; Juvenal, 6.250.

280 *Scriptores Historiae Augustae*, 'Elagabalus' 6.6–7.

281 *Magazine of Art*, 1894, pp.272–3.

282 It has been identified by Dominic Montserrat as an original of the first century AD (Antikensammlung, Berlin) which belonged to the Viennese collector, Theodor Graf. Graf amassed a collection of Fayum portraits which were sold with an accompanying catalogue written by Alma-Tadema's friend, Georg Ebers. See Dominic Montserrat, 'To Make Death Beautiful: The Other Life of the Fayum Portraits', *Apollo*, July 1999, pp.22–3.

283 See John D'Arms, *Romans on the Bay of Naples* (Cambridge MA, 1970).

284 Statius, 2.2.

285 See Christie's, London, *Victorian Pictures*, 13 June 2000, no. 40.

286 Seneca, *Epistles*, 51.

287 Propertius, 1.2.27–30, trans. Guy Lee (Oxford, 1994).

288 Frédéric Bastet, 'Een gunstig uitkijkpunt op Capri', *Origine*, 6, 1995, pp.81–2; see Axel Munthe, *The Story of San Michele* (London, 1929).

289 Seneca, *Epistles*, 51.12.

290 Cicero, *Pro Caelio*, 15.35.

291 Frank Benson, *My Memoirs* (London, 1913), p.119.

292 See Jenkyns (1996), pp.303–8, and Fiona Macintosh, 'Tragedy in Performance' in P. E. Easterling, ed., *The Cambridge Companion to Greek Tragedy* (Cambridge, 1997).

293 See Richard Phené Spiers, 'The Architecture of "Coriolanus" at the Lyceum Theatre', *Architectural Review*, July 1901, pp.2–21; S. Rosenfeld, 'Alma-Tadema's designs for Henry Irving's 'Coriolanus', *Deutsche Shakespeare-Gessellschaft West Jahrbuch*, 1974, pp.84–95.

294 Standing, p.92

295 According to David Mayer, *Playing Out the Empire: Ben-Hur and other Toga Plays* and *Films 1883–1908: A Critical Anthology* (Oxford, 1994) p.2, the term 'toga play' was coined between 1895 and 1896 and in general use by 1898.

296 Ibid., p.194.

297 See pp.131–2.

298 A typical example is *The Theatre*, 1 Feb. 1893, p.105.

299 Standing, p.93.

300 Letter to Ebers, 21 Jan. 1892, quoted in Swanson (1990), p.81.

301 *The Sketch*, 1 March 1893, p.301.

302 See p.185.

303 Lady Constance Benson, *Mainly Players: Bensonian Memoirs* (London, 1926), p.89.

304 In 1889 Alma-Tadema had also advised Frank Benson's *Julius Caesar* in Oxford.

305 Standing, p.93

306 Frederick Dolman, 'Illustrated Interviews: LXVIII, Sir Lawrence Alma-Tadema', *Strand Magazine*, Dec. 1899,p.607.

307 George Bernard Shaw, *Our Theatres in the Nineties* (London, 1931) vol.3, p.318.

308 *Daily Telegraph*, 24 Jan. 1898.

309 Bram Stoker, *Personal Reminiscences of Henry Irving*, 2 vols. (London, 1906), vol. 2, p.66.

310 Harker, p.245, presumably referring to *The Finding of Moses*; see p.186.

311 See Mario Amaya, 'The Painter Who Inspired Hollywood', *Sunday Times Magazine*, 18 Feb. 1968, pp.26–7 and Caroline Dunant, 'Olympian Dreamscapes, the photographic Canvas: The Widescreen Paintings of Leighton, Poynter and Alma-Tadema' in J. Bratton, J. Cook and C. Gledhill, eds., *Melodrama: Stage, Picture, Screen* (London, 1994), pp.82–93.

312 *Academy*, 8 May 1880, p.348.

313 MacColl's campaigns were, frankly, invidious in that he singled out individuals – usually Poynter and Blake Richmond – for particular abuse.

314 George Moore, *Modern Painting* (London, 1893), p.54 (reprinted from an article in the *Spectator*).

315 Quoted in Swanson (1990), p.80.

316 18 Sept. 1897, ibid., p.83.

317 Quoted in Leonée Ormond, *George Du Maurier* (London, 1969), p.102.

318 See p.155.

319 Modern authorities agree that Paula had embraced Christianity before Jerome's arrival in Rome. See Joan M. Peterson, *Handmaidens of the Lord: Holy Women in Late Antiquity and the Early Middle Ages* (Michigan, 1996), pp.123–5.

320 *Magazine of Art*, 1898, p.467.

321 Dolman (1899), p.604.

322 G. A. Blouet, *Restauration des Thermes d'Antonin Caracalla* (Paris, 1828).

323 S. A. Iwanoff and C. Huelsen, *Architektonische Studien aus den Thermen des Caracalla* (Berlin, 1898).

324 My thanks to Ronald Higginson for this suggestion.

325 E. Paulin, *Restauration des monuments antiques. Thermes de Dioclétian* (Paris, 1890).

326 *Athenaeum*, 29 Apr. 1899, p.536.

327 See pp.134–7.

328 Pliny, *Natural History*, 34.61–5.

329 Dolman (1901), p.1.

330 Swanson (1990), p.99.

331 Dolman (1901), p.1.

332 Surely a parody of Horace's *Carmen Saeculare*.

333 Standing, p.107.

334 B. Guinaudeau 'La Décennale anglaise', *L'Aurore*, Aug. 1900, quoted in *1900: Art at the Crossroads* (Royal Academy of Arts, London, 2000), p.67.

335 *The Saturday Review*, 17 Nov. 1900, pp.613–14.

336 *The Oxford Book of Modern Verse, Chosen by W. B. Yeats* (London, 1936), Introduction.

337 Quoted in Swanson (1990), p.88.

338 See Christopher Pick, *Egypt: A Traveller's Anthology* (London, 1992).

339 The lines were previously misquoted in the title of a painting by P. H. Calderon as *Her Eyes Are With her Heart and That is Far Away*. See Edward Morris, *Victorian and Edwardian Paintings in the Walker Art Galleries and Sudley House* (London, 1996), p.60.

340 Quoted in Leonée Ormond, *George Du Maurier* (London, 1969), p.438.

341 Cicero, *Ad. Atticum*, 1.18.6, 1.19.6, 1.20.3, 2.1.7.

342 Tacitus, *Annals*, 13.20, trans. Michael Grant (Harmondsworth, 1971).

343 Pliny, *Natural History*, 9.173, trans. H Rackham.

344 See also *Water Pets* (1874), *Water Pets* (1875), *Water Pets* (1900).

345 *Nation*, 18 Jan. 1913, p.667

346 *Journal of the RIBA*, 30 June 1906, p.437.

347 See p.109.

348 Frederick Goodall, *The Finding of Moses* (1885), Edwin Long, *The Finding of Moses* (1886).

349 For further discussion, see Barrow, (1998), pp.188–9.

350 Edward Gibbon, *The History of the Decline and Fall of the Roman Empire*, ed. J. B. Bury (London, 1909), vol.1, p.148.

351 The present author (Barrow (1998)) mistakenly suggested that Geta stood in the background and Caracalla showed himself to the crowd. For the artist's own identification of the characters, see Lawrence Alma-Tadema, *Caracalla and Geta, A Vision of the Coliseum, by Sir L Alma Tadema*, Arthur Tooth and Sons (London, 1907). My thanks to Charlotte Garner for this observation.

352 Alma-Tadema had previously painted a reconstructed exterior of the Colosseum in *The Parting Kiss* (1882) and *The Coliseum*; see p.155.

353 *Caracalla and Geta, A Vision of the Coliseum, by Sir L Alma Tadema*,

Arthur Tooth and Sons (London, 1907).
354 Sections of *Caracalla and Geta* are repeated in *Maenianum Secundum et Summum Coliseum* (1911) and *Preparations in the Coliseum*, see p.194, neither of which have a historical narrative.
355 See p.61.
356 *Horace: The Complete Odes and Epodes*, trans. David West (Oxford, 1997).
357 In *Sir Lawrence Alma-Tadema* (cat. 84), the present author mistakenly suggested that the building was a construction of different rooms from the Stabian baths and not as is now apparent an amalgamation of two different bath houses at Pompeii. My thanks to Caroline Carter for this observation.
358 For a discussion of the Chantrey controversy see S. Hynes, *The Edwardian Turn of Mind* (London, 1991), pp.314–24 and Maureen Borland, *D. S. MacColl: Painter, Poet, Art Critic* (Harpenden, 1995), pp.136–51.
359 Oscar Wilde, 'The Grosvenor Gallery 1877', *Dublin University Magazine*, July 1877.
360 *Athenaeum*, 14 May 1910, p.588.
361 See pp.147–50.
362 See Edwin Becker, 'The Soul of Things: Alma-Tadema and Symbolism' in *Sir Lawrence Alma-Tadema*.
363 Swanson (1990), cat.432.
364 Ibid., p.94.
365 The collection was moved to the University of Birmingham in 1947.
366 *Saturday Review*, 18 Jan. 1913, pp.77–8; *Burlington Magazine*, 22, 1913, p.286; *Studio*, 58, Feb. 1913, p.56; *Connoisseur*, 35, Feb. 1913, pp.113–15. Two favourable reviews were from the traditional art critic, Cosmo Monkhouse (*Academy*, 8 March 1913, pp.311–12), and Richard Phené Spiers (*Architectural Review*, March 1913, pp.45–8), who presented a detailed examination of the artist's archaeological sources.
367 *Athenaeum*, 9 Dec. 1912, pp.778–80.
368 *Nation*, 18 Jan. 1913, pp.666–7.
369 *Nation*, 15 Feb. 1913.
370 *The Times*, 7 Jan. 1913, p.9, 8 Jan., p.10, 21 Jan., p.8.
371 *National Review*, Feb. 1913, p.945.
372 *Nineteenth Century*, March 1913, pp.597–607.
373 *The Times*, 5 May, 1913, p.5.
374 Lecture given to students of the Royal Academy, 30 June 1883, in J. Wyse Jackson, ed., *Aristotle at Afternoon Tea: the Rare Oscar Wilde* (London, 1991).
375 For a full list, see Vern G. Swanson, *John William Godward: The Eclipse of Classicism* (Woodbridge, Suffolk, 1997), pp.141–5.
376 Letter to *The Times* (21 March 1995, p.17) from Bernard G. Hart, former director of M. Newman Ltd.
377 Dolman (1899), p.607.
378 I.50-51. Trans. *The Works of Stefan George Rendered into English by Olga Marx and Ernst Morwitz* (North Carolina, 1974).
379 Stephen Phillips, *Nero* (London 1906), pp. 56-7.
380 *Gladiator: The Making of the Ridley Scott Epic* (London, 2000).

BIBLIOGRAPHY

EXHIBITIONS

Tooth and Sons, London 1907 = *Caracalla and Geta, A Vision of the Coliseum, by Sir L. Alma Tadema*, exhibition catalogue, London: Arthur Tooth & Sons.

Williamstown 1991 = *Empires Restored, Elysium Revisited: The Art of Sir Lawrence Alma-Tadema*, exhibition catalogue, ed. Jennifer Gordon Lovett and William R. Johnston, Massachusetts: Sterling and Francine Clark Institute, Williamstown and Baltimore: Walters Art Gallery.

Bristol 1996 = *Imagining Rome: British Artists and Rome in the Nineteenth Century*, exhibition catalogue, ed. Michael Liversidge and Catharine Edwards, Bristol: City Museum and Art Gallery.

Amsterdam 1996 = *The Colour of Sculpture 1840–1910*, exhibition catalogue, ed. Andreas Bluhm, Amsterdam: Van Gogh Museum and Leeds: Henry Moore Institute.

Amsterdam 1996 = *Sir Lawrence Alma-Tadema*, exhibition catalogue, ed. Edwin Becker *et al.*, principal author Elizabeth Prettejohn, Amsterdam: Van Gogh Museum and Liverpool: Walker Art Gallery.

BOOKS AND ARTICLES

Alma-Tadema, Lawrence, 'Laurens Alma-Tadema, RA', T. P. O'Conner, ed., *In The Days of my Youth* (London, 1901).

——, 'Marbles: Their Ancient and Modern Application', *Journal of the RIBA*, 14 (1907), pp.168–180.

——, 'My Reminiscences', *Strand Magazine*, 37 (1909), pp.286–95.

Amaya, Mario, 'The Painter Who Inspired Hollywood', *Sunday Times Magazine*, 18 Feb. 1968, pp.26–7.

Asleson, Robyn, *Classic into Modern: The Inspiration of Antiquity in English Painting 1864–1918*, Yale University Ph.D. thesis, 1993.

Barrow, Rosemary, 'The Scent of Roses: Alma-Tadema and the Other Side of Rome', *Bulletin of the Institute of Classical Studies*, 42 (1998), pp.183–202.

——, *British Classical-Subject Painting 1860–1910*, University of London Ph.D. thesis, 1999.

Boucher, Bruce, 'Lawrence Alma-Tadema, Edward Poynter and the Redecoration of the Athenaeum Club', *Apollo*, Oct. 1999, pp.21–9.

Boyes, J. F., 'The Private Art Collections of London: Mr John Aird's in Hyde Park Terrace', *Art Journal*, 1891, pp.135–140.

Carr, Joseph Comyns, *Coasting Bohemia* (London, 1914).

Carr, Philip, 'Alma-Tadema and his Friends', *The Listener*, 9 Dec. 1954, pp.1013–14.

Catalogue of the Well-known and Interesting Collection of Antique Furniture and Objects d'art formed by the Late Sir Lawrence Alma-Tadema including Valuable Pictures and the Archaeological Library (Hampton & Sons, June 9–16, London, 1913).

De Cordova, Rudolph, 'The Panels in Sir Lawrence Alma-Tadema's Hall', *Strand Magazine*, Dec. 1902, pp.615–30.

Dirks, Rudolf , 'Sir Lawrence Alma-Tadema', *Art Journal Christmas Number* (London, 1910).

Dolman, Frederick, 'Illustrated Interviews: LXVIII, Sir Lawrence Alma-Tadema', *Strand Magazine*, Dec. 1899, pp.602–14.

——, 'Pictures Preferred by their Painters', *Strand Magazine*, July 1901, p.1.

Ebers, Georg, *Lorenz Alma Tadema: His Life and Works*, trans. Mary J. Safford (New York, 1886)

Edmonds, Fred, 'Boys Who Have Risen; the Boyhood of Alma-Tadema', *Boys Own Paper*, 1 Mar.1890, pp.347–50.

Fry, Roger, 'The Case of the late Sir Lawrence Alma Tadema', *The Nation*, 18 Jan.1913, pp.666–7.

Gosse, Edmund, 'Lawrence Alma-Tadema RA', F. G. Dumas, ed., *Illustrated Biographies of Modern Artists* (London, 1882).

Hedreen, Guy, 'Lawrence Alma-Tadema's *Women of Amphissa*', *The Journal of the Walters Art Gallery, Baltimore* 52/3 (1994/5), pp.79–92.

Jenkyns, Richard, *The Victorians and Ancient Greece* (Oxford, 1980).

——, *Dignity and Decadence: Victorian Art and the Classical Inheritance* (London, 1996).

Kestner, Joseph A., *Mythology and Misogyny: The Social Discourse of Nineteenth-Century British Classical-Subject Painting* (Madison,Wisconsin, 1989).

Lippincott, Louise, *Lawrence Alma-Tadema: Spring* (Malibu, California, 1990).

Maas, Jeremy, *Gambart: Prince of the Victorian Art World* (London, 1975).

Meynell, Wilfred, 'Our Living Artists: Laurens Alma-Tadema', *Magazine of Art*, 1879, pp.193–7.

——, 'Mr Alma-Tadema. Seven Years Ago and Now', *Magazine of Art*, 1881, pp.94–6.

——, 'Artists' Homes: Mr Alma-Tadema's at North Gate, Regent's Park', *Magazine of Art*, 1882, pp.184–8.

Montserrat, Dominic, 'To Make Death Beautiful: The Other Life of the Fayum Portraits', *Apollo*, July 1999, pp.18–25.

Morris, Edward, *Victorian and Edwardian Paintings in the Lady Lever Art Gallery* (London, 1994).

——, *Victorian and Edwardian Paintings in the Walker Art Galleries and Sudley House* (London, 1996).

'Presentation to Sir Lawrence Alma-Tadema, The Royal Gold Medal', *Journal of the RIBA*, 30 June 1906, pp.437–41.

Prettejohn, Elizabeth, 'Lawrence Alma-Tadema and the Modern City of Ancient Rome', Andrew Hopkins, ed., *Responding to the Antique* (Cambridge, forthcoming).

Raven, Maarten, 'Alma-Tadema als Amateur-Egyptolog', *Bulletin van het Rijksmuseum*, 27 (1980), pp.103–17.

Richmond, William Blake, 'A Great Artist and his Little Critics', *The National Review*, Feb. 1913, pp.943–53.

Rosenfeld, S., 'Alma-Tadema's Designs for Henry Irving's *Coriolanus*', *Deutsche Shakespeare-Gessellschaft West Jahrbuch*, 1974, pp.84–95.

'Sir Lawrence Alma-Tadema's Reply', *Journal of the RIBA*, 30 June 1906, pp.441–3.

Spiers, Richard Phené, 'The Architecture of *Coriolanus* at the Lyceum Theatre', *Architectural Review*, July 1901, pp.2–21.

——, 'Archaeological Research in the Paintings of Sir Lawrence Alma-Tadema', *Archaeological Review*, 33 (1913), pp.45–8.

Standing, Percy Cross, *Sir Lawrence Alma-Tadema* (London, 1905).

Stephens, F. G., *Lawrence Alma-Tadema, A Dedication to Bacchus, Companion to the Famous Picture The Vintage Festival* (Lefèvre Gallery, London, 1889).

——, *Laurence Alma Tadema: A Sketch of his Life and Work* (London, 1895).

——, *Selected Works of Sir Laurence Alma-Tadema, O.M. RA* (London, 1901).

Swanson, Vern G., *Sir Lawrence Alma-Tadema: The Painter of the Victorian Vision of the Ancient World* (London, 1977).

——, *The Biography and Catalogue Raisonné of the Paintings of Sir Lawrence Alma-Tadema* (London, 1990).

Tomlinson, Richard, *The Athens of Alma-Tadema* (Stroud, Gloucestershire, 1991).

Van Wickervoort Crommelin, H. S. N., 'Laurens Alma Tadema RA', Max Rooses, ed., *Dutch Painters of the Nineteenth Century* (London, 1898–1901).

Wood, Christopher *Olympian Dreamers: Victorian Classical Painters 1860–1914* (London, 1983).

Walkley, Giles, *Artist's Houses in London 1764–1914* (Aldershot, 1994).

West, David, 'Death by Roses', *ad familiares*, 13, Autumn 1997.

Zimmern, Helen, 'Lawrence Alma-Tadema', *Art Annual*, 1886.

——, *Sir Lawrence Alma-Tadema* (London, 1902).

CLASSICAL TEXTS

Athenaeus, *The Deipnosophists*, text and trans. C. B. Gulick (Loeb Classical Library, Cambridge MA and London, 1993–8) .

Catullus, text and trans. Guy Lee, *The Poems of Catullus* (Oxford, 1990).

Cicero, *Pro Caelio*, text and trans. R. Gardner (Loeb Classical Library, Cambridge MA and London, 1987) .

Cicero, *De Re Publica*, text and trans. Clinton Walker Keyes (Loeb Classical Library, Cambridge MA and London, 1966) .

Dio Cassius, *Dio's Roman History*, text and trans. Earnest Cary (Loeb Classical Library, Cambridge MA and London, 1970–82) .

Hesiod, *Works and Days*, trans. S. Lombardo (Indianapolis, 1993).

Horace, text and trans. David West, *The Complete Odes and Epodes* (Oxford, 1997).

Josephus, *The Jewish War*, text and trans. H. St. J. Thackeray (Loeb Classical Library, Cambridge MA and London, 1997).

Juvenal, *Satires*, trans. Peter Green (Harmondsworth, 1967).

Livy, text and trans. E. T. Sage, B. O. Foster, F. G. Moore, A. C. Schlesinger (Loeb Classical Library, Cambridge M.A and London, 1982–8).

Martial, *Epigrams*, trans. D. R. Shakleton Bailey (Loeb Classical Library, Cambridge MA and London, 1993) .

Ovid, *Ars Amatoria*, trans. A.D. Meriville, *The Love Poems* (Oxford, 1990).

Ovid, *Fasti*, text and trans. J. G. Frazer (Loeb Classical Library, Cambridge MA and London, 1976) .

Petronius, *Satyricon*, trans. J. P. Sullivan (Harmondsworth, 1986).

Pliny, *Natural History*, text and trans. H. Rackham (Loeb Classical Library, Cambridge MA and London, 1989–91).

Plutarch, *Moralia*, text and trans. F. C. Babbit, W. C. Helmbold *et al.* (Loeb Classical Library, Cambridge MA and London, 1989–95).

Propertius, text and trans. Guy Lee (Oxford, 1994).

Scriptores Historiae Augustae, text and trans. D. Magie (Loeb Classical Library, Cambridge MA and London, 1982); *Lives of the Later Caesars*, trans. A. Birley (Harmondsworth, 1976).

Seneca, *Epistles*, text and trans. Richard M. Gummere (Loeb Classical Library, Cambridge MA and London 1991).

Statius, *Silvae*, text and trans. J. H. Mozley (Loeb Classical Library, Cambridge MA and London, 1982) .

Suetonius, text and trans. J. C. Rolfe (Loeb Classical Library, Cambridge MA and London 1989).

Tacitus, *Annals*, trans. Michael Grant, *The Annals of Imperial Rome* (Harmondsworth, 1986).

Tacitus, *The Histories*, trans. W. H. Fyfe (Oxford, 1997).

Tibullus, *Elegies*, text and trans. Guy Lee (Leeds, 1990).

Vitruvius, *On Architecture*, text and trans. F. Granger (Loeb Classical Library, Cambridge MA and London, 1995).

INDEX OF WORKS

Plate references are in **bold**

GENERAL INDEX

Plate references are in **bold**

PICTURE CREDITS

Acropolis Museum, Athens Acr.670 **88**
Amsterdams Historisch Museum **4**
Archaeological Museum, Naples negative no. M.N./C.1735 **25**, negative no.M.N./B.2405 **33**, negative no. M.N./A.5842 **46**, negative no.H.N./A.5594 **117**, negative no.M.N./A. 6131 **151**, negative no.M.N./B. 1473 **152**, catalogue no.9511 **160**
Art Gallery of Ontario, Toronto gift from the Junior Women's Committee Fund 1969 **189**
Birmingham Museums and Art Gallery **36**, **141**
Bridgeman Art Library, London **12**, **26**, **32**, **57**, **72** (Chris Beetles, London), **105**, **106**, **134**, **142**, **143**, **159**, **179**, **180**, **183**, **184**, **186**, **188**, **192**, **194**, **196**
Bridgeman/Bristol City Museum and Art Gallery **146**
Bridgeman/Fine Art Society, London **185**
Bridgeman/Forbes Magazine Collection, New York **86**, **118-119**, **137**
Bridgeman/Guildhall Art Gallery, Corporation of London, UK **40**, **77**
Bridgeman/Manchester City Art Galleries, UK **35**
Bridgeman/Peter Willi **193**
Bridgeman/Townley Hall Art Gallery and Museum, Burnley, Lancashire **69**
British Library, London: shelfmark PP1931PCI **91**, **120**, **168**; PP1931pc **121**, **122**, **135**
British Museum, London: GR Sculpture 2193 **45**, 1875.10-12.8 **66**, BM1206 **71**
British Museum/Royal Watercolour Society **107**;
Capitoline Museum, Rome/photog. Maria Theresa Natale **132**, **138**
Cartwright Hall Art Gallery, Bradford **60**, **157** (Private collection on loan)
Christie's Images, London **5**, **10**, **43**, **50**, **52**, **79**, **94**, **96**, **109**, **123**, **125**, **126**, **131**, **154**, **162**, **163**, **166**
Colindale Newspaper Library **170**
Dordrechts Museum, Dordrecht **6**
Exeter City Museums and Art Gallery **81**
Faringdon Collection Trust **65**
Fitzwilliam Museum, Cambridge **99-101**
Fogg Art Museum, Harvard University Art Museums, gift of Samuel D.Warren **7**
Frances Lehman Loeb Art Center gift of Mrs Avery Coonley **29**;
Fries Museum, Leeuwarden, Holland **2**, **11**, **53**
Gemaldegalerie der Akademie der bildenden Kunste, Vienna **8**
Groninger Museum, Groningen/photog. John Stoel **9**
Hamburger Kunsthalle, Hamburg/photog. Elke Walford **44**, **67**, **136**
By kind permission of the Harris Museum and Art Gallery, Preston **14**
Hood Museum of Art, Dartmouth College, Hanover, New Hampshire: gift of Arthur M. Loew, class of 1921A **70**
J. Paul Getty Museum, Malibu, California **149-150**, **164**
Johannesburg Art Gallery, South Africa **13**
John Constable Esq., England **3**
London Borough of Hammersmith and Fulham **103**
MacConnal-Mason, London **175**
Manchester City Art Galleries **73**, **165**, **181**
Milwaukee Art Museum, Layton Art Collection **41**
Montreal Museum of Fine Arts, Montreal, Canada: Horley and Annie Townsend Bequest/ photog. Christine Guest **30**
Museo Nacional del Prado, Madrid **39**
Robert Dawson Evans Collection, 1917 courtesy of Museum of Fine Arts, Boston **27**
Museums and Arts Section, East Ayrshire Council **74**
National Archaeological Museum, Athens: catalogue no.216 **182**
National Gallery of Scotland, Edinburgh **144**
National Museums and Galleries on Merseyside/Lady Lever Art Gallery, Port Sunlight **93**, **139**
National Museum in Warsaw **127**
By courtesy of the National Portrait Gallery, London **63**
Philadelphia Museum of Art: George W. Elkins Collection **124**;
RIBA, London **104**
Photo RMN **102**, **112**
Rijksmuseum, Amsterdam **17**, **55**, **56**
Royal Academy of Arts, London **62**, **84**
Royal Collections, The Hague **111**
Sotheby's Picture Library, London **16**, **64**, **85**, **95**, **109**, **145**, **161**, **174**
Sotheby's, New York **20**, **28**
State Hermitage Museum, St Petersburg **21**
Stedelijk Museum, Amsterdam **110**
Sterling and Francine Clark Institute, Williamstown, MA **130**
Tate London 2001 **190**
Trustees of the Cecil Higgins Art Gallery, Bedford, UK **108**
Tyne and Wear Museums/Laing Art Gallery **140**
Ufizzi Gallery, Florence **172-3**
University of Birmingham: catalogue no.123.11161 **19**, catalogue no.81.E2172 **38**, catalogue no.14.8085 **47**, catalogue no.35.8833 **58**, catalogue no.75.9799 **89**, catalogue no.82.10039 **90**, catalogue no.136.11604 **113**, catalogue no.117.E2625 **114**, catalogue no.138.E2792 **115**, catalogue no.84.E2309 **129**, catalogue no.66.9433 **133**, catalogue no.70.9618 **148**, catalogue no.11.7983 **155**, catalogue no.10.7954 **176**, catalogue no.66.9431 **187**, catalogue no.10.7962 **191**
University of Birmingham/Archaeological Museum, Naples: catalogue no.120.11100 **23**, catalogue no.81.EE2219 **51**, catalogue no.70.9605 **153**
University of Birmingham/British Museum, London: catalogue no.36.E1488 **15**, catalogue no.77.9966 **37**, catalogue no.36.E1429 **59**, catalogue no.152.12178 **156**
University of Birmingham/Church of S.Maria degli Angeli, Rome: catalogue no.10.7952 **178**
University of Birmingham/Conservatori Museum, Rome: catalogue no.67.9499 **80**, catalogue no.140.11727 **83**
University of Birmingham/Capitoline Museum, Rome: catalogue no.117.11008 **24**
University of Birmingham/Vatican Museums, Rome: catalogue no.82.10007 **31**, catalogue no.81.9994 **42**, catalogue no.134.11511 **76**, catalogue no.140.11722 **177**
University of Bristol: Theatre Collection, HBT/D/000 0007/16 **171**
Van Gogh Museum, Amsterdam: **61**, **68**
Victoria and Albert Museum, London: **48-49**, **167**, **195**
Walters Art Museum, Baltimore **54**, **78**, **87**, **116**, **169**
Werner Forman Archive, London **147**
William Morris Gallery, London E17 **82**
Witt Library/Courtauld Institute of Art: negative no.948/16(35) **92**, negative no.938/1 (B) **98**, **18**
Yale University Art Gallery: Mary Gertrude Abbey Fund **34**, **97**